Biodiversity Litigation

Biodiversity Litigation

Edited by

GUILLAUME FUTHAZAR

Max Planck Institute for Comparative Public Law and International Law

SANDRINE MALJEAN-DUBOIS

Centre national de la recherche scientifique and Aix-Marseille University

JONA RAZZAQUE

Bristol Law School, University of the West of England

OXFORD
UNIVERSITY PRESS

OXFORD
UNIVERSITY PRESS

Great Clarendon Street, Oxford, OX2 6DP,
United Kingdom

Oxford University Press is a department of the University of Oxford.
It furthers the University's objective of excellence in research, scholarship,
and education by publishing worldwide. Oxford is a registered trade mark of
Oxford University Press in the UK and in certain other countries

First Edition published in 2023

Published in the United States of America by Oxford University Press
198 Madison Avenue, New York, NY 10016, United States of America

British Library Cataloguing in Publication Data

Data available

Library of Congress Control Number: 2022941397

ISBN 978–0–19–286546–5

DOI: 10.1093/oso/9780192865465.001.0001

Printed and bound by
CPI Group (UK) Ltd, Croydon, CR0 4YY

Foreword

Dr David R Boyd
UN Special Rapporteur on human rights and the environment

Humanity Depends on Biodiversity

Earth is the only planet in the universe known to support life. On this unique and miraculous blue-green planet, evolution has produced a mind-boggling diversity of life, with millions of species, from elephants, redwood trees, and blue whales to axolotls, butterflies, and cacti. Biological diversity includes ecosystems, species, and differences in genes within a single species. An ecosystem is a group of organisms together with the physical environment where they live. The biosphere (or nature) is the sum of all ecosystems, the zone of life on Earth.

Nature's contributions to people are immense and irreplaceable. There are many compelling reasons to protect, conserve, and sustainably use biodiversity, based on a wide spectrum of values: ecological, social, economic, scientific, educational, cultural, recreational, and aesthetic. While some speak of natural capital and ecosystem services, others refer to nature's gifts and intrinsic value.[1]

All human rights ultimately depend on a healthy biosphere. Without healthy, functioning ecosystems, which depend on healthy biodiversity, there would be no clean air to breathe, safe water to drink, or nutritious food to eat. Plants, on land and in water, produce oxygen through photosynthesis. One type of phytoplankton, *Prochlorococcus*, is so small that millions can fit in a drop of water, yet the tiny organisms generate countless tons of oxygen. A teaspoon of healthy soil contains billions of microorganisms—algae, bacteria, fungi, nematodes, and protozoa—that process organic matter into rich, dark humus to feed plants and help to protect them from pests and pathogens.

Healthy ecosystems also regulate the Earth's climate, filter air and water, recycle nutrients, and mitigate the impact of natural disasters. Wetlands remove pollutants, shield coastlines, store carbon, absorb water, and contribute

[1] Unai Pascual and others, 'Valuing Nature's Contributions to People: The IPBES Approach' (2017) 26–27 Current Opinion Environmental Sustainability 7.

to the food supply (eg rice, fish, and seaweed). Marine and terrestrial ecosystems absorb 60 per cent of the carbon dioxide emissions produced by humans, slowing the pace of climate change. Healthy ecosystems also provide a renewable supply of timber, fibre, food, fish, and other goods. Insects, bats, and birds pollinate more than 75 per cent of crops, including fruits, vegetables, almonds, cocoa, and coffee.

Billions of persons rely on natural medicines for their health care. More than half of prescription drugs and 70 per cent of cancer-fighting drugs are natural or derived from nature. Spending time in nature provides people with physical, mental, emotional, and spiritual benefits. Nature's contributions to people affect almost every aspect of life and are essential to fulfilling almost all of the Sustainable Development Goals. Although many believe that it is impossible or unwise to place an economic value on nature, economists have estimated the annual value of ecosystem goods and services to be $125 trillion.[2]

The Global Biodiversity Crisis

Unfortunately, instead of treating the Earth—this unique, life-supporting, and irreplaceable home—with care, respect, and reverence, humans are inflicting catastrophic damage on ecosystems and biodiversity, undermining nature's extraordinary contributions to human well-being and prosperity. In 2019, in the most comprehensive assessment of the state of nature undertaken, the Intergovernmental Science-Policy Platform on Biodiversity and Ecosystem Services (IPBES) summarized the destruction of nature by human activities as follows:[3]

(a) wildlife populations (including amphibians, birds, fish, and mammals) have plummeted an average of 60 per cent since 1970;
(b) the rate of extinction is hundreds of times higher than the average over the past ten million years and is accelerating, with one million species at risk;
(c) nearly three-quarters of the Earth's land surface has been altered significantly;

[2] Monique Grooten and Rosamunde Almond (eds), *Living Planet Report 2018: Aiming Higher* (World Wildlife Fund 2018).
[3] See IPBES/7/10/Add.1.

(d) two-thirds of the Earth's ocean realm is experiencing adverse impacts, including acidification, deoxygenation, and a loss of sea ice;
(e) more than half of the world's accessible freshwater flows are appropriated for human use;
(f) more than 85 per cent of the planet's wetlands have been destroyed;
(g) 420 million hectares of forest have been lost since 1990 through conversion to other land uses;
(h) the global biomass of large predatory fish targeted by fisheries has fallen by two-thirds over the past hundred years.

Despite conservation efforts at the international and national levels, the decline in nature's diversity and abundance during the past fifty years is unprecedented in human history. Scientists believe that humans are causing the sixth mass extinction in the history of life on Earth.[4]

The human activities directly responsible for the rapid decline in ecosystem health and biological diversity are, in order of global importance, changes in land and sea use (eg conversion of forests to agriculture), direct exploitation of species (eg fishing, hunting, poaching, illegal wildlife, and the timber trade), climate change, pollution, and invasive species. Climate change is a risk multiplier that exacerbates the impact of the other drivers, with potentially devastating short-term impacts on coral reefs, tropical forests, and Arctic ecosystems.[5]

The five direct drivers are propelled by an array of underlying root causes—indirect drivers of change—including production and consumption patterns, human population growth, trade, technological innovations, and societal values. In the past fifty years, the human population has doubled, the global economy has quadrupled, and global trade has grown by a factor of ten, sending demand for energy and materials skyrocketing. Agriculture is the largest single factor in the destruction of ecosystems and the decline in biological diversity. Deforestation is driven by the demand for beef, soy (mostly for livestock feed), and palm oil, as well as the expansion of subsistence agriculture.[6] Wealthy people are disproportionately responsible for overconsumption and the associated pressure on nature.

[4] Gerardo Ceballos, Paul R Ehrlich, and Peter H Raven, 'Vertebrates on the Brink as Indicators of Biological Annihilation and the Sixth Mass Extinction' (2020) 17(24) Proceedings of the National Academy of Sciences 13596.

[5] See IPBES/7/10/Add.1.

[6] Navin Ramankutty and others, 'Trends in Global Agricultural Land Use: Implications for Environmental Health and Food Security' (2018) 69 Annual Review of Plant Biology 789.

Scientists have warned society of the downward spiral of ecosystems and biodiversity for more than fifty years, since the publication in 1962 of Rachel Carson's *Silent Spring*. In 1992, more than 1,700 scientists warned, 'Human activities ... put at serious risk the future that we wish for human society and the plant and animal kingdoms, and may so alter the living world that it will be unable to sustain life in the manner that we know.'[7] In 2005, the Millennium Ecosystem Assessment concluded that humans were having potentially irreversible impacts on ecosystems and biodiversity, on a scale unprecedented in human history.[8] In 2017, more than 15,000 scientists from 184 states observed that 'humanity has generally failed to make sufficient progress in solving these foreseen environmental challenges, and alarmingly, most of them are getting far worse.'[9] In 2019, the United Nations Environment Programme (UNEP) concluded that the ongoing destruction of nature was 'compromising planetary integrity and Earth's capacity to meet human needs.'[10] According to IPBES, the current negative trends in biodiversity and ecosystems will undermine progress towards 80 per cent of the targets of Sustainable Development Goals related to poverty, hunger, health, water, cities, climate, oceans, and land.

International Biodiversity Law

States have created hundreds of treaties and declarations pledging to protect nature. The most important, the Convention on Biological Diversity (1992), has three overarching objectives: conservation, sustainable use, and the equitable sharing of benefits. Other cornerstones of international protection for nature include the Convention on International Trade in Endangered Species of Wild Fauna and Flora; the World Charter for Nature; the United Nations Framework Convention on Climate Change; the United Nations Convention to Combat Desertification in Those Countries Experiencing Serious Drought and/or Desertification, Particularly in Africa; the Convention on the Conservation of Migratory Species of Wild Animals; the Convention on Wetlands of International Importance especially as Waterfowl Habitat; and the Convention for the Protection of the World Cultural and Natural Heritage.

[7] Union of Concerned Scientists, 'World Scientists Warning to Humanity' (16 July 1992).

[8] Millennium Ecosystem Assessment, *Ecosystems and Human Well-Being: Synthesis* (Island Press 2005).

[9] William J Ripple and others, 'World Scientists Warning to Humanity: A Second Notice' (2017) 67(12) Bioscience 1026.

[10] UNEP, *Global Environmental Outlook: GEO 6—Healthy Planet, Healthy People* (2019) 4 and 8.

In 2002, parties to the Convention on Biological Diversity pledged 'to achieve by 2010 a significant reduction of the current rate of biodiversity loss at the global, regional and national level as a contribution to poverty alleviation and to the benefit of all life on Earth'.[11] In 2010, parties to the same convention established the Aichi Biodiversity Targets, comprising five strategic goals and twenty targets to be achieved by 2020.[12] In 2015, nations pledged to achieve seventeen Goals through the 2030 Agenda for Sustainable Development. A deadline of 2020 was set for some targets pursuant to Goals 14 (life under water) and 15 (life on land), including to sustainably manage and protect marine and coastal ecosystems to avoid significant adverse impacts, to ensure the conservation, restoration, and sustainable use of terrestrial and inland freshwater ecosystems and their services, to halt deforestation, and to halt the loss of biodiversity.

States have failed to meet any of the goals that they established for protecting and conserving ecosystems and biodiversity. None of the 2010 targets of the Convention on Biological Diversity, the 2020 Aichi targets, or the 2020 commitments of the Sustainable Development Goals have been achieved,[13] although there has been modest progress. As of 2021, 16.64 per cent of the world's terrestrial areas and 7.74 per cent of its oceans are protected.[14] Some species threatened with extinction, from bald eagles to humpback whales, have recovered. However, incremental progress towards protecting specific places and species has been overwhelmed by exponential growth in human impacts on nature.

States have not responded with appropriate urgency to the increasingly dire warnings issued by the world's leading scientists. On the contrary, states encourage damage to ecosystems and biodiversity, providing more than $500 billion annually in subsidies that harm nature, more than five times what they spend to protect biodiversity.[15] Efforts to protect nature are undermined by prioritizing economic growth, trade, and corporate profits over environmental protection and failing to address weaknesses in the rule of law (eg corruption and weak institutions), poverty, armed conflict, limited civic space, the criminalization of human rights defenders, and the failure to recognize the rights of indigenous peoples and local communities.

[11] See UNEP/CBD/COP/6/20, Annex I, Decision VI/26, para 11 (Strategic Plan for the Convention on Biological Diversity).

[12] See UNEP/CBD/COP/10/27, Annex II, Decision X/2 (Strategic Plan for Biodiversity 2011–2020).

[13] United Nations, The Sustainable Development Goals Report 2020 (United Nations No E.20.I.7).

[14] UNEP and others, *Protected Planet Digital Report* (2020).

[15] Organization for Economic Cooperation and Development (OECD), 'A Comprehensive Overview of Global Biodiversity Finance' (April 2020).

There is a huge implementation and enforcement gap, acknowledged by states, as actions fall short of commitments made through treaties and legislation. Laws, regulations, and policies are paper tigers because governments turn a blind eye to corporate activities that are detrimental to ecosystems and biodiversity. The overall impact of humanity continues to increase, intensifying pressure on the planet's life-support systems and reflecting our dysfunctional relationship with nature.[16]

The Urgent Need for Transformative Change

In 2019, scientists united in their calls for urgent and transformative change.[17] As stated by IPBES, 'Goals for conserving and sustainably using nature and achieving sustainability ... may only be achieved through transformative changes across economic, social, political and technological factors.'[18] According to UNEP, 'Urgent action at an unprecedented scale is necessary to arrest and reverse this situation, thereby protecting human and environmental health and maintaining the current and future integrity of global ecosystems.'[19] The Food and Agriculture Organization of the United Nations concluded, 'Transformational change is needed in the way we manage our forests and their biodiversity, produce and consume our food and interact with nature.'[20]

Transformative change requires rethinking the goals of society, what makes us happy, how we generate and use energy, the food that we eat and how we produce it, the way that we manufacture goods, how we design our cities, and how we can reduce and eliminate waste. The Sustainable Development Goals, as well as the vision of the Convention on Biological Diversity of living in harmony with nature by 2050, embody a vision of a transformed world. Scientists estimate that unless we begin to make transformative changes in the next ten years it could take millions of years for biodiversity on Earth to recover, forcing future generations to live in a biologically impoverished world.[21] However, it is not too late. As IPBES concluded, 'Acting immediately and simultaneously on

[16] David R Boyd, 'Human Rights Depend on a Healthy Biosphere', Report of the UN Special Rapporteur on human rights and the environment to the General Assembly, UN Doc A/75/161 (15 July 2020).

[17] Sandra Diaz and others, 'Pervasive Human-Driven Decline of Life on Earth Points to Need for Transformative Change' (2019) 366(6471) Science.

[18] See IPBES/7/10/Add.1.

[19] UNEP Nairobi, *Global Environmental Outlook: GEO6—Summary for Policymakers* (2019) 4.

[20] FAO and UNEP, *The State of the World's Forests 2020* (2020).

[21] Eric Dinerstein and others, 'A Global Deal for Nature: Guiding Principles, Milestones and Targets' (2019) 5(4) Science Advances.

the multiple indirect and direct drivers has the potential to slow, halt and even reverse some aspects of biodiversity and ecosystem loss.'[22]

Turning to the Courts

In response to the compelling evidence of the collapse of global biodiversity and the repeated failure of governments and businesses to fulfil their promises to protect nature, a growing number of individuals, communities, and institutions have turned to the courts in search of accountability. This encyclopaedic book represents a pioneering effort to understand the big picture of biodiversity litigation at the national, regional, and international levels.

The authors ask what kind of lawsuits are being filed, by whom, using what legal theories, to achieve what remedies, and in front of which judicial bodies. They canvas not only biodiversity law, but also criminal law and law related to trade and investment, human rights, constitutions, corporate due diligence, taxation, and contracts. Are these cases successful or unsuccessful? What are the key factors contributing to the effectiveness, or lack thereof, of litigation strategies to improve the conservation and sustainable use of biodiversity and ensure equitable sharing of the benefits? What is the role of international biodiversity instruments, both hard law and soft law types? What developments are occurring at the confluence of biodiversity law and human rights law, especially regarding the right to a clean, healthy, and sustainable environment and the rights of indigenous peoples? What are the appropriate roles of judges, lawyers, and civil society? What advances are occurring at the frontiers of biodiversity law, involving issues such as the rights of nature, future generations, and biopiracy? To answer these questions, individual chapters provide deep dives into the jurisprudence of Australia, Brazil, Canada, China, France, India, South Africa, the United Kingdom, and the United States, as well as international litigation globally and within the European Union.

The lessons articulated, although preliminary and pending future research are important for lawyers, judges, policymakers, and people who are passionate about finding ways to protect and restore the diversity of life that provides the irreplaceable foundation of human well-being. Lawyers are expanding the field of biodiversity litigation beyond the initial focus on endangered species and protected areas. Courts are increasingly incorporating biodiversity law and biodiversity science in their decisions. These are timely and significant

[22] IPBES/7/10/Add.1, para C4.

developments, with fascinating parallels to, and differences with, the equally vital and more recent but widely studied field of climate litigation.

If we fail to protect the biosphere, future generations will live in an ecologically impoverished world, deprived of nature's critical contributions to human well-being, ravaged by increasingly frequent pandemics, and riven by deepening environmental injustices. Biodiversity litigation could be a catalyst for transformative changes that enable humans to achieve a just and sustainable future where people live happy, healthy, and fulfilling lives in harmony with nature. This book helps to chart the course forward.

Preface

The elaboration of international environmental policies or expediting the implementation of multilateral environmental agreements by setting goals and targets seemed to have become common practice over the last few decades. What has also become common is how the achievement of these goals and targets remained elusive. As projected by the most recent edition of the Global Biodiversity Outlook, by the end of 2020 none of the globally agreed Aichi Biodiversity Targets was fully met, although at national level some progress was made on some of them. It is now evident that the exponential growth of international environmental law is not accompanied by the right amount of energy, dedication, and enforcement to keep the promises made either in the treaties, or goals and targets within strategic plans or frameworks which are mostly adopted as soft law.

In what looks like an effort to counterbalance the discrepancy between the international commitments made by states and their lacklustre national-level implementation, international courts and arbitral tribunals are increasingly being called upon to deal with or resolve environmental disputes or claims against non-performance. This, in turn, is resulting in the expansion of the role and contribution of courts, judges, and arbitrators in elaborating obligations under international environmental treaties and customary international rules and in affirming their effective implementation by the parties concerned. For example, there is a trend, particularly in the field of climate change mitigation and adaptation, of giving more emphasis to enforcement of standards and commitments by seeking judicial remedies. The Paris Agreement has spurred—to the credit of civil society, including the youth and their consistent engagement—climate litigation in a remarkable way and offered national courts the opportunity to position themselves as key players of climate governance.

Inspired by the rising prominence of climate change litigation, the editors of this volume sought to take a side step and analyse how courts deal with biodiversity-related matters. International climate law has been instrumental in the rise of climate change litigation. Can the same be said about international biodiversity law? This simple question had not thus far been addressed in depth by legal scholarship. Moreover, such a question also opens the space to analyse the particularities of biodiversity litigation as a potential subcategory of environmental litigation.

The editors chose to explore this topic in a comparative fashion, with case studies from all continents. As highlighted by the editors, this is only the first step in what should become a more systematic investigation of the topic. Nevertheless, the findings of this book, and especially its synthesis, offer a better understanding of the trends in biodiversity litigation and the role international law plays in court. On a positive note, it does appear that litigation plays a role in the effectiveness of biodiversity law and policies, although this depends largely on the legal and institutional context. This volume also pushes for an entrenchment of the notion of biodiversity litigation, which was quasi non-existent a few years ago and is now starting to be more common.

As we enter a new phase in the development of international biodiversity law, such research is timely. It allows us to better understand the subtle interplay between the national and international legal orders, specifically in a field where notions of local and global become so intertwined. Time will tell whether the adoption and implementation of soft law instruments such as the decisions of the Conference of the Parties to the Convention on Biological Diversity, including the global biodiversity framework, could become increasingly important considerations along with the provisions of biodiversity-related treaties, by courts or arbitral tribunals in their adjudication of biodiversity litigations.

Elizabeth Maruma Mrema
United Nations Assistant Secretary General &
Executive Secretary, Secretariat of the Convention
on Biological Diversity

Acknowledgements

The idea for this project saw light in the corridors of UNESCO, during the seventh plenary of the Intergovernmental Science-Policy Platform for Biodiversity and Ecosystem Services (IPBES). It took three years to turn this idea into a complete book, and this was only possible thanks to the collaboration and support of many people.

Especially, we would like to thank Mingzhe Zhu for his help in organizing the workshops that allowed us to continuously refine our understanding of biodiversity litigation. We wish also to thank all the participants in these preparatory workshops, particularly, Randianina Radilofe who shared fascinating insights on biodiversity litigation in Madagascar.

We thank Luise Wilde, Jack McNichol, and the editorial team at Oxford University Press who accompanied us at each step of the publication process.

We thank the Max Planck Institute for Comparative Public Law and International Law for its support of the project. Particularly, the introduction to this book benefited from the brilliant collective intelligence of Professor Anne Peters and her research team at the Institute.

Every book benefits from the immeasurable help of invisible hands. Without the help of Cleverline T Brown, this volume would not have been finalized in time. We also wish to express our gratitude to Helen Cecil for her careful proofreading of the synthesis of this book. The introduction to this book also benefited from the brilliant collective intelligence of Professor Anne Peters and her research team at the Max Planck Institute for Comparative Public Law and International Law.

To conclude, we are most grateful to Elizabeth Maruma Mrema and David Boyd who accepted to share their insights on the topic.

We hope this book will provide valuable insight to the legal community.

Contents

List of Abbreviations

ABS	Access and benefit sharing
ACCC	Aarhus Convention Compliance Committee
AEWA	Agreement on the Conservation of African-Eurasian Migratory Waterbirds
APL	Administrative Procedure Law
ASEAN	Association of Southeast Asian Nations
BMC	Biodiversity management committees
BPBES	Brazilian Platform for Biodiversity and Ecosystem Services
CBD	Convention on Biological Diversity
CCP	Chinese Communist Party
CERD	Committee on the Elimination of Racial Discrimination
CFP	Common Fisheries Policy
CITES	Convention on International Trade in Endangered Species of Wild Fauna and Flora
CJEU	Court of Justice of the European Union
CMS	Convention on the Conservation of Migratory Species of Wild Animals
CNPA	Canadian National Parks Act
CONAMA	Conselho Nacional do Meio Ambiente (Brazil National Council for the Environment)
COP	Conference of the Parties
COP26	26th Climate Change Convention Conference of the Parties
COSEWIC	Committee on the Status of Endangered Wildlife in Canada
CPAWS	Canadian Parks and Wilderness Society
CPR	Civil Procedure Rules
DEA	Department of Environmental Affairs
DEFF	Department of Forestry, Fisheries and the Environment
DEFRA	Department for Environment, Food & Rural Affairs
EA	Environmental assessment
EC	Ecological civilization
	European Community
ECHR	European Court of Human Rights
ECJ	European Court of Justice
EDO	Environmental Defenders Office
EEA	European Environment Agency
EEZ	Exclusive economic zone
EIA	Environment impact assessment
EIS	Environmental impact statement

EMP	Environmental Management Programme
EPA	Environmental Protection Agency
EPBC Act	Environmental Protection and Biodiversity Conservation Act
EPL	Environmental Protection Law
ESA	Endangered Species Act
EU	European Union
FDA	Food and Drug Administration
FPIC	Free prior informed consent
FWS	Fish and Wildlife Service
GATT	General Agreement on Tariffs and Trade
GHG	Greenhouse gas
GMO	Genetically modified organisms
HIS	Humane Society International
IACtHR	Inter-American Court of Human Rights
IBA	Important Bird Areas
IBL	International biodiversity law
ICHR	Inter-American Court of Human Rights
ICJ	International Court of Justice
ICPE	Installations Classées pour l'Environnement
ILC	International Law Commission
ILO	International Labour Organization
IPBES	Intergovernmental Science-Policy Platform on Biodiversity and Ecosystem Services
IPCA	Indigenous Protected and Conserved Areas
IPCC	Intergovernmental Panel on Climate Change
IPLC	Indigenous peoples and local communities
IRS	Internal Revenue Service
ITLOS	International Tribunal for the Law of the Sea
IUCN	International Union for Conservation of Nature
JNCC	Joint Natural Conservation Council
LIFE	L'Instrument Financier pour l'Environnement
MAT	Mutually agreed terms
MBTA	Migratory Bird Treaty Act
MHSCL	Maharashtra Hybrid Seeds Company Ltd
MMPA	Marine Mammal Protection Act
MNES	Matters of national environmental significance
MOU	Memorandum of understanding
NAFTA	North American Free Trade Agreement
NBA	National Biodiversity Authority
NBP	National Biodiversity Policy
NBSAP	National Biodiversity Strategy and Action Plan
NEB	National Energy Board
NEMA	National Environmental Management Act
NEMBA	National Environmental Management Biodiversity Act
NEMPA	National Environmental Management Protected Areas Act

NEPA	National Environmental Policy Act
NERCA 2006	Natural Environment and Rural Communities Act 2006
NGO	Non-governmental organization
NGT	National Green Tribunal
NPA	National Prosecuting Authority
NPAES	National Protected Area Expansion Strategy
NPC	National People's Congress
NSW	New South Wales
NSWLEC	Land and Environment Court of New South Wales
NT	Northern Territory
PIC	Prior informed consent
PIL	Public interest litigation
RSPB	Royal Society for the Protection of Birds
SACEP	South Asia Co-operative Environment Program
SADC	South African Development Community
SANBI	South African National Biodiversity Institute
SARA	Species at Risk Act
SBPC	Society for the Progress of Science
SCA	Supreme Court of Appeal
SCA 1981	Senior Courts Act 1981
SDG	Sustainable Development Goals
SEPP	State Environmental Planning Policy
SLA	Submerged Lands Act
SNUC	National System of Protected Areas
SPC	Supreme People's Court
SPCA	Society for the Prevention of Cruelty to Animals
SPP	Supreme People's Procuratorate
STF	Supremo Tribunal Federal
STJ	Superior Tribunal de Justiça
SWG	Scientific Working Group
TAC	Total allowable catch
TCA	Trade and Cooperation Agreement
TEU	Treaty on European Union
TFEU	Treaty on the Functioning of the European Union
TRFs	Tribunais Regionais Federais
UAS	University of Agricultural Sciences
UNCCD	United Nations Convention to Combat Desertification
UNCLOS	United Nations Convention on the Law of the Sea
UNECE	United Nations Economic Commission for Europe
UNEP	United Nations Environment Programme
UNESCO	United Nations Educational, Scientific and Cultural Organization
UNFCCC	United Nations Framework Convention on Climate Change
WHC	World Heritage Convention
WTO	World Trade Organization
WTO DSB	World Trade Organization Dispute Settlement Body

List of Contributors

Charles-Hubert Born is a Professor at the Université Catholique de Louvain (UCLouvain) and lawyer at the Bar of Nivelles (Belgium). He is a Doctor of Legal Science and has degrees in biology and in environmental management sciences. He teaches introduction to law, land use planning law, and environmental law. He performs and leads research on various topics in environmental and planning law and especially in biodiversity law at the Seminar of Environmental and Land-Use Planning Law (SERES). He has published several scholarly books and articles on these subjects. He is the managing editor of the Belgian French-speaking leading journal on planning and environmental law. He is the co-chair of the Observatoire Juridique Natura 2000.

David R Boyd was appointed as the UN Special Rapporteur on human rights and the environment for a three-year term commencing 1 August 2018. He is an Associate Professor of Law, Policy, and Sustainability at the University of British Columbia. His career has included serving as the executive director of Ecojustice, appearing before the Supreme Court of Canada, and working as a special advisor on sustainability for Canadian Prime Minister Paul Martin. He has advised many governments on environmental, constitutional, and human rights policy and co-chaired Vancouver's effort to become the world's greenest city by 2020. He is a member of the World Commission on Environmental Law, an expert advisor for the UN's Harmony with Nature Initiative, and a member of ELAW, the Environmental Law Alliance Worldwide. He is also the author of nine books and over 100 reports and articles on environmental law and policy, human rights, and constitutional law. His most recent books include *The Rights of Nature* (ECW Press 2017), *The Optimistic Environmentalist* (ECW Press 2015), *Cleaner, Greener, Healthier: A Prescription for Stronger Canadian Environmental Laws and Policies* (UBC Press 2015), and *The Environmental Rights Revolution: A Global Study of Constitutions, Human Rights, and the Environment* (UBC Press 2012).

Larissa Suassuna Carvalho Barros is a Federal Attorney, member of the Brazilian Attorney General's Office (Advocacia-Geral da União—AGU). She has a Master in Law, State and Constitution from University of Brasília (UnB). Larissa is a specialist in constitutional law at the University for the Development of the State and the Pantanal Region (Uniderp). She is also a Member of the IUCN World Commission on Environmental Law and Protected Areas. She is a researcher at the Study Group on Law, Natural Resources and Sustainability (GERN/UnB) and the Environmental Law and Sustainable Development Research Group (UniCEUB), with participation in research on environmental justice, marine resources, and protected areas. She acted as the General Coordinator of Legal Affairs at the Ministry of the Environment (2018–19), was Vice-Chief Attorney at Chico Mendes Institute for Biodiversity Conservation

(2017–18), and was Federal Attorney at the Brazilian Institute of the Environment (2011–16).

Carina Costa de Oliveira is a Professor of International and Environmental Law, Law Faculty, University of Brasília, Brazil. She is a Visiting Scholar at the C-EENRG, University of Cambridge, and the University of Adelaide, Australia. She has a PhD in International Law from Panthéon-Assas, France. She acts as the Coordinator of the Research Group on Law, Natural Resources and Sustainability (Gern-UnB). Her research areas include public and private international law, environmental law, and conservation and sustainable use of marine resources.

Lucas Dermenghem is a lawyer at the Bar of Lille (France). In December 2016, after professional experiences with the French Ministry of Environment and the Douai Administrative Court of Appeal, he was sworn in and started his career at the Paris Bar. He now practises mainly in environmental law and urban planning law within the law office 'Géo Avocats', which he joined in March 2022 as a partner. He regularly publishes in legal journals.

Márcia Dieguez Leuzinger is a Public Attorney for the State of Parana, Brazil and a Professor of Environmental Law at Brasilia University Center (CEUB). She graduated in Law, MSc in Public Law, PhD in Sustainable Development at the University of Brasilia (UnB), and completed her postdoctoral studies on Environmental Law. She is an Adjunct Professor at the University of New England, Australia and a Member of the IUCN World Commission on Environmental Law. She leads the Research Group on Environmental Law and Sustainable Development and has published several books and articles on environmental law.

Guillaume Futhazar is a Senior Research Fellow at the Max Planck Institute for Comparative Public Law and International Law (Heidelberg, Germany). His research focuses mainly on international biodiversity law, and particularly, within that field, on the relationship between law and science and the evolutions of normative trends. He holds a PhD from Aix-Marseille University for a thesis on regional international environmental law in the Mediterranean. He is currently based in La Réunion (France) where he advises the Centre Sécurité Requin on environmental-related matters and risk management.

Joshua Ginsberg is a lawyer at Ecojustice, Canada's largest environmental law charity. He has represented environmental groups and First Nations in the courts of Ontario, Quebec, Saskatchewan, and Alberta, in federal court, and in the Supreme Court of Canada. His litigation experience includes appearing as counsel in the constitutional reference cases on Canada's carbon pricing and environmental assessment legislation. He has also appeared before House of Commons and Senate committees to provide testimony on proposed environmental legislation. Josh is a part-time professor at the University of Ottawa Faculty of Law, Common Law Section where he directs the Ecojustice Environmental Law Clinic, training the next generation of public interest environmental lawyers. Josh lives and works in Ottawa, the unceded territory of the Algonquin people.

Arpitha Kodiveri is a postdoctoral scholar at the Center for Human Rights and Global Justice at NYU School of Law. She received her doctoral degree in law from the European University Institute as a Hans Kelsen Fellow. Her research examines land conflicts and legal mobilization by forest-dwelling communities in India. She has previously practised as an environmental lawyer in India supporting forest-dwelling communities. She has an LLM from UC Berkeley as a Fulbright Nehru Fellow and a BSL LLB from ILS Law College, Pune.

Willem Daniël Lubbe is a senior lecturer at North-West University, Faculty of Law, South Africa. He specializes in environmental law with a specific focus on regional biodiversity law, wildlife crimes, protected areas, and the law–science interface.

Sandrine Maljean-Dubois is a Directeur de Recherche (senior researcher) at the CNRS. She teaches international and European environmental law at the Faculty of Law and Political Sciences at Aix-Marseille University (France). Her research focus is on international environmental law, in particular on biodiversity and climate change law. She is the author of several books and numerous articles on these topics. During the summer of 2019, she lectured at the Hague Academy of International Law on the topic 'International law and biodiversity' (Collected Courses, Brill/Martinus Nijhoff, 2020, vol 407, forthcoming publication in English). She serves as a member of the IUCN World Commission on Environmental Law.

Elizabeth Maruma Mrema is the executive secretary of the UN's Convention on Biological Diversity (CBD). She is a Tanzanian lawyer and diplomat who worked for the UN Environment Programme (UNEP) for more than two decades, as director of the law division and deputy director of the ecosystem division. On 31 March, she was awarded the 2022 Kew International Medal. From 2009 to 2012, she served as the Executive Secretary of the UNEP/Secretariat of the Convention on the Conservation of Migratory Species of Wild Animals and as the Acting Executive Secretary of the UNEP/ASCOBANS (Agreement on the Conservation of Small Cetaceans of the Baltic, North East Atlantic, Irish and North Seas) as well as Interim Executive Secretary of the UNEP/Gorilla Agreement, all based in Bonn, Germany. Before joining UNEP, she worked with United Republic of Tanzania's Ministry of Foreign Affairs and International Cooperation.

Elisa Morgera is a Professor of Global Environmental Law at the University of Strathclyde Law School, Glasgow, UK. She specializes in international biodiversity law and its linkages with human rights, notably the rights of indigenous peoples and small-scale fishing communities, everyone's right to health and science, and business responsibility to respect human rights. She is the director of the One Ocean Hub, a global inter-disciplinary research collaboration of research institutions that is pioneering research on human rights and the marine environment with a view to better connecting marine and social sciences, and the arts, to support fair and inclusive decision-making for a healthy ocean whereby people and planet flourish.

Frederic Perron-Welch is a Doctoral Fellow at the Grotius Centre for International Legal Studies at Leiden Law School, Visiting Fellow at the United Nations Research Institute for Social Development (UNRISD), and member of the IUCN World Commission on Environmental Law. He has been involved in international biodiversity negotiations since 2009, representing intergovernmental, private sector, and civil society organizations. He serves on the board of the Canadian Branch of the International Law Association and served on the ILA Committee on the Role of International Law in Sustainable Natural Resources Management for Development from 2015 to 2020. He was called to the Bar of Ontario in 2011.

Jona Razzaque is a Professor of Environmental Law at Bristol Law School, University of the West of England (UWE Bristol, UK) and a barrister. Her research focuses on environmental law in the global south, natural resource governance, and environmental justice. She acted as a Coordinating Lead Author of the IPBES Global Assessment on Biodiversity and Ecosystem Services (2019). She is a member of the Advisory Board of the Journal of Environmental Law and serves as a member of the IUCN World Commission on Environmental Law. She has published extensively on participatory rights, biodiversity conservation, nature protection law, ecosystem services, water management, and forest conservation.

Hendrik Schoukens is a Professor of Environmental Law at the Department of European, Public and International Law of Ghent University. He received his PhD, which focused on the legal aspects of eco-restoration within EU law, in 2017 (Ghent University). In 2016, he co-edited a handbook on the EU Habitats Directive and frequently publishes on EU nature conservation law, access to justice, and climate change. He is a practising lawyer at the Bar of Brussels, where he represents NGOs in strategic lawsuits in the realm of environmental governance. Hendrik is city councillor competent for the environment and urban planning.

William J Snape, III is a Professor, assistant dean for adjunct faculty, and director of the Program on Environmental and Energy Law at American University's Washington College of Law. He is also a senior counsel with the Center for Biological Diversity, a non-profit advocacy group. He has authored numerous articles on natural resource conservation. Snape is also general counsel of the Board for the US Climate Action Network and is President of US CAN's political action arm. He received his BA in History *magna cum laude* from the Honors College at the University of California, Los Angeles, and his JD from George Washington University.

Paul Stookes is a solicitor-advocate at Richard Buxton Solicitors specializing in environmental law. He is also the Law and Policy Advisor at the UK Environmental Law Association (UKELA) working on law reform. Paul also lectures part-time at the Open University, the University of Hertfordshire, City University, and is currently supervising UK-wide climate emergency research linking international law and human rights. He sits on the Professional Standards Committee of the Institute of Environmental Management and Assessment (IEMA) and is a lead assessor for IEMA's Full Member and Chartered Environmentalist programme. He is an experienced mediator and publishes widely and regularly. He has been involved in a number of leading environmental cases in the UK and Europe.

Chris Tollefson is a Professor of Law at the University of Victoria. He is the founding executive director of the Pacific Centre for Environmental Law and Litigation (CELL), Canada's only charity devoted to training aspiring public interest environmental litigators. He is also founding principal at Tollefson Law, a litigation boutique that represents indigenous and public interest clients. He served for fifteen years as a director of Ecojustice, including four years as Chair and national President. Chris publishes on a range of environmental and resource law topics including species at risk, resource management and governance, contaminated sites, and SLAPPs (Strategic Lawsuits Against Public Participation).

Ella Vines is a PhD candidate at the University of Melbourne, researching legal pathways to halt or phase out coal extraction and consumption in Australia. She holds an LLM from the University of Melbourne, an LLB from Deakin University, and a Diploma of Languages (Indonesian), and is admitted as a barrister and solicitor of the Supreme Court of Victoria. Prior to commencing her PhD, she worked as a commercial lawyer in litigation and dispute resolution and business and not-for-profit structuring. In 2022, Ella was appointed as a Melbourne Law School Teaching Fellow, teaching Global Human Rights Law.

Margaret A Young is a Professor at the University of Melbourne and a Fellow of the Australian Academy of Law. Her award-winning research has included recognition from the International Union for Conservation of Nature (IUCN) Academy of Environmental Law Junior Scholar Prize in 2012 and a Certificate of Merit from the American Society of International Law in 2019. Admitted as a barrister and solicitor, Margaret is a former associate to the Chief Justice of the Federal Court of Australia. She holds a PhD and an LLM from the University of Cambridge and a BA/LLB (Hons) from the University of Melbourne.

Mingzhe Zhu works at Law Faculty of the University of Antwerp (Belgium) as a Senior Postdoctoral Researcher. He obtained his PhD in Law from Sciences Po de Paris in 2015 and works as a historian and philosopher of law. Mingzhe's primary line of research focuses on the relation between political authority, society, and nature in the Anthropocene, with particular attention to contesting power imbalance and social inequality in environmental governance. He teaches various courses, including Legal Philosophy, Chinese Legal History, Comparative Law, and Law & Ecology in several Chinese and European universities.

1
Introduction
Setting the Scene

Guillaume Futhazar, Sandrine Maljean-Dubois, and Jona Razzaque

1. Introduction

In 2020, the cognitive dissonance of environmental governance was made painfully clear. At the same time that the pandemic shed light on the disastrous and direct consequences of environmental degradation for the well-being of humans worldwide,[1] environmental exploitation and mismanagement nevertheless continued, mostly in a ruinous 'business as usual' fashion.[2]

The most recent edition of the Global Biodiversity Outlook is clear: 'none of the Aichi Biodiversity Targets[3] will be fully met'.[4] This assessment is unfortunately similar to the outcome of the 2002 Strategic Plan for the Convention on Biological Diversity (CBD)[5] that ended in 2010 on the same observation.[6] These failures are not uncommon in international environmental law, and the field inevitably carries a sense of pessimism. It is now a truism to point out that the exponential growth of this branch of international law stands in stark

[1] In October 2020, the Intergovernmental Science-Policy Platform on Biodiversity and Ecosystem Services (IPBES) issued a special report highlighting the links between biodiversity loss and the occurrence of pandemics. IPBES, *IPBES Workshop on Biodiversity and Pandemics Executive Summary* (IPBES 2020).

[2] This state of affairs was highlighted with stark words by the UN Secretary-General during a speech at Columbia University in December 2020: 'The state of the planet is broken', 'Humanity is Waging War Against Nature' ... such were the words used by António Guterres on this occasion. <www.un.org/en/climatechange/un-secretary-general-speaks-state-planet> accessed 9 March 2022.

[3] CBD, Decision X/2, The Strategic Plan for Biodiversity 2011–2020 and the Aichi Biodiversity Targets (2010).

[4] Secretariat of the Convention on Biological Diversity, *Global Biodiversity Outlook 5—Summary for Policy Makers* (2020) 4. The Aichi Targets were a set of objectives to be met by 2020 in order to ensure the conservation and sustainable use of biodiversity worldwide.

[5] Convention on Biological Diversity (opened for signature 5 June 1992, entered into force 29 December 1993) 1760 UNTS 79. For the 2010 plan, see CBD, Decision VI/26, Strategic Plan for the Convention on Biological Diversity (2002).

[6] CBD, UNEP/CBD/COP/10/8, Implementation of the Convention and the Strategic Plan and Progress Towards the 2010 Biodiversity Target (2010) §85.

Guillaume Futhazar, Sandrine Maljean-Dubois, and Jona Razzaque, *Introduction* In: *Biodiversity Litigation*. Edited by: Guillaume Futhazar, Sandrine Maljean-Dubois, and Jona Razzaque, Oxford University Press. © Guillaume Futhazar, Sandrine Maljean-Dubois, and Jona Razzaque, 2023. DOI: 10.1093/oso/9780192865465.003.0001

contrast to the factual situation. In many ways, international environmental law is fraught with unfulfilled promises.

But necessity is the mother of invention. And we have witnessed legal developments in the past years that have the potential to facilitate better implementation of international environmental law.[7]

For instance, at the global level there are ongoing and concerted efforts to improve the overall effectiveness of international biodiversity law (IBL).[8] As we enter the new decade, several multilateral environmental agreements will have landmark conferences of the parties (COPs) paving the way for the future of IBL. The most important of which being arguably the fifteenth COP of the CBD—which was postponed several times due to the pandemic and is now scheduled for the fourth quarter of 2022—which intends to set the tone for the next decade of international efforts for the conservation and sustainable use of biodiversity. A new 'post 2020' framework is expected to be endorsed for this purpose,[9] potentially cementing the coherence and synergies of this field as did the previous strategic plan.[10]

In some ways, this current trajectory for global biodiversity governance is akin to the momentum that preceded the adoption of the Paris Agreement in 2015.[11] In the years leading up to its adoption, there was consensus on the shortcomings of the current climate regime on the necessity to advance it further by establishing a new and better suited legal framework. The adoption of such a framework was seen as a diplomatic success[12] and welcomed with cautious optimism by observers.[13]

[7] These innovations are carefully monitored by institutions working in the field of environmental conservation and sustainable development. See eg UN Environment, *Global Environment Outlook 6 Summary for Policy Makers* (CUP 2019) 17–18.

[8] In the context of this project, we understand International Biodiversity Law as 'the branch of international law that comprises all of the rules related to biodiversity (the variability among living organisms from all sources and the ecological complexes of which they are part)'. This introduction will expand on this definition in the first section.

[9] CBD, CBD/WG2020/3/3, First Draft of the Post-2020 Global Biodiversity Framework (2021), 'Note by the Co-Chairs'.

[10] Guillaume Futhazar, 'The Diffusion of the Strategic Plan for Biodiversity and its Aichi Biodiversity Targets Within the Biodiversity Cluster. An Illustration of Current Trends in the Global Governance of Biodiversity and Ecosystems' (2014) 35 Yearbook of International Environmental Law 133.

[11] Paris Agreement (opened for signature 12 December 2015, entered into force 4 November 2016) UNTS I-54113.

[12] Fiona Harvey, 'Paris Climate Change Agreement: The World's Greatest Diplomatic Success', *The Guardian* (London, 14 December 2015).

[13] This can be seen in the articles that followed the adoption of the agreement. See eg Annalisa Savaresi, 'The Paris Agreement: A New Beginning?' (2016) 34 Journal of Energy & Natural Resources Law 16; Jorge Viñuales, 'The Paris Agreement on Climate Change: Less is More' (2017) 59 German Yearbook of International Law 12. This feeling soon faded as the assessments on GHG emissions and states' commitments highlighted that we were not on track to meet the objectives. UNEP, *Emissions Gap Report 2020* (2020).

However, if one is to compare the future development of international biodiversity law with what happened in the climate regime, then the outcomes do not look promising. Evidently, the Paris Agreement has become a central instrument to strengthen the global response to the threat of climate change. Policymakers worldwide will generally incorporate references to climate change mitigation and/or adaptation in their decisions, projects, and programmes.[14] Yet, despite this centrality in the political discourse, the recent global assessments show that the concentration of greenhouse gas (GHG) is still on the rise.[15] Without radical and swift change, the very purpose of the climate regime is unlikely to be met.[16] If the climate regime is failing to meet its objective, why would it be any different for the biodiversity regime?

One has to keep in mind that the management of global environmental problems is not only dealt through international legal instruments and institutions; innovative solutions can come from other actors and at different levels. In the case of climate change mitigation and adaptation, judges are increasingly contributing to counterbalance the discrepancy between the international commitments of states and their lacklustre implementation.[17]

The year 2019 offered a spectacular illustration of this role with the final act of the Urgenda saga.[18] Here, the Dutch Supreme Court interpreted the national and international commitments of the Netherlands through the prism of international climate law and issued a decision compelling the Dutch state to reduce its GHGs by at least 25 per cent by 2020. To reach this conclusion, the United Nations Framework Convention on Climate Change (UNFCCC) and its protocols, its COP decisions, and the reports of the Intergovernmental Panel on Climate Change all came to bear on how to interpret and implement the articles of the European Convention on Human Rights. The Urgenda case

[14] eg climate change is mentioned on numerous occasions in the documents produced for the ongoing reform for the EU Common Agricultural Policy. See, inter alia, Regulation (EU) 2020/2220 of the European Parliament and of the Council of 23 December 2020 laying down certain transitional provisions for support from the European Agricultural Fund for Rural Development (EAFRD) and from the European Agricultural Guarantee Fund (EAGF) in the years 2021 and 2022.

[15] IPCC, *Global Warming of 1.5°C. An IPCC Special Report 2018: Summary for Policymakers* (2018); UNEP Nairobi, *Emissions Gap Report 2021: The Heat Is On—A World of Climate Promises Not Yet Delivered* (2021).

[16] Paris Agreement, art 2: 'This Agreement, in enhancing the implementation of the Convention, including its objective, aims to strengthen the global response to the threat of climate change, in the context of sustainable development and efforts to eradicate poverty, including by: (a) Holding the increase in the global average temperature to well below 2°C above pre-industrial levels and pursuing efforts to limit the temperature increase to 1.5°C above pre-industrial levels, recognizing that this would significantly reduce the risks and impacts of climate change.'

[17] Matthias Petel, 'Analyse de l'usage stratégique des droits humains au sein du contentieux climatique contre les États' (2020) MPIL Research Paper Series No 2020-33.

[18] Supreme Court of the Netherlands, Judgment19/00135 of 20 December 2019.

is but the 'spectacular' tip of the iceberg of a legal trend that has been ongoing for several years.[19] These numerous cases indicate that the developments that occurred at the global level for the mitigation of climate change are correlated with a rise in the number of legal disputes concerning climate change. We also witness an emerging trend of cases where international developments on climate change have been used as part of the arguments of the claimants and the reasoning of the judges.[20] Indeed, the Paris Agreement, thanks to the involvement of civil society, has provided fuel for climate litigation in a decisive manner and offered national courts the opportunity to position themselves as key players of climate governance.[21]

This development is a welcome one. It opens up new means to act for civil society, which in recent years has shown a growing, massive, rejuvenated, and sometimes even radicalized mobilization to defend the environment—one that can help to defeat the general feeling of pessimism that stems from the obvious 'reality schism' that is at play in the field of international environmental law.[22] In some circumstances, judges are utilizing the connections that allow international environmental law to overcome its structural ineffectiveness. Judges can link the national and the global levels by allowing international environmental law to permeate, explicitly or implicitly, their reasoning and decisions. They can also influence other judges, thus pushing for converging approaches on this matter.[23] And, most importantly, they often have the ability to deliver decisions that will actually bind states or compel individuals to act.

[19] The Sabin Center for Climate Change Law has been referencing these cases for several years now. See <https://climate.law.columbia.edu/> accessed 9 March 2022. Some authors have argued that the cases referenced by the Sabin Center are only but a fraction of the cases that might have an impact on climate change. On this question of framing, see Kim Bouwer, 'The Unsexy Future of Climate Change Litigation' (2018) 30 Journal of Environmental Law 483.

[20] eg in recent cases of civil disobedience in Switzerland and France, the parties invoked the international commitments of the states, and their subsequent failure to act, as a justification for their action. See Saskia Stucki, 'In Defence of Green Civil Disobedience Judicial Courage in the Face of Climate Crisis and State Inaction' (2020) Verfassunblog <https://verfassungsblog.de/in-defence-of-green-civil-disobedience/> accessed 30 October 2020.

[21] Sandrine Maljean-Dubois, 'Climate Litigation: The Impact of the Paris Agreement in National Courts' (2022) Taiwan Law Review 211–12; Anna-Julia Saiger, 'Domestic Courts and the Paris Agreement's Climate Goals: The Need for a Comparative Approach' (2020) 9(1) Transnational Environmental Law 37–54; Lys Kulamadayil, 'Between Activism and Complacency: International Law Perspectives on European Climate Litigation' (2021) 10(5) European Society of International Law Reflections 1–7.

[22] Stefan Aykut and Amy Dahan, *Gouverner le climat 20 ans de négociation internationale* (Presses de Sciences Po 2015) 399

[23] In the Urgenda case, the Urgenda Foundation made several references to other cases in its arguments. The same approach can be observed in currently ongoing disputes in France. See *L'Affaire du Siècle*, written pleadings <https://laffairedusiecle.net/argumentaire-memoire-complementaire/> accessed 9 March 2022 and Judgment of the Paris Administrative Court, Case Nos 1904967, 1904968, 1904972, 1904976/4-1, 14 October 2021.

This edited volume draws from this observation and seeks to ask similar questions with regard to biodiversity. If the rise of climate change litigation is correlated with the development of international climate law, can we find a biodiversity litigation correlated with the development of international biodiversity law?

Surprisingly, this question has not, to our knowledge, been explored in a systematic way by legal scholarship. That is not to say that the topic of environment and the courts is an unexplored one, far from it.[24] But a glance at the available literature shows that the focus is mainly articulated around two main lines of questioning:[25] either climate change before the courts, or the environment, as a whole, before the courts. In the case of climate change, obstacles and litigation strategies are explored,[26] while scholarship on the environment focuses on the practices of judges when dealing with environmental matters and also on how this topic might have reshaped procedures (expertise, evidence, legal standing, and so on).[27]

Yet, biodiversity has unique characteristics that warrant a more specific investigation as a topic of legal scholarship.

First, biodiversity combines spatial scales in a remarkable way. Elements of biodiversity may exist only locally, yet the conservation of biodiversity as a whole is simultaneously considered as a common concern of mankind.[28] In other words, the loss of a species located in the confines of a single state will be considered a loss for the entirety of the international community. This interplay between local and global stands in contrast with climate which is by its very nature global and less tangible.

Also, in comparison to climate change law, international biodiversity law is far older and denser.[29] It has therefore had many more opportunities to influence litigation in different contexts.

[24] For recent examples see the edited volumes by Christina Voigt (ed), *International Judicial Practice on the Environment: Questions of Legitimacy* (CUP 2019) and *Courts and the Environment* (Edward Elgar 2018).

[25] Of course, exceptions to these two trends exist. See eg the Claws and Laws project that focuses specifically on the conservation of large carnivores: <www.clawsandlaws.eu/> accessed 9 March 2022.

[26] A summary of the debates can be found in the last UNEP report on the topic, UNEP, *Global Climate Litigation Report: 2020 Status Review* (2021).

[27] eg Eve Truilhé-Marengo (ed), La relation juge-expert dans les contentieux sanitaires et environnementaux (La Documentation Française 2012); Mathilde Hautereau-Boutonnet and Ève Truilhé (eds), *Le procès environnemental. Du procès sur l'environnement au procès pour l'environnement* (Dalloz 2021); Hendrik Schoukens, 'Access to Justice Before EU Courts in Environmental Cases Against the Backdrop of the Aarhus Convention Balancing Pathological Stubbornness and Cognitive Dissonance?' in Voigt (n 24) 74.

[28] Preamble to the CBD.

[29] This characteristic of international biodiversity will be further explored in Section 2.

Moreover, biodiversity is inherently dynamic and complex. Our knowledge of the topic never ceases to evolve, and so does our realization of the remaining knowledge gaps.[30] This scientific uncertainty is paired with a plurality of socio-cultural values associated with biodiversity, making an objective and decontextualized approach to the field both problematic and impossible.[31] The fleeting nature of biodiversity makes it difficult to be seized by law. It does not fare well with the notion of legal certainty[32] and calls for appropriate legal and conceptual innovation in order to achieve adequate conservation and sustainable use.[33]

To summarize, the purpose of this edited volume is twofold. First, we seek to identify what we label as 'biodiversity litigation'. To do so, we will follow a comparative approach in order to understand its trends in different contexts and reframe it in the more general context of environmental litigation. Secondly, we also want to understand how international biodiversity law might have influenced biodiversity litigation. Understanding this correlation will help us to better grasp the full impact of international biodiversity law on states and will suggest paths to improve its overall effectiveness.

Doing so requires that several elements be defined with more precision in this introduction.

To this end, the next section will focus on explaining our understanding of international biodiversity law in the context of this project. We will highlight how this branch of international law is far-reaching both in terms of topics and in terms of temporality. This section will discuss the current centrality of the CBD for IBL as a whole and the unfortunate lack of effectiveness of this branch.

Section 3 will then turn to biodiversity litigation as a potential tool for tackling this lack of effectiveness. The section will define biodiversity litigation by taking the concepts of the CBD as a point of reference in order to identify what may actually be covered by such legal disputes. It will highlight that biodiversity litigation can refer to disputes concerning the conservation of biodiversity, the sustainable use of biodiversity, and/or access and benefit sharing.

Finally, Section 4 will present the methodology we have chosen to answer our research questions. Specifically, we will discuss the rationale for the

[30] See Intergovernmental Science Policy Platform on Biodiversity and Ecosystem Services, *Global Assessment Report on Biodiversity and Ecosystem Services* (2019).

[31] On the downfalls of claimed objectivity in environmental governance, see Douglas A. Kysar, *Regulating from Nowhere: Environmental Law and the Search for Objectivity* (Yale UP 2001).

[32] Being roughly understood here as the clarity, accessibility, and predictability of law. For more insight on this notion, see Mark Fenwick, Mathias Siems, and Stefan Wrbka (eds), *The Shifting Meaning of Legal Certainty in Comparative and Transnational Law* (Hart 2017).

[33] On these numerous innovations, see eg Elisa Morgera and Jona Razzaque (eds), *Biodiversity and Nature Protection Law* (Edward Elgar 2017).

selection of our case studies and expose the set of questions that our contributing authors have been asked to answer and to explain their relevance for our investigation.

2. International Biodiversity Law: A Broad and Far-Reaching Field

The section will start by presenting our definition of international biodiversity law for the purpose of this edited volume (2.1). It will then discuss the emergence of this branch of international law by explaining how something as local as biodiversity nevertheless became the subject of international cooperation and regulation (2.2). Unfortunately, international biodiversity law suffers from a clear lack of effectiveness, particularly regarding its implementation at the national level. In this context, we postulate that biodiversity litigation could help to achieve a better implementation of international biodiversity law (2.3).

2.1 The Heterogeneity of International Biodiversity Law

We understand international biodiversity law as the branch of international law that comprises all of the rules related to biodiversity (defined as the variability among living organisms from all sources and the ecological complexes of which they are a part).[34]

This seemingly obvious, even tautological, definition is less straightforward than it seems once we start to unpack it. Indeed, this understanding implies several layers, both thematic and temporal.

International biodiversity law comprises international instruments that predate the global consecration of the notion of biodiversity. In other words, what we refer to as being international biodiversity law is uncorrelated with the history of biodiversity as a scientific notion.[35] Indeed, several international agreements managed or protected biodiversity, at least partially, even before

[34] We draw this understanding of biodiversity from art 2 of the CBD.

[35] For a brief overview of the history of this notion, see Patrick Blandin, 'La diversité du vivant avant (et après) la biodiversité: repères historiques et épistémologiques' in Elena Casetta and Julien Delord (eds), *La biodiversité en question* (Editions Matériologiques 2014); Sandrine Maljean-Dubois, *Le droit international de la biodiversité* (Brill/Martinus Nijhoff 2021); Désirée McGraw, 'The Story of the Biodiversity Convention: from Negotiation to Implementation' in Philippe Leprestre (ed), *Governing Global Biodiversity: The Evolution and Implementation of the Convention on Biological Diversity* (Ashgate 2004) 7.

the concept of biodiversity became a staple of environmental governance. We can mention, for instance, the Washington Convention on International Trade in Endangered Species of Wild Fauna and Flora (CITES) adopted in 1973,[36] the Ramsar Convention on Wetlands of International Importance Especially as Waterfowl Habitat adopted in 1971,[37] or the Bonn Convention on the Conservation of Migratory Species of Wild Animals.[38] These instruments continue to play an important role today for the conservation and sustainable use of biodiversity,[39] alongside the more recent ones that rely explicitly on the notion of biological diversity.[40]

Thematically, international biodiversity law is not strictly limited to conservation and sustainable use. It also refers to all rules that have a direct impact on biodiversity. Because of the all-encompassing nature of biodiversity, these rules are abundant. One can mention international rules on fishing, hunting, and biosafety, but also the access to genetic resources and the sharing of the benefits arising out of their utilization. In this respect, international biodiversity law sits at the intersection of numerous regimes such as international trade, investment, or human rights. Consequently, the boundaries of international biodiversity law are inherently blurry. But this blurriness is a common characteristic in a global environmental landscape that is both dense and complex.

Thus conceived, international biodiversity law is a broad field with an abundance of international instruments, both binding and soft. It is, moreover, still a scattered area, the conceptualization of which is at an early stage.

2.2 The Convention on Biological Diversity as the Compass of IBL

International biodiversity law was built in a scattered and disconnected fashion. The first IBL treaties concerned specific species or areas and only engaged a limited number of states. For instance, the 1902 Convention for the Protection

[36] Convention on International Trade in Endangered Species of Wild Fauna and Flora (opened for signature 3 March 1973, entered into force 1 July 1975) 993 UNTS 243.

[37] Convention on Wetlands of International Importance Especially as Waterfowl Habitat (opened for signature 2 February 1971, entered into force 21 December 1975) 996 UNTS 245.

[38] Convention on the Conservation of Migratory Species of Wild Animals (opened for signature 23 June 1979, entered into force 1 November 1983) 1651 UNTS 333.

[39] eg in 2019 the parties to the Ramsar Convention adopted a resolution on the 'Restoration of Degraded Peatlands to Mitigate and Adapt to Climate Change and Enhance Biodiversity and Disaster Risk Reduction' (Resolution XIII.13). The theme of this resolution illustrates how the convention can contribute to the achievement of the goals of more recent multilateral environmental agreements.

[40] eg the International Treaty on Plant Genetic Resources for Food and Agriculture (opened for signature 3 November 2001, entered into force 29 June 2004) 2400 UNTS 303.

of Birds Useful to Agriculture[41] had ten signatories from Europe and aimed at the protection of certain species only because of their instrumental value. The 1936 Convention relative to the Preservation of Fauna and Flora in their Natural State[42] only sought to establish national parks in Africa at a time when the continent was still mainly under colonial domination.

As our conceptions evolved and our knowledge improved, states became involved in numerous regional and global conventions protecting certain species, groups of species, and natural areas. CITES and the Ramsar Convention, mentioned earlier, are representative of this broader approach. The 1979 Bonn Convention on the Conservation of Migratory Species of Wild Animals (CMS), also mentioned above, is similarly illustrative of a systemic understanding of biodiversity rather than a fragmented one.

This progressive broadening of the scope culminated in the adoption of the Convention on Biological Diversity in 1992, which has become, to some extent, the cornerstone of this body of law. With 196 parties, it is the only convention covering all species and all activities throughout the planet. It is an omnibus convention for 'all life on Earth'. The Convention has three explicit objectives that reflect what earlier instruments sought to achieve but in a less comprehensive way: the conservation of biological diversity, the sustainable use of its components, and the fair and equitable sharing of the benefits arising out of the utilization of genetic resources (often referred to as 'access and benefit sharing').[43] To this end, it contains numerous obligations, most of which are tempered by the expression 'as far as possible and as appropriate'. This phrasing makes the CBD a relatively weak legal instrument in terms of binding power.[44]

The CBD is supplemented by various protocols. In 2000, the parties adopted the Cartagena Protocol on biosafety in 2000,[45] itself supplemented by the Nagoya–Kuala Lumpur Supplementary Protocol on Liability and Redress in

[41] Convention for the Protection of Birds Useful to Agriculture, 19 March 1902 (accessible online at <www.ecolex.org>).

[42] Convention Relative to the Preservation of Fauna and Flora in their Natural State, 8 November 1933 (accessible online at <www.ecolex.org>).

[43] We use both terms interchangeably throughout this introduction.

[44] As stressed by the International Court of Justice in 2015 when it declared that art 14 of the CBD on impact assessment 'does not create an obligation to carry out an environmental impact assessment before undertaking an activity that may have significant adverse effects on biological diversity'. See *Certain Activities Carried Out by Nicaragua in the Border Area* (*Costa Rica v Nicaragua*) and *Construction of a Road in Costa Rica along the San Juan River (Nicaragua v Costa Rica)*, Judgment [2015] ICJ Rep 665, para 164.

[45] Cartagena Protocol on Biosafety to the Convention on Biological Diversity (opened for signature 29 January 2000, entered into force 11 September 2003) 2226 UNTS 208.

2010.[46] The same year, the parties also adopted the Nagoya Protocol on Access to Genetic Resources and the Fair and Equitable Sharing of Benefits Arising from their Utilization.[47] Additionally, the CBD is complemented by a wealth of COP decisions that thicken[48] its normative framework. On its own, the CBD system is thus already highly complex.

Unlike the two other conventions adopted following the 1992 Rio Conference,[49] the CBD arrived in an already crowded legal field. As mentioned earlier, several IBL treaties were in force at that time. Yet, during the negotiation for the CBD the consensus was that the existing international rules were insufficient to curb extinctions and that a new tool was needed to strengthen cooperation and, above all, to link all the pre-existing regimes.[50] To ensure proper legal coexistence, article 22 of the CBD states that its provisions 'shall not affect the rights and obligations of any Contracting Party deriving from any existing international agreement, except where the exercise of those rights and obligations would cause a serious damage or threat to biological diversity'.

The adoption of the CBD did not mean that the earlier conventions had lost their *raison d'être*. The text of the Convention remains very general in its content and is only weakly normative. The other instruments, past and future, thus complement it with more precise and more suited provisions with a narrower scope *ratione loci* and/or *ratione materiae*.

This intricate framework where the CBD coexists with a multitude of other treaties forms a 'regime complex'[51]—a network of international regimes that relate to a common subject matter, exhibit overlapping membership, and generate substantive interaction.[52] In this legal constellation, the CBD appears as a legal and political backbone that sets the tone for biodiversity governance and influences the development of other treaties. As such, even though IBL

[46] Nagoya–Kuala Lumpur Supplementary Protocol on Liability and Redress to the Cartagena Protocol on Biosafety (opened for signature 15 October 2010, entered into force 5 March 2018) UNTS A-30619.

[47] Nagoya Protocol on Access to Genetic Resources and the Fair and Equitable Sharing of Benefits Arising from their Utilization to the Convention on Biological Diversity (opened for signature 29 October 2010, entered into force 12 October 2014) UNTS A-30619.

[48] Annecoos Wieserma, 'The New International Law-Makers? Conferences of the Parties to Multilateral Environmental Agreements' (2009) 31 Michigan Journal of International Law 231.

[49] United Nations Framework Convention on Climate Change (opened for signature 9 May 1992, entered into force 21 March 1994) 1171 UNTS 107; United Nations Convention to Combat Desertification in those Countries Experiencing Serious Drought and/or Desertification, Particularly in Africa (opened for signature 14 October 1994, entered into force 21 December 1996) 1954 UNTS 3.

[50] See UNEP/Bio.Div.1/3, Report of the Ad Hoc Working Group on the work of its first session (1988).

[51] On this notion, see, inter alia, Amandine Orsini, Jean-Frédéric Morin, and Oran Young, 'Regime Complexes: A Buzz, a Boom, or a Boost for Global Governance?' (2013) 19 Global Governance 27.

[52] ibid 29.

cannot and should not be reduced to the CBD as its sole representative, the Convention is currently the driving conceptual force of this branch.

The architects of the CBD also intend it to have an impact on non-environmental regimes.[53] It was expected that the objectives, principles, and standards of the CBD would become commonly agreed references. Indeed, this outreach is crucial as several drivers of biodiversity decline are dealt with by specialized regimes that are not part of IBL per se (climate change, chemicals, urbanization, transport, armed conflicts, trade, etc).

From this point of view—ie the mainstreaming of biodiversity issues—the strategic plan adopted in 2010 by the COP of the CBD, which defines a set of strategic objectives known as the 'Aichi Targets',[54] has been a real success at the international level. Its adoption represented a concrete step forward, effectively allowing a strategic refocusing of conventional activities around the Aichi Targets.[55] The Convention, which had hitherto been rather marginalized in international governance,[56] was able to assert itself further. Indeed, the United Nations Environment Programme (UNEP) supported the implementation of the targets, considering them to be 'an important global policy framework for reversing the ongoing decline in biodiversity and ecosystem services'. The strategic framework has subsequently been adopted by the other conventions related to biodiversity and ecosystems.[57] But its influence goes far beyond the biodiversity cluster,[58] since the Rio + 20 Conference also built on these objectives. Biodiversity and ecosystems do indeed occupy a major place in the UN Sustainable Development Goals (SDGs) and associated targets, in particular SDGs 14 (marine biodiversity) and 15 (terrestrial biodiversity), but also as a cross-cutting issue in most of the SDGs.[59]

To summarize, while IBL emerged in a fragmented way, the adoption of the CBD added a centre of gravity to this branch of international law. While the

[53] As illustrated by the numerous COP decisions on cooperation with other sectors. Eg CBD, Decision 14/3, Mainstreaming of biodiversity in the energy and mining, infrastructure, manufacturing and processing sectors (2018).

[54] CBD, Decision X/2, The Strategic Plan for Biodiversity 2011–2020 and the Aichi Biodiversity Targets (2010).

[55] Futhazar (n 10).

[56] ibid. The 2002 Strategic Plan had met explicit resistance from the permanent bodies of other biodiversity-related convention. UNEP, *International Environmental Governance*, Report of the Executive Director, UNEP/IGM/1/2 (3 April 2001).

[57] ibid.

[58] The group of self-identified conventions that focus mainly on biodiversity matter. See UNEP-WCMC, *Promoting Synergies Within the Cluster of Biodiversity-related Environmental Multilateral Agreements* (2012).

[59] CBD, FAO, The World Bank, UNEP, and UNDP, 'Biodiversity and the 2030 Agenda for Sustainable Development: Technical Note' (2017) <www.cbd.int/development/doc/biodiversity-2030-agenda-technical-note-en.pdf> accessed 9 March 2022.

CBD itself is not the most relevant instrument in terms of binding and specific rules, its influence within and outside IBL illustrates that it has become an important conceptual pillar.

This dynamic development of IBL stands in stark contrast with the current biodiversity crisis.

2.3 The Ineffectiveness of IBL in a Context of Global Biodiversity Crisis

At first glance, the biodiversity crisis may seem less global than the threat posed by climate change. Why should, for instance, the disappearance of a local species be considered a global threat? Such an understanding ignores two key characteristics of biodiversity: first, the vital interconnections between its elements and, secondly, the numerous equally vital contributions that biodiversity brings to human beings.

On the first characteristic, one has to keep in mind that biological diversity covers the diversity of life, from fauna and flora to bacteria, genes, and ecosystems including all ordinary biodiversity made up of common and not necessarily remarkable organisms. Thus, biodiversity is evaluated and measured from the macro to the micro, at different levels (genes, species, ecosystems) and on different scales (biocenosis, landscape, biosphere). It is therefore a unifying concept. Thinking about biodiversity and no longer 'wildlife' or 'nature' leads to a change of perspective, a more detailed and encompassing one. From this perspective, elements of biodiversity are connected, and the loss of one element can have consequences for the system of which it was part. With less biological diversity, these systems are less resilient to changes and shocks and may therefore collapse. Currently, this risk of collapse is high for the entirety of biological diversity. As highlighted by Johan Rockström and others,[60] the level of biological diversity can be considered as a planetary boundary which, when reached, leaves humanity in an unsafe 'operating space'. In a world with a too low degree of biological diversity, humanity is threatened.

These risks come from the fact that humanity benefits from numerous services—commonly referred to as ecosystem services[61]—that are provided by biological diversity. For instance, pollination is crucial for agriculture—and, by

[60] Johan Rockström and others, 'A Safe Operating Space for Humanity' (2009) 461 Nature 472.

[61] On this notion, see the TEEB Initiatives (The Economics of Ecosystems and Biodiversity): <http://teebweb.org/> accessed 9 March 2022.

extension, food security—and is made possible by biological diversity (ie the existence of numerous pollinators).[62] These ecosystem services cannot all be replaced and may disappear if the decline of biological diversity continues. If such were the case, it is uncertain whether human societies would be resilient enough to withstand the effects of such an event.[63]

If we compare the impressive development of international biodiversity law, which began more than a century ago, to the worsening state of biodiversity regularly described in environmental reports,[64] it is obvious that the proliferation of rules has not led to the intended outcome. Admittedly, international biodiversity law has led to an increase in international cooperation among states. However, most of the rules and instruments defined at the international level must be implemented at the national level and then applied locally. Despite the efforts of various COPs to promote it, international biodiversity law still suffers from a lack of implementation at the domestic level.

The parties to multilateral environmental agreement are often under the obligation to provide periodic reports on the local implementation of their international commitments.[65] These reports are self-assessments and therefore should not be read uncritically. For instance, the observations of NGOs and international organizations may differ vastly. Nevertheless, even these reports highlight that IBL instruments suffer from a lack of implementation at the local level. For instance, the progress report from the CMS has stressed that more effort is needed in some countries to establish an appropriate governance framework for the conservation of migratory species.[66] The latest progress report for the implementation of the Ramsar Convention on Wetlands paints a sombre picture with regard to implementation,[67] while the Standing Committee of CITES highlights that a significant number of parties still have an inappropriate legislative framework for the implementation of the convention.[68]

[62] IPBES, *Assessment Report on Pollinators, Pollination and Food Production* (2016).

[63] The Millennium Ecosystem Assessment had already highlighted in 2005 that many of these services were in decline. All the volumes of the Millennium Ecosystem Assessments are available online: <www.millenniumassessment.org/> accessed 9 March 2022.

[64] IPBES, Global Assessment Report on Biodiversity and Ecosystem Services (2019); Sandra Diaz and others, 'Pervasive Human-Driven Decline of Life on Earth Points to the Need for Transformative Change' (2019) 336(6471) Science.

[65] eg art 26 of the CBD or art VIII of CITES.

[66] CMS, UNEP/CMS/COP13/Doc.14.1, Annex 2, Strategic Plan for Migratory Species 2015–2023—Progress Report (2019).

[67] Ramsar Convention, Ramsar COP13 Doc.11.1, Report of the Secretary General on the implementation of the Convention: Global implementation (2018): 'With the Exception of Strategies Relating to Biodiversity, the Incorporation of Wetland Benefits into National Strategies and Planning Processes is Progressing Slowly, if at all.' See also Ramsar Convention, *Global Wetlands Outlook* (2021): <www.global-wetland-outlook.ramsar.org/> accessed 9 March 2022.

[68] CITES, SC70 Doc. 25 (Rev. 1) (2018): 'While progress and commitment may seem significant with well over half of the Parties with legislation in Category 1, there is still a total of 75 Parties with

The same goes for the CBD and the Aichi Targets. Target 17 specifically specified that 'By 2015 each Party has developed, adopted as a policy instrument, and has commenced implementing an effective, participatory and updated national biodiversity strategy and action plan.' However, the final assessment carried out by the CBD Secretariat and based on the parties' sixth national reports shows that 'none of the 20 targets have been fully achieved, though six targets have been partially achieved' and suggests that 'despite all the measures taken to date in support of conservation, sustainable use and sharing the benefits of biodiversity, a continuing decline in biodiversity can be expected based on the pressures currently faced by the world's ecosystems. It also supports the conclusion that an improvement in current trends requires a fundamental change of approach that addresses the underlying drivers of change.'[69]

The CBD's treaty bodies are reflecting on ways to strengthen the national implementation of the global targets. A new agreement is due to be reached in 2022 at COP 15 in Kunming, China, concluding a negotiation process launched at COP 14. It is envisaged, inter alia, to draw inspiration from the Paris Agreement by requiring parties to prepare 'nationally determined contributions' as well. Such contributions would be accompanied by monitoring systems established at the international level to follow their level of implementation and encourage raising the ambition of national policies over time.

In this volume, we seek to explore another approach for effectiveness by determining if litigation could also be used to strengthen the effectiveness of IBL.

2.4 Biodiversity Litigation as a Tool for Effectiveness?

Climate litigation demonstrates the possible role of national courts for the realization of states' international commitments. The rapid development of this litigation trend could lead to national trials for other global environmental threats, such as the loss of biodiversity. Moreover, international provisions promoting broad access to justice in environmental matters could support such developments.[70]

legislation placed in Category 2 or 3, many of which have been Parties to the Convention for decades' (Categories 2 and 3 refers to legislation that does not meet all the requirements of the Convention).

[69] Secretariat of the Convention on Biological Diversity, *Global Biodiversity Outlook 5—Summary for Policy Makers* (2020).

[70] Particularly the Aarhus Convention, and more recently the Escazu Agreement. See Convention on Access to Information, Public Participation in Decision-Making and Access to Justice in Environmental Matters (opened for signature 25 June 2001, entered into force 30 October 2001) 2161 UNTS 447 and Regional Agreement on Access to Information, Public Participation and Justice in Environmental

Such an approach would be particularly appropriate for the implementation of the CBD and its protocols, especially if parties choose to rely on nationally determined contributions in the future framework. We can imagine cases where a judge may find a state responsible for not acting with due diligence to meet its target. This could also concern the implementation of sectoral conventions on wetlands, migratory species, international trade in wild fauna or flora, etc, or even regional conventions. Additionally, judges may have to interpret these different regimes in a consistent manner and thus be in a position to promote better coherence between them.

At the same time, regional—particularly within the European Union—and international disputes relating to biodiversity are also developing.[71] Complementing national litigation, they can help to clarify the commitments of states by interpreting treaty provisions, identifying customary rules, and clarifying their content. They can also provide guidance for coordinating international biodiversity law with other branches of international law. The development of international litigation could thus inspire, or even guide, national judges who may have difficulties engaging with an unfamiliar and complex legal landscape.

Biodiversity litigation has the potential to strengthen the effectiveness of international biodiversity law and to push states and businesses to commit themselves further to tackle the current biodiversity crisis. This is the wager we make in this volume, which leads us to see in biodiversity litigation a particularly relevant and promising field of research.

3. The Versatility of Biodiversity Litigation

In this edited collection, we define biodiversity litigation as *any legal dispute at the national, regional or international level that concerns conservation of, sustainable use of and access and benefit-sharing to genetic resources, species, ecosystems and their relations.*

In this section, we will explain why we chose the conceptual apparatus of the CBD to frame our definition of biodiversity litigation (3.1). We will then

Matters in Latin America and the Caribbean (opened for signature 4 March 2018, entered into force 22 April 2021): <www.cepal.org/en/escazuagreement> accessed 9 March 2022.

[71] See Chapter 11 on the European Union and Chapter 12 on International Biodiversity Litigation in this volume.

discuss potential disputes arising from the three objectives of the CBD: conservation, sustainable use, and access and benefit sharing (3.2).

3.1 Understanding Biodiversity Litigation Through the CBD Lens

There are several reasons to align the definition of biodiversity litigation with the CBD.

First, the CBD promotes conservation of three types of diversity: ecosystem, species, and genetic.[72] By including genetic and ecosystem diversity in its definition of biodiversity, the CBD goes further than earlier treaties on nature protection, which aim to protect enumerated species or areas from human threats and destruction or extinction. It also supports a balance between conservation and sustainable use and defines legal concepts such as biodiversity, ecosystems, genetic resources and biotechnology, benefit sharing, and traditional knowledge. Therefore, using the CBD as a point of reference for our definition of biodiversity litigation allows us to encompass the multiplicity of legal disputes that may have an impact on biodiversity. We will not limit the analysis to cases concerning species, or cases concerning protected areas, but try to adopt a transversal reading of biodiversity before the courts.

Secondly, at its core, the CBD strikes a balance between the sovereignty of states to exploit their own resource and the imperious need for conservation and sustainable use. We expect to witness this balance, or tension, within biodiversity litigation at all levels (local, national, global) and within all elements (genes, species, ecosystems).

Thirdly, as highlighted earlier, the CBD has become a conceptual cornerstone of biodiversity governance and, as such, other biodiversity-related conventions work closely with the CBD. Framing biodiversity litigation through the conceptual lens of the CBD allows us to consider cases that may refer to other biodiversity-related conventions. In other words, our definition of biodiversity litigation stems from the CBD but permeates all international biodiversity law.

For all these reasons, the CBD is a useful reference point for our framing of biodiversity litigation as it encompasses the complexity of biodiversity, carries

[72] Article 2 of the CBD defines biodiversity as '... the variability among living organisms from all sources including, inter alia, terrestrial, marine and other aquatic ecosystems and the ecological complexes of which they are a part, this includes diversity within species, between species and of ecosystems'.

the different interests at stake in the conservation and sustainable use of biodiversity, and allows us to study the influence of the entirety of IBL.

The next sections will highlight the tensions that may arise from the three goals of the CBD: conservation, sustainable use, and access and benefit sharing.

3.2 Conservation, Sustainable Use, and Access and Benefit Sharing: Tensions Within the Objectives of the CBD

To understand the remit of biodiversity litigation, it is crucial to unpack the three key objectives of biodiversity protection: *conservation, sustainable use, and access and benefit sharing*. In this section, we will explore the potential disputes that may arise within these objectives and at their intersection.

The three objectives of the CBD reflect the path on which IBL was at the time of its adoption. They carry the core principles and values of this branch of international law. Moreover, these objectives are interlinked, mutually reinforcing, and, to a large extent, interdependent. A number of CBD provisions consider conservation and sustainable use together.[73] For example, article 6 calls for the development of national strategies, plans, or programmes for the conservation and sustainable use of biological diversity[74] and the integration of conservation and sustainable use with the relevant sectoral or cross-sectoral plans, programmes, and policies.[75] In addition, the link between the two objectives is explicit in the definition of sustainable use (ie 'not lead to the long-term decline of biological diversity' and maintain 'its potential to meet the needs and aspirations of present and future generations').[76] Similarly, the conservation and sustainable use aspirations could be achieved simultaneously through access and benefit sharing (ABS) and the goods and services flowing from biological diversity could provide an incentive for its conservation. Thus, sustainable use offers a strategy for promoting conservation, provided that there is a fair and equitable sharing of benefits resulting from such uses. However, sustainable use and the ABS objectives of biodiversity are often dictated by political

[73] Article 6 (general measures for conservation and sustainable use); art 7 (identification and monitoring); art 8 (in situ conservation); art 10 (sustainable use of components of biological diversity), art 11 (incentive measures); and art 13 (promotion of education and public awareness with respect to the conservation and sustainable use of biological diversity).

[74] Article 6(a).

[75] Article 6(b).

[76] CBD, UNEP/CBD/SBSTTA/5/13, Sustainable Use of the Components of Biological Diversity (1999).

priorities and economic development. This led, to a large extent, to the marginalization of the strictly ecocentric conservation aims of the CBD.[77]

In the following section, we will explore potential tensions between these objectives and how biodiversity litigation may arise from these tensions.

3.2.1 Tensions between conservation and sustainable use

Exploring the potential tensions first requires us to precisely define conservation and sustainable use.

3.2.1.1 Conservation

The meaning of conservation is not just to protect in isolation certain elements of biodiversity, but also to 'conserve and enhance the ability of ecosystems to develop and regenerate themselves as living systems'.[78] At the same time, the CBD encourages parties to '[e]ndeavour to provide the conditions needed for compatibility between present uses and conservation of biological diversity and the sustainable use of its components'.[79] While 'conservation' is not defined in the CBD, the traditional meaning of conservation includes 'the functions of protection and maintenance'.[80] The principal mechanism in the CBD for achieving conservation is the set of obligations associated with in situ and ex situ conservation.[81] Ex situ conservation means the conservation of components of biological diversity outside their natural habitats. In situ conservation is the conservation of ecosystems and natural habitats and the maintenance and recovery of viable populations of species in their natural surroundings.[82] According to Smagadi, in situ and ex situ conservation in the CBD include 'protectionist' goals as well as 'sustainable use' objectives.[83]

3.2.1.2 Sustainable use

The CBD defines 'sustainable use' as 'the use of components of biological diversity in a way and at a rate that does not lead to the long-term decline of

[77] Sarah Laird and others, 'Rethink the Expansion of Access and Benefit Sharing' (2020) 367 Science 1200, 1202.

[78] Aphrodite Smagadi, 'Analysis of the Objectives of the Convention on Biological Diversity: Their Interrelation and Implementation Guidance for Access and Benefit Sharing' (2006) 31 Columbia Journal of Environmental Law 243 at 253.

[79] Article 8 of the CBD.

[80] Douglas Edgar Fisher, 'Legal and Paralegal Rules for Biodiversity Conservation: A Sequence of Conceptual, Linguistic, and Legal Problems' in Michael I Jefferey, Jeremy Firestone, and Karen Bubnalitic (eds), *Biodiversity Conservation: Law and Livelihoods Bridging the North South Divide* (CUP 2008) 105.

[81] Article 2 of the CBD.

[82] ibid.

[83] Smagadi (n 78) 253–54.

biological diversity, thereby maintaining its potential to meet the needs and aspirations of present and future generations.'[84]

The first part of the definition refers to biological sustainability, and the second part focuses on social and financial sustainability.[85] According to the Intergovernmental Science-Policy Platform on Biodiversity and Ecosystem Services (IPBES), sustainable use refers to 'a rational use of the natural resources without undermining the capabilities of regeneration of natural resources.'[86] This definition is built on the CBD definition and emphasizes the need to acknowledge multiple and diverse values (anthropocentric and non-anthropocentric types of value).[87]

To ensure the sustainable use of biological resources, parties are encouraged to consider ex situ and in situ measures together, ensure collaboration between biodiversity users, develop supportive incentive measures, and cooperate with other parties in the case of transboundary resources.[88]

3.2.1.3 Potential tensions between conservation and sustainable use

According to the CBD, Member States are required to develop national strategies, plans, or programmes for the conservation and sustainable use of biodiversity, or to adapt existing plans or programmes for this purpose.[89] Parties are to identify for themselves components of biodiversity important for conservation and sustainable use.[90]

At the national level, such measures may give rise to several tensions leading to legal claims in relation to, for instance, wildlife protection, protected areas/ecosystems, or illegal trade. Cases on land conservation may include forest conservation, habitat protection, and illegal wildlife trade (eg Africa, Southeast Asia, Europe).[91] Examples of marine conservation claims include marine

[84] Article 2 of the CBD. Sustainable use of biological diversity and its components is mentioned in most of the substantive articles of the Convention as well as Annex I and several preambular paragraphs.

[85] Eleanor Jane Milner-Gulland and Marcus J Rowcliffe, *Conservation and Sustainable Use: A Handbook of Techniques* (OUP 2007) 4. Biological sustainability implies that 'the activity does not compromise the integrity of biological systems'; Social sustainability requires 'cultural appropriateness, social support and institutions'; and financial sustainability implies that 'the activity outcompetes unsustainable alternative activities in profit generation.'

[86] IPBES, Preliminary Guide Regarding Diverse Conceptualization of Multiple Values of Nature and its Benefits, Including Biodiversity and Ecosystem Functions and Services', IPBES/4/INF/13 (2015), 93.

[87] ibid 21–22.

[88] Addis Ababa Principles and Guidelines for the Sustainable Use of Biodiversity, Decision VII/12, Annex II, COP-7 (2004).

[89] Article 6(a).

[90] Article 7.

[91] Giovanni Broussard, 'Building an Effective Criminal Justice Response to Wildlife Trafficking: Experiences from the ASEAN Region (2017) 26(2) Review of European, Comparative & International Environmental Law 118; Melanie Wellsmith, 'Wildlife Crime: The Problems of Enforcement' (2011) 17 European Journal of Criminal Policy and Research 125; Patricia Kameri-Mbote and others (eds), *Law, Environment, Africa* (Nomos 2019).

parks, coastal development, aquaculture, wetlands, heritage, and marine pollution. For instance, in India since the 1980s, we can mention several cases dealing with forest conservation, protection of wildlife, bird habitat, wetland conservation, conservation of biodiversity, aquaculture, and coastal zone development.[92] Similarly, in Africa,[93] examples of illegal wildlife trade and wildlife crime cases are abundant.

These cases highlight several trends.

First, at the national level, 'conservation' can be treated differently from 'sustainable use'.[94] Trade-offs[95] at the national level are evident between the protection of nature and sustainable use of natural resources (eg management of protected areas[96]).

Secondly, various uses of biodiversity and values can lead to trade-offs among intrinsic, biophysical, instrumental, and relational values (eg protection of ancient woodlands,[97] indigenous people and local communities, and forest management[98]).[99]

[92] Shyam Divan and Armin Rosencranz, *Environmental Law and Policies in India* (OUP 2002) chs 7 and 8; Jona Razzaque, *Public Interest Environmental Litigation in India, Pakistan and Bangladesh* (Kluwer 2004) chs 1 and 2.

[93] Examples from Kenya: Kofi Ernest Abotsi, Paolo Galizzi, and Alena Herklotz, 'Wildlife Crime and Degradation in Africa: An Analysis of the Current Crisis and Prospects for a Secure Future' (2016) 12(3) Fordham Intellectual Property Media & Entertainment Law Journal 394; Juma Salum and others, 'Wildlife Crime Promoted by Weak Governance' (2018) 56(1) African Journal of Ecology 101; Margit Hellwig-Bötte, *Wildlife Crime in Africa—A Global Challenge: Successful Countermeasures Must Involve Local Populations* (Stiftung Wissenschaft und Politik 2014).

[94] Jens Jetzkowitz and others, 'The Significance of Meaning: Why IPBES Needs the Social Sciences and Humanities' (2018) Innovation: The European Journal of Social Science Research 31 (sup 1) 38; Sam Johnston, 'The Convention on Biological Diversity: The Next Phase' (1997) 6 Review of European, Comparative & International Environmental Law 219; Kent Redford and Brian D Richter, 'Conservation of Biodiversity in a World of Use' (1999) 13 Conservation Biology 1246.

[95] According to IPBES, '[a] trade-off is a situation where an improvement in the status of one aspect of the environment or of human well-being is necessarily associated with a decline in or loss of a different aspect. Trade-offs characterize most complex systems and are important to consider when making decisions that aim to improve environmental and/or socio-economic outcomes.' Available at: <https://ipbes.net/glossary/trade> accessed 9 March 2022.

[96] Thomas O McShane and others, 'Hard Choices: Making Trade-offs Between Biodiversity Conservation and Human Well-being' (2011) 144 Biological Conservation 966; Charles Victor Barber, Kenton Miller, and Melissa Boness (eds), *Securing Protected Areas in the Face of Global Change: Issues and Strategies* (IUCN 2004).

[97] Jona Razzaque and Claire Lester, 'Why Protect Ancient Woodlands in the UK? Rethinking the Ecosystem Approach' (2020) 10 Transnational Environmental Law 135. This article highlights the tension surrounding the economic value of a large infrastructure project and the intrinsic value of ancient woodlands.

[98] eg *Saramaka People v Suriname*, Judgment of 28 November 2007 (Preliminary Objections, Merits, Reparations, and Costs), Inter-American Court of Human Rights (IACtHR). This case does not deal with CBD-related issues. However, the tension surrounding the economic and cultural value dimension is reflected in the case.

[99] Unai Pascual and others, 'Valuing Nature's Contributions to People: The IPBES Approach' (2017) 26–27 Current Opinion in Environmental Sustainability 7; Adam Hejnowicz and Murray Rudd, 'The Value Landscape in Ecosystem Services: Value, Value Wherefore Art Thou Value?' (2017) 9 Sustainability 850.

Thirdly, tensions arise when biodiversity policies and decisions prioritize economic growth without consideration of damage to ecosystems and the rights of nature. This has led to remarkable cases where the rights of nature has been acknowledged.[100] To prevent these tensions, some countries have even adopted specific legislative or constitutional provisions recognizing the rights of nature.[101]

While the CBD offers conceptual guidance that envisions disputes centred around conservation and sustainable use, many other IBL instruments might be involved in such disputes. For instance, any dispute concerning the conservation and sustainable use of wetlands might be resolved by relying on the Ramsar Convention.[102] On the matter of sustainable use, we witness similar tension within CITES on the controversial topic of the legal ivory trade.[103]

3.2.2 The tensions within fair and equitable benefit sharing of genetic resources, species, ecosystems, and their relations

3.2.2.1 The rationale of fair and equitable benefit sharing

While the first two objectives aim to conserve and sustain biodiversity, the third is to balance the costs of conservation and to support the socio-economic development of biodiverse countries of the global south, by sharing monetary or non-monetary benefits that arise from the utilization of genetic resources with the original providers of biological material. Although the rationale of fair and equitable sharing is present across most IBL instruments,[104] the concrete legal rules related to it are found mostly within the framework of the CBD and its Nagoya Protocol.

The underlying philosophy of the CBD is that providing access to genetic resources should be done in exchange for a share of the benefits. Resource-user countries need to share the results of research and development as well as

[100] This was the case, inter alia, for the Ganges and the Yamuna Rivers in India. See High Court of Uttarakhand, *Nainital, Mohd Salim v State of Uttarakhand & others*, Writ Petition (PIL) No 126 of 2014, 20 March 2017.

[101] New Zealand being a famous example: Te Awa Tupua (Whanganui River Claims Settlement) Act 2017, Public Act no 17, 20 March 2017.

[102] eg an infrastructure project near the Gediz Delta in Turkey (classified as a Ramsar site) was dropped following a ruling by a Turkish court. See <https://dibird.com/news/2739/> accessed 9 March 2022.

[103] During the last COP, several states pushed for a declassification of certain elephant populations in order to engage in the ivory trade. This led to particularly visible tensions that can be witnessed in the official documentation prepared for that meeting. See eg CITES, CoP18 Doc. 11, Review of the Convention (document prepared by Democratic Republic of the Congo, Namibia, South Africa and Zimbabwe) (2019). See also CITES, CoP18 Prop. 10, Consideration of proposals for amendment of appendices I and II (2019).

[104] The rationale being that differences in economic development should lead to appropriate rules on how to conserve and sustainably use biodiversity.

the benefits arising from commercial and other uses of the resources with the provider country upon mutually agreed terms.[105] Resource-provider countries are required to facilitate access to such use of genetic resources and minimize restrictions on access. Provider countries can benefit from participation in scientific research, access to technology, and other forms of benefit sharing.[106] To achieve fair and equitable sharing, the CBD introduced the concept of prior informed consent (PIC) for access and mutually agreed terms (MAT) for the utilization of genetic resources in bilateral agreements between providers and users.

The benefit-sharing provisions are contained principally in articles 15, 16, and 19. According to the CBD, where a country provides genetic resources, it should receive a share of any benefits derived from the use of those resources.[107] The CBD does not spell out the meaning of 'fair and equitable'[108] and there is a wide margin of discretion for the Member States to apply this objective at the national level. This objective is to be achieved by appropriate access to genetic resources, appropriate transfer of relevant technologies, and funding.[109] Genetic materials extracted from plants and animals provide the basis of research by, for example, pharmaceutical, chemical, and agricultural seed companies. Products generated from this research are often protected by patents and marketed worldwide. The CBD recognizes that state parties with sovereign rights over their natural resources have 'the authority to determine access to genetic resources rests with the national governments and is subject to national legislation'.[110] In order for the sharing of benefits to be fair and equitable, the user of the genetic resources must have prior informed consent and such consent to access genetic resources shall 'be on mutually agreed terms'.[111] The source country providing access to genetic resources must know in advance what will be done with the resource, and what benefits will be shared. Where a party provides genetic resources to another party, the receiving party 'shall endeavour to develop and carry out scientific research based on [those] genetic resources … with the full participation of, and where possible in, [the providing party]'.[112]

[105] Alan Boyle and Catherine Redgwell, *Birnie, Boyle, and Redgwell's International Law and the Environment* (4th edn, OUP 2021) 702–03.
[106] Articles 15(7), 16(3), 19(1) and (2). Ibid 631–32.
[107] Lyle Glowka and others, 'A Guide to the Convention on Biological Diversity: A Contribution to the Global Biodiversity Strategy', IUCN Environmental Policy and Law Paper No 30 (1994),.
[108] Article 15 (7) of the CBD.
[109] Article 16 deals with the transfer of technology. Articles 20 and 21 deal with financial resources.
[110] Article 15(1).
[111] Articles 15(4) and 15(5).
[112] Article 15(6).

State parties are asked to take appropriate measures to provide for the effective participation in biotechnological research by the parties, especially developing countries that provide the genetic resources for such research.[113] In general, each party shall take measures 'with the aim of sharing in a fair and equitable way the results of research and development and the benefits arising from the commercial and other utilization of genetic resources with the [party] providing such resources'.[114] Parties are required to 'take all practicable measures to promote and advance priority access on a fair and equitable basis' for parties providing genetic resources, especially developing countries, 'to the results and benefits arising from biotechnologies based upon genetic resources ... on mutually agreed terms'.[115]

The CBD also provides a broad framework for Member States' policies concerning access, development, and transfer of technologies.[116] Each party shall take measures, 'with the aim that Contracting Parties, in particular those that are developing countries, which provide genetic resources are provided access to and transfer of technology which makes use of those resources, on mutually agreed terms including technology protected by patents and other intellectual property rights'.[117]

The implementation of this intricate system encounters many hurdles, either locally or transnationally, and is prone to generate controversies and legal disputes.

3.2.2.2 Tensions regarding access and benefit sharing that may give rise to biodiversity litigation

At the domestic level, there are tensions between the state and resource holder regarding the access and benefit sharing of biological resources.

First, even though the three objectives of the CBD should be complementary, the national laws of access and benefit sharing may fail to take into account the conservation and sustainable use of biological diversity.[118] Moreover, access-related national laws may not always ensure equitable sharing of benefits, thus limiting the ability of poorer communities to obtain benefits from access laws.[119] In addition, not all stakeholders may be included in the process

[113] Article 19(1).
[114] Article 15(7).
[115] Article 19(2).
[116] Article 16.
[117] Article 16(3).
[118] ibid.
[119] ibid.

of determining access and use rights to genetic resources. For example, the national seed laws may not have adequate protection for indigenous varieties and may not ensure access rights of the indigenous and local communities.[120] These national rules related to ABS need to provide sufficient information to the community regarding the aims, risks, and implications of using the biological resources, and include clear rules and procedures for 'prior informed consent' and 'mutually agreed terms'.[121]

Secondly, the issue of biopiracy[122] shows the tension between the private and public good aspects of biological resources. Privatization of biological resources can lead to restricted access, greater poverty, and unsustainable exploitation of biological resources. Granting private property rights over traditional knowledge raises serious questions in respect of 'prior art',[123] and can also be viewed as biopiracy, that is, 'the illegal appropriation of life—micro-organisms, plants, and animals—and the traditional cultural knowledge that accompanies it'.[124] Biopiracy allegations are frequent: a US patent granted for the healing properties of turmeric, known for centuries in India; a US patent on the 'ayahuasca' plant considered sacred and used for medicinal purposes by Amazon's indigenous peoples; Hoodia, an appetite suppressant, and the patent that capitalized the traditional knowledge of the San people in South Africa; and a patent application by Nestec SA in 2010 in respect of the use of South African rooibos and honeybush for the treatment of hair, skin, and some other inflammatory disorders.[125] Such tension regarding biopiracy and intellectual property rights gives rise to the potential for biodiversity litigation.

[120] Keith Aoki, 'Weeds, Seeds and Deeds: Recent Skirmishes in the Seed War' (2003) 11 Cardozo Journal of International and Comparative Law 247; Zayaan Khan, 'The tragic loss of seed culture', *Mail and Guardian* (9 December 2021) online: <https://mg.co.za/friday/2021-12-09-the-tragic-loss-of-seed-culture/> accessed 9 March 2022).

[121] Articles 6, 12, and 13 of the Nagoya Protocol.

[122] Understood as the illegal appropriation of life—micro-organisms, plants, and animals—and the traditional cultural knowledge that accompanies it. See Marcia Ellen DeGeer, 'Biopiracy: The Appropriation of Indigenous Peoples' Cultural Knowledge' (2002) 9(1) New England Journal of International & Comparative Law 179. Many academics have termed this as 'biocolonialism' or 'bioprospecting' whereby companies or institutions from the industrialized countries appropriate the genetic resources and traditional knowledge in biodiversity-rich countries and become the new owner of these resources. See Lakshmi Sarma, 'Biopiracy: Twentieth Century Imperialism in the Form of International Agreements' (1999) 13 Temple International and Comparative Law Journal 107; Loïc Peyen, *Droit et biopiraterie Contribution à l'étude du partage des ressources naturelles* (LGDJ, 2018). Daniel Robinson, *Confronting Biopiracy: Challenges, Cases and International Debates* (Routledge 2010).

[123] 'Prior art' is the body of knowledge that exists prior to the invention. It helps to determine whether or not the invention is 'new' and 'non-obvious'.

[124] DeGeer (n 122).

[125] Ashish Kothari and RV Anuradha, 'Biodiversity and Intellectual Property Rights: Can the Two Co-Exist?' (1999) 2(2) Journal of International Wildlife Law and Policy 204–23; Commission on Intellectual Property Rights, *Integrating Intellectual Property Rights and Development Policy* (2002), ch 4 (Traditional Knowledge and Geographical Indications). Examples from Africa can be found in African Centre for Biosafety, 'Pirating African Heritage: The Pillaging Continues', Briefing Paper (2009).

Thirdly, states need to provide adequate legal protection for biological resources and traditional knowledge.[126] At the national level, traditional knowledge can be protected through conventional intellectual property laws, or through *sui generis* laws, such as laws for the protection of traditional knowledge associated with genetic resources. Effective national legislation is crucial because of the role traditional knowledge plays in the economic and social life of these communities. The link between genetic resources and traditional knowledge is inextricable in the sense that any access to genetic resources inevitably involves access to traditional knowledge.[127] Examples of traditional knowledge include the use of *plao-noi* by Thai traditional healers to treat ulcers and the use *argyapaachya* by the Kani people in southern India to suppress fatigue and reduce stress. Countries such as Brazil, Ethiopia, India, and the Philippines have national laws to protect the traditional knowledge rights of indigenous peoples.[128] In addition, the ABS framework at the regional level (eg European Union, African Union, Andean Community) entails obligations that need to be implemented nationally by their respective Member States.[129] Tensions arise when the national laws fail to provide adequate protection associated with the traditional knowledge, restrict the misuse or misappropriation of traditional knowledge, reflect the expectations of the knowledge holder, acknowledge indigenous and customary rights and practices, contain the principle of free prior informed consent, and ensure effective participation of traditional knowledge holders in the decision making.[130] There is a growing jurisprudence regarding indigenous peoples' rights, especially in relation to the rights over their lands and territories and the right to participate in any decision making affecting them. The decisions from the Inter-American Court of Human Rights[131] and the African Commission on Human and Peoples

[126] UN Environment World Conservation Monitoring Centre, *Access to Genetic Resources and Benefit-sharing: A Review of Existing Frameworks* (CUP 2019).

[127] The relationship between access and use of genetic resources and associated or non-associated traditional knowledge is dealt with in arts 15 and 8(j) of the Biodiversity Convention. Articles 7 and 12 of the Nagoya Protocol.

[128] 'ECOLEX: The Gateway to Environmental Law', available at <www.ecolex.org/>.

[129] Jorge Cabrera Medaglia, Frederic Perron-Welch, and Freedom Kai Phillips, *Overview of National and Regional Measures on Access and Benefit Sharing and Opportunities in Implementing the Nagoya Protocol* (Technical Report, October 2014). Eg Regulation (EU) No 511/2014 of the European Parliament and of the Council on compliance measures for users from the Nagoya Protocol on Access to Genetic Resources and the Fair and Equitable Sharing of Benefits Arising from their Utilization in the Union; African Union Model Law for the Protection of the Rights of Local Communities, Farmers and Breeders and for the Regulation of Access to Biological Resources.

[130] ibid 117–19. UN Environment World Conservation Monitoring Centre (n 126) 188–200.

[131] IACtHR, *Yakye Axa Indigenous Community v Paraguay*, Judgment of 17 June 2005, Series C No 125; IACtHR, *Mayagna (Sumo) Awas Tingni Community v Nicaragua*, Judgment of 31 August

Rights[132] can shed light on implementation options concerning key provisions of the Nagoya Protocol related to the rights of indigenous and local communities, including the right to grant free prior and informed consent[133] for using genetic resources located within their lands.

Fourthly, because the CBD and the Nagoya Protocol use a broad, sometimes even vague, language, key definitions remain unclear. Therefore, national implementation as well as compliance have to rely on juridical interpretation and commentaries at the expense of legal certainty.[134] For instance, both the CBD and the Nagoya Protocol fail to define 'access' and 'fair and equitable'. Interpretation of what is covered by an ambiguous definition of genetic resource, access, traditional uses, commercial utilization, and exemptions could lead to tension among the users and providers of genetic resources and traditional knowledge, and may lead to biodiversity litigation at the national level.

In sum, because of the different and opposing interests that coexist in the realm of fair and equitable sharing, legal disputes are likely to abound. Here again, even though the CBD and its protocol are a useful guide for conceptualizing such disputes, it is important to keep in mind that other international instruments might be relevant for settling such disputes. For instance, the International Treaty on Plant Genetic Resources for Agriculture is an obvious point of references in disputes touching upon the rights of farmers.

Now that we have laid down the main elements of our investigation—international biodiversity law and biodiversity litigation—we can turn to our methodology for understanding how biodiversity litigation might be affected by IBL.

2001, Series C No 79; *Maya Indigenous Community of the Toledo District v Belize*, Case 12.053; IACtHR, Report No 40/04, OEA/Ser.L/V/II.122, doc. 5 rev. 1 (2004) at 727; IACtHR, *Saramaka People v Suriname*, Judgment of 28 November 2007 (Preliminary Objections, Merits, Reparations, and Costs), Series C No 172; IACtHR, *Kichwa Indigenous People of Sarayaku v Ecuador*, 2012, Series C No 245 [186].

132 African Commission on Human and Peoples' Rights, 276/03 Centre for Minority Rights Development (Kenya) and Minority Rights Group International on behalf of *Endorois Welfare Council v Kenya*, paras 162 and 291 (May 2009).

133 Jona Razzaque, 'A Stocktaking of Free Prior Informed Consent in International Environmental Law' in Stephen J Turner and others (eds), *Environmental Rights—The Development of Standards* (CUP 2019) 195–221.

134 Dirk Neumann and others, 'Global Biodiversity Research Tied Up by Juridical Interpretations of Access and Benefit-Sharing' (2017) 18(1) Organisms Diversity & Evolution 1.

4. Methodology

Studying the evolution of biodiversity litigation and how international biodiversity may have influenced it requires a comparative approach framed by a specific set of questions.

4.1 Selection of Case Studies

For this project, we have invited authors from nine countries to present biodiversity litigation in their respective jurisdiction. These national case studies are from, in alphabetical order: Australia, Brazil, Canada, China, France, India, South Africa, the UK, and the United States.

We have chosen to focus mainly on mega-diverse countries in which the abundance and uniqueness of biodiversity are likely to lead to legal disputes with crucial outcomes for the preservation of biodiversity as a whole. Biodiversity litigation is obviously not limited to these countries and we have also added case studies for global north countries that are particularly active in international fora dealing with biodiversity. The results of biodiversity litigation in Canada, France, and the UK may have effects on the global governance of biodiversity as cases potentially reshape international policies.

These national cases are admittedly too few to allow a true grasp of the reality of biodiversity litigation worldwide. However, this selection aims at representativeness by studying countries with different degrees of development and with different legal traditions (common law, civil law, and all the other possible nuances).

In parallel with these national case studies, we have also added an analysis of case law at the international level. Chapter 12 is dedicated to biodiversity litigation before the international courts and dispute settlement bodies. The idea is that these bodies are likely to influence the interpretation of IBL at the national level in potential cases. Chapter 11 focuses on the case of the Court of Justice of the European Union (CJEU) as the regional court with the most developed case law on environmental matters. The European Union being a major norm entrepreneur at the global level, with a clear ambition to shape the governance of biodiversity,[135] studying biodiversity litigation at this level, and how it is influenced by IBL, will yield interesting findings. Moreover, the practice of the

[135] EU Commission, EU Biodiversity Strategy for 2030 Bringing Nature Back into Our Lives, COM (2020) 380 final, 20.

CJEU exerts considerable influence on the interpretation and implementation of environmental law at the national level in the Member States.

4.2 Research Questions

The topic of biodiversity litigation, as described in this introduction, is vast. In order to identify trends, it is therefore necessary to have a framework that will guide the investigation for each case study. To this end, the contributors to this project have been provided with a set of questions that will guide their studies.

These questions are divided along two main lines. First, what is the observable influence of IBL in biodiversity litigation? And, secondly, have we witnessed a paradigm shift in biodiversity litigation?

These questions are broad, and each of them has been complemented by sub-questions. The following sections will present these sub-questions and explain their rationale.

4.2.1 What is the observable influence of IBL in biodiversity litigation?

If we are to measure the impact of IBL on biodiversity litigation, then a set of basic questions need to be answered first.

- Can judges make direct or indirect use of international biodiversity law?

The first question has an obvious constitutional nature. Indeed, this possibility will be directly linked to the monist or dualist nature of the state where the dispute unfolds. As such, this first inquiry is directly tied to the broader theme of international law before the domestic court which is to this day a topic of varied scholarly discussion in law.[136]

More than a matter of constitutional law, the question also relates to which part of IBL can be used directly by judges. Even if their constitutional system allows them to rely on IBL, we have seen that this legal branch is characterized by its heterogeneity. Its rules are diverse and some may not be meant to be used by judges while others can have direct applicability in certain disputes. Identifying which type of IBL rules are used directly by the courts could then be a useful tool in the hands of lawmakers for the future design of new IBL instruments.

[136] See, inter alia, Andre Nollkaemper and others (eds), *International Law in Domestic Courts: A Casebook* (OUP 2018).

But the influence of IBL in the courts does not have to be a strictly direct one. Indeed, the influence of international law on domestic legal systems can manifest itself in numerous ways. One of the most obvious is the translation of international rules into domestic legal rules. Witnessing the influence of IBL in biodiversity litigation can also mean analysing the importance of domestic rules inspired by IBL in the context of litigation. If a biodiversity litigation case involves a domestic rule adopted in accordance with IBL, then we have a clear illustration of the influence of international biodiversity law, albeit an indirect one.

This question requires engaging in a survey of the legislative activity as a reaction to the evolution of IBL, and the relevance of norms thus produced in the context of litigation. Their eventual impact will be a demonstration of how influential IBL can be. A clear example could come from the different National Biodiversity Strategy and Action Plans adopted by parties to the CBD. Have these national policies ever been used in the context of a legal dispute?

- Have other branches of international law (eg investment, trade, sea, human rights) played a role (direct/indirect) in biodiversity litigation?

Understanding the influence of IBL on biodiversity litigation can also be done by observing other branches of international law. First of all, we can question if IBL is the most important body of international rules in the context of biodiversity litigation. How about other branches of international law? How have international human rights, international trade rules, or even investment treaties impacted biodiversity litigation? It may be that legal regimes that only indirectly concern biodiversity have a greater impact on legal dispute concerning diversity. If this proves to be the case, then such a finding will prompt a re-examination of the legal functions of IBL. If these legal regimes influence biodiversity litigation as much as IBL itself, then this will be a clear illustration of the all-encompassing nature of biodiversity as a topic than spans way beyond its dedicated regimes.

- Have international procedural obligations (access to information, participation, access to justice) played a role in biodiversity litigation?

Finally, when discussing the matter of biodiversity before the courts, one cannot ignore the importance of rules dealing with procedure. Have these types of norms, embodied in the aforementioned Aarhus Convention,[137] served or have the potential to serve as a catalyst for biodiversity litigation?

[137] Also, the Escazu Agreement that entered into force in 2021.

4.2.2 Have we witnessed a paradigm shift in biodiversity litigation?

This line of questioning seeks less to assess the legal role of IBL within the disputes. Rather, the purpose of these questions is to establish whether there is a correlation between the evolution of the global governance of biodiversity and the ways in which judges have dealt with biodiversity over the years. For instance, has the emergence of new concepts (eg ecosystem services, ecosystem approach) had an influence on the arguments of the parties and on the reasoning of the judges?

The main questions boil down to this: have judges and parties to disputes considered non-human life in a different perspective over the years? Is this change correlated with the evolution of IBL?

- What is the nature of biodiversity disputes?

For instance, do disputes concerning biodiversity fall mainly within the private sphere or within the public sphere? Is it something that happens mainly between private individuals, as a result of state action against individuals, or as a result of individual action against the state? In any event, these trends can shed light on the underlying paradigm that manifests itself in the national laws for biodiversity. For instance, it may be expected that a dispute concerning genes will mainly fall in a private setting as it seems that nowadays genes are mainly considered as an object of private ownership despite the existence of rules acknowledging their public and common nature. The nature of disputes can also be linked to the potential remedies ordered by the court. The award of damage to an individual may not have the same beneficial impact as an order to act addressed to the state. Therefore, the nature of the disputes matters in terms of concrete outcome for the conservation, sustainable use, and ABS of biodiversity.

- How are rights (human and non-human) used within biodiversity litigation?

In recent years, we have witnessed a regime collision between the environment and human rights,[138] and this collision was manifest in the recent Urgenda case

[138] On the interaction between these regimes, see inter alia Annalisa Savaresi, 'Climate Change and Human Rights: Fragmentation, Interplay and Institutional Linkages' in Sebastien Duyck, Sebastien Jodoin, and Alyssa Johl (eds), *Routledge Handbook of Human Rights and Climate Governance* (Routledge 2018). More generally, on regime interaction, see Margaret Young (ed), *Regime Interaction in International Law* (CUP 2012).

where the international human rights obligations of a state were the legal basis for the court to order mitigation by the state. Human rights are now present in most international environmental regimes, and vice versa, environmental concerns are ever present in human rights discourse. With this in mind, our study aims to identify occurrences of human rights discourses in biodiversity litigation in order to determine whether this regime collision at the international level has also occurred before the courts.

Another important conceptual change that has occurred in the governance of biodiversity is the apparition of new legal subjects. Recently, legal personality was awarded to ecosystems and even nature as a whole, thus denoting a shift in how the environment was considered in legal texts. This shows that biodiversity is no longer considered only in its physical aspect, but the cultural and spiritual values it carries are also being acknowledged. In this sense, it can be useful to observe how this broader understanding of biodiversity has entered the realm of legal disputes. For instance, do we see a prevalence in the use of different notions referring to biodiversity. One can imagine that the notion of Nature, or its other names (Pacha Mama, Gaia), has entered the discourse of judges and parties. If this is the case, it can be useful to see where this has happened, and what the consequences of such discursive shifts have been.

Additionally, with the rise of non-human rights, one wonders if the way judges deal with biodiversity matters has evolved. The cases are well documented and it may be useful to draw a parallel between their rise and the conceptual evolution of biodiversity. For instance, how does the rise of the legal status of the individual animal correlates with the evolution of international biodiversity law? If these two phenomena are disconnected, how then can we explain this disconnection? Are animals, legally, a special element of biodiversity?

- Is biodiversity litigation linked to climate change litigation?

In the same vein of regime collision, one may also wonder how the interplay of biodiversity and climate might have influenced legal disputes. The inherent ties between the two topics have brought different regimes closer.[139] Numerous institutional partnerships and legal synergies are illustrative of the complementarity of the two topics.[140] Has biodiversity been protected in the name of climate change before the courts, and vice versa?

139 See eg Franck Maes and others (eds), *Biodiversity and Climate Change Linkages at International, National and Local Levels* (Edward Elgar 2013).

140 For a recent example, see the report of the workshop co-organized by the IPCC and the IPBES: <www.ipcc.ch/site/assets/uploads/2021/07/IPBES_IPCC_WR_12_2020.pdf> accessed 9 March 2022.

- Do we witness strategic litigation in the field?

More than the substance of the disputes, another interesting element to investigate is the instrumentation of these disputes. For instance, climate change litigation is a field where strategic litigation is an obviously powerful tool for promoting systemic and broader change. Is this something that we witness for biodiversity, too? If not, does that mean that biodiversity fails to create the same popular momentum as does climate change?

4.2.3 Does biodiversity litigation contribute to the effectiveness of IBL?

Finally, after all these questions, it is crucial to ask: does biodiversity litigation contribute to a greater effectiveness of biodiversity law? This question is crucial in order to determine whether courts are actually equipped to enforce biodiversity law and contribute in a meaningful way in halting the current crisis.

Each case study addresses this set of questions which were intended as guidelines rather than a fixed frame. Therefore, each chapter is structured as the authors saw fit, depending on the relevance of certain questions. The results are presented in Chapter 13, in which we identify the similarities and divergences between the case studies and highlight the main trends of biodiversity litigation. In the synthesis, we also suggest future research questions. This volume intends to set the path for a new research agenda, with fascinating theoretical and practical aspects that can be of use for decision-making processes affecting biodiversity at all levels. We hope researchers and practitioners will join us in this effort: the field is immense and the prospects for biodiversity promising.

2

Biodiversity Litigation in Australia

Constrained Efforts to Protect Beauty, Rich and Rare

Margaret A Young and Ella Vines

1. Introduction

Australia is a self-described land that 'abounds in nature's gifts of beauty rich and rare'.[1] Yet its world-renowned biological diversity faces grave threats. People around the globe witnessed the unprecedented Australian megafires of 2019–20, which destroyed vast swathes of habitat for a large number of threatened species[2] and caused the death or displacement of at least 3 billion animals.[3] Over the longer term, 100 species endemic to the Australian continent have become extinct since white settlement, with at least one species already wiped out by the effects of climate change.[4] Significant population declines in Australian mammals and birds, as well as other animal and plant groups, have been caused by climate change,

[1] This phrase is from the Australian national anthem.

[2] The area affected the habitat of 832 species of native vertebrate fauna: see Michelle Ward and others, 'Impact of 2019–2020 Mega-Fires on Australian Fauna Habitat' (2020) 4 Nature Ecology and Evolution 1321.

[3] Lily van Eeden and others, 'Impacts of the unprecedented 2019–20 bushfires on Australian animals', report prepared for WWF-Australia, Sydney, 2020. The full impact of the fires is still unknown, but the conservation of many species will need to be reassessed: Helen Murphy and Stephen van Leeuwen, 'Biodiversity: Climate Change' in Commonwealth of Australia, *State of the Environment 2021*, DOI: 10.26194/ren9-3639 For example, the status of the koala in Queensland, New South Wales, and the Australian Capital Territory is now listed as endangered: Department of Agriculture, Water and the Environment 2022, 'Conservation Advice for the *Phascolarctos cinereus* (Koala)', Canberra.

[4] John CZ Woinarski and others, 'The Contribution of Policy, Law, Management, Research, and Advocacy Failings to the Recent Extinctions of Three Australian Vertebrate Species' (2017) 31 Conservation Biology 13, 15 (noting the Bramble Cay myelomas (*Melomys rubicola*), a small rodent in the Torres Strait, whose extinction was likely caused by storm surges). A press release noting the extinction from then Federal Environment Minister Melissa Price of 19 February 2019 was subsequently removed from the internet archive: <www.environment.gov.au/minister/price/media-releases/mr20 190218a.html>. On the implications for environmental law of extinctions, see Afshin Ahktar-Khavari, Michelle Lim, and Katie Woolaston, 'Environmental law's extinction problem' (2020) 29(4) Griffith Law Review 493.

Margaret A Young and Ella Vines, *Biodiversity Litigation in Australia* In: *Biodiversity Litigation*. Edited by: Guillaume Futhazar, Sandrine Maljean-Dubois, and Jona Razzaque, Oxford University Press.
 DOI: 10.1093/oso/9780192865465.003.0002

invasive species, and habitat loss and degradation,[5] with high rates of deforestation[6] and land clearing continuing.[7]

What is the relevance of litigation to the dire state of Australia's biodiversity?[8] The question is timely, not just because of the utility of the comparative approach of this volume, but because threats to Australian biodiversity are rapidly escalating, as highlighted by the recent megafires. Moreover, Australia's national legislation, the Environment Protection and Biodiversity Conservation Act 1999 (Cth) (EPBC Act),[9] has been formally assessed as inadequate to its task of protecting Australia's natural environment.[10] The latest statutory review of the EPBC Act recommended, amongst other things, the development and implementation of legally enforceable national environmental standards. With a new federal government elected in 2022 (after nine years of power of the former ruling coalition), there is hope for an executive and legislative response to these recommendations.[11] A review of the activities of the judicial branch is important in this context.

This chapter provides analysis of Australian practice and experience through a survey of Australian cases over the last few decades. The dominant legal challenges have been to land clearing and forestry, mining, marine exploitation, and climate change, and the analysis is structured along these topics. The chapter provides the context of the legal challenges at the federal level, while also noting developments within the subnational jurisdictions (the 'states and territories' of Australia, such as Victoria and New South Wales). Traditional avenues for judicial review sit alongside novel claims including duties of care. The chapter also

[5] Murphy and van Leeuwen, 'Biodiversity: Key Findings' in *State of the Environment 2021* (2021) (n 3) <https://soe.dcceew.gov.au/biodiversity/key-findings> accessed 25 July 2022. We note that Australia's 'State of the Environment' report is published every five years. The ruling Coalition government had not released the report by the time of the May 2022 election, at which it was replaced by the incoming Labor Party. The new Department of Climate Change, Energy, the Environment and Water released the 2021 SoE report on 19 July 2022.

[6] CJA Bradshaw, 'Little Left to Lose: Deforestation and Forest Degradation in Australia since European Colonization' (2012) 5 Journal of Plant Ecology 109.

[7] Note that 13.2 per cent of Australia's native vegetation has been replaced for urban, production and extractive uses of the land. Nine of the ten threatened species that have lost habitat to clearing have occurred in Queensland: see Murphy and van Leeuwen, 'Biodiversity: Industry' in State of the Environment (n 3).

[8] We concentrate on 'biodiversity litigation', defined by the editors as 'any legal dispute at the national, regional or international level that concerns conservation of, sustainable use of and access and benefit-sharing to genetic resources, species, ecosystems and their relations': see Chapter 1, Section 3 in this volume. We note that indigenous perspectives tend not to use the word 'biodiversity', but rather emphasize 'Country', as 'everything all living together': Fiona Walsh, Peter Christophersen, and Sandra McGregor, 'Indigenous Perspectives on Biodiversity' in Steve Morton, Andy Sheppard, and Mark Lonsdale (eds), *Biodiversity: Science and Solutions for Australia* (CSIRO Publishing 2014) 81, 84.

[9] Environment Protection and Biodiversity Conservation Act 1999 (Cth). See further Section 2.3.

[10] Australian Government Department of Agriculture, Water and the Environment, Graeme Samuel, *Independent Review of the EPBC Act* (Final report, October 2020), ii (hereafter Samuel Review).

[11] At the time of the federal election in May 2022, the ruling Liberal and National Party Coalition had not responded to the Samuel Review.

considers whether human rights and other rights discourses, which have little by way of express protection in the Australian constitutional context, are growing in prevalence; unlike many countries, Australia has no constitutional or statutory bill of rights at the national level. In parallel, the chapter seeks to determine the influence of international biodiversity law in biodiversity litigation.

Section 2 of the chapter sets out the dualist relationship between public international law and the Australian domestic legal system and provides background to Australia's ratification of the Convention on Biological Diversity (CBD),[12] as well as Australia's National Biodiversity Strategy and Action Plan and relevant statutes. Section 3 moves to an analysis of the relevant case law from the federal and state courts, to provide the context in which biodiversity has been considered by judges. The emphasis in this chapter is on cases that have been heard, although Australian lawyers have been creative in reimagining biodiversity litigation within a more protective 'wild law' frame.[13] Section 4 concludes on the question of whether Australian biodiversity litigation contributes to the effectiveness of biodiversity law.

2. International Law in Australian Domestic Law

Australia's Constitution, which in 1901 established the federation,[14] is based largely on the British common law system, with many of its federal arrangements also inspired by the United States. This section provides a brief introduction to the legal paths through which international environmental law applies to Australia. It thereby describes the constitutional basis for Australia's biodiversity laws, including the federal government's powers with respect to external affairs.

2.1 Constitutional Basis for Biodiversity Laws

According to Australian constitutional law, Australia's executive branch enters into treaties that bind Australia under public international law. Australia has been a party to the CBD since 1993. At the level of domestic law, legislation is

[12] Convention on Biological Diversity (opened for signature 5 June 1992, entered into force 29 December 1993) 1760 UNTS 79.

[13] Nicole Rogers and Michelle Maloney (eds), *Law as if Earth Really Mattered: The Wild Law Judgment Project* (Routledge 2017).

[14] Commonwealth of Australia Constitution Act 1900 (Imp) 63 & 64 Vict, c 12, s 9.

required to incorporate treaties before they have direct legal effect in Australia.[15] Australian judges therefore do not 'apply' international law, but may refer to it in constitutional or statutory interpretation. This was done most famously in the environmental context by the High Court of Australia,[16] which upheld the constitutional validity of Commonwealth legislation purporting to implement the World Heritage Convention,[17] thus allowing the Commonwealth to override Tasmania's plans to construct a hydro-electric dam which would have flooded world heritage-protected areas. More recently, an Australian court has accepted public participation as a feature of the protection and conservation of matters of national environmental significance, as informed, inter alia, by articles 8 and 14 of the CBD.[18]

The federal nature of Australia's legal system means that litigation occurs within different jurisdictions. Under Australia's Constitution, the central 'Commonwealth' has express powers 'with respect to external affairs',[19] while the states and territories have residual powers relating to land and natural resource management. It will already be apparent that development of international biodiversity law can shift the balance between the Commonwealth and states in significant ways: when Australia ratified the CBD (or other treaties such as the World Heritage Convention),[20] the Commonwealth assumed wider powers over those issues vis-à-vis the states and territories. The Commonwealth's powers also flow from its responsibility for the oceans seaward from the territorial sea to the exclusive economic zone, as well as from its greater control over tax revenue. Prior to Australia's ratification of the CBD, concerns about the conservation of the natural environment were mounting.[21] According to an advocate appearing in the *Tasmanian Dams* case, the public were beginning to be concerned about international aspects of the environment, including whales and whaling and atmospheric nuclear tests.[22] An

[15] *Minister for Immigration and Ethnic Affairs v Teoh* (1995) 183 CLR 273, 286–87. See also Stephen Donaghue, 'International Law' in Cheryl Saunders and Adrienne Stone (eds), *The Oxford Handbook of the Australian Constitution* (OUP 2018) 237, 241.

[16] *Commonwealth v Tasmania* (1983) 158 CLR 1 (hereafter *Tasmanian Dam case*). See also Ann Genovese, 'Critical Decision 1983: Remembering *Commonwealth v Tasmania*' (2015) 24 Griffith Law Review 1; The Hon Sir Anthony Mason (AC KBE GBM), 'Reflections on Legal Issues in the *Tasmanian Dams Case*' (2015) 24 Griffith Law Review 16.

[17] Convention Concerning the Protection of the World Cultural and Natural Heritage (opened for signature 16 November 1972, entered into force 17 December 1975) 1037 UNTS 151.

[18] *The Wilderness Society (Tasmania) Inc v Minister for the Environment* [2019] FCA 1842, [125].

[19] Commonwealth of Australia Constitution Act 1900 (Imp) 63 & 64 Vict, c 12, ss 9 and 51(xxix).

[20] See especially *Tasmanian Dam case* (n 16).

[21] The Hon Michael Black AC QC, 'The *Tasmanian Dam Case*: An Advocate's Memoir' (2015) 24 Griffith Law Review 22, 25.

[22] ibid 26.

appropriate starting point for considering the development of biodiversity law in Australia is Australia's ratification of the CBD in June 1993.

2.2 Convention on Biological Diversity and the National Biodiversity Strategy and Action Plan

In line with its obligations under article 26 of the CBD, Australia has released six National Reports to the Convention on Biological Diversity, the latest in 2020.[23] Australia signed but did not ratify the Nagoya Protocol, and has stated that its actions are already consistent with Nagoya.[24] There have been no cases heard by Australian courts relating to access and benefit sharing,[25] and one case citing the Cartagena Protocol on Biosafety to the Convention on Biological Diversity.[26]

Australia has released three versions of its National Biodiversity Strategy and Action Plan (although only the first and second versions are available on the CBD website).[27] The first version was released in 1998. The second version, released in 2010, purported to cover the period 2010–30. It contained three national priorities for action: (1) engaging all Australians in biodiversity conservation; (2) building ecosystem resilience in a changing climate; and (3) getting measurable results (including through implementing robust national monitoring, reporting, and evaluation).[28] In 2016, a biodiversity working group convened under a meeting of Australia's federal and state environment ministers

[23] Australian Government, 'Australia's Sixth National Report to the Convention on Biological Diversity 2014–2018' (24 March 2020).

[24] Australian Government, 'The Nagoya Protocol: Convention on Biological Diversity' <www.environment.gov.au/science-and-research/australias-biological-resources/nagoya-protocol-convention-biological#:~:text=The%20Nagoya%20Protocol%20was%20adopted,are%20consistent%20with%20the%20Protocol> accessed 11 March 2022.

[25] Section 301 of the EPBC Act (n 9) allows the Environment Protection and Biodiversity Conservation Regulations 2000 (Cth) to provide for 'the equitable sharing of the benefits arising from the use of biological resources in Commonwealth areas': Part 8A relates to this. There is no record of litigation in relation to access and benefit sharing arising from the EPBC Act and Regulations.

[26] Cartagena Protocol on Biosafety to the Convention on Biological Diversity (opened for signature 29 January 2000, entered into force 11 September 2003) 2226 UNTS 208. Although Australia is not a party to the Cartagena Protocol, it was referred to in *Brimcove Pty Ltd v Director General of Dept of Agriculture and Food Western Australia* [2015] WASAT 30. This case related to a request to import table grapes to Australia. The tribunal referred to the Cartagena Protocol in the context of defining the scope of the International Plant Protection Convention (opened for signature 6 December 1951, entered into force 3 April 1952) 150 UNTS 67. The International Plant Protection Convention was the main multilateral instrument analysed in this case.

[27] Convention on Biological Diversity, 'National Reports and NBSAPS' <www.cbd.int/reports/search/?country=au> accessed 11 March 2022.

[28] Natural Resource Management Ministerial Council, 'Australia's Biodiversity Conservation Strategy 2010–2030' (2010) 8–9.

conducted a review of the first five years of the 2010–30 strategy.[29] It reported that the strategy itself was not 'a strong driver' of this progress, and had not 'effectively influenced biodiversity conservation activities'.[30] A non-government review of the 2010–30 strategy, conducted by Humane Society International, expressed concern about the ability to monitor the progress towards the biodiversity outcomes of the strategy, and identified a gap in alignment between the strategy and the Aichi biodiversity targets used to assess progress in implementing the UN's Strategic Plan for Biodiversity 2011–20.[31]

The third version of the National Strategy and Biodiversity Action Plan was released in 2019 by the Australian federal, state, and territory governments. It replaced the 2010 strategy with Australia's Strategy for Nature 2019–30.[32] The 2019 strategy is noticeably less detailed than the 2010 strategy, does not contain measurable targets or mention a date on which it will be reviewed,[33] and has been criticized by national environmental groups as inadequate.[34] The 2019 strategy does not, for example, reflect calls for a nationally coordinated approach to environmental data collection, monitoring, evaluation, and reporting.[35]

2.3 The EPBC Act 1999 and other relevant statutes

The Environment Protection and Biodiversity Conservation Act 1999 (Cth) is the framework national legislation that implements Australia's obligations under the CBD in addition to other treaties including the World Heritage Convention. It refers to these treaties directly in many of its provisions.[36] Its objects are, inter alia:[37]

[29] Australian Government, 'Report on the Review of the First Five Years of Australia's Biodiversity Conservation Strategy 2010–2030' (2016).

[30] ibid 1, 47.

[31] Humane Society Internationale, 'Australia's Biodiversity Conservation Strategy 2010–2030: An Independent Review of Progress' (April 2015) 6, 8.

[32] Australian Government, *Australia's Strategy for Nature 2019–2030* (2019).

[33] In contrast to the 2010 strategy, which expressly stated that the strategy would be reviewed every five years: see '2010 Strategy' (n 28) 64.

[34] Emma Jukić and Margaret Young, 'Australia' (2018) 29 Yearbook of International Environmental Law 363, 366.

[35] The Australian Panel of Environmental Experts, 'Blueprint for the Next Generation of Australian Environmental Law' (2017).

[36] See eg EPBC Act (n 9) s 528, which is the definitions section, s 305 which gives the Commonwealth Environment Minister the power to enter into conservation agreements, and s 12 relating to the requirement for approval of activities with a significant impact on a declared World Heritage property. See generally EPBC Act Pt 13A, which regulates the international movement of wildlife specimens.

[37] ibid s 3.

(a) to provide for the protection of the environment, especially those aspects of the environment that are matters of national environmental significance; and
(b) to promote ecologically sustainable development through the conservation and ecologically sustainable use of natural resources; and
(c) to promote the conservation of biodiversity; and ...
(e) to assist in the co-operative implementation of Australia's international environmental responsibilities; ...

The passage of the EPBC Act has been interpreted 'as an expression of the agreement amongst governments of the federation to co-operate in their shared responsibilities in respect of the environment'.[38] Courts in Australia have thus had to determine how its implementation of international treaties operates alongside the allocation of roles and powers between the Commonwealth and Australia's states and territories; for some, the EPBC Act is 'not concerned generally with the protection of the environment' but rather with 'matters of national environmental significance'.[39] While matters of national significance include listed endangered species, they do not necessarily extend to all threats to biodiversity. In general, and especially regarding climate change, the boundaries of the constitutional division of powers are a matter of considerable legal and political debate. A tendency to defer action to protect the environment to a different unit within the federation has enduring and negative consequences.[40] The 2019–20 bushfires provide a powerful message that 'whole of nation' or 'whole of society' cooperation is necessary to address environmental catastrophe.[41]

The EPBC Act undergoes a statutory review every decade, and the second and latest review, chaired by Professor Graeme Samuel, published its results in October 2020.[42] It concluded that the EPBC Act requires fundamental reform, including with respect to new, legally enforceable national environmental standards. The report recommended the establishment of a new independent

[38] *Minister for the Environment v Sharma* [2022] FCAFC 35, [43] (Allsop CJ).
[39] ibid [44].
[40] Laura Schuijers and Margaret Young, 'Climate Change Litigation in Australia: Law and Practice in the Sunburnt Country' in Ivano Alogna, Christine Bakker, and Jean-Pierre Gauci (eds), *Climate Change Litigation: Global Perspectives* (Brill 2021) 47, 53.
[41] Margaret Young, 'Climate Change and Law: A Global Challenge for Legal Education' (2021) 40(3) University of Queensland Law Journal 351, 365.
[42] Samuel Review (n 10). The review was contemporaneous with the work of the Intergovernmental Science-Policy Platform on Biodiversity and Ecosystem Services: see Michelle Lim, 'How do we address unprecedented biodiversity decline?—the IPBES Global Assessment and the opportunities for Australian law and policy' (2019) 34(6) Australian Environment Review 103, 107.

Office of Compliance and Enforcement which would have modern regulatory powers and tools.[43]

The EPBC Act allows for development harmful to nationally significant biodiversity to proceed in some cases where there is compensation for residual adverse impacts. The practice surrounding the use of offsets was criticized in the Samuel Review, which recommended the EPBC Act be reformed to provide that biodiversity offsets 'only be considered after all possible measures to avoid and mitigate the impacts of an action have demonstrably been taken'.[44] This suggested reform addresses the finding that the current offsets policy under the EPBC Act contributes to environmental decline despite the fact that offsets are intended as a tool to limit such decline resulting from development.[45] While the suggested reform—if implemented—could stop offsetting from being a so-called 'saviour for inappropriate development',[46] it does not address some underlying critiques that have emerged in the Australian context. One such critique—framed around Australia's iconic koala—argues that the biocentrist logic of environmental markets does not pertain to sentient organisms in the way that it does to fungible commodities like greenhouse gas.[47] An additional critique recognizes that any baseline for Australia's biodiversity has been decimated by the unprecedented impact of the wildfires. Australia's not-for-profit community legal service, the Environmental Defender's Office (EDO), is currently investigating legal mechanisms to pause biodiversity offset decisions 'until there has been a reassessment of what has been lost to fires'.[48]

Aside from the federal statute addressing matters of national environmental significance, Australian state and territory laws respond to the need for conservation, often in statutes predating the CBD.[49] The Victorian Flora and Fauna Guarantee Act 1988 (Vic) and the New South Wales Biodiversity Conservation Act 2016 (NSW), for example, support strategic planning frameworks for conserving threatened species in those jurisdictions. In addition, at the local level,

43 Samuel Review (n 10) 147, 153 (Recommendation 30).
44 ibid 140 (Box 28), 141 (Recommendation 27).
45 ibid 138.
46 David Takacs, 'Are Koalas Fungible: Biodiversity Offsetting and the Law' (2017) 26 NYU Environmental Law Journal 161, 185, citing Australian Senate Environment and Communications References Committee, *Environmental Offsets* (Report, June 2014) [3.4].
47 Takacs (n 46) 186.
48 Elaine Johnson, 'A State of Emergency: EDO Is Stepping In' (Environmental Defender's Office, 9 January 2020) <www.edo.org.au/2020/01/09/a-state-of-emergency-edo-is-stepping-in/> accessed 11 March 2022.
49 A list of all state and territory laws is contained in Appendix 4 to the National Biodiversity Strategy and Action Plan.

planning authorities have a range of roles relating to land use planning, environmental management, and climate change adaptation.

The form of litigation and remedies are often specific to jurisdictions. At the Commonwealth level, for example, judicial review plays the central role. In 2009, the first review of the EPBC Act chaired by Dr Allan Hawke made recommendations about broadening the scope for merits review under the EPBC Act.[50] Calls for broader merits review were also made (particularly by Environment Defenders Offices—EDOs)[51] in submissions to the Australian Senate Environment and Communications References Committee leading to its 2019 interim report on Australia's faunal extinction crisis.[52] This issue was also prominent in the Samuel Review, which advised against 'full' merits review, but nevertheless recommended a narrow expansion of its scope.[53]

2.4 Standing to Bring Claims

Procedural obligations relating to access to justice are of major importance to biodiversity litigation. Australian law does not extend to standing for non-human entities. This absence was made clear by Chief Justice Brian Preston in a fictitious judgment provided for the 'Wild Law Project', in which green sea turtles successfully challenged Commonwealth and Queensland government approvals of coal mines, on the basis of harm to their habitat caused by anthropogenic climate change.[54] Yet mechanisms for initiating public interest biodiversity litigation do exist under the EPBC Act, and can be said to be consistent with Australia's international obligations.[55] Of particular importance are the provision of public interest legal services by organizations such as the EDOs

[50] Australian Government Department of the Environment, Water, Heritage and the Arts, *The Australian Environment Act: Report of the Independent Review of the Environment Protection and Biodiversity Conservation Act 1999* (Final report, October 2009) II ('Hawke Review') 40.

[51] Brendan Sydes, 'The Challenges of Putting Wild Law into Practice: Reflections on the Australian Environmental Defenders Office Movement' in Michell Maloney and Peter Burdon (eds), *Wild Law: In Practice* (Routledge 2014) 58.

[52] Senate Environment and Communications References Committee, 'Australia's Faunal Extinction Crisis: Interim Report' (April 2019) 57 (hereafter Australia's Faunal Extinction Crisis).

[53] Samuel Review (n 10) 11, 93–95 (recommending that merits review only be available to litigants with standing, that the scope of the review be limited to the material available at the time of the original decision, that only approval decisions or decisions in relation to approval conditions be available for review, and that the review must relate to consideration of decisions where the exercise of discretion was incorrect or unreasonable in the circumstances).

[54] Brian Preston, 'Green Sea Turtles by Their Representative, *Meryl Streef v The State of Queensland and the Commonwealth of Australia*' in Nicole Rogers and Michelle Maloney (eds), *Law as if Earth Really Mattered: The Wild Law Judgment Project* (Routledge 2017) 31.

[55] See eg art 13 of the CBD relating to public education and awareness: see Felicity Millner, 'Access to Environmental Justice' (2011) 16 Deakin Law Review 189.

established in Sydney, Melbourne, and other cities,[56] alongside other non-governmental organizations.

The extent of standing provisions under the EPBC Act has been a topic of controversy in Australia in recent years. Section 487 of the EPBC Act provides legal standing to Australian individuals or groups that engage in environmental protection, conservation, or research activities, who may apply for judicial review of decisions made under the EPBC Act. This is alongside common law rules relating to standing, which have evolved to require parties to have a connection and interest in the subject matter of the action—a situation that is often easier to satisfy in private rather than public interest cases.[57] Of the sixteen Australian cases from 2000 to 2020 citing the CBD, six were brought by an EDO.

For some commentators, business lobby groups, and governments opposed to climate and associated litigation, public interest litigants are engaging in 'green lawfare'[58] and have abused the mechanism of judicial review to disrupt and delay development projects.[59] Under the leadership of the Coalition, the Commonwealth government endorsed this view by introducing the Environment Protection and Biodiversity Conservation Amendment (Standing) Bill 2015,[60] which sought to repeal section 487 of the EPBC Act.[61]

The repeal of section 487 was sought by the Coalition government despite the fact that there was little evidence to support the contention that the section opened a floodgate to vexatious and frivolous litigation.[62] The Bill passed the House of Representatives and was sent to the Senate,[63] but ultimately lapsed at the prorogation of Parliament on 17 April 2016.[64] However, the broader issue

[56] Sydes (n 51).

[57] The general rule is that for a party to bring an action, they must have a real connection and interest in the matter in dispute: see *Australian Conservation Foundation v Commonwealth* (1980) 146 CLR 493, 527 (Gibbs J).

[58] Annika Reynolds, Andrew Ray, and Shelby O'Connor, 'Green Lawfare: Does the Evidence Match the Allegations?—An Empirical Evaluation of Public Interest Litigation under the EPBC Act from 2009 to 2019' (2020) 37 Environmental and Planning Law Journal 497; Andrew Macintosh and others, 'Delays, Stoppages and Appeals: An Empirical Evaluation of the Adverse Impacts of Environmental Citizen Suits in the New South Wales Land and Environment Court' (2018) 69 Environmental Impact Assessment Review 94; Rachel Pepper and Rachael Chick, 'Ms Onus and Mr Neal: Agitators in an Age of "Green Lawfare"' (2018) 35 Environmental and Planning Law Journal 177.

[59] This debate intensified following the Mackay Conservation Group's successful challenge to the approval of the Adani Carmichael coal project in 2015, following which the Commonwealth government attempted to reduce the number of proceedings in relation to the mine by limiting the parties who had standing to apply for judicial review of decisions made under the EPBC Act: Department of Parliamentary Services (Cth), Bills Digest (Digest No 37 of 2015–16, 3 November 2015) 3.

[60] ibid.

[61] EPBC Act (n 9) s 487; Department of Parliamentary Services (Cth), Bills Digest (n 59) 3–4.

[62] Department of Parliamentary Services (Cth), Bills Digest (n 59) 6–9.

[63] Environment Protection and Biodiversity Conservation Amendment (Standing) Bill 2015 (Parliament of Australia).

[64] ibid.

to which the proposed repeal of section 487 of the EPBC Act relates—that the EPBC Act must be reformed to 'tackle' the 'green tape' prevalent in this complex legislation—endured within the Coalition government.[65] Indeed, 'making decisions simpler, including reducing unnecessary regulatory burdens for Australians, businesses and governments' was identified as a guiding principle informing the Samuel Review and was supported in proposed legislation before the change in government in 2022.[66]

The final report of the Samuel Review found 'courts already have the capacity to deal with baseless or vexatious litigation' and recommended the current standing provisions under the EPBC Act be retained.[67] This recommendation aligns with empirical evidence that shows concerns in relation to 'green lawfare' are unfounded.[68] However, the Samuel Review also recommended that 'legal challenges should be limited to matters of outcome, not process, to avoid litigation that does not have a material impact on the outcome'.[69] With a new government in power, it remains to be seen whether there will be changes to the types of litigation pursued at the federal level.

3. Evolution of Biodiversity Litigation in Australia

Having described the legal framework for Australian biodiversity protection and conservation, this section moves to a survey of the cases. These are divided according to the following subject areas underlying the cases: land clearing and deforestation; mining and related climate change litigation (extending to recent claims relating to public duties); and marine cases. The rise in discourses surrounding rights and the use of scientific data is also discussed.

3.1 Land Clearing and Deforestation

A significant number of biodiversity cases in Australia relate to deforestation and land clearing. Habitat loss due to vegetation clearing is considered the

[65] Sussan Ley (MP), 'Graeme Samuel to Lead Environment Review' (Media Release, Australian Government Department of the Environment and Energy, 29 October 2019).

[66] Australian Government Department of the Environment and Energy, *Independent Review of the EPBC Act* (Discussion Paper, 2019) 2. See also Environment Protection and Biodiversity Conservation Amendment (Streamlining Environmental Approvals) Bill 2020 (Parliament of Australia) (not supported by the then opposition Labor party during various Senate processes).

[67] Samuel Review (n 10) 93, 95.

[68] See Reynolds, Ray, and O'Connor (n 58) 502, 505–06.

[69] ibid 81. See also at 93.

most significant driver of population decline and species extinctions.[70] Since European settlement of Australia in the late eighteenth century, Australia has lost nearly 40 per cent of its forests, resulting in the remaining native vegetation being highly fragmented.[71] Accordingly, protecting these fragments has been identified by scholars as the necessary foundation of Australia's forest conservation policy. Attempts at aligning Australia's environmental legislation with this requirement have been made through biodiversity litigation.

The decision of the Federal Court in *Friends of Leadbeater's Possum Inc v VicForests* reflects one such attempt.[72] The case related to the status of intergovernmental agreements between the Commonwealth and state governments. These 'regional forestry agreements' support commercial timber-harvesting activities by statutory agencies, which seek to harvest timber from state native forests in accordance with ecologically sustainable management. Forestry operations undertaken in accordance with these regional forestry agreements are exempt from certain provisions of the EPBC Act.[73] The case was brought against the Victorian statutory agency whose purpose is to manage and sell the timber resources of Victorian state forests. The Friends of Leadbeater's Possum sought declaratory and injunctive relief, submitting that VicForests had breached the EPBC Act when undertaking actions with a significant impact on listed threatened species or endangered communities, including the endangered greater glider and Leadbeater's possum species.

The primary judge ruled in favour of the Friends of Leadbeater's Possum.[74] Her Honour found that the exemption from the EPBC Act did not apply. Amongst other things, Her Honour ruled that obligations for threatened species to be 'maintained' according to the EPBC Act extended to a recognition that biodiversity decline must be arrested and reversed.[75] Her Honour made orders restraining VicForests from undertaking forestry operations in specific coupes of significance to the threatened species.[76]

The orders of the primary judge were set aside on appeal.[77] The Full Court held that, according to the correct statutory construction of the EPBC Act, the

[70] Bradshaw (n 6) 110; see also n 7 and accompanying text.

[71] ibid 109.

[72] *Friends of Leadbeater's Possum Inc v VicForests (No 4)* [2020] FCA 704; *VicForests v Friends of Leadbeater's Possum Inc* [2021] FCAFC 66; see also *MyEnvironment Inc v VicForests* [2012] VSC 91; *Environment East Gippsland Inc v VicForests* [2010] VSC 335; *Forestry Tasmania v Brown* [2007] FCAFC 186; *Bob Brown Foundation Inc v Commonwealth of Australia* [2021] FCAFC 5.

[73] EPBC Act (n 9) s 38.

[74] *Friends of Leadbeater's Possum (No 4)* (n 72).

[75] ibid [630].

[76] ibid; *Friends of Leadbeater's Possum Inc v VicForests (No 6)* [2020] FCA 1199.

[77] *VicForests v Friends of Leadbeater's Possum* (n 72).

conduct of VicForests did not lead it to lose its exemption.[78] The Full Court emphasized, however, that the primary judge's findings of fact were not disturbed on appeal (ie that VicForests had contravened state legislative instruments with respect to the endangered greater glider and Leadbeater's possum species). In addition, the Full Court rejected VicForests' ground for appeal on the inapplicability of the precautionary principle.[79] The 'public interest' nature of the litigation, and the rejection by the Full Court of most of VicForests' grounds of appeal, were noted by the Full Court in its discretionary costs order, which was in terms favourable to Friends of Leadbeater's Possum.[80] Although the Friends of Leadbeater's Possum sought leave to appeal to the High Court of Australia, this application was refused.[81]

The litigation concerning regional forestry agreements is a good example of the complexity of federal arrangements in the environmental sphere, and the lack of a coherent national approach to biodiversity protection. Since the *Leadbeater's Possum* case was launched against Victorian forestry practices, a parallel set of cases have been brought in relation to Tasmania. These were dismissed by the Full Federal Court,[82] signalling resistance from this court to interrogate whether the conduct of state-based forestry activities conform to biodiversity obligations. It should be noted that the final report of the Samuel Review recommended that national environmental standards be developed, and that the Commonwealth require Australia's state governments to ensure that regional forestry agreements are consistent with these standards.[83] The Samuel Review also recommended that the regional forestry agreement exemption which allowed the logging challenged in *Friends of Leadbeater's Possum* and the Tasmanian cases, should be replaced by a requirement for accreditation against national environment standards.[84]

In other contexts, litigation at the state and territory levels indicates some success in upholding commitments to biodiversity protection. In litigation in the Northern Territory (NT), also supported by the EDO, an application by the Environment Centre was made to review a decision of the NT Environment Protection Authority (EPA), which had held that an environment impact statement was unnecessary regarding an application to clear

[78] ibid [130].
[79] ibid [134]–[144].
[80] *VicForests v Friends of Leadbeater's Possum Inc (No 2)* [2021] FCAFC 92.
[81] *Friends of Leadbeater's Possum Inc v VicForests* [2021] HCATrans 215 (10 December 2021).
[82] *Bob Brown Foundation* (n 72) [2].
[83] Samuel Review (n 10) 30 (Recommendation 15).
[84] The review recommended that this accreditation process be overseen by a new Environment Assurance Commissioner: ibid, viii.

vegetation from 237.95 km^2 of land. The NT Supreme Court found that the EPA's decision was invalid.[85] In Queensland, the resources company Boral Resources (Qld) Pty Ltd challenged a decision of the Gold Coast City Council refusing a development permit for a change in land use to develop a quarry, which would have involved the clearing of koala habitat. The Queensland Court of Appeal dismissed the appeal and the decision to reject the development was upheld.[86]

3.2 Mining and Other Links to Climate Change Litigation

Mining-related litigation is significant in Australia, and it often links biodiversity protection with obligations relating to climate change mitigation. Prominent cases involving Australian biodiversity have been brought to address the impacts of mining.[87] There are also examples of miners violating their social licence to operate through eroding public opinion, as occurred in the 2020 destruction of the culturally significant Juukan Gorge site by the mining company Rio Tinto.[88] While biodiversity claims have yet to permanently halt the development of a mine, some have significantly delayed the approval process.[89]

The case of *Bulga* at the NSW Land and Environment Court is perhaps most noteworthy for its acceptance of a new term to the corpus of environmental harm: namely, 'solastalgia'.[90] This term was used by Chief Justice Preston to describe the distress and suffering experienced by the residents who lived close to

[85] *The Environment Centre Northern Territory v The Northern Territory Environment Protection Authority and Anor* [2019] NTSC 69.

[86] *Boral Resources (Qld) Pty Ltd v Gold Coast City Council* [2018] QCA 75.

[87] See eg Paul Martin, Márcia Dieguez Leuzinger, and Solange Teles da Silva, 'The Issues, Methods and Evidence' in Paul Martin and others (eds), *Achieving Biodiversity Protection in Megadiverse Countries: A Comparative Assessment of Australia and Brazil* (Routledge 2020) 1, 50.

[88] Joint Standing Committee on Northern Australia, 'Inquiry into the Destruction of 46,000 Year Old Caves at the Juukan Gorge in the Pilbara Region of Western Australia'. See also Emma Jukić and Margaret Young, 'Australia' (2020) 30 Yearbook of International Environmental Law 363–73.

[89] See eg *Bulga Milbrodale Progress Association Inc v Minister for Planning and Infrastructure and Warkworth Mining Ltd* [2013] NSWLEC 48 and appeal; *Adani Mining Pty Ltd v Land Services of Coast and Country Inc* [2015] QLC 48; *Mackay Conservation Group v Commonwealth of Australia* (Federal Court of Australia, NSD33/2015, commenced 12 January 2015); *New Acland Coal Pty Ltd v Ashman and Chief Executive, Department of Environment and Heritage Protection (No 4)* [2017] QLC 24; *Upper Mooki Landcare Inc v Shenhua Watermark Coal Pty Ltd and Minister for Planning* [2016] NSWLEC 6; *Tarkine National Coalition v Minister for the Environment* [2015] FCAFC 89; *Tarkine National Coalition Inc v Minister for Sustainability Environment Population and Communities* [2013] FCA 694.

[90] *Bulga* (n 89). On the emergence of the term, see Glenn Albreacht and others, 'Solastalgia: The Distress Caused by Environmental Change' (2007) 15 Australasian Psychiatry S95; see also Amanda Kennedy, 'A Case of Place: Solastalgia Comes before the Court' (2016) 12 Philosophy Activism Nature 23.

an open-cut coal mine which was seeking expansion.[91] The desolation tied to their sense of place could be further extrapolated to the biodiversity context in future litigation.

Faced with the limited capacity of Australia's environmental laws to address climate change, litigants have opposed mining developments on biodiversity grounds. Often in these cases, the submissions in relation to biodiversity have been more material to the outcome of slowing down development approval than submissions made in relation to climate change. This is attributable to the fact that Australia's national political leaders have been less reluctant to legislate in relation to biodiversity than they have been in relation to climate change.[92] For example, the EPBC Act prohibits actions that will have a significant impact on 'matters of national environmental significance' (MNES) from being carried out without the approval of the Commonwealth Minister for the Environment.[93] There are nine MNES under the EPBC Act which are colloquially referred to as 'triggers'.[94] These include actions which may affect: world heritage properties;[95] listed threatened species and ecological communities listed;[96] and the Great Barrier Reef Marine Park.[97] These MNES are clearly underpinned by biodiversity concerns. In contrast, actions that will cause high greenhouse gas emissions are not included in the list of MNES and climate change is treated as incidental to the nine existing MNES.[98] In practice, this means that emissions associated with a proposed development are considered in ministerial decision making under the EPBC Act, but are not sufficient to halt the approval of the development.[99]

91 *Bulga* (n 89) [404], [420]–[430].

92 Australia introduced a carbon-pricing mechanism introduced 2011, but this was repealed in 2014. For an overview of the changes, see Emma Jukic and Margaret Young, 'Australia' in (2017) 28 Yearbook of International Environmental Law 404; (2016) 27 Yearbook of International Environmental Law 399; (2015) 26 Yearbook of International Environmental Law 390; (2014) 25 Yearbook of International Environmental Law 471; (2013) 24 Yearbook of International Environmental Law 512; (2012) 23 Yearbook of International Environmental Law 512; (2011) 22 Yearbook of International Environmental Law 566.

93 EPBC Act (n 9) ss 12, 15B, 16, 18, 20, 21, 23, 24B, 24D; 'Australia's Faunal Extinction Crisis' (n 52) 6.

94 'Australia's Faunal Extinction Crisis' (n 52) 6.

95 EPBC Act (n 9) s 12.

96 ibid s 18.

97 ibid s 24B.

98 Environmental Defenders Office NSW and Humane Society International Australia, *Next Generation Biodiversity Laws: Best Practice Elements for a New Commonwealth Environment Act* (2018) 54.

99 eg *Australian Conservation Foundation Incorporated v Minister for the Environment* [2016] FCA 1042; *Australian Conservation Foundation Incorporated v Minister for the Environment and Energy* [2017] FCAFC 134.

Since the enactment of the EPBC Act, politicians and scholars have debated whether it should be amended to include a climate change trigger.[100] The most recent consideration of this issue was during the Samuel Review. The review did not recommend a climate change trigger be included, but it did recommend that national environmental standards be developed to require development proposals to 'explicitly consider the likely effectiveness of avoidance or mitigation measures on nationally protected matters under specified climate change scenarios' and 'transparently disclose the full emissions of the development'.[101]

The lack of a climate change trigger under the EPBC Act explains why emissions-intensive developments are often opposed on grounds including the impacts on listed species. The successful challenge brought by Mackay Conservation Group (supported by the EDO) to the approval of the Adani Carmichael coal project in 2015 is an example.[102] The applicant claimed that the decision to grant the mining lease should be set aside on the basis that the minister failed to consider the impact of the greenhouse gas emissions from the proposed mine on the Great Barrier Reef. This issue was left unresolved by the court.[103] Instead, the court set aside the mining licence on the grounds that the minister failed to consider the impact of the mine on the yakka skink and the ornamental snake—two endangered species listed under the EPBC Act.[104] The minister had not been provided with the correct conservation advice in relation to these species, therefore the approval decision did not comply with the requirements of the EPBC Act.[105] Thus, even though it did not permanently stop the development of the mine, the yakka skink and ornamental snake slowed down the approval process by necessitating a second ministerial approval.[106] This case exemplifies that due to the insufficiency of the EPBC Act to address climate change, biodiversity claims can and have strengthened climate change litigation in Australia.

A less successful example of this was *Tarkine National Coalition v Minister for Sustainable Environment Population and Communities*,[107] a claim brought

[100] See Chris McGrath, 'Regulating Greenhouse Gas Emissions from Australian Coal Mines' (2008) 25 Environmental and Planning Law Journal 240, 259. The Hawke Review of the EPBC Act recommended the inclusion of a climate change trigger in the EPBC Act: see Hawke Review (n 50) 116.

[101] Samuel Review (n 10) 26 (Recommendation 2).

[102] Federal Court of Australia, NSD33/2015, commenced 12 January 2015.

[103] A Grech, RL Pressey, and JC Day, 'Coal, Cumulative Impacts, and the Great Barrier Reef' (2016) 9 Conservation Letters 200, 204.

[104] Order of Justice Katzmann in *Mackay Conservation Group v Commonwealth of Australia* (Federal Court of Australia, NSD33/2015, 4 August 2015); Grech, Pressey, and Day (n 103) 204.

[105] EPBC Act (n 9) s 139(2); Grech, Pressey and Day (n 103) 204;

[106] ibid.

[107] [2013] FCA 694; *Tarkine National Coalition v Minister for the Environment* [2015] FCAFC 89.

against the minister's decision to approve a proposed action to develop and operate a mine in northwest Tasmania. The applicants claimed that the minister failed to have regard to the approved conservation advice for the Tasmanian devil (Australia's iconic meat-eating marsupial).[108] Although the applicant was ultimately unsuccessful in the case, this was for reasons other than the ground of review relating to the CBD.

Other cases demonstrating links between biodiversity and climate change litigation include *Spencer v Commonwealth of Australia*,[109] in which a farmer challenged NSW laws restricting the clearing of vegetation. Mr Spencer considered the laws made his land unsuitable for commercial farming, effectively amounting to an acquisition or expropriation of his interests in it. He was concerned that the Commonwealth was attempting to fulfil international obligations relating to climate mitigation through the land clearing laws, and that his proprietary interests had been accordingly acquired on other than just terms. The Federal Court dismissed his arguments.

In *Two Rocks Investments Pty Ltd*,[110] review was sought of a Western Australian Planning Commission's decision not to approve a plan for residential development along approximately 2.6 kilometres of coastline. The court upheld the Planning Commission's decision, rejecting the development on the basis that it did not have the appropriate safeguards to account for sea level rises anticipated by climate change. While this case is primarily classifiable as a 'climate change' case, biodiversity and ecosystem integrity of the coastline were important considerations.

Before turning to novel claims relating to the duties of the executive to act to avert climate change, it is important to note a further link between cases that relate to biodiversity protection and climate change: namely, the observable failure of Australia's environmental legislation in addressing cumulative impacts. The difficulty of assessing cumulative impacts that harm the environment plagues law and regulatory approaches.[111] Biodiversity litigation, like climate change litigation, is based on challenges to proposed activities that are assessed by the courts in a vacuum,[112] leading to significant limitations.

[108] See 'Approved Conservation Advice for *Sarcophilus harrisii* (Tasmanian Devil)' (19 May 2009).
[109] [2018] FCAFC 17, (2018) 262 FCR 344.
[110] [2019] WASAT 59, [124].
[111] See Ayodele Olagunju and others, 'Cumulative Effects Assessment Requirements in Selected Developed and Developing Countries' in Jill AE Blakley and Daniel M Franks (eds), *Handbook of Cumulative Impact Assessment* (Edward Elgar 2021) 21–38.
[112] Brian Preston, 'Adapting to the Impacts of Climate Change: The Limits and Opportunities of Law in Conserving Biodiversity' (2013) 30 Environmental and Planning Law Journal 375, 383.

3.3 Duties of the Executive in Statute or Tort Law

Two cases are significant for the development of public duties in the climate context, which can be extrapolated to the biodiversity context and thus merit discussion here. The first, in the federal jurisdiction, relates to claims for a duty of care to children held by the Commonwealth Environment Minister;[113] the second, in the NSW Land and Environment Court, targets the NSW environmental regulatory authority by bushfire survivors.[114] A third case, brought by a group of indigenous peoples, is on foot. The cases can be contrasted to mooted ideas about how the 'public trust' doctrine could be used in relation to climate change impacts.[115] Yet they diverge significantly, and there is persistent uncertainty about whether an Australian government might be deemed by a court through litigation to hold a duty of care to Australian citizens, breached by climate action failure.[116]

The case of *Sharma* was based on a novel conception of a duty of care founded in tort law, owed to children, and argued to flow from the minister's responsibilities under the EPBC Act. The primary judge held that the Commonwealth Environment Minister owed a duty of care to Australian children not to cause them harm from climate change when deciding whether to approve the extension of a coal mine under the EPBC Act.[117] This finding of May 2021 appeared to herald a significant shift of the kind reached by the Dutch Urgenda case.[118] Subsequent developments make this outcome less likely. In September 2021, the Commonwealth Environment Minister proceeded to approve the coal mine extension.[119] In reaching this decision, the minister considered the duty of care found by the court and determined that this duty would be discharged if the mine was approved. The minister considered the approval of the proposed action unlikely to cause harm to human safety, and that the contribution of the

[113] *Minister for the Environment v Sharma* [2022] FCAFC 35 (Allsop CJ, Beach and Wheelahan JJ).

[114] *Bushfire Survivors for Climate Action Inc v Environment Protection Authority* [2021] NSWLEC 92. The case was brought under the Protection of the Environment Administration Act 1991 (NSW), which requires the EPA to 'develop environmental quality objectives, guidelines and policies to ensure environment protection'.

[115] Bruce Thom, 'Climate Change, Coastal Hazards and the Public Trust Doctrine' (2012) 8 Macquarie Journal of International and Comparative Environmental Law 21.

[116] Scholars have considered duty-based tort claims against governments to face significant challenges in Australia: Jacqueline Peel, Hari Osofsky, and Anita Foerster, 'Shaping the "Next Generation" of Climate Change Litigation in Australia' (2017) 41 Melbourne University Law Review 793, 805. But see, in a reimagined judgment on public nuisance obligations as part of the wild law project, Preston (n 54).

[117] *Sharma by her litigation representative Sister Marie Brigid Arthur v Minister for the Environment* [2021] FCA 560, [490]–[491].

[118] *Urgenda Foundation v State of Netherlands* (Hoge Raad—Dutch Supreme Court) ECLI:NL:HR:2019:2007 (C/09/00456689) (delivered 20 December 2019).

[119] Sussan Ley (MP), 'Approval: Vickery Extension Project, Gunnedah, NSW (EPBC 2016/7649)'.

mine to global greenhouse gas emissions was outweighed by the claimed social and economic benefits of the mine.[120]

The minister also appealed the decision by the primary judge. In March 2022, the Full Federal Court overturned the primary judge's finding of a duty of care for various reasons including that in the court's view the judiciary should not intervene in relation to climate change policy.[121] Though the science and impending risk of climate change was not disputed, the Full Court reversed the primary judge's findings regarding the minister's duties towards private individuals. As stated by Allsop CJ:

> we all rely on an elected government to develop and implement wise policy in the interests of all Australians, in one sense especially the children of the country who are its future. That is not the foundation of the law of torts. It is the foundation of responsible democratic government.[122]

His Honour expressed a view, common amongst the judiciary, that the judicial branch is unsuitable for matters of climate policy, due in part to the consideration that the impending catastrophe 'can only be addressed by global co-ordinated policy and action'[123] and due also to a need for decisions that are based on 'political and democratic choices involving relationships of interests incommensurable by reference to any legal standard' (ie decisions of the political branches).[124] These views of Allsop CJ are somewhat at odds with the practical incapacities of the other branches of power to act on climate change, observed in Australia and elsewhere (and not put before the court in *Sharma*).[125]

The applicants in *Sharma* did not seek leave to appeal to the High Court.[126] Despite initial concerns that the Full Court's decision would hinder public trust doctrine arguments in future claims,[127] a later order relating to issue estoppel noted that harm to the litigants from climate change could eventuate decades from now, 'at which time any number of facts and circumstances, and the state

[120] Sussan Ley (MP), 'Statement of Reasons for Approval under the Environment Protection and Biodiversity Conservation Act 1999', paras 163–282.
[121] *Minister for the Environment v Sharma* (n 113).
[122] ibid [344].
[123] ibid [227].
[124] ibid [238].
[125] Young (n 41) 366.
[126] Statement by litigants, '"They will not forget our names": no appeal, but a vow to keep pushing for climate action', available on the website of Equity Generation Lawyers—the law firm representing the applicants <https://equitygenerationlawyers.com/cases/sharma-v-minister-for-environment/> accessed 18 July 2022.
[127] Jacqueline Peel and Rebekkah Markey-Towler, 'Today's disappointing federal court decision undoes 20 years of climate litigation progress in Australia', *The Conversation* (15 March 2022).

and development of the law of negligence in Australia or the relevant law area in Australia, could dictate a different result'.[128] There is keen interest in litigation relating to alleged violations of public duties commenced by a group of Torres Strait Islanders against the Commonwealth in October 2021, in which the claimants have noted that '[b]iodiversity loss disproportionately impacts those communities and societal groups that are most directly dependent on nature'.[129] This augments existing international petitions on behalf of Torres Strait Islanders at the Human Rights Committee in relation to Australia's responsibilities to address climate change.[130]

The second decided case of relevance to public trust was litigated in the jurisdiction of the NSW Land and Environment Court, and contrasts with *Sharma* in legal basis and result. A group who survived the NSW bushfires successfully challenged the NSW EPA. The group was granted an order compelling the EPA 'to perform a statutory duty to develop environmental quality objectives, guidelines and policies to ensure the protection of the environment from climate change'. The duty was found in the Protection of the Environment Administration Act 1991 (NSW).[131]

It is possible to translate these cases to a more specific biodiversity context, including at the state level. For example, a report published by the Victorian Auditor General's Office has found that action plans have been prepared for only 20 per cent of listed species.[132] These action plans are required to be prepared under Victorian legislation, and set out past and planned conservation efforts in relation to listed threatened species or endangered communities.[133] While rights-based arguments on behalf of the remaining 80 per cent of listed species are not currently possible, it is at least conceivable that litigation could be brought against the relevant government department for breach of the requirement to prepare action statements for all listed species in a timely manner.[134] It should be noted,

[128] *Minister for the Environment v Sharma (No 2)* [2022] FCAFC 65 (14 April 2022), [11]
[129] *Pabai Patai and Anor v Commonwealth of Australia* (Federal Court of Australia, VID622/2021, Statement of Claim (Form 17—Rule 8.06(1)(a)) (VID622/2021), filed 26 October 2021, 10.
[130] See Young (n 41) 358; see further Matthew Rimmer, 'The Torres Strait Eight: Climate Litigation, Biodiversity, Human Rights, and Indigenous Intellectual Property' in Charles Lawson, Michelle Rourke, and Frances Humphries (eds), *Access and Benefit Sharing of Genetic Resources: Problems and Solutions* (Taylor Francis 2022).
[131] *Bushfire Survivors* (n 114); see further Laura Schuijers, 'Compelled by the Court to Act on Climate Change: *Bushfire Survivors for Climate Action Incorporated v Environment Protection Authority* [2021] NSWLEC 92' (2022) 34 *Journal of Environmental Law* 223.
[132] Victorian Auditor General's Office, 'Protecting Victoria's Biodiversity, Independent assurance report to Parliament 2021–22:07 (October 2021).
[133] See also Flora and Fauna Guarantee Act 1988 (Vic), s 19.
[134] Victorian Auditor General Office (n 132) 45.

however, that this requirement does not extend to implementing the action plans.[135]

3.4 Marine Cases

Australian cases in the marine context are notable in demonstrating connections between international and domestic litigation. At the international level, the marine context gives rise to examples of litigation protecting 'global public goods' including biodiversity.[136] For example, Australia's litigation against Japan at the International Court of Justice led to a ruling for the protection of whales.[137] Although underpinned by Japan's violations of the International Convention on the Regulation of Whaling, the original application by Australia also alleged violations of the CBD and other international biodiversity laws.[138] In another series of cases brought by Australia and New Zealand against Japan, allegations centred on the over-exploitation of southern blue fin tuna and violations of the law of the sea.[139] The subject matter of these claims has featured in domestic Australian litigation.

The marine context gives rise to domestic constitutional complexity in Australia, which is outside the scope of the present chapter. It is sufficient to note that the Constitution vests to the Commonwealth sovereignty over all offshore areas (aside from areas that were part of a state at federation), although state powers have been conferred through agreements. Constitutional litigation has determined the jurisdiction of subnational governments vis-à-vis the Commonwealth.[140] Consistent with the UN Convention on the Law of the Sea, the Commonwealth has jurisdiction extending to the exclusive economic zone (EEZ).[141]

135 ibid.

136 But see Margaret A Young, 'International Adjudication and the Commons' (2019) 41 University of Hawai'i Law Review 353.

137 *Whaling in the Antarctic (Australia v Japan: New Zealand Intervening)* (Judgment) (International Court of Justice, General List No 148, 31 March 2014).

138 ibid; see also Margaret A Young and Sebastian Rioseco Sullivan, 'Evolution through the Duty to Cooperate: Implications of the Whaling Case at the International Court of Justice' (2015) 16 Melbourne Journal of International Law 310, also Chapter 12 in this volume on international biodiversity litigation.

139 *Southern Bluefin Tuna (New Zealand v Japan; Australia v Japan)* (Provisional Measures, Order of 27 August 1999) [1999], ITLOS Reports 280; *Southern Bluefin Tuna (Australia and New Zealand v Japan)*, Award on Jurisdiction and Admissibility, 23 RIAA 1, para 65 (Arb Trib 2000).

140 See eg the important constitutional case concerning a rock lobster fishery in the waters off the South Australian and Victorian coast lines: *Port MacDonnell PFA Inc v South Australia* (1989) 63 ALJR 671.

141 On the EEZ, see United Nations Convention on the Law of the Sea (opened for signature 10 December 1982, entered into force 16 November 1994) 1833 UNTS 3, arts 2–3, Pt V.

The domestic litigation against whaling was brought against Japanese whalers by an NGO.[142] The Humane Society International (HSI) successfully invoked the EPBC Act, submitting that a Japanese whaling firm violated the federal environmental law in the Australian Whale Sanctuary of the Australian Antarctic Territory. The Full Court upheld the ability of HSI to bring the claim even though service was likely to be ineffective.[143] This case was avowedly different from the international litigation: the latter avoided any focus on Australia's claims over Antarctic waters. In addition, HSI was careful not to bring contempt proceedings against the Japanese whaling company until well after the conclusion of the case before the International Court of Justice.[144]

Two further cases brought by HSI sought to develop the principles underpinning Australian legislation. The first comprised an application to review the classification of the export of southern bluefin tuna as an approved wildlife trade operation under the EPBC Act.[145] While HSI was ultimately unsuccessful in challenging the export, the tribunal affirmed that the provisions of the EPBC Act relating to the listing of threatened species 'appears to be a direct response to Australia's obligations' under article 14 of the CBD.[146] In the second case, involving a review of a shark control programme,[147] the Federal Court upheld a decision of the Administrative Appeals Tribunal applying the precautionary principle and ordered that shark control programmes be carried out in a manner that avoided, to the greatest extent possible, the lethal take of shark species.[148] This was consistent with the main object of the legislation under which the permits were issued—to 'provide for the long term protection and conservation of the environment, biodiversity and heritage values of the Great Barrier Reef Region'.[149]

There are a broad range of other fisheries matters that have been heard by Australian courts, often brought by companies seeking to safeguard their commercial interests.[150] A major event occurred in Tasmanian waters in 2012

[142] *Humane Society International Inc v Kyodo Senpaku Kaisha Ltd* [2006] FCAFC 116.
[143] ibid [29].
[144] Henry Burmester, 'Civil Society and the Instigation of International Court Litigation: The Australian Experience' (2021) 21(3) Melbourne Journal of International Law 772, 787.
[145] *Humane Society International v Minister for the Environment and Heritage* [2006] AATA 298.
[146] ibid [11].
[147] *Humane Society International (Australia) Inc and Department of Agriculture & Fisheries (Qld)* [2019] AATA 617.
[148] *State of Queensland (Department of Agriculture and Fisheries) v Humane Society International (Australia) Inc* [2019] FCAFC 163 (hereafter *Qld Shark Control Programme*).
[149] Great Barrier Reef Marine Park Act 1975 (Cth), s 2A.
[150] See eg *Triabunna Investments Pty Ltd v Minister for Environment and Energy* [2019] FCAFC 60; *Huon Aquaculture Group Ltd v Minister for the Environment* [2018] FCA 1011; *Seafish Tasmania Pelagic Pty Ltd v Burke, Minister for Sustainability, Environment, Water, Population and Communities (No 2)* [2014] FCA 117; *Minister for Sustainability, Environment, Water, Population and Communities v Woodley* [2012] FCA 957.

when a 'supertrawler', a Dutch vessel that was apparently the world's second largest fishing trawler, was brought to fish for mackerel and redbait within Australia's 'small pelagic fishery' zone. Although the supertrawler was ostensibly aiming to fish only the allocated quota, there were significant concerns about the environmental impact of this supertrawler and its impacts on the local fishing industry. The Commonwealth government was sympathetic to these concerns and responded by amending the EPBC Act to allow for the prohibition of the supertrawler's activities.[151] The owner of the supertrawler commenced judicial review proceedings against the Commonwealth Environment Minister, but these were dismissed by the Federal Court.[152] The submission that the minister should have given more consideration to the financial and reputational damage sustained by the owner was not accepted by the court.[153] By contrast, the commercial interest of a swordfish wholesaler was upheld in the Federal Magistrates Court.[154] The minister had refused to grant a permit, required under the EPBC Act, to export CITES II-listed freshwater sawfish to an aquarium in Dubai. The minister noted that the aquarium was not for 'primarily conservation purposes'. The court held that the decision making was flawed, as the minister ought to have instead considered whether it was an appropriate and acceptable facility to house the sawfish,[155] consistently with determinations of the CITES Conferences of the Parties. The minister's decision was quashed and remitted back to the minister for redetermination.

The marine cases demonstrate how the key biodiversity legislation in Australia—primarily, the EPBC Act—continues to underpin litigation that involves wrangling over state or Commonwealth jurisdiction, interpretative guidance from multilateral environment agreements, high political and financial stakes, and escalating species loss. The cases have often been instigated by citizen suits, although litigation is also used by companies seeking to exploit marine biodiversity for commercial gain.

[151] See Environment Protection and Biodiversity Conservation Amendment (Declared Commercial Fishing Activities) Bill 2012; Bill McCormick, 'Commonwealth Legislating to Ban Large Trawler' (Parliament of Australia, 13 September 2012).

[152] *Seafish Tasmania Pelagic Pty Ltd v Burke, Minister for Sustainability, Environment, Water, Population and Communities (No 2)* [2014] FCA 117. The grounds of appeal included the argument that the environment minister was prevented from considering submissions from the broader public in making the decision to prohibit the supertrawler's activities. The court dismissed this ground and held that not only could the minister consider public submissions, but also that it was a matter for ministerial discretion as to the weight to be given to such submissions—see [86].

[153] ibid [88]–[91].

[154] *Anzbrook Pty Ltd trading as Cairns Marine Aquarium Fish v Minister for the Environment, Heritage and the Arts (Cth)* [2010] FMCA 34.

[155] ibid [52].

3.5 Rights Discourses and Other Developments

In Australia, there is no constitutional or statutory bill of rights at the national level.[156] Human rights or rights of nature have not featured in biodiversity litigation, although such developments are emerging in the climate litigation context.[157] While the utility of pursuing a human rights approach to the protection of ecosystems is contested,[158] the trend is important to track.

With human rights charters now operating at the subnational level,[159] there is an expanded opportunity to bring claims. These claims would depend upon connecting the civil and political rights protected by those charters to biodiversity loss—including through concepts such as solastalgia, mentioned earlier.[160] In the climate context, proceedings have been filed by a group of young people being represented by the EDO against a Queensland coal mine based on the human rights of Queensland youth.[161] A NSW planning case referenced 'environmental rights' as part of an overview of the principles of 'ecologically sustainable development',[162] but this case was not upheld on appeal.[163] Moreover, there is significant scope for the influence of indigenous approaches to help to develop alternative concepts of relations between humanity and nature.[164] The link between rights discourses and the 'public trust' doctrine may also strengthen in the future.[165]

[156] See generally Scott Stephenson, 'Rights Protection in Australia' in Cheryl Saunders and Adrienne Stone (eds), *The Oxford Handbook of the Australian Constitution* (OUP 2018) 905.

[157] Schuijers and Young (n 40) 61–65.

[158] Benoit Mayer, 'Climate Change Mitigation as an Obligation Under Human Rights Treaties?' (2021) 115(3) American Journal of International Law 409, 419; Office of the UN High Commissioner for Human Rights, Report on the Relationship Between Climate Change and Human Rights, UN Doc. A/HRC/10/61 (15 January 2009) para 70; Lavanya Rajamani, 'Human Rights in the Climate Change Regime' in John Knox and Ramin Pejan (eds), *The Human Rights to A Healthy Environment* (CUP 2018) 236, 250; Alan Boyle, 'Climate Change, the Paris Agreement and Human Rights' (2018) 67(4) International and Comparative Law Quarterly 759, 777; Fanny Thornton, 'The Absurdity of Relying on Human Rights Law to Go After Emitters' in Benoit Mayer and Alexander Zahar (eds), *Debating Climate Law* (CUP 2021) 159.

[159] Charter of Human Rights and Responsibilities Act 2006 (Vic); Human Rights Act 2004 (ACT); Human Rights Act (2019) (Qld).

[160] See n 90 and accompanying text.

[161] The case is supported by the EDO: see Environmental Defenders Officer, 'Clive Palmer's Galilee Coal Project Faces Human Rights Challenge' (13 May 2020). This case is yet to proceed to a full hearing. An application from the mining company to have the case struck out was unsuccessful: see *Youth Verdict Ltd v Waratah Coal Pty Ltd* [2020] QLC 33; *Youth Verdict Ltd v Waratah Coal Pty Ltd* [2021] QLC 4. See also Justine Bell-James and Briana Collins, 'Queensland's Human Rights Act: A New Frontier Climate Change Litigation?' (2020) 43 University of New South Wales Law Journal 36.

[162] *Walker v Minister for Planning* [2007] NSWLEC 741, [60].

[163] *Minister for Planning v Walker* [2008] NSWCA 224.

[164] Sandra Diaz and others, 'Pervasive Human-Driven Decline of Life on Earth Points to the Need for Profound Change' (2019) 366 Science eaax3100.

[165] See further Section 3.3 earlier.

In other legal developments, 'rights for nature' discourses may become more prominent. One area of significance in Australia is in recognition of rivers and other natural entities as legal persons or living entities. For example, legal personality has been established to hold and manage Victoria's environmental water rights; the Victorian Environmental Water Holder is a newly established entity with the capacity and responsibility to hold water rights for the purpose of maintaining and improving the health of the aquatic environment.[166] Conferring legal personhood on the aquatic environment has had mixed and paradoxical outcomes in relation to balancing the dual objectives of conservation and sustainable use of water.[167] There is evidence to suggest that the operation of environmental water rights-holders may drive law reform that weakens cultural narratives that support protection of the environment. Often, the rights are symbolic, and have not translated to substantive protections.[168] For biodiversity litigation, the rivers' powers are thus limited in protecting their flows and ecosystems.

Public participation features in Australian environmental litigation but there are not the same protections as there are in Aarhus Convention countries.[169] For example, in 2020, the Federal Court dismissed an appeal brought by an aboriginal community which had been excluded from voting on a proposed nuclear waste-disposal facility in rural South Australia. Barngarla native title holders were excluded from the ballot by the local government authority as not satisfying the eligibility criteria. In *Barngarla Determination Aboriginal Corporation RNTBC v District Council of Kimba*,[170] the Full Federal Court upheld the finding of White J. It found that the passing of resolutions for the ballot by the local government authority was not unlawful by reason of the Racial Discrimination Act 1975 (Cth).[171]

A recent federal case brought by a group supporting feral horses (known as brumbies) gave rise to significant questions about clashes between cultural heritage and the preservation of natural ecosystems.[172] The applicants sought an

[166] Erin L O'Donnell and Julia Talbot-Jones, 'Creating Legal Rights for Rivers: Lessons from Australia, New Zealand, and India' (2018) 23 Ecology and Society 7.

[167] Erin O'Donnell, *Legal Rights for Rivers, Competition, Collaboration and Water Governance* (Routledge 2019) 151–53.

[168] Erin O'Donnell, 'Rivers as Living Beings: Rights in Law, But No Rights to water?' (2020) 29(4) Griffith Law Review 643.

[169] Convention on Access to Information, Public Participation in Decision-Making and Access to Justice in Environmental Matters (opened for signature 25 June 1998, entered into force 30 October 2001) 2161 UNTS 447 (hereafter Aarhus Convention). Australia is not a party to this Convention, notwithstanding that any UN Member State is allowed to accede: see art 19(3).

[170] [2020] FCAFC 39.

[171] ibid [62]–[64].

[172] *Australian Brumby Alliance Inc v Parks Victoria Inc* [2020] FCA 605.

injunction to restrain the managing authority from removing wild horses from the alpine national park. Their application, which rested on interpretations of the CBD in addition to the 'ecosystem approach', was dismissed. The Federal Court found that cultural and social values (in this case, transhumant grazing, aesthetic value, pioneering identity value, and 'Australian writers' value), did not fall within the scope of article 8 of the CBD. The court found the applicant had selectively chosen provisions relating to the ecosystem approach, and the court instead referred to CBD materials relating to invasive alien species. The court held that article 8 of the CBD is concerned with the conservation of biological diversity, not cultural values.[173]

The CBD also featured in an appeal against a decision relating to the import of live specimens of the Savannah cat. In *Parker v Minister for Sustainability, Environment, Water, Population and Communities*,[174] the appellant sought a declaration that an instrument preventing the import of the specimens was invalid. The Federal Court noted that there was a 'real connection' between Australia's obligations under the CBD and the minister's power to prevent the introduction of species that threaten ecosystems, habitats, or species.[175] This use of the CBD to interpret domestic legislation was uncontroversial, perhaps due to the fact that the court's decision and the Commonwealth government's policy in relation to the Savannah cat were in alignment in this case.

While litigation is clearly important for groups seeking to enforce the CBD and other treaties at the domestic level, it is but one of several approaches. For example, for 2020, the EDO's public campaign to protect the koala included: engaging in the development of a draft strategy on koala conservation for south-east Queensland; calling for revisions to the NSW State Environmental Planning Policy—Koala Habitat (Koala SEPP) to be finalized (including that the Koala SEPP be strengthened to identify and protect habitat and corridors that will support koalas' resilience to more extreme heat and natural disasters); and engaging in the NSW Parliamentary Inquiry on koala habitats and populations.[176] Any assessment of biodiversity litigation in Australia must be aware of how it intersects with other forums of engagement, public education, protest, and activism.[177]

173 ibid [199]–[217].
174 [2012] FCAFC 94.
175 ibid [81].
176 Johnson (n 48). On 12 February 2022, the koala (combined populations of Queensland, NSW, and the ACT) was listed as endangered under the EPBC Act: Department of Agriculture, Water and the Environment (n 3).
177 See eg Nicole Rogers, 'Duck Rescuers and the Freedom to Protest: *Levy v Victoria*' in Nicole Rogers and Michelle Maloney (eds), *Law as if the Earth Really Mattered: The Wild Law Judgements Project* (Routledge 2017) 340.

3.6 Expert Evidence and the Use of Scientific Data

The availability of sufficient expert witnesses has been identified as an essential ingredient for successful public interest environmental litigation in Australia.[178] As noted by Chief Justice Preston of the NSW Land and Environment Court, 'increasingly, it is being recognised that a court with special expertise in environmental matters is best placed to play this role in the achievement of ecologically sustainable development'.[179] This claim has been borne out in the cases examined for this chapter. Of the fifty-seven Australian cases involving biodiversity claims between 2010 and 2020, twenty-three were originally claims heard in the NSW Land and Environment Court. An advantage of a specialist court is that it brings both judges and non-lawyer specialists who act as internal experts together to create a 'centre of excellence' for environmental law.[180] Panels of officers with diverse specialist expertise, including environmental scientists, are assembled by the court to advise and assist judges in hearing environmental cases, thus facilitating interdisciplinary decision making.[181]

Australian courts more generally have developed a concept known as 'hot-tubbing' which is also known as 'concurrent evidence'.[182] Pursuant to this approach, each side to a litigation selects its own expert witness, and these experts testify side-by-side, as though in a hot tub, with experts giving concurrent statements on their views.

The concept of hot-tubbing and the existence of specialist environmental courts elevate the prominence of scientific evidence in biodiversity litigation in Australia. Scientific evidence has been material to the judgment in many cases. For example, in the shark drum case discussed earlier,[183] the court referred to the 'overwhelming' scientific evidence that the lethal component of the shark control programme did not reduce the risk of unprovoked shark interactions.[184] Further, in the brumby case,[185] expert evidence in relation to the genetics of the brumbies was invoked to support the conclusion that the

178 Chris McGrath, 'Flying Foxes, Dams and Whales: Using Federal Environmental Laws in the Public Interest' (2008) 25 Environmental and Planning Law Journal 324, 328.

179 Brian Preston, 'Operating an Environment Court: The Experience of the Land and Environment Court of New South Wales' (2008) 25 Environmental and Planning Law Journal 385, 386.

180 ibid; Brian J Preston, 'Characteristics of Successful Environmental Courts and Tribunals' (2014) 26 Journal of Environmental Law 365, 379.

181 ibid.

182 Elizabeth Reifert, 'Getting into the Hot Tub: How the United States Could Benefit from Australia's Concept of Hot Tubbing Expert Witnesses' (2011) 89 University of Detroit Mercy Law Review 103, 113.

183 *Qld Shark Control Programme*; see n 148 and surrounding text.

184 ibid [33].

185 *Australian Brumby Alliance* (n 172).

proposed removal of brumbies from the alpine national park was appropriate to give effect to Australia's obligations under article 8 of the CBD. This was because the culling programme would not remove a population that was likely to carry some unique genetic features.[186] Further, a planning challenge against the construction of a steel fabrication workshop and distribution facility was brought on the basis of threats to a threatened species of honeyeater. Expert evidence provided to the court to assist in the application of the precautionary principle referred to the 'long term decline in the genetic diversity of the species within the locality'.[187] This evidence contributed to the court's decision to set aside the development consent. As threats of extinction escalate in Australia, the need for court processes to support the use of scientific data and expert evidence will continue.

4. Conclusion

This chapter has assessed the constitutional basis, influence of international law, and range of terrestrial and marine contexts for biodiversity litigation in Australia. Cases have sought to protect iconic native species, including the Tasmanian devil,[188] possums threatened by forestry,[189] and sharks subject to culls.[190] Cases have also related to introduced or invasive species, including Australian brumbies[191] and a desired imported cat species.[192] We have demonstrated that Australian courts have been relatively constrained in protecting biodiversity, due to dominant interpretations of the separation of powers and limited direct applicability of international environmental law. Moreover, Australia's federal structure limits the Commonwealth's ability to intervene in circumstances concerning federally listed species, which is required to implement Australia's obligations under international environmental treaties. Yet there is increasing recognition by judges, especially within subnational, specialist jurisdictions, of the need to enforce biodiversity law and educate broader society about the needs and even rights of non-human species.

186 ibid [82].

187 *Friends of Tumblebee Inc v ATB Morton Pty Ltd (No 2)* [2016] NSWLEC 16, [43], [181]–[185].

188 *Tarkine National Coalition* (n 107).

189 *Friends of Leadbeater's Possum (No 4)* (n 72).

190 *Qld Shark Control Programme* (n 148). For the imagined case involving sea turtles, see Preston (n 54).

191 *Australian Brumby Alliance* (n 172).

192 *Parker v Minister for Sustainability, Environment, Water, Population and Communities* (n 174).

We have based our analysis in this chapter on a discussion of land clearing and forestry, mining, marine species, climate change, and rights discourses, as these have been the major contexts of the cases before the Australian courts. We have shown that Australian biodiversity litigation takes account of Australia's international environmental treaty obligations in various ways. Although there is no direct applicability of international law, courts have interpreted statutes with reference to the principles of the CBD[193] or CITES.[194] For example, while the Full Court appeal in *Leadbeater's Possum* overturned part of the Federal Court's judgment, the Federal Court's findings in relation to the precautionary principle stand as an example of the influence of CBD principles in Australian environmental law. Indeed, while it is too early to assess general trends in Australian biodiversity litigation, the prevalence of arguments based on the precautionary principle is important. So, too, is the move by litigants towards legal claims based on the duties of government departments.

Cases have been brought by public interest law firms and citizens groups to protect the intrinsic value of biodiversity but also by commercial entities seeking to utilize biodiversity for aquariums or breeding purposes. In relation to the former aim, the activity of the 'Environment Defenders Offices' across Australia's jurisdictions is significant. As mentioned previously, of the sixteen cases citing the CBD in Australian courts in the last twenty years, six were brought by an EDO on behalf of individual citizens, community groups, or conservation organizations.[195] The participation of other NGOs, including Humane Society International, has also played a vital role in biodiversity litigation.[196] Yet litigation is only one of several strategies from public interest groups seeking to integrate CBD principles in Australian law and better support Australia's biodiversity. Moreover, the explosion in private claims that are observable in the Australian climate context (including with respect to risk assessment and disclosure obligations of corporations) is not as apparent in Australian biodiversity claims.

The high esteem with which the Australian public holds its biodiversity has not yet translated to enhanced political action or legal protection. Biodiversity litigation in Australia faces a major barrier from the primary federal statute,

[193] See eg *Australian Brumby Alliance Inc v Parks Victoria Inc* (n 172).

[194] *Cairns Marine Aquarium Fish* (n 154).

[195] See eg *Friends of Leadbeater's Possum (No 4)* (n 72); *The Wilderness Society (Tasmania) Inc* (n 18); *Wildlife Preservation Society of Queensland Proserpine/Whitsunday Branch Inc v Minister for the Environment and Heritage* [2006] FCA 736; *Minister for the Environment and Heritage v Queensland Conservation Council Inc* [2004] FCAFC 190; *Booth v Bosworth* [2001] FCA 1453. Regarding the EDO's engagement with community organizations and individual citizens more generally, see Sydes (n 51).

[196] See eg *Humane Society International* (n 145).

the EPBC Act. The Act's shortcomings have been highlighted by the recent independent statutory review, which recommended legally enforceable national environmental standards be adopted,[197] including a specific standard for indigenous engagement and participation in decision making.[198] The need for better provision of information about Australian biodiversity data has been recognized in successive National Biodiversity Strategies and Action Plans and by the Australian Academy of Science.[199] The review also recommended the Commonwealth publish a response to the 2021 State of the Environment Report,[200] together with annual reporting on the implementation of a strategic national plan. The review recommended that within twelve months the EPBC Act be amended to strengthen the Commonwealth's environmental reporting requirements, including requiring a set of national environmental-economic accounts to be tabled annually in the Commonwealth Parliament.[201] With a new Australian federal government in 2022, it is possible that the needed transformations will be made within the executive and legislative branches. Improving the legal framework will help support the role of litigation in generating and sustaining community awareness and action, and ensure the courts of Australia can play their part in addressing the calamitous threats to biodiversity on and around this wondrous and vulnerable continent.

197 Samuel Review (n 10) 49–56. See especially Recommendation 3.

198 ibid 57–72 (Recommendations 5–8). This proposed reform would better align Australia's biodiversity laws with art 8(j) of the CBD.

199 Australian Academy of Science, 'Environment Reform Must Include a "Biodiversity BOM"' (14 October 2020).

200 Samuel Review (n 10) 190 (Recommendation 35).

201 ibid Recommendation 36.

3

Biodiversity Litigation in Brazil

A Strategic Tool to Ensure the Effectiveness of Biodiversity Protection

Carina Costa de Oliveira, Márcia Dieguez Leuzinger, and Larissa Suassuna Carvalho Barros

1. Introduction

The worrying levels of biodiversity loss in Brazil reveal that environmental protection rules are often not spontaneously enforced and fail to produce the expected legal effects. Biodiversity and ecosystem services are decreasing, especially due to changes in land use (pressures from agricultural and farming sectors).[1] Brazil is a megadiverse country and hosts around 10–15 per cent of the known species of global biodiversity. It houses six terrestrial biomes (Amazon, Caatinga, Cerrado, Atlantic Forest, Pampas, and Pantanal), two of which are biodiversity hotspots (Atlantic Forest and the Cerrado). Brazil also has three large marine ecosystems, the largest continuous stretch of mangroves in the world (1.3 million hectares), and the largest reef habitats in the Western South Atlantic.[2]

Biodiversity litigation[3] is an important tool to maintain this megadiversity, ensure compliance with the biodiversity legal framework, and guarantee

[1] Despite the reduction in annual rates of habitat loss due to deforestation in Brazilian biomes in the last decade, especially in the Amazon biome, the conversion of natural ecosystems remains high, especially in the Cerrado biome (236,000 km^2 between 2000 and 2015) and in the Caatinga biome (conversion of 45 per cent of the original coverage). Even in the Atlantic Forest, the deforested area—about 29,000 hectares from 2015 to 2016—substantially exceeds the restored area in the period. In recent years, forest loss in the country has exceeded at least three times all restoration pledges made in the period. Only the recognition that the future of agricultural production depends on maintaining the integrity of ecosystems will allow a definitive reconciliation between socio-economic growth and environmental conservation. See on this issue: Carlos Alfredo Joly and others, *Sumário para tomadores de decisão do relatório de avaliação da Plataforma Brasileira de Biodiversidade e Serviços Ecossistêmicos* (BPBES 2018) 16.

[2] CBD, *Sixth National Report for the Convention on Biological Diversity—Brazil* (29 April 2020) <www.cbd.int/doc/nr/nr-06/br-nr-06-en.pdf> accessed 11 March 2022.

[3] This chapter follows the definition of biodiversity litigation found in Chapter 1, Section 3 in this volume.

Carina Costa de Oliveira, Márcia Dieguez Leuzinger, and Larissa Suassuna Carvalho Barros, *Biodiversity Litigation in Brazil*
In: *Biodiversity Litigation*. Edited by: Guillaume Futhazar, Sandrine Maljean-Dubois, and Jona Razzaque,
Oxford University Press.
DOI: 10.1093/oso/9780192865465.003.0003

its proper interpretation. This argument will be addressed by explaining the particularities of the Brazilian context (Section 2) before turning to the influence of international biodiversity law (IBL) on biodiversity litigation in Brazil (Section 3). We will then assess the legal and strategic impacts of biodiversity litigation in Brazil (Sections 4 and 5).

2. The Particularities of the Brazilian Context

The particularities of the Brazilian context are: the dualist model of incorporation and application of international law, including IBL, into domestic law; a consolidated internal biodiversity legal framework; the sufficient remedies available and the plurality of parties entitled to litigate for biodiversity protection; the unfinished implementation of the Aichi Targets; and the actions and diagnosis of the National Biodiversity Strategy and Action Plan (NBSAP) and of the Brazilian Platform for Biodiversity and Ecosystem Services (BPBES). These aspects of the Brazilian context will be discussed before presenting the methodology adopted for this chapter.

The incorporation of IBL into the Brazilian national legal system, in the case of hard law instruments, requires an internalization process. IBL can only be applied and enforced after an approval and a ratification procedure by the legislative and executive branches. In this sense, Brazil adopts a dualist approach.[4] A legislative decree, approved by the Congress, authorizes the ratification of treaties before their formal ratification by the President who sends the ratification instrument to the treaty's Secretary and to the Secretary-General of the United Nations. The President also adopts an executive decree which enables treaties to enter into force internally.[5] There may be a large gap between the two decrees (weeks or even years). It is therefore possible that treaties enter into force at the international level without being implemented at the national level.

Almost all the important biodiversity international treaties have already been internalized in Brazil,[6] with some exceptions.[7] IBL has an indirect

[4] Marcelo Dias Varella, *Direito internacional público* (6th edn, Saraiva 2016).

[5] The competence of the executive, represented by the President, is based on art 84, VIII of the 1988 Federal Constitution.

[6] See Table 3.1 at the end of the chapter, which lists the main global and regional biodiversity-related treaties signed and ratified by Brazil.

[7] Main Global and Regional Biodiversity-Related Treaties signed but not ratified by Brazil: Nagoya–Kuala Lumpur Supplementary Protocol on Liability and Redress to the Cartagena Protocol on Biosafety (opened for signature 15 October 2010, entered into force 5 March 2018) A-30619 UNTS; Agreement on Port State Measures to prevent, deter and eliminate illegal, unreported and unregulated fishing (opened for signature 22 November 2009, entered into force 5 June 2016) 3161 UNTS I-54133; Convention for

influence on biodiversity litigation in the country, as it is applied through the national laws that internalized it. However, during the litigation process, the parties and judges interestingly refer to the treaty title and not to the executive decree as such, preferring a direct reference to international law. This occurs mainly as an *obiter dictum* and not as a *ratio decidendi*[8] but illustrates the persuasive value given to international law instruments during litigation.

The internal biodiversity legal framework, mostly based on public law, is quite diverse and wide. There are laws on the protection of species, sites, habitats, ecosystems, forests, special protection for specific biomes, and biodiversity.[9] Article 225 of the 1988 Federal Constitution states that everyone has the right to an ecologically balanced environment and that public authorities have the obligation to preserve and to restore essential ecological processes, to promote the management of species, genetic resources, and ecosystems, to establish specially protected territorial spaces, and to protect the fauna and flora. In addition, some ecosystems have acquired the status of national heritage such as the Amazon rainforest, the Mata Atlântica, the Serra do Mar, the Pantanal, and the Coastal Zone.[10] In terms of regulation, there are specific national policies on biosafety and on sustainable development for aquaculture and fisheries.[11] There are also important rules at the infra-legal level,[12] adopted to implement the main laws, such as the decrees on the national strategic plan for protected areas and the national programme for biological diversity.[13]

The creation of specially protected territorial spaces is one of the best strategies for the conservation of biological diversity in situ in Brazil.[14] The country is committed to meeting Aichi biodiversity target 11,[15] which calls for the

the Conservation of Southern Bluefin Tuna (opened for signature 10 May 1993, entered into force 20 May 1994) 1819 UNTS I-31155.

[8] Some examples are: REsp 1549459 (STJ, 9 May 2017); RE 835558 (STF, 9 February 2017); AG 0006114-14.2005.4.01.0000 (TRF1, 16 September 2009).

[9] Law no 5197 1967 (protection of fauna); Law no 12651 2012 (protection of native vegetation); Law no 9985 2000 (National Protected Areas System); Law no 11284 2006 (management of public forests); Law no 11428 2006 (protection of native vegetation in the Atlantic Forest Biome); Law no 11460 2007 (planting of genetically modified organisms in protected areas); and Law no 13123 2015 (access to genetic heritage and benefit sharing).

[10] Federal Constitution 1988, art 225, para 4.

[11] Law no 11105 2005 (National Biosafety Policy) and Law no 11959 2009 (National Policy for the Sustainable Development of Aquaculture and Fisheries).

[12] Norms issued by the executive endowed with generality and abstraction.

[13] Decree no 5758 2006 (National Strategic Plan for Protected Areas) and Decree no 10235 2020, which amends Decree no 4703 2003 (National Program for Biological Diversity—PRONABIO).

[14] Katrina Brandon, 'Natural Protected Areas and Biodiversity Conservation' in *Anais II Congresso Brasileiro de Unidades de Conservação*, vol 1 (Rede Nacional Pró-Unidades de Conservação and Fundação O Boticário 2000) 1–10.

[15] CBD, 'Aichi Biodiversity Targets' <www.cbd.int/sp/targets> accessed 11 March 2022.

conservation of 'at least 17% of terrestrial and inland water areas and 10% of coastal and marine areas'.[16] The national target 11[17] mirrors the Aichi target 11 and aims to expand and implement the national protected areas system. This target states that 'by 2020, at least 30% of the Amazon, 17% of each of the other terrestrial biomes, and 10% of the marine and coastal areas, especially areas of particular importance for biodiversity and ecosystem services, are conserved through protected areas'. In the Sixth National Report to the Convention on Biological Diversity (CBD), Brazil classified the progress towards the implementation of this target as 'on track to achieve target'.[18]

Brazil started the process of internalizing the Aichi Targets and defining its national biodiversity goals with the approval of the National Biodiversity Strategy and Action Plan 2011–20, which enabled the construction and adoption of the first NBSAP (2016–20).[19] This version was published in 2017 and contains 721 actions under the responsibility of fifty-two institutions, including the federal government, state governments, universities, research institutes, NGOs, and inter-governmental organizations.[20] During the monitoring and evaluation process in 2018, the institutions reported complementary actions and identified the need to adjust the NBSAP. The updated version has become a database with information on 1,032 actions distributed among the twenty biodiversity targets. The monitoring of the implementation of actions in the NBSAP, including actions reported in 2018, revealed that only 12 per cent of actions were concluded, 54 per cent are under implementation, 15 per cent are at the planning phase or initial implementation, and 7 per cent have not yet started.[21] However, the NBSAP has not been used by courts as a basis for their decisions in cases dealing with biodiversity.

Another diagnosis on the state of biodiversity in Brazil was carried out by the Brazilian Platform for Biodiversity and Ecosystem Services (BPBES). This platform was initially constituted as a Working Group of the Brazilian Society

[16] In 2015, Brazil reaffirmed this commitment at the launch of the UN 2030 Agenda for Sustainable Development, in Sustainable Development Goal 14 (SDG14): Conservation and sustainable use of the oceans, seas and marine resources for sustainable development. In 2017, Member States reiterated their commitment to achieving the SDG14 targets on time, in the final document of the Conference on the Oceans.

[17] This is one of the National Targets for Biodiversity established by the National Biodiversity Commission in 2013 through Resolution no 6 2013.

[18] CBD, *Sixth National Report* (n 2).

[19] ibid.

[20] The current biodiversity action plan reflects a diversity of actors working for nature conservation in Brazil. The federal government accounts for 40.8 per cent of actions, state governments for 37.4 per cent, civil society for 13.7 per cent, the private sector for 5.2 per cent, academia for 2.8 per cent, and municipalities for 0.1 per cent. Brazil, Ministry of Environment, *Estratégia e Plano de Ação Nacionais para a Biodiversidade (EPANB)* (2017) <bit.ly/3wJLbXx> accessed 11 March 2022.

[21] CBD (n 2).

for the Progress of Science (SBPC) and it has been developing its activities since 2015. As a result, a first Brazilian Diagnosis of Biodiversity and Ecosystem Services and five more thematic reports were released in 2019.[22]

In its Executive Summary for Decision Makers, the First Brazilian Biodiversity & Ecosystems Services Diagnosis from BPBES states that 'Brazil has a wide variety of policy instruments and options for socio-environmental governance, as well as commitments assumed globally (SDG, Aichi, Paris), which refer to the possibility of a sustainable future. On the other hand, inefficiency in control, management or low incentive to comply all of the rules imply risks to the consolidation of that future.'[23] It also underpins the fact that the low implementation rate of protected areas, the discontinuation of financial incentive systems for conservation and poverty reduction, and the problems with environmental licensing processes of projects reflect the insufficiency of public policies to ensure the conservation and sustainable use of biodiversity and associated ecosystem services in the country.[24] This BPBES diagnosis, however, is not mentioned in any of the decisions analysed in this study.

The main remedies available to safeguard biodiversity-related rights in the civil sphere are collective actions, mostly brought by the entities of the federal states, their environmental agencies, or the Public Prosecutor's Office (*Parquet*). However, citizens and non-governmental organizations can also bring claims in some situations.[25] In the criminal sphere, the Public Prosecutor's Office is the only one authorized to prosecute environmental crimes regarding biodiversity. Given the constant presence of these public entities, biodiversity litigation is primarily governed by the public law regime and in the pursuit of the public interest. Access to the courts is not expensive. The fees normally correspond to only about 1 per cent of the economic value of the case and people with insufficient resources to pay costs and lawyers are entitled to free access to justice. The main procedural obstacles are the excessive duration of lawsuits due to widespread inaction in the Brazilian judiciary[26] and the lack of expertise

[22] BPBES, 'Quem somos' <www.bpbes.net.br> accessed 11 March 2022.

[23] BPBES, *1º Diagnóstico Brasileiro de Biodiversidade & Serviços Ecossistêmicos. Sumário para Tomadores de Decisão* (2019), <bit.ly/3IGaJJM> accessed 11 March 2022.

[24] ibid.

[25] Law no 4717 1965 (popular action) and Law no 7347 1985 (public civil action).

[26] A lawsuit in Brazil lasts, on average, two years and six months in the first instance. In the higher courts, the average is one year and two months, and there is still time to process ordinary appeals at the second instance and to execute the final sentence. See on this issue, A Richter, 'Pesquisa do CNJ aponta 80 milhões de processos em tramitação no país' (Agência Brasil, 27 August 2018), <bit.ly/3c78Fw4> accessed 11 March 2022.

of the judges, since there are few specialized sections on environmental issues in the courts.[27]

The methodology adopted in this chapter is of a qualitative and exploratory type, based on extensive research to identify and analyse administrative, civil, and criminal biodiversity cases before the Brazilian superior and federal courts.[28] Different topics/keywords[29] regarding terrestrial and marine biodiversity were used to select forty-seven[30] leading cases decided between 2003 and 2020.[31] The influence of IBL on biodiversity litigation (Section 3) will be analysed before the biodiversity litigation impacts in Brazil (Sections 4 and 5).

3. The Influence of International Biodiversity Law on Biodiversity Litigation in Brazil

The influence of IBL on biodiversity litigation in Brazil depends on the subject. This influence is more evident in conceptual aspects, such as the definition of biodiversity, as well as in cases related to subjects such as genetic resources, species, flora, and the illegal wildlife trade than in those related to forests and protected areas. The international negotiations on environment and human development impacted the Brazilian institutional framework despite the resistance of Brazilian diplomats in supporting environmental protection during international negotiations.[32] For instance, the first environmental protection federal body[33] was created in 1973, just after the United Nations Conference on Human Environment that took place in Stockholm in 1972.[34] It also influenced the adoption of the law which instituted the National Environmental Policy[35] and even the environmental chapter of the 1988 Federal Constitution.

[27] Andreia Mendonca Agostini and Vladimir Passos de Freitas, 'A especialização da jurisdição ambiental como garantia de efetividade do direito fundamental ao meio ambiente ecologicamente equilibrado' (2012) 39 Revista da Ajuris 297.

[28] The Brazilian high/superior courts are the Supremo Tribunal Federal (STF) as the constitutional court and the Superior Tribunal de Justiça (STJ) as the federal law court. At the regional level, there are five federal tribunals around the country, the so-called Tribunais Regionais Federais (TRFs), in charge of ruling on any federal law cases in that region.

[29] Human rights, animal rights, forests, protected areas, species, genetic resources, bioinvasion, climate change, crimes relating to the illegal trade in wildlife and endangered species, environmental harms, environmental crimes, procedural obligations, and competence.

[30] See all the analysed cases in Table 3.2 at the end of the chapter.

[31] The selection of cases in this period is due to a growing increase in actions since 2003, the period of creation of the first specific federal environmental agency in charge of biodiversity management in the country (2007), and of an increase in active litigation by environmental-related actors.

[32] See Andre Aranha Correa do Lago, *Conferências de Desenvolvimento Sustentável* (Funag 2013).

[33] Decree no 73030 1973, which created the Secretaria Especial do Meio Ambiente (SEMA).

[34] United Nations, *Stockholm Declaration and Action Plan for the Human Environment* (1972) <www.un.org/en/conferences/environment/stockholm1972> accessed 11 March 2022.

[35] Law no 6938 1981.

The main argument of this section is twofold. It will first address the conceptual influence of IBL, notably its impacts on definitions in the Brazilian legislation and litigation. It will then highlight the variability of IBL's influence depending on the area of biodiversity law concerned in the case. Particularly, cases related to genetic resources, species, and the illegal wildlife trade are more currently impacted than cases related to protected areas and forests.

3.1 The Conceptual Influence of IBL

The conceptual influence of IBL definitions on Brazilian legislation is direct, as terms such as biodiversity, biological diversity, and ecosystem were internalized in domestic law thanks to IBL. However, the conceptual influence of IBL definitions on subjects such as forests and animal rights is limited, as national legislation on these matters is older than the most important biodiversity treaties. Moreover, other international law fields, such as human rights and trade law, have also contributed to shaping Brazilian biodiversity concepts related to other social or economic issues such as public participation. This section will examine this conceptual influence, the role of other fields of international law in biodiversity legislation and litigation, as well as the impact of international procedural obligations on national litigation.

The conceptual influence of IBL on the Brazilian legislation started in 1998 with the first norm to introduce the term biodiversity.[36] Although the term biodiversity was only inserted in the Brazilian legal framework in 1998 by the executive decree that internalized the CBD,[37] the concern with the protection of forests and other natural resources and ecosystems arose long before that time. In 1934, the first Brazilian Forest Code was issued by decree.[38] The second Forest Code was adopted in 1965 by means of a statute,[39] which was one of the most important environmental laws in Brazil for forty-seven years. It was replaced in 2012 by Law 12651,[40] that represented a flagrant setback for the protection of forests and other native Brazilian ecosystems. In this sense, the influence of IBL on forests and protected areas issues is limited, as these fields have been regulated in Brazil since 1934. More recently, Law 9985/2000[41]

[36] Executive Decree no 2519 1998, after Legislative Decree no 02 1994.
[37] ibid.
[38] Decree no 23793 1934.
[39] Law no 4771 1965.
[40] Law no 12651 2012.
[41] Law no 9985 2000, art 2, III.

instituted the National System of Protected Areas (SNUC) and Decree 4339/2002 instituted the National Biodiversity Policy (NBP)[42] and elaborated on the role of protected areas in biodiversity conservation.

The impact of IBL on Brazilian litigation is also limited. In most cases, the concepts provided by treaties are mentioned only as *obiter dicta*. They are not used as a *ratio decidendi*. Many biodiversity litigation cases are not isolated, but rather connect to and impact on other fields of litigation related to social and economic issues. As the following discussion shows, some of the cases are connected to human rights with topics such as a healthy quality of life and procedural obligations with issues such as public participation. International trade law is also often linked to biodiversity litigation. The recognition of the protection of animal rights is likewise a trend in Brazilian jurisprudence, but this trend is not directly influenced by IBL.

The most important influence of international law regarding definitions connected to human rights derives from decisions of the Inter-American Court of Human Rights (IACtHR) that deal with the topic of the right to a healthy quality of life and healthy environment.[43] On this issue, of 146 cases judged from 1988 to 2020 by the Supremo Tribunal Federal (SFT, the Brazilian Constitutional Court), only four directly mentioned the cases of the IACtHR.[44] In this sense, the express mention of IACtHR cases by STF jurisprudence is quite sparse.[45]

One important case related to trade law highlighted the effects of the right to a healthy quality of life on the ban of used and retreaded tyres.[46] The ban, which applied to different countries such as Uruguay, was considered constitutional, based on the afore-mentioned right. The disposal of used tyres causes enormous damage to biodiversity due to pollution. Indeed, in Brazil, there are no landfills in cities which, in turn, leads to disposal in open dumps.

[42] Decree no 4339 2002.

[43] ADPF 747 (STF, 28 October 2020); ADPF 748 (STF, 28 October 2020); ADPF 749 (STF, 28 October 2020; RE 654833 (STF, 20 April 2020). See Chapter 12 in this volume on international biodiversity litigation.

[44] The cases mentioned were: *Povo Indígena Kichwa de Sarayaku v Equador* (IACtHR, 27 June 2012); *Comunidades Indígenas Miembros De La Asociación Lhaka Honhat (Nuestra Tierra) v Argentina* (IACtHR, 6 February 2020); Opinião Consultiva no 23 (IACtHR, 2017).

[45] See Carina Costa de Oliveira and Pedro Henrique Saad Messias de Souza, 'O Direito à sadia qualidade de vida: contribuições da Corte Interamericana de Direitos Humanos às decisões do Supremo Tribunal Federal' in Jose Rubens Morato Leite and Flavia Franca Dinnebier (eds), *Estado de direito Ecológico: conceito, conteúdo e novas dimensões para a proteção da natureza* (Instituto o Direito por um Planeta Verde 2017) 809–35.

[46] ADPF 101 (STF, 24 June 2009).

The international law instruments mentioned in this case were the CBD, the United Nations Framework Convention on Climate Change (UNFCCC),[47] and the United Nations Convention to Combat Desertification (UNCCD),[48] as well as soft law instruments such as the Rio Declaration on Environment and Development[49] and Agenda 21.[50] It is important to highlight that the analysis of this issue mainly concerns international environmental law, even though biodiversity issues were brought in the case.

As for the procedural obligations—specifically the definition of participation—the International Labour Organization Convention No 169 on Indigenous and Tribal Peoples[51] was mentioned in important STF cases such as 'Petition' 3388.[52] This case analysed the compatibility between indigenous lands and protected areas following a popular action filed by a senator against the state. He argued that the criteria used for the demarcation of the indigenous land called Raposa Serra do Sol were illegal. The STF ruled that there was perfect compatibility between the indigenous lands and areas of environmental 'conservation' and 'preservation', based on the relevant relationship between the indigenous lands and environmental protection. The Indigenous and Tribal Peoples Convention was used to point out that consultation with indigenous people was a central element in the case, but the right to participate in decision making can be limited by other issues such as national security. In this sense, the right to participate is not absolute.[53] The fundamental right to a healthy environment was also noted by the court.[54]

With regard to animal rights, their welfare and the fight against cruel treatment have been at the heart of some important cases before the STF. However, there was no direct influence of IBL in those decisions. One emblematic case discussed the unconstitutionality of a state law that regulated the practice of

[47] UN General Assembly, United Nations Framework Convention on Climate Change: Resolution adopted by the General Assembly, 20 January 1994, A/RES/48/189.

[48] UN General Assembly, Implementation of the United Nations Convention to Combat Desertification in those Countries Experiencing Serious Drought and/or Desertification, particularly in Africa: Resolution adopted by the General Assembly, 18 February 1999, A/RES/53/191.

[49] UN General Assembly, Rio Declaration on Environment and Development: Resolution adopted by the General Assembly, 12 August 1992, A/CONF.151/26 (vol I).

[50] UN General Assembly, Report of the United Nations Conference on Environment and Development: Resolution adopted by the General Assembly, 13 August 1992, A/CONF.151/26 (vol II).

[51] International Labour Organization (ILO), Indigenous and Tribal Peoples Convention, C169, 27 June 1989, 28(6) ILM 1382.

[52] Petition 3388 (STF, 19 March 2009). Another important case on the issue is ADI 3573 (STF, 1 December 2005).

[53] ibid 66–70.

[54] ibid 44.

vaquejada as a sporting and cultural activity.[55] *Vaquejada* is a type of rodeo that takes place in different arenas in north-eastern Brazil whereby cowboys chase and try to bring down an ox by pulling it by the tail. Several studies and technical reports have proved that the animal's tail is generally broken or even pulled off during the event, which can gather thousands of spectators and generate millions of reais (the local currency). The main argument of the claimant was based on the violation of the right of animals. The STF recognized the constitutional protection of animals and forbade *vaquejada* in the country, ruling that the practice brings unnecessary suffering to these animals, due to a supposed cultural tradition. In another notable case, the STF considered unconstitutional the state laws that authorized the creation, exposure, and holding of competitions between combatant birds (cockfighting), since its practice constituted cruelty to those animals.[56] None of the two decisions explicitly mentioned IBL.

In summary, the conceptual influence of IBL definitions on Brazilian legislation is a direct one because the domestic laws and institutions use the concepts of IBL in practice. However, in biodiversity litigation this influence is limited to subjects such as forests and animal rights; and indirect, as the definitions of IBL are referred to only as *obiter dicta* and not as *ratio decidendi.* Areas of law, such as human rights and trade law, make more reference to IBL than those on animal rights. Hence, it is notably difficult to distinguish between biodiversity litigation and environmental dispute settlement in Brazil.

This conceptual influence is coupled with a variable influence depending on the area of biodiversity law.

3.2 A Variable Influence Depending on the Area of Biodiversity Law

Some issues are more connected to the internalization of biodiversity treaties than others. For instance, IBL is mentioned in cases related to genetic resources, species, and the illegal wildlife trade but is not mentioned in cases related to protected areas and forests.

Some cases expressly mention the Convention on International Trade in Endangered Species of Wild Fauna and Flora (CITES)[57] to provide a higher

[55] ADI 4983 (STF, 6 October 2016).

[56] ADI 2514 (STF 29 June 2005).

[57] Convention on International Trade in Endangered Species of Wild Fauna and Flora (opened for signature 3 March 1973, entered into force 1 July 1975) 993 UNTS 243 (CITES).

level of protection for flora species, such as a decision that endorsed the refusal of the environmental agency to authorize the export of mahogany because it violated the CITES Convention.[58] In relation to fauna, an interesting case from the Superior Tribunal de Justiça (STJ) considered the use of endangered animals in advertising as abusive if they were included in CITES lists.[59] The tribunals also use the inclusion of an animal in the CITES official lists as an argument to increase fines of administrative violations of killing, chasing, hunting, catching, collecting, or using specimens of wild fauna without or in contravention of a licence.[60] However, in these instances the treaties were mentioned as *obiter dicta* and not as *ratio decidendi*.

IBL impacted a case in which the STF established the binding rule that crimes of illegal trade in wildlife are always international crimes. It was argued in that decision that international agreements such as CITES and the CBD highlight the interests of protecting and conserving biodiversity and national biological resources.[61] Similarly, IBL played an important role in a judgment that ruled that the insignificance principle[62] is not applicable to environmental crimes if they are committed against endangered species.[63] With regard to genetic resources, it is quite common for parties and the tribunals to use the CBD to strengthen the argument that Brazil has ratified the Convention and that, consequently, the administrative procedures to obtain an authorization to explore genetic resources must be facilitated.[64]

In summary, the influence of IBL in Brazil is limited because it is mainly presented as *obiter dicta*. It is not therefore possible to affirm that there is a widespread influence because the impact is quite different depending on the subject.

It is worth analysing the legal impacts of biodiversity litigation in Brazil on issues related to material and procedural law, as well as its strategic use.

[58] AG 0006114-14.2005.4.01.0000 (TRF1, 16 September 2009).

[59] REsp 1549459 (STJ, 9 May 2017).

[60] AC 0800486-03.2012.4.05.8100 (TRF5, 30 January 2014).

[61] RE 835558 (STF, 9 February 2017).

[62] The insignificance principle, equivalent to the '*de minimis* principle', means that the law does not take into account matters of little or no value or importance. This principle does not have a legal source in Brazilian law, but the STF has established conditions for its application, which are widely followed by all other Brazilian courts. See Cleber Masson, *Direito penal esquematizado* (6th edn, Editora Método 2012) 25.

[63] AgRg REsp 1847810 (STJ, 19 May 2020).

[64] AI 559568 (TRF3, 21 October 2015) and SLS 1438 (STJ, 9 May 2011).

4. The Legal Impacts of Biodiversity Litigation in Brazil

Biodiversity litigation is an important tool for increasing the effectiveness of biodiversity protection in Brazil because it seeks to guarantee compliance with the legal framework. From a quantitative point of view, the number of claims in the Brazilian judiciary is increasing. This increase is linked to the worsening of the environmental crisis, growing public awareness, and the rise of biodiversity-related rights. From a qualitative standpoint, judges and parties are specializing by building new legal theses and interpretations and by elaborating claims and decisions in more technical depth. This search for increased technicity greatly impacts biodiversity litigation in Brazil. The impact can be material (4.1), procedural (4.2), or strategic (4.3).

4.1 The Material Impacts

From the perspective of material law, the impacts of biodiversity litigation can be administrative, civil, and criminal. Therefore, three types of sanction can be assigned to the author of an act or omission which affects biodiversity. Biodiversity litigation can result in both an increase or a decrease in biodiversity protection though, on average, most cases lead to an increase in protection.

4.1.1 The impacts on administrative issues

The impacts on biodiversity litigation concerning administrative issues, such as public control of authorizations, administrative responsibility, and environmental licensing, can be seen in different fields, such as genetic resources, fauna, protected areas, and forests. The following discussion will present a variety of cases with examples leading to better protection of biodiversity, but also examples where the outcome of litigation has exacerbated a decline in biodiversity.

With regard to genetic resources, some cases have confirmed the mandatory nature of an authorization to explore genetic resources economically.[65] Moreover, there are cases related to the confirmation of fines applied to companies that have not shared the benefits of their economic exploitation of genetic resources.[66] One particular case confirmed the necessity of environmental studies to authorize the use of such organisms.[67] These decisions were

[65] See AI 559568 (TRF3, 21 October 2015) and SLS 1438 (STJ, 9 May 2011).
[66] AC 5013440-40.2012.4.04.7200 (TRF4, 26 May 2015).
[67] REsp 1387921 (STJ, 15 December 2015).

key in ensuring that public authorities duly take into account the protection of biodiversity while authorizing activities which exploit it. In addition, the centrality of scientific evidence has also been reinforced in cases where environmental studies were required.

Two interesting cases on the protection of wild fauna and flora can be highlighted. An administrative violation of killing, chasing, hunting, catching, collecting, or using specimens of wild fauna without or in contravention of the licence of the competent authority is punishable with a fine of 500 reais (USD$92) per species. However, the fine is ten times higher (USD$920) if the species is on one of the official lists of Brazilian fauna threatened with extinction, such as CITES.[68] Brazilian courts have been observing this rule and consider fines according to these amounts to be legal.[69] Another decision of the First Federal Court endorses the Environmental Agency's refusal to authorize the export of mahogany and expressly states that the refusal complies with CITES, ensuring the compliance of wild flora exploitation for international trade.[70]

The following discussion focuses on two cases concerning protected areas that are representative of the positive impacts of administrative decisions on biodiversity protection. In the first case,[71] the STJ recognized buffer zones as a transition space designed to ensure the health of the protected area and to reduce the vulnerability of biodiversity within its ambit. This interpretation on the importance of buffer zones is extremely relevant to biodiversity preservation in protected areas. The reason is related to the need to reduce the edge effects caused by anthropic activities outside the area limits.

The second example is a statement made by the STJ on the necessity of elaborating a management plan to preserve a protected area.[72] Such a plan would establish rules about the use of the area and the management of its natural resources, including the implementation of the physical structures necessary for its management. Therefore, an omission by the state in the elaboration of a management plan for the Baleia Franca Environmental Protection Area (a type of Brazilian protected area) put the protected area's integrity at risk and violated the state's fundamental duty to protect the environment.

In another case on the protection of forests, the STJ[73] pointed out that the Forest Code[74] establishes the minimum criteria for the protection of forests

[68] Decree no 6514 2008, art 24.
[69] AC 0800486-03.2012.4.05.8100 (TRF5, 30 January 2014).
[70] AG 0006114-14.2005.4.01.0000 (TRF1, 16 September 2009).
[71] REsp 1406139 (STJ, 7 November 2016).
[72] REsp 1163524 (STJ, 17 August 2011).
[73] AREsp 1312435 (STJ, 13 November 2012).
[74] Law no 12651 2012.

and regulates the use of land in the country. In that sense, the court emphasized that the Forest Code provisions do not establish the maximum limits of the environmental protection required, clarifying that the municipalities were not allowed to undermine and restrictively interpret its provisions in order to reduce the protective threshold. In this case, the decision specifically mentioned that it was up to the municipal legislation to intensify the degree of environmental protection, or at least to maintain the level of protection, proposed under federal law.

Nevertheless, biodiversity litigation on administrative matters can also lead to biodiversity loss. In Brazil, if the state intends to expropriate a private area, it must issue a decree of public use and, within two or five years depending on the type of expropriation, carry out concrete acts aimed at transferring the property to the state. Two cases on protected areas serve as examples of where such decrees have expired.[75] According to these decisions, the decree which declares the public utility of the area for expropriation purposes expires five years after its issue if no concrete acts of expropriation are forthcoming. This interpretation is very worrying since many protected areas created on private property do not have their land tenure status legalized within five years of their creation due to multiple problems, such as budget shortfalls, ignorance of the real landowners, lack of documentation by the landowners, etc. If this interpretation prevails, several protected areas, including those with a higher level of environmental protection, will be considered extinct in practice due to the lack of land regularization. This, in turn, could lead to incalculable damage to the preservation of biodiversity.

4.1.2 The impacts on civil issues

Biodiversity litigation can also have an impact on civil issues, such as liability, and such cases can have a great impact on biodiversity protection. The most important cases relate to protection of fauna, flora, and biodiversity reparation instruments, such as those concerning liability.

There are interesting cases involving publicity and advertising with wild animals. The STJ considers the participation of endangered animals included in the CITES list in advertisements to be abusive, whether these be Brazilian or exotic fauna. According to the court, these advertisements[76] may stimulate

[75] EREsp 191656 (STJ, 2 August 2010) and AgInt no REsp 1781924 (STJ, 10 June 2019).
[76] Law no 8078 1990, art 37, para 2.

both national and international trade in illegal wildlife because they humanize the animals and trivialize their exploration.[77]

One important example regarding biodiversity protection is related to marine bioinvasion caused by ballast water and biofouling. The tribunals have been highly active in naming those responsible for repairing the damage caused to marine biodiversity. Since the golden mussel invasion (*Limnoperna fortunei*) in Brazil in 1999, efforts have been made to prevent bioinvasion caused by this type of mussel by evaluating the effectiveness of the disposal of ballast water in the high seas.[78] Brazilian courts recognized the state's duty to control golden mussel bioinvasion in 2017,[79] based on civil and constitutional norms. Other bioinvasions due to ballast water and biofouling are occurring in Brazil. The sun coral (*Tubastraea*) identified in different states in Brazil, such as Rio de Janeiro and Alagoas, is causing a series of imbalances in the environment.[80] Multidisciplinary working groups were formed at the national and the state levels to study the issue, aiming to shed more light on the scientific uncertainties and the consequences for marine biodiversity.[81]

Expertise and evidence are key to the science-based decisions of the courts in complex biodiversity-related disputes. It is quite common to see amicus briefs[82] and expertise produced during civil procedures.[83] This was recently seen cases concerning the construction of a hydroelectric plant and also bioinvasion, for instance.[84] Brazil has general procedural norms that provide the basis for producing evidence before the courts. In cases related to the interpretation of the precautionary principle, it is quite common to see reports

[77] REsp 1549459 (STJ, 9 May 2017). One different decision can be noted: AC 1147173 (TRF3, 18 December 2014).

[78] Eliane Bee Boldrini and Leticia Knechtel Procopiak, *Projeto Água de Lastro. Diagnóstico, Dificuldades e Medidas Preventivas Contra a Bioinvasão de Espécies Exóticas por Água de Lastro de Navios nos Terminais Portuários da Ponta do Félix S.A. Porto de Antonina-PR* (Projeto Água de Lastro, MMA 2012).

[79] AC 5049424-26.2014.4.04.7100 (TRF4, 1 August 2017).

[80] Luiz Ricardo Santana de Araujo Júnior and Liziane Paixão Silva Oliveira, 'A bioinvasão por bioincrustação pelo Coral-Sol e a responsabilidade civil ambiental no direito brasileiro' in Carina Costa de Oliveira and others (eds), *Meio ambiente marinho e direito: a gestão sustentável da investigação, da exploração e da explotação dos recursos marinhos na zona costeira, na plataforma continental e nos fundos marinhos*, vol 2 (Juruá 2018) 541–62.

[81] See AI 0008256-41.2017.4.02.0000 (TRF 2, 30 June 2020). In Pernambuco, a state law was promulgated on the issue: Decree no 52351 2021. At the federal level, a National Plan was published by the Portaria no 3642 2018.

[82] Law no 9869 1999, art 7; Law no 9882 1999, art 6; Law no 13105 (Civil Procedural Code, 2015), art 138; Law no 11416 2006, art 3.

[83] It can be required by the parties or by the judges. Law no 13105 (Civil Procedural Code, 2015, art 370). The parties can also have technical assistants to provide evidence for their arguments (Civil Procedural Code, 2015, art 470).

[84] AREsp 1285871 (STJ, 30 October 2019) and AI 0008256-41.2017.4.02.0000 (TRF 2, 30 June 2020).

from different international bodies used as parameters for such decisions. One leading case[85] regarding electromagnetic fields pointed out that the evidence used in the case demonstrated that the impact of these fields on health and the environment was in conformity with national norms,[86] based on World Health Organization parameters. In this case, higher parameters, based on foreign rules, were put forward as more suitable parameters for the issue. However, the court considered that the national parameters were sufficient, without requiring further demonstration by different experts. Another interesting case highlighted that experts could be called to given evidence in proceedings even before the occurrence of damage. This occurred in a case related to oil exploration by hydraulic fracturing (fracking) fluids.[87] However, even though expertise does seem to play a central role in biodiversity litigation, judges may not always rely on it to settle disputes.[88]

Civil solidary liability[89] is an important contribution to environmental law, and it has been consolidated by biodiversity litigation. Whatever the legal status of the polluter may be—public or private—civil liability in Brazil for environmental damage is objective, solidary, and unlimited, based on the polluter pays principle. In compliance with Law 6938/1981,[90] the priority of such liability is the complete reparation of the damage.[91] The STJ has also stated that public entities are responsible for urban-environmental damage due to the omission of their duty to control and inspect; an omission which contributes directly or indirectly to the environmental degradation or to its aggravation, consolidation, or perpetuation. The public agents in charge of implementing this duty may also suffers disciplinary, criminal, and civil action if they act without due diligence. In this 2010 judgment,[92] it was stated that the so-called solidary civil liability of subsidiary execution means that the state must compensate the damages if the polluter does not. The government, after paying the compensation, can then sue the polluter to try to reclaim the money.

[85] RE 627189 (STF, 8 June 2016).

[86] Law 11934 2009.

[87] AI 5012993-50.2014.4.04.0000 (TRF4, 18 November 2014).

[88] See ACP 02030948119944036104 (TRF 3, 23 May 2001). Larissa Maria Medeiros Coutinho, 'Limites às funções da responsabilidade civil ambiental por danos marinhos causados pela navegação' (Master's Degree dissertation, Law Faculty of the University of Brasília 2017).

[89] Solidary civil liability means that any person, natural or legal, who has caused, directly or indirectly, damage to the environment, will be jointly and severally liable to repair or indemnify the damage. Objective and joint civil liability is provided for in arts 3, IV and 14, § 1 of Law no 6.938/1981.

[90] Law no 6938 1981.

[91] REsp 1071741 (STJ, 16 December 2010).

[92] ibid.

4.1.3 The impacts on criminal issues

The impacts of biodiversity litigation on criminal issues concern the interpretation of principles such as the insignificance and the definition of cases where granting a pardon should be avoided.

One of the biggest impacts of biodiversity litigation on criminal issues is linked to the insignificance principle,[93] which can, if applied, exclude the very existence of a crime. The rationale of this principle is that the criminal law should not deal with irrelevant matters, incapable of harming the protected legal good. The STF established that it is possible to exclude any crime when the following objective elements are present in the case: minimal offence, low degree of disapproval, and lack of social danger of the conduct, as well as a low threshold of harm. However, subjective elements must also be considered, such as the importance of the good to the victim in terms of their economic condition and sentimental value, the circumstances, and the outcome of the crime.[94]

In accordance with that interpretation, the STJ initially authorized an application of this principle and excluded the crime in a biodiversity-related dispute.[95] Fortunately, the court has apparently changed its position in the last six years and has dismissed the application of the principle in two cases involving environmental crimes because they were committed in marine protected areas.[96] Although IBL did not have a direct influence on these judgments, it did have an important role in a judgment that ruled that the insignificance principle is not applicable to environmental crimes against endangered species.[97]

Still on this issue, there is another relevant decision on granting a pardon involving crimes against endangered species. The law authorizes a judge to waive the application of a penalty for crimes involving non-threatened wild animals which are kept for domestic purposes.[98] Nevertheless, in this instance the judge granted the defendant a pardon in a case involving an endangered species. The court later amended the decision by faithfully applying the law and ruled that the granting of a judicial pardon does not apply in cases of endangered species[99] kept for domestic purposes. A number of decisions from another regional court viewed that the guardianship of parrots in domestic environments for a long period without any evidence of mistreatment could not be interpreted as the facilitation of predatory hunting or trade in wildlife.[100]

93 On this principle, see n 62.
94 Cleber Masson, *Direito penal esquematizado* (6th edn, Editora Método 2012) 25.
95 REsp 905864 (STJ, 11 March 2008).
96 REsp 1626599 (STJ, 14 March 2017) and AgRg no REsp 1503896 (STJ, 17 September 2015).
97 AgRg no REsp 1847810 (STJ, 19 May 2020).
98 Law no 9605 1998, art 29, para 2.
99 AG 0108242-70.2014.4.02.0000 (TRF2, 27 April 2016).
100 AC 544293 (TRF5, 16 August 2012).

In addition to material impacts, procedural impacts can also be highlighted.

4.2 The Procedural Impacts

Biodiversity litigation in Brazil had procedural impacts on competence issues, participation, access to information, and access to justice.

The competence to rule on crimes in the illegal trade in wildlife is an important procedural matter. In Brazil, not all environmental crimes are prosecuted by federal courts as, for some biodiversity-related cases, the STF has transferred this competence from state to federal jurisdictions for all crimes involving wild animals, endangered species, exotic species, or any other species protected by international agreements.[101] The STF specified that such crimes should be considered as international because of the agreements signed by the country, such as the Convention on Nature Protection and Wildlife Preservation in the Western Hemisphere,[102] CITES, and the CBD. This decision does not mean that the STF has directly applied the obligations stated in the treaties. In fact, the court simply considers that those crimes must be determined by the federal courts and not by state courts, based on the importance of the legal question.

Another important procedural consequence of biodiversity litigation is the necessity of public consultation for an increase of a protected area's limits.[103] A decree[104] extended the limits of the Chapada dos Veadeiros National Park without a new public consultation and the expansion decree was therefore considered illegal by the STF. According to the decision, the consultation of the park management council did not replace the need for public consultation; that is, the need to consult the population affected or potentially affected by the expansion of the protected area. However, there are other interpretations of the same legal question, such as that stated in the STF decision MS 24665.[105] In this case, a decree[106] had extended the limits of the Taim Ecological Station (a category of protected area). The main finding in the case was that public consultation is not mandatory for the creation of ecological stations. The jurisprudence that emerged from the case created an illogical position in which there was no legal requirement for public consultation for the creation of an

[101] RE no 835558 (STF, 9 February 2017).

[102] Convention on Nature Protection and Wildlife Preservation in the Western Hemisphere (opened for signature 12 October 1940, entered into force 1 May 1942) XXX.

[103] MS 24184 (STF, 13 August 2003).

[104] Decree of 27 February 2001.

[105] MS 24665 (STF, 1 December 2004).

[106] Decree of 5 June 2003.

ecological station whereas there is such a requirement for the expansion of a protected area.

Regarding participation and access to information, Belo Monte is a case in point.[107] In this case,[108] the right of prior and informed consent of the indigenous communities before the construction of the Belo Monte hydropower plant was one of the main concerns. The STF analysed the constitutionality of the decree[109] which authorized the construction and decided that it could not analyse the constitutionality of the decree because it did not have the nature of a general norm. Therefore, the merits of the case were not analysed. Other cases regarding the violation of indigenous communities' rights during the Belo Monte construction were brought before different tribunals.[110] However, the main decisions argued that community consent was not mandatory for the decision to construct the Belo Monte plant. Even if other cases stated that public consultation was mandatory,[111] as per other legal sources, the public administration does not have to take public concerns into account. The Belo Monte case highlights the limited impact of the rights of access to information and participation regarding biodiversity protection when large construction projects are implemented in Brazil. The necessity of public consultation of the affected population has been recognized, but the requirement of their consent is not mandatory.

From a procedural point of view, biodiversity litigation has also initiated techniques to facilitate access to justice; for instance, the reversal of the burden of proof in favour of environmental victims as a result of the precautionary principle.[112] This has been applied by different courts since 2009, but was consolidated in 2018 when the STJ published the *Súmula* 618 stating that the 'reversal of the burden of proof is applicable to actions related to the environmental degradation'.[113] There is an important impact on biodiversity litigation

[107] ADI 3573 (STF, 1 December 2015).

[108] See Carina Costa de Oliveira, 'Ação Direta de Inconstitucionalidade 3.473 (caso "Belo Monte")' in Alberto do Amaral Jnr and Joao Henrique Ribeiro Roriz (eds), *O direito internacional em movimento: jurisprudência internacional comentada*, vol 1: *Corte Internacional de Justiça e Supremo Tribunal Federal* (IBDC 2016) 251–73; Carina Costa de Oliveira and Fernanda Castelo Branco Araujo, 'Avanços e limites no cumprimento de obrigações conectadas ao direito de acesso à informação ambiental de alguns órgãos federais no Brasil: exemplo do caso Belo Monte' in Nitish Monebhurrun and Pierre Gautreau (eds), *Direito à informação ambiental: uma agenda de pesquisa interdisciplinar* (Prismas 2018) 373–407.

[109] Decree no 788 2005.

[110] eg AI 2006.01.00.017736-8 (TRF 1, 13 December 2006) and RCL 14404 (STF, 23 August 2012).

[111] MS 24184 (STF, 13 August 2003).

[112] REsp 972902 (STJ, 25 August 2009).

[113] See Carina Costa de Oliveira and Gabriela Garcia Batista Lima Moraes (eds), *A interpretação do princípio da precaução pelos tribunais: análise nacional, comparada e internacional* (Pontes Editores 2019).

because this decision facilitates access to justice, and whoever is accused of having caused the damage will have to prove that they are not the author or that the damage did not occur.

Nevertheless, the procedural impacts are less representative in biodiversity litigation than the material ones. Overall, there is a lack of public participation and access to information that must be improved in Brazil. After having explored the material and procedural impact of biodiversity litigation, the discussion now focuses on the strategic use of biodiversity litigation in Brazil.

5. The Strategic Use of Biodiversity Litigation in Brazil

In Brazil, biodiversity litigation has been evolving with the purpose of raising awareness. Biodiversity litigation can be seen as public interest litigation. This has become more evident in the last few years due to the regression of the environmental protection in the country since 2018. Some examples of this regression in the field of biodiversity protection will be discussed before addressing how biodiversity litigation has been used strategically to reduce this impact.

Several institutional changes adopted by the current government have weakened biodiversity management. For instance, Federal Law No 13.844 of 2019 stated that the Ministry of Agriculture is the new institution in charge of the Brazilian Forestry Service, a task previously undertaken by the Ministry of the Environment. Many other obligations carried out by the Ministry of the Environment were also allocated to other ministries such as the management of fisheries.

Other examples of legislative changes and regressions can be given:[114] the change in parameters to protect native vegetation in the country, such as the protection of coastal ecosystems; the reduction of Brazil's annual greenhouse

[114] See Felipe Werneck and others, *Passando a boiada: o segundo ano de desmonte ambiental sob Jair Bolsonaro* (Observatório do Clima 2021); Joana Pereira and Eduardo Viola, 'Close to a Tipping Point? The Amazon and the Challenge of Sustainable Development under Growing Climate Pressures' (2020) 52(3) Journal of Latin American Studies 467–94; Suely Mara Vas Guimaraes de Araújo, 'Environmental Policy in the Bolsonaro Government The Response of Environmentalists in the Legislative Arena' (2020) 14(2) Brazilian Political Science Review 1–20 <www.scielo.br/pdf/bpsr/v14n2/1981-3821-bpsr-14-2-e0005.pdf> accessed 12 March 2022; Mariana Vale and others, 'The Covid-19 Pandemic as an Opportunity to Weaken Environmental Protection in Brazil' (2021) Biological Conservation 255; Luciana Gomes Barbosa, Maria Alice Santos Alves, and Carlos Eduardo Viveiros Grelle, 'Actions Against Sustainability: Dismantling of the Environmental Policies in Brazil' (2021) Land Use Policy 104.

gas (GHG) emissions targets; the increase in the authorization of the use of some pesticides classifying them as less dangerous or without a specific category; and temporary fishing authorization for all fishermen who claim to practise industrial fishing.

This context increases the necessity to use biodiversity litigation in a strategic way to avoid regression. Despite the absence of an administrative or legislative provision on the non-regression principle,[115] it has been used by the courts in Brazil to interrupt normative changes.[116] During 2019 and 2020, its contribution was one of the only means of avoiding the regression of topics such as: the maintenance of important administrative regulations; the guarantee of public hearings on climate change issues; the confirmation of the imprescriptibly of environmental damages; and the protection of animals during cosmetic experiments.

It is important to note that, in Brazil, the possibility of filing lawsuits is restricted to limitation periods established by law. Once that period has expired, it is no longer possible to file an action. However, there are exceptions, such as the possibility of filing actions to repair environmental damage. In such a case, it does not matter when the damage occurred.

The following discussion focuses on various interpretations of the non-regression principle. One example is a case[117] which analysed the constitutionality of a provisional measure[118] that altered several protected areas in the Amazon. Provisional measures are adopted by the President and are eventually enacted by the legislature. According to the STF, this provisional measure, when enacted, caused a decrease in the protected areas' ecosystems and infringed the non-regression principle since it breaches the fundamental right to a balanced environment, guaranteed by the Federal Constitution.

[115] One possible definition of the principle is the following: 'The principle of non-regression prohibits any recession of environmental law or existing levels of environmental protection, and comprises its protective norms in the category of non-revocable and intangible legal rules, in the common interest of humanity' <https://globalpact.informea.org/glossary/principle-non-regression> accessed 11 March 2022. See Michel Prieur, 'Le principe de non-régression en droit de l'environnement, condition du développement durable' (2013) Revue Africaine de Droit de l'Environnement 17.

[116] Ingo Wolfgang Sarlet and Tiago Fensterseifer, 'Breves considerações sobre o princípio da proibição de retrocesso em matéria ambiental à luz do atual cenário de flexibilização da legislação ecológica brasileira' in Flavia Franca Dinnebier and Jose Rubens Morato Leite (eds), *Estado de Direito Ecológico: conceito, conteúdo e novas dimensões para a proteção da natureza* (Inst O direito por um Planeta Verde 2017) 414; Barbara Lucchesi Ramaciotti and others, 'O Princípio da Proibição do Retrocesso Ambiental Aplicado às Políticas Públicas Ambientais' (2020) 6(2) Revista Estudos Institucionais 685, 706.

[117] ADI 4717 (STF, 15 February 2019).

[118] Provisional Measure no 558 2012, converted into Law no 12678 2012.

One of the competent institutions to regulate environmental issues in Brazil is the Conselho Nacional do Meio Ambiente (CONAMA). This institution has been weakened which led to the repeal[119] of important norms such as the licensing process of irrigation activities,[120] the protection of ecosystems such as mangroves and sand bars,[121]and the establishment of standards to protect artificial reservoirs.[122] The STF stated in a decision connected to decision ADPF 749[123] that the revocation of these norms was unconstitutional since there was no replacement by another similar protective norm. The decision mentioned the regression concerning the protection of fundamental rights to life, health, and the environment. Therefore, these norms had their validity re-established.

Though not directly linked to biodiversity litigation, the rise of climate litigation before different tribunals in Brazil should be mentioned. In 2021, these cases did not reach any conclusion, but important measures such as public hearings were summoned to include climate change in the legal discussions. Decision ADPF 708[124] was the first opportunity for the STF to discuss climate change issues with society in general. The action was proposed by some political parties which argued that the National Fund on Climate Change must be re-established, after have been at a standstill since 2019. A sum of more than $500 million[125] was being blocked which could have been used to fight deforestation and wildfires. Other actions have been brought to the same tribunal on this issue.[126] At present, it is not clear how these cases might influence biodiversity litigation.

Another important decision concerns the environmental reparation of damages. As already mentioned, judicial action to repair environmental damages does not have a limitation period. The STF,[127] based on the necessity of guaranteeing integral reparation for environmental damage for present and future generations, considered that reparation for environmental damages is a fundamental right and can take place at any time after its occurrence.

119 Resolution no 500 2020.
120 Resolution 84 2001.
121 Resolution 303 2002.
122 Resolution 302 2002.
123 ADPF 749 (STF, 30 November 2020).
124 ADPF 708 (STF, 15 September 2019).
125 2.9 billion Brazilian Reais.
126 ADO 59 (STF, 5 June 2020).
127 RE 654833 (STF, 20 April 2020).

Moreover, another decision refers to the constitutionality of a state regulation on the prohibition of the use of animals in cosmetic product experiments. In that case, the state of Amazonas prohibited the use of animals for developing cosmetic products.[128] That competence was recognized by the STF,[129] based on the concurrent competence to legislate, to allow states to legislate in a more protective way than the federal state.

Finally, with regard to the maintenance of environmental licensing in Brazil, there are federal and state initiatives to weaken the licensing procedure and the STF has been engaged in trying to block these licensing initiatives. One good example is the declaration on the unconstitutional nature of the flexibility of environmental licensing in the Amapá state.[130] Such flexibility had simplified the procedure of activities such as agriculture, raising cattle and other animals, fisheries, and similar activities.

In summary, in Brazil, there are impacts of biodiversity litigation on administrative, civil, and criminal issues but the impacts are less procedural than material. There is a lack of public participation and access to information that must be improved. In this sense, the strategic use of biodiversity litigation is crucial for addressing these questions as well as the administrative and legislative regression that biodiversity law has been facing since 2018.

6. Conclusion

Biodiversity litigation is an important tool for ensuring compliance and technical interpretation of the environmental legal framework as well as for raising awareness of biodiversity concerns. In this sense, biodiversity litigation can increase the effectiveness of biodiversity protection in Brazil. This shows the limited influence of IBL, but IBL has impacted material and procedural issues as well as strategic litigation in Brazil.

Our research shows that IBL has a limited influence on biodiversity litigation in Brazil. Considering that its impact is quite diverse and depends on the subject, it is not possible to affirm that there is a considerable influence on Brazilian biodiversity litigation. The influence is more evident in conceptual matters, such as biodiversity definition, as well as in cases related

[128] State Law (Amazonas) no 289 2015.
[129] ADI 5996 (STF, 15 April 2020).
[130] ADI 5475 (STF, 20 April 2020).

to subjects such as genetic resources, species, flora, and the illegal trade in wildlife rather than in those related to forests and protected areas. In addition to this, other international fields such as human rights and trade law have contributed to consolidating Brazilian concepts regarding biodiversity in relation to other social and economic issues. Subjects such as animal rights and climate change have not yet had a direct connection with biodiversity litigation.

There are material, procedural, and strategic impacts of biodiversity litigation in Brazil. For the first aspect, administrative, civil, and criminal issues can be highlighted. Court decisions have been relevant for guaranteeing that public power must take into account biodiversity protection while authorizing biodiversity exploitation activities. In addition, scientific evidence has also been reinforced in the cases where environmental studies were required. Civil issues, related to biodiversity litigation, are based on liability concerns; they contribute to ensuring compliance with the biodiversity legal framework and guarantee its proper interpretation. Criminal issues have impacted on the interpretation of important principles such as the insignificance principle. The procedural impacts of biodiversity litigation must also be pointed out—there are some impacts on competence issues and access to justice, but limited impacts on participation and access to information.

In Brazil, biodiversity litigation can be seen as a form of public interest litigation and this has become more evident in the last few years. However, there are many procedural barriers that must be overcome, such as the excessive duration of the cases and the lack of expertise of judges.

The next step in this research is to analyse if the reason why IBL has had little impact on Brazilian litigation is related to the vague content of international obligations related to biodiversity or if it is related to a resistance of national tribunals to refer to international law. Moreover, there is a need for more research on the connection between biodiversity law and other areas, such as trade, human rights, and climate change, through instruments, rights, and principles such as public participation, the right to a healthy quality of life and healthy environment, and the non-regression principle. The research must proceed to consolidate the subject and design other legal instruments and techniques to strengthen biodiversity arguments within the judiciary. See Table 3.1 for the key treaties signed and ratified by Brazil and Table 3.2 for biodiversity-related cases analysed by subject.

Table 3.1 Global and regional biodiversity-related treaties signed and ratified by Brazil

Treaty	Entry into force in international law	Approval by domestic law (legislative decree)	Ratification by domestic law (executive decree)
Convention on Biological Diversity (CBD)—Rio de Janeiro, 1992	29 December 1993	No 2 1994	No 2519 1998
Cartagena Protocol on Biosafety to the Convention on Biological Diversity (Biosafety Protocol)—Cartagena, 2000	11 September 2003	No 908 2003	No 5705 2006
Convention on Wetlands of International Importance especially as Waterfowl Habitat (Ramsar Convention)—Ramsar, 1971	21 December 1975	No 33 1992	No 1905 1996
United Nations Convention to Combat Desertification in those Countries Experiencing Serious Drought and/or Desertification, particular in Africa (UNCCD)—Paris, 1994	26 December 1996	No 28 1997	No 2741 1998
Nagoya Protocol on Access to Genetic Resources and their Fair and Equitable Sharing of Benefits Arising from their Utilization to the Convention on Biological Diversity (Nagoya Protocol)—Nagoya, 2010	12 October 2014	No 136 2020	X
Kyoto Protocol to the United Nations Framework Convention on Climate Change (Kyoto Protocol)—Kyoto, 2005	16 February 2005	No 144 2002	No 5445 2005
Agreement for the Implementation of the Provisions of the United Nations Convention on the Law of the Sea relating to the Conservation and Management of Straddling Fish Stocks and Highly Migratory Fish Stocks—New York, 1995	11 December 2001	No 5 2000	No 4361 2002
Convention for the Conservation of Antarctic Seals—London, 1972	11 February 1972	No 37 1990	No 66 1991
Convention on the Conservation of Antarctic Marine Living Resources (CCAMLR)—Canberra, 1980	7 April 1982	No 33 1985	No 93935 1987
Protocol to the Antarctic Treaty on Environmental Protection (Madrid Protocol)—Madrid, 1991	14 January 1998	No 88 1995	No 2742 1998

(*continued*)

Table 3.1 Continued

Treaty	Entry into force in international law	Approval by domestic law (legislative decree)	Ratification by domestic law (executive decree)
International Convention for the Regulation of Whaling—Washington, 1946	10 November 1948	No 14 1950	No 28524 1950
Protocol to the International Convention for the Regulation of Whaling—Washington, 1956	14 May 1959	No 14 1958	No 46873 1959
Convention on International Trade in Endangered Species of Wild Fauna and Flora (CITES)—Washington, 1973	1 July 1975	No 54 1975	No 76623 1975 No 3607 2000
Amendment to the Convention on International Trade in Endangered Species of Wild Fauna and Flora—Art XXI (Gaborone amendment)—Gaborone, 1983	29 November 2013	No 35 1985	No 92446 1986 No 3607 2000
Convention on the Conservation of Migratory Species of Wild Animals (CMS)—Bonn, 1979	1 November 1983	No 387 2013	No 9080 2017
Agreement on the Conservation of Albatrosses and Petrels (ACAP)—Cape Town, 2001	1 February 2004	No 187 2008	No 6753 2009
International Tropical Timber Agreement—Geneva, 2006	7 December 2011	No 68 1997	No 2707 1998
International Treaty on Plant Genetic Resources for Food and Agriculture (ITPGR)—Rome, 2001	29 June 2004	No 70 2006	No 6476 2008
Stockholm Convention on Persistent Organic Pollutants (Stockholm Convention)—Stockholm, 2001	17 May 2004	No 204 2004	No 5472 2005
Convention on the Prevention of Marine Pollution by Dumping of Wastes and Other Matter (London Convention)—London, 1972	30 August 1975	No 10 1982	No 87566 1982
Basel Convention on the Control of Transboundary Movements of Hazardous Wastes and their Disposal (Basel Convention)—Basel, 1989	5 May 1992	No 34 1992	No 875 1993
Convention concerning Indigenous and Tribal Peoples in Independent Countries—Geneva, 1989	5 September 1991	No 143 2002	No 5051 2004

Table 3.2 Biodiversity-related cases analysed by subject

Subject	Case	Judgment date	Court
Human rights	ADPF 747	28 October 2020	STF
	ADPF 748	28 October 2020	STF
	ADPF 749	28 October 2020	STF
	ADPF 101	24 June 2009	STF
	RE 627189	8 June 2016	STF
	AG 2006.01.00.017736-8	13 December 2006	TRF1
	RCL 14404	23 August 2012	STF
Animal rights	ADI 4983	6 October 2016	STF
	ADI 2514	29 June 2005	STF
Procedural obligations	Petition 3388	19 March 2009	STF
	MS 24184	13 August 2003	STF
	ADI 3573	1 December 2005	STF
	REsp 972902	25 August 2009	STJ
Forests	AREsp 1312435	13 November 2012	STJ
Climate change	ADPF 708	15 September 2019	STF
	ADO 59	5 June 2020	STF
Species	AG 0006114-14.2005.4.01.0000	19 September 2009	TRF1
	REsp 1549459	9 May 2017	STJ
	AC 0800486-03.2012.4.05.8100	30 January 2014	TRF5
Illegal wildlife trade crimes and endangered species	RE 835558	9 February 2017	STF
	AgRg REsp 1847810	19 May 2020	STJ
	AC 1147173	18 December 2014	TRF3
	AG 0108242-70.2014.4.02.0000	27 April 2016	TRF2
	AC 544293	16 August 2012	TRF5
Genetic resources	AI 559568	21 October 2015	TRF3
	SLS 1438	9 May 2011	STJ
	AC 5013440-40.2012.4.04.7200	26 May 2015	TRF4
	REsp 1387921	15 December 2015	STJ
Bioinvasion	AC 5049424-26.2014.4.04.7100	1 August 2017	TRF4
	AC 0008256-41.2014.4.02.0000	30 June 2020	TRF2
Protected areas	REsp 1406139	7 November 2016	STJ
	ADI 3646	2 December 2019	STF
	AREsp 155302	20 November 2012	STJ
	REsp 1163524	17 August 2011	STJ
	EREsp 191656	2 August 2010	STJ
	AgInt no REsp 1781924	10 June 2019	STJ
	AREsp 1285871	30 October 2019	STJ
	MS 24665	1 December 2004	STF
	ADI 4717	15 February 2019	STF

(*continued*)

Table 3.2 Continued

Subject	Case	Judgment date	Court
Environmental harms	ACP 02030948119944036104	23 May 2001	TRF3
	AC 5012993-50.2014.4.04.0000	18 November 2014	TRF4
	RE 654833	20 April 2020	STF
Environmental crimes	REsp 905864	11 March 2008	STJ
	REsp 1626599	14 March 2017	STJ
	AgRg no REsp 1503896	17 September 2015	STJ
Competence	ADI 5996	15 April 2020	STF
	ADI 5475	20 April 2020	STF

4

Biodiversity Litigation in Canada

In Quest of Accountability

Frederic Perron-Welch, Chris Tollefson, and Joshua Ginsberg

1. Introduction

In December 1992, Canada[1] became the first industrialized country to ratify the Convention on Biological Diversity (CBD). It entered into force domestically on 29 December 1993 simultaneously with its entry into force internationally (Table 4.1 at the end of the chapter shows a list of biodiversity treaties to which Canada is a party).[2] Since then, at least on paper, Canada has continued to work domestically to promote the CBD's goals, finalizing a variety of agreements and strategy documents. These include the federal Canadian Biodiversity Strategy in 1995,[3] the federal, provincial, and territorial Accord for the Protection of Species at Risk in 1996,[4] the 2006 Biodiversity Outcomes Framework,[5] the 2007 National Framework for Species at Risk Conservation,[6] and the 2020 Biodiversity Goals and Targets for Canada[7] adopted in 2015. Canada has also

[1] While it is not considered to be a 'megadiverse' country, Canada contains globally significant biodiversity, natural habitats, and ecosystems. These range from Arctic tundra to deserts, lakes, mountains, oceans, prairies, rainforests, taiga, evergreen and broadleaf forests, and wetlands, among others. It also holds more intact forest landscape than any other place on Earth—estimated at 25 per cent of the world's remaining primary forest; see Boreal Leadership Council, *Canadian Boreal Forest Conservation Framework* (International Boreal Conservation Campaign 2015), 1.

[2] Canada has not ratified either the Cartagena Protocol on Biosafety or the Nagoya Protocol on Access and Benefit-sharing.

[3] Government of Canada, *Canada Biodiversity Strategy: Canada's Response to the Convention on Biological Diversity* (1995) <www.cbd.int/doc/world/ca/ca-nbsap-01-en.pdf> accessed 10 March 2022.

[4] Government of Canada, *Protection of Species at Risk: Federal, Provincial and Territorial Accord* (2014) <www.canada.ca/en/environment-climate-change/services/species-risk-act-accord-funding/protection-federal-provincial-territorial-accord.html> accessed 10 March 2022.

[5] Government of Canada, *A Biodiversity Outcomes Framework for Canada* (2006) <www.cbd.int/doc/world/ca/ca-nbsap-oth-en.pdf> accessed 10 March 2022.

[6] Government of Canada, *Species at Risk Conservation National Framework* (2014) <www.canada.ca/en/environment-climate-change/services/species-risk-act-accord-funding/conservation-national-framework.html> accessed 10 March 2022.

[7] Government of Canada, '2020 Biodiversity Goals and Targets for Canada', < <www.biodivcanada.ca/national-biodiversity-strategy-and-action-plan/2020-biodiversity-goals-and-targets-for-canada> accessed 10 March 2022.

Frederic Perron-Welch, Chris Tollefson, and Joshua Ginsberg, *Biodiversity Litigation in Canada* In: *Biodiversity Litigation*.
Edited by: Guillaume Futhazar, Sandrine Maljean-Dubois, and Jona Razzaque, Oxford University Press.
 DOI: 10.1093/oso/9780192865465.003.0004

Table 4.1 List of biodiversity treaties to which Canada is party

Bilateral Biodiversity Treaties

- 1916 Convention between the United Kingdom and the United States for the Protection of Migratory Birds in Canada and the United States and 1995
- 1956 Great Lakes Fisheries Convention
- 1987 Agreement between the Government of Canada and the Government of the United States of America on the Conservation of the Porcupine Caribou Herd
- 1995 Protocol between the Government of Canada and the Government of the United States of America amending the 1916 Convention between the United Kingdom and the United States of America for the Protection of Migratory Birds in Canada and the United States

Multilateral Biodiversity Treaties

- Agreement on Conservation of Polar Bears
- Convention for the Protection of the World Cultural and Natural Heritage
- Convention on Biological Diversity
- Convention on International Trade in Endangered Species of Wild Fauna and Flora
- Convention on Wetlands of International Importance especially as Waterfowl Habitat
- International Plant Protection Convention
- International Treaty on Plant Genetic Resources for Food and Agriculture

negotiated and joined various international biodiversity treaties including the Convention on International Trade in Endangered Species of Wild Fauna and Flora (CITES),[8] the Polar Bear Agreement,[9] the Ramsar Convention,[10] and the World Heritage Convention.[11]

On the ground, however, Canada has struggled to meet the challenge of biodiversity loss.[12] Canada met some of its domestic biodiversity targets,[13] but in a number of cases, domestic targets were less ambitious than the Aichi Targets, or some were not established at all (eg a target on ending or reforming incentives harmful to biodiversity under Aichi Target 3). Overall, the record of Canadian governments at all levels has been lacklustre. In the words of one assessment: 'Canada's federal, provincial and territorial governments are doing

[8] Convention on International Trade in Endangered Species of Wild Fauna and Flora (opened for signature 3 March 1973, entered into force 1 July 1975) 993 UNTS 243.

[9] Agreement on the Conservation of Polar Bears (opened for signature 15 November 1973, entered into force 26 May 1976) 2898 UNTS 243.

[10] Convention on Wetlands of International Importance Especially as Waterfowl Habitat (opened for signature 2 February 1971, entered into force 21 December 1975) 996 UNTS 245.

[11] Convention for the Protection of the World Cultural and Natural Heritage (opened for signature 16 November 1972, entered into force 17 December 1975) 1037 UNTS 151.

[12] The Wild Species Report 2015 indicates that 'a total of 1659 species have been ranked as presumed extirpated, possibly extirpated, critically imperilled, and imperilled at the national level in Canada'. See Canadian Endangered Species Conservation Council, *Wild Species 2015: The General Status of Species in Canada* (Government of Canada 2016) 102.

[13] Government of Canada, *Summary of Canada's 6th National Report to the Convention on Biological Diversity* (2019) <www.biodivcanada.ca/reports/national-reports-to-cbd/6th-national-report> accessed 10 March 2022.

an abysmal job protecting our at-risk species and the habitat they need to survive and recover.'[14]

The reasons for this gap between aspiration and outcome are complicated. As in many jurisdictions, it reflects a perceived tension between economic growth and environmental protection, a tension that is exacerbated by the political influence of business interests that have enjoyed success, in various governmental venues, in lobbying against robust protection for areas and species.[15] In many instances, these business interests are active in the industries that are the main direct drivers of biodiversity loss in Canada—agriculture, forestry, fisheries, and non-renewable resource extraction (mining and oil and gas). Overall, some scholars have contended that this influence has led to regulatory capture, and an undermining of Canadian environmental law and ambition in recent decades.[16]

The failure to meet the challenge of biodiversity loss is also structural. Of particular consequence has been the nature of Canada's federation.[17] Like other federations, while Canada's national government is vested with arguably ample constitutional authority to tackle the biodiversity crisis, the suite of powers and proprietary rights vested in the provinces, and the tradition of cooperative federalism, has meant that federal species protection laws have often been framed in a more timid and discretionary fashion than many would argue is necessary to tackle the daunting challenge of biodiversity loss. But while Canada's biodiversity laws are certainly wanting, this has not deterred species protection champions from relying on litigation to hold government to account. And, despite their usually deferential posture, in many of the early biodiversity cases argued before them Canadian courts have rendered rulings that have enhanced the efficacy of Canadian species laws, and been surprisingly critical of government's failure to vigorously discharge its legal obligations to species. Indeed, as discussed later, many of these decisions cite Canada's commitment to the CBD and ancillary concepts such as the precautionary principle. To gain a fulsome picture of the biodiversity litigation in Canada, however, it is important to take into account litigation in related areas. Key in this regard are lawsuits arising in relation to parks and protected areas,

[14] Sean Nixon and others, *Failure to Protect: Grading Canada's Species at Risk Laws* (Ecojustice 2012) 23.

[15] Stepan Wood, Georgia Tanner, and Benjamin J Richardson, 'What Ever Happened to Canadian Environmental Law?' (2010) 37 Ecology Law Quarterly 981, 1025–27.

[16] Jason MacLean, 'Regulatory Capture and the Role of Academics in Public Policymaking: Lessons from Canada's Environmental Regulatory Review Process' (2019) 52 University of British Columbia Law Review 479, 480, 498–514, 526–32, 536–37.

[17] For an illuminating reflection on the relationship between biodiversity protection and federalism, see A Dan Tarlock, 'Biodiversity Federalism' (1995) 54 Maryland Law Review 1315.

environmental assessments, and, importantly, in relation to constitutionally protected Aboriginal rights asserted by Canada's indigenous peoples.[18]

The structure of this chapter is as follows. In Section 2, we offer a short overview of Canada's constitutional arrangements. This is accompanied by a discussion of the process, and rules that govern, the reception of international obligations, such as those under the CBD, into domestic law. Section 3 explores the influence of the CBD on domestic litigation outcomes in several selected areas of biodiversity litigation, as it is the predominant international biodiversity law instrument influencing biodiversity litigation in Canada. This exploration, although not comprehensive, tackles the topics of litigation under the federal species at risk law, litigation in relation to parks and protected areas, and litigation brought by indigenous groups to protect their constitutionally protected rights. It also seeks to understand how the architecture of the legal frameworks within which these cases are brought, and other contextual factors including political pressures and constitutional imperatives, can help to explain the biodiversity litigation picture to date.

2. Background

2.1 Constitutional Division of Powers

Part VI of the Constitution Act, 1867 allocates different legislative powers to the federal and provincial governments. In consequence, the '[j]urisdiction to implement Canadian treaty obligations is split between Parliament and the provincial legislatures according to the subject-matter distribution ...'[19] The Supreme Court of Canada has determined that environmental competencies are divided between the federal government and the provinces.[20] This recognition of concurrent jurisdiction to legislate is relevant to the implementation of international environmental treaties, particularly the CBD.[21] Many of the

[18] In this chapter, we refer to 'Aboriginal rights' as the legal rights (including the right to Aboriginal title) that are constitutionally protected under s 35 of the Canadian Constitution. 'Aboriginal law' is the body of post-colonial law that governs the legal situation of the Aboriginal peoples of Canada; 'indigenous law' refers to the law of a particular Aboriginal group, as defined and applied by the group: see Jim Reynolds, *Aboriginal Peoples and the Law* (UBC Press 2018).

[19] Gib van Ert, 'The Domestic Application of International Law in Canada' in Curtis A Bradley (ed), *The Oxford Handbook of Comparative Foreign Relations Law* (OUP 2019) 508.

[20] Diana Jung, 'Canada's Patchwork Environmentalism' (2019) 12 Journal of Parliamentary and Political Law 797, 800; *R v Crown Zellerbach Canada Ltd* [1988] 1 SCR 401; *Friends of the Oldman River Society v Canada (Minister of Transport)* [1992] 1 SCR 3; *R v Hydro-Québec* [1997] 3 SCR 213.

[21] Wood, Tanner, and Richardson (n 15) 1019.

obligations that Canada took on under the CBD required the provincial enactment and enforcement of relevant laws on natural resources like forests, and on lands owned by the provinces.[22] However, provincial legislatures have exclusive competence over lawmaking on the development, conservation, and management of forestry resources in their jurisdiction, including on the rate of primary production.[23] In consequence, the federal government sought provincial endorsement before ratifying the CBD, reducing the potential for jurisdictional conflicts and improving the chances of meeting its international obligations.[24]

2.2 Reception of International Law in Canada

Like many former British possessions, 'the rules governing international law's reception in Canada originate in British constitutionalism and English common law'.[25] These rules require that international law be implemented domestically before it can be applied in domestic courts. This approach is founded on the respective powers of the federal executive (to carry out foreign relations and conclude treaties) and the federal and provincial legislatures (the power to legislate).[26] The federal and provincial legislatures can use numerous techniques for treaty implementation,[27] such as the adoption of measures giving legal force to specific treaty provisions, measures ensuring performance of the treaty without directly adopting its wording, or measures empowering the government to implement treaty obligations by regulation.[28] Where measures make no mention of an underlying treaty, extrinsic sources can be relied upon to determine whether a provision was adopted to implement a treaty.[29] Another technique is use existing laws to perform treaty obligations, which is fairly common in practice.[30]

[22] Michelle L Campbell and Vernon G Thomas, 'Constitutional Impacts on Conservation' (2002) 32 Environmental Policy and Law 223, 225.
[23] Constitution Act, 1867, s 92A(1)(b).
[24] Campbell and Thomas (n 22) 227.
[25] van Ert (n 19) 501.
[26] Charles-Emmanuel Côté, 'Federalism and Foreign Affairs in Canada' in Curtis A Bradley (ed), *The Oxford Handbook of Comparative Foreign Relations Law* (OUP 2019) 278–80, 282–83, 291–93, 295.
[27] Hugo Cyr and Armand de Mestral, 'International Treaty-Making and Treaty Implementation' in Peter Oliver, Patrick Macklem, and Nathalie Des Rosiers (eds), *The Oxford Handbook of the Canadian Constitution* (OUP 2017) 608 notes that 'implementation is accomplished by at least 13 different approaches in current Canadian practice'.
[28] van Ert (n 19) 508.
[29] ibid 508–09.
[30] ibid 509.

Canadian courts interpret laws in the light of their text, context, and purpose. The values and principles of customary and conventional international law enter as part of the context, especially where a law has been enacted to implement a treaty.[31] International law can also help at the stage of determining legislative purpose where legislation was enacted in response to treaty commitments.[32] The starting point for interpretation is the presumption that laws should be interpreted in a manner consistent with Canada's international obligations.[33] For policy reasons, courts tend to avoid interpretations that would violate these obligations.[34] When examining international law for context, or to determine legislative purpose, Canadian courts often rely on the customary rules of interpretation established by Articles 31 and 32 of the Vienna Convention on the Law of Treaties.[35]

Biodiversity litigation in Canada typically proceeds by way of a petition seeking judicial review of a statutory decision maker's application of the relevant law or regulation. While Canadian courts rarely advert directly to international law, they nonetheless recognize both the constraining effect and interpretive value of international legal principles. For instance, in the Supreme Court of Canada's landmark administrative law decision *Vavilov v Canada*, the majority discusses the manner in which international law constrains administrative decision making.[36] International law is also relevant to judicial interpretation. The presumption of conformity means that an administrative decision maker cannot reasonably interpret a domestic provision inconsistently with Canada's international obligations.[37] Furthermore, treaties may inform whether a decision was a reasonable exercise of administrative power even where the agreement has not been implemented by statute.[38] Thus, while the *direct* effects of international law on domestic legal outcomes are not always readily apparent, its *indirect* effects can be quite profound.

[31] *B010 v Canada (Citizenship and Immigration)* [2015] SCC 58, para 47; *Canada (Minister of Citizenship and Immigration) v Vavilov* [2019] SCC 65, para 114, ibid 501. In the case under appeal, *Vavilov v Canada (Citizenship and Immigration)* [2017] FCA 132 (upheld), Stratas JA reminded that '[i]t is trite that … [the provision in question] should be interpreted in accordance with relevant principles of customary and conventional international law … This is all the more where the provision to be construed has been enacted with a view towards implementing international principles or against the backdrop of those principles …'

[32] *R v Appulonappa*, 2015 SCC 59, para 33.

[33] van Ert (n 19) 511.

[34] *B010 v Canada (Citizenship and Immigration)* (n 31) paras 47–48.

[35] Vienna Convention on the Law of Treaties (open for signature 23 May 1969, entered into force 27 Jan 1980) 1155 UNTS 331. See *Febles v Canada (Citizenship and Immigration)*, 2014 SCC 68, para 11.

[36] *Canada (Minister of Citizenship and Immigration) v Vavilov* [2019] SCC 65, para 114.

[37] ibid.

[38] ibid.

2.3 Canada's Response to the Convention on Biological Diversity

Canada and the provinces responded in domestic law and policy to the ratification of the CBD. In some cases, the relevant federal and provincial frameworks pertinent to biodiversity preceded the entry into force of the CBD for Canada, particularly in the case of in situ conservation obligations,[39] and impact assessment obligations.[40] Many of these laws were subsequently amended or replaced, in some cases bringing them closer to the spirit of the CBD.[41] Other laws were adopted subsequent to ratification in order to directly and indirectly implement the CBD's provisions both at the federal and provincial/territorial levels.[42] In other cases, provinces declared that their existing legal framework would be used to satisfy CBD obligations.[43]

3. Biodiversity Litigation

3.1 Species at Risk

Overall, Canada's approach to protecting species at risk may charitably be regarded as a patchwork. While the majority of its provinces and two of its three territories (Northwest Territories and Nunavut, but not the Yukon) have enacted species at risk legislation, with some exceptions this legislation is generally considered to be weak, reactive, and ad hoc.[44] Notably, as well, in some of Canada's most resource-dependent jurisdictions, including in its three most western provinces (BC, Alberta, and Saskatchewan), provincial governments have vigorously resisted passing species at risk legislation, preferring to rely on outdated wildlife laws principally intended to regulate hunting and fishing.

In this section of the chapter, we focus on biodiversity litigation at the federal level. A direct legacy of the CBD, the Species at Risk Act[45] (SARA) has now

[39] Such as the National Parks Act, RSC 1985, c N-14; Canada Wildlife Act, 1985; Canadian Environmental Protection Act, 1988; Act Respecting Threatened or Vulnerable Species, CQLR c E-12.01.

[40] Canadian Environmental Assessment Act, SC 1992, c 37 (repealed, 2012, c 19, s 66).

[41] Such as the integration of the ecosystem approach in the National Parks Act, SC 2000, c 32.

[42] Including the federal Oceans Act, SC 1996, c 31 and Species at Risk Act, SC 2002, c 29; Nova Scotia's Endangered Species Act, SNS 1998, c 11; Ontario's Endangered Species Act, 2007, SO 2007, c 6; Quebec's Act Respecting the Conservation and Development of Wildlife, CQLR C C-61.1.

[43] Such as British Columbia: see Paul M Wood and Laurie Flahr, 'Taking Endangered Species Seriously? British Columbia's Species-at-Risk Policies' (2004) 30 Canadian Public Policy 381.

[44] Nixon and others (n 14).

[45] Species at Risk Act, SC 2002, c 29 (SARA).

been in force for over two decades and is by far Canada's most important biodiversity protection law. Its development followed the commitment in the 1995 Canadian Biodiversity Strategy that 'Federal, provincial and territorial governments will review their current legislation to determine if improvements are required in order to protect species-at-risk and their habitats, determine the benefits and costs of a more harmonized legislative approach and pursue harmonization where appropriate and practical.'[46] After a decade of negotiations and failed attempts to pass a federal species law following Canada's ratification of the CBD, expectations amongst species protection advocates for SARA were tempered. In key respects, addressed in more detail later, the architecture of SARA represents a compromise reflective of the wide range of competing interests and perspectives out of which it was born.

A key factor militating towards compromise in SARA is the division of powers within the Canadian federation.[47] Under Canada's federal model, ownership and control over most public lands rests with the provinces. Unlike some other federal jurisdictions such as the United States, only a small percentage of Canada's land mass is under federal jurisdiction. Nor is there a clear and obvious plenary federal jurisdiction that would vest in the federal government authority to legislate in relation to biodiversity protection. This has meant that the federal government has generally tried to discharge its biodiversity obligations under the CBD using soft diplomacy, often referred to as 'cooperative federalism' rather than employing a more adversarial enforcement approach, particularly with respect to species inhabiting non-federal lands.[48] In contrast, the legal protections conferred on species that inhabit federal lands (most notably in Canada's northern territories) or otherwise fall within federal jurisdiction (aquatic species and migratory birds), are notably more proactive.

The preference of Canadian lawmakers for a cooperative approach also meant that a legislative choice was made not to include within the SARA architecture action-forcing citizen suit provisions. Citizen suit provisions, a common feature of US environmental statutes, empower citizens to secure standing to enforce the law in the face of persistent non-compliance on the part of governments or private entities.[49] They are broadly credited for efficacy and durability of the US Endangered Species Act[50] (ESA).

46 Government of Canada (n 7) para 1.21.

47 On the mismatch between federalism and biodiversity protection, see Tarlock (n 17).

48 Matthew D Zinn, 'Policing Environmental Regulatory Enforcement: Cooperation, Capture, and Citizen Suits' (2002) 21 Stanford Environmental Law Journal 81.

49 Meinhard Doelle and Chris Tollefson, *Environmental Law: Cases and Materials* (3rd edn, Carswell 2019) 477–82.

50 Barton H Thompson Jr, 'The Continuing Innovations of Citizen Enforcement' (2000) 2000 University of Illinois Law Review 185.

Twenty years after its enactment, it is now generally believed that SARA has outperformed, in at least some key respects, initial expectations. While it lacks citizen suit provisions, SARA has nonetheless spurred action by governments and courts alike, which have in turn been encouraged to implement both the letter and spirit of SARA through the work of dedicated scientists and public interest lawyers. This is not to suggest, however, the role of science and scientists under SARA is settled or uncontroversial. Nor have government lawyers always welcomed the judicial spotlight that public interest SARA lawsuits have sought to shine. As well, the last two decades have likewise demonstrated the need to better integrate SARA requirements and aspirations into the broader machinery of government decision making, particularly in relation to the environmental impact assessment of major projects.

In this section, we explore these tensions and trends in four key areas of Canadian species protection law: species assessment and listing (3.1.1); designation of critical habitat, recovery strategies, and action plans (3.1.2); safety net and emergency orders (3.1.3); and species protection and project assessment/permitting (3.1.4).

3.1.1 Species assessment and listing

A key battleground in the decade or so that it took Parliament to enact SARA was the process by which species were assessed as to whether they were in need of protection (*assessment*), and subsequently how species were to be listed for legal protection (*listing*). Species protection proponents argued that both the assessment and listing decisions should be vested exclusively in scientific experts. Conflict over this issue presaged similar conflicts over the role of science and politics, and the division of labour between scientists and politicians. Comparable battles over this issue have likewise been fought in the United States.[51] The dominant approach under ESA, at least in theory, has skewed to delegating both assessment and listing powers to arm's length scientists.

In Canada, long before SARA came into force, scientists had worked collaboratively to assess the status of species under the auspices of COSEWIC (the Committee on the Status of Wildlife in Canada).[52] In the lead-up to the adoption of SARA, an eleventh-hour compromise was reached. Under this so-called

[51] Robin S Waples and others, 'A Tale of Two Acts: Endangered Species Listing Practices in Canada and the United States' (2013) 63 BioScience 723.

[52] Established in 1977 as a result of a decision made at the Conference of Federal-Provincial-Territorial Wildlife Directors held in 1976, see COSEWIC, 'Brief history: Committee on the Status of Endangered Wildlife in Canada' <www.cosewic.ca/index.php/en-ca/about-us/brief-history.html> accessed 10 March 2022.

'negative option' compromise, COSEWIC is given exclusive authority to conduct listing assessments. Thereafter, its listing recommendations will be legally binding unless they are explicitly rejected by Cabinet.[53] A Cabinet decision to reject a listing recommendation must occur within nine months, and be accompanied by reasons for the decision.[54]

The Canadian government has exercised its negative option to reject COSEWIC recommendations in what commentators have called 'a taxonomically and geographically non-random' fashion.[55] Marine and northern species have tended to be denied listing, particularly where harvesting is perceived to be of significant economic value, or habitats overlap with resource-based economic activities. Indeed, as an aid to listing decisions, the federal government has implemented a cost–benefit analysis protocol which critics argue frequently underestimates the ecological and other benefits of recommended species' listings.[56]

While, in practice, Canada's negative option listing approach has prompted some well-justified criticism, in principle it is one that some species at risk experts would defend. In particular, Moers has argued that it is an approach that 'allows for the transparent separation of science and policy, providing the opportunity for accurate and science-based assessments as well as an unequivocal government response'.[57] In other respects, as we shall see, SARA decision making has neither been transparent nor have the respective roles of science and policy (and law) been clearly demarcated.

3.1.2 Designation of critical habitat, recovery strategies, and action plans

Species experts concur that the efficacy of species protection legislation is closely linked to the efficacy with which it succeeds in protecting critical habitat. Under SARA, whether and how critical habitat is designated is governed by a highly discretionary process that commences with the development of a recovery strategy and culminates in the implementation of an action plan.

The definition of 'critical habitat' drives much of the biodiversity litigation in this area. SARA defines it as 'the habitat that is necessary for the survival or recovery of a listed wildlife species and that is identified as the species' critical habitat in the recovery strategy or in an action plan for the species'.[58] Recovery

[53] See Doelle and Tollefson (n 49) 756–59.
[54] ibid.
[55] Arne O Mooers and others, 'Science, Policy, and Species at Risk in Canada' (2010) 60 BioScience 843, 845.
[56] C Scott Findlay and others, 'Species Listing under Canada's Species at Risk Act (SARA)' (2009) 23 Conservation Biology 1609.
[57] Mooers and others (n 55).
[58] SARA (n 45) s 2(1).

strategies and action plans are conceived of as sequential steps on the road towards the survival and recovery of a species. A recovery strategy establishes the overall scientific framework within which recovery will be implemented; it is intended to be exclusively science-based. Action plans 'detail the specific projects or activities that must be implemented to enable species recovery'.[59] These plans engage the efforts of a range of experts and stakeholders who draw upon scientific guidance from the recovery strategy and are entitled to weigh socio-economic and other factors.

The legal requirements associated with recovery strategies are more prescriptive than for action plans and include a requirement that the minister responsible identify the '*species' critical habitat, to the extent possible, based on best available information*'.[60] For newly listed species, SARA requires recovery strategies to be completed within one year. There is no time limit for the completion of action plans.

The mandatory language with respect to habitat identification under section 41(1)(c) has generated some important precedents that affirm the legislative requirement of deferring to the best available science where science and policy come into conflict. Both of the leading cases were decided in 2009: *Alberta Wilderness Association v Canada*[61] and *Environmental Defence Canada v Canada*.[62] The first of these cases related to a terrestrial species, the greater sage grouse, which inhabits areas in southern Alberta and Saskatchewan. In the second, the subject of the challenge related was a species known as the nooksack dace, a small minnow whose habitat is a small group of freshwater streams in southern British Columbia. In both cases, the complaint was that minister responsible had failed to identify critical habitat that COSEWIC scientists had determined existed.

In both cases, civil society groups argued that the federal government had acted unlawfully in failing to identify critical habitat where the evidence of COSEWIC scientists suggested that such an identification could be made. Moreover, in both cases the Federal Court interpreted the habitat designation obligation as reflecting and embodying the precautionary principle,[63] concluding that the government's failure to designate habitat was not only inconsistent with the precautionary principle but also unlawful.[64] Both decisions

[59] Mooers and others (n 55).
[60] SARA (n 45) s 41(1)©.
[61] 2009 FC 710.
[62] 2009 FC 878.
[63] SARA (n 45) s 38 incorporates the precautionary principle as a mandatory decisional consideration in the preparation of a recovery strategy, action plan, or management plan.
[64] *Alberta Wilderness Association v Canada (Environment)*, 2009 FC 710 and *Environmental Defence Canada v Minister of Fisheries and Oceans*, 2009 FC 878.

also reject the argument, often raised by the federal government, that courts should eschew engaging with relevant scientific evidence when coming to their decision.[65] As expressed in *Alberta Wilderness*, while acknowledging that courts should avoid becoming 'academies of science', to discharge their duty of determining whether the minister's actions were reasonable courts must evaluate the available evidence, even if that evidence is predominantly scientific in nature.

Indeed, *Environmental Defence* goes further by explicitly linking SARA and the CBD, observing that the precautionary principle is an important feature of the CBD, and holding that SARA must be interpreted in a way that conforms to the values and principles of the CBD. Further, in its view, this obliges courts to avoid any interpretation that could put Canada in breach of its obligations.[66] The Federal Court has subsequently affirmed the relationship between the CBD and the precautionary principle as articulated in SARA. For example, in 2011, in *Adam v Canada*,[67] the Federal Court observed that SARA effectively codified the precautionary principle that 'cost-effective measures to prevent the reduction or loss of [a] species should not be postponed for lack of full scientific certainty' and that these provisions of SARA were enacted to fulfil Canada's obligations under the CBD.[68]

Once a recovery strategy has been completed, what happens next depends upon whether the species is a federal one (aquatic or migratory bird) or inhabits federal lands, or whether it falls outside this category. If the latter, SARA confers initial responsibility for implementing the recovery strategy on the provinces and territories in respect of which the critical habitat has been identified. This is a deliberate legislative decision intended to respect the constitutional authority of the provinces and territories in relation to what are referred to colloquially as 'non-federal species'. As is discussed later, implementation of species protection by the provinces and territories has been mixed, leading to calls for the federal government to step in and exercise its 'safety net' and 'emergency' order powers.[69]

65 See the discussion on 'academies of science' in Martin Olszynski and Meinhard Doelle, '*Ontario Power Generation Inc v Greenpeace Canada*: Form over Substance Leads to a "Low Threshold" for Federal Environmental Assessment' (22 September 2015) ABlawg <https://ablawg.ca/2015/09/22/ontario-power-generation-inc-v-greenpeace-canada-form-over-substance-leads-to-a-low-threshold-for-federal-environmental-assessment/> accessed 10 March 2022.

66 *Alberta Wilderness Association v Canada (Environment)* (n 64).

67 *Adam v Canada (Environment)*, 2011 FC 962.

68 ibid para 71.

69 See eg Emily Chung, 'Why Canada's endangered species are declining faster than ever: Effectiveness of Species at Risk Act depends on government enthusiasm, scientists say', CBC News (14 September 2017) <www.cbc.ca/news/technology/wwf-living-planet-sara-1.4290024> accessed 10 March 2022: Nicole Thompson, 'Environmental groups call on federal government to protect caribou in

On the other hand, for species falling within federal jurisdiction, SARA requires time-limited federal action. For species falling within this category, section 58 of SARA requires the federal government, within 180 days of a recovery plan being completed, to confirm appropriate protection measures are in place either by means of issuing a 'protection order' under section 58(4), or a 'protection statement' under section 58(5)(b). The latter describes how critical habitat is already protected by provisions in, or measures under, other Acts of Parliament.[70]

The adequacy of the federal government's response in this context has also led to litigation, most notably in the 2010 *David Suzuki Foundation v Canada*[71] case in relation to the Southern resident orca habitat on Canada's west coast. In this case, the federal government claimed that it was complying with its obligations under section 58 of SARA by issuing a protection statement, or alternatively by making a protection order that failed to address the biophysical attributes essential to the orcas' survival and recovery, including its requirements with respect to environmental quality and prey availability, and instead was primarily focused on the geophysical location of that habitat. Both the trial court and the Federal Court of Appeal held that the federal government's approach was contrary to SARA. Relying on the reasoning in *Environmental Defence*, it held that the federal government's duty under SARA to identify and protect critical habitat does not just connote a location, but rather both the location and biophysical components of critical habitat.[72]

In *Environmental Defence*,[73] the court had given strong weight to the applicants' argument that CBD provisions should be relied on in analysing SARA's requirement to identify critical habitat. This involved interpreting section 41(1)(c) in the light of the CBD definition of 'ecosystem', which includes both biotic and abiotic components, and the application of article 7(a) and (b) of the CBD on identifying and monitoring components of biodiversity that are important for conservation, in order to promote the protection of ecosystems, natural habitats, and the maintenance of viable populations of species in natural surroundings.[74]

northern Ontario', The Canadian Press (14 November 2018) <https://globalnews.ca/news/4663051/northern-ontario-caribou-protection> accessed 10 March 2022.

[70] *David Suzuki Foundation v Canada (Fisheries and Oceans)*, 2010 FC 1233, varied on other grounds, 2012 FCA 40, para 31.

[71] ibid.

[72] ibid para 70.

[73] 2009 FC 878, para 62.

[74] ibid para 55; CBD, art 8(d).

3.1.3 Safety net and emergency orders

As part of the legislative compromise surrounding the enactment of SARA, two key provisions were incorporated to provide a 'backstop' in the event that a species was facing a dire situation that required immediate action by the federal minister. These two backstop provisions are intended to deal with slightly different scenarios, although in certain circumstances both may be deemed to apply.

The safety net provision is intended to allow the federal government to step in and assume lead responsibility for protection of a 'non-federal' species under its section 58 powers where the minister forms the opinion that the 'laws of the province or territory do not effectively protect' the critical habitat of that species. This safety net provision, the effect of which is to confer broad federal authority to regulate within a province or territory to protect a non-federal species, has yet to be invoked by the federal government.

To date, the federal government has been extremely reluctant to invoke its safety net powers, even in egregious cases, preferring to negotiate voluntary and non-binding agreements with recalcitrant provinces or territories. A case in point arose in 2019 when two environmental groups and two First Nations applied to the Federal Court to compel the Minister of the Environment to recommend a safety net order for five critically endangered populations of boreal woodland caribou.[75]

The minister did not dispute that he had formed the opinion that existing laws did not effectively protect the caribou. This dispute centred on whether, notwithstanding that opinion, the minister was required—at the time of the lawsuit or at all—to recommend a safety net order to Cabinet. The case was discontinued after the minister informed the applicants that he had made a recommendation for a safety net order, but the federal government opted not to accept it.

Instead, Cabinet chose to rely on a conservation agreement with the province to protect the caribou.[76] Under the plan, the provincial government is responsible for delivering protection plans for caribou within five years. In the interim, the caribou remains unprotected. While it is implied that a safety net

[75] Bob Weber, 'First Nations, environmental groups take legal action to protect endangered Alberta caribou', The Canadian Press (24 January 2019) <https://globalnews.ca/news/4885539/alberta-first-nations-environmentalists-caribou-lawsuit/> accessed 10 March 2022.

[76] Ecojustice, 'Protecting boreal caribou in Alberta' (24 January 2019) <https://ecojustice.ca/case/protecting-boreal-caribou-in-alberta/> accessed 10 March 2022.

order will be implemented if the province does not deliver, that is not explicitly set out in the agreement and not legally enforceable.

For species that have been imperilled by dilatory or inadequate action by the provinces or territories, species advocates have instead tended to rely on the other backstop provision: the emergency order power. This is an order power that accords a species priority protection under section 80(2) of SARA where the minister forms the opinion that it faces 'imminent threats to its survival or recovery'. As a result of ongoing litigation and provincial inaction, the first ever emergency order was made in relation to the greater sage grouse in 2013.[77] Species protection advocates have also gone to court on several occasions in an attempt to compel the minister to make such an order in circumstances in which the minister's position was that they were not of 'an opinion' that an imminent threat existed.

Perhaps the best-known example of this is the *Adam*[78] case involving boreal caribou, one of Canada's most iconic species and a species whose habitat spans all three Canadian territories and most of its provinces. In this case, various First Nation bands and environmental organizations sought a court order to require the minister to take steps to recommend an emergency order due to long delays in completing a recovery strategy arising from consultations with various affected provinces and territories. While the Federal Court ultimately did not make the order sought, it did set aside the minister's determination that the caribou populations were not facing an imminent threat on the basis that such a conclusion was unreasonable.

Just four years later, the Federal Court went even further in a case involving threats to the western chorus frog arising from a housing development that would destroy its critical habitat.[79] The decision opines at some length on the linkage between SARA and the CBD, and their shared commitment to the precautionary principle. According to the court, it was unreasonable for the minister not to form the opinion that the species was facing imminent threats, and it ordered the minister to reconsider and render a new decision within six months. The developer's legal challenge to the resulting emergency order was unsuccessful at both the Federal Court and the Federal Court of Appeal, and was denied leave to appeal to the Supreme Court of Canada.[80]

[77] Emergency Order for the Protection of the Greater Sage-Grouse, SOR/2013-202.

[78] *Adam v Canada* (n 67).

[79] *Centre Québécois du droit de l'environnement v Canada* [2015] FC 773.

[80] *Groupe Maison Candiac Inc v Canada (Attorney General)*, 2018 FC 643; *Groupe Maison Candiac Inc v Canada (Attorney General)*, 2020 FCA 88; leave to appeal refused in 2020 CarswellNat 5311.

3.1.4 Species protection and project assessment/permitting

Often species protection laws are criticized for adopting an emergency room model which focuses mainly on the needs of species in imminent peril. While understandable, this approach risks failing to anticipate potential future harms from species-associated, project-related decisions that are made by other government agencies. A reactive, emergency room approach can also fail to capitalize on the biodiversity-enhancing opportunities that front-end collaboration with other agencies and decision makers can offer. Instead, a proactive, anticipatory approach to biodiversity-related decision making aligns closely with commitments to the precautionary principle found in the CBD and SARA.

SARA has provisions intended to promote a proactive approach to decision making that promotes collaboration between governmental agencies with authority to make decisions that can affect biodiversity protection. These provisions require government decision makers empowered to approve licences or permits that may result in the destruction of critical habitat or harm to a listed species to consider 'all reasonable alternatives' to avoid the harm and minimize its impact.[81] Where a federal environmental assessment discloses that a project may have these effects, the assessment agency is required to notify the minister responsible for the project of the impact on the species or its critical habitat. If the project is carried out, decision makers with authority over the project must also ensure that appropriate mitigation measures are in place and are consistent with SARA recovery strategies and action plans.[82]

These provisions became headline news in a 2018 case involving a heavy oil pipeline expansion project from Alberta's tar sands to the coast of British Columbia. The federal agency responsible for the environmental assessment (the National Energy Board or NEB) recommended that the project be allowed to proceed even though it would have likely cause significant adverse environmental effects on Southern resident orcas. Cabinet agreed and granted approval to the project. Neither Cabinet nor the NEB took steps to ensure that measures were in place to mitigate these harms contrary to SARA. A challenge to Cabinet's approval was brought on this basis. Ultimately, the Federal Court of Appeal quashed the approval both on this ground and on the basis that project-related consultation with affected First Nations was inadequate.[83]

[81] SARA (n 45) s 77.

[82] ibid s 79.

[83] *Tsleil-Waututh Nation v Canada*, 2018 FCA 153 and see generally Doelle and Tollefson (n 49) 826–34.

3.2 Protected Areas

The past three decades have seen a proliferation of litigation to preserve the integrity of Canada's protected spaces. Environmental groups have had some success in enforcing limits to development in national parks, and indigenous peoples have acted to preserve spaces critical to the exercise of their inherent rights and rights conferred by treaty. However, despite the updating of Canada's national parks legislation, the National Parks Act,[84] to prioritize 'ecological integrity' as the first priority for management in section 8(2),[85] the courts are increasingly apt to defer to administrative decisions that encroach on the environment for non-ecological purposes. This is a disturbing reality, particularly at a time where Canada struggled to meet its 2020 Biodiversity Goals and Targets for Canada and has stated its intent to conserve 25 per cent of both Canada's land and oceans by 2025, working toward 30 per cent of each by 2030.[86] Canada aimed to, by 2020, protect at least 17 per cent of terrestrial areas and inland water and 10 per cent of marine and coastal areas, through networks of protected areas and other effective area-based measures.[87] While the percentage of oceans designated as protected appears to have reached the 2020 targets, Canada fell considerably short of its terrestrial protection goal.[88] Furthermore, tolerance for encroachment on parkland for non-conservation purposes renders uncertain whether the biodiversity of protected areas will truly be preserved.

3.2.1 Litigation to protect parks: a mixed record

A review of the major cases brought to preserve federally protected spaces demonstrates that, while Canadian courts have accepted that commercial logging has no place in national parks, they have hesitated to enforce the broader statutory mandate to preserve their ecological integrity. Uncertainty about the ecological integrity of putatively protected areas may undermine

[84] RSC 1985, c N-14 (National Parks Act).

[85] This did not stem from the Canadian Biodiversity Strategy, but rather from the findings of the Panel on the Ecological Integrity of Canada's National Parks established in 1998. See Parks Canada, 'Report of the Panel on the Ecological Integrity of Canada's National Parks' <www.pc.gc.ca/en/docs/pc/rpts/ie-ei/report-rapport_1> accessed 10 March 2022, in particular, vol II, *Appendix C: Report of the Sierra Legal Defense Fund to the Panel. Improving the National Parks Act to Support Ecological Integrity.*

[86] Office of the Prime Minister, 'Minister of Environment and Climate Change Mandate Letter', 13 December 2019 <https://pm.gc.ca/en/mandate-letters/2019/12/13/minister-environment-and-climate-change-mandate-letter> accessed 10 March 2022.

[87] 2020 Biodiversity Goals and Targets for Canada (n 9) Target 1.

[88] Canada's Conserved Areas <www.canada.ca/en/environment-climate-change/services/environmental-indicators/conserved-areas.html> accessed 10 March 2022.

Canada's accounting of its terrestrial protection, resulting in further setbacks in achieving its targets and the CBD more broadly.

In 1991, the Canadian Park and Wilderness Society (CPAWS) brought a lawsuit aimed at ending commercial logging in Canada's largest national park.[89] Spanning an area larger that Switzerland in northern Alberta and southern Northwest Territories, Wood Buffalo National Park protects the pristine northern boreal plain, some of Canada's last remaining bison herds, and the last known nesting area of the endangered whooping crane. Created in 1922, the park was declared a UNESCO world heritage site in 1987.

In the 1950s, the federal government began to license commercial logging in the park notwithstanding its importance for conservation.[90] In one of its earliest cases, the Sierra Legal Defence Fund (now Ecojustice) brought an application for judicial review of the planned logging, on the basis that it contravened the National Parks Act.[91] The Act, as it then read, prohibited public lands within the park from being 'disposed of or located or settled upon ... except under the authority of this Act or its regulations'.[92] Sierra argued that forestry constituted a prohibited 'disposition'. In an apparent effort to avoid an adverse court ruling, the minister consented to settle the case by issuing an order that the logging was 'invalid and unauthorized by the provisions of the National Parks Act or any regulations thereunder'.[93] No commercial logging has since taken place in Canada's national parks.

Not all litigation aimed at curbing harmful resource development in Canada's national parks has been as successful. In subsequent years, development pressures in parks—such as recreation facilities, businesses catering to tourism, and roads—continued to encroach on protected spaces. Responding to public pressure to dedicate Canada's national parks to the preservation of nature, and having studied the issue for several years after the entry into force of the CBD, Parliament enacted new parks legislation in 2000.[94] The new Canada National Parks Act made clear that the maintenance and restoration of ecological integrity, through the 'protection of natural resources and natural processes', is the first priority in 'all aspects of the management of parks'.[95] The Act defines 'ecological integrity' as 'a condition that is determined to be characteristic of its

[89] Kevin Timoney, 'The Logging of a World Heritage Site: Wood Buffalo National Park, Canada' (1996) 72 The Forestry Chronicle 485.

[90] ibid 485.

[91] ibid 489.

[92] National Parks Act, RSC 1985, c N-14, s 6(1).

[93] *Canadian Parks and Wilderness Society v Canada (Minister of the Environment)* [1992] FCJ No 553.

[94] Shaun Fluker, 'Ecological Integrity in Canada's National Parks: The False Promise of the Law' (2010) 29(1) Windsor Review of Legal and Social Issues 89.

[95] Canada National Parks Act, SC 2000, c 32 (CNPA), s 8(2).

natural region and likely to persist, including abiotic components and the composition and abundance of native species and biological communities, rates of change and supporting processes'.[96]

The ecological integrity mandate can be read as a kind of constitutional baseline for park management—the highest ('first') principle on which no management decision may trample. That interpretation was certainly the one envisioned by the proponents of the change. However, while the legislative language implies a laser focus on preserving the natural integrity and diversity of parks above all else, park management practices have not always worked that way. As a result, environmental groups have litigated to enforce the ecological integrity mandate. Unfortunately, those cases have met with little success, with courts deferring to the administrative jurisdiction of the relevant minister and park authorities.

The leading case on the interpretation of the ecological integrity mandate also arose in Wood Buffalo National Park. A winter road was proposed to run through the park, bisecting a bison wintering range and requiring clearing of trees and vegetation that would not regrow for decades. The minister approved the road, having reviewed an environmental assessment and concluded that its effects were likely to be 'insignificant'.[97] Ecological integrity was mentioned nowhere in the approval decision. Again, CPAWS—represented by Sierra Legal Defense Fund—brought a judicial review, arguing that the minister had no jurisdiction to approve a road for non-park purposes and had failed to discharge the ecological integrity mandate.

While the litigants were initially successful, obtaining an interim injunction to halt the road construction,[98] the trial court ultimately denied the application, a decision upheld on appeal.[99] The trial court took a narrow view of the implications of the newly adopted ecological integrity mandate. According to the court, 'ecological integrity' was to be weighed by the minister as one of many factors in a delicate 'balancing' exercise, mindful of the statutory direction that national parks are 'dedicated to the people of Canada for their benefit, education and enjoyment'.[100] In the court's view, this language should be read to recognize the 'benefit and enjoyment of those living in, and in close

[96] ibid s 2(1).
[97] *Canadian Parks and Wilderness Society v Canada (Minister of Canadian Heritage)* [2003] FCA 197, para 23.
[98] *Canadian Parks and Wilderness Society v Canada (Minister of Canadian Heritage)* [2001] FCJ No 1961.
[99] *Canadian Parks and Wilderness Society v Copps* [2001] FCT 1123; aff'd 2003 FCA 197 (Wood Buffalo Trial).
[100] CNPA (n 96) s 4(1).

proximity to, Wood Buffalo National Park' whose interests 'overrode the first priority given to ecological integrity where impairment of such integrity can be minimized to a degree that the Minister concludes is consistent with the maintenance of the Park for the enjoyment of future generations'.[101]

The Court of Appeal adopted a similar approach, affording 'considerable deference to the view of park officials that particular action was not inconsistent with the due discharge of the broad statutory duties to leave parks unimpaired and to give the first priority to ecological integrity'.[102] Accordingly, the court found that it was not 'patently unreasonable' for the minister to have concluded that the road proposal was compatible 'with maintaining as the first priority the ecological integrity of the Park through the protection of natural resources and natural processes'.[103] Of course, the minister did not actually come to that conclusion. Rather, the court was prepared to imply that conclusion owing to the 'polycentric' nature of the determination.[104]

The sympathetic nature of the putative road users—two isolated communities with few winter transportation options—clearly swayed the court in the Wood Buffalo road case. However, the result is that ecological integrity can be traded away where other considerations are perceived to be more important. Degradation through small encroachments on protected areas, like Wood Buffalo, that preserve Canada's diverse and most at-risk ecosystems does not bode well for the achievement of Canada's biodiversity goals.

In 2016, the Federal Court dismissed another application for judicial review of a development in a national park. The superintendent of Jasper National Park approved a proposal to build tent cabins at Maligne Lake.[105] Again, CPAWS argued that the superintendent had failed to give first priority to ecological integrity, since there was evidence that the development would further impair the recovery of critically endangered caribou. The application was dismissed on the grounds that the approval was not final, and thus it did not constitute a contravention of the Act or the park's management plan, which supported the maintenance of ecological integrity. Although the application was dismissed on the narrow ground of prematurity, the decision did help to solidify the legal standing of park management plans, stating that 'project proposals cannot be

[101] Wood Buffalo Trial (n 100) para 53.
[102] ibid para 45.
[103] ibid para 78. The standard of 'patent unreasonableness' has since been overturned and excised from review of federal decisions, which are now reviewed on a 'robust' standard of reasonableness, which focuses on the adequacy of reasons. This would have been an important factor, since the reasons in this case did not even mention ecological integrity.
[104] ibid para 70.
[105] *Canadian Parks and Wilderness Society v Maligne Tours Ltd* [2016] FC 148.

accepted or implemented unless they comply with a validly enacted and/or amended management plan'.[106] In that sense, the case may provide some support for enforcement of the ecological integrity mandate.

3.2.2 Protected areas and indigenous rights

While environmentalists were pressing their case against the encroachment into Wood Buffalo Park, the Mikisew Cree First Nation, on whose traditional territory the park is situated, was also in court challenging the proposed road.[107] The Mikisew have inhabited the area that is now Wood Buffalo for over 8,000 years, and many community members subsist by hunting, fishing, and trapping within the its boundaries. As much as the environmentalists were concerned that the road threatened the ecological integrity of the park, the Mikisew worried that it would threaten the integrity of their traditional way of life, which depends on undisturbed land and fauna and had been guaranteed to them by treaty in 1899.[108] Their case ultimately found it way to the Supreme Court of Canada, which quashed the road approval on the basis that the Mikisew had not been adequately consulted about its impacts.[109]

In finding for the Mikisew, the Supreme Court of Canada took a markedly different approach than did the Federal Court in the parallel 'ecological integrity' lawsuit discussed earlier, neither dismissing the impacts as *de minimis* nor suggesting that they could be traded off against other interests. The court's solicitude for the constitutionally protected rights of the Mikisew is to be lauded, and reflects a well-founded judicial concern for reconciliation, and for the need to redress the historical and ongoing breaches of the 'honour of the Crown' in the Crown's dealings with indigenous people. The different outcomes in these closely related legal challenges, on their face, suggest that while the courts will tend to defer to the executive action that is arguably inconsistent with parliamentary direction (here a statutory prioritization of conservation), they are less likely to be deferential where executive action is said to violate the constitutional rights of indigenous peoples. Subsequent Federal Court authority, however, has tended to display an increasingly deferential judicial posture even where it is alleged that a governmental decision has breached the section

[106] ibid para 100.

[107] Brian P Schwartz and Darla L Rettie, 'The Long and Winding Road: Case Comment on *Mikisew Cree First Nation v Canada (Minister of Canadian Heritage)*' (2006) 34 The Supreme Court Law Review 465.

[108] Treaty no 8 made 21 June 1899 and adhesions, reports, etc (Queen's Printer 1966) <www.rcaanc-cirnac.gc.ca/eng/1100100028813/1581293624572> accessed 10 March 2022.

[109] Mikisew Cree First Nation v Canada (Minister of Canadian Heritage) [2005] SCC 69, [2005] 3 SCR 388.

35-based right of an affected First Nation to be consulted and accommodated. For instance, in its recent decision in *Coldwater First Nation v Canada*,[110] the Federal Court of Appeal held that the adequacy of such a process should not be measured against a legal 'correctness' standard, but rather on whether in all the circumstances it could be said to be justified under a more deferential 'reasonableness' standard.[111]

Among the historical injustices to which courts and policymakers are now beginning to respond is the use of protected areas as tools of dispossession and colonialism. Many (likely most) parks and protected areas in Canada were created without the consent of the indigenous peoples on whose territory they were situated and, in egregious cases, indigenous peoples were removed from their homes to establish parks.[112] A recent response to such historical injustices is the creation of Indigenous Protected and Conserved Areas (IPCAs): lands and waters where indigenous governments have the primary role in protecting and conserving ecosystems through indigenous laws, governance, and knowledge systems.[113] In addition to promoting reconciliation, IPCAs emerged as a key component of Canada's contribution to achieving the global Aichi Biodiversity Targets. However, establishing IPCAs has not always been easy. In one notable example, an indigenous community engaged in protracted litigation in order to win protection for its land.

Jumbo Valley in British Columbia's Purcell Mountains is sacred to the Ktunaxa First Nation, who call it Qat'muk. The Ktunaxa consider Qat'muk to be home to Kławła Tukłułakʔ is, or the Grizzly Bear Spirit, one of the most important aspects of their religious practice. The Ktunaxa therefore opposed a proposed ski resort at Qat'muk, which they said would compromise their ability to receive Grizzly Bear Spirit's guidance.[114] The Ktunaxa sued, claiming that the development would breach their constitutional right to freedom of religion under the Canadian Charter of Rights and Freedoms[115] and the protection of Aboriginal interests under section 35 of the Constitution Act, 1982. The Supreme Court disagreed, concluding that the Ktunaxa's claim fell outside the scope of the protection of freedom to hold and manifest religious beliefs. According to the Court, neither the Ktunaxa's freedom to hold their beliefs

[110] 2020 FCA 34.

[111] *Dene Tha' First Nation v Canada* (2006) FC 1354; aff'd (2008) FCA 20.

[112] Parks Canada, *We Rise Together: Achieving Pathway to Canada Target 1 Through the Creation of Indigenous Protected and Conserved Areas in the Spirit and Practice of Reconciliation: The Indigenous Circle of Experts' Report and Recommendations* (Government of Canada 2018).

[113] ibid.

[114] Factum of the Appellants, Ktunaxa Nation Council et al, SCC file no 36664.

[115] Canadian Charter of Rights and Freedoms in the Constitution Act, 1982, being Sch B to the Canada Act 1982 (UK), c 11.

nor their freedom to manifest those beliefs were infringed by the decision to approve the ski resort: the state's constitutional duty is not to protect the *object* of beliefs, such as Grizzly Bear Spirit. Rather, 'the state's duty is to protect everyone's freedom to hold such beliefs and to manifest them in worship and practice or by teaching and dissemination'.[116]

Rebuffed in their attempt to protect the religious significance of Qat'muk, the Ktunaxa worked in parallel with environmental groups represented by Ecojustice to challenge a key permit for the ski resort project. In that litigation, the British Columbia Court of Appeal upheld a 2015 decision from the province's Minister of Environment, who found that the company had failed to 'substantially start' construction by a ten-year deadline, resulting in the expiry of the project's environmental assessment certificate.[117] With the ski resort project sent back to square one after almost thirty years of controversy, the Ktunaxa had an opportunity to negotiate an IPCA for Qat'muk. In January 2020, the Ktunaxa, the federal government, and the government of British Colombia agreed to turn Jumbo Valley and the surrounding mountains into the Qat'muk IPCA, foreclosing the possibility of a ski resort and other development, and leaving the Ktunaxa in charge of stewarding and managing the area.

In addition to the planned Qat'muk IPCA, approximately 160,000 km^2 of land and water have been placed under indigenous-led conservation management using the IPCA model since 2017. Four IPCAs have so far been established in the Northwest Territories and Nunavut: Thaidene Nene National Park Reserve,[118] Ts'udé Niljné Tuyeta (Ramparts),[119] Edéhzhíe Dehcho Protected Area,[120] and Tallurutiup Imanga National Marine Conservation Area.[121] As of

[116] Ktunaxa Nation v British Columbia (Forests, Lands and Natural Resource Operations) [2017] SCC 54, [2017] 2 SCR 386, para 71.

[117] Glacier Resorts Ltd v British Columbia (Minister of Environment) [2019] BCCA 289.

[118] Thaidene Nene protected areas permanently protect 26,376 km^2 of nationally significant boreal forest, tundra, and freshwater ecosystems in and around the East Arm of Great Slave Lake, sustaining the culture and livelihood of the Łutsël K'é Dene First Nation, other First Nations, and Métis. See Parks Canada, 'Thaidene Nene National Park Reserve' (July 2020) <www.pc.gc.ca/en/pn-np/nt/thaidene-nene> accessed 10 March 2022.

[119] Ts'udé Niljné Tuyeta (Ramparts), is 10,060 km^2 in size and protects the biodiversity of the Taiga Plains and Taiga Cordillera in the Northwest Territories and is a sacred place and harvesting area of the K'asho Got'jnę. See the Government of Northwest Territories, Environment and Natural Resources, 'Conservation Network Planning: Ts'udé Niljné Tuyeta' (2019) <www.enr.gov.nt.ca/en/services/conservation-network-planning/tsude-niline-tuyeta> accessed 10 March 2022.

[120] Edéhzhíe Dehcho Protected Area covers 14,218 km^2 in the Horn Plateau in Northwest Territories. It is an important hunting place, as well as a spiritual gathering place, for Dehcho and Tłįchô Dene. See Government of Canada, 'Edéhzhíe Protected Area' (April 2019) <www.canada.ca/en/environment-climate-change/services/national-wildlife-areas/locations/edehzhie.html> accessed 10 March 2022.

[121] Tallurutiup Imanga National Marine Conservation Area is located in the northeastern region of Nunavut and encompasses 108,000 km^2 of Arctic seascape that is critical habitat for the polar bear, bowhead whale, narwhal, and beluga whale. It is vital to the economic and cultural practices of the Inuit living in the region. See Government of Canada, 'Tallurutiup Imanga National Marine Conservation Area' <www.pc.gc.ca/en/amnc-nmca/cnamnc-cnnmca/tallurutiup-imanga> accessed 10 March 2022.

November 2020, dozens more IPCAs are in the proposal or planning stages in every region of the country, which will contribute to Canada's stated goal of conserving 25 per cent of its land and 25 per cent of its oceans by 2025.[122] This is a significant achievement, despite the 'wicked problems' confronting indigenous communities, governments, and other stakeholders in implementing indigenous-led protection.[123]

3.3 Sustainable Customary Use

Like all other CBD parties, under article 10(c) Canada has committed to, 'as far as possible and as appropriate, protect and encourage customary use of biological resources in accordance with traditional cultural practices that are compatible with conservation or sustainable use requirements'. Target 12 of Canada's 2020 Biodiversity Goals and Targets aims that, by 2020, 'customary use by Aboriginal peoples of biological resources is maintained, compatible with their conservation and sustainable use'.[124] The 2018 interim assessment of the goals and targets did not demonstrate that Canada is on track to meet this target by 2020.

Although not explicitly defined as such, a right similar to that expressed in article 10(c) has developed in Canada as a corollary to decades of litigation by indigenous peoples asserting their rights to continue traditional cultural practices founded on the customary use of biological resources. A considerable part of the case law is the result of 'conflict between those activities and government regulation purportedly enacted for conservation purposes'.[125]

Litigation over the use of biological resources by Canada's indigenous peoples has primarily occurred under the aegis of section 35 of the Constitution Act, 1982, that both recognizes and affirms existing Aboriginal and treaty rights, including rights that exist or may be acquired under land claims agreements.[126] Most 'existing rights' so far identified by the courts have related to the

[122] Government of Canada, 'Canada Target 1 Challenge' (12 June 2020) <www.canada.ca/en/environment-climate-change/services/nature-legacy/canada-target-one-challenge.html> accessed 10 March 2022.

[123] Melanie Zurba and others, 'Indigenous Protected and Conserved Areas (IPCAs), Aichi Target 11 and Canada's Pathway to Target 1: Focusing Conservation on Reconciliation' (2019) 8(1) Land 10.

[124] Government of Canada, 'Canada Target 12' <www.biodivcanada.ca/national-biodiversity-strategy-and-action-plan/2020-biodiversity-goals-and-targets-for-canada/canada-target-12canada-target-12> accessed 10 March 2022.

[125] Lynda M Collins and Meghan Murtha, 'Indigenous Environmental Rights in Canada: The Right to Conservation Implicit in Treaty and Aboriginal Rights to Hunt, Fish and Trap' (2010) 47 Alberta Law Review 959, 967.

[126] Constitution Act, 1982, s 35(1)–(4).

harvesting or use of a specific biological resource, and have been affirmed case by case, community by community.[127] They protect the contemporary version of the custom, practice, or tradition relating to the resource—which must have been an integral part of the indigenous group's culture prior to contact—as well as certain activities incidental to participation in it.[128] Such rights are communal in nature,[129] and typically site-specific, only protecting access to a prescribed resource in specific areas.[130]

The use of section 35 is often defensive, invoked in response to action by the Crown that threatens these constitutionally protected indigenous rights. Many such cases have arisen in the context of harvesting fish, game, and timber, with courts regularly finding an indigenous right to harvest a biological resource for food, social, or ceremonial reasons.[131] An incidental inter-generational right has also been found 'to teach such a practice, custom and tradition to a younger generation to ensure the continuity of aboriginal practices, customs and traditions'.[132] Despite their importance for indigenous communities, and traditional medicines in particular, no litigation has tested the merits of claims to harvest or gather berries, roots, and medicinal plants.[133] Indigenous communities are generally successful in these cases where 'they have been able to show that their ancestral communities were present, and hunting and/or fishing, in the geographic area to which the claim of right pertains'.[134]

To date, judicial recognition of indigenous rights to commercial use of biological resources has been limited.[135] Often, cases have foundered on the basis that whatever trade took place prior to contact with Europeans was purely incidental to the social and ceremonial activities of the indigenous group making

[127] Canadian Encyclopedic Digest, Aboriginal Law III.4(a)(ii)A, §§742–43.

[128] ibid §§743–44; *R v Sappier*, 2006 SCC 54.

[129] *Behn v Moulton Consulting* [2013] SCC 26 clarifies that: 'despite the critical importance of the collective aspect of Aboriginal and treaty rights, rights may sometimes be assigned to or exercised by individual members of Aboriginal communities, and entitlements may sometimes be created in their favour. In a broad sense, it could be said that these rights might belong to them or that they have an individual aspect regardless of their collective nature.'

[130] Canadian Encyclopedic Digest, Aboriginal Law III.4(a)(ii)A, §743; *R v Adams* [1996] 3 SCR 101; *R v Côté* [1996] 3 SCR 139; *R v Powley* [2003] SCC 43.

[131] eg *R v Adams* [1996] 3 SCR 101; *R v Côté* [1996] 3 SCR 139; *R v Powley* [2003] SCC 43; *R v Morris* [2006] SCC 59; *R v Sappier* [2006] SCC 54; *R v Beer* [2012] MBPC 45; *R v Francis* [2009] NBCA 75; *Tolko Industries Ltd v Okanagan Indian Band* [2010] BCSC 24.

[132] *R v Côté* [1996] 3 SCR 139, para 56.

[133] Canadian Encyclopedic Digest, Aboriginal Law III.4(a)(ii)C, §755.

[134] ibid B.1, §746.

[135] Only two cases have established a right to commercial fisheries: *R v Gladstone* [1996] 2 SCR 723, finding that the Heiltsuk people have an Aboriginal right to trade herring spawn on kelp, and *Ahousaht Indian Band v Canada (Attorney General)* [2013] BCCA 300, leave to appeal refused, 2014 CarswellBC 231 (SCC), which addressed the fishing rights of five indigenous (Nuu-chah-nulth) bands on the west coast of Vancouver Island, British Columbia.

the claim.[136] It is more common to find, as was notably done in the *Marshall* case, for the right to use a biological resource to be limited to securing a moderate livelihood and not 'the open-ended accumulation of wealth'.[137] The meaning of a right to a 'moderate livelihood' remains very contested on the ground.[138]

In order to succeed in upholding a restrictive measure in a section 35 case, the government must justify its limitation on an indigenous right due to the need to conserve a resource or for a pressing and substantial public purpose. The merits 'may vary from resource to resource, species to species, community to community and time to time'.[139] There must also be appropriate consultation with the indigenous community, and the restrictions must go no further than required to meet their purpose.[140] The government may be required to make accommodations, as indigenous concerns and proposals must be taken into account, and this can lead to different conservation and management techniques in respect of the exercise of the section 35 right.[141]

4. Conclusion

The last three to four decades have been transformative for the Canadian legal landscape governing biodiversity protection. Certainly, the most powerful driver for change has been the assertion of Aboriginal rights that, since 1982, have been expressly affirmed and recognized under the Canadian Constitution. Not only has this created new space for robust national conversations about post-colonial political arrangements, it has also empowered traditionally deferential Canadian courts to take a more hands-on role in constitutional and public interest litigation.[142] Canada's ratification of the CBD and a growing

136 *R v NTC Smokehouse Ltd* [1996] 2 SCR 672; *R v Van der Peet* [1996] 2 SCR 507; *R v Bernard* [2005] 2 SCR 220; *Lax Kw'alaams Indian Band v Canada (Attorney General)* [2011] 3 SCR 535.

137 *R v Marshall* [1999] 3 SCR 456, para 7.

138 See eg Alex Cooke, 'Mi'kmaw fishermen launch self-regulated fishery in Saulnierville', CBC News (17 September 2020) <www.cbc.ca/news/canada/nova-scotia/mikmaw-fishermen-self-regulated-fishery-lower-saulnierville-1.5727920> accessed 10 March 2022; Emma Davie, 'Fishermen haul up, dump Mi'kmaw lobster traps to protest moderate livelihood fishery', CBC News (21 September 2020) <www.cbc.ca/news/canada/nova-scotia/mikmaw-commercial-fishermen-alleged-lobster-buyer-1.5732357> accessed 10 March 2022.

139 *R v Marshall* [1999] 3 SCR 533, paras 19 and 22 (*Marshall II*).

140 ibid para 44.

141 ibid.

142 Numerous organizations now exist in Canada that dedicate a significant part of their practice to public interest environmental litigation, including the Canadian Environmental Law Association (CELA), Centre québécois du droit de l'environnement (CQDE), Ecojustice, and the Pacific Centre for Environmental Law and Litigation (CELL).

awareness of its globally important role in protecting biodiversity has also been critical to this evolving picture, and is a reality about which Canadian courts and tribunals are becoming increasingly well informed.

While these same courts and tribunals continue to display deep deference for the actions of other branches of government, increasingly this reflexive deference is being challenged, particularly where it conflicts with Canada's international commitments or with prevailing science. One consequence of this is that the range of what is deemed relevant in biodiversity and other public interest litigation has expanded despite traditionalist objections to reliance on international law arguments, and concerns about transforming courtrooms into 'academies of science'.

The battle over enacting SARA, and more recently its interpretation, is emblematic of the tension between the more traditional versus emerging visions of Canada. Canadian constitutional arrangements and practices have tended to exacerbate rather than quell these tensions. How and whether Canada will be able to reconcile its long-standing commitment to resource development and the fossil fuel economy, with its constitutional obligations to its indigenous peoples and its international commitments to biodiversity—increasingly being undermined by its failure to take meaningful action on climate change—remains to be seen.

5

Biodiversity Litigation in China

Confronting Degradation from All Sides in the Era of Ecological Civilization

Mingzhe Zhu[*]

1. Introduction

In the context of promoting 'ecological civilization',[1] biodiversity law is increasingly attracting attention in China. China—one of the world's twelve mega-biodiverse countries[2]—signed the Convention on Biological Diversity (CBD)[3] in 1992 and ratified it in 1993, making it one of the first state parties to do so. By that time, the National People's Congress (NPC) had already ratified the Convention for the Conservation of Antarctic Marine Living Resources[4] (in 1980); later on, it ratified the Cartagena Protocol on Biosafety[5] (2005) and the Nagoya Protocol[6] (2016). China has also been a member of the Convention on International Trade in Endangered Species of Wild Fauna and Flora (CITES)[7] since 1981, the Convention on Wetlands of International Importance (Ramsar Convention)[8] since 1992, the United Nations Framework Convention on

* This research is funded by the Research Foundation—Flanders (File number: 76473). The author is grateful to the research assistance provided by Ms Lisha Yu and Ms Yikai Li.

1 The Seventeenth National Congress of the Chinese Communist Party (CCP) in 2007 identified the promotion of 'ecological civilization' as an explicit goal. The constitutional amendment in 2018 further adopted this term in the Constitution.

2 See <www.cbd.int/countries/profile/?country=cn#facts> accessed 12 March 2022.

3 Convention on Biological Diversity (opened for signature 5 June 1992, entered into force 29 December 1993) 1760 UNTS 79.

4 Convention on the Conservation of Antarctic Marine Living Resources (open to signature 20 May 1980, entered into force 7 April 1982), 1329 UNTS 47.

5 Cartagena Protocol on Biosafety to the Convention on Biological Diversity (open to signature 29 January 2000, entered into force 11 September 2003) 2226 UNTS 208.

6 Nagoya Protocol on Access to Genetic Resources and the Fair and Equitable Sharing of Benefits Arising from their Utilization to the Convention on Biological Diversity (open to signature 29 October 2010, entered into force 12 October 2014) UNTS A-30619.

7 Convention on International Trade in Endangered Species of Wild Fauna and Flora (opened for signature 3 March 1973, entered into force 1 July 1975) 993 UNTS 243.

8 Convention on Wetlands of International Importance Especially as Waterfowl Habitat (opened for signature 2 February 1971, entered into force 21 December 1975) 996 UNTS 245.

Mingzhe Zhu, *Biodiversity Litigation in China* In: *Biodiversity Litigation*. Edited by: Guillaume Futhazar, Sandrine Maljean-Dubois, and Jona Razzaque, Oxford University Press. © Mingzhe Zhu, 2023.
DOI: 10.1093/oso/9780192865465.003.0005

Climate Change (UNFCCC)[9] since 1994, and the United Nations Convention to Combat Desertification (UNCCD)[10] since 1997. China has also forged bilateral agreements, as in the case of its 2012 treaty with Russia regulating fishing.[11] As this chapter will highlight, the CBD and CITES stand out among these instruments as having the most practical value in biodiversity litigation in China.

The chapter's main body is divided into four sections, Section 2 briefly introduces China as a megadiverse country and examines the domestic transformation of the international instruments concerning biodiversity. Section 3 details the application of scientific expertise and indirect use of international biodiversity law (IBL) in Chinese judicial practice, as well as the main channels through which the dynamics of biodiversity litigation mostly unfold. Section 4 confirms the potential value of IBL and clarifies the challenges that China's environmental justice system must handle, and, finally, Section 5 explores two fronts of biodiversity litigation in China that have been discussed only rarely: the reliance on scientific evidence and the role of prosecutorial preliminary procedures.

2. Particularities of the Chinese Context

2.1 A Mega-Biodiverse Country in Difficulties

China contains a variety of ecosystem types, among which grasslands, forests, deserts, and agricultural ecosystems are most common, covering 87.7 per cent of all ecosystem areas.[12] In terms of individual species, China is home to the third highest number in the world for vascular plants and 13.7 per cent of the world's total for vertebrates.[13] The geographic distribution of China's ecosystems and species are shaped by its landscapes: mammals and vascular plants densely populate South China and the mountain regions, for example, but are less common in North China and in the plains.[14] River and lake basins in the

[9] United Nations Framework Convention on Climate Change (opened for signature 9 May 1992, entered into force 21 March 1994) 1771 UNTS 107.

[10] United Nations Convention to Combat Desertification in those Countries Experiencing Serious Drought and/or Desertification, Particularly in Africa (opened for signature 14 October 1994, entered into force 26 December 1996) 1954 UNTS 3.

[11] Cooperation Agreement between the People's Republic of China and the Russian Federation to Prevent, Deter and Eliminate Illegal, Unreported and Unregulated Fishing (2012).

[12] The Ministry of Environmental Protection of China, *China's Fifth National Report on the Implementation of the Convention on Biological Diversity* (China Environmental Press 2014) 16.

[13] ibid 16.

[14] ibid 16.

south are also home to amphibians, reptiles, and inland fishes.[15] Most of the birds in China are migratory, travelling along the coastal areas and appearing in the mountainous areas of Southwest China.[16] More than 28,000 marine species are present, accounting for roughly 11 per cent of the world's total.[17] As a country with a long agricultural tradition, China also grows and raises the world's largest variety of cultivated crops, fruit trees, and domesticated animals.[18]

The conservation of this biodiversity is facing critical challenges. Within China, 34.7 per cent of invertebrate species, 35.9 per cent of vertebrates, and 10.9 per cent of higher plant species are endangered.[19] The national authority identifies degradation (loss of habitat), overexploitation of natural resources, pollution, large-scale monoculture (single-species agriculture), invasive species, and climate change as the major causes of biodiversity loss.[20] From a broader, historical perspective, biodiversity loss in China has also been a result of the vast landscape transformation that has taken place since 1949. Even as the centralized administrative system adopted measures to encourage reforestation and prevent land erosion, it also felled massive forests to fuel steel furnaces, filled lakes to create rice paddies, and supported agriculture in previously pastoral regions.[21] And, in 1978, when market mechanisms were newly introduced in China, they raised not only economic growth[22] but also resource extraction and ecological loss to new heights.[23]

In 2007, as awareness of the importance of ecological challenges grew, the term 'ecological civilization' (EC) entered the Chinese legal and political domain when the promotion of EC was identified as an explicit goal by the Seventeenth National Congress of the Chinese Communist Party (CCP).[24] The elevation of EC as a national priority embodied China's political determination

[15] ibid 19.
[16] ibid 18–19.
[17] ibid 19.
[18] ibid 19.
[19] ibid 19.
[20] ibid 20–21.
[21] Judith Shapiro, *Mao's War Against Nature: Politics and the Environment in Revolutionary China* (CUP 2001).
[22] Justin Yifu Lin, *Demystifying the Chinese Economy* (CUP 2011).
[23] Elizabeth C Economy, *The River Runs Black: The Environmental Challenge to China's Future* (Cornell UP 2019).
[24] Coraline Goron, 'Ecological Civilisation and the Political Limits of a Chinese Concept of Sustainability' (2018) 4 China Perspectives 39. It is worthy of note that the initial official translation of '生态文明' in English was 'conservation culture'. See Report to the Seventeenth National Congress of the Communist Party of China on 15 October 2007, available at <www.chinadaily.com.cn/china/2007-10/24/content_6204564_5.htm> accessed 12 March 2022.

to shift its focus from economic exploitation to sustainability,[25] and indeed, in 2018, the NPC integrated the term to the preamble to the Chinese Constitution.

2.2 Ambiguous Judicial Value of International Treaties

As China's Constitution lacks a specific clause on the value and applicability of international law, it is difficult to categorically label China as a monist or dualist state.[26] Article 67 of the Constitution recognizes the powers of the Standing Committee of the NPC to enact and amend laws that do not concern fundamental civil or penal institutions or the organization of state institutions. Article 67 also recognizes the power of the NPC to ratify and abrogate treaties, though it does not stipulate where treaties fall in the hierarchy of norms. In practice, the applicability of international instruments is decided either by laws enacted by the NPC or by the judicial policy of the Supreme People's Court (SPC). At one time, the automatic incorporation and supremacy of international treaties were the rule, being confirmed by many individual statutes. For instance, in private international law, international treaties prevailed over national legislation in foreign-related civil relations, as provided for in Article 142 of the General Principles of Civil Law (1986), among other provisions. Such was also the case for the Environmental Protection Law (EPL) before its 2015 amendment.[27]

Today, the rule of necessary transformation seems to be replacing that of automatic incorporation. The 2015 amendment of the EPL repealed the clause that granted supremacy to international law. The new Civil Code, voted on in May 2020, does the same in the domain of civil law.[28] Still, the SPC can, via its judicial policy, individually determine how certain international treaties are applied.[29] For instance, the SPC rejects the direct application of World Trade

[25] Mingzhe Zhu, 'Sturm und Drang of Ecological Civilization' (2021) 11 IUCN AEL Journal of Environmental Law 67.

[26] On the applicability of international law in Chinese justice in general, see Keyuan Zou, 'International Law in the Chinese Domestic Context' (2010) 44 Valparaiso University Law Review 935; Congyan Cai, 'International Law in Chinese Courts During the Rise of China' (2016) 110 The American Journal of International Law 269.

[27] Article 46, Environmental Protection Law (1989/2015). In the Chinese context, a law can be substantially different from its original text after several revisions, while keeping the initial title. When citing such laws, this chapter indicates both the dates of promulgation and the last revision.

[28] Cai (n 26) 274.

[29] The Organic Law of the People's Courts (1979/2018) provides that the SPC can decide judicial policy on the interpretation and application of specific statutory provisions (Art 18), but it is the SPC itself that promulgated the Provisions of the SPC on Judicial Explanation (最高人民法院关于司法解释工作的规定) in 2007. In practice, the SPC publishes several 'explanations' that are de facto binding in judicial practice. Although many of them merely provide more detailed instructions to the judges, it

Organization (WTO) law but instructs the judiciary to interpret domestic law so that it is consistent with WTO law.[30] Meanwhile, it stipulates that judges can refer directly to the appendices to CITES in criminal cases that concern endangered species.[31] In 2018, in a case concerning the damage arising from hydrocarbon pollution caused by the collision of two foreign ships, the SPC ruled that if a legislative text is adopted to incorporate the rules of an international treaty, then the court must interpret that domestic law in conformity with the treaty it incorporates.[32] The question of whether this method of conformity can be generalized to other situations remains unanswered. With all this in mind, it becomes clear that scholarship on biodiversity litigation in China inevitably involves studying the legislative texts inspired by the CBD and their interpretations in judicial practice. At the same time, it is equally important to note that a directly applicable text is more likely to be referred to before the court than a text that serves only for interpretative purposes, the reason being that the application of the latter depends largely on the judge's knowledge of legislative history and international law.

2.3 Selective Transformation of IBL in Legislation

China has incorporated IBL through both national policy and national law. Before examining this incorporation in detail, we will first take a brief look at the overall landscape of biodiversity regulation in China. Until quite recently, China had no comprehensive law on biodiversity. In October 2020, during the pandemic, the Biosecurity Law was enacted,[33] and the National Park Law was in the drafting process.[34] Numerous laws contain provisions concerning

is not uncommon for a judicial policy in the name of explanation or interpretation to substantially alter the requirements of the statutory rules. See Vai Io Lo, 'Towards the Rule of Law: Judicial Lawmaking in China' (2016) 28 Bond Law Review 149. The judicial explanations cited in this chapter are judicial policy of this type.

[30] 《最高人民法院关于审理国际贸易行政案件若干问题的规定》法释[2002]27号 [Regulation on Administrative Procedure Concerning International Trades (2002)].

[31] International expertise will be discussed later in this chapter.

[32] 运输部上海打捞局、普罗旺斯船东2008-1有限公，中华人民共和国最高人民法院（2018）最高法民再368号 [*Shanghai Bureau of Salvage v Provence Shipowner 2008-1 Ltd*, Supreme Court (2018)]. The cases cited in this chapter can be found on the official website of the judicial system at China Judgements Online: <https://wenshu.court.gov.cn/> accessed 12 March 2022.

[33] Law on Biodiversity (2020) <www.npc.gov.cn/npc/c30834/202010/bb3bee5122854893a69acf4005a66059.shtml> accessed 12 March 2022.

[34] <www.npc.gov.cn/npc/c30834/202001/a6a83ce994e244d39b369ce2d9ad338c.shtml> accessed 12 March 2022.

biodiversity.[35] The most commonly applied of these is the Penal Code's section on environmental crimes, particularly Articles 340 (on maritime protection), 341 (on illicit hunting, transport, purchase, and sale of endangered wild animals), 344 and 345 (on illicit logging and damage of plants). Article 30 of the EPL, as amended in 2015, clarifies the state's duty to conserve biodiversity; the Wild Animal Protection Law (1988/2018), meanwhile, requires that ecosystems' interests be balanced and contains provisions on managing alien species and biological–genetic resources. Other laws related to environmental protection and agriculture, such as the Seed Law (2000/2013) and Forest Law (1984/2019), have also been revised in response to treaty obligations.[36] Further regulations are set to appear in the coming years—the framework of reserves constructed around national parks by the administration, for example, will be put into perspective when the corresponding legislation is promulgated. Many of China's domestic laws concerning biodiversity were enacted or amended after the ratification of one or both of the CBD and CITES. Before a Bill is first read, the entity in charge of drafting sends a representative to speak to the NPC.[37] Typically, when the entity in question is a ministry or other governmental body, this representative, or rapporteur, is a leading official who explains what inspired and motivated the draft. Frequently, when explaining such motives, rapporteurs highlight the need 'to fulfil China's international obligation' or 'to adapt to international law'. In reply to the NPC's request for the drafting of the Law on Biosecurity, for instance, the Ministry of Ecology and Environment clearly stated that the law would incorporate both the CBD and the Cartagena Protocol.[38] Later, when explaining the draft of the law, the rapporteur also emphasized the legislation's importance in honouring the international commitment that China made when it ratified the CBD and other international instruments.[39] Such comments suggest that IBL is, at the very least, an inspiration in Chinese domestic environmental law. Although it may not always be clear how particular treaties and pieces of legislation correspond, we can

[35] For an overall review of China's biodiversity legislation, see Jason Czarnezki and Yu Wenxuan, 'Challenges to China's Natural Resources Conservation and Biodiversity Legislation' (2013) 43 Pace Law Faculty Publications 125.

[36] See China's Sixth National Report for the Convention on Biological Diversity: 5 <https://chm.cbd.int/database/record?documentID=241353> accessed 12 March 2022.

[37] Article 29(2) of the Law on Legislation (2000/2015).

[38] 生态环境部：《对十三届全国人大一次会议第008、150号议案的答复意见》（环建函〔2018〕16号）[Ministry of Ecology and Environment, Response to the Motions Nos 008 and 150 of the Thirteenth NPC's 1st Meeting (Huanjianhan 2018 (16))]，<www.mee.gov.cn/gkml/sthjbgw/jytafw_new/201809/t20180926_629621.htm> accessed 12 March 2022.

[39] 高虎城：《关于<中华人民共和国生物安全法（草案）>的说明》[Hucheng Gao, Report on the Draft of the Biosecurity Law]，<www.npc.gov.cn/npc/c30834/202010/a2d515b5158c4216b9e1d83038b5c820.shtml> accessed 12 March 2022.

nevertheless identify certain cases in which international law has directly inspired the domestic law—both by examining the comments of rapporteurs and by recognizing straightforward textual similarities between the two.

With respect to inspiring domestic law, CITES is the international instrument most frequently cited before the NPC on biodiversity conservation. As early as 1988, the Wild Animal Protection Law stipulated (through Art 24) that the executive branch's approval is necessary for the import or export of any wild animal subject to an international treaty restriction. The rapporteur for this Bill specifically explained to the NPC that the provision was intended to fulfil China's international obligation under CITES.[40] The clause remained untouched by two revisions to the law, one in 2004 and the other in 2009, and its eventual revision in 2016 continued to defer to international regulation: the 2016 amendment directed the authority in charge of wildlife imports and exports to publish a directory of animals whose trade is restricted by international law.[41] Another example of the legislative adaptation of CITES is the 1998 amendment to the Forest Law, Article 38 of which stipulates that the Administration of Forestry must be consulted before each trade of 'precious trees and their products and derivatives, the export of which is forbidden or restricted, and the annual export quantitative restrictions'. The Minister of Forestry at the time described this clause as a response to the requirement of CITES.[42]

In addition to taking the general measures for conservation and sustainable use prescribed by article 6 of the CBD, China's environmental legislation particularly highlights five of the CBD's requirements.

First, and arguably the most evident example, is the domestic adoption of the duty to identify and monitor (art 7 of the CBD). This duty is reflected in the Forest Law (Art 27), the Wild Animal Protection Law (Arts 11, 12, 14, and 16), and the Grassland Law (Arts 6, 25, 30, 54), all of which instruct various levels of government to monitor biological resources and formulate a directory of protected species and their habitats.[43]

[40] 《关于<中华人民共和国野生动物法（草案）>的说明》（1988年8月29日在第七届全国人民代表大会常务委员会第三次会议上）[Report on the Draft of the Wild Animal Protection Law before the Standing Committee of the NPC (1988)] <www.npc.gov.cn/wxzl/gongbao/2000-12/26/content_5002181.htm> accessed 12 March 2022.

[41] Article 35 of the Wild Animal Protection Law. Although the law does not specifically designate which organ is in charge, the directory in question is published and updated by the National Forestry and Grassland Administration.

[42] 《关于〈中华人民共和国森林法修正案（草案）>的说明》（1997年10月29日在第八届全国人民代表大会常务委员会第二十八次会议上）[Report on the Draft of the Amendment of the Forest Law before the Standing Committee of the NPC (1997)] <www.npc.gov.cn/wxzl/gongbao/2000-12/17/content_5003927.htm> accessed 12 March 2022.

[43] As is suggested by the titles of the laws, it is the national and local organs of forestry and grassland administration that identify and monitor.

Second is the requirement of in situ (on-site) conservation (art 8 of the CBD) by several provisions in the domestic law governing zoning and maintenance in protected areas. The domestic versions of this requirement are exemplified by the EPL (Art 29), the Forest Law (Arts 31 and 35), the Wild Animal Protection Law (Art 12), the Seed Law (Art 10), and the Law on Animal Husbandry (Art 13).

Third is the establishment of incentive and support mechanisms (arts 7 and 20 of the CBD). Most of the laws mentioned in the previous paragraph contain general provisions on the state's duty to incentivize, through proper policy, biodiversity conservation by individuals and social organizations.[44] They also stipulate that the state shall facilitate conservation research and provide subsidies, remedies, or long-term loans to conservation activities.

Fourthly, to promote public education and awareness (art 13 of the CBD), the EPL, Forest Law, and Wild Animal Protection Law designate public education and awareness as a general principle of Chinese biodiversity law. The clauses in question show high textual similarity with the CBD's article 13(a).

Fifth and finally, the assessment of impacts and minimization of adverse impacts provided for by article 14 of the CBD are embodied in various domestic provisions. The general environmental impact process is instituted by Article 19 of the EPL, and even more specifically, Article 13 of the Wild Animal Protection Law requires 'analysis, prediction, and assessment of the proposed projects that are likely to have impacts on wild animals and their habitats to avoid or minimize such effects'. This clause is almost a word-for-word translation of article 14(a) of the CBD, though references to public participation are missing.[45] Article 34 of the Forest Law (as amended in 2019) further incorporates article 14(e) of the CBD, requiring the government to enact emergency response plans.

Other examples of positive responses to the CBD include the state's duty to restore habitat and prevent the growth of invasive alien species, as prescribed by Article 12 of the Wild Animal Protection Law and Articles 60 and 81 of the Law on Biosecurity. Indeed, in comparison with other domains of law, international norms play a substantial role in inspiring the law of the land when it comes to biodiversity. However, the provisions inspired by the CBD's general

[44] Articles 12, 44, and 45 of the Forest Law; Arts 4, 5, and 8 of the Wild Animal Protection Law; Arts 7 and 9 of the Law on Environmental Protection.

[45] Article 53 of the Law on Environmental Protection provides that citizens shall have access to environmental information, and participate and oversee environmental protection. On public participation in Chinese environmental law, see Xiao Zhu and Kaijie Wu, 'Public Participation in China's Environmental Lawmaking: In Pursuit of Better Environmental Democracy' (2017) 29 Journal of Environmental Law 389.

requirements do not usually prescribe any substantial legal consequence for non-compliance and, therefore, they are rarely applied by the judiciary.

China's incorporation of CBD-prescribed obligations at the national level is a selective process not a comprehensive one, which is clear in China's partial acceptance of the CBD's objectives. The EPL highlights the conservation of biological diversity and biosecurity in its Article 30, and fragments of germplasm resource conservation can be found in the Seed Law (Arts 8 and 9), Forest Law (Art 31), Law on Agriculture (Arts 18 and 64), Law on Animal Husbandry (Arts 9–14 and 18), Wild Animal Protection Law (Arts 17 and 25), and the Regulation on Wild Plant Protection (Arts 14 and 15). However, it is difficult, if not impossible, to identify any clause that transforms 'the fair and equitable sharing of the benefits arising out of the utilization of genetic resources' (art 1 of the CBD). On the contrary, the legislature is concerned with the foreign threat to China's germplasm resources. When the Seed Law was amended in 2015, the rapporteur explained that 'some foreign individuals, corporations, or other organizations can easily have access to the germplasm resources of our country under the disguise of scientific research'.[46] As a result, Article 56 of the Law on Biosecurity reaffirms state sovereignty over germplasm and requires the State Council's approval for any international research project on utilizing germplasm resources. President Xi Jinping echoed this concern in 2020 when he underlined the centrality of biosecurity as part of overall national security.[47]

China's emphasis on sovereign rights and national security is deeply rooted in its national history as a colonized nation and its self-perception as a third-world country faced with consistent exploitation by the global north.[48] This mentality has led to a constitution that insists on a typically 'modernist' ontology of nature in two senses.[49] First, it maintains the absolute distinction of human beings from non-human ones by virtue of their inherent qualities, and it insists that the former shall own the latter. Article 9(1) reverently prescribes that 'all mineral resources, waters, forests, mountains, grasslands, unreclaimed land, beaches, and other natural resources' are owned by the state (except those legally owned by local collective economic organizations). In other words,

[46] 《关于<中华人民共和国种子法（修订草案）>的说明》（2015年4月20日在第十二届全国人民代表大会常务委员会第十四次会议上）[Report on the Draft of the Amendment of the Seed Law before the Standing Committee of the NPC (2015)] <www.npc.gov.cn/wxzl/gongbao/2016-01/05/content_1958845.htm> accessed 12 March 2022.

[47] 《习近平谈总体国家安全：把生物安全纳入国家安全体系》[Jinping Xi on Biosecurity as a Component of General National Security] <http://cpc.people.com.cn/n1/2020/0414/c164113-31673157.html> accessed 12 March 2022.

[48] Maria Adele Carrai, *Sovereignty in China: A Genealogy of a Concept since 1840* (CUP 2019) 82; Chih-yu Shih, *Navigating Sovereignty: World Politics Lost in China* (Palgrave Macmillan 2004).

[49] Philippe Descola, *Par-Delà Nature et Culture* (Gallimard 2005).

Chinese law establishes state ownership of natural resources, of which the elements of biodiversity are considered part. Secondly, the Constitution also draws a clear distinction between public authority and civil society. Article 89(6) entrusts the State Council, the central government, with the authority to implement 'ecological civilization'. Within this constitutional framework, which seeks to avoid 'the tragedy of the commons'[50] by clarifying the state's sovereign ownership of nature, China's state-centric approach to biodiversity is only logical.

This constitutional ontology further explains the absence of a 'rights turn' in China's biodiversity and environmental litigation at large. Despite years of petitioning by environmental lawyers, including certain preeminent ones,[51] recent constitutional and legislative amendments have not included the term 'environmental right(s)'. Environmental protection and improvement instead remain state duties championed by constitutional lawyers.[52]

Since neither the Constitution nor statutory law recognizes a state obligation to respect or judicially protect an individual or collective right to environmental protection, ordinary citizens' initiatives are marginalized in the realm of environmental litigation. According to Article 12 of the Administrative Procedure Law (APL), concerned citizens cannot sue the government for failing to perform its legal duty unless such a failure violates a specific right.[53] However, an alternative instrument for holding the government accountable is made available by procedural law. As this chapter will discuss later, Article 25(3) of the APL provides that prosecutors can urge the executive branch to fulfil its environmental duties by way of public interest litigation (PIL). This mechanism, known as prosecutorial PIL, is one of the means by which Chinese magistrates can respond to the urgent need for biodiversity preservation, and through it they have developed an alternative to rights discourse. To that end, Chinese judges tend to conceive of the environment as a public good and of ecological degradation as a threat to the public interest.

[50] Garrett Hardin, 'The Tragedy of the Commons' (1968) 162 Science 1243–48.

[51] eg吕忠梅：《环境权入宪的理路与设想》，《法学杂志》2018年第1期，第23–40页[Zhongmei Lyu, 'Pathway and Reasons for the Addition of Environmental Right into the Constitution' (2018) 1 Law Science Magazine 23–40]. The author is the president of the China Society of Environmental Law.

[52] Articles 9(2) and of the Constitution. See 张翔：《环境宪法的新发展及其规范阐释》，《法学家》2018年第3期，第90–97页 [Xiang Zhang 'New Development of Environmental Constitution and Its Normative Value' (2018) 33(3) Jurist 90–97].

[53] Christopher Stone has discussed the magnitude of right discourse. Although not of precisely the same subject matter, I find that the same discussion can apply to human being's right to a safe and healthy environment. See Christopher D Stone, 'Should Trees Have Standing?—Toward Legal Rights for Natural Objects' (1972) 45 Southern California Law Review 450.

3. The Marginal Role of IBL and Pathways of Biodiversity Litigation

3.1 Science Sans Frontière

Compared with the legislature's emphasis on national sovereignty and vigilance in transplanting international law, the universalism and attachment to scientific objectivity of the SPC's epistemology are remarkable. Indeed, the SPC's judicial policy requires judges to refer to lists formulated by international institutions when determining whether a species is 'precious' or 'endangered'. The most typical example of this is a judicial explanation issued in 2000, Article 1 of which stipulates that the phrase 'precious and endangered wild animal', where it appears in the Penal Code, shall be interpreted to include all animal species in Appendices I and II to CITES.[54] The same article defined the coverage of 'wild animal' as sufficiently broad to include specimens born to domesticated parents. In a controversial 2016 criminal case, the court found a man guilty for breeding and selling some dozens of parakeets that had been born and raised in the man's apartment.[55] A less well-known example can be found in a judicial explanation on smuggling jointly issued by the SPC and the Supreme People's Procuratorate (SPP).[56] Article 10 of the explanation repeats the wording of the 2000 judicial explanation and directs judges to consider both wild and domesticated animals appearing in CITES Appendices I and II as 'precious animals' under Article 151(2) of the Penal Code. Similarly, Article 12 of the 2016 explanation considered the plants protected by CITES to be 'precious plants' under the Penal Code, Article 151(2).

It remains a matter of debate whether the full weight and severity of criminal law will be the instrument deployed in the name of biodiversity conservation to punish trading in domesticated animals. We can imagine that a textualist interpreter of the statutory law would disapprove of the SPC's policy, which alters the plain and ordinary meaning of the word 'wild'. The matter of statutory interpretation is discussed in Section 4, but more critical here is to appreciate

[54] 《最高人民法院关于审理破坏野生动物资源刑事案件具体应用法律若干问题的解释》（法释[2000]37号）[Judicial Explanation of the Supreme Court on Application of Law in Criminal Litigation Concerning Wild Animal Resource (2000)].

[55] 王某、谢某福非法收购、运输、出售珍贵、濒危野生动物、珍贵、濒危野生动物制品罪，深圳市中级人民法院（2017）粤03刑终1098号二审刑事判决书 [*Prosecutor v Wang and Xie*, Intermediate Court of Shenzhen Municipality (2017)], abbreviated as 'Parakeets case'.

[56] 《最高人民法院、最高人民检察院关于办理走私刑事案件适用法律若干问题的解释》（法释[2014]10号）[Judicial Explanation of the Supreme Court on Application of Law in Criminal Litigation Concerning Smuggling (2014)].

the SPC's role in policymaking, without which we cannot understand how the regulatory landscape is constructed in environmental matters.

As established by Article 10 of the Law on the Organization of the People's Courts, the SPC supervises the judicial system. Similarly, Article 10 of the Law on the Organization of the People's Procuratorates dictates that the SPP 'leads' the prosecutorial system.[57] These laws also grant their corresponding entities the competence to exercise disciplinary power via guiding cases and judicial explanations. Some explanations go so far as to modify the substance of the legislative text that they are meant to clarify, and whether these explanations have the binding force of law has been the subject of continuous scholarly discussion.[58] In 2007, the SPC enacted a self-empowering provision Article 10 of which provides that the judiciary shall regard judicial explanations as law.[59] Since 2015, the SPC and SPP have issued several explanations and responses, circulars, notices, and recommendations concerning environmental litigation. For instance, the Recommendations on Judicial Protection of Environment establish specific jurisdiction in biodiversity cases, which supports the creation of new, special divisions for biodiversity conservation.

The creative force of judicial explanation has made CITES one of the most cited international treaties before Chinese courts. Chinese judges use its appendices to determine whether the hunting, owning, selling, purchasing, or smuggling of certain animals is punishable by criminal law, and neither the SPC nor local judges seem to be particularly suspicious of the reliability of the international scientific bodies or the correctness of their determinations. Evidence even more revealing of judges' attitudes is their judicial use of the Red List of the International Union for Conservation of Nature (IUCN). Unlike the appendices to CITES, application of which is at least stipulated by judicial policy, the IUCN Red List is not referred to in any regulation. Nevertheless, criminal tribunals consistently cite the list of endangered or precious species cases. The Red List is typically cited alongside the CITES appendices but, even so, they are two different lists with different contents, and we can even identify

[57] In China's constitutional framework, the prosecutors are neither component of the judicial power nor that of the executive power.

[58] See 王成：《最高法院司法解释效力研究》，《中外法学》2016年第1期，第263–79页 [Cheng Wang, 'Binding Force of the Judicial Explanation of the SPC' (2016) 1 Peking University Law Journal 263–79].

[59] Provisions of the Supreme People's Court on the Judicial Explanation (2007). Despite the more common use of 'judicial interpretation', I insist on the term 'explanation', saving 'interpretation' for the application of law in concrete case. Even if the Constitution and Law on Legislation do not grant the Supreme Court with legislative power and the explanations have merely the status of internal disciplinary instruments within the judicial systems, they are de facto the norms that the court will observe in a trial. We will cite them as binding law in the following sections.

at least a dozen criminal cases since 2015 in which the amici curiae simply inform the judges that the animals in question appear on the Red List. In most of these cases, the judges found the suspects guilty because the animals they had hunted or traded were also on the national conservation-priority list. In one extreme case, the court even ruled that the Alexandrine parakeet was 'precious and protected', despite it only being listed as 'near threatened' by the IUCN.[60] It is true that a considerable number of the birds in question (471 to be precise) were transported, but regardless, the species is not technically protected under Chinese criminal law. This rare and exceptional case unexpectedly demonstrated just how willing the Chinese judicial system is to accept the judgements of established scientific authorities.[61]

3.2 Indirect Application of IBL

Besides exercising their semi-legislative power, the SPC and SPP also guide judicial activities by deciding which precedents are 'models' that should be followed in future cases. The SPC has published about 140 guiding cases since 2012, each with an accompanying note explaining its selection; all thirteen of the most recent cases are related to environmental law.[62] Moreover, in 2017, the SPC issued ten model cases on environmental PIL to help to manage the introduction of PIL to civil and administrative procedures.[63] In 2018, the SPP similarly selected its own ten model cases related to prosecutorial PIL, including comments and highlights attached to each case.[64] Though these guiding and model cases have no binding force per se, they still serve as useful indicators of the possible evolution of judicial practice.

One particular precedent sheds light on the possible indirect application of IBL. The China Biodiversity Conservation and Green Development Foundation, an environmental NGO that brings numerous environmental protection cases before the Chinese courts, routinely cites the CBD in its pleas to justify its stance on PIL.[65] In one of the guiding cases on environmental law,

[60] 陈兴华非法运输珍贵、濒危野生动物案永仁县人民法院一审刑事判决书，（2015）永刑初字第60号[*Prosecutor v Xinghua Chen*, Court of the Yongren County (2015)].

[61] Compare Sheila Jasanoff, 'A New Climate for Society' (2010) 27 Theory, Culture & Society 233.

[62] The English translation of most cases can be found on the website of Stanford Law School's China Guiding Cases Project <https://cgc.law.stanford.edu/> accessed 12 March 2022.

[63] 《最高法发布十件环境公益诉讼典型案例》[The SPP Publishes Ten Model Cases of Environmental Public Interest Litigation]，<www.chinacourt.org/article/detail/2017/03/id/2573898.shtml> accessed 12 March 2022.

[64] ibid.

[65] 中国生物多样性保护与绿色发展基金会诉深圳市速美环保有限公司、浙江淘宝网络有限公司，杭州市中级人民法院（2016）浙01民初1269号一审民事判决书 [*China Biodiversity*

the SPC cited the definition of biodiversity provided by the CBD and concluded that an organization specializing in biodiversity conservation should be considered an 'environmental organization' and therefore had standing in PIL.[66] The SPC did nothing more here than highlight a common perception that the phrase 'environmental protection' encompasses biodiversity conservation. But not only does this action suggest that the judiciary will interpret the term 'environmental protection' broadly, it also indicates that an international treaty can be cited as persuasive authority, if not as a legal ground for deciding a case.

The SPC later normalized the practice that judges should elaborate their complete arguments with legal and non-legal considerations, as well as direct and indirect ones.[67] These recommendations on judicial decision-writing encourage the judiciary to do more than simply justify their decisions in the light of the law: they must also show that their judgments are further motivated by underlying pragmatic considerations. The SPC suggests that judges can use scientific evidence and everyday experience to achieve this goal.[68] Since the normalization of the practice, the consideration of biodiversity has expanded in environment-related criminal justice. In the context of China's enthusiasm for ecological civilization—but also of China's hosting of the CBD's Fifteenth Conference of the Parties meeting in Kunming in 2021—Chinese judges' and citizens' knowledge and awareness of IBD might increase.

3.3 Three Channels of Biodiversity Litigation

Today, the Chinese judicial system intervenes in biodiversity conservation mostly through three channels: criminal justice, public interest litigation, and civil adjudication. Cases brought before the courts in these ways can help researchers to verify whether the relevance of IBL is indeed growing.

Conservation and Green Development Foundation v Sumei Environmental Protection Ltd and Taobao Ltd, Intermediate Court of Hangzhou (2016)]；中国生物多样性保护与绿色发展基金会环境污染责任纠纷，最高人民法院（2016）最高法民再51号审判监督民事裁定书[*Decision on Action Brought by China Biodiversity Conservation and Green Development Foundation*, SPC (2016)].

[66] 中国生物多样性保护与绿色发展基金会诉宁夏瑞泰科技股份有限公司环境污染公益诉讼案，最高人民法院（2015）民再47号民事裁定书 [Decision on *China Biodiversity Conservation and Green Development Foundation v Tairui Ltd*, SPC (2015)].

[67] 《关于加强和规范裁判文书释法说理的指导意见》（2018） Recommendations on Strengthening and Standardising Arguments in Judicial Decision (2018).

[68] Recommendation 13, Recommendations on Strengthening and Standardising Arguments in Judicial Decision (2018).

3.3.1 Criminal justice and the rise of biodiversity consideration

Although Articles 341, 344, and 345 of the Penal Code criminalize the hunting, transporting, trading, and logging of the habitats of endangered species, they mainly target damage done to individuals, not to local ecosystems. The 2000 judicial explanation mentioned earlier further fortified this tendency by providing a scale for determining the length of an offender's prison term according to the number of plants or animals harmed and the amount of money involved.[69]

Recently, on the SPC's recommendation, judges have begun to consider the functions of a given species at issue in a case in connection with other elements of its local ecosystem. In a simple criminal case of illicit logging, the court ruled that the felling of three endangered yews threatened local biodiversity and therefore harmed the public interest.[70] In March 2020, the SPP and the SPC co-issued a judicial explanation that requires prosecutors and judges to consider the extent of the ecological loss when applying Article 344 of the Penal Code.[71] Likewise, in publishing the model cases of environmental offences, the SPP praised the efforts of judicial power in preserving biodiversity.[72] During the last few years, Chinese judges have already acquired a new ritual: beginning their rulings with a paragraph on the importance of biodiversity and the place in the ecosystem of the particular species at issue.[73] This ritual was further generalized in the context of the Covid-19 outbreak. For example, the judge in an illicit hunting case in March 2020 spent half of the very concise decision lecturing on the ecological significance of weasels and squirrels (the animals hunted in the case) and on the enormous threat to public health posed by poaching them.[74]

[69] Articles 3, 4, 5, and 6 of the Judicial Explanation of the Supreme Court on Application of Law in Criminal Litigation Concerning Wild Animal Resource (2000).

[70] 雅安市人民检察院诉郑涛非法采伐、毁坏国家重点保护植物罪，雅安市中级人民法院（2019）川18刑初7号刑事判决书[*Prosecutor v Tao Zheng*, Intermediate Court of Ya'an (2019)].

[71] 最高人民法院、最高人民检察院关于适用《中华人民共和国刑法》第三百四十四条有关问题的批复，法释〔2020〕2号 [SPC and SPP, *Response Regarding the Application of Art 344 of the Penal Code* No 2 (2020)].

[72] 徐盈雁：《最高检发布10起检察机关加强生态环境司法保护典型案例》，《检察日报》2015年6月17日 [Yingyan Xu, 'The SPP Publishes 10 Model Cases on Ecology and Environment Protection', 17 June 2015, Prosecutors' Journal], <www.spp.gov.cn/zdgz/201506/t20150617_99553.shtml> accessed 12 March 2022.

[73] See 徐州市云龙区人民检察院诉张爱民、李楠等非法收购、运输、出售珍贵、濒危野生动物、珍贵、濒危野生动物制品罪，徐州市鼓楼区人民法院（2016）苏0302刑初189号刑事判决书[*Prosecutor v Aimin Zhang and Nan Li*, Court of Gulou District (2006)]；重庆市万州区人民检察院诉杜发国、杜发田等非法收购、运输、出售珍贵、濒危野生动物、珍贵、濒危野生动物制品罪上诉案刑事判决书，重庆市第二中级人民法院（2018）渝02刑终1号刑事判决书[*Prosecutor v Faguo Du et al*, Second Intermediate Court of Chongqing (2018)].

[74] 宜兴市人民检察院诉王杰非法狩猎罪，苏州市姑苏区人民法院（2020）苏0508刑初91号刑事判决书[*Prosecutor v Jie Wang*, Court of Gusu District, Suzhou (2020)].

In the light of rising public concern with biosecurity, the judiciary may incorporate biodiversity considerations in their decisions more often.

3.3.2 Public interest litigation

The double amendment in 2017 of the Law on Administrative Procedure and the Law on Civil Procedure, along with the EPL (as amended in 2015), creates the legal framework for environmental PIL. Article 55(1) and (2) of the Civil Procedure Law recognizes NGOs and prosecutors' standing in civil PIL, Article 58 of the EPL further stipulates the qualification of suitable NGOs, and Article 25(4) of the APL endows prosecutors with the competence to sue the government.

Environmental NGOs are succeeding in attracting public attention to biodiversity loss. The most recent example is the Green Peafowl Case.[75] In March 2017, during its investigation in a rainforest in Yunnan Province, the NGO Wild China, whose objective is to document endangered natural reserves and species, discovered that the construction of a hydropower station would destroy the largest green peafowl habitat in China and probably result in the bird's regional disappearance. The corresponding lawsuit, investigated and reported by the dominant state-owned television network China Central Television, had generated immense attention it began.[76] The case represented a perfect combination of factors that together helped sympathetic citizens to visualize the abstract concept of habitat loss: a species with high aesthetic value, a habitat known for its rich biodiversity and mysterious rainforest, a threat to that habitat from a giant monopoly, and, finally, the case being broadcast by an investigative programme that enjoyed a high level of credibility among the educated audience.

Another environmental NGO, the Friends of Nature Institute, sued the grid company and the company that designed the hydropower station before a local court on the ground of biodiversity loss prevention. In the light of its lack of experience in environmental matters, the court of presumed territorial jurisdiction asked the High Court to reassign the case, and the High Court complied, reallocating it to the jurisdiction of the Municipal Court of Kunming.[77] On

[75] 自然之友环境研究所与中国水电顾问集团新平开发有限公司、中国电建集团昆明勘测设计研究院有限公司裁定案，云南高级法院（2017）云民辖23号民事裁定书 [*Friends of Nature Institute v Xinping Development Co Ltd*, Decision on jurisdiction, High Court of Yunnan Province (2017)].

[76] 《因为绿孔雀》[For the Sake of Grean Peafowls] <http://m.news.cctv.com/2019/05/19/ARTIFbRLfZwClqrmtMouKTHU190519.shtml> accessed 12 March 2022.

[77] 自然之友环境研究所与中国水电顾问集团新平开发有限公司、中国电建集团昆明勘测设计研究院有限公司裁定案，云南高级法院（2017）云民辖23号民事裁定书 [*Friends of Nature Institute v Xinping Development Co Ltd*, Decision on jurisdiction, High Court of Yunnan Province (2017)].

20 March, 2020, the court ruled against the defendant and halted the project until a further environmental impact assessment (EIA) could be completed.[78] However, the plaintiff was dissatisfied because it suspected that the new EIA would again approve the construction. The value of this judgment symbolized more than just the conservation of a rainforest: not only did it satisfy the public's demand that rare and remarkable birds be saved, it further raised awareness of the environmental risks of power plant construction in general. The power sector, meanwhile, currently expects an increase in lawsuits because numerous similar projects are endangering the habitats of other species, albeit perhaps ones less often considered so beautiful.[79] Both parties have appealed the judgment, and the disputes now focus on the validity of the original EIA, which had previously given the project the green light.

Since 2017, prosecutorial PIL has become the procuratorates' centre of gravity, especially in the realm of environmental protection.[80] Through 2019, more than half of the public interest prosecution cases concerned environmental protection and resources, totalling 118,012 such cases.[81] The results of these lawsuits include the removal of more than 31 million tons of solid waste and the reparation 4.5 billion Renminbi (RMB) in ecological damage.[82] Meanwhile, the SPP focuses its efforts on environmental governance involving the conservation of ecosystems, such as protecting river and maritime ecosystems.[83]

3.3.3 Civil action in the light of the new Civil Code

The reparation of environmental and ecological damage will become one of the most discussed topics in the coming years. As the Civil Code promulgated in 2021 establishes a complex mechanism governing reparations for environmental damages—a system that involves victims, NGOs, and the state—it will be interesting to see how judges determine the nature and cost of alleged

[78] 自然之友环境研究所诉中国水电顾问集团新平开发有限公司，昆明市中级人民法院（2017）云01民初2299号民事判决书 [*Friends of Nature Institute v Xinping Development Co Ltd*, Intermediate Court of Kunming Municipality (2017)].

[79] 《停建！！涉及"绿孔雀案"的水电站一审被宣判停止建设》[The Court Ordered the Suspension of the Hydropower Station that Concerns the Green Peafowls]，<http://news.bjx.com.cn/html/20200323/1056569.shtml> accessed 12 March 2022.

[80] On the list of model cases of prosecutorial PIL published by the SPP, fifteen out of twenty-three concern environmental protection. The complete list is available at <www.spp.gov.cn/xwfbh/wsfbt/202109/t20210915_529543.shtml#2> accessed 12 March 2022.

[81] 张军：《最高人民检察院关于开展公益诉讼检察工作情况的报告》[Procurator-General's Discourse before the Standing Committee of the National People's Congress, 23 October 2019] <www.spp.gov.cn/spp/tt/201910/t20191024_435925.shtml> accessed 12 March 2022.

[82] ibid.

[83] ibid. It seems that the SPP specifically relates 'environmental governance' to ecosystem protection that involves several provincial or municipal jurisdictions.

damage. More importantly, chapter 7 of the book on civil liability recognizes the idea of pure ecological loss and therefore goes beyond the previous paradigm, which focused on pollution. Biodiversity contributes to the introduction of ecological damage through a disputed case from decades ago that concerned the damage caused by an environmental improvement effort. That case is discussed below.

In 1995, the transport authority of Hubei Province began to plant Chinese junipers alongside the national highway as a measure to optimize the environment. Quite ironically, this would become poison to local tree growers since, though juniper is native to China, it was not common in that area and, since the planting began, the productivity of pear trees continuously decreased in the area surrounding the highway. Even worse, in 2003 and 2004, an outbreak of pear rust caused 14,000 acres of pear orchards to completely fail to produce; the junipers were later proven to be the primary carrier of the attacking fungus. Some 2,000 households of pear growers sued the transport authority for damaging the local ecosystems by failing to consider the negative impact of junipers on the surrounding agriculture. The court ruled against the pear growers, finding that the spread of disease did not fit the pollution-based concept of damage described by the General Provisions of Civil Law.[84] Since then, the pear growers' failed case has raised awareness of biosecurity among legal professionals, and it became one of the incentives for the inclusion of 'ecological degradation' alongside 'environmental pollution' as a source of civil liability.[85] So formulated, Article 1229 allows the victims of adverse ecological impacts other than pollution, such as biodiversity loss and invasion by non-native species, to demand a remedy.

The innovative efforts of this chapter of the Civil Code on environmental liability are not limited to escaping the paradigm of pollution. Article 1232 institutes punitive remedies in cases of intentional environmental offences that cause severe consequences, and Article 1234 further stipulates that where remediable ecological degradation is caused by a violation of national provisions but no personal harm is identifiable, the state (or other organizations authorized by law to do so) can demand that the responsible person proceed with remediation. These provisions are at odds with the continental legal tradition, which recognizes liability only when personal harm is identifiable and which rejects punitive remedies.

[84] 2227户梨农诉交通委员会等七被告生态侵权案，见吕忠梅主编：《环境法案例评析》，高等教育出版社2006年版，第84–85页[*Pear Growers v Transport Authority et al*, in Zhongmei Lyu (ed), *Caselaw of Environmental Law* (Higher Education Press 2006) 84–85].

[85] Article 1229 of the Civil Code.

Article 9 of the Civil Code states: 'When conducting a civil activity, a person of the civil law shall act in a manner that facilitates conservation of resources and protection of the ecological environment.'[86] This provision, together with other 'ecological provisions' of the Code,[87] can—if we paraphrase Otto von Gierke—be 'drops of ecocentric oil' in anthropocentric civil law.[88] We can expect that the Chinese judiciaries will further constrain property and contractual liberty in the name of ecological good. However, it is premature to hope for a self-aware ecocentric approach. After all, statutory rules cannot predetermine their application, and 'the law' is also a matter of how lawyers understand environmental governance and the role of civil law therein. So far, the mainstream civil law doctrine still resents the inclusion of ecological considerations, seeing them either as black sheep that trouble the purity of the civil law system or as repetitions of the principle of *ordre public*.[89]

4. The Need for Further Elaboration of International Biodiversity Law

If we analyse the previous sections, we can see that ecological concerns and the relevance of IBL are growing simultaneously in Chinese judicial practice. In this context, Chinese judiciaries will face the challenge of balancing the mandates of conservation, the rule of law, and other aspects of sustainability. Careful elaboration of IBL, and especially its relationship with other regimes of law, will be necessary as judges manage these often-competing requirements.

Because the vast majority of Chinese biodiversity litigation is tried before criminal tribunals, determining how IBL should be correctly applied can serve a vital function in maintaining the rule of law in environmental justice. Biodiversity consideration can encourage judges to leave overkilling behind as a standard for environmental harm and to instead evaluate damage in terms of ecosystem or habitat conservation, therefore improving the

[86] The provision does not distinguish between natural and legal persons. Therefore, we shall interpret 'person' as used in the ordinary term.

[87] Besides Art 9, ecological considerations can be found in Arts 286, 326, 346, 509(3), 621, and 1229–35.

[88] Mingzhe Zhu, 'The Ecologization of the Chinese Civil Code' (2020) 64 (4) Pravovedenie 511–25.

[89] 苏永钦：《现代民法典的体系定位与建构规则》，载《交大法学》（第1卷），上海交通大学出版社2011 年版，第59–93 页[Yongqin Su, 'The Systematization and Rules of Construction of Modern Civil Codes' (2010) 1 Shanghai Jiaotong University Law Review 59–93]；尹田：《民法基本原则与调整对象立法研究》，载《法学家》2016年第5期，第10–19页[Tian Yin, 'Review on Basic Principles of General Principles of Civil Code' (2016) 5 Jurist 10–19].

efficiency with which biodiversity loss is prevented.[90] At the same time, reliance on a scientific concept that has no clear legal status is likely to be criticized, especially in the name of *nulla poena sine lege*.[91] For instance, in the Parakeets case, the defendant's lawyer challenged the legality of the judicial explanation of 2000 over its broadening of the applicability of a crime by removing the qualifying word 'wild'. The biologists, through their amici curiae, expressed a different view: they testified that tolerating the domestication of members of the endangered species would encourage their capture and eventually lead to habitat destruction.[92] The court of appeal ultimately found the defendant guilty, but it sentenced him to two years in prison instead of the five provided for by the Penal Code.[93] Similar decisions opened discussions on the role of IBL within the Chinese legal system amongst criminal lawyers. For example, Professor Guangquan Zhou, an authority on criminal law and an eminent member of the Constitution and Law Committee of the NPC, has argued in a short essay that the judiciaries should recognize that CITES does not, in itself, fall into the regime of criminal law and that incriminating any trade that involves species in the CITES appendices puts proportionality at risk.[94] In this sense, we can predict the growing relevance of IBL in Chinese environmental justice.

Meanwhile, habitat conservation cases that target clean energy projects such as hydropower stations reveal the complicated and problematic trade-off between renewable energy and biodiversity. The development of large-scale renewable projects will almost inevitably involve occupying and transforming vast landscapes in the wild.[95] In other words, China's energy transition will, at

[90] James Chen, 'The Fragile Menagerie: Biodiversity Loss, Climate Change, and the Law' (2018) 93 Indiana Law Journal 303, 304.

[91] Clearly, legal concepts cannot avoid ambiguity. Still, empirical research demonstrates that a degree of legal certainty is achievable in practice. John Hasnas, 'Back to the Future: From Critical Legal Studies Forward to Legal Realism, Or How Not to Miss the Point of the Indeterminacy Argument' (1995) 45 Duke Law Journal 84; Brian Bix, 'Doctrine, Data, and High Theory' (2016) 6 UC Irvine Law Review 137.

[92] 深圳市宝安区人民检察院诉王某、谢某福非法收购、运输、出售珍贵、濒危野生动物、珍贵、濒危野生动物制品罪，深圳市中级人民法院（2017）粤03刑终1098号二审刑事判决书 [*Prosecutor v Wang and Xie*, Intermediate Court of Shenzhen Municipality (2017)].

[93] 深圳市宝安区人民检察院诉王某、谢某福非法收购、运输、出售珍贵、濒危野生动物、珍贵、濒危野生动物制品罪，深圳市中级人民法院（2017）粤03刑终1098号二审刑事判决书 [*Prosecutor v Wang and Xie*, Intermediate Court of Shenzhen Municipality (2017)]. Article 63(2) of the Penal Code provides that the court can mitigate the penalty with the approval of the SPC.

[94] 周光权：《危害人工繁育珍贵、濒危野生动物的罪与非罪》，《法治日报》2021年11月3日第10版[Guangquan Zhou, 'Criminality and Discrimination of Domestically Raised Animals' 3 November 2021 Journal of the Rule of Law].

[95] Jordi López-Pujol and Ming-Xun Ren, 'Biodiversity and the Three Gorges Reservoir: A Troubled Marriage' (2009) 43 Journal of Natural History 2765; Mingyue Pang and others, 'Ecological Impacts of Small Hydropower in China: Insights from an Emergy Analysis of a Case Plant' (2015) 76 Energy Policy 112; Hongzhang Xu and others, 'Limiting the Effects of Hydropower Dams on Freshwater Biodiversity: Options on the Lancang River, China' (2019) 70 Marine and Freshwater Research 169.

least in the short term, jeopardize its biodiversity—a fact that makes renewables projects the targets of biodiversity PIL. In 2016, the China Environmental Protection Foundation filed a public interest complaint before the Municipal Court of Yantai, Shandong Province against a wind-farm project on Changdao Island for disturbing seasonal bird migration.[96] Though this wind farm had been a symbol of the paradigm shift in the local economy from highly polluting industries to clean power and was operated by state-owned enterprises, the settlement reached by the parties mandated the removal of all wind turbines and the reforestation of the island.[97]

Of course, this is not to say that Chinese environmentalists favour biodiversity over mitigating climate change. The very same NGO that first advocated for climate change litigation in China has also sued enterprises over causes of biodiversity. The so-called 'first climate change litigation in China', a case against the State Grid Corporation for excessively abandoning wind power, was filed by the Friends of Nature Institute, which was also the plaintiff in the green peafowl case.[98] However, biodiversity conservation lawyering is, at least for now, much more visible. Despite urban residents' increasing public awareness of climate change,[99] Chinese judges may still find no legislative instruments with which to urge more radical governmental measures or impose further limitation on private sector emissions. The SPC has announced that climate mitigation and the emissions trade will be the focus in the coming years, making it vital for the Chinese government and eco-aware citizens to balance the subtle and often competing interests of emission reduction and habitat conservation.

[96] 中华环保基金会诉长岛联凯风电发展公司环境破坏案，山东省烟台市中级人民法院（2016）鲁06民初373号民事调解书 [*CEPF v Kailian Wind Power Ltd*, Court of Yantai Municipality (2016)].

[97] See 徐光明、孙航、郭宏伟：《旧产能退出去，新经济走进来——山东烟台法院服务新旧动能转换工作纪实》，《人民法院报》2018年7月30日 第1版 [Guangming Xu, Hang Sun, and Hongwei Guo, 'From Old Productivity to New Economy' *Journal of People's Court* (Beijing 30 July 2018)].

[98] 自然之友环境研究所诉国家电网宁夏公司案，甘肃省高级人民法院（2018）甘民终679号民事裁定书 [*The Friends of Nature Institute v Ningxia State Grid*, High Court of Gansu Province (2018)].

[99] The China Center for Climate Change Communication has conducted two national surveys entitled *Climate Change in the Chinese Mind*, retrospectively in 2012 and 2017. The percentage of respondents who know as least a little about climate change grew from 6 to 92.7 per cent Binbin Wang, Yating Shen, and Yangyang Jin, 'Measurement of Public Awareness of Climate Change in China: Based on a National Survey with 4,025 Samples' (2017) 15 *Chinese Journal of Population Resources and Environment* 285–91.

5. Neglected Fronts of Biodiversity Litigation

Legal scholarship often focuses on the application and interpretation of sources of law, taking for granted that judges are the princes of the law's empire. In order to fully grasp the dynamics of biodiversity litigation in China, we will explore the use of scientific expertise in trials and the role of prosecutors.

5.1 Science in Robes

The SPC designates the judicial protection of the environment and natural resources as one of three 'tough battles' to win in its *Essential Tasks for the Judicial Reform in 2020*.[100] Specific measures in this 'battle' include the reorganization of jurisdiction over environmental and natural resources cases, the definition of boundaries between ecological damage and PIL, and the exploration of punitive damages in cases concerning ecological loss.[101] In several more developed provinces (such as Shandong and Jiangsu), the institutional perspective on this task may include transforming the environmental chamber into a separate court that exercises jurisdiction over civil, criminal, and administrative litigation related to environmental issues. The SPC seems to have confidence—based on five years of experience and 1 million first-instance cases—in the tribunals' competence to manage environmental litigation.[102]

This structural turn may help a new model of judicial reasoning to flourish in environmental justice: submitting scientific evidence to argue the necessity of conservation.[103] The first indicator of the rise of science before the court is the increasing reliance in trials on scientific expertise on biodiversity. Before 2014, Chinese courts did consult scientists on environmental issues to identify which species of plant or animal had been captured, killed, or traded and to determine the nature of pollutants or waste. However, the opinions given by these experts usually did little more than inform the court whether the creature in question could be found on one of the national or

[100] 最高人民法院：《2020年人民法院司法改革工作要点》[SPC, *Key Tasks of Judicial Reform in 2020*].

[101] 刘峥：《对<2020年人民法院司法改革工作要点>的解读》，《人民法院报》2020年2月27日 [Zheng Liu, 'Understanding the Key Tasks of Judicial Reform in 2020', 27 February 2020, Journal of People's Courts].

[102] 《最高法召开环境资源审判庭成立五周年发布会》[Press Release on the Occasion of the Fifth Anniversary of the Establishment of the Environmental Chamber], <www.court.gov.cn/zixun-xiangqing-173942.html> accessed 12 March 2022.

[103] Benoit Mayer, '*The State of the Netherlands v Urgenda Foundation*: Ruling of the Court of Appeal of The Hague (9 October 2018)' (2019) 8 Transnational Environmental Law 167.

international directories, or whether the volume of the emission surpassed the regulation or technical standards. This information was sufficient to decide the offence, and among sixty-eight first-instance cases regarding illicit hunting in 2013, not a single judge asked for an evaluation of the relevant ecological impact. Since 2015, judges have gradually developed the habit of summoning experts to evaluate the particular species' bigger-picture value. For instance, a research institute testified in 2018 before a court in the Hunan Province that the capture of Chinese hwamei (*Garrulax canorus*) would cause significant damage to the local ecosystem.[104] As a response to the Standing Committee's decision discussed in the next paragraph, on 24 February 2020 the SPP published six model cases of prosecutorial wildlife protection, of which four involved expert witnesses. In categories of environmental offences that depend more on experts' discretion, such as pollution and natural resources damages, the princes of the law's empire are more than willing to seek scientific assistance.

The second indicator of the possible ascendancy of scientific evidence is the growing emphasis on biosecurity. In the context of the initial Covid-19 outbreak's alleged origination from a wet market in Wuhan and its association with the consumption of wildlife,[105] the Standing Committee of the National People's Congress enacted the Decision on Full Prohibition of Wildlife Trade and Alimentary Use for the Sake of People's Life and Health Security.[106] This eight-article text relates the necessity of wildlife protection to biosecurity, ecological security, and public health. Technically speaking, this decision of the legislative body is not a proper legal text, but given the gravity of the pandemic and the dramatic global quarantine, the concern conveyed by the decision with biodiversity and its linkage to hunting and eating will dominate the revision of the Wildlife Protection Law, as well as the judicial interpretation of the relevant statutes. Indeed, the magnitude of epidemiological discourse has already directed judges' attention to the relationship between culinary habits and public health.

[104] 王某某、吴某某非法狩猎罪，湖南省宁乡市人民法院（2018）湘0124刑初497号刑事判决书[*Prosecutor v Wang and Wu*, Court of Ningxiang (2018)].

[105] For a broader account of wildlife and the epidemic, see John Vidal, '"Tip of the Iceberg": Is Our Destruction of Nature Responsible for Covid-19?' *The Guardian* (18 March 2020) <www.theguardian.com/environment/2020/mar/18/tip-of-the-iceberg-is-our-destruction-of-nature-responsible-for-covid-19-aoe> accessed 12 March 2022.

[106] 《全国人民代表大会常务委员会关于全面禁止非法野生动物交易、革除滥食野生动物陋习、切实保障人民群众生命健康安全的决定》[NPC Standing Committee's Decision on Total Prohibition of Wild Life Trade and Consummation]，<www.npc.gov.cn/npc/c30834/202002/c56b129850aa42acb584cf01ebb68ea4.shtml> accessed 12 March 2022.

5.2 The Role of Prosecutorial Preliminary Procedure and the Effectiveness of Biodiversity Law

As we have mentioned in the previous section, prosecutors have become active in PIL but their activism may eventually block the access of civil society. Compared with the total of 118,012, the number of environmental cases brought by NGOs is almost negligible—no more than a few dozen per year.[107] In fact, though about 700 NGOs have standing to engage in environmental litigation, only twenty-five had brought cases by 2018.[108] Even in 2019, which the SPC considers a landmark year in terms of NGO-filed public interest actions, the total count was just 179, less than one-tenth of the number of prosecutorial PIL cases.[109] The practical utility of initiatives originating in civil society is even more suspect if we consider the fact that many of China's ecology-oriented NGOs have their roots in the public sector.[110] One of the key actors in biodiversity litigation, for example China Biodiversity Conservation and Green Development Foundation, was established in 1985 by the initiative of a number of vice presidents of the Political Consultative Conference, the political legislative advisory body.

Prosecutors' true force, however, stems from their authority to oversee the executive branch by way of preliminary procedure before actual prosecution. Article 55(2) of the Civil Procedure Law and Article 25(4) of the APL establish a mandatory preliminary procedure before prosecution.[111] These provisions direct the prosecutor to first advise the executive-branch body in charge of the subject at hand of its duty and urge it to perform that duty before filing a suit before the court. In practice, the executive branch follows the prosecutors' advice in an overwhelming 99.5 per cent of cases;[112] only on very exceptional

[107] 陈杭平、周晗隽：《公益诉讼"国家化"的反思》，载《北方法学》2019年第6期，第70-79页[Hangping Chen and Hanjun Zhou, Reflection on the Nationalization of Public Interest Litigation (2019) 6 Northern Law Review 70–79].

[108] 王琳琳：《保障社会组织开展公益诉讼需精准施策》，载《中国环境报》2018 年3月14日[Linlin Wang, 'Access of NGOs to Public Interest Litigation Needs to Be Assured by Policy Accuracy', 14 March 2018 Chinese Journal of Environment].

[109] 《中国环境资源审判（2019年）》[White Paper on Environmental Justice (2019)] <www.court.gov.cn/zixun-xiangqing-228341.html> accessed 12 March 2022.

[110] On the government organization of environmental NGOs, see Guobin Yang, 'Environmental NGOs and Institutional Dynamics in China' [2005] The China Quarterly 46; Jonathan Schwartz, 'Environmental NGOs in China: Roles and Limits' (2004) 77 Pacific Affairs 28.

[111] To be precise, the text of the Civil Procedure Law does not mention the preliminary procedure but a notice issued jointly by the Supreme Court and the Supreme Procuratorate in November 2019 makes it clear that this procedure is mandatory in prosecutorial public interest litigation through civil action. See 《最高人民法院、最高人民检察院关于人民检察院提起刑事附带民事公益诉讼应否履行诉前公告程序问题的批复》，法释〔2019〕18号[SPC and SPP's Response Concerning the Preliminary Procedure of Public Interest Litigation Filed by the Prosecutor (fashi No 18, 2019)].

[112] 张军：《最高人民检察院关于开展公益诉讼检察工作情况的报告》[Procurator-General's Discourse before the Standing Committee of the National People's Congress, 23 October 2019].

occasions do prosecutors actually need to sue the government for non-compliance. Of ten model PIL cases selected by the SPP, seven were resolved without prosecution. In the remainder, the prosecutors used their authority to orchestrate collaboration between different governmental departments and protect public interests.[113]

The active role of the prosecutor as the biodiversity conservator is not without drawbacks. Prosecutors, especially those at the county level, are rarely versed in environmental knowledge and, in practice, their advice is not always realistic.[114] In fieldwork, officials of the local Bureau of Environmental Protection told us that they had no choice but to obey the prosecutors' requests because an implicit chain of command constructed by bureaucratic disciplinary measures places the prosecutors in the de facto superior position.

The positive side of prosecutorial intervention is that it contributes to the effectiveness of biodiversity law in a regime dependent on executive discretion and regulation. Indeed, the effectiveness of environmental law is a complicated matter, and we can distinguish at least three forms of effectiveness: legal effectiveness, meaning that the law is respected; behavioural effectiveness, meaning that the law changes people's behaviour; and problem-solving effectiveness, meaning that the aim of the legal provisions is achieved.[115] If we accept the premise that biodiversity law's effectiveness can be improved by two avenues, namely better legislation and better implementation, it is possible to argue that Chinese prosecutors walk both paths towards more effective biodiversity law through their exercise of prosecutorial preliminary procedure.

In terms of rule-making, prosecutors can urge local governments to enact local regulations. Most of the current provisions concerning biodiversity entrust the executive branch with the power and duty to act but prescribe no legal consequences for inaction, an arrangement that gives governments too much discretion. When local governments fail to adopt regulatory norms, prosecutorial intervention can limit this overabundance of administrative discretion. In 2016, for instance, the prosecutor's office of Jilin Province issued prosecutorial advice effectively mandating that the provincial Five Year Plan would include

113 《最高检发布检察公益诉讼十大典型案例》[Ten Model Cases of Prosecutorial Public Interest Litigation], <www.spp.gov.cn/spp/zdgz/201812/t20181225_403407.shtml> accessed 12 March 2022.

114 刘建新：《论检察环境公益诉讼的职能定位及程序优化》，载《中国地质大学学报（社会科学版）》2021年第4期[Jianxin Liu, 'On the Function Orientation and Procedure Optimization of Environmental Public Interest Litigation Filed by the Prosecutor' (2021) 4 Journal of China University of Geosciences 28–41].

115 Sandrine Maljean-Dubois, 'Introduction. The Effectiveness of Environmental Law: A Key Topic' in Sandrine Maljean-Dubois (ed), *The Effectiveness of Environmental Law*, vol 3 (Intersentia 2017) 4–5.

measures devised to improve protection of the Yidong River.[116] This isolated and rather anecdotal case demonstrates the weight of preliminary procedure, which allows prosecutors to review the governments' policymaking.

When it comes to rule implementation, prosecutors behave as coordinators and help to resolve the challenges of interdepartmental cooperation. Of the ten model prosecutorial public interest cases, two concerned issues of interdepartmental coordination. In the Shuimoxi Wetland Nature Reserve case, the industrial park planned by the county overlapped with the reserve, and its construction had altered the function of the wetland ecosystem. The prosecutor of the Municipality of Chongqing decided to take over and initiated the preliminary procedure, as a result of which the county major accepted the prosecutor's advisory opinion and, under the prosecutor's supervision, paid the private enterprises in the industrial park to leave.[117] In the other case, a villager had illicitly maintained a fishery on the Cihu Lake. The illegal fishing activity has continued for more than fourteen years because it fell within the jurisdiction of five offices with no efficient practice of coordination. At the demand of the office in charge of land management, the municipal prosecutor intervened in May 2018 by issuing its advisory opinion and holding a workshop to orchestrate the fishery-closing operation among the five offices (and roughly 150 officers) in question.[118]

6. Conclusion

While biodiversity remains unfamiliar to Chinese courts, and indeed is not yet a well-defined legal term, the judicial system is becoming more active in conservation efforts. Because Chinese judges rarely apply international law and the provisions that have adopted CBD requirements do not prescribe any concrete consequences for violation, IBL has almost no visible direct application in Chinese justice. Indeed, the truth is that the normative foundation of biodiversity litigation is built by domains other than 'environmental law'. In

[116] See《吉林公益诉讼推动河流综合治理，省检察院向省政府发检察建议》[Prosecutor in Jilin Province Promoting River Improvement Projects Through Public Interest Litigation]，<www.thepaper.cn/newsDetail_forward_1629027> accessed 16 June 2020.

[117]《重庆市石柱县水磨溪湿地自然保护区生态环境保护公益诉讼案》[Case Concerning Ecology and Environment Protection of Shuimoxi Wetland Nature Reserve in Shizhu District, Chongqing City]，<www.spp.gov.cn/spp/zdgz/201812/t20181225_403407.shtml> accessed 12 March 2022.

[118]《湖北省黄石市磁湖风景区生态环境保护公益诉讼案》[Case Concerning Ecology and Environment Protection of Cihu Lake Scenic Area in Huangshi City, Hubei Province]，<www.spp.gov.cn/spp/zdgz/201812/t20181225_403407.shtml> accessed 12 March 2022.

criminal cases, it has for a long time been the policy of the SPC to rely on the CITES appendices as sound scientific evidence to determine whether a species is endangered and therefore protected by the Penal Code. Over the last decade, scientific expertise has been gaining authority before the tribunal of law as judges have begun to invite biologists and environmental scientists to testify as to the value of a species to the local ecosystem. The conservation effort stands to benefit from judges transcending the paradigm of overkill in biodiversity conservation—just as they left behind the paradigm of pollution in environmental protection—and taking habitat and ecosystem conservation into consideration. Argumentative strategy, in turn, must be improved in order to avoid jeopardizing the certainty of the law, particularly criminal law.

Judges, prosecutors, and NGOs serve different functions in biodiversity litigation. Outside narrowly defined legal rights and causality, judges are more concerned with the social impacts of their judgments, and they act to promote eco-awareness. While environmental NGOs win some well-reported cases and help to raise public awareness of habitat protection, the number of their actions remains marginal, even negligible. In contrast, the supervisory power of prosecutors—exercised not through litigation itself but by through preliminary procedure—runs the whole gamut of environmental governance, from forming outlooks to evaluating outcomes. In this context, prosecutorial advice seems a fitting mechanism by which both the rule-making and the rule-implementing effectiveness of biodiversity law may be improved.

6
Biodiversity Litigation in France
The Quest for Balance

Guillaume Futhazar and Lucas Dermenghem

1. Introduction

Biodiversity litigation—understood here as legal disputes before the courts concerning the conservation, the sustainable use, and/or access and benefit-sharing of biodiversity[1]—is becoming quite common in France. The year 2021 had numerous examples of such litigation. For instance, several NGOs initiated proceedings against the French state for its lack of appropriate action in regulating the approval of pesticides for the French markets, thus leading to important damage to ecosystems across France.[2] Similarly, the Ligue de Protection des Oiseaux, an NGO specialized in the conservation of birds, initiated civil proceedings against Bayer and Nufarm for their alleged responsibility in the decline of field birds due to the effect of the pesticides these companies produce.[3] In June 2021, an administrative court issued an order compelling the state to issue an appropriate action plan against the accumulation of green algae on the coast of Britany.[4] The list could go on.

The all-encompassing nature of biodiversity implies that biodiversity litigation will take on many different faces, from disputes on the conservation of species to ones concerning the management of entire ecosystems. The purpose of this chapter is to draw a portrait of the current state of biodiversity litigation in France. In doing so, we will also determine what role international biodiversity law (IBL) plays in this field. To do so, the chapter is structured as follows.

[1] See Chapter 1 in this volume.
[2] 'Pollinis and our Affair to All Launch Legal Action Against the State' <www.pollinis.org/publications/justice-pour-le-vivant-pollinis-et-notre-affaire-a-tous-attaquent-letat/> accessed 31 March 2022.
[3] 'The LPO Accuses Agrochemical Manufacturers of Having Decimated the Birds of the Fields' <www.lpo.fr/qui-sommes-nous/toutes-nos-actualites/articles/actus-2021/la-lpo-accuse-des-industriels-de-l-agrochimie-d-avoir-decime-les-oiseaux-des-champs> accessed 31 March 2022.
[4] TA Rennes, 04/06/2021, no 1806391.

Guillaume Futhazar and Lucas Dermenghem, *Biodiversity Litigation in France* In: *Biodiversity Litigation*. Edited by: Guillaume Futhazar, Sandrine Maljean-Dubois, and Jona Razzaque, Oxford University Press.
 DOI: 10.1093/oso/9780192865465.003.0006

In Section 2, we present the French context by briefly discussing its physical and legal particularities in terms of biodiversity. Section 3 contains the bulk of our analysis, with a discussion on biodiversity cases in France. In this section, we will first present some of the general features of biodiversity litigation (who, what, where), before turning to specific cases on species, habitats, and protected areas. This section will, inter alia, highlight that biodiversity litigation is, from a quantitative point of view, a phenomenon that mostly falls within public and criminal law and that the most influential cases for the implementation and evolution of biodiversity law are usually those dealt with by administrative judges. Biodiversity litigation is also a fragmented field of litigation due to the equally fragmented nature of environmental law in the French system. Section 4 of the chapter will address one of the main research questions of this edited volume: the importance of IBL for French biodiversity litigation. In this section, we will demonstrate that although IBL has little to no direct legal relevance in biodiversity litigation, it still has a significant indirect influence through the laws that implement IBL and through its importance as a conceptual tool for the interpretation of rules and facts in certain cases. Section 5 will question the relevance of the concept of biodiversity litigation within the French context. Is it possible to distinguish, within the broader theme of environmental litigation, a subset that could be labelled as biodiversity litigation and what would be the added value of such an approach? The conclusion of the chapter will discuss the potential future of biodiversity litigation based on current national, regional, and international trends.

2. Biodiversity in France

This section will first describe the state of biodiversity in France, before turning to the existing legal system.

2.1 The Biological Diversity Covered by the French Legal System

As in most parts of the planet,[5] the state of biodiversity is worrying in France.[6] Be it on the continent or in its overseas territories, recent environmental

[5] IPBES, *Global assessment report on biodiversity and ecosystem services of the Intergovernmental Science-Policy Platform on Biodiversity and Ecosystem Services* (2019).

[6] Ministère de la Transition écologique et solidaire, *L'environnement en France—édition 2019*, Rapport de synthèse (2019) 12.

assessments all point towards a continuous erosion of biological diversity. For instance, bird and insect populations have been continuously declining over the past decades.[7]

France is not among the list of megadiverse countries, but through its presence in the Indian Ocean, the Pacific, the Caribbean, the South American continent, and in the vicinity of both polar Circles, it exercises its sovereignty in multiple biogeographical regions. Its insular territories host many endemic species, most of which are threatened by invasive alien species or habitat destruction.[8]

This multiplicity of overseas territories across the globe makes France the second biggest actor in terms of maritime domain (with more than 10 million km^2 of maritime space under its influence).[9] As such, France also exercises its sovereignty and sovereign rights over a significant proportion of marine biodiversity. Combined with the action of the European Union in terms of fisheries,[10] the legal choices of the French state can lead to significant impacts on the marine environment.

Consequently, the French legal framework for the protection of biodiversity is not only relevant for its environment on the European continent, but actually has a significant impact for the preservation of biodiversity globally.

2.2 The Evolution of French Biodiversity Law

2.2.1 France and international biodiversity law

France is party to numerous biodiversity-related treaties. At the global level, the French state has signed the main instruments of IBL.[11] These global

[7] Académie des Sciences, *Le déclin des insectes: il est urgent d'agir* (Avis du 26 mars 2021); Ligue pour la protection des oiseaux, Office français de la biodiversité, MNHN, *Suivi des oiseaux communs en France 1989–2019: 30 ans de suivis participatifs* (Ministère de la Transition écologique et solidaire 2021).

[8] Number of endemic species in France <https://naturefrance.fr/indicateurs/nombre-despeces-endemiques-de-france> accessed 31 March 2022.

[9] See the Context <https://limitesmaritimes.gouv.fr/pour-en-savoir-plus/le-contexte> accessed 31 March 2022.

[10] Ernesto Peñas, *The Common Fishery Policy: The Quest for Sustainability* (Wiley Blackwell 2016).

[11] Also referred to as 'biodiversity-related conventions': inter alia, the Plant Treaty, the Convention on Biological Diversity, the Convention on Migratory Species, the Ramsar Convention on Wetlands, CITES, the World Heritage Convention, the International Treaty on Plant Genetic Resources for Food and Agriculture (opened for signature 3 November 2001, entered into force 29 June 2004) 2400 UNTS 303; the Convention on Biological Diversity (opened for signature 5 June 1992, entered into force 29 December 1993) 1760 UNTS 79; the Convention on Wetlands of International Importance Especially as Waterfowl Habitat (opened for signature 2 February 1971, entered into force 21 December 1975) 996 UNTS 245; the Convention on International Trade in Endangered Species of Wild Fauna and Flora (opened for signature 3 March 1973, entered into force 1 July 1975) 993 UNTS 243; the Convention for the Protection of the World Cultural and Natural Heritage (opened for signature 16 November 1972, entered into force 17 December 1975) 1037 UNTS 151.

commitments are supplemented by regional ones, specific to the European, Mediterranean, and Caribbean environment.[12]

France's Constitution gives prevalence to international law over its national laws.[13] French judges are therefore competent to examine whether a law or a regulatory act is compatible with France's international commitments.[14] Should a law be considered incompatible with international commitments, it will not be applicable in the context of the dispute.[15] In this monist system, judges are able to directly implement international law. They often do so for EU norms, even more so since national judges of the EU are meant to be the ordinary judge of EU law.[16] However, when it comes to general international law, the conditions for its applicability in a dispute are more restrictive. Specifically, judges will only directly implement international law when an international commitment creates direct rights and/or obligations for individuals in a sufficiently precise manner.[17] This approach to international law within the national legal system therefore excludes the direct application of most IBL treaties in disputes. This has been highlighted on numerous occasions by administrative judges in relation to the Convention on Biological Diversity (CBD) and the Ramsar Convention.[18] As we will see in Section 4, this entails that IBL can only exert its influence on French biodiversity litigation through indirect paths (though some cases blur the lines).[19] Therefore, at the national level, IBL mainly exerts its influence through the various laws that serve as a means for its implementation. These laws are usually passed after the signature and ratification of treaties, in order to incorporate their dispositions in the national legal system.[20] These laws sometimes predate treaties and can be used as a means to comply with the new international commitments, through slight modification in their interpretation and implementation.[21] National

[12] eg the Convention for the Protection of the Mediterranean Sea Against Pollution (opened for signature 16 February 1976, entered into force 12 February 1978) 1102 UNTS 27 or the Convention for the Protection and Development of the Marine Environment of the Wider Caribbean Region (opened for signature 24 March 1983, entered into force 11 October 1986) 1506 UNTS 157.

[13] Article 55 of the Constitution.

[14] See for a recent example in which the Conseil d'État partially annulled the provisions of Decree No 2018-435 of 4 June 2018, for non-compliance with Directive 2011/92/EU of the European Parliament and of the Council of 13 December 2011 on the assessment of the effects of certain public and private projects on the environment: CE, 15 April 2021, no 425424.

[15] Judges' powers depend, however, on the nature of the act in question: the modification or annulment of a law is the exclusive competence of the French Parliament in virtue of art 24 of the Constitution, but an administrative judge has the power to annul an act of a regulatory nature, totally or partially.

[16] As recalled, eg, in CE, 30 October 2009, no 298348.

[17] See Section 4 of this chapter.

[18] ibid.

[19] ibid.

[20] eg arts L.411-4 to L.411-6 of the French Environmental Code for CITES.

[21] eg all the rules related to protected areas in the French legal system can be seen as tools for implementing the in situ conservation requirements of the CBD.

laws related to biodiversity therefore carry the influence of IBL, and the impact of these laws on national biodiversity litigation illustrates an indirect impact of IBL. However, one has to bear in mind that the French legal system is not simply reacting to IBL. It can sometimes be more advanced, and subsequently influence the development of international law, as was the case for Integrated Coastal Zone Management in the Mediterranean region.[22]

A second important element to keep in mind is that France's national legal system is greatly impacted by the norms adopted at the EU level.[23] These norms (directives and regulations) are themselves part of the EU's efforts to implement IBL and can be directly implemented by French judges.[24] This double influence of IBL and EU law on the legislative development of biodiversity law can make it hard to distinguish which element has had more influence on newly adopted national norms. However, from a practical point of view, this question is not so important as IBL and EU law are not opposing forces and tend to develop in a coherent and mutually reinforcing manner.

2.2.2 France's national laws for biodiversity

The French laws regarding biodiversity have been constantly evolving over the past fifty years. They now form a dense and complex system that cannot be presented in detail within the confines of a single chapter.[25] Among the long list of legislative reforms, two stand out in particular. The first law specifically devoted to nature, enacted in 1976,[26] and the most recent law dealing with biodiversity, enacted in 2016.[27]

The 1976 law did not refer to biological diversity, which had not yet been coined as a concept of environmental governance.[28] Rather, the law referred more broadly to 'nature' and established several frameworks for the protection of endangered species and the creation of protected areas.[29] It

[22] Michel Prieur, 'Le Protocole de Madrid à la Convention de Barcelone relatif à la gestion intégrée des zones côtières de la Méditerranée' (2011) Vertigo Hors Serie 9 https://journals.openedition.org/vertigo/10933 accessed 18 June 2022.

[23] Though France has shown some reluctance to incorporate some EU environmental regulations, as illustrated by the long saga of disputes on the implementation of the Habitats Directive. See Julien Bétaille, 'L'ours dans les Pyrénées: la carence fautive de l'État dans la mise en œuvre de la directive Habitats' (2018) 41 Actualité Juridique Droit Administratif 2344.

[24] Regulations are directly applicable in the legal order of the Member States. The judge also controls, under certain conditions, respect of the directives by laws and administrative acts (see CE, 30 October 2009, no 298348 for individual administrative acts).

[25] For a detailed presentation, see, inter alia, Michel Prieur and others, *Droit de l'environnement* (8th edn, Dalloz 2019).

[26] Loi no 76-629 du 10 juillet 1976 relative à la protection de la nature.

[27] Loi no 2016-1087 du 8 août 2016 pour la reconquête de la biodiversité, de la nature et des paysages.

[28] See Chapter 1 in this volume.

[29] Jean Untermaier, 'Une innovation durable: la protection de la faune et de la flore dans la loi du 10 juillet 1976' (2011) 41 Revue Juridique de l'Environnement 647.

modernized pre-existing instruments, such as parks, and also established new legal mechanisms—basically a system of lists—for the protection of endangered species. It also modernized the system for the protection of the environment against potentially harmful infrastructures. The framework for the Installations Classées pour l'Environnement (ICPE—classified installations for the protection of the environment) is to this day one of the most influential piece of environmental legislation, both in terms of rules and litigation.[30]

The most recent overarching law on biodiversity was adopted in 2016: The Loi pour la reconquête de la biodiversité, de la nature et des paysages (Law for the reclaiming of biodiversity, nature and landscape). This law was adopted to modernize the French legal landscape with regards to biodiversity.[31] For instance, new concepts and approaches were added to the legal framework, such as ecosystem services and ecological damage. This law also aims at getting rid of partial concepts—such as the simplistic notions of animals or plants—in favour of a more holistic understanding of biodiversity, one that also takes into consideration 'ordinary biodiversity'.[32]

This law has led to a profound modification of the French legal and institutional landscape for the environment.[33] On the normative side, it has added new principles for the preservation and sustainable use of the environment. It also further entrenched an economical approach to biodiversity conservation with the consecration of offsetting mechanisms and contractual approaches to conservation.[34] (See Table 6.1 for a list of the environment law principles in the French legal system.)

Relevant legal norms related to biodiversity are not centralized, they permeate several codes that each form specialized fields of law. While, obviously, the Environmental Code will contain most of the norms related to biodiversity, other codes will also contain relevant norms (eg the Urban Code,[35] the Civil Code,[36] the Forest Code, etc).[37] In this sense, the transversal and ubiquitous

[30] David Deharbe, 'Réflexions, sans fétichisme ni désenchantement sur la police des ICPE 40 ans après la loi du 19 Juillet 1976' (2016) 41 Revue Juridique de l'Environnement 665.

[31] As mentioned in the *travaux préparatoires* for the law. See Rapport no 607 (2014–15) (Sénat).

[32] ibid. Ordinarily biodiversity broadly refers to non-protected or non-'remarkable' biodiversity. On the conceptual and legal intricacies of this notion, see Aline Treillard, *L'appréhension juridique de la nature ordinaire* (Université de Limoges 2019).

[33] See Chantal Cans and Olivier Cizel (eds), *Loi biodiversité Ce qui change en pratique* (Editions Legislative 2017).

[34] Agathe Van Lang, 'La compensation des atteintes à la biodiversité: de l'utilité technique d'un dispositif éthiquement contestable' (2016) 38 Revue de Droit Immobilier 586. On the contractual approach to preserve biodiversity, see art L.132-3 of the Environmental Code.

[35] eg article R.111-26 of the Urban Code on Environmental Concerns.

[36] Article 1247 of the Civil Code on Ecological Damage.

[37] Article L.112-1 of the Forest Code on the Conservation of Forest Biodiversity.

Table 6.1 Environmental law principles

List of environmental law principles in the French system (art L110-1 of the Environmental Code)
• Environmental protection is a public interest • The precautionary principle • The prevention principle • The polluter pays principle • The access to environmental information principle • The participation principle • The ecological solidarity principle[a] (added in 2016) • The sustainable use principle (added in 2016) • The complementarity principle[b] (added in 2016) • The non-regression principle[c] (added in 2016)

[a] This principle requires that any public decision having a significant impact on the environment be taken on the basis of a global view and taking into account, in particular, the interactions between ecosystems, living beings, and natural or developed environments.

[b] This principle conveys the idea of complementarity, from the point of view of ecosystem services, between the environment, agriculture, aquaculture, and sustainable forest management.

[c] The principle provides that the protection of the environment, ensured by the legislative and regulatory provisions relating to the environment, can only be subject to constant improvement, taking into account the available scientific and technical knowledge.

nature of biodiversity is logically correlated with its normative diffusion within the entire legal system.

In 2005, the Charte pour l'Environnement was added to the constitutional bloc, thus cementing the place of the environment as a central element in the French legal system.[38] Biodiversity is mentioned in the preamble to the Charter as an element affected by our 'current mode of consumption', however the Charter itself does not contain specific provisions on biodiversity. A constitutional reform to add a reference to state action for climate and biodiversity was recently debated before being abandoned.[39]

In sum, there is a clear correlation between France's involvement in the development of IBL and the evolution of its national legal system for biodiversity. The aforementioned rules are far more impactful than the several National Biodiversity Strategies and Action Plans (NBSAP) France adopted in

[38] It is frequently used in legal disputes, eg Simon Jolivet and Julie Malet Vigneaux, 'La Charte de l'Environnement devant les juges administrative et judiciaire (Juillet 2020–Juin 2021)' (2021) 46 Revue Juridique de l'Environnement 777.

[39] Draft constitutional law, presented on 20 January 2021, completing art 1 of the Constitution and relating to the preservation of the environment (JUSX2036137L).

compliance with article 6 of the CBD. We have not found evidence of these documents having an impact in the courts or on the interpretation of existing norms. Their overall influence might be best assessed through other lenses than the legal discipline.

This overview leads us to our main inquiry: how does this legal system translate from the perspective of litigation?

3. Biodiversity Litigation in France: The Administrative Judge as an Arbitrator of Interests

In this section, we will first discuss our methodology for the selection of cases. We will then offer a general overview of the main characteristics of biodiversity litigation, before discussing in more detail cases that are representative of biodiversity litigation in France.

3.1 Methodology

The sheer volume of cases that deal directly or indirectly with biodiversity makes it difficult to engage in a thorough quantitative analysis of biodiversity litigation in France. For instance, in 2018, it is estimated that approximately 18,000 cases dealt with environmental matters before the administrative courts.[40] Among these 18,000 cases, distinguishing the cases that deal directly with biodiversity is difficult as many cases can have an impact on biodiversity without mentioning related key terms.

Moreover, environmental litigation also occurs before the criminal courts and civil courts. Several thousand environmental cases were dealt by criminal courts in 2018.[41] Alongside administrative courts, criminal courts have been instrumental in shaping the evolution of environmental law in France. In the landmark decision on the Erika oil spill,[42] the Criminal Chamber of the Cour de Cassation recognized the notion of ecological damage, thus disconnecting its reparation from the specific interests of individuals or associations. This notion was later incorporated in the Civil Code, following the adoption of the 2016 Law on biodiversity.[43] In comparison, environmental cases are far less

[40] Bruno Cinotti and others, *Une justice pour l'environnement* (Ministère de la Transition Ecologique et Solidaire 2019) 22.
[41] ibid 17–21.
[42] Cass, crim, 25 September 2012, no 10-82.938.
[43] Article 1246 of the Civil Code.

common before the civil courts, though there is clearly an emerging trend of environmental litigation before civil judges.[44]

All in all, commentators tend to agree that environmental litigation is mainly a matter of administrative law.[45] This is due to the rationale of the French legal system where, often, acts that will have an impact on biodiversity—the constructions of large infrastructure, the opening of the hunting seasons, the reintroduction of a species, and so on—are subjected to administrative authorizations. These authorizations can then be contested in the administrative courts. Also, the consequences of these administrative acts can lead to the responsibility of the French state under certain circumstances.

To be able to offer a faithful account of what biodiversity litigation looks like in 2021, and has evolved over the years, we have chosen to mainly focus on cases that occurred after the adoption of the latest biodiversity law in 2016. This law intended to modernize the French system in the light of the evolution of IBL, therefore litigation that has taken place since then can be of particular interest to highlight the potential influence of IBL. Also, we also mainly narrowed our scope to cases dealt with before the Conseil d'État, the highest court in the French administrative system. We used several key terms,[46] related to the scope of this project, in different databases[47] in order to extract relevant cases. In parallel, we have relied on scholarship to identify the cases that had an important echo among legal commentators. This led to a set of approximatively sixty cases that we refer to throughout this chapter.

In this analysis, we will occasionally mention cases that fall outside this scope to highlight evolutions or singularities in the way that French judges deal with biodiversity-related cases.

Finally, in analysing the cases for this study, we have focused on the non-procedural elements of disputes to describe how judges take the physical aspects of biodiversity into account. Procedure is key for environmental litigation in France. Has an impact assessment been appropriately conducted? Were the public effectively consulted in the preparation of a project? Was an act effectively publicized? These elements are often decisive in settling environmental cases.[48] However, for the purpose of this project, we wanted to see how

[44] Mathilde Hautereau-Boutonnet, *Le Code civil, un code pour l'environnement* (Dalloz 2021).

[45] Christian Huglo, *JurisClasseur Fasc 4980 Contentieux Administratif de l'Environnement* (Lexis Nexis 2020) para 2.

[46] Mostly terms that are commonly found in IBL instruments, eg biodiversity, ecosystem, genetic resources, access and benefit sharing, endangered species.

[47] Ariane (Conseil d'État), Doctrine, Lexis Nexis, Dalloz.

[48] Moreover, France is party to the Aarhus Convention: Convention on Access to Information, Public Participation in Decision-Making and Access to Justice in Environmental Matters (open for signature 25 June 1998, entered into force 30 October 2001) 2161 UNTS 447.

judges dealt with the physical aspects of the disputes they had to settle; in other words, biodiversity itself. This distinction between procedural and substantive elements is illustrated by the notions of external legality and internal legality. In a case, the judge will often examine the external legality (procedural requirements) first before turning to the internal legality (substantial requirements). This focus on internal legality should allow us to discern patterns in how judges perceive the inherent complexity of biodiversity once the procedural elements have been removed from the picture.

3.2 The General Structure of Biodiversity Litigation in France

Here, we will discuss the main characteristic of biodiversity litigation before turning to more specific cases. This subsection answers the general questions. Who is involved in biodiversity litigation? Where does biodiversity litigation take place and what can judges do? What is covered by biodiversity litigation?

3.2.1 A litigation driven by 'associations'

Environmental litigation in France, and consequently biodiversity litigation, is mainly driven by private persons, among which 'associations' have a prominent place.[49] Under French law, these are private entities created by individuals to pursue a common interest, without seeking to reap a benefit.[50] In the context of legal dispute, their standing is dependent on two elements. First, their official registration as an association and, secondly, their statute, which indicates their purposes and operations. Environmental associations will therefore have standing in cases where there is an alleged violation of their interests as indicated in their statutes.

Environmental associations are the driving force of environmental litigation and also play a fundamental role in the implementation of environmental laws, alongside French public institutions. As such, environmental associations are both partners and critics of the French state and its environmental policies. This role in the implementation, control, and evolution of environmental law has been acknowledged through the adoption of an accreditation system for environmental associations.[51] Accredited environmental associations can act to defend their interests before the courts—they are presumed to have

[49] See, inter alia, Louis Dutheillet de Lamothe, 'Le contentieux en droit de l'environnement mené par les associations devant le Conseil d'État' (2019) HS19 Revue Juridique de l'Environnement 39.

[50] Article 1 Loi du 1er juillet 1901 relative au contrat d'association.

[51] Article L.141-1 of the Environmental Code.

standing—and can also act on behalf of victims of environmental damages, if such action corresponds with their statutes.

Environmental associations often engage in what could be labelled as strategic litigation, understood here as the use of litigation in broader political contexts. For instance, large infrastructure projects, which may be considered as superfluous and too damaging for the environment, are often contested on several levels, through protests, lobbying, and litigation. This was recently the case for the Notre Dame des Landes airport project and Sivens dam project which led to several forms of protest and numerous cases before the administrative courts.[52]

3.2.2 The powers of the administrative judge

The French administrative court system is highly centralized, with the Conseil d'État sitting at its top as the highest court. At the first instance level are the forty-two Tribunaux Administratifs where most of the daily environmental litigation takes place (construction permits, environmental police, and so on). At the appellate level are the nine Cours Admistratives d'Appel. Finally, cases can go before the Conseil d'État which will give a definitive legal interpretation of the matter at hand.

Biodiversity cases that reach the Conseil d'État are therefore only the tip of a vast contentious iceberg. Nevertheless, these rulings are fundamental as they carry legal interpretations that solidify the existing legal framework and also allow for its evolution. French public law is historically the product of legal disputes before the administrative judge, and is still, to this day, evolving through dispute resolution.

Administrative judges have varying degrees of power depending on the dispute they have to settle. In other words, the available remedies differ according to the type of dispute: disputes on legality, full litigation, or urgency procedures.

In the context of disputes on legality—where the legality of an administrative act is contested through a *recours en excès de pouvoir*—they have the power to annul the contested act, or moderate some of elements of the act that are deemed illegal.[53] In this context, the environmental impact of the decision is indirect.

[52] CE, 28 November 2014, no 377232; CAA Nantes, 14 November 2016, nos 15NT02883, 15NT02884, 15NT02864, 15NT02860, 15NT02858, 5NT02859, 15NT02851, 15NT02847, 15NT02386, and 15NT02863 for the Notre Dame des Landes airport project. TA Toulouse, 30 June 2016, no 1400853 for the Sivens dam project.

[53] In disputes on legality, this power of moderation is, however, limited.

In the event of a 'full litigation' request, an administrative judge has more extensive powers. Not only can the judge annul the administrative act before them but also reform it, modify it, or substitute a new decision. A full litigation judge can also order the administration to pay damages (contractual or tort liability of the administration).[54] This variety of powers explains why the judge is referred to as an 'administrator judge' in this context. Since a 2017 reform—the 'unique environmental authorization',[55] which streamlines a previously fragmented procedural landscape—full litigation is even more prevalent in environmental litigation.

Lastly, administrative judges can act in the context of emergencies; there are various emergency procedures provided for by French law, but the most used in environmental matters is the *référé suspension* where the judge is asked to rule on the prima facie legality of an administrative act that could lead to serious environmental damage.[56] In such cases, an administrative act can be temporarily suspended until its legality is formally determined in the context of a *recours en excès de pouvoir* or full litigation. This emergency procedure is particularly relevant for environmental matters where administrative acts can lead to irreparable damage.[57] Therefore, the ability to freeze such decisions is crucial in the context of disputes. As such, many examples of biodiversity litigation cases are drawn from this form of procedure.

3.2.3 A litigation on species and habitats

As the next paragraph will show, biodiversity litigation mainly occurs along the demarcation of species and spaces[58] (habitats and/or protected areas). This is how the protection of biodiversity has been historically organized in French law,[59] and even though the 2016 Law on biodiversity has tried to modernize this approach by considering the systemic nature of biodiversity (its constitutive elements and their connections), litigation still seems to uphold the

[54] Ecological damage and its specific reparation are acknowledged by the French legal system; however, to this day, courts are hesitant to incorporate this notion when deciding on remedies. See TC Marseille, 06 March 2020, no 18330000441. See Grégoire Leray and others, 'Réflexions sur une application jurisprudentielle du préjudice écologique' (2020) 27 Recueil Dalloz 1553.

[55] Ordonnance no 2017-80 du 26 Janvier 2017 Relative à l'autorisation environnementale.

[56] According to the expression provided for by art L.521-1 of the Code of Administrative Justice, a judge examines whether there is 'serious doubt' on the legality of the decision.

[57] See for recent examples: TA Toulouse, Ord, 17 February 2022, no 2200362 (suspension of administrative authorizations allowing work for the construction of a logistics warehouse and the destruction of protected species); TA Grenoble, 4 October 2021, nos 2105744 and 2105745 (suspension of an environmental authorization for the renewal and extension of a quarry).

[58] We use the term 'space' as some areas are not protected on the basis of environmental considerations.

[59] See the 1976 law (n 26).

demarcation between species and spaces.[60] This leaves out of the picture several elements of biodiversity: local and indigenous communities and access and benefit sharing of biodiversity.

The topic of local and indigenous communities, which is central to international biodiversity law, sits at odds with the French legal system. Indeed, under French constitutional law, the French population is considered as being one.[61] This constitutional concept of unity prevents French national laws from recognizing specific legal categories that would create a demarcation between different citizens in terms of rights.[62] This stands in stark contrast, for instance, with countries such as Canada or Bolivia, where indigenous communities have a specific status.[63] The consequence of this constitutional configuration is that there are no cases involving the rights of indigenous and local communities relating to biodiversity.[64]

To our knowledge, there have been no cases involving access and benefit sharing of genetic resources before the French courts. There is, however, a case involving a French national research institution (Institut de Recherche pour le Développement) and the indigenous communities in Guyana that has been deferred to the European Patent Office.[65] The topic of genes—often linked to access and benefit sharing—is a topic of litigation in France, but specifically for genetically modified organisms (GMOs).[66]

3.3 Biodiversity Litigation, a Balancing Exercise

Here, we will examine in closer detail cases that have dealt directly with biodiversity. We understand these cases as those where the crux of the dispute concerned the interpretation of biodiversity-related facts (what is the state of biodiversity?) or the interpretation of biodiversity-related rules (what it the content of a norm?). This presentation of biodiversity litigation will be centred around two themes. First, cases that deal directly with the management of

[60] Simon Jolivet, 'Espaces naturels: les nouvelles frontières de la protection' (2016) 41 Revue Juridique de l'Environnement 629.

[61] Article 1 of the 1958 Constitution.

[62] This was highlighted by the Conseil Constitutionnel with regard to Corsica, C Const, 09 May 1991, Decision no 91-290 DC.

[63] See Chapter 4 on Canada in this volume.

[64] Though traditional practices have been acknowledged in Guyana, see CE, 17 November 1999, no 196531.

[65] The patent was, in the end, delivered; see European Patent Office, European Patent Register, EP2443126. On this saga, see Philippe Karpe and Catherine Aubertin, 'Une occasion manquée pour les droits des autochtones (et au-delà) . . .' (2019) 44 Revue Juridique de l'Environnement 313.

[66] For a recent example, see CE, 15 April 2016, no 376809 (annulment of prohibition of certain GMOs).

species, where judges will have to settle disputes on the life, or death, of certain species. Secondly, the protection of spaces, either as a mean to preserve species or as a conservation objective in its own right.

As this paragraph will show, it can be said that biodiversity litigation before an administrative judge is often a question of the balancing of interests. On the one hand, environmental interests recognized by law and, on the other hand, economic and societal interests. However, despite a legislative attempt at having a system that favours the environment, it appears that biodiversity is often on the losing side of this balancing exercise.

3.3.1 Managing species

By managing species, we refer to the different actions that the French state will allow or undertake and that will have an effect on the population and individual well-being of species. This covers, inter alia, derogations from the statute of protected endangered species, decisions to reintroduce certain individuals to a species to enhance its conservation status, and the management of invasive alien species. These cases are prime examples of biopolitics, where the state exercises its authority and governance over both the life and death of living elements on its territory.[67] The cases that are illustrative of this approach are too numerous to mention here. In this section, we will focus on two sides of the same coin: cases where judges had to examine the legality of reintroducing species in the French environment and cases where judges had to examine the legality of an authorization to destroy members of a protected species under French law.

3.3.1.1 Reintroducing species

The reintroduction of bears (*Ursus arctos*) within French borders is emblematic of this species management and the disputes to which it can lead. Pyrenean bears have been the topic of public policies since the 1980s in France, but their presence has been met with opposition from shepherds who feared for their livestock. As the bear population was reaching a critical point, the French government, in the context of the LIFE programme, decided to collaborate with the Slovenian government to reintroduce bears. This led to several attempt at reintroduction that were often contested by local actors.[68] One dispute on reintroduction took place following a 2006 decision by the Ministry for the

[67] On this theme, see, inter alia, Vito De Lucia, 'Beyond Anthropocentrism and Ecocentrism: A Biopolitical Reading of Environmental Law' (2017) 11 Journal of Human Rights and the Environment 224.

[68] eg TA Pau, 2 July 1996, no 97-42; CE, 20 May 2005, no 261564.

Environment which was, yet again, contested by associations and municipalities which feared for the security of livestock. In examining the legality of the decision to reintroduce the bear population, the Conseil d'État considered several factors, for instance the lack of prior evaluation or consultation, and the internal legality of a reintroduction decision.[69] The judge highlighted that while the bear population was not declining overall at the European level, it was indeed in the French Pyrenees.[70] As such, preventing the disappearance of the bear in that region had to be considered as a public interest objective in accordance with article L.110-1 of the Environmental Code.[71] Arguments on the danger of the bear to humans and livestock were discarded as no bear attack had been recorded for over 150 years, and the government had taken several preventive measures to reduce the risk of attacks on livestock.[72] Here, the judge favoured environmental interests over the fears of certain local communities as such fears had not been found to be grounded in objectivity.

3.3.1.2 Destroying or protecting species?

In the same way that the state can reintroduce a species because it is deemed to be threatened and declining, so can it allow for the destruction of individuals of a protected species under certain circumstances. Endangered species are protected under French law by article L.411-1 of the Environmental Code.[73] This article not only prohibits destruction but also bans any action that could have a detrimental effect on the species and ecosystems listed as protected under French law, for instance intentional perturbations, captures, purchases, etc. Importantly, this article also extends the legal protection to the habitats of protected species. Certain areas will be protected not for their own sake, but for the sake of the species within them.[74]

There are, however, exceptions to this protection. Article L.411-2. §.4 of the same code allows for derogations in certain situations, for instance if a species is threatening agriculture,[75] or if the derogation is made in the context of a project which has been deemed to be of 'major public interest'.[76] Whatever the reason for the derogation may be, it has to be strictly demonstrated that there were no other alternatives and that the derogation does not harm the

[69] CE, 23 February 2009, no 292397.
[70] ibid.
[71] ibid.
[72] ibid.
[73] This article results from the transposition of arts 16 et seq of Directive 92/43/EC of 21 May 1992.
[74] This is the purpose of the *arrêté biotope* which can be taken by local authorities to preserve the habitat of endangered species. See Décree no 2018-1180, 19 December 2018.
[75] Article L.411-2, 4th, b) of the Environmental Code.
[76] Article L.411-2, 4th, c) of the Environmental Code.

keeping in a favourable conservation status of the species concerned in their natural area.[77] Derogations to article L.411-1 are administrative acts that are frequently contested by environmental associations and there is a profuse case law on that matter.[78] These cases offer insights in how administrative judges interpret and assess facts in biodiversity cases. In this section, we will offer examples where derogations have been deemed legal as well as cases where the judge has declared that the necessary conditions for the derogation have not been met. Specifically, we will examine derogation for agricultural reasons and public interest reasons.

The legal saga of wolves in the Pyrenees is emblematic of how a judge will consider the legality of such derogations. Particularly, two recent cases offer an interesting insight into the clash of interests that can occur in the field of conservation. In 2018, an *arrêté* was taken by the Ministry for the Environment in order to determine the number of wolves that could be destroyed each year. This *arrêté* was taken in compliance with article L.411-2 of the Environmental Code. It was contested on both sides: by shepherds and municipalities who considered that it did not do enough to protect agricultural interests, and by environmental associations which considered that it was a threat to the conservation of wolves in the region. Both requests were rejected by the Conseil d'État which gave a detailed analysis of the law and facts in both cases. In the case initiated by shepherds and municipalities, the Conseil d'État mainly discussed the legality of the *arrêté*, highlighting, inter alia, that it did not conflict with other rights claimed by the plaintiff (eg an alleged 'right to hunt').[79] The case by the environmental associations offers a more detailed view of how judges examine the conditions for derogation. In a 2021 case,[80] the judge successively determined that the cause of the derogation was genuine (the threat to livestock), that no other alternatives were available, and that the derogation were not a threat to the conservation of wolves in the region. On the first element, the judge highlighted that attacks on livestock had occurred on numerous occasions in the region and that some livestock were located in areas labelled as 'colonization fronts' for wolves, thus making them particularly vulnerable.[81] On the element of absence of alternatives, the judge highlighted that

[77] These conditions being cumulative and distinct: CE, 30 December 2021, no 439766; CAA Lyon, 21 March 2017, no 14LY03096.

[78] According to an analysis of the case law conducted by DREAL Occitanie over the period from 2010 to January 2020, 56 per cent of 'protected species' derogations were suspended or cancelled by the administrative judge (seventy out of 125).

[79] CE, 8 July 2020, no 423342, para 17.

[80] CE, 15 February 2021, no 434933.

[81] ibid para 15.

the destruction of wolves by means of shooting was only allowed under strict conditions, for instance if it has been deemed by an expert organization that the livestock could not be protected by other means due to its particularities, or its proximity to colonization fronts.[82] Finally, on the threat to conservation, the Conseil d'État referred to expertise produced by several public institutions that documented the growth rate of wolf populations in the region.[83] It came to the conclusion that the percentage of destruction allowed by the government (10 to 12 per cent) was not a threat considering the overall health of the wolf population.

Derogations for projects of 'major public interest' are also often contested and lead to disputes where the judges will have to determine whether a project is indeed of major public interest. This concept is interpreted strictly by the administrative judge; the existence of an indisputable public interest around a project is not necessarily sufficient to characterize it as of 'major public interest'[84] and the project must be of such importance that it can be balanced with the objective of conserving natural habitats, wild fauna, and flora.[85] Economic and social considerations can be considered as constitutive of a major public interest. This examination varies greatly depending on each case thus creating legal uncertainty where it may be difficult to anticipate the relative importance placed on it by the judges.

For instance, a road project that was intended to alleviate traffic and shorten the time needed to traverse the town was considered as not being of major public interest.[86] A derogation from the protection of endangered species for the construction of the road was consequently declared illegal. Larger road projects, particularly highways, are more often seen as fulfilling the condition of major public interest. In 2010, the Conseil d'État considered that a highway project that was intended to enhance the fluidity of regional and national traffic, while also increasing security for drivers, fulfilled the condition of public interest.[87] This highlighted that in addition to serving a public interest, the project was accompanied by several measures aimed at limiting its environmental impact on protected species.[88] The same balancing exercise can

[82] ibid para 22.
[83] ibid para 28.
[84] TA Dijon, ord, 27 February 2013, no 1300303, confirmed by CE, 29 October 2013, no 366803.
[85] CE, 3 June 2020, no 425395.
[86] CE, 28 December 2018, no 419918.
[87] CE, 16 April 2010, no 320667. For similar cases involving highways, and with a similar outcome, see CE, 17 December 2020, no 439201; TA Toulouse, 6 September 2018, no 1502207; TA Orléans, 15 April 2021, no 1803356.
[88] CE, 16 April 2010, no 320667.

be seen in a project for waste management,[89] for the production of energy,[90] for the construction of shopping centres,[91] and mining projects.[92]

The cases on renewable energy are particularly interesting as they highlight that different environmental objectives can clash, with, on the one hand, an attempt to move away from fossil fuel and, on the other hand, the necessity to preserve endangered species and biodiversity more generally.[93] This echoes the often-made observation that in the fight against climate change, biodiversity is still the loser in most scenarios.[94]

What becomes obvious when reading these cases is that biodiversity law does not trump economic and social development but necessitates that such development is made within environmentally acceptable limits. However, even though such legal limits exist, they have not been sufficient to stop the erosion of biodiversity in France. For instance, the artificialization of France's soil—one of the main drivers of biodiversity loss—is ongoing[95] and it seems that such a legal framework amounts to additional procedural burdens for the designers of infrastructure projects than an actual conservation tool.

3.3.2 Protecting habitats and other spaces

Numerous legal classifications exist in French law to preserve the habitats of endangered species, sensitive areas, or remarkable environment.[96] Some are only meant to be tools for better knowledge of the environment,[97] while others prohibit certain activities within an area[98] or impose a positive restoration obligation.[99] Within this array of conservation tools, some are only intended for ecosystems that are considered as particularly important, such as coastal areas, mountains ecosystems, or forests. Some areas will be protected by virtue of the

[89] CAA Marseille, 12 July 2016, nos 16MA00072 and 16MA00071.

[90] eg a project for the construction of wind turbines that were expected to disturb a population of protected bats was declared of major public interest. CE, 15 April 2021, no 430500. The same approach can be seen in CE, 10 March 2022, no 439784.

[91] CE, 24 July 2019, no 414353.

[92] CE, 3 June 2020, no 425395.

[93] See eg CE, 15 April 2021, no 430500 (n 90).

[94] IPBES and IPBES-IPCC cosponsored workshop 'Biodiversity and Climate Change Scientific Outcomes' (IPBES 2021) section 3.

[95] See Artificialisation des sols <www.ecologie.gouv.fr/artificialisation-des-sols> accessed 31 March 2022.

[96] For a complete analysis, see Michel Prieur and others, *Droit de l'environnement* (n 25) 461–624.

[97] eg the *Zone naturelle d'intérêt écologique, faunistique et floristique* (Natural area of ecological, faunistic and floral interest) (art L.411-5 of the Environmental Code).

[98] eg natural reserves.

[99] Such as the priority areas for biodiversity (Zones Prioritaires pour la Biodiversité). Décree no 2017-176 du 13 février 2017 relatif aux zones prioritaires pour la biodiversité.

presence of protected species.[100] Such habitat protection operates through the legal framework described earlier, complemented by specific regulatory acts.

In this section, we will focus on two different types of disputes concerning protected areas. First, the disputes relating to protected areas where the environment is protected as such, irrespective of a specific conservation objective for endangered species. Secondly, we will examine cases concerning areas that are protected irrespective of environmental considerations, for instance for aesthetic considerations. Natura 2000 areas are also important as are the national areas, but litigation in these areas is more often dealt with at the EU level, while national courts focus on other legal instruments.[101]

What is obvious in all these cases is that judges do not really engage with the merit of establishing such protected areas. Rather, the bulk of the legal reasoning will concern procedural.

3.3.2.1 Spaces in themselves: the establishment of protected areas

The various protected areas that exist in French law are important tools for meeting the international objectives set in the context of the CBD.[102] However, the creation of parks, natural reserves, and other types of protected areas, is often met with defiance from the local communities who will have to change their behaviour in and around these newly established zones. This has led to frequent legal disputes on the creation of parks or reserves where various elements can be contested. Often, the rules on activities within those protected areas will be seen as unfavourable by certain associations. For instance, in May 2021 the Conseil d'État requested a modification of the decree establishing the Chastreix–Sancy natural reserve, as it prohibited in a disproportionate manner the pastimes of alpinism and rock climbing. To reach such a decision, the court took into consideration several reports highlighting that while rock climbing was indeed a threat to species within the reserve, the prohibition of alpinism during the winter was not grounded in convincing scientific data.[103]

Sometimes it is the very creation of such a protected area that will be at the heart of a dispute. Here, the case law is mainly centred on procedural aspects relating to the appropriate information and consultation with the public. With regard to discussing the actual merits of establishing a protected area (park or natural reserve), an administrative judge tends to acknowledge the relevance

[100] *Arrêtés biotopes* (n 74).
[101] See Chapter 11 on the EU in this volume.
[102] CBD, 2021, CBD/WG2020/3/3, First draft of the post-2020 global biodiversity framework, 2030 action targets, target 3.
[103] CE, 5 May 2021, no 433553.

of creating such zones as highlighted by the scientific and factual elements submitted during the dispute. For instance, in 2017 the French government created a marine natural park in Martinique, a French overseas territory.[104] The decision was opposed by the local municipality which argued that the consultation with local actors had not been properly conducted and that the decision to create such a park was unnecessary as several management measures were already in place at the time. On this last element, and after having verified the relevance of the consultation procedures, the Conseil d'État stated that no elements submitted in the dispute indicated that the protection of the marine environment in Martinique did not warrant the creation of a park. Consequently, the decision could not be annulled on that basis.[105]

It seems that disputes relating to these types of protected areas are much more about procedures than they are about scientific relevance. We have not found a single case where an administrative judge considered that the creation of a protected area was unjustified after considering the available scientific knowledge.

3.3.2.2 Spaces for humans: landscape and world heritage

In some cases, biodiversity can be protected through a strictly anthropocentric lens, irrespective of any environmental considerations. This can be the case when certain areas are protected because of the value they hold in the eyes of humans; for instance, world heritage sites or landscapes that have been classified as protected. These spaces may be important for biodiversity but are not primarily protected for that reason. Nevertheless, the restrictions imposed in those areas can be beneficial for species and their habitats.

The protection of such spaces is often connected to international commitments such as the World Heritage Convention or the European Landscape Convention,[106] although the French legal system had already envisioned the protection of landscapes and monuments prior to those instruments.[107] Disputes related to these elements will often concern either the decision to classify an area as protected because of its value as a landscape or for world heritage reasons or the decision to allow modifications to such areas.

For instance, in November 2020 the Conseil d'État had to consider whether the decision to classify the landscape of the Canal du Midi as a protected

[104] Decree no 2017-784 of 5 May 2017.
[105] CE, 15 May 2019, no 412087.
[106] European Landscape Convention (opened for signature 20 October 2000, entered in force 1 March 2004) 2296 UNTS 141.
[107] Untermaier, Une innovation durable (n 29).

site was legal.[108] The decision was contested by several municipalities which claimed that the decision was not actually meant to protect a landscape but, rather, to influence agricultural and urbanistic practices. After having analysed whether the procedural requirements had been met, the Conseil d'État then examined whether the decision was in line with the objectives of article L.341-1 of the Environmental Code. In doing so, it considered that the classification of 'non-remarkable' sites was meant to ensure the coherence of the protected landscape as a whole and did not constitute a subversion of article L.341-1 for other purposes. Therefore, as a protected landscape, the area was less likely to be subject to further urbanization, thus alleviating a potential driver of biodiversity loss.

3.4 Conclusion: An Overall Assessment of Recent Trends in French Biodiversity Litigation

These examples of biodiversity litigation are far from exhaustive. More could be said on the management of forests,[109] fisheries,[110] mines,[111] or agriculture.[112] What is constant, however, is the fact that biodiversity litigation is a balancing exercise between environmental interests and other interests and also that the litigation highlights that the French state not only protects species and habitats but it also manages them, controlling both their existence and destruction through administrative acts. As a result, it cannot be said that a French administrative judge is clearly pro or anti-environment. Our study has shown that all will depend on the elements that are provided for the balancing exercise.

This observation leads us to the question the place of expertise in this jurisprudence. In the cases before administrative courts, this expertise is somewhat 'invisible'. Judges will often use the sentence '*les éléments du dossier*' (elements of the case) to indicate that their analysis is based on reports and documents provided by the claimant and the defendant. In the French system, administrative judges have inquisitorial powers, meaning that they have the possibility of various investigative measures, including seeking expertise, to determine the

108 CE, 4 November 2020, no 416017.
109 See, inter alia, CE, 11 May 2007, no 272091 (on codes of good practice for forest management).
110 See, inter alia, CE, 23 December 2021, no 459225 (on the bycatch of dolphins).
111 See, inter alia, CE, 25 February 2019, no 410170 (on a mining project in Guyana).
112 See, inter alia, CE, ord, 15 Mach 2021, no 450194 (on the use of pesticides and their impact on bees).

facts. However, in practice, judges rarely use these powers and essentially rely on elements provided by the claimants in each case. Claimants benefit from the principle of 'freedom of proof', meaning that they can back up their claims by any means, and the judge will then assess their credibility.[113] However, this process is not made explicit in the available text of the cases. Nevertheless, what we do see in the above-mentioned litigation examples, is that administrative judges will base their decisions on reports by scientific bodies, thus showing a willingness to engage with scientific knowledge.[114]

Finally, it seems that biodiversity litigation remains very much litigation concerned with remarkable or endangered biodiversity. Most of the cases we have analysed for this chapter involved endangered species or remarkable areas. We are yet to see litigation of 'ordinary biodiversity'[115] even though the 2016 law intends to extend legal protection to this type of biodiversity.

4. The Ambivalent Place of International Biodiversity Law in French Biodiversity Litigation

In this section, we will provide an analysis of one of the main questions of this edited volume: what is the influence of IBL on national biodiversity litigation? To answer this question, we will first expand on an observation made in the opening sections of the chapter: IBL, due to its characteristics, is unlikely to be directly implemented by national judges in France. However, this does not mean that IBL is absent from their analysis and, as such, it does exercise a form of conceptual influence on several cases. After having made these observations, we then ask an opening question: what would be the added value of directly implementing IBL in biodiversity-related disputes? We argue that in the French context, there is only a slight added value to such a possibility. Indeed, IBL does not seem to have many legal or regulatory gaps to fill. It would, however, bring more coherence to the jurisprudence if judges refer to IBL when relevant rather than excluding its application for unconvincing reasons.

[113] Hervé de Gaudemar, 'La preuve devant le juge administratif' (2009) 6 Droit Administratif 12.

[114] For recent studies on this matter, see Anne Jacquemet-Gauché, 'Le juge administratif face aux connaissances scientifiques' (2022) 8 Actualite Juridique Droit Administratif 443 and Elisanda Malaret, 'Le rôle des juges face à la fiabilité des données et à la qualité de leur traitement dans les procédures décisionnelles de l'administration' (2020) 173 Revue Française d'Administration Publique 19.

[115] Understood as biodiversity that is not explicitly protected under French law (n 32).

4.1 The Restrictive Conditions for the Use of International Law by National Judges

In France, international treaties are immediately applicable in the French legal system, as per the French Constitution.[116] However, this immediate effect does not mean that all treaties will have direct effect. This distinction between immediate and direct effect is an important one for understanding the potential legal influence of IBL on litigation. Immediate effect implies that a treaty will be incorporated in the French legal system without first having to be translated into law. This is one of the consequences of a monist legal system. But even though all ratified treaties become part of the legal system, this does not mean that they can be directly invoked by persons in the context of litigation. Judges will control whether laws or regulatory acts comply with international law,[117] but will only directly apply international law if it satisfies certain conditions.[118]

The first condition is that the international norm invoked is sufficiently precise and non-conditional for the judge to directly rely on it. For instance, article 12 of the International Covenant on Economic, Social and Cultural Rights[119] was considered by the Conseil d'État as not being sufficiently precise and non-conditional to be invoked by a claimant.[120]

The second condition for international law to be invoked by judges is that it is considered as intended to create rights for individuals. This means that the treaty invoked in a dispute is not meant simply to regulate relations between states, but also to create rights for individuals. Following this logic, French judges have determined that article 6 of the Aarhus Convention[121] could be directly invoked by claimants and defendants in courts.[122]

These conditions leave out of the courtroom most instruments of IBL. For instance, the substantial environmental obligations of the CBD are notoriously vague.[123] This approach is quite common in international environmental law

[116] Article 55.

[117] The seminal cases being CE, 20 October 1989, no 108243 (Nicolo), C Cass, 24 May 1975, no 73-13.556 (Jacques Vabre).

[118] See CE, 11 April 2012, no 322326. As previously mentioned, this does not apply to EU law, which is directly implemented by French judges as ordinary judges for the EU legal order.

[119] International Covenant on Economic, Social and Cultural Rights (opened for signature 16 December 1966, entered in force 3 January 1976) 993 UNTS 3.

[120] CE, 26 November 2005, no 248357. Still on the same covenant, see CE, 5 March 1999, no 194658. The same conditions apply before the ECJ (see Chapter 11 on the EU in this volume).

[121] Article 6 on public participation in decisions on specific activities.

[122] CE, 15 November 2021, no 434742.

[123] So much so that some have been deemed as not creating any obligations at all by the International Court of Justice, ICJ, *Certain Activities Carried Out by Nicaragua in the Border Area (Costa Rica v Nicaragua)* and *Construction of a Road in Costa Rica along the San Juan River (Nicaragua*

where many treaties share this characteristic. Consequently, the Conseil d'État has explicitly rejected direct effect for the CBD and the Ramsar Convention on numerous occasions. In 1995, the Conseil d'État rendered a decision determining whether the public interest status of a high-speed rail project had been lawfully determined.[124] The associations disputing this decision argued that the envisioned project would be contrary to the obligations of the Ramsar Convention as it would damage protected wetlands. The court in considering this argument, stated that the Ramsar Convention creates rights and obligations between states but does not create rights for private persons. Therefore, it could not be invoked by the associations contesting the legality of the administrative decision in question. The same analysis, this time concerning the CBD, can be seen in the case previously mentioned on the reintroduction of the bear in the Pyrenees.[125] Here, the Conseil d'État also stated that the CBD only created obligations between states and could not be invoked by private persons in a legal dispute.

Though it would seem that the direct legal influence of IBL is simply not conceivable in the French legal systems, we have found some cases that blur the lines. In February 2020, the Conseil d'État had to examine the legality of an implicit rejection by the administration of a modification request of a decision containing the list of protected species in the Caribbean overseas territories and the modalities of their protection.[126] The associations disputing the decision invoked the fact that the current decision was contrary to the Kingston Protocol[127] of the Cartagena Convention. In this case, the Conseil d'État effectively engaged in an analysis of the decision in regard to France's international commitment and concluded that it had failed to meet it. Therefore, it had to be modified accordingly.[128]

We can also mention a 2019 case on the creation of a marine reserve in Martinique.[129] Here, the administrative judge had to determine whether the

v Costa Rica) (Judgment) [2015] ICJ Rep 665, para 164. See Chapter 12 on international biodiversity litigation in this volume.

[124] CE, 17 November 1995, no 159855.

[125] CE, 23 February 2009, no 292397.

[126] CE, 5 February 2020, no 422631.

[127] Protocol concerning specially protected areas and wildlife to the Convention for the protection and development of the marine environment of the wider Caribbean region (opened for signature 18 January 1990, entered in force 17 June 2000) 2180 UNTS 101.

[128] This decision highlights the intricacies of French administrative law as, here, the decision in dispute was not the decision itself, but the implicit refusal to modify it. The examination of this implicit refusal led to a legal analysis of the decision, but the conclusion of this case is that the implicit refusal—that constitutes in itself an administrative act—had to be annulled and that therefore the government had to modify the decision.

[129] See n 105.

park would constitute a violation of the United Nations Convention on the Law of the Sea (UNCLOS). It concluded that it did not, but the reasoning indicates that international law was use in the case.

4.2 A Different Function: International Biodiversity Law as an Elements of Legal and Factual Interpretation

The absence of direct legal relevance does not leave IBL entirely out of the frame of biodiversity litigation in France. Several cases show that IBL has an impact on how judges will interpret laws and facts in biodiversity-related cases. In such situations, IBL is not meant to be implemented; rather it serves as part of the reasoning in assessing the facts. Therefore, there is no limitation in the nature of norms being used, and both hard law and soft law may be mobilized, as the following examples highlight.

In 2020, the Ministry for the Environment issued a decision that authorized the hunting of the European turtle dove for the 2020–21 period. The Ligue de Protection des Oiseaux contested the decision, arguing that the dove was in an unfavourable state of conservation and it initiated a *référé* procedure to suspend the decision. In that context, the Conseil d'État had to evaluate whether there was indeed an urgency and any serious doubt about the legality of the act.[130] On this second condition, the court examined whether the contested act was compliant with articles L.424-1 and L.425.16 of the Environmental Code that specify that the ministry can take a decision to preserve and enhance the population of birds and that 'adaptive management' has to be implemented to that end. To interpret these articles, the court first noted that expert reports by several organizations, both national and international, highlighted the endangered status of the European turtle dove. With regard to 'adaptive management', the court referred to an action plan adopted by the parties to the AEWA[131] in 2018,[132] that indicated the criteria that adaptive management should follow. It then went on to note that the final decision adopted by the ministry disregarded both that international action plan and the recommendations of a national committee specifically set up to issue recommendations on adaptive

[130] CE, ord, 11 September 2020, no 443482.

[131] Agreement on the Conservation of African-Eurasian Migratory Waterbirds (opened for signature 15 August 1996, entered in force 1 November 1999) 2365 UNTS 203.

[132] European Commission, International Single Species Action Plan for the Conservation of the European Turtle Dove *Streptopelia turtur* (2018 to 2028), LIFE14 PRE/UK/000002 Project. This action plan was adopted in the context of AEWA, 2012, Resolution 5.8 Adoption and Implementation of International Single Species Action Plans and Species Management Plans.

management. Therefore, the contested act was suspended in accordance with articles L.425-16 and L.425-17 of the Environmental Code interpreted in the light of an action plan; that is, a soft law instrument of IBL.[133] The difference between direct implementation and interpretative influence appears to be minimal in practical terms: in this case, IBL could exert its influence because of national norms that opened the way for its influence.

Interestingly, IBL can also serve as a tool for assessing the vulnerability of species or habitats. It then becomes a tool of factual analysis rather than legal interpretation. This has been demonstrated in numerous cases on wetlands. For instance, in 2011 the Conseil d'État examined whether the annulment of a declaration of public utility by the Appellate Administrative Court was appropriate.[134] In this case, the Appellate Court had annulled a declaration of public utility for a resort project that was likely to have a serious impact on some particularly sensitive areas which were listed under the Ramsar Convention. In the factual analysis of the sensitivity of these areas, the judge indicated that their listing under several international, regional, and national zones (among which the Ramsar Convention) was indicative of their 'environmental quality'.[135] Other types of areas which benefit from international protection are often mentioned in environmental litigation; for instance, areas labelled as 'World Common Heritage' under the UNESCO Convention. In many disputes concerning 'declarations of public utility' which can then lead to derogation from legal protection of biodiversity, judges have taken into consideration the fact that areas that could be affected by such projects came under the UNESCO regime. This was the case, for instance, in a wind farm project which was going to be close to the Causse du Larzac, which is labelled as a World Common Heritage site.[136]

As a tool for factual interpretation, the level of normativity of IBL becomes irrelevant; it is referenced alongside scientific assessments and soft declarations.[137] Also, its use by judges is unpredictable, with some cases being surprisingly silent with regard to IBL. For instance, a case on the legal definition of wetlands under French law made no mention of the Ramsar Convention even though its influence was obviously looming over the legal analysis by the judge.[138]

[133] Other examples of such an approach can be seen in CE, Ord 6 February 2019, no 427504.
[134] CE, 20 May 2011, no 325552.
[135] ibid.
[136] CAA Bordeaux, 19 May 2020, no 19BX00504.
[137] eg the UICN Red List, CE, ord 26 August 2019, no 433434.
[138] CE, 22 February 2017, no 386325.

4.3 The Added Value of Implementing International Biodiversity Law in National Disputes

As we have just seen, IBL is not designed in a way that allows for its direct implementation, even though a few cases might create some confusion as to the attitude of judges with regard to international environmental law. However, as a tool for legal and factual interpretation, IBL can have a considerable impact on the analyses of judges; so much so that the difference with direct implementation, in practical terms, might become irrelevant.

This raises a question: should IBL be directly applicable in biodiversity litigation cases? Two elements indicate that this approach would be welcomed. First, the literature on the use of international law by French judges is already quite critical of their attitude towards conditions for direct implementation. Authors stress that this attitude might weaken international instruments within the national context.[139] Secondly, claimants in biodiversity litigation cases very often make reference to IBL to strengthen their arguments. This strategy seems to imply that, despite the already known attitude of administrative courts towards IBL, the use of international law in legal arguments is nevertheless considered as impactful.

We believe that the effectiveness of biodiversity law would benefit from the direct implementation of IBL by judges, although the gain would only be at the margins. Judges are already interpreting national rules in the light of IBL, and we believe that this attitude should become more frequent in order to ensure more coherence between France's commitments at the global level and the national legal system. The direct implementation of IBL would only serve the purpose of filling eventual legal gaps in the framework for biodiversity. However, as we discussed earlier, such gaps are bound to be scarce as the legal framework for biodiversity is already significantly dense and complex. In practical terms, this type of direct application would assist in cases where the legality of an administrative act would have to be determined in relation to IBL if no national rules yet existed on the matter. In full litigation, this could be used to determine the responsibility of the state if the damage resulted from a disregard of

[139] Hélène Tigroudja, 'Le juge administratif français et l'effet direct des engagements internationaux' (2003) 1 Revue Française De droit Administratif 154; Marie Gautier, 'L'effet direct des conventions internationales' (2012) 3 Revue Française de droit Administratif 560; Delphine Burriez, 'Retour sur les critères de l'effet direct depuis l'arrêt GISTI du Conseil d'État du 11 avril 2012' (2015) 5 Revue Française de droit Administratif 1031; Xavier Domino, 'Les aléas de l'effet direct' (2012) 17 Actualité Juridique Droit Administratif 936. This approach to the applicability of international law has even been referred to as 'disguised dualism', CE, 19 November 2020, no 427301, Conclusions of Public Rapporteur Stéphane Hoynck.

IBL. This was the case at the EU level when France was declared responsible of breaching the Barcelona Convention and its protocols because of the pollution of the Étang de Berre.[140]

Finally, the consistent use of IBL in disputes would ensure that national norms that are in obvious violation of international rules would be annulled or not implemented in the context of disputes. Although such an occurrence would be rare considering the vagueness of many IBL rules, this would at least ensure legal certainty and coherence within biodiversity law.

5. The Relevance of Biodiversity Litigation as a Concept in the French Context

Biodiversity litigation is far from being an innovation in the French legal context. In a way, biodiversity litigation is probably as old as public litigation itself in France, which laws deal with pollution since, at least, the nineteenth century.[141] More generally, it seems that biodiversity litigation is undiscernible from environmental litigation in the discourse of scholars and practitioners alike. This stands in stark contrast to climate change litigation which recently saw some landmark cases in France[142] and is gaining a great deal of attention as a field of litigation in its own right.[143]

So what would be the added value of using such a concept? We believe that it could accelerate the modernization of judges' reasoning in cases dealing with biodiversity. We see in the jurisprudence that recent cases dealing with biodiversity showcase the fact that French administrative judges now take full consideration of the systemic nature of the environment. For instance, in a recent case dealing with 'pests', the judge annulled part of an administrative act authorizing the destruction of certain species.[144] In doing so, the judge provided a case-by-case analysis of the conservation status of those species, their actual harmful impact, and also their role in the ecosystem they occupy. However, it

140 ECJ, Case C-213/03 *Commission v France* (2004) ECLI:EU:C:2004:464 (Pêcheurs de l'étang de Berre).

141 Décret impérial du 15 October 1810 relatif aux Manufactures et Ateliers qui répandent une odeur insalubre ou incommode.

142 TA Paris, 14 October 2021, nos 1904967, 1904968, 1904972, and 1904976/4-1 (also known as '*l'affaire du siècle*'). CE, 19 November 2020, no 427301. For a commentary on these cases and what they entail for the future of climate change litigation in France, see, inter alia, Marta Torre-Schaub, 'Le contentieux climatique: du passé vers l'avenir' (2022) 1 Revue Française de droit Administratif 75.

143 See Christel Cournil and Leandro Varison (eds), *Les procès climatiques: entre le national et l'international* (Pedone 2018).

144 CE, 7 July 2021, no 432485.

seems that the modernization of the approach of judges is inextricably linked to the semantics of the applicable law. For instance, we see that the use of the term 'ecosystem' only became widespread once it had been incorporated in various codes.[145] In a sense, the conceptual leeway of judges in France seems bounded by what is contained in the texts. We believe that engaging explicitly in 'biodiversity litigation' could open this conceptual toolbox and allow for legal reasoning that is more open to the complex and dynamic nature of biodiversity.

Also, recognizing 'biodiversity litigation' as a concept could help to bring more attention to an environmental crisis that is sometimes overshadowed by climate change. It is well established that climate and biodiversity are interlinked and that climate change will have an impact of biodiversity. However, even if we were to tackle climate change effectively in the near future, it does not seem that it would necessarily mean that biodiversity would be significantly preserved. Indeed, it has been highlighted that biodiversity is often on the losing end of environmental effort. In other words, promoting the concept of biodiversity litigation could help to keep this priority afloat while we are also focusing our efforts on climate change mitigation and adaptation.

6. Conclusion: The Future of Biodiversity Litigation in France

To envision the future of biodiversity litigation in France, it is necessary to consider the evolution of IBL, the main environmental policy choices of the French government, and the current trends in litigation.

With regard to the first element, and as we noted in the presentation of biodiversity law in France, the strategic plan for biodiversity and the national action plans do not seem to have an influence on biodiversity litigation. It is therefore unlikely that the post-2020 global framework for biodiversity will influence litigation. What would have an impact is either the adoption of new national laws for the better implementation of IBL (as a continuation of the 2016 effort) or the adoption of new international instruments which can have an influence on litigation, although an unpredictable one.

Beyond this uncertain future, it seems that a source of tension, and therefore litigation, will be between competing environmental objectives. As we have mentioned, renewable energy projects are sometimes at the heart of

[145] The Ariane database of the Conseil d'État shows that the use of the concept of an ecosystem only became common in the mid-2000s.

biodiversity-related disputes and this creates a dilemma between mitigation objectives and conservation objectives. As the climate urgency keeps growing, and with the multiplicity of commitments to leave fossil energy behind, France is bound to invest massively in renewable energy and nuclear energy in the future. The open question is now on the compatibility of such a trajectory with the conservation of certain endangered species. In this context, judges will surely have to continue their balancing exercise and it is difficult to anticipate which element they will favour.

Another aspect of the future of biodiversity litigation is in the development of civil cases. We chose to focus on administrative courts in this chapter for the reasons stated earlier. However, biodiversity litigation is likely to become more and more transversal, allowing for the intervention of different types of judges in this matter that was traditionally set in the realm of criminal and public law. With the development of contractual tools for conservation and sustainable use of biodiversity, this might become a major mutation of biodiversity litigation in the future.

Finally, it might be possible to see in the future cases similar to the major climate cases that we have seen in recent years, although it will be difficult to determine the role IBL will play in those case. Currently, a case is pending on the question of pesticide use and its impact on biodiversity.[146] Specifically, the French government is accused of not acting appropriately in controlling such substances.[147] However, a case akin to the climate change example is unlikely as there are no specific targets for the protection of biodiversity. There is no '2 degree' equivalent in biodiversity, thus making it difficult to determine whether or not policies are appropriate for the conservation of biodiversity. IBL does have, however, several sectoral targets which could be mobilized in a similar fashion (eg the 30 per cent objective for protected areas). The 'big' biodiversity cases will therefore likely be more situated than climate change cases.

Though the assessment of biodiversity law and litigation may seem bleak, the constant efforts of civil society in France to battle environmental degradation on all grounds is often met with success. The future may hold decisive cases where creative legal reasoning and persistence from environmental lawyers will yield powerful results.

[146] See n 2.
[147] ibid.

7

Biodiversity Litigation in India

A Typology of Cases and Varieties of Environmentalism

Arpitha Kodiveri

1. Introduction

'The dilemma of conserving biodiversity is not about saving individual species or geographies, it is an ethical choice of how we conserve, how we decide to balance rights and ensure that the poor are not marginalized' said a senior lawyer who has been practising before the Supreme Court in India for many years.[1] Biodiversity litigation in India has been an area of contestation over conserving individual species, geographies, and recognizing the rights of communities dependent on them. The courts in India, as will be argued in this chapter, are left to choose between a variety of environmentalism that permeates the cases that are filed before them and deployed by environmental movements in India.[2] Environmentalism in this chapter refers to an approach to protect the environment and its associated philosophical, ecological, and political underpinnings.[3] An example of this is environmentalism of the poor which refers to the need to consider the right to livelihood, resources, and the culture of the poor when decisions to conserve or protect the environment are taken.[4]

This chapter provides a schematic overview of the legal framework that governs biodiversity in India and a typology of cases concerning biodiversity. The question addressed in this chapter is how courts choose between the varieties of environmentalism and how does that shape biodiversity litigation and jurisprudence in India. The chapter will also address the role of international biodiversity law in informing the development of domestic biodiversity

[1] Interview with a senior lawyer by Arpitha Kodiveri in New Delhi in August 2019.

[2] Arpitha Kodiveri, 'Climate Change Litigation in India: Possibilities and Associated Challenges' in Cesar Rodriguez Garavito (ed), *Litigating the Climate Emergency: How Human Rights, Courts, and Legal Mobilization Can Bolster Climate Action* (CUP 2021).

[3] Ramchandra Guha, *Environmentalism: A Global History* (Penguin Books 2016).

[4] Joan Martínez-Alier, *The Environmentalism of the Poor* (Edward Elgar Publishing 2002).

Arpitha Kodiveri, *Biodiversity Litigation in India* In: *Biodiversity Litigation*. Edited by: Guillaume Futhazar, Sandrine Maljean-Dubois, and Jona Razzaque, Oxford University Press. © Arpitha Kodiveri, 2023.
DOI: 10.1093/oso/9780192865465.003.0007

jurisprudence. In addition, it will briefly examine the relationship between biodiversity litigation and climate change litigation, which is nascent in India.

The argument this chapter makes is that there are lessons to be drawn from the experience of biodiversity litigation which apply to present and future efforts of climate change litigation. While the courts in biodiversity litigation have reinforced the idea of exclusionary conservation, they have nonetheless developed jurisprudence that recognizes the participation of forest-dwelling communities and adopted ecocentric approaches.[5] The investigation at the intersection of environmentalism and biodiversity litigation sheds light on a similar struggle within international biodiversity law of exclusionary conservation, community participation, and ecocentric approaches. These jurisprudential pathways provide an antidote to the dilemma that the senior lawyer alluded to earlier which is a framework for making choices on biodiversity conservation that balance rights and secure the rights of marginalized communities.

The chapter begins in Section 2 with an overview of the Indian context and the specific legal regime to regulate biodiversity. The chapter will then highlight the role of the courts and the methodology used in case selection in Section 3. Section 4 will then provide an overview of the typology of cases and an analysis of the varieties of environmentalism and biodiversity litigation. Section 5 will explore the limitations in biodiversity litigation and the progressive shifts in biodiversity jurisprudence. Section 6 then provides a brief note on the relationship between biodiversity litigation and climate litigation.

2. Particularities of the Indian Context

2.1 India's Biodiversity

India is a megadiverse country that is rich in both species and geographical diversity and is reported to be home to 7–8 per cent of the globally recorded species. The diversity in landscapes includes wetlands, forests, mangroves, and marine environments. In terms of species diversity, too, India is blessed with 7.6 per cent of the world's mammalian population, 12.6 per cent of birds, and 6.2 per cent of the world's reptiles.[6] Many of these species are being threatened

[5] Abhayraj Naik, 'Law's Nature: Transformative Environmental Constitutionalism in the Supreme Court of India', *Seminar* (September 2019).

[6] Convention on Biological Diversity, Country Profile—India <www.cbd.int/countries/profile/?country=in> accessed 12 March 2022.

by habitat destruction and aggressive economic growth.[7] India has four of the thirty-six biodiversity hotspots which have been identified.[8] The sixth report submitted by the Indian government to the Secretariat of the Convention on Biological Diversity (CBD) chronicles how India is well on its way to meeting the Aichi Targets as well as the national biodiversity targets which have been set.[9] In a detailed analysis of budgetary allocations and schemes for biodiversity conservation, it identifies '116 public schemes from 24 ministries and 29 departments as biodiversity relevant' and underlines that 'technical work is under progress to identify workable solutions for raising additional resources for biodiversity'.[10]

The report identifies that the challenge with biodiversity regulation in India has been balancing development prerogatives, rights of local communities, and biodiversity conservation. The fifth report submitted by the Indian government to the Secretariat, identified habitat loss, fragmentation, and degradation as major threats to biodiversity.[11] These threats have, however, far from disappeared and India's political economy which is dependent on industrialization and rapid urbanization has only aggravated these threats. The newly approved National Mission on Biodiversity and Human Well-Being[12] is an ambitious effort to bring biodiversity conservation to the forefront of India's science and policy to document India's biodiversity, promote ecological restoration, and provide early warning systems for zoonoses. These steps are working to advance the mechanisms available for regulating biodiversity but, as the next section on the law will demonstrate, they remain in the realm of soft law.[13]

Another particularity about the Indian context is the varieties of environmentalism that shape legal and executive decision making. It becomes important to locate these different approaches of environmentalism to understand where biodiversity fits into the frame in the decision-making process. India and other countries in the global south subject to British colonial

[7] Tilker A Abrams and others, 'Habitat Degradation and Indiscriminate Hunting Differentially Impact Faunal Communities in the Southeast Asian Tropical Biodiversity Hotspot' (2019) 2(1) Communications Biology 396.

[8] Mukunda Dev Behera, Soumit Kumar Behera, and Subrat Sharma, 'Recent Advances an Biodiversity and Climate Change Studies in India' (2019) 28 Biodiversity and Conservation 1943–51.

[9] Sixth National Report submitted by India to the Biodiversity Secretariat <https://chm.cbd.int/database/record?documentID=241351> accessed 12 March 2022.

[10] ibid.

[11] Fifth National Report submitted by India to the Secretariat <www.cbd.int/doc/world/in/in-nr-05-en.pdf> accessed 12 March 2022.

[12] Kamaljit S Bawa and others, 'Securing Biodiversity, Securing Our Future: A National Mission on Biodiversity and Human Well-Being for India' (2021) 253 Biological Conservation 1.

[13] Anusha Krishnan, 'National Mission on Biodiversity and Human Well Being: For a Greener, Healthier and More Sustainable Way of Life', NCBS News (March 2020).

rule inherited forest laws from that period which were founded on an exclusionary notion of conservation. Forests and areas rich in biodiversity were also part of ecosystems on which the most marginalized communities depended for their livelihoods, particularly *Adivasi* or indigenous[14] communities.[15] As a way to accommodate the concerns of these communities, the environmentalism of the poor[16] became a dominant lens through which protest movements were organized. This variety of environmentalism brought the concerns of ecology and equity together.[17] The tension between exclusionary conservation and a more inclusive approach plays out in the realm of environmental law and jurisprudence. In more recent times, environmentalism of the ecosystem where nature's inherent value is preserved gained appreciation in environmental law and jurisprudence. Though it is in the nascent stages, it can be seen developing further in the future through the rights of nature framework.[18] On biodiversity conservation, the varieties of environmentalism are seen to be playing out. The exclusionary form of conservation is seen in campaigns and cases being filed for the protection of a particular species, such as the Asiatic lion, which will be discussed in Section 4.

Similarly, the environmentalism of the poor can be seen in the decentralized biodiversity governance framework and the involvement of the community in decision making. The ecosystem approach is providing a new frame to bring these concerns together as seen in the *Niyamgiri* judgment.[19]

2.2 Biodiversity Law and Governance in India

India is formally recognized as a dualist country; however, the judiciary, especially in matters of the environment, displays some tendencies of monism. The incorporation of international legal principles has made its way into environmental jurisprudence through public interest litigation filed before the courts.[20] With regard to biodiversity law and governance,

[14] Adivasi communities refers to the original inhabitants in the forest areas of India and refers to the indigenous communities in India.
[15] Ramchandra Guha, *Environmentalism: A Global History* (Penguin Books 2016).
[16] Martínez-Alier (n 4).
[17] ibid.
[18] Naik (n 5).
[19] *Odisha Mining Corporation v Ministry of Environment and Forests and Others* (Writ Petition) (Civil) No 180 of 2011).
[20] Aparna Chandra, 'India and International Law: Formal Dualism, Functional Monism' (2017) 57 Indian Journal of International Law 25.

however, India has abided by its dualist foundations and passed the Biological Diversity Act 2002[21] to incorporate the treaty provisions of the CBD in domestic law.[22]

India is has quasi-federal structure with more powers concentrated at the federal level. The Constitution divides jurisdiction over law and governance issues through lists between the centre or federal level and the state. In relation to biodiversity governance, the quasi-federal structure is present in the governance arrangement of the national biodiversity authority in the centre and the state biodiversity boards at the subnational level. There are a total of twenty-nine state biodiversity boards.[23] The centre continues to retain more power in terms of rule-making within the Act while the state biodiversity boards have considerable power in implementation within the borders of the subnational units.[24]

Regionally, India belongs to the South Asian Association of Regional Cooperation which has been active with biodiversity conservation through the South Asia Co-operative Environment Program (SACEP) which set up the regional Clearing House Mechanism to better share the information and technology needed to conserve biodiversity.[25] The SACEP is also involved in providing capacity-building and assistance in updating the national biodiversity action plans. These regional policies shape domestic decision making within India such as the presence of the Clearing House Mechanism.[26]

India is party to many international legal instruments for biodiversity conservation. The challenge with India and its relationship with international biodiversity law is where it has seen more uptake when it comes to aspects of access and benefit sharing and less in terms of biodiversity conservation through the creation of protected areas.[27] At the international level, India has been active in shaping biodiversity law especially in approaches to the recognition of

[21] Biological Diversity Act 2002 <www.indiacode.nic.in/bitstream/123456789/2046/1/200318.pdf> accessed 12 March 2022.

[22] ibid.

[23] Details of the State Biodiversity Boards are available at <http://nbaindia.org/text/13/StateBiodiversityBoards.html> accessed 12 March 2022.

[24] Sujit Choudhury, Pratap Bhanu Mehta, and Madhav Khosla (eds), *The Oxford Handbook of the Indian Constitution* (OUP 2016).

[25] Details of the Clearing House Mechanism can be found at <www.sacep.org/programmes/biodiversity-conservation> accessed 12 March 2022.

[26] ibid.

[27] Kabir Bavikatte and Daniel F Robinson, 'Towards a People's History of the Law: Biocultural Jurisprudence and the Nagoya Protocol on Access and Benefit Sharing' (2011) 7(1) Law, Environment and Development Journal 35–51.

Table 7.1 International legal instruments

International legal instruments	Year India ratified the treaties
Convention on International Trade in Endangered Species of Wild Fauna and Flora	1975
Convention on Biological Diversity	1994
Ramsar Convention	1982
Cartagena Protocol	2003
Nagoya Protocol	2011

traditional knowledge as well as the involvement of local communities in biodiversity conservation[28]. Table 7.1 shows the international legal instruments that the courts have referred to in their judgments.[29]

The Biodiversity Act of 2002 puts in place a three-tiered institutional structure for biodiversity governance. It establishes the national biodiversity board at the central level, the state biodiversity boards at the subnational level, and biodiversity management committees at the village level. This decentralized governance architecture has been beneficial in documenting traditional knowledge and making more localized decisions.[30] The national biodiversity authority is entrusted with the mandate of advising the central government on biodiversity conservation, the equitable sharing of benefits, and the sustainable use of biodiversity.[31] The state biodiversity board performs a similar function in advising the state governments. The biodiversity management committees at the local level are charged with promoting biodiversity conservation, chronicling local knowledge of biodiversity, and conservation of landraces, folk varieties, and domestic breeds of livestock.[32]

India's domestic biodiversity law is not restricted to the Biodiversity Act alone and includes laws that regulate forests and wildlife protection. Table 7.2 lists the other legal frameworks that make up domestic biodiversity law in

[28] Shalini Bhutani and Ashish Kothari, 'The Biodiversity Rights of Developing Nations: A Perspective from India' (2002) 32 Golden Gate University Law Review.

[29] Kanchi Kohli and Shalini Bhutani, 'Access to India's Biodiversity and Sharing Its Benefits' (2015) 50(31) Economic and Political Weekly 19–22.

[30] Madhav Gadgil and others, 'New Meanings for Old Knowledge: The People's Biodiversity Registers Program' (2000) 10(5) Ecological Applications 1307–17.

[31] ibid.

[32] Sections 18, 23 and 41 of the Biodiversity Act, 2002.

Table 7.2 Domestic biodiversity law

Domestic biodiversity laws	Nature and purpose of the law
Indian Forest Act, 1927	To create protective categories for forests and establish the forest department
Wildlife Protection Act, 1972	To protect wildlife and facilitate the creation of protected areas
Forest Conservation Act, 1980	To regulate decisions on the use of forest land for development
Forest Rights Act, 2006[a]	To recognize the rights of forest-dwelling communities over forest land, minor forest produce, and conservation

[a] Sections 18, 23, and 41 of the Biodiversity Act, 2002.

India. This chapter, however, will focus on the Biodiversity Act which directly addresses the challenges of biodiversity conservation while these other laws are also mentioned in the cases studied in this chapter.

The story of how India came to develop its National Biodiversity Action Plan is an interesting one. It began with a grant from the United Nations Development Programme and Global Environment Facility in 1999 to the Ministry of Environment and Forests. The Ministry of Environment and Forests engaged with the Kalpavriksh Environment Action Group, an NGO to assist it in preparing the National Biodiversity Strategy and Action Plan (NBSAP).[33] What then ensued was an elaborate process of ensuring participation from the marginalized communities in determining the contents of the plan. The lengthy and well-orchestrated inclusive process concluded with a technical report. To the dismay of Kalpavriksh, nine years after the process began, the Indian government released its NBSAP without including any of the recommendations from the technical report.[34] The NBSAP has since been amended in 2014 to align it with the Aichi Targets with the introduction of new national targets. The NBSAP works as a guiding document for executive decision making but functions more like a soft law instrument.[35] The Biodiversity Act is seen as the harder law for the regulation of biodiversity conservation.

[33] Ashish Kothari and Kanchi Kohli, 'National Biodiversity Action Plan' (2009) 44(20) Economic and Political Weekly 13–16.

[34] ibid.

[35] India's National Biodiversity Action Plan is available at <www.cbd.int/doc/world/in/in-nbsap-v3-en.pdf> accessed 12 March 2022.

2.3 The Role of Courts and Biodiversity Conservation in India

Environmental governance in India is a complex maze of multiple authorities with overlapping jurisdictions and has been plagued with regulatory failures. Regulatory failure caused by the inaction of the governing bodies is a pervasive issue experienced from the regulation of pollution to biodiversity loss.[36] The courts have then been asked to step in by civil society actors by filing cases to ensure that the executive fulfils its obligations. Courts have thus become an important component of the set of institutional actors engaged in environmental governance in India. They are described as levers of change to combat the issue of regulatory failure.[37] The loosening of the requirements for standing with the emergence of public interest litigation in the 1970s made the courts accessible to citizens to bring legal claims on biodiversity loss and environmental issues.[38] The nature of remedies delivered by the courts in the context of biodiversity loss has ranged from strengthening the protected area framework, forest conservation laws, and limiting the scale and nature of development projects.[39]

With the innovation of public interest litigation (PIL), the courts became a viable venue for civil society members. Geetanjoy Sahu, in his work, assesses how the making of environmental jurisprudence in India is a product of many PILs filed by passionate environmental lawyers and non-profit organizations. PILs reshaped the nature of environmental jurisprudence in India and infused it with many international legal principles, such as the polluter pays principle, public trust doctrine, and international biodiversity law. These cases also changed the legal landscape on which future environmental laws were made.[40]

While PILs have contributed significantly to the development of environmental jurisprudence, in a seminal study Anuj Bhuwania shows how they have further marginalized the rights of the poor. In the example of the Delhi pollution case, he highlights how the factories being moved out of the city caused the poor labourers who worked in them to be shifted to ghettos on the outskirts of Delhi.[41] Similarly, a case filed by a non-profit organization called Wildlife First, which challenged the constitutionality of the Forest Rights Act 2006, resulted in an oppressive order which called for the relocation of forest-dwelling

[36] Sharachchandra Lele and others, 'A Structure for Environment Governance: A Perspective' (2010) 45(6) Economic and Political Weekly 13–16.

[37] Geetanjoy Sahu, 'Public Interest Environmental Litigations in India: Contributions and Complications' (2008) 69(4) The Indian Journal of Political Science 745–58.

[38] ibid.

[39] ibid.

[40] ibid.

[41] Anuj Bhuwania, *Courting the People: Public Interest Litigation in Post-Emergency India* (CUP 2016).

communities from the forest areas.[42] Legal mobilization can result in the perpetuation of a strain of environmentalism which Amita Baviskar terms as bourgeois environmentalism, where a certain class interest and its idea of environmentalism prevails while marginalizing the rights of the poor.[43] Thus, PILs have been a pertinent source for transforming environmental law but they have their limitations too with their ability to marginalize the rights of the poor. The courts are left to choose between varieties of environmentalism that pervade decision making on environmental issues in India. Here we see the environmentalism of the poor being placed on the backburner and being replaced by bourgeois environmentalism and exclusionary conservation.[44] An example of such a case is the Wildlife First case where a group of organizations challenged the constitutionality of the Forest Rights Act 2006, on the grounds that recognition of forest rights would result in the fragmentation of forest land. The case continues to be heard before the Supreme Court. However, the court did pass an order which called for the eviction of forest-dwellers in February 2018 which was later stayed by the court in response to mass protests by the forest-dwelling communities. This case is an example of how the varieties of environmentalism remain contested.[45]

The courts, including the National Green Tribunal, have sometimes been described as overreaching as they interfere with the executive's functioning concerning the environment. An instance is the *Godavarman* judgment, discussed in Section 4.1. In this case, the court took over executive decision making on how forest land was being used and conserved.[46] It created a quasi-judicial committee, called the Central Empowered Committee, to investigate decisions of forest land diversion. The judiciary, which is an important actor in the environmental governance architecture, can become overbearing in its influence yet provide the necessary oversight to check executive decision making. The courts have an important role to play in designing such post-judgment monitoring mechanisms such as the Central Empowered Committee.[47]

The National Green Tribunal, which was established in 2010, is a specialized tribunal that hears cases concerning environmental matters. It was set up

[42] Arpitha Kodiveri, 'Changing Terrain of Environmental Citizenship in India's Forests' (2016) 12(2) NLS Socio-Legal Review 74.

[43] Amita Baviskar, *Uncivil City: Ecology, Equity and the Commons in Delhi* (Sage 2020).

[44] ibid.

[45] *Wildlife First and Others v Ministry of Environment and Forest and others* <https://indiankanoon.org/doc/58553838/> accessed 12 March 2022.

[46] Armin Rosencranz and Sharachchandra Lele, 'Supreme Court and India's Forest' (2008) 43(5) Economic and Political Weekly 11–14.

[47] *TN Godavarman v Union of India Air* (1997) SC 1228.

to provide an avenue for hearing environmental disputes which require a specialized panel consisting of judges and experts. The tribunal has become an important node in the governance of biodiversity and is the site where multiple cases discussed in the chapter are heard.[48] The courts and the tribunal on biodiversity law and governance have been key in combatting regulatory failure, providing clarity on the applicability of the laws, and challenging the loss of biodiversity. The Biodiversity Act provides the national and state biodiversity boards with powers to approach the courts for violations of the Biodiversity Act 2002.[49] The courts in cases concerning biodiversity are used by the government departments as well as concerned citizens and NGOs. As we examine the role of courts in biodiversity conservation, we will draw from Benjamin Ewing and Douglas Kysar's work on climate change litigation in the United States where they argue that courts act as a prod and a plea for better governance outcomes. We will also rely on the work by Anuj Bhuwania and Amita Baviskar to offer an analysis of the role of the courts being in a dual position of a site of struggle and also as a source of disempowerment.[50]

Courts can provide essential prods and pleas but can equally disempower the most marginalized in their struggle for rights over resources. This double register of the courts is contingent on the choice that courts make in the varieties of environmentalism available to them, as courts are still unable to work out complex interpretive tools to balance conflicting rights. What we see is an ad hoc prioritization of rights by the judiciary that compromises the rights of nature or those dependent on these ecosystems. The chapter demonstrates this double register of the courts in biodiversity litigation, too.

3. Methodology for the Selection of Cases

The work began by creating a database of thirty cases where the terms biodiversity, biodiversity conservation, and biodiversity loss had appeared across the central and subnational jurisdictions. It then arrived at the following criteria to select the cases for analysis. They are:

[48] The National Green Tribunal Act No 19 2010 <https://greentribunal.gov.in/sites/default/files/act_rules/National_Green_Tribunal_Act,_2010.pdf> accessed 12 March 2022; Geetanjali Gill, *Environmental Justice in India: The National Green Tribunal* (Routledge 2018).

[49] Shalini Bhutani and Kanchi Kohli, 'Litigating India's Biodiversity Act 2002: A Study of Legal Cases' <https://docplayer.net/54604536-Litigating-india-s-biological-diversity-act-a-study-of-legal-cases-by-shalini-bhutani-kanchi-kohli.html> accessed 12 March 2022.

[50] Benjamin Ewing and Douglas A Kysar, 'Prods and Pleas: Limited Government in an Era of Unlimited Harm' (2011) 121(2) The Yale Law Journal 350–424.

- *Litigating the Biodiversity Act and reference to international biodiversity law*: to understand how the Biodiversity Act of 2002 was being interpreted and argued before the courts. Cases that were significant on aspects of applicability of the Act and the diverse set of issues of biodiversity governance that were argued were chosen. These cases also refer to international legal instruments in specific ways.
- *Public interest litigation*: the Indian judiciary with its unique feature of PIL enables anyone to approach the courts on matters of public interest. Issues of biodiversity have been important and PILs have been the route taken by civil society actors to approach the courts. This category of cases was included to understand how civil society actors were mobilizing the law concerning biodiversity.
- *Multiple venues*: to inquire into cases that were across jurisdictions and judicial venues which include the High Court, the Supreme Court, and the National Green Tribunal which is a specialized tribunal that examines questions relating to the environment.
- *Influence on environmental governance beyond the case*: a few cases whose impact on environmental governance is significant have been chosen. The significance here is in how they have recrafted the governance architecture on regulating forests and biodiversity. A total of twelve cases across different geographies and jurisdictions are based on the following criteria.

4. A Typology of Cases

In the selection of cases, a typology started to emerge in terms of the nature of legal issues before the courts. This typology is an analytical framework to navigate the twelve cases being discussed. They are not exhaustive but illustrative of the diverse nature of legal issues that come within the ambit of biodiversity. This section will provide a brief description of the cases being analysed and the typologies under which they sit. Aspects of this typology are derived from the extensive study of biodiversity litigation undertaken by Shalini Bhutani and Kanchi Kohli who examined cases up to 2016.[51] The typology of cases is within the following categories: landmark cases, cases concerning the regulation of GMOs, protection of specific species, declaration of biodiversity heritage sites and protection of ecosystems, cases which seek to fill the enforcement gap, and, lastly, cases concerning access and benefit sharing of biodiversity.

[51] Bhutani and Kohli (n 49).

4.1 Landmark Cases

Landmark cases refer to cases that had a significant influence on the biodiversity governance of India's forests. Two cases are particularly striking in this respect: the *Godavarman* case and the *Niyamgiri* case. Both these cases speak of the need to conserve biodiversity, but their approaches differ.[52] The *Godavarman* case was a case filed by TN Godavarman Thirumulkpad to prevent illegal timber operations in the Niligiri hills in the western ghats. The case, which began with examining forest conservation in the Niligiri hills, evolved into a continuing mandamus.[53] The case specifically refers to India having adopted the CBD and its applicability. It states:

> A few decisions taken at the Convention on Biological Diversity dated 5th June 1992 would be relevant. The Preamble, inter-alia, contains the following: 'Concerned that biological diversity is being significantly reduced by certain human activities. Aware of the general lack of information and knowledge regarding biological diversity and of the urgent need to develop scientific, technical, and institutional capacities to provide the basic understanding upon which to plan and implement appropriate measures. Noting that it is vital to anticipate, prevent and attack the causes of significant reduction or loss of biological diversity at the source. Noting further that the fundamental requirement for the conservation of biological diversity is the in-situ conservation of ecosystems and natural habitats and the maintenance and recovery of viable populations of species in their natural surroundings.'[54]

The reason the *Godavarman* case was chosen is because of this explicit reference to international biodiversity law and the integration of concerns of biodiversity loss with forest conservation. This landmark case defined forests as the dictionary meaning of forests and led to the creation of quasi-judicial committees to oversee executive decision making on deforestation. It resulted in a reconfiguration of the governance architecture with the Central Empowered Committee that undertook investigations on proposed forest land diversion.

[52] *TN Godavarman v Union of India Air* (n 47) 1228 and *Odisha Mining Corp v Ministry of Environment and Forests and Others* (n 19).

[53] This is a writ used in an environmental case which requires the government or concerned executive body to perform an act or a series of acts as decreed by the court in an order or final judgment.

[54] *TN Godavarman v Union of India Air* (n 47) 1228.

The committee has played a significant role in preventing the loss of forests and biodiversity.[55]

The second case is the *Niyamgiri* case; here the PIL was filed by three concerned citizens to prevent the mining of bauxite in the sacred Niyamgiri hills where the forest-dwellers, the Dongria Khond, had been living. In this landmark case, the Supreme Court ruled, acknowledging the sacred relationship shared between the Dongria Khond and the Niyamgiri hills, that decision of whether mining should take place rested with the forest-dwelling community.[56] It was the first time that power was devolved to the village assembly on decision making on the diversion of forest land. The impact of this case was in its recognition of the sacred relationship shared with the mountain, and in its judgment by devolving power to the village assembly it implied the recognition of the procedural right of prior informed consent.[57] The case referred to biodiversity loss in the following manner:

> The impact on ecological and biodiversity values of the Niyamgiri hills upon which the Dongaria Kondh and Kutia Kondh depend on. FAC [Forest Advisory Committee] opined that it was a fit case for applying the precautionary principle to obviate the irreparable damage to the affected people and recommended for the temporary withdrawal of the in-principle/State I approval accorded.[58]

Here the court highlights that the precautionary principle has to be applied in instances where development will result in irreparable damage to the affected people. This strengthens the progressive biodiversity jurisprudence in India by requiring the strict application of principles such as the precautionary principle in deciding on deforestation.

4.2 Regulation of Genetically Modified Organisms (GMOs)

The other set of cases brought before the High Courts has been on issues concerning the regulation of GMOs. GMOs were under the 1989 'Rules for the

[55] Ashish Pathak Kothari and others, 'Forests, Rights and Conservation: FRA Act 2006, India' in Henry Scheyvens (ed), *Critical Review of Selected Forest-Related Regulatory Initiatives: Applying a Rights Perspective* (Institute for Global Environmental Strategies 2011) 20–50.
[56] *Odisha Mining Corp v Ministry of Environment and Forests and Others* (n 19); Naik (n 5).
[57] *Odisha Mining Corp*, ibid, paras 58 and 60.
[58] ibid para 14.

manufacture, use, import, export & storage of hazardous microorganisms, genetically engineered organisms or cells' which formed the Genetic Engineering Approval Committee.[59] With the passing of the 2002 Biodiversity Act, the National Biodiversity Authority (NBA) and state biodiversity boards became another regulatory mechanism for GMOs.[60]

In two interesting cases, PILs were filed challenging the use of local plant varieties for the creation of GMOs. They invoked the 2002 Biodiversity Act to prevent the use of such local varieties with differing legal outcomes. In the petition in the *Environment Support Group* case, the NGO argued that the NBA had failed to fulfil its regulatory function as the Tamil Nadu Agricultural University and University of Agricultural Sciences (UAS) had not sought permission from the NBA as they worked with the Maharashtra Hybrid Seeds Co Ltd (MHSCL)—the Indian subsidiary of Monsanto—in developing BT brinjal. The High Court of Karnataka issued a notice to the NBA stating that it had been callous in protecting India's biodiversity.[61] The case went on to be transferred to the National Green Tribunal and the special leave petition before the Supreme Court which ruled in favour of the NBA.[62] In response to this petition, the NBA filed a criminal complaint against UAS and MHSCL in Dharwad.[63]

In another PIL filed by the NGO Research Foundation for Science Technology and Ecology, the granting of a patent by the European Patent Office against an Indian variety of wheat was challenged. What was significant about this case was its identification of a gap in the regulation of GMOs and called for a committee or board to be set up with the inclusion of civil society members to coordinate with international patent offices to be able to check the granting of such patents and issues of biopiracy. The petition was, however, dismissed. The court ordered that there was no need for such a body and that the government was doing all in its power to preserve India's biodiversity.[64]

[59] Section 3, Rules for the Manufacture, Use, Import, Export and Storage of Hazardous Micro Organisms, Genetically Engineered Organisms or Cells. New Delhi, 5 December, 1989 <https://biosafety.icar.gov.in/rules-for-the-manufacture-use-import-export-and-storage-of-hazardous-microorganisms-genetically-engineered-organisms-or-cells/> accessed 12 March 2022.

[60] Section 2(f) and Ch II of the Biological Diversity Act, 2002 <http://nbaindia.org/uploaded/Biodiversityindia/Legal/31.%20Biological%20Diversity%20%20Act,%202002.pdf> accessed 12 March 2022.

[61] *Environment Support Group & Another v NBA & Others* (Writ Petition) (No 41532 of 2012) <https://indiankanoon.org/doc/169940544/> accessed 12 March 2022.

[62] ibid.

[63] ibid.

[64] *Research Foundation for Science, Technology & Ecology & Another v Union of India & Others* (Writ Petition) (Civil) No 64 of 2004.

4.3 Protection of Specific Species

Several cases in India deal with the legal demands of protecting specific species. Among the cases filed, the following three stood out given their ecocentric approach. The first case is part of the elaborate *TN Godavarman* judgment where the court considered whether specific protection had to be granted to the red sanders tree under the Wildlife Protection Act and the Biodiversity Act.[65] In it, as it refers to the Biodiversity Act, it speaks of a need to shift to an ecocentric approach to environmental law. It states:

> Biological Diversity Act, 2002 was also enacted by the Parliament with the object of conserving biological diversity, sustainable use of its components, and for fair and equitable sharing of the benefits arising out of the utilization of genetic resources. Biological diversity includes all the organisms found on our planet viz., plants, animals, and microorganisms. When we examine all those legislations in the light of the constitutional provisions and various international conventions like the Convention on International Trade in Endangered Species of Wild Fauna and Flora 1973 (CITES), the Convention of Biological Diversity 1992 (CBD) evidently, there is a shift from environmental rights to ecological rights, though gradual but substantial.[66]

Similarly, in the judgment by the Supreme Court in the *Asiatic Lion* case, a PIL had been filed to conserve the lion. The court highlights the need to conserve species as an important piece of the puzzle for conserving biodiversity. It includes the need to protect all living beings as an essential element of preventing the loss of biodiversity. It states:

> Biodiversity and biological diversity include all the organisms found on our planet i.e. plants, animals, and micro-organisms, the genes they contain, and the different eco-systems of which they form a part. The rapid deterioration of the ecology due to human interference is aiding the rapid disappearance of several wild animal species.[67]

These cases refer to international biodiversity law and provide an ecocentric lens through which to read biodiversity laws and expand the understanding

[65] *TN Godavarman v Union of India Air* (n 47) paras 18 and 19.
[66] ibid para 18.
[67] *Centre for Environment Law, WWF-I v Union of India* (2013) 8 SCC 234, paras 48 and 49.

of biological diversity to include the need to protect all living beings. They also highlight the influence of anthropogenic activities that are causing the loss of biodiversity. In the context of marine biodiversity and the protection of fish, the Goa Federation case is an interesting example where a PIL was filed to protect fish and the rights of fish workers from mechanized fishing and trawlers. In its judgment, the High Court of Bombay called for the state of Goa to arrive at a detailed set of guidelines for the implementation of the fishing ban that was in place.[68]

4.4 Biodiversity Heritage Sites and Protecting Ecosystems

Among the cases that were surveyed for this chapter a fascinating set of cases emerged on the declaration of areas as biodiversity heritage sites. Under the Biodiversity Act of 2002, the state biodiversity boards have the power to declare areas as biodiversity heritage sites. These areas are subject to protection and can act as a barrier to land acquisition and development activities.[69] The most comprehensive of these cases is one filed by the Biodiversity Management Committees (BMC) in Keoti village in Madhya Pradesh, where the BMC called for the restriction of construction, illegal mining, and trading of tendu leaves by the contractors. In this case, filed before the National Green Tribunal, a progressive decision was made where the state of Madhya Pradesh was asked to draft guidelines and a strategy to document and preserve such biodiversity-rich areas. A pertinent observation made in the case is the linkage between human survival and biodiversity: it states that '[b]iodiversity is the foundation of ecosystem services to which human wellbeing is intimately linked'.[70] Another instance of moving away from an ecocentric approach highlighting the continuing contestation over different environmentalisms.

Another interesting case before the Kerala High Court concerned whether an area declared as a biodiversity heritage site (in this case, a private coffee estate) could be acquired by the state to set up a food park. The court ruled that the state biodiversity boards had the power to restrict activities, including acquisition, to protect biodiversity. This has not, however, been sufficiently deployed by the state biodiversity boards.[71] Interestingly, the court here does

[68] *Goa Environment Federation v State of Goa & Others* (2002) INHCB 298.

[69] Section 32 of the Biodiversity Act, 2002.

[70] The BMC of Keoti Village in Rewa district of Madhya Pradesh had filed a case before the NGT's CZ Bench in 2014 (Original Application no 06/2014 (CZ).

[71] *M/s Chembra Peak Estates Ltd v State of Kerala & Others* (Writ Petition) (Civil) No 3022 of 2008 6.

not refer to the United Nations Education, Social and Cultural Organization Conventions on the setting up of heritage sites.

4.5 Filling the Enforcement Gap in Biodiversity Law and Conservation

As argued in Section 2.2 on locating the courts, the courts are approached to be able to fill the enforcement gap in the implementation of environmental laws. The Biodiversity Act is no different, as shown in a case filed by Chandra Bhal Singh before the principal Bench of the National Green Tribunal (NGT) inquiring into the slow implementation of the Act.[72] In particular, the case raises the concern of inadequacy in the creation of Biodiversity Management Committees (BMCs) at the village level where the village assembly has decision-making power over biodiversity conservation. As the case was being heard, the NGT started to oversee compliance with the Act and called for periodic compliance reports to be filed by the NBA. In its most recent compliance report submitted in 2020, it was noted that compliance with the formation of BMCs was at 90 per cent and the drafting of a peoples' biodiversity register stood at 39 per cent. This delay in the implementation of the Act is indicative of the enforcement gap created by the executive. The oversight role of the courts acts as a catalyst for speedy implementation of this law. As the court states: 'The Act was enforced in 2002. The Rules came into force in 2004. Any further delay is not conducive to the rule of law.'[73]

4.6 Access and Benefit Sharing and Levying Fees

Access and benefit sharing (ABS) is an aspect of biodiversity regulation that has been heavily litigated.[74] In two cases, the applicability of the Biodiversity Act was investigated. In the *Divya Pharmacy* case,[75] the Uttarakhand High Court examined whether Indian companies could be subject to the requirements of

[72] *Chandra Bhal Singh v Union of India & Others*, OA No 347 of 2016.

[73] ibid.

[74] Gitanjali Gill, Nupur Choudhury, and Nidhi Shrivastava, 'Biodiversity and the Indian Judiciary: Tracing and Trajectory' <https://researchportal.northumbria.ac.uk/ws/portalfiles/portal/51882064/Gita_Gill_and_others_BLJ_BIODIVERSITY_ARTICLE_MAY_2021.pdf> accessed 10 February 2022.

[75] *Divya Pharmacy v Union of India* (Writ Petition) (M/S) No 3437 of 2016 <https://indiankanoon.org/doc/140341868/> accessed 12 March 2022.

ABS as the Act provides for such an exception. The court ruled that the pharmaceutical company which was engaged in manufacturing ayurvedic medicines was liable to share the benefits with the state biodiversity board and the local communities.[76] A poignant observation made in this judgment is the understanding that biodiversity is as much the property of the nation-state as it is of the local community.[77]

In another interesting case, the question asked by the BMC in Eklahara before the NGT was whether coal is a bioresource. The BMC, in its petition, sought to recognize coal as a bioresource so that it could levy fees for its extraction by the state-owned company Southeastern Coal Ltd. The court concluded that coal was not a bioresource and thus did not require payment of fees or attract the legal requirements of the Biodiversity Act. The case is illustrative of how contested are the definitions within the Act and the role of courts in restricting the scope of these definitions to enable extraction.[78]

5. Analysis and Key Findings

The typology of cases reveals three analytical threads that can be seen across the cases. When biodiversity loss and conservation are deliberated in the courts, the courts are asked to choose between the varieties of environmentalism that inform biodiversity law both domestically and internationally, the regulation of biodiversity, and the governance architecture, and how these cases draw from international biodiversity law.

5.1 Varieties of Environmentalism and Biodiversity Litigation

On biodiversity litigation, the court has been asked to choose between these competing normative frameworks (eg exclusionary conservation and ecocentric approaches to environmental law) of environmentalism. These competing frameworks are not exhaustive in capturing the changing landscape of environmentalism which is actively being shaped and reshaped by vibrant social

[76] ibid.
[77] ibid.
[78] BMC Eklahara sought NGT intervention to declare coal as a bioresource to be able to insist on benefit sharing by coal companies (Application No 28 of 2013(CZ) and Application No 17 of 2014(CZ) THC), see paras 35 and 36 at <www.casemine.com/judgement/in/574989a8e56109100ce98676> accessed 12 March 2022.

movements on the ground. The varieties of environmentalism that are visible in these cases are derived from those who brought the petitions, the remedy and legal interpretations that these petitions seek, and the impact they have on the rights of the poor. The varieties of environmentalism seen in this collection of judgments are bourgeois environmentalism, environmentalism of the poor, and ecocentrism.[79] In international biodiversity law, too, these tensions of exclusionary conservation, ecocentrism, and environmentalism of the poor play out. The Kunming Declaration which lays the foundation for the post-2020 global biodiversity framework advocates for the increase in the recognition of protected areas which has gathered criticism from indigenous communities who have been marginalized by the recognition of protected areas globally and argues for a rights-based approach to conservation.[80]

Bourgeois environmentalism refers to environmentalism that emerges from the middle-class interest of seeing nature as pristine. Amita Baviskar arrives at this variety of environmentalism through her extensive work on examining environmental movements and jurisprudence in the city of Delhi.[81] Bourgeois environmentalism can be seen in the *Godavarman* case where the case was filed by TN Godavarman who was part of a princely family in Kerala and is referred to as 'The Green Man'. The *Godavarman* judgment is known for the efforts of the Supreme Court in conserving the forests in question but with it came a set of orders to evict forest-dwelling communities who were dependent on those ecosystems for their livelihood. The order caused grave injustice to the forest-dwellers who were already marginalized by exclusionary conservation practices.[82] Bourgeois environmentalism is closely tied to this idea of exclusionary conservation and these cases seldom acknowledge the rights of communities who are dependent on ecosystems, such as the Wildlife First case. Thus, biodiversity conservation from the viewpoint of exclusionary conservation fails to address the rights of the poor.[83] The marginalization of forest-dwelling and indigenous communities due to exclusionary conservation is not an isolated experience in the biodiverse-rich forests of India, as seen in other countries that were subject to colonial forest policies by the British and other European powers like Sri Lanka, Singapore, and Myanmar to name but a few.[84]

[79] Ramchandra Guha, *Environmentalism: A Global History* (Penguin Books 2016).

[80] Kunming Declaration <www.cbd.int/doc/c/df35/4b94/5e86e1ee09bc8c7d4b35aaf0/kunmingdeclaration-en.pdf> accessed 11 March 2022.

[81] Amita Baviskar, *Uncivil City: Ecology, Equity and the Commons in Delhi* (Sage 2020).

[82] ibid.

[83] ibid.

[84] Richard Grove, *Green Imperialism: Colonial Expansion, Tropical Island Edens and the Origin of Environmentalism 1600–1860* (Australian National University 1996).

Environmentalism of the poor is where the considerations of the rights of communities dependent on ecosystems form an integral part of biodiversity jurisprudence.[85] The *Niyamgiri* judgment is an example of where considerations of ecology and equity come together. The Supreme Court recognized the sacred rights of the Dongria Kondh community and their relationship with the Niyamgiri mountain. This recognition transferred decision-making power on deforestation to the community. This was an important shift as it decentralized decision making on conservation and the acquisition of forest land. Similarly, the case brought by the biodiversity management committee in Keoti village is another example of how local communities took control of decision making in the area declared as a biodiversity heritage site. Environmentalism of the poor pushes for more inclusive decision making on biodiversity conservation.[86]

Ecocentrism is a nascent variety of environmentalism making its way into biodiversity jurisprudence in India. This variety of environmentalism comes with an understanding of nature having an intrinsic value and the need to conserve the natural environment and particular species with this ethical underpinning. The *Asiatic Lion* case and the *Red Sanders* case are examples of ecocentrism making its way into biodiversity jurisprudence.[87] Ecocentrism being nascent has not adequately addressed the challenges that come with exclusionary conservation practice. As a consequence of the *Asiatic Lion* judgment, villages within the forest area were relocated. The forest-dwellers and their rights were marginalized again.[88]

The courts in India are seen as reinforcing one variety of environmentalism to the deprivation of another variety. Biodiversity jurisprudence has not been able to reconcile these competing varieties of environmentalism in a way that interpretive tools for reconciling conflicting rights can be forged both domestically and internationally. This perhaps demands the reimagination of environmentalism that underlies the framing of biodiversity law. Sharchchandra Lele calls for a movement back to democratic environmentalism when he states that:

> Such environmentalism embraces multiple societal goals, including material and spiritual well-being, justice, sustainability and democracy. It acknowledges that both biotic and abiotic nature play a role in meeting these goals,

85 Guha (n 79).
86 *Odisha Mining Corp v Ministry of Environment and Forests and Others* (n 19).
87 *TN Godavarman v Union of India Air* (n 47) 18.
Centre for Environment Law, WWF-I v Union of India (n 67).
88 Naik (n 5).

but that there is no one way of managing nature that will achieve all goals for everyone.[89]

The lack of reconciliation from the perspective of democratic environmentalism demands that there is room for negotiating between these competing environmentalisms in the courts without a predisposition for prioritizing exclusionary conservation. Biodiversity jurisprudence has marginalized the rights of forest-dependent communities by reinforcing exclusionary conservation practices. A biodiversity jurisprudence from below akin to democratic environmentalism akin to the *Niyamgiri* judgment and the *Keoti* case can act as an antidote to this reinforcement of exclusionary conservation practice.

5.2 Biodiversity Regulation: Filling the Regulatory Gap

Courts have the ability to fill the enforcement gap and push the executive into action. The courts can be seen performing this role in the *Chandra Bhal* case before the NGT where the formation of biodiversity management committees was scrutinized, thus showing that the courts can push the national and state biodiversity boards into action to speed up the implementation of the Biodiversity Act.[90] The courts, when it comes to biodiversity regulation, do something else which is interesting: they fulfil the role of monitoring the implementation of the Biodiversity Act by demanding periodic reports from the national and state biodiversity boards on the formation of biodiversity management committees. This judicial oversight highlights the role of courts among the regulatory actors engaged in biodiversity conservation.[91]

In the cases concerning GMOs, the courts are approached as a venue for filling the regulatory gap for GMOs as well as holding the national biodiversity boards accountable for their role in regulating GMOs. The courts are viewed by civil society actors as a venue where demands for alternative governance arrangements can be made as has been shown. The courts continue to fulfil the key function of filling the enforcement gap generated by bureaucratic lethargy in relation to biodiversity conservation. PIL has been the dominant pathway for making these claims before the courts.[92]

[89] Sharachchandra Lele, 'From Wildlife-ism to Ecosystem-service-ism to a Broader Environmentalism' (2021) 48(1) Environmental Conservation 5–7.

[90] *Chandra Bhal Singh v Union of India & Others* (n 72).

[91] Geetanjoy (n 37) 745–58.

[92] ibid.

5.3 Role of International Biodiversity Law in Domestic Biodiversity Jurisprudence

International biodiversity law has directly influenced judicial decision making. Courts, and particularly the Supreme Court, have been instrumental in infusing environmental jurisprudence with international law. Biodiversity jurisprudence has been shaped directly by international biodiversity law; namely, the CBD and CITES. In the typology of cases listed previously, what can be seen is how the cases focusing on the protection of particular species and ecocentric approaches to jurisprudence rely on international law.

International biodiversity law also influences the discourse on environmentalism domestically. International biodiversity law has emerged as an important space to push for the recognition of the rights of indigenous communities and the participation rights of local communities in conservation.[93] Kabir Bavikatte in his book *Stewarding the Earth* argues that international biodiversity law has generated a new subset of biocultural rights recognizing rights over property and the knowledge of biocultural communities.[94] This has propelled discussions in India on approaches to community-based conservation and locally driven biodiversity conservation which is visible in the Biodiversity Act 2002.[95]

In the *Godavarman* case, CITES along with existing environmental laws are seen as a way of reasserting the need to view ecological rights and understand the role of biodiversity jurisprudence as one conserving the whole ecosystem including particular species.[96] The *Asiatic Lion* case relies on the CBD to make the argument that the influence of humans on biodiversity is adverse and there is a need to curb human activity in such ecological landscapes. International biodiversity law is both a source of inspiration to push for ecocentric approaches to biodiversity conservation, but it also plays a supplementary role in supporting the courts' decisions.[97] International biodiversity law concerning the protection of species tends to recognize an ecocentric approach to environmentalism.[98]

In the context of access and benefit sharing, international biodiversity law—namely, the CBD and the Nagoya Protocol—are referred to, while decisions

[93] Bavikatte and Robinson (n 27) 35.
[94] Kabir Bavikatte, *Stewarding the Earth: Rethinking Property and the Emergence of Biocultural Rights* (OUP 2014).
[95] Kohli and Bhutani (n 29) 19–22.
[96] *TN Godavarman v Union of India Air* (n 47) para 18.
[97] Naik (n 5).
[98] ibid.

on the equitable and fair sharing of benefits are put forward. Biodiversity jurisprudence and the laws in India are derived and influenced by international biodiversity law.[99] Courts have been the primary avenue for the entry of international biodiversity law into the domestic environmental jurisprudence. It is this tendency by the courts to use international law in their judgments that has made some scholars argue that India depicts monist practices when it comes to the entry of international law into the domestic legal framework.[100]

5.4 Limitations of Courts in Shaping Biodiversity Jurisprudence and Law

Despite the courts playing an active role in shaping biodiversity jurisprudence, there are two limitations. These limitations, noticeable in biodiversity jurisprudence, are its ability to reinforce exclusionary conservation practices and its inability to effectively challenge development projects that cause biodiversity loss. These limitations cannot be located in jurisprudence alone but exist in biodiversity laws, too. The courts have been inconsistent in their approach to the rights of local communities dependent on the ecosystems they seek to conserve and in challenging the development paradigm.

The *Godavarman* and *Asiatic Lion* judgments have adversely impacted the rights of the forest-dwellers. This reinforcement of exclusionary conservation practice is a pressing issue, particularly concerning forest areas.[101] In a recent case on the Aravalli forests that surround Delhi, slum dwellers who had come to occupy forest land were being brutally evicted in order to conserve the forests. Forest conservation has always shared a tenuous relationship with recognizing the rights of forest-dwellers. This tenuous relationship is replicated in biodiversity conservation concerning forests. The courts have prioritized exclusionary conservation to the exception of the rights of forest-dwellers with a few notable exceptions, for example the *Niyamgiri* judgment.[102]

Biodiversity jurisprudence has not been able to challenge development projects which cause biodiversity loss, such as mining or other extractive activities.

[99] Ali Mehdi, 'Climate Change and Biodiversity: India's Perspective and Legal Framework' (2010) 52(3/4) Journal of the Indian Law Institute 343–65; Sandip Verma, 'The Biodiversity Convention and Intellectual Property Rights: A Study in Sustainable Development' (1995) 51(1) India Quarterly 5–18.

[100] Aparna Chandra, 'India and International Law: Formal Dualism, Functional Monism' (2017) 57 Indian Journal of International Law l, 25.

[101] Arpitha Kodiveri, 'Wildlife First, People Later?—Towards an Experimentalist Governance Approach' (2018) 9 Journal of Indian Law and Society 39–63.

[102] Kanchi Kohli and Manju Menon, SC order to Raze Khori Gaon is a jarring example of coercive environmentalism', *The Indian Express* (August 2021).

The failure of this cannot be attributed to the courts alone but can be seen in biodiversity laws that provide limited scope for challenging such projects. The available avenue in the law is the identification of biodiversity heritage sites.[103] In the typology of judgments, what can be seen is a few cases where this provision has been used to prevent development activities that result in biodiversity loss. In the future, it will be important for the courts to infuse biodiversity jurisprudence with a set of principles and interpretations to be able to challenge such projects. A significant limitation in biodiversity litigation in terms of challenging development projects has been that it has focused more on holding the state accountable. The question of corporate accountability for biodiversity loss has been restricted to the regulation of GMOs.[104]The *Niyamgiri* judgment was one example where the Orissa Mining Corporation and Vedanta Resources Private Ltd were held accountable for the loss of biodiversity by opening up a bauxite mine.[105]

5.5 Shifts in Biodiversity Jurisprudence in India

The decisive shifts in biodiversity jurisprudence can be seen in its recognition of ecocentric approaches and the innovation in procedural rights of the participation of local communities. These changes are poignant as they usher in new ways of handling the difficult questions raised by biodiversity loss. The contours of this jurisprudential evolution are still indeterminate until more cases on aspects of biodiversity conservation are brought before the courts.

The courts have begun to think of ecological rights when they encounter questions of species conservation as was seen in the *Godavarman* and *Asiatic Lion* judgments. In both cases, the definitive shift to look at the ecosystem as a unit of rights and not merely humans and species ushers in the beginning of jurisprudence that accounts for the web of life and its connections. These conceptual variations are still in the making and the influence they will have on the future of biodiversity jurisprudence is yet to be seen. The logistics of how an ecocentric jurisprudence will be realized without marginalizing the rights of the poor is still a work in progress. The ecocentric approach offers a new lens

[103] An example of the case discussed earlier of a coffee plantation owner wanting to avoid acquisition by the state by declaring the area as a biodiversity heritage site in *M/s Chembra Peak Estates Limited v State of Kerala & Others* (Writ Petition) (Civil) No 3022 of 2008.

[104] Manju Menon and Kanchi Kohli, 'Environmental Decision-Making: Whose Agenda?' (2007) 42(26) Economic and Political Weekly 2490–94; Kachi Kohli and Shalini Bhutani, 'The Legal Meaning of Biodiversity. (2013) 48(33) Economic and Political Weekly 15–17.

[105] ibid.

to examine more complex questions on the relationship between humans and the non-human world and biodiversity jurisprudence which is trapped in the framework of competing varieties of environmentalism. Ecocentrism can be a way to reconcile these competing varieties of environmentalism and find ways to balance human and non-human rights.[106]

The procedural innovations in the right to participation have again been a noticeable shift in biodiversity jurisprudence. The involvement of local and forest-dwelling communities in conservation and decisions on deforestation is seen in the *Niyamgiri* judgment. These procedural rights can effectively challenge exclusionary conservation practices and development projects. The drawback of these procedural rights has been their inadequate implementation and their inability to influence state decision making on biodiversity conservation.[107] Since the *Niyamgiri* judgment, there have not been other examples of cases where the local or forest-dwelling community has been able to assert their procedural right to free, prior and informed consent adequately. Both ecocentrism and procedural rights of participation are jurisprudential tools that can address the limitations of exclusionary conservation and the need to challenge the dominant development paradigm. The loss of biodiversity cannot be addressed by marginalizing the rights of the poor or by allowing for development projects to continue unscrutinized.[108]

6. A Note on Climate Change Litigation and Biodiversity Litigation

Some cases have used climate change as an issue to draw the attention of the judiciary to environmentally destructive practices. The key cases that emerge are before the High Courts of Delhi and Allahabad and the NGT. For example, in *Manushi Sangathan v Government of Delhi and Others*,[109] the petitioners were fighting a ban on cycle rickshaws by using the Intergovernmental Panel on Climate Change's fourth assessment report which encouraged policies that emphasized the use of more fuel-efficient vehicles.[110] The High Court went on

[106] In India, the right of nature was recognized in the context of the rights of the rivers Ganga and Yamuna in *Lalit Miglani v State Of Uttarakhand and Others* on 2 December 2016 (Writ Petition) (PIL) No 140 of 2015.

[107] Chitrangada Choudhury and Aniket Aga, 'Manufacturing Consent: Mining, Bureaucratic Sabotage and the Forest Rights Act in India' (2020) 31(2) Capitalism Nature Socialism 70–90.

[108] Kodiveri (n 2).

[109] Writ Petition (Civil) 4572 of 2007.

[110] Fourth Assessment Report of the Intergovernmental Panel on Climate Change <www.ipcc.ch/assessment-report/ar4/> accessed 12 March 2022.

to rule that the restriction on the plying of trade for cycle rickshaws was arbitrary and the legal basis for it was a violation of the right to livelihood for the cycle rickshaw drivers.

In *We the People v Union of India*,[111] the petitioners argued against the cutting down of trees for the expansion of roads in Uttar Pradesh which was contributing to global warming. They further argued that trees were not being planted elsewhere to compensate for the loss of these trees. The Allahabad High Court held that trees needed to be planted to compensate for the loss of the trees which had been cut down.

Lastly, in 2017, Ridhima Pandey, a nine-year-old from Uttarakhand, filed a case before the NGT challenging government inaction in the area of climate change. The grounds on which the case were filed were as follows:

> The Applicant is invoking the principle of sustainable development and the precautionary principle, as envisaged under Section 20 of the National Green Tribunal Act, 2010, as well as the inter-generational equity principle and the Public Trust Doctrine. The application also raises the issue of non-implementation of various environmental laws, more particularly non-implementation of the Forest (Conservation) Act, 1980, the Air (Prevention and Control of Pollution) Act, 1981, the Environment (Protection) Act, 1986, and the Environmental Impact Assessment Notification, 2006, which has led to adverse impacts of climate change across the country.[112]

This case is being heard before the NGT with no significant decisions having yet been made although the case has attracted significant media attention which has not translated into concrete policy changes.

The cases are too few to draw any meaningful comment on the role that the judiciary has played in climate change, but what these cases provide is an insight into the way climate change concerns have been argued in the courts. The latter case also alerts us to the integral link between biodiversity conservation and climate change with the adverse impact of cutting down trees.

Climate change has been invoked by the petitioners on grounds of air pollution, cutting down of trees, and government inaction. Climate change litigation is still in its early stages of development in India. As climate change litigation is a trend across the globe, in India environmental cases continue to examine more

[111] Order of the Allahabad High Court in Misc Bench No 5750 of 2010, 16 June 2010 <www.indiankanoon.org/doc/1558452/> accessed 12 March 2022.

[112] Petition of Ridhima Pandey <http://climatecasechart.com/non-us-case/pandey-v-india/> accessed 12 March 2022.

traditional questions of environmental justice, forest conservation, and biodiversity loss; unlike biodiversity loss, which has been an issue that the courts have encountered since the 1970s and which have developed a complex set of jurisprudential principles to be able to tackle it.[113] Climate change as an issue is being brought before the courts now and the courts have yet to pronounce significant judgments on the issue. In both genres of environmental litigation, the challenge before the courts of choosing between the varieties of environmentalism and the legacy of exclusionary conservation remains. The influence of the strain of ecocentrism present in international biodiversity law can provide important legal mechanisms and interpretive guidance in balancing these competing forms of environmentalism. As climate change litigation picks up steam in India, there are lessons to be drawn from biodiversity litigation particularly on the development of an ecocentric approach and the expansion of procedural rights to include local and forest-dwelling communities.

7. Conclusion

In this chapter, after an overview of biodiversity litigation in India, what can be seen is that courts are an important site for the deliberation of pertinent questions on the environment and development and the varieties of environmentalism. The potential for biodiversity litigation is subject to the limitations of the judiciary as it has failed to curtail developmental activities which harm the environment and the marginalizing discourse of exclusionary conservation.

The chapter tries to problematize the role of courts when viewed through the lens of competing environmentalisms. The challenge of competing environmentalisms as this chapter argues is not restricted to Indian biodiversity law alone but in the framing and implementation of international biodiversity law, too. The tensions between these varieties of environmentalism can be productive if the exercise of reconciliation is through a democratic and deliberative process as Sharachchandra Lele puts forth. The fact that biodiversity jurisprudence in India is skewed towards exclusionary conservation has reduced the scope for negotiation and a democratic reconciliation among the varieties of environmentalism.

As India sees rapid deforestation and biodiversity loss, the role of biodiversity litigation will continue to gain salience. The choices that the judiciary makes in terms of the varieties of environmentalism will determine how

[113] Bhutani and Kohli (n 49).

conflicting rights are reconciled. In Khori village, the local communities were forcefully pushed out by the state in a bid to conserve the Aravalli forests and their biodiversity. As decisions on biodiversity conservation continue to exclude the most marginalized and the courts support such evictions, the insight shared by the senior lawyer at the beginning of the chapter of how the role of the courts as an empowering force will be shaped by how they seek to balance conflicting rights.

8

Biodiversity Litigation in South Africa

A Rich Legal Landscape for Litigation

Willem Daniël Lubbe

1. Introduction

Biodiversity provides jobs, water security, food, and many other benefits that humankind depends on, especially in South Africa,[1] one of seventeen megadiverse countries in the world.[2] It is therefore crucial that law, policy, practitioners, and the judiciary remain aware of the important link between biodiversity and humankind. Even more so since, in a developing economy, there is a direct correlation between the quality of the environment and human dignity.[3] Although we have extreme developmental needs, the environment needs to be considered as a primary concern when aiming to further our developmental needs.

In this regard, Bosselmann argues that sustainable development should be seen in a hierarchical order: first the environment, then people, and finally the economy.[4] Bosselmann further argues that 'nature as a whole has never been on the radar of legal systems'.[5] He indicates that the focus of legal systems has been on components of nature rather than the holistic whole.[6] It is difficult to refute such an observation and much has been written about the fragmented nature of environmental law and law in general.[7] An example may shed light on the potential pitfalls of policy fragmentation.

[1] South African National Biodiversity Institute *National Biodiversity Assessment 2018: The Status of South Africa's Ecosystems and Biodiversity: Synthesis Report* (SANBI 2019) 31.

[2] ibid 3–11.

[3] Michael Kidd, *Environmental Law* (2nd edn, Juta 2011) 73; Dina Lupin Townsend, 'The Place of Human Dignity in Environmental Adjudication' (2017) 3 Oslo Law Review 27.

[4] Klaus Bosselmann, 'Grounding the Rule of Law' in Christina Voigt (ed), *Rule of Law for Nature: New Dimensions and Ideas in Environmental Law* (CUP 2013) 77.

[5] ibid 82.

[6] ibid 82–83.

[7] John Carter Morgan, 'Fragmentation of International Environmental Law and the Synergy' (2016) 18 Vermont Journal of Environmental Law 134; Anne Peters, 'Fragmentation and Constitutionalization' in Anne Orford and Florian Hoffmann (eds), *The Oxford Handbook of the Theory of International Law* (OUP 2016) 1011; Andreas Fischer-Lescano and Gunther Teubner, 'Regime-Collisions: The Vain Search

Willem Daniël Lubbe, *Biodiversity Litigation in South Africa* In: *Biodiversity Litigation*. Edited by: Guillaume Futhazar, Sandrine Maljean-Dubois, and Jona Razzaque, Oxford University Press.
DOI: 10.1093/oso/9780192865465.003.0008

A call for a blanket ban on wildlife trade seems to consecrate environmental and ecosystem health as primary concerns. Does such a call, however, recognize that certain people depend on legal trade to sustain their livelihoods?[8] In this context, it needs to be remembered that conservation in South Africa has an unfortunate legacy where, in many instances, people were removed from their ancestral land to free up space for conservation areas.[9] The human rights impacts of such removals are well documented.[10] Ignoring the importance of the interrelationship between humankind and the environment (in this case, a specific cultural connection as well) has left a lasting antagonism between indigenous communities and conservation authorities. This is, even though countries like South Africa and Australia have, to some extent, tried to rectify the wrongs by returning some of the land.[11]

A country like South Africa, where people depend on biodiversity both directly and indirectly to sustain their livelihoods, provides a complex backdrop for biodiversity conservation. This context must be kept in mind when discussing law, biodiversity, and conservation. This chapter aims to discuss biodiversity litigation in South Africa by answering two main questions:[12] (1) what is the observable influence of international biodiversity law (IBL) in biodiversity litigation; and (2) have we witnessed a paradigm shift in biodiversity litigation? To start, Section 2 will provide a legal and scientific overview of biodiversity in South Africa and give an overview of the institutional structure of the legal system. After that, Section 3 will aim to discuss the influence of IBL using a theme-by-theme approach. This section will tackle issues from sustainable development to animal welfare, among others, by discussing relevant case law. Section 4 highlights observed trends and general observations in biodiversity litigation. Sections 5 and 6 discuss and provide a brief synthesis of the key

for Legal Unity in the Fragmentation of Global Law' in Gunther Teubner and Diana Göbel (eds), *Critical Theory and Legal Autopoiesis* (Manchester UP 2019) 237; Dionysia-Theodora Avgerinopoulou, *Science-Based Lawmaking: How to Effectively Integrate Science in International Environmental Law* (Springer 2019) 75.

[8] Rosie Cooney and Paul Jepson, 'The International Wild Bird Trade: What's Wrong with Blanket Bans?' (2006) 40 Oryx 18 for the potential effect that blanket bans can have on equity. See also Diana S Weber and others, 'Unexpected and Undesired Conservation Outcomes of Wildlife Trade Bans—An Emerging Problem for Stakeholders?' (2015) 3 Global Ecology and Conservation 389; Dilys Roe, *Making a Killing or Making a Living? Wildlife Trade, Trade Controls, and Rural Livelihoods* (IIED 2002).

[9] Daniel Brockington and James Igoe, 'Eviction for Conservation: A Global Overview' (2006) 4 Conservation and Society 424; Marcus Colchester, 'Conservation Policy and Indigenous Peoples' (2004) 7 Environmental Science and Policy 145.

[10] Michael Cernea and Kai Schmidt-Soltau, 'Biodiversity Conservation Versus Population Resettlement: Risks to Nature and Risks to People' in Center for International Forestry Research, *International Conference on Rural Livelihoods, Forests and Biodiversity* (CIFOR 2003) 19–23; Lindsay Hossack and John Nelson (eds), *Indigenous Peoples and Protected Areas in Africa* (Forest Peoples Programme 2003).

[11] Brockington and Igoe (n 9) 452.

[12] Cf Chapter 1 in this volume.

findings. Finally, Section 7 provides some comments and observations on the way forward.

2. Biodiversity in South Africa: An Overview

This section aims to provide a brief overview of the different stakes related to biodiversity in South Africa. The focus will be on the specific characteristics of biodiversity, the challenges to biodiversity, and the implementation of the Aichi Targets. From a geopolitical point of view, the focus will fall on the structure of South Africa as a nation-state and its geopolitical place and role within the African continent. Also, this section will highlight South Africa's participation in IBL, specifically the Convention on Biological Diversity (CBD), and how IBL has been implemented at the national level. Finally, this section will explain the methodology used to select the cases used for this chapter.

2.1 Our Biodiversity and Its Value

Biodiversity supports and maintains ecological infrastructure and is therefore crucial to sustain and provide ecological goods and services essential to human livelihoods.[13] Moreover, various 'biodiversity hotspots' are found in southern Africa.[14]

Hotspots contain biodiversity found nowhere else on the planet, and the biodiversity in hotspots is therefore irreplaceable.[15] Generally, hotspots are selected according to strict criteria. To qualify as a hotspot, a region must hold an exceptional number of endemic species and must face critical threats. Each of the thirty-five selected hotspots worldwide has already lost 70 per cent of its original vegetation.[16] Another significant indicator of the importance of hotspots is that they collectively host 50 per cent of the world's plant species.[17] Moreover, 42 per cent of all terrestrial vertebrate species are endemic to the identified hotspots. Simply put, hotspots host the highest concentrations of endemic biodiversity in the world and consequently also face the most critical threats, such as climate

[13] Alexander Ross Paterson, 'Biological Diversity' in Hendrik Andries Strydom, Nicholas King, and Francois Retief (eds), *Environmental Management in South Africa* (3rd edn, Juta 2018) 532.

[14] Conservation International, 'Hotspots' <www.conservation.org/priorities/biodiversity-hotspots> accessed 14 February 2022. Also see Sean Sloan and others, 'Remaining Natural Vegetation in the Global Biodiversity Hotspots' (2014) 177 Biological Conservation 12.

[15] ibid.

[16] ibid.

[17] ibid.

change, pollution, unsustainable use and overexploitation, and habitat fragmentation and transformation, among other things. Southern Africa is host to six of the eight hotspots in Africa.[18] South Africa has three of the six (sub-regionally) and thirty-four global biodiversity hotspots and is a recognized megadiverse country. South Africa is also considered to be the only megadiverse country to have assessed its entire flora.[19]

2.1.1 Threats and status of biodiversity in South Africa

According to the latest National Biodiversity Strategy and Action Plan (NBSAP), all or most of South Africa's terrestrial, riverine, wetlands, estuaries, coastal, and inshore, as well as offshore ecosystems, are threatened.[20] Loss of natural habitat is the single biggest threat to terrestrial ecosystems and species.[21] Agriculture, mining, plantation forestry, infrastructure development, and urban expansion are the main drivers of this loss.[22]

As a result, loss of ecosystem services, weakened resilience to climate change impacts, loss of livelihoods (for those depending directly on biodiversity), negative impacts on food security, and negative impacts on biodiversity tourism are some of the implications coupled to biodiversity loss.[23] Invasive alien species, illegal wildlife harvesting and trafficking, and climate also contribute to the decline of biodiversity loss.

Maintenance or preservation of biodiversity (the species element, for example) is causally linked to the existence of intact natural habitat (the ecosystem element).[24] The current figures alarmingly indicate that very little natural vegetation is left intact in South Africa, rendering the conservation of biodiversity of critical importance in the region. The conservation of naturally intact vegetation is therefore crucial to conserve, as both the species and genetic elements rely on its existence. Moreover, as most of the identified hotspots in southern Africa traverse sovereign borders, supranational law and policy are crucial to the conservation of biodiversity. Overall, South Africa faces many challenges in conserving

[18] The six hotspots include: the Cape floristic region; the coastal forests of eastern Africa; the Maputaland-Pondoland-Albany region; the succulent Karoo region; Madagascar and the Indian Ocean islands; and the eastern Afromontane. Apart from the Cape floristic region and Madagascar and the Indian Ocean Islands, all of the regions reach across borders within the southern African region.

[19] Department of Environmental Affairs, *National Biodiversity Strategy and Action Plan* (Pretoria 2015) 13.

[20] The extent to which these are threatened differ. See ibid 18, Fig 9.

[21] Paterson (n 13) 530.

[22] ibid.

[23] NBSAP (n 19) 18.

[24] Barry W Brook and others, 'Momentum Drives the Crash: Mass Extinction in the Tropics' (2006) 38 Biotropica 302; Thomas M Brooks and others, 'Habitat Loss and Extinction in the Hotspots of Biodiversity' (2002) 16 Conservation Biology 909; Fangliang He and Pierre Legendre, 'On Species-Area Relations' (1996) 148 American Naturalist 719.

biodiversity. The aforesaid notwithstanding, South Africa—through the continued efforts of the South African National Biodiversity Institute (SANBI)[25] makes great efforts to conserve and manage its biodiversity.

2.1.2 Progress on the implementation of the Aichi Targets

The implementation of the Aichi Targets is hard to quantify. Nonetheless, the NBSAP tables how the strategic objectives of the plan align with the targets. Table 8.1 is a tabulation of the strategic objectives and the Aichi Targets which they aim to effect. This tabulation is a compilation of data deduced from Annex 1, Table 5 of the NBSAP.[26]

Moreover, in terms of the national targets agreed to by South Africa in its Sixth National Report for the Convention on Biological Diversity (Sixth National Report),[27] South Africa seems to take serious cognizance of the targets and aims to achieve these as far as possible through its NBSAP and other biodiversity-related policies. An example can be made of the target aimed to address Aichi Targets 5 and 11: '[b]y 2028, in protected areas: 10.8 m land-based hectares, 353

Table 8.1 Strategic objectives of the NBSAP and its relevance to the Aichi Targets[a]

Strategic objective	Aichi Targets aimed to give effect to
1. Management of biodiversity assets and their contribution to the economy, rural development, job creation, and social well-being is enhanced	6, 11, 12, 13, 14, 15, 16
2. Investments in ecological infrastructure enhance resilience and ensure benefits to society	9, 11, 14, 15
3. Biodiversity considerations are mainstreamed into policies, strategies, and practices of a range of sectors	2, 3, 4, 7, 8, 9, 16, 20
4. People are mobilized to adopt practices that sustain the long-term benefits of biodiversity	1, 4
5. Conservation and management of biodiversity is improved through the development of an equitable and suitably skilled workforce	All Aichi Targets
6. Effective knowledge foundations, including indigenous knowledge and citizen science, support management, conservation, and sustainable use of biodiversity	Underpins all targets

[a] The original figure in the NBSAP contains sub-objectives and further information. See NBSAP (n 19) 64–66, Table 5.

[25] South African National Biodiversity Institute, 'Biodiversity' (2022) <www.sanbi.org/biodiversity/> accessed 12 February 2022.

[26] NBSAP (n 19) 64–66.

[27] Clearing-House Mechanism of the Convention on Biological Diversity, 'Sixth National Report: South Africa' (CBD, 2018) <https://chm.cbd.int/database/record?documentID=241240> accessed 12 February 2022.

km inshore, 210 000 km^2 marine offshore in SA's EEZ plus 93 300 km^2 marine offshore in Prince Edward Islands EEZ.'[28] This target stems from the National Protected Area Expansion Strategy, 2008 (NPAES). This target exceeds the targets set by the CBD. Another example of South Africa's commitment to the Aichi Targets is found in national Target 7 found in the Sixth National Report: 'By 2030, a 10% increase in average annualized GDP growth rate of the SA bioprospecting and wildlife sectors.'[29] This national target directly aims to address Aichi Targets 2 and 3. Supporting this national target is the National Biodiversity Economy Strategy developed by the (then known as) Department of Environmental Affairs (DEA),[30] currently known as the Department of Forestry, Fisheries and the Environment (DEFF). Also, these targets are supported by the Biodiversity Economy Lab (developed under Operation Phakisa)[31] aimed at supporting the revitalization of the agriculture and agro-processing value chain, supporting small, medium, and micro-enterprises. From these two examples, it is clear that South Africa is serious about implementing the Aichi Targets. Most of the goals and targets set are, however, long-term and it remains to be seen to what extent they will be met. The Aichi Targets again enjoy attention in the latest Draft Revised National Biodiversity Framework.[32] It is clear that the DEFF is committed to achieving the targets even after 2020.[33] An example of this is found in the NPAES. Although already aligned with Aichi Target 11, the targets for expansion of protected areas are set to be updated and revised every five years. The biodiversity framework is not static and it is clear that the DEFF sees the Aichi Targets not as end-goals, but rather as waymarkers on the road towards sustainability.[34]

2.2 South Africa from a Legal and Institutional Perspective

This section aims to briefly discuss the legal and institutional structure of South Africa and how this structure accommodates the implementation of IBL. In doing so, the following elements will be addressed: South Africa's approach to

[28] ibid 4.

[29] ibid 9.

[30] Currently the Department of Forestry, Fisheries and the Environment.

[31] Operation Phakisa is a programme aimed at fast-tracking specific areas in need of critical developmental assistance. Included in these areas are, among others, oceans economy, mining health, tourism, and basic education. For more information, see Department of Planning, Monitoring and Evaluation, 'Operation Phakisa' <www.operationphakisa.gov.za/Pages/Home.aspx> accessed 12 February 2022.

[32] Department of Environment, Forestry and Fisheries, 'Draft Revised National Biodiversity Framework 2019–2024' (2021), published for comment in N 171 in GG 44229 of 5 March 2021.

[33] ibid 18–39, Table 4.

[34] Author's personal observation. It must be noted that the success of the biodiversity framework lies in the hands of the executive. In other words, the framework needs to be translated into grassroots action by the implementation thereof.

the implementation of international law; a tabulation of the most important IBL instruments to which South Africa is party; the status of South Africa's NBSAP; and a brief exposition of the implementation of IBL instruments at the national level. Finally, this section will present the methodology used to select the cases for this particular chapter.

2.2.1 Institutional structure and legal approach

South Africa is a unitary state consisting of three spheres of government: national, provincial, and local.[35] These spheres are described as distinctive, interdependent, and interrelated.[36] South Africa follows a dualistic approach to the domestication of international law. In brief, international legal instruments need to be ratified *and* subsequently incorporated into national law before being domestically binding.[37] South Africa is further divided into three branches: the executive, legislative, and judiciary. It is important to note that the judiciary functions on the precedent system observing a hierarchy among courts. Figure 8.1 explains.[38]

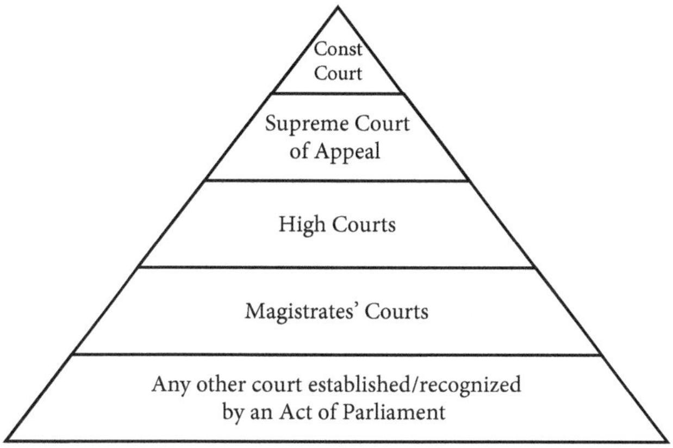

Figure 8.1 Hierarchy of the judicial system in South Africa[a]

[a] Note that in terms of s 166(c) of the Constitution, High Courts can also act as courts of appeal for any courts of similar status as the High Court of South Africa. Also note the lowest level as depicted in the figure may (depending on its type) assume the powers of any level in the hierarchy—apart from the Supreme Court of Appeal and the Constitutional Court. For a further discussion on the court system, see PG Du Toit, 'A Critical Evaluation of the Prohibition on the South African Prosecuting Authority to Appeal against Decisions on Questions of Fact' (2019) 30 Criminal Law Forum 451.

[35] Section 40(1) of the Constitution of the Republic of South Africa, 1996.

[36] ibid. See Anél A Du Plessis, 'Understanding the Legal Context' in Alexander R Paterson and Louis J Kotzé, *Environmental Compliance and Enforcement in South Africa: Legal Perspectives* (Juta 2009) 30–33.

[37] See s 231 of the Constitution and specifically s 231(4) stating: '(4) Any international agreement becomes law in the Republic when it is enacted into law by national legislation; but a self-executing provision of an agreement that has been approved by Parliament is law in the Republic unless it is inconsistent with the Constitution or an Act of Parliament.'

[38] This figure is based on s 166 of the Constitution.

Table 8.2 Selection of IBL instruments ratified by South Africa[a]

Instrument	Date of ratification/accession/signature
The CBD	1996 (R)
• Cartagena Protocol	2003 (A)
• Nagoya Protocol on access and benefit sharing	2013 (R)
Ramsar Convention	1975 (S)
Bonn Convention	1983 (S)
• CMS	1991 (S)
• AEWA	2002 (S)
• ACAP	2003 (S)
• Atlantic turtles	MoU signatory 2007
• IOSEA marine turtles	MoU signatory 2005
• Birds of prey (raptors)	MoU signatory 2008
• Sharks	MoU signatory 2011
CITES	1975 (R)
WHC	1977 (R)
International Plant Protection Convention	1956 (R)
International Whaling Convention	1948 (R)

[a] A list selected specifically for this chapter. The list is not exhaustive.

South Africa has a strong commitment to IBL,[39] as reflected by its signature and ratification of many multilateral environmental agreements which are shown in Table 8.2.

Mere involvement and membership should not, however, be seen as a success story. Success should ultimately be measured against the extent to which

[39] Apart from the general institutional structure elaborated on earlier, South Africa is a member of the regional organization the African Union (AU) and a member of the sub-regional Southern African Development Community (SADC). Both organizations create supranational law and South Africa actively takes part in and plays a leading role in both organizations. Unfortunately, South Africa's contribution in this regard is not always positive. In 2014, the SADC Summit issued a protocol rendering the SADC Tribunal ineffective. This decision was supported and signed by former President Jacob Zuma. This action by the SADC Summit led to, amongst other things, litigation in the South African courts challenging the legality of the former President's action. In *Law Society of South Africa v President of the Republic of South Africa* (2019) (3) SA 30 (CC), para 52, Chief Justice Mogoeng Mogoeng described the action as follows: 'Our President's signature is symbolic of a warm welcome by South Africa of the stealthy introduction of impunified disregard for and violation of fundamental rights or key Treaty provisions. It inadvertently but in reality reassures all others that we would turn a blind eye to human rights abuses and non-adherence to the rule of law in their jurisdictions even if it affects our people.' Given the important link between human rights and the environment, this example of 'regional interaction' is troubling. Environmental law of the AU and SADC contains general provisions and has not yet been the subject of national litigation.

these instruments are effected through their enforcement and implantation through national legislation.

2.2.2 Legal framework implementing IBL

As already pointed out, South Africa follows a dualist approach to the domestication of international law.[40] A constitutional duty is placed on the judiciary to interpret legislation in a manner consistent with international law.[41] The aforementioned duty is important when keeping in mind what the influence of IBL *should be* on domestic law in South Africa. Bearing this in mind, all environmental legislation and policy in South Africa are informed by section 24 of the Constitution:

> Everyone has the right—
> (a) to an environment that is not harmful to their health or wellbeing; and
> (b) to have the environment protected, for the benefit of present and future generations, through reasonable legislative and other measures that—
>   (i) prevent pollution and ecological degradation;
>   (ii) promote conservation; and
>   (iii) secure ecologically sustainable development and use of natural resources while promoting justifiable economic and social development.

To give effect to section 24, the National Environmental Management Act (NEMA) was promulgated to serve as umbrella legislation in terms of which sector-specific legislation is adopted.[42] Complementing the NEMA is, among others, the NEMA: Biodiversity Act (NEMBA),[43] the NEMA Protected Areas Act (NEMPA),[44] the NEMA: Integrated Coastal Management Act (NEMICM),[45] the NEMA: Air Quality Act (NEMAQA),[46] and the NEMA: Waste Act (NEMWA).[47] This list contains the main national

[40] Section 231(1)–(4) of the Constitution. Section 232 of the Constitution determines that customary international law is deemed to be law in the Republic unless it is inconsistent with the South African Constitution.

[41] Section 233 of the Constitution determines that when interpreting any legislation every court must prefer any reasonable interpretation of the legislation that is consistent with international law over any alternative interpretation that is inconsistent with international law.

[42] Act 107 of 1998.

[43] Act 10 of 2004.

[44] Act 57 of 2003.

[45] Act 24 of 2008.

[46] Act 39 of 2004.

[47] Act 59 of 2008.

instruments for environmental governance in South Africa. It is not an exhaustive list and it is complemented by myriad provincial laws and local government by-laws.[48]

2.2.2.1 *Implementation of IBL at the national level*

Because South Africa follows the dualist approach to international law, biodiversity-related conventions[49] are effected and implemented by national legislation. In general, this is provided for in section 25 of NEMA.[50] An example is found in section 5 of NEMBA stating that '[t]his Act gives effect to ratified international agreements affecting biodiversity to which South Africa is a party, and which bind the republic'. The best example is found in the World Heritage Convention Act (WHCA)[51] which was promulgated to specifically implement the World Heritage Convention (WHC).

2.2.3 Methodology for selection of cases

The method used to select the cases was based on a database search of all reported judgments in South Africa refined by cases that are relevant to the IBL instruments mentioned in this chapter. Preference was given to cases that were decided in the Constitutional Court and courts in the upper parts of the judicial hierarchy since these set the tone and precedent for future legal interpretation.[52] The sample of cases was divided into six themes to structure the

[48] The true complexity of the South African environmental legal landscape cannot be explained within the confines of this chapter. For further reading on this issue see, in general, Hendrik Andries Strydom, Nicholas King, and Francois Retief (eds), *Environmental Management in South Africa* (3rd edn, Juta 2018).

[49] See Table 8.2.

[50] Section 25(3) specifically provides:

> The Minister may introduce legislation in Parliament or make such regulations as may be necessary for giving effect to an international environmental instrument to which the Republic is a party, and such legislation and regulations may deal with inter alia the following—
> (a) the co-ordination of the implementation of the instrument.
> (b) the allocation of responsibilities in terms of the instrument, including those of other organs of state.
> (c) the gathering of information, including for the purposes of compiling and updating reports required in terms of the instrument and for submission to Parliament.
> (d) the dissemination of information related to the instrument and reports from international meetings.
> (e) initiatives and steps regarding research, education, training, awareness raising and capacity building.
> (f) ensuring public participation.
> (g) implementation of and compliance with the provisions of the instrument, including the creation of offences and the prescription of penalties where applicable; and
> (h) any other matter necessary to give effect to the instrument.

[51] Act 49 of 1999.

[52] See Figure 8.1.

discussion and was limited since it is not possible to include all case law in a single chapter.[53]

3. Biodiversity Litigation in South Africa

3.1 Introduction

This section aims to discuss selected litigation relevant to the IBL discussed earlier. Because South Africa follows the dualist approach to international law,[54] the courts seldom directly mention or refer to IBL.[55] This is balanced by the fact that international law is incorporated in the national legal framework. To structure the following discussion, a themed approach will be followed. Two main themes are: specific environmental litigation (3.2) and rights-based litigation (3.3). The cases discussed here are only representative of litigation trends and not meant to be a complete list of cases.

3.2 Specific Environmental Litigation

This section will discuss themes that can be considered environmental-specific and are relevant to biodiversity conservation. The sub-themes addressed will be: sustainable development, wildlife crime, protected areas, total allowable catch and precaution, and animal welfare.

3.2.1 Sustainable development

In *Fuel Retailers Association of SA (Pty) Ltd v Director-General, Environmental Management, Mpumalanga*,[56] the Constitutional Court considered the concept

[53] South Africa has a vast number of legal cases and it would be impossible to include them all. This chapter is a selection of the many available cases filtered by a very specific mandate.

[54] Various pieces of legislation and policy were adopted as a direct result of the CBD (opened for signature 5 June 1992, entered into force 29 December 1993) 1760 UNTS 69. Also, South Africa complies with the duties set forth in arts 6 and 26 of the CBD and submits her NBSAP as required. The NBSAP serves as a roadmap for the implementation and strategic goals within which legislation and policy operate. See NBSAP (n 19) for the 2015–25 NBSAP.

[55] In *Willemse v Patelia* [2007] 2 BLLR 164 (LC), the labour court, in a case concerning employment equity, made special mention of the involvement of the applicant in South Africa's responsibilities resulting from the ratification of the CBD. Although not stated explicitly, it is deduced that the court held in high regard the applicant's connection to the CBD and by implication a high regard for the CBD itself. The involvement of the applicant with the CBD was considered in the light of his suitability for the post of Director: Biodiversity Management in the Department of Environmental Affairs and Tourism.

[56] 2007 (6) SA 4 (CC).

of sustainable development in the context of an application to erect a filling station. The Constitutional Court explicitly referred to the concept of sustainable development as developed in international law including the Stockholm Conference,[57] the Brundtland Report,[58] the instruments flowing from the 1992 United Nations Conference on Environment and Development,[59] and the World Summit on Sustainable Development.[60] It would seem that the court held in high regard the international legal context of sustainable development. Moreover, the court gave an opinion on the general role of the courts in the protection of the environment:[61]

> [t]he role of the courts is especially important in the context of the protection of the environment and giving effect to the principle of sustainable development. The importance of the protection of the environment cannot be gainsaid. Its protection is vital to the enjoyment of the other rights contained in the Bill of Rights; indeed, it is vital to life itself. It must therefore be protected for the benefit of the present and future generations. The present generation holds the earth in trust for the next generation. This trusteeship position carries with it the responsibility to look after the environment. It is the duty of the Court to ensure that this responsibility is carried out. Indeed, the Johannesburg Principles adopted at the Global Judges' Symposium underscore the role of the Judiciary in the protection of the environment.

The importance of the above passage, coming from the highest court in South Africa, cannot be overstated. By referring to the important benchmark international legal developments alluded to above, the court underlines the importance of international environmental law when considering the interpretation of national environmental law.[62]

[57] Declaration of the United Nations Conference on the Human Environment, UN Doc A/CONF.48/14/Rev.1 (1972).

[58] World Commission on Environment and Development, *Our Common Future* (OUP 2009).

[59] The United Nations Conference on Environment and Development was held in Rio de Janeiro, Brazil, on 3–14 June 1992. The court only referred to 'instruments' and did not specify any apart from the Rio Declaration.

[60] Held in Johannesburg, South Africa, 2002.

[61] *Fuel Retailers* case (n 57) para 102. The court goes further and refers to some of the principles adopted at the Global Judges' Symposium. See paras 102–04.

[62] For an in-depth discussion of the case, see Tumo Murombo, 'From Crude Environmentalism to Sustainable Development: *Fuel Retailers*' (2008) 125 South African Law Journal 488; Loretta Feris, 'Sustainable Development in Practice: *Fuel Retailers Association of Southern Africa v Director-General Environmental Management, Department of Agriculture, Conservation and Environment, Mpumalanga Province*: Case Comments' (2008) 1(1) Constitutional Court Review 235, among others.

3.2.2 Wildlife crime

It is perhaps prudent to first refer to a remark made in the Supreme Court of Appeal (SCA)[63] in *S v Lemthongthai*.[64] In a case concerning rhino poaching, Navsa ADP elaborates on the constitutional duty placed on the judiciary by section 24, stating:[65]

> [t]he duty resting on us to protect and conserve our biodiversity is owed to present and future generations. In so doing, we will also be redressing past neglect. Constitutional values dictate a more caring attitude towards fellow humans, animals and the environment in general.

Considering this remark, it is clear that the court takes its constitutional duty seriously and that the court is aware of topical environmental discourse. Still, given the strong position taken by the Constitutional Court in the *Fuel Retailers* case, a more progressive interpretation could have been given to section 24. That notwithstanding, the court is bound by the arguments before it and since this was an appeal against a sentence there was little room, apart from the *obiter* remark above, to provide any further elaboration that may have alluded to IBL. Redress, as alluded to by the court, would seem to be in the form of the sentence imposed by the Supreme Court of Appeal. Although the sentence here was reduced from thirty to thirteen years, the court found that proportionality was important when considering the sentence.[66]

In a case in 2021, *S v Ndlovu*,[67] the sentencing for ten incidents of rhino poaching came under the spotlight.[68] The High Court[69] had to hear an appeal against a sentence and had to consider whether or not the trial court had imposed sentences that were 'shockingly disproportionate' under the circumstances.[70] After meticulous consideration of the foundational sentencing principle[71] as well as stating that the trial court 'correctly found that the interests of the community must be accorded the necessary weight and that it

[63] Many cases related to wildlife crime exist in South Africa but only a few can be included here.

[64] *S v Lemthongthai* 2015 (1) SACR 353 (SCA). The Supreme Court of Appeal is the second highest court in South Africa, the Constitutional Court being the highest.

[65] ibid para 20.

[66] ibid para 21.

[67] 2021 (1) SACR 299 (ECG).

[68] The court also considered a question related to the admissibility of evidence which will not be discussed here.

[69] Eastern Cape division, Makhanda.

[70] *Ndlovu* case (n 68) para 1.2.

[71] ibid para 61: 'the punishment must fit the criminal as well as the crime, be fair to society, and be blended with a measure of mercy'.

would not be served by sentences which are disproportionately light in comparison with the seriousness of the offences',[72] the court held that the sentence of twenty-five years' direct imprisonment was indeed appropriate. It is important to note that the court considered the bigger picture of poaching and environmental sustainability when it considered the appropriateness of the sentence.

3.2.3 Protected areas

In 2021, in *Mining and Environmental Justice Community Network of South Africa v Uthaka Energy (Pty) Ltd*[73] Davis J considered an application by a conglomerate of NGOs to review and set aside the permission that was given to conduct coal-mining activities in protected wetland areas. Davis J considered section 24 of the Constitution, NEMA, NEMBA, NEMPA, and various other Acts before setting aside two of the decisions and remitting one back to the relevant ministers for reconsideration. Referring to the trusteeship role of the state, the High Court stated:[74]

> NEMPAA provides in section 3 thereof that 'in fulfilling the rights contained in section 24 of the Constitution, the State, through the organs of state implementing legislation applicable to protected areas, must act as the trustee of protected areas in the Republic'. Although the principle of sustainable development finds application, it is subject to more scrutiny than otherwise if the area in which the proposed development, in this case, underground coal mining, is to take place, is a protected environment. The MPE comprises of wetlands and grasslands which, ... have largely been classified as 'Irreplaceable Critical Biodiversity Areas'.

Considering an argument related to the applicability of the precautionary principle, the court takes the view that, where a protected environment is concerned, it is the duty of the court to 'err on the side of protection of possible harm and to prevent the occurrence of harm which may be irreversible'.[75] In so doing, mining activities were halted in the protected area pending the outcome of various other reviews and appeals.[76]

[72] ibid para 66.
[73] (11761/2021) [2021] ZAGPPHC 195 (30 March 2021) (hereafter *Mabola* case).
[74] ibid para 6.12.
[75] ibid para 6.22. This was stated in response to the respondents that precaution meant that 'to err on the side of caution thus means to insist on mitigation measures despite uncertainty and not to veto development because of uncertainty'.
[76] ibid para 9.

3.2.4 Total allowable catch and precaution

In *WWF South Africa v Minister of Agriculture, Forestry and Fisheries*,[77] the High Court had to decide on the lawfulness of the total allowable catch (TAC) for west coast rock lobster. In brief, the TAC was set at the same tonnage as the previous season. This was done against the recommendation of the Scientific Working Group (SWG) established by the department to significantly reduce the TAC.[78] The court found that South Africa is party to both the United Nations Convention on the Law of the Sea (UNCLOS) and the SADC Protocol on Fisheries and that both of these instruments point to the inclusion of best scientific evidence in decision making, which in this case was ignored.[79] In declaring the TAC unlawful, the court gave a full exposition of the precautionary and risk-averse approach by not only discussing the South African legal framework, but also referencing and discussing European, Canadian, Indian, and Australian jurisprudence.[80] In so doing, the court sent a clear message as to the importance of the precautionary approach in environmental decision making.

3.2.5 Animal welfare

In *National Council of the Society for Prevention of Cruelty to Animals v Minister of Environmental Affairs* (*Lion Bone* case),[81] the High Court[82] needed to establish whether the export quota set for lion bones was unlawful. In brief, the court found that the export quota, as established by the Minister of DEFF (then DEA), was an administrative action subject to administrative review. In a decision heavily favouring a welfare interpretation, the export quota was declared unlawful and unconstitutional. Kollapen J remarked:[83]

> if as a country we have decided to engage in trade in lion bone, which appears to be the case for now, then at the very least our constitutional and legal obligations that arise from Section 24, NEMBA and the Plan require the consideration of animal welfare issues.

The court specifically focused on the welfare of lions in captivity and stated that this welfare was not considered when the export quote was set.[84]

77 2019 (2) SA 403 (WCC).
78 The SWG suggested that the TAC be lowered from 1924.8 tons to 790 tons.
79 *WWF* case (n 78) para 117.
80 ibid paras 100–16.
81 2019 (4) All SA 249 (GP).
82 Gauteng division.
83 *Lion Bone* case (n 82) para 74.
84 The court further explained and unpacked how CITES influences the decision making where a quota is set. This starts with the regulations published to effect CITES and the synergy between NEMBA, the minister, and CITES. See *Lion Bone* case (n 82) paras 15–23.

In *National Council of Societies for the Prevention of Cruelty to Animals v Openshaw*, the SCA had to consider an application for an interdict where live prey was fed to tigers.[85] The SCA found that no evidence was placed before it creating the likelihood of future transgressions and therefore dismissed the application.[86] In a dissenting opinion, however, Cameron JA highlighted the importance of animal welfare and made reference to the sentience of animals that make them worthy of being protected from 'human ill-treatment'.[87]

3.3 Rights-Based Litigation

This section investigates environmental litigation primarily brought in terms of fundamental or procedural rights. Crucially, through the recognition of a right to a healthy environment in the South African Constitution, it is possible for biodiversity litigation to be 'elevated' to constitutional litigation. Consequently, fundamental rights refer to litigation based on constitutional rights and procedural rights to matters procedural in nature. Cost orders and public participation being two examples. It is important to note that the distinction made here can be misleading as many procedural rights (such as public participation) are embedded in the South African Constitution.

3.3.1 Procedural rights

3.3.1.1 Access to information and cost

In *Trustees, Biowatch v Registrar: Genetic Resources*,[88] Biowatch—an NGO dedicated to the implementation and monitoring of the CBD in South Africa—applied for a mandamus[89] to obtain information on genetically modified organisms (GMOs). The main issue in the case revolved around access to information and whether the Genetically Modified Organisms Act[90] could, in certain circumstances, limit the constitutionally protected right to access to information.[91] Biowatch only partially succeeded in its application and received an unfavourable cost order. Biowatch appealed this decision through various courts and eventually came before the Constitutional Court. In *Biowatch Trust*

[85] 2008 (5) SA 339 (SCA), paras 1–6.
[86] In the High Court, it was found that Openshaw contravened the Animals Protection Act 71 of 1962.
[87] *Openshaw* case (n 86) para 38.
[88] 2005 (4) SA 111 (T).
[89] A mandamus is an interdict to force a party to do something.
[90] Act 15 of 1997.
[91] Section 32 of the Constitution.

v Registrar, Genetic Resources,[92] the Constitutional Court decided only on cost orders, clarifying especially what should happen in matters where public interest litigation is at play. Importantly, the court remarked that in constitutional litigation cost orders should, as a primary consideration, contemplate 'the way in which a costs order would hinder or promote the advancement of constitutional justice'.[93] The Constitutional Court further underlined the principle that where private parties litigate against the state, the state should bear its own costs where it wins, and where it loses it should pay the costs of the private party.[94]

3.3.1.2 Locus standi, rationality, and public participation

In *Landev (Pty) Ltd v Black Eagle Project Roodekrans*,[95] various important findings related to public interest litigation were made. Landev sought an order[96] that would effectively bring to a halt the litigation by Black Eagle opposing the authorization of development in an area that, according to expert testimony, endangered the survival of raptors.[97] Landev argued that Black Eagle was unable to meet any adverse cost order, their litigation was reckless, and that they lacked *locus standi* in the matter. The High Court[98] found against Landev on all three arguments. Importantly, the court underlined both section 38 of the Constitution and section 32 of NEMA relating to *locus standi*. Concerning section 32 of NEMA, the court stated:[99]

> The right of a public interest group to litigate in respect of a breach or threatened breach of the provisions of NEMA is provided for in section 32(1) of that Act.... In my view, section 32(1) of NEMA confers locus standi to approach a court for relief in respect of any breach or threatened breach of NEMA either because it is in that group of persons' own interest or in the interest of or on behalf of the person who is for practical reasons unable to institute such proceedings or if it is in the public interest or in the interests of protecting the environment.

[92] 2009 (6) SA 232 (CC).
[93] ibid para 16.
[94] ibid para 22.
[95] *Landev (Pty) Ltd v Black Eagle Project, Roodekrans In re Black Eagle Project, Roodekrans v MEC, Department of Agriculture, Conservation & Environment, Gauteng Provincial Government* 2010 JOL 25241 (GSJ).
[96] ibid para 7.
[97] ibid para 39.
[98] South Gauteng division, Johannesburg.
[99] *Landev* case (n 96) para 40.

In more recent litigation in *The Black Eagle Project Roodekrans v The MEC: Department of Agriculture, Conservation and Environment, Gauteng Provincial Department*,[100] Black Eagle partially succeeded in challenging a decision taken by the MEC.[101] Still dealing with the matter of development (as alluded to in the *Landev* case earlier) in the area crucial to the survival of raptors, the Black Eagle Project opposed a decision taken by the MEC that allowed Landev to increase the number of residential units from 358 to 1,064 in the ecologically sensitive area. The High Court, because there was no public participation informing the decision by the MEC or any reasons given for the decision, set it aside.[102] The court connects provision of reasons to rationality and uses the SCA for authority:[103]

> As to rationality, I think it is rather cynical to say to an affected individual: you have a constitutional right to a rational decision but you are not entitled to know the reasons for that decision.

The court further reaffirmed the principle that a private party bringing a matter to court asserting a constitutional right should not be mulcted with costs should they be unsuccessful.[104]

In *Federation of South African Fly Fisheries v Minister of Environmental Affairs*,[105] an application was brought by the Federation of South African Fly Fishers (FOSAF) to declare invalid the draft regulations on alien and invasive species.[106] The effect of the proposed changes to the species listed would be that both brown and rainbow trout would be listed as alien and invasive. It was argued by FOSAF that the minister had failed to comply with the public participation requirements as set out in NEMBA.[107] One of the concerns raised

[100] 2019 JDR 0337 (GJ).

[101] Member of the Executive Council. This normally refers to the members forming the cabinet of a provincial government in South Africa. They are headed by the Premier.

[102] *Black Eagle* case (n 101) para 50.

[103] *Judicial Service Commission v Cape Bar Council* 2013 (1) SA 170 (SCA) para 44.

[104] *Black Eagle* case (n 101), para 49; *Biowatch Trust v Registrar, Genetic Resources and others* 2009 (6) SA 232 (CC), paras 21–25.

[105] (62486/2018) [2021] ZAGPPHC 575 (10 September 2021).

[106] These regulations were published in GN 112 and GN 115 in GG 41445 of 16 February 2018. Interestingly, the court referred to the CBD in the context of the regulation of biological diversity. However, it only mentioned the CBD and thereafter proceeded to discuss the NEMBA as one of the Acts adopted to manage and conserve biodiversity. See the *FOSAF* case (n 106) para 1.

[107] *FOSAF* case (n 106), para 14. Section 99 of NEMBA deals with the consultation of relevant parties and s 100 deals with public participation. Section 100 determines:

> (1) The Minister must give notice of the proposed exercise of the power referred to in section 99—
> (a) in the *Gazette*; and
> (b) in at least one newspaper distributed nationally, or if the exercise of the power may affect only a specific area, in at least one newspaper distributed in that area.

by FOSAF was that the minister did not provide sufficient information in the notices to enable meaningful public participation.[108] The court tellingly noted that public participation:

> in democratic processes is not the exclusive preserve of educated members of society who can read English or the privileged few who have access to the internet. Participative democracy is one of the foundational values of the Constitution and everyone should be encouraged and enabled to participate. Section 100 gives effect to the notion of participative democracy and should be interpreted in a manner which is consistent with the notion.[109]

Given this view of meaningful participation in participative democracy, the court declared the publishing of the draft regulations invalid.[110]

3.3.2 Fundamental rights

3.3.2.1 Right to property and freedom of expression

In *Petro Props (Pty) Ltd v Barlow*,[111] the High Court had to consider the rights of campaigners to oppose the erection of a service station in a wetland area. The applicant argued that it had applied for and received permission for construction and contended that its fundamental property rights under section 25 of the Constitution had to prevail over the respondent's fundamental right to freedom of expression under section 16 of the Constitution. The applicant argued that their only remedy was through administrative appeals. This argument was rejected by the High Court. Importantly, the court found that the right to freedom of expression outweighed the constitutional property right in this specific context dealing with the environment. Consequently, the

(2) The notice must—
  (a) invite members of the public to submit to the Minister, within 30 days of publication of the notice in the *Gazette*, written representations on, or objections to, the proposed exercise of the power; and
  (b) contain sufficient information to enable members of the public to submit meaningful representations or objections.
(3) The Minister may in appropriate circumstances allow any interested person or community to present oral representations or objections to the Minister or a person designated by the Minister.
(4) The Minister must give due consideration to all representations or objections received or presented before exercising the power.

[108] *FOSAF* case (n 106) para 45.

[109] ibid para 66.

[110] It should be noted that the decision was not on the content of the regulations but on the conduct of the minister in how the regulations were published. See the *FOSAF* case (n 106) para 68.

[111] 2006 (5) SA 160 (W).

application by Petro Props was dismissed and the respondent could continue to campaign against the erection of the service station.[112]

3.3.2.2 Right to a healthy environment and right to language and culture

In *Sustaining the Wild Coast NPC v Minister of Mineral Resources and Energy* (*Shell* case),[113] the High Court was approached for an interim interdict to stop Shell from proceeding with a seismic survey off the eastern coast of South Africa. The applicants consisted of non-profit companies, natural persons, and a communal property association.[114] The application was brought in two parts: Part A, to interdict the seismic survey pending the relief sought under Part B; and Part B sought to interdict the respondents from proceeding with the seismic survey 'unless and until' an environmental authorization had been granted under the NEMA.[115] To secure an interdict under A, the applicants had to satisfy the court that they had established, among others, at least a prima facie right and reasonable apprehension of irreparable and imminent harm of the right if the interim interdict was not granted.[116] To satisfy that requirement, the applicants claimed that three of their constitutional rights were implicated in the proposed seismic survey. These were sections 24, 30, and 31 of the Constitution.[117] The court had clear empathy with the local communities and their connection to the land. This empathy manifested in the recognition by the court of the importance of the land to the communities' socio-economic and cultural well-being.[118] Moreover, the court found that the consultation process followed by Shell was inadequate.[119] This was based, among other reasons, on the fact that publication of the Environmental Management Programme

[112] ibid paras 75–76.

[113] (3491/2021) [2021] ZAECGHC 118 (28 December 2021).

[114] ibid para 2 of the decision for a full list of applicants.

[115] *Shell* case (n 114) para 1.

[116] Furthermore, that the balance of convenience favours the granting of the interim interdict; and that they have no other satisfactory remedy. See *Shell* case (n 114) para 7.

[117] The content of s 24 of the Constitution has already been covered in Section 2.2.2. Section 30 protects language and culture: 'Everyone has the right to use the language and to participate in the cultural life of their choice, but no one exercising these rights may do so in a manner inconsistent with any provision of the Bill of Rights'; and s 31 deals with the rights related to cultural, religious, and linguistic communities:

> (1) Persons belonging to a cultural, religious or linguistic community may not be denied the right, with other members of that community—
> (a) to enjoy their culture, practise their religion and use their language; and
> (b) to form, join and maintain cultural, religious and linguistic associations and other organs of civil society.
>
> (2) The rights in subsection (1) may not be exercised in a manner inconsistent with any provision of the Bill of Rights.

[118] See generally the *Shell* case (n 114) paras 12–19.

[119] ibid para 22.

(EMP) was done only in English and Afrikaans while the affected communities of the affected communities were mostly isiZulu and isiXhosa.[120] Very interestingly the court also recognized the fact that the consultation route followed by Shell was culturally inappropriate.[121] In so doing, the court recognized and gave effect to indigenous law. The court eloquently stated:[122]

> I accept that the customary practices and spiritual relationship that the applicant communities have with the sea may be foreign to some and therefore difficult to comprehend. How can ancestors reside in the sea and how can they be disturbed, may be asked. It is not the duty of this court to seek answers to those questions. We must accept that those practices and beliefs exist. What this case is about is to show that had Shell consulted with the applicant communities, it would have been informed about those practices and beliefs and would then have considered, with the applicant communities, the measures to be taken to mitigate against the possible infringement of those practices and beliefs. In terms of the [C]onstitution those practices and beliefs must be respected and where conduct offends those practices and beliefs and impacts negatively on the environment, the court has a duty to step in and protect those who are offended and the environment.

The court granted the interim relief and postponed Part B of the application to a later date. This case is recognition of the linkage between biodiversity, culture, and socio-economic well-being. Pending Part B of the application, the affected local communities, at least for the present, enjoy protection.

4. Biodiversity Litigation Trends: General Observations

4.1 Introduction

South Africa is endowed with a comprehensive, yet sector-specific, environmental framework. As a result, courts usually deal with matters in a sector-specific way. Biodiversity, as a holistic concept, is not necessarily used or decided upon in cases. A definite trend can be seen in the attitude of certain judges relating to biodiversity. Remarks in cases such as the *Lion Bone* case

[120] ibid para 22.
[121] ibid para 26.
[122] ibid para 32.

about the welfare of animals as well as the recognition of the state of rhinos (both globally and nationally) in the *Ndlovu* case show an awareness by judges of topical biodiversity-related issues. The South African legal system allows for expert evidence to be presented and considered. This evidence usually takes the form of reports produced by experts.[123] It is standard practice for judges to engage with and consider such reports. It should be considered here that the judicial system is accusatorial and not inquisitorial. Especially in civil cases, the court will be bound by the evidence before it unless it is found to be necessary to obtain more.[124] In criminal cases, however, the court may, in specific circumstances, ask a witness to present evidence where the parties before the court have presented reports and evidence that are contradictory.[125]

4.2 Public or Private Law

The law in South Africa provides an opportunity to institute both criminal and civil litigation for environmental purposes. For clarity, public law normally refers to a situation where the law regulates the relationship between the state and the citizenry[126] and private law usually refers to the situation where the law regulates the relationship between natural persons.[127] Normally, where an act has been transgressed, the state will institute criminal proceedings if such contravention is a criminal offence.[128] However, the law provides an opportunity for actors other than the state to litigate on behalf of the environment. This stems from the fact that the state merely serves as a custodian for the environment.[129] With this idea as a basis, this section will briefly unpack the standing for litigation in general as well as private criminal prosecutions.

123 Rule 24 of the *Rules Regulating the Conduct of the Proceedings of the Magistrates' Courts of South Africa* (GN R740 in GG 33487 of 23 August 2010), for example.

124 Rule 29 of the Rules Board for Courts of Law has, under s 6 of the Rules Board for Courts of Law Act 107 of 1985, read with s 9(6)*(a)* of the Jurisdiction of Regional Courts Amendment Act 31 of 2008.

125 Louis Theodor Christian Harms, 'Demystification of the Inquisitorial System' (2011) 14 Potchefstroom Electronic Journal Law Journal 1. Also see DWM Broughton, 'Accusatorial (Adversarial) Process as a Mechanism for Engendering or Promoting Judicial Impartiality in the Face of Adverse Pre-Trial Publicity' (2019) 82 Tydskrif vir Hedendaagse Romeins-Hollandse Reg (Journal for Contemporary Roman-Dutch Law) 363; *Banana v Attorney-General* (1999) (1) BCLR 27 (ZS) on the impartiality of a presiding officer and a fair trial.

126 This can be described as a vertical relationship: eg state v individual.

127 Horizontal application of the law, in other words.

128 Where the state does not prosecute, private parties can also institute prosecution. See eg the *NSPCA* case discussed later at n 138.

129 Section 2(4)(o) of NEMA: '[t]he environment is held in public trust for the people, the beneficial use of environmental resources must serve the public interest and the environment must be protected as the people's common heritage'.

A theme covered throughout this section will be the relief sought in the form of damages as well as the possibility of forfeiture of assets.

4.2.1 Legal standing

When aiming to litigate, one of the primary concerns is whether or not the litigant will be allowed to appear in the matter at hand. In plain terms: does that litigant have standing before the court? Section 32 of NEMA regulates legal standing for private individuals. This section allows people or groups of people to litigate:

(a) in that person's or group of person's own interest;
(b) in the interest of, or on behalf of, a person who is, for practical reasons, unable to institute such proceedings;
(c) in the interest of or on behalf of a group or class of persons whose interests are affected;
(d) in the public interest; and
(e) in the interest of protecting the environment.

This section of NEMA is complimented by section 38 of the Constitution which provides generously for legal standing and, of specific interest to biodiversity litigation, is the determination that anyone acting in the public interest protecting a right in the Bill of Rights[130] can approach a competent court.

4.2.2 Private prosecution and civil litigation

4.2.2.1 Private prosecution in general

Where the state decides not to prosecute an alleged offence, section 33 of NEMA allows for private prosecution provided that the proper procedure was followed as set out in the Criminal Procedure Act.[131] In this instance, individuals may take it upon themselves to prosecute alleged criminals. It should be made clear that private prosecution is not only limited to individuals but that legal entities (like non-profit organizations) can also institute such proceedings. What can be claimed *if* prosecution should succeed? Section 34 of NEMA indicates that a party must provide proof of the amount of the loss or damage and, upon proof, the court may then render a judgment. This judgment will have the same effect in terms of its execution as a civil action. Where

[130] This is ch 2 of the Constitution containing all of the human rights, including s 24, the environmental right.
[131] Section 7 of the Criminal Procedure Act 51 of 1977 regulates private prosecution on certificate *nolle prosequi*.

a conviction is obtained under, for example transgressions in terms of the NEMBA, the court may investigate and assess the monetary value of the advantage gained or likely to be gained. Based on this assessment, the court may award damages or compensation equal to the assessed amount or rule that remedial measures be taken by the convicted party. Also of relevance is the aspect of forfeiture. In terms of section 34D of NEMA, the court may order 'any specimen, container, vehicle, vessel, aircraft or document that was used for the purpose of or in connection with the commission of the offence and was seized under the provisions of this Part, to be forfeited to the State'. The forfeited asset(s) will be placed under the supervision of the state. This, however, raises the question of whether or not an application can be made by a private individual or entity other than the state to take control of the items seized. If this is allowed, the items could be liquidated for the benefit of conservation and anti-poaching initiatives. Theoretically, such an application could be argued to be in the public interest and should be allowed, should our courts not be overly conservative in their interpretation of the law, and if they are aware of the current crisis faced by nature.[132]

4.2.2.2 Private prosecution: animal cruelty

To criminally prosecute (privately) alleged crimes under the Society for the Prevention of Cruelty to Animals Act (SPCA Act),[133] a person requires a certificate *nolle prosequi* from the National Prosecuting Authority (NPA). Historically, the NPA did not issue such certificates to the SPCA when attempting to privately prosecute matters related to animal cruelty.[134] After various attempts challenging the constitutionality of the conduct of the NPA, the matter landed in the Constitutional Court. In *National Society for the Prevention of Cruelty to Animals v Minister of Justice and Constitutional Development*,[135] the court, although not addressing the constitutionality aspect, found:[136]

> The historical development of the protection of animal welfare, and the role of the NSPCA in upholding this mandate, illustrates why the NSPCA plays a critical and unique role in our polity ... For this reason, and in the context of

[132] Such remedies may greatly contribute to biodiversity conservation efforts but require an invested and progressive judiciary. The awareness of the judiciary can definitely be seen to be on the increase. See eg the *Shell* case (n 114) discussed earlier.

[133] Act 169 of 1993.

[134] Jan-Harm De Villiers, 'Law and the Question of the Animal: A Critical Discussion of *National Society for the Prevention of Cruelty to Animals v Minister of Justice and Constitutional Development*' (2019) 136 South African Law Journal 207.

[135] 2017 (4) BCLR 517 (CC).

[136] ibid para 61.

> the statutory regime that now exists, a contextual and purposive reading of the SPCA Act must be taken to include the right to prosecute. It is unusual, but not entirely novel, for a body to have powers to police, investigate and prosecute.

After the *NSPCA* case, the right to prosecute (privately) can accordingly be exercised through the SPCA Act. It should, however, be made clear that animal law (or animal welfare law) remains distinct from biodiversity law. Also, the South African courts are yet to enter into the debate of animal rights. It remains to be seen whether this will happen in the future.

4.2.3 Civil litigation and potential challenges

Section 24 of the Constitution creates a right to an environment that is not harmful to health or well-being. This right reflects an anthropocentric formulation, yet it still creates an important causality between human health, human well-being, and the environment. This right forms the basis for the environmental law framework giving effect to it and providing a framework in which the lawfulness of actions can be determined for civil litigation. Civil litigation in the form of a delictual action requires the following to be proved:[137]

- damage was suffered;
- the damage caused was as a result of the defendant's actions (causation);
- the conduct was unlawful (unlawfulness);
- the defendant was at fault (through negligent or intentional conduct); and
- the defendant had the capacity to carry out the action.

In brief, a delict seeks to compensate victims of conduct that, according to the law, is wrongful or unlawful. One of the remedies available where damage is suffered is the *action legis aquiliae*.[138] This is available where damage is caused (according to the aforementioned list) to the person or property of another. In the poaching scenario, this may provide some challenges. Where rhinos are poached from a private individual who has ownership over the rhinos in question, the action for damages is theoretically available. More challenging, though, is the situation where poaching causes harm not necessarily directly related to private law interests or rights. A good example of this is rhinos

[137] Richard Summers, 'Common-Law Remedies for Environmental Protection' in Alexander R Paterson and Louis J Kotzé, *Environmental Compliance and Enforcement in South Africa: Legal Perspectives* (Juta 2009) 341.

[138] Common law action for damages.

traversing national borders in transfrontier conservation areas. Summers[139] states that delictual liability for such 'pure environmental damage will arise only where harm is contemporaneously occasioned to individual interests'. Summers uses the example of atmospheric pollution causing damage to a natural person as a manifestation of delictual damage.[140]

An important caveat to consider is that a claim based on delict largely falls within the confines of private law finding an application in matters concerning the relationship between individuals. Applying a delict in the public interest as argued above would therefore enter the domain of public law. Or more simply put—individuals start to usurp the role of government.[141] In *Company Secretary of Arcelor Mittal South Africa v Vaal Environmental Justice Alliance*,[142] the SCA, in the context of an application for access to information, dealt with a similar question. The SCA emphasized the importance of individuals in protecting the environment in various passages and effectively found that, in this instance, did not usurp the government's role to directly enforce regulatory provisions of environmental legislation. Navsa ADP stressed that:

> It is clear, therefore, in accordance with international trends, and constitutional values and norms, that our legislature has recognized, in the field of environmental protection, inter alia the importance of consultation and interaction with the public. After all, environmental degradation affects us all. One might rightly speak of collaborative corporate governance in relation to the environment.

Apart from the fact that legal standing clearly allows the public to litigate in the interest of the environment, the court in the *Arcelor* case emphasizes the role of the public not only as a right-bearer but as a partner in collaborative corporate governance.[143]

The following explanation may provide clarity: private law is aimed at protecting the private interests of the individual and public law is directed at upholding and protecting the public interest. Regarding environmental conservation, there is a clear overlap between the interests. In fact, they seem intertwined. Protecting these interests should then not be confined to either

139 See Summers (n 138) 342.
140 ibid.
141 This blurs the otherwise strict outlook on horizontal and vertical application of private and public legal governance.
142 2015 (1) SA 515 (SCA).
143 In the context of biodiversity, we already see private corporate governance in the form of private nature reserves and private service delivery in urban and rural areas, to name only two examples.

the public or public law sphere. In the field of delict, the Constitutional Court in *Mashongwa v Passenger Rail Agency of South Africa*[144] confirmed that it may be possible to apply the law of delict in a broader sense. In this case, a delictual action against a public entity allegedly failing to protect both public and private interests. The court allowed Mashongwa to claim damages but it did state that this remedy was an action of last recourse. Put differently, no other remedies should be available to the claimant. This decision potentially plants the seeds required to institute a delictual claim where ecological degradation in terms of section 24 of the Constitution or section 28 of NEMA is caused. Some intelligent footwork will be required in arguing this especially since it seems that the delictual claim is a remedy of last resort. However, there is a clear message from our courts that change in traditional thinking (and therefore methods) is needed. In *Director: Mineral Development, Gauteng Region v Save the Vaal Environment*, Olivier JA stated that: 'together with the change in the ideological climate must also come a change in the legal and administrative approach to environmental concerns'.[145] Although this decision specifically relates to administrative processes, the court did not restrict the foregoing statement to only administrative processes related to environmental concerns. Furthermore, the importance of civil society in protecting the public interest was stressed in the *Biowatch* constitutional case. In this case, Sachs J remarked that 'the protection of environmental rights will not only depend on the diligence of public officials, but also on the existence of a lively civil society willing to litigate in the public interest'.[146] It should be clear that a change in *legal* and administrative processes to environmental concerns is required according to the court.

From the above, it is argued that change is not only needed but required. Civil litigation may face hurdles but, where and if it succeeds, become a very useful tool for aiding conservation funding. After all, the courts do have a constitutional mandate to promote the spirit, purport, and objects of the Bill of Rights when developing the common law.[147] Apart from the constitutional mandate, the development of the common law is not foreign to South African jurisprudence. Already in 1909, Innis J had acknowledged that the common law had to be modified to keep in touch with the changing context, such as legal ideas and changing conditions.[148]

144 2016 (3) SA 528 (CC).
145 1999 (2) SA 209 (SCA), para 20.
146 *Biowatch Trust v Registrar, Genetic Resources and others* 2009 (6) SA 232 (CC), para 19.
147 Section 39(2) of the Constitution.
148 *Blower v Van Norden* (1909) TS 890.

5. Key Findings

The South African litigation landscape is ripe for innovative approaches to litigate. This landscape is already exploited by NGOs and pressure groups. The possibilities created by a legal framework welcoming public interest litigation welcomes litigation on behalf of the environment. South Africa, through a vigilant environmental advocacy landscape, has plenty of relevant examples of how biodiversity litigation is used to benefit current and future generations. Some key aspects can again be highlighted as strong points of the South African legal framework:

- *locus standi*: ample opportunity is provided for NGOs and individuals to litigate on behalf of the environment and provision is also made for amicus briefs and leading scientific evidence where litigants bring such to the courts;[149]
- cost orders: courts will favourably look at litigants that litigate in the interest of the environment (save where there is frivolous litigation) aiming to encourage litigation in this regard. Large opposing companies and expensive cost orders should thus not inhibit litigants to enforce their environmental rights;
- sound legal framework: South Africa has a sound legal framework incorporating environmental principles and allowing a landscape where the public can litigate in their best interests and the court holds procedural rights and fairness in high regard. The Constitution, with the environmental right, bolsters and elevates environmental concerns to the level of a human right. This is important since it results in constitutional litigation and precedent-setting at the highest level; and
- place of IBL: because of the sound national legal framework in place (incorporating IBL), reference is not always made to the IBL instruments themselves in the case law or litigation. Despite this, South Africa has diligently submitted country reports to the CBD and, through SANBI, actively engages in the processes within the CBD. From this, it can be deduced that South Africa is serious in its commitments to the CBD in particular, and IBL in general. Since a lot of environmental litigation revolves around administrative law, it may appear that IBL and the previously mentioned reports do not receive the required attention.[150] Special

[149] Note, again, of the accusatorial nature of the legal system as discussed earlier.
[150] In various cases, however, scientific reports on potential environmental impacts play a major role in determining the outcome thereof. The *Shell* case (n 114) discussed earlier is an example.

mention should be made of the incorporation of the precautionary principle as applied in the *Shell*, *Mabola*, and *WWF* cases. These are prime examples of South African courts taking to heart a principle of IBL as a result of it being brought into the national legal framework.

One case worthy of note that made headlines in South Africa is *Earthlife Africa Johannesburg v Minister of Environmental Affairs*[151] where the High Court pointed to the international obligations of South Africa under the Paris Agreement.[152] The court ordered that climate change impacts had to form part of the impact assessment report even though it was not expressly included in the NEMA.[153] In so doing, the court highlighted the importance of South Africa's international commitments.

6. Synthesis of Key Findings

In sum, the chapter highlights the following key findings: (1) in South Africa, the influence of IBL can be seen as strong—although not direct. This means that the IBL instruments have been incorporated well into the legal system making specific reference to it unnecessary in most case law; (2) an increase of PIL is observed putting pressure on both the state and corporate companies to protect biodiversity and to comply with environmental law; and (3) biodiversity litigation, in general, contributes to the effectiveness of biodiversity law. The only real limitation to using litigation is that it is an expensive route to follow and is usually met with opposition from deep corporate pockets that can draw out legal proceedings. Nonetheless, the cost-order incentives as discussed earlier provide some relief in this regard.

7. The Way Forward

The South African legal framework is substantial when considering biodiversity-related issues. If anything, too many laws and fragmentation make for complex biodiversity governance. Nonetheless, ample room and opportunity are provided for litigants to engage with biodiversity issues. Biodiversity

[151] [2017] 2 All SA 519 (GP).
[152] Although these were not yet promulgated into national law at the time of the decision.
[153] Section 240 of NEMA. See the *Earthlife* case (n 152) para 124 of the judgment.

litigation is mostly driven by NGOs and organizations acting on behalf of the environment. Although this is positive and can be seen as an encouraging sign, the general public also needs to be educated about the value of biodiversity. In this context, two proposals can be offered.

First, education about the value of biodiversity in general and the negative effects of the loss thereof need to be highlighted to the general public. The negative effects on human rights, for example, should be highlighted. A lack of clean drinking water and food security may be two tangible examples. Education of the judiciary and counsel dealing with biodiversity litigation is also important. Counsel, to present proper arguments before the court, should not only rely on the presentation of scientific reports but should have a working knowledge of the issues at hand—not only the law.

Education should, in theory, lead to behavioural change. This leads to the second proposal, where behavioural change should, however, be encouraged with incentives. Incentivizing responsible environmental citizens should lead to a more sustainable future. Currently, tax incentives encourage small and large businesses to be energy efficient.[154] A key example of a programme with incentives for biodiversity is the Working for Water (WfF) programme that was established to clear catchments and riparian zones of invasive alien species.[155] This is an excellent example of payments for ecosystem services (PES). PES should be looked at more prominently since it is viewed as potentially effective and can be implemented by an already active non-governmental society. All in all, South Africa is well positioned to accommodate litigation from various angles and litigants are well endowed with the opportunity to litigate on behalf of the environment.

[154] Mareli Dippenaar, 'The Role of Tax Incentives in Encouraging Energy Efficiency in the Largest Listed South African Businesses' (2018) 21 South African Journal of Economic and Management Sciences 1.

[155] See Jane Turpie, Chris Marais, and James Nelson Blignaut, 'The Working for Water Programme: Evolution of a Payments for Ecosystem Services Mechanism that Addresses Both Poverty and Ecosystem Service Delivery in South Africa' (2008) 65 Ecological Economics 788.

9

Biodiversity Litigation in the UK

A Complex Set of Environmental Law Norms Grappling with a Diverging and Fragmented Legal Justice System

Paul Stookes

1. Introduction

The UK ratified the Convention on Biological Diversity (CBD) in 1994.[1] Prior to ratification, UK Prime Minister John Major, along with over 150 other heads of state, signed the Convention at the Rio Earth Summit in 1992 in order to 'express a shared belief that action must be taken to halt the worldwide loss of animal and plant species and genetic resources'.[2] However, this has not prevented a severe loss of species and decline in biodiversity in the UK since Rio[3] and there is increasing concern about the failure to avoid biodiversity harm particularly in public decision making. The 2021 House of Commons Environmental Audit Committee report: *Biodiversity in the UK: bloom or bust*[4] explained that:

> The world is witnessing a colossal decline in global biodiversity. One million animal and plant species are threatened with extinction. Most terrestrial biomes are damaged. Since 1970 there has been a 68 percent decrease in population sizes of mammals, birds, amphibians, reptiles, and fish. This global picture is reflected in the UK, one of the most nature-depleted countries in the world. 15 percent of UK species are threatened with extinction. Of the G7 countries, the UK has the lowest level of biodiversity remaining. At a

[1] United Nations Treaties Collection <https://treaties.un.org/pages/ViewDetails.aspx?src=TREATY&mtdsg_no=XXVII-8&chapter=27#EndDec> accessed 12 March 2022.

[2] *Biodiversity: The UK Action Plan* (HMSO 1994) 3. More recent government action includes the publication of the *25 Year Environment Plan* (HMSO 2018), the introduction of the Environment Bill (2019–21), and the associated law, policy, and governance that is intended to flow from this (discussed later).

[3] See eg *State of Nature 2019* (State of Nature Partnership 2019) and the Sixth National Report to the United Nations Convention on Biological Diversity: United Kingdom of Great Britain and Northern Ireland March 2019 (DEFRA March 2019) discussed later.

[4] House of Commons (HC 136, June 2021).

Paul Stookes, *Biodiversity Litigation in the UK* In: *Biodiversity Litigation*. Edited by: Guillaume Futhazar, Sandrine Maljean-Dubois, and Jona Razzaque, Oxford University Press. © Paul Stookes, 2023.
DOI: 10.1093/oso/9780192865465.003.0009

minimum, the UK has failed to meet 14 of the 19 Aichi biodiversity targets, the global nature goals the UK committed to meet by 2020.

There is also increasing public disquiet and distrust in decisions, acts, or omissions relating to the environment[5] and prompts individuals, communities, and NGOs turning to the courts to help to protect biodiversity. Recent cases with an emphasis on biodiversity loss include: *Wild Justice v Natural Resources Wales*[6] which alleged that licences granted to kill certain species of wild birds was unlawful; *R (RSPB) v Natural England*[7] claiming that the approach to the management of hen harriers, a protected species, was unlawful; and *R (Langton) v Secretary of State for the Environment, Food and Rural Affairs*[8] which challenged the government's approach to the culling of badgers. However, as becomes clear from this chapter, the effectiveness of litigation in helping to conserve and enhance biodiversity is unclear.

This chapter reviews how international biodiversity law (IBL) and litigation form part of biodiversity litigation in the UK and how aspects of the UK legal justice system influence this. It considers the role of international environmental law more widely and whether there has been a shift in biodiversity litigation over the last twenty years. The methodology in undertaking a review of the role of IBL in the UK was defined by attempting to convey the complex structure of the UK legal justice system, complicated further by the UK leaving the European Union on 1 January 2021 (Brexit). It was impracticable to provide a comprehensive study of all relevant cases. Instead, key cases, legislation, and policy have been discussed to illustrate the current position using recent examples where possible and in an effort to provide a snapshot of the legal landscape as it is in 2022. That said, there has been no specific start or cut-off date for the analysis. However, discussion of the position before the ratification of the CBD is limited. The cases and legislation are selected from the author's own legal and academic practice and experience[9] and an extensive review of specialist legal databases[10] as well as government databases.

The chapter sets the legal landscape, outlining the complexity of the UK legal justice system including the concepts of the common law and constitutional

[5] eg the very public act of civil disobedience with five members of Insulate Britain jailed for defying injunctions banning their protest blockades of the M25 motorway, *The Guardian* <www.theguardian.com/environment/2022/feb/02/> accessed 11 March 2022.

[6] [2021] EWHC 35 (Admin).

[7] [2019] EWHC 585 (Admin).

[8] [2019] EWCA Civ 1562.

[9] With research and review support from colleagues (and, in particular, Paul Wyard at Richard Buxton Solicitors).

[10] These include Westlaw and LexisNexis.

principles as well as the divergence of law across the UK. It then explores biodiversity policy and post-Brexit provisions. There is then a review of IBL in the context of biodiversity litigation with an analysis of the influence of IBL and the role of other international environmental law provisions, the role of regulation and also the influence of private rights and human rights. The chapter concludes by presenting an air of uncertainty in how biodiversity litigation including IBL may develop.

2. Setting the Legal Landscape

2.1 The Complexity of the UK Legal Justice System

This section explores the complexity of the UK legal justice system including the role of the common law legal system, the principle of parliamentary sovereignty, and the divergence of environmental law across the four nations of England, Northern Ireland, Scotland, and Wales.

2.1.1 A common law system

In order to understand the role of IBL and biodiversity litigation, it is essential to recognize the complex legal and regulatory landscape within the UK. First, international law has to engage with a common law legal system that has developed over more than 800 years[11] whereby judicial precedent helps to shape the law. Next, since 1972, the UK's common law system has been interacting with the civil code-based law of the EU[12] which has been developing an expanding system of laws. It is generally accepted that prior to Brexit around 80 per cent of UK environmental legislation derived from the EU.[13]

The marriage between the UK and the EU was not without tension, with regular allegations of inadequate transposition of EU environmental provisions.[14]

[11] eg in *St Helen's Smelting Co v Tipping* [1865] 11 HLC 642, the court held that noxious fumes and gases emitted from a copper-smelting works causing damage to a neighbour's trees and shrubs amounted to material injury to property and for which the smelting works was liable.

[12] See Chapter 11 in this volume on the European Union.

[13] See eg the UK government's Environmental Audit Committee (EAC) report, *The Future of the Natural Environment after the EU Referendum* (HMSO December 2016) 15; and reference to evidence submitted to the EAC by the European Environment Bureau.

[14] See eg the wealth of litigation challenging the correct application of environmental assessment provisions requiring numerous amendments to domestic law that had attempted to transpose the associated EU provisions; see eg *Berkeley v Secretary of State* [2001] 2 AC 603; Case C-201/02 *Wells v Secretary of State* (2004) ECLI:EU:C:2004:12; *Barker v Secretary of State* [2007] 1 AC 470; *Baker v BANES* [2010] 1 P & CR 4; and *Loader v Secretary of State* [2013] PTSR 406.

Another consequence of the obligation to integrate EU jurisprudence into the UK common law was that if international law was referenced in law and litigation it has tended to have had an EU reference or basis. On 1 January 2021, the UK left the EU and forty-nine years of supranational law, policy, and governance ended; the consequence of this is considered later.

2.1.2 The principle of parliamentary sovereignty

The UK common law system is also tied into the constitutional principle of parliamentary sovereignty, which means that the UK courts are not required to determine disputes or issues in accordance with international law.[15] This does not mean that one never finds reference to international law in UK litigation: see, for example, Principle 15 of the Rio Declaration on Environmental and Development 1992 expressly referred to in the 2020 case of *R (Plan B Earth) v Secretary of State Transport*[16] (at [259]). However, the general approach in UK litigation has been that if a particular piece of international law had been transposed into EU law, EU law is cited because that sets the obligation to act or not to act.

2.1.3 Divergence of environmental law across the four UK nations

Added to the melange of EU and common law is an ever-increasing divergence of law between the UK four nations; England, Northern Ireland, Scotland, and Wales with environmental priorities not always being aligned. For example, section 1 of the Nature Conservation (Scotland) Act 2004 (NCSA 2004) requires every Scottish public body to 'further the conservation of biodiversity so far as is consistent with the proper exercise of those functions' and in so doing must have regard to any biodiversity strategy published under section 2(1) of the NCSA 2004 and the CBD. In England, there is a duty for English public bodies to have regard to the purpose of conserving biodiversity under section 40 of Natural Environment and Rural Communities Act 2006 (NERCA 2006). Section 1 of the Wildlife and Natural Environment Act (Northern Ireland) 2011 places a duty on Northern Irish public bodies to further the conservation of biodiversity but does not mention the CBD. While in Wales, section 6 of the Environment (Wales) Act 2016 (EWA 2016) provides that Welsh public

[15] This was a critical argument of those voting for Brexit and that the UK Parliament was bound by the decisions of the EU. A poll by Lord Ashcroft on referendum day (24 June 2016) noted that: 'Nearly half (49%) of leave voters said the biggest single reason for wanting to leave the EU was 'the principle that decisions about the UK should be taken in the UK.' One-third said the main reason was that leaving 'offered the best chance for the UK to regain control over immigration and its own borders. . . .' <http://lordashcroftpolls.com/2016/06/how-the-united-kingdom-voted-and-why/> accessed 13 March 2022.

[16] [2020] PTSR 1446.

bodies must 'seek to maintain *and enhance* biodiversity in the exercise of functions in relation to Wales', and where section 6(4)(a) requires central government departments and ministers (but not other public bodies) to have regard to the CBD.

All four distinct legislative provisions are consistent in that they have clauses that weaken any potential biodiversity protection considerably by:

(1) stating that the various public bodies need only 'have regard' to conserving biodiversity; and
(2) by qualifying the 'have regard' duty by stating that this only necessary 'so far as consistent with the proper exercise of those functions'.[17] This is a balancing exercise whereby a public body can prioritize other non-biodiversity considerations in policymaking and decision taking. Litigation relating to the 'have regard to biodiversity' provisions is discussed later. What is evident from the outset is that four different legislative provisions, all seeking to confer some biodiversity protection, are distinct in what they attempt to do. Moreover, apart from a passing reference to the CBD in some of the provisions (but not all) there appears to be no attempt to align or coordinate biodiversity law between the four nations.

Similarly, what may reasonably be regarded as the most influential environmental regulatory regime across the four UK countries, land use planning, is based upon entirely separate legislation, policy, and guidance: something highlighted in the National Assembly for Wales research paper, 'Comparison of the planning system in the four UK countries', which notes that:

> Although the basic structures of the four systems are similar there are differences in the detail and in how each system works. Recent changes introduced by the UK Coalition Government (2010–2015) have seen a greater divergence between the system in England and the other three countries in the last couple of years. England, Scotland, Northern Ireland and Wales now each have their own primary planning legislation. The system in Northern Ireland has been changed significantly recently with passing of planning functions to local Councils. (page 1)[18]

[17] All four legislative provisions provide similar text but see eg s. 6(1) of the EWA 2016 as cited.
[18] <https://commonslibrary.parliament.uk/?s=> accessed 3 February 2022.

2.1.4 A multi-layered approach to environmental law

In addition to the common law collision with the EU, the distinct national legal frameworks, and the concept of parliamentary sovereignty, UK biodiversity protection laws and policy are multi-layered. They are found in some specific nature conservation legislation (as seen earlier) as well as cross-cutting regulatory mechanisms such as environmental impact assessment (EIA). The public bodies responsible for protecting, maintaining, and enhancing biodiversity (including having the power to pursue legal action) are similarly diverse and include, among others, the Environment Agency, Natural England, Natural Resources Wales, the Northern Ireland Environment Agency, the Scottish Environmental Protection Agency, NatureScot,[19] local authorities at both district and county levels, the Department for Environment, Food & Rural Affairs (DEFRA), the Joint Nature Conservation Council (JNCC), and Police Wildlife Crime Officers.[20] In addition, biodiversity litigation is pursued by individuals and NGOs. This may be through challenging public decision making, for example by judicial review or by pursuing private prosecutions of wildlife crime.[21]

2.2 Biodiversity Policy

Government policy also has an important role to play in biodiversity management and governance. The UK is understood to have been the first country to produce a national biodiversity strategy and action plan, publishing *Biodiversity: The UK Action Plan*[22] in order to comply with article 6(a) of the CBD. However, as explained previously, UK devolution has resulted in divergence and, in order to implement the Aichi Plan, there was a need by 2012 to publish a common framework setting out an agreed UK purpose and vision.[23] Consistent with the Aichi Plan, the Common Framework provided that:

> By 2050, biodiversity is valued, conserved, restored and wisely used, maintaining ecosystem services, sustaining a healthy planet and delivering benefits essential for all people.

19 Formerly Scottish Natural Heritage.

20 This is not an exhaustive list but goes to illustrate the range of agencies and organizations involved in biodiversity and litigation.

21 *R (Kent) v Teesside Magistrates Court* (28 November 2019, unreported).

22 HMSO 1994.

23 Published by JNCC and DEFRA on behalf of the Four Countries' Biodiversity Group (2012).

The Common Framework explained that biodiversity and the natural environment were devolved responsibilities[24] and so, for example, DEFRA published for England: *Biodiversity 2020* as a national strategy for England's wildlife and ecosystem services, while Wales published the *Nature Recovery Action Plan for Wales* (December 2015),[25] the Scottish government published *2020 Challenge for Scotland's Biodiversity*,[26] and Northern Ireland published the *Biodiversity Strategy for Northern Ireland to 2020*.[27] In January 2018, the UK government published: *A Green Future: Our 25 Year Plan to Improve the Environment*[28] which included a proposal to implement the UK's international commitments by publishing a new strategy for nature. This encapsulates the fragmented nature of environmental law and policy, including biodiversity, by noting in the executive summary that:

> Since the UK Government is responsible for a number of policies and programmes which affect sectors across the UK and internationally, some aspects of the Plan will apply to the UK as a whole. In other areas where environmental policy is devolved and responsibility rests with the Scottish Government, Welsh Government and Northern Ireland Executive, the proposals in this Plan apply to England only.

The various plans, frameworks, and strategies that have been published since 1992 fall squarely within the category of 'soft law'. There are no sanctions for a failure to comply with or meet any targets set by or associated with the targets. Moreover, up until the introduction of the Environment Act 2021, there was no domestic legislative basis for environmental targets in the UK. Any biodiversity indicators that may have been published can reasonably be said to comply with international obligations under the CBD although these may be categorized as progress reports on any biodiversity strategies.[29] This becomes clear through the separate areas of action towards achieving the Aichi Targets; a core part of each of the nations' biodiversity action plans.

24 ibid 2.
25 <https://gov.wales/nature-recovery-action-plan> accessed 13 March 2022.
26 Scottish Government (2013).
27 Department of the Environment, Northern Ireland (2015).
28 JNCC and DEFRA (n 23) 9.
29 See eg Scottish Biodiversity Strategy Report to Parliament 2017–2019 (Scottish Government June 2020).

2.3 Post-Brexit Biodiversity Law

From 1 January 2021, UK biodiversity law and policy have had to accommodate the complexity of divorce from the EU. A starting point to ascertain where post-Brexit biodiversity law and policy stands is to consider the commitment to the principle of non-regression of environmental law. This is found in the EU–UK Trade and Cooperation Agreement (24 December 2020) (TCA) with article 7.2.2 of Title XI, 'Level playing field for open and fair competition and sustainable development' providing:

> A Party shall not weaken or reduce, in a manner affecting trade or investment between the Parties, its environmental levels of protection or its climate level of protection below the levels that are in place at the end of the transition period, including by failing to effectively enforce its environmental law or climate level of protection.[30]

However, some legislative provisions on litigation already enacted may be inconsistent with this TCA non-regression promise: see, for example, the European Union (Withdrawal) Act 2018 (Relevant Court) (Retained EU Case Law) Regulations 2020[31] which provide that the higher appellate courts across the UK[32] have the power to depart from retained EU case law. This may be contrasted with section 6(4) of the EU (Withdrawal) Act 2018 which limited that power to the Supreme Court only.

A further concern on regression has been the failure to provide environmental governance mechanisms to replace the European Commission. This was caused, in part, by delay in enacting the Environment Act 2021 and the establishment of the Office for Environmental Protection to cover environmental governance in England and Northern Ireland. In Wales, the European Commission 'replacement' is an interim Environmental Protection Assessor who has no investigative powers. This assessor was appointed in February 2021 for two years during which time the Welsh government will develop a permanent environmental governance body.[33] While a new body, Environmental Standards Scotland in place since October 2021, is monitoring the effectiveness

[30] https://ec.europa.eu/info/strategy/relations-non-eu-countries/relations-united-kingdom/eu-uk-trade-and-cooperation-agreement_en accessed 20 June 2022.
[31] SI 2020/1525.
[32] eg the Court of Appeal in England and Wales.
[33] <https://gov.wales/welsh-government-appoints-new-environmental-protection-assessor> accessed 13 March 2022.

of Scottish environmental law although this body does not provide a complaints mechanism on particular cases equivalent to, say, the ability to petition the European Parliament who may then refer a matter to the European Commission.

Notwithstanding the difficulties in getting governance measures in place, there are some encouraging signs for post-Brexit UK environmental law. There has, for instance, been a renewed focus on tackling climate change, driven, without doubt, by the UK hosting the Climate Change Convention Conference of the Parties (COP26) in Glasgow in November 2021. This has seen, for instance, an apparent political abandonment of coal as an energy source[34] and a drive towards a low carbon economy.[35] It is less clear whether this will have a positive or negative influence on biodiversity and what may flow from this in terms of biodiversity litigation. It appears common ground that the problem of climate change and the prognosis for biodiversity and ecosystems is generally not good. See, for instance, the series of articles entitled 'Climate change and ecosystems: threats, opportunities and solutions'[36] which note by way of introduction that anthropogenic greenhouse gas (GHG) emissions, which drive climate change and ocean acidification, increasingly threaten the viability and resilience of natural ecosystems and human societies. In recent years, the threats have become clearly observable with projections suggesting an increased likelihood of negative consequences.

The UK government cannot be said to be ignoring biodiversity in its pursuit of a climate change imperative. For instance, key provisions in the Environment Act 2021 aim to support nature and biodiversity. Part 1 of the Act on environmental governance confers power on relevant government ministers to set long-term targets in four priority areas of: (1) air quality; (2) water; (3) biodiversity; and (4) resource and waste reduction. There is also a provision in Part 6 of the Act in relation to: biodiversity net gain; extending the duty under section 40 of the NERCA 2006 from having regard to 'conserving biodiversity' to 'conserving *and enhancing* biodiversity and revising the obligations for public bodies' (emphasis added); biodiversity reporting; local nature recovery strategies, and tree felling and planting.

[34] See the decision on Highthorn opencast coal mine and the call-in of the Cumbria coal mine.

[35] See eg Energy White Paper, 'Powering our Net Zero Future' (HMSO December 2020) and setting the Sixth UK Carbon Budget to reduce greenhouse gas emissions by 78 per cent by 2035 of 1990 emission levels as recommended by the UK Climate Change Committee and considered by the UK to be 'the most ambitious in the world'; see eg the Queen's Speech 2021 (11 May 2021) and <www.theccc.org.uk/publication/sixth-carbon-budget/> accessed 13 March 2022.

[36] Malhi Yadvinder and others, 'Climate Change and Ecosystems: Threats, Opportunities and Solutions' (2020) 375 Philosophical Transactions of the Royal Society 1794. <https://royalsocietypublishing.org/doi/pdf/10.1098/rstb.2019.0104> accessed 13 March 2022.

Moreover, it is possible to point to key areas of existing domestic legislation areas that play a prominent role in biodiversity litigation including, for example, the Conservation of Species and Habitats Regulations 2017, the EIA Regulations, the Wildlife and Countryside Act 1981, and the National Planning Policy Framework (NPPF). And this is perhaps the key to understanding biodiversity litigation in the UK which is that while the law and policy on wildlife and nature make many grand statements, often this is just 'hot air' or 'hollow words' whereby the protection and enhancement of biodiversity in fact fails to materialize. Thus, much of the biodiversity litigation in the UK is attempting to enforce the potentially effective laws and policy when policymakers and decision takers ignore nature in preference for, say, economic growth.

3. The Influence of IBL on UK Biodiversity Litigation

Section 2 set out the current UK legal landscape, while this section provides some of the key ways in which IBL engages with UK environmental law, including:

(1) the interaction with the dualist system of UK law whereby international law and domestic law can operate independently from one another;
(2) the direct influence of IBL where, for example, direct reliance on international law is in play;
(3) the indirect influence of IBL by the transposition of international law into domestic law through either primary or secondary legislation;
(4) the influence of general international environmental law, rights, obligations, and principles impacting on biodiversity indirectly, for instance whereby prosecutions for a breach of a permit to limit discharges to watercourse or regulatory waste disposal may have an indirect effect on biodiversity; and
(5) the role of private rights and human rights, exploring how other rights in civil society may have an indirect impact on biodiversity.

3.1 The Dualist System in the UK

As noted earlier, the four legal jurisdictions enable judges to refer to and apply international law, although they are not obliged to determine matters in accordance with international law. In 2017 in *R (Miller & another) v Secretary of State for Exiting the European Union*,[37] the Supreme Court explained that:

> the so-called dualist theory, which is based on the proposition that international law and domestic law operate in independent spheres. The prerogative power to make treaties depends on two related propositions. The first is that treaties between sovereign states have effect in international law and are not governed by the domestic law of any state. … The second proposition is that, although they are binding on the United Kingdom in international law, treaties are not part of UK law and give rise to no legal rights or obligations in domestic law.

Thus, IBL such as the CBD may be referred to and potentially applied but any challenge to government acts or omissions based upon non-compliance with international law is unlikely to succeed. In *Venn v Secretary of State for Communities & Local Government*,[38] the government successfully appealed a claimant's costs protection order in land use planning litigation with Lord Justice Sullivan noting:

> 34. For these reasons I would allow the appeal. I do so with reluctance. In the light of my conclusion on article 9(3), and the decisions of the Aarhus Compliance Committee and the CJEU in *Commission v UK* [2014] QB 988 referred to in para 24 above, it is now clear that the costs protection regime introduced by CPR [Civil Procedure Rules] r 45.41 is not Aarhus-compliant in so far as it is concerned to applications for judicial review, and excludes statutory appeals and applications. …
>
> 35. This court is not able to remedy that flaw by the exercise of a judicial discretion. If the flaw is to be remedied action by the legislature is necessary. …

3.2 The Direct Influence of IBL

There is very little evidence of express and direct influence of IBL on law and policy in the UK. This, in the author's view, is because of: (1) the dualist legal

[37] [2017] UKSC 5, [55] and [56]. In *Miller*, the UK government was held to have acted beyond its powers when giving notice to the EU to withdraw from the Union under Art 50 of the Treaty of the European Union by not giving notice through primary legislation.

[38] [2015] 1 WLR 2328.

system (discussed earlier); (2) the need to comply with EU law for nearly fifty years; (3) the overriding principle of parliamentary sovereignty; and (4) the desire to transpose non-domestic provisions into domestic law, driven by the concept of parliamentary sovereignty. Thus, it has either been unnecessary, undesirable, or unarguable to refer to or rely upon international legislation in UK litigation; and those attempting to do so are almost always doomed to fail.

3.3 The Indirect Influence of IBL

Following on from above, if IBL is influencing UK law it will almost certainly be transposed into UK domestic law. Thus, IBL has indirect rather than direct influence. That said, through transposition into domestic law, IBL has played a prominent role in litigation, although how successful it has been in conserving and enhancing biodiversity is less clear. Pre-Brexit transposed EU directives drew international legislation into UK law.[39] There is some direct reference to IBL (as distinct from EU law) but its application by public bodies may reasonably be regarded as 'weak' when seen through the litigation lens. For instance, prior to very recent amendments by the Environment Act 2021, section 40 of NERCA 2006 placed a duty on public bodies in England to have regard to conserving biodiversity although the claims placing reliance upon that duty were largely unsuccessful. In *Morge v Hampshire County Council*,[40] the court held that the absence of a reference to section 40 of NERCA 2006 did not render a decision defective and that 'awareness' of that section can be assumed in the decision makers.[41] A similar approach was taken in 2009 in *R (Buglife: The Invertebrate Conservation Trust) v Thurrock Thames Gateway Development Corp*[42] by the Court of Appeal.

The transposition of IBL, via the Habitats Directive[43] has prompted considerable litigation;[44] and where focus has often been on the adequacy of

[39] See eg the Convention on the Conservation of European Wildlife and Natural Habitats 1979 (the Bern Convention), transposed by Directive 92/43/EEC on the conservation of natural habitats and of wild fauna and flora (the Habitats Directive) which is then transposed into UK law to a large extent by the Conservation of Habitats and Species Regulations 2017 (SI 2017/1012, the Habitats Regulations 2017).

[40] [2009] EWHC 2940 (Admin).

[41] The High Court judgment was appealed and later dismissed by the Supreme Court in *R (Morge) v Hampshire County Council* [2011] 1WLR 268.

[42] [2009] EWCA Civ 29.

[43] Council Directive 92/43/EEC of 21 May 1992 on the conservation of natural habitats and of wild fauna and flora]1992] OJ L206/7.

[44] See eg *R (Wingfield) v Canterbury City Council* [2019] 7 WLUK 363; *R (Plan B Earth) v Secretary of State for Transport* [2020] EWCA Civ 214; and *R (Hudson) v Windsor and Maidenhead Royal Borough Council* [2019] 12 WLUK 364.

the appropriate assessment required under regulation 63 of the Habitat's Regulations 2017 (as amended). This provides that:

> A competent authority, before deciding to undertake, or give any consent, permission or other authorization for, a plan or project which—
> (a) is likely to have a significant effect on a European site or a European offshore marine site (either alone or in combination with other plans or projects), and
> (b) is not directly connected with or necessary to the management of that site,
> must make an appropriate assessment of the implications of the plan or project for that site in view of that site's conservation objectives.

In *Wealden DC v Secretary of State for Communities & Local Government*,[45] the Court of Appeal affirmed that a planning inspector's conclusion was flawed, insufficiently reasoned, and therefore unlawful in concluding that an 'appropriate assessment' required by regulation 61 of the Conservation of Habitats and Species Regulations 2010[46] (the earlier provisions) was unnecessary. The inspector's decision was consequently quashed. While in *Natural England v Warren*,[47] the Upper Tribunal upheld a stop notice issued to prohibit the appellant releasing and shooting birds on land designated as a Site of Special Scientific Interest and European protected area. In reaching her conclusion, Judge Markus QC held that the lower court was bound to apply the precautionary principle in order to comply with the Habitats Directive. It should be noted that the precautionary principle which is a familiar IBL principle has recently been included in primary legislation in the UK and is one of the environmental principles found within section 17 of the Environment Act 2021.[48]

The influence of the Court of Justice of the European Union (CJEU) cannot be ignored in biodiversity litigation with judgments such as Case C-323/17 *People Over Wind v Coillte Teoranta*[49] being relied upon by the courts to determine

[45] [2018] Env LR 5, [2017] EWCA Civ 39.

[46] SI 2020/490.

[47] [2020] PTSR 565, [2019] UKUT 300 (AAC).

[48] Section 16 of the European Union (Withdrawal Agreement) 2018 also included the precautionary principle although this section was repealed in the light of the then emerging provisions in the Environment Bill 2019–21.

[49] ECLI:EU:C:2018:244, [2018] PTSR 1668. In *People Over Wind*, the CJEU held that measures to mitigate harm could not be relied upon when deciding whether or not to carry out an appropriate assessment as required by Art 6 of the Habitats Directive.

domestic decisions: see, for example, the judgments in 2019 in the joined cases of *Canterbury City Council v SSHCLG*.[50]

3.4 The Role of the Aarhus Convention on UK Biodiversity Litigation

Another important aspect of IBL in the UK is the influence and adoption of general international environmental law provisions which may indirectly influence biodiversity litigation. For example, Part 45.41–45.44 of the Civil Procedure Rules 1998 seeks to provide adverse costs protection in environmental judicial review. The rationale for environmental costs protection can be traced back to Principle 10 of the Rio Declaration which provides that:

> Environmental issues are best handled with the participation of all concerned citizens, at the relevant level. . . . Effective access to judicial and administrative proceedings, including redress and remedy, shall be provided.

Principle 10 is transposed into national law via the Aarhus Convention 1998 with CPR 45.41 noting:

> This section provides for the costs which are to be recoverable between the parties in Aarhus Convention claims.
>
> In this Section; (a) 'Aarhus Convention claim' means a claim brought by one or more members of the public by judicial review or review under statute which challenges the legality of any decision, act or omission of a body exercising public functions, and which is within the scope of Article 9(1), 9(2) or 9(3) of [the Aarhus Convention]; (b) references to a member or members of the public are to be construed in accordance with the Aarhus Convention. . . .

In this context, it is evident that the UK courts do draw upon international law and practice. For instance, the 2019 *ex tempore* judgment of Mr Justice Freedman in *R (Kent) v Teesside Magistrates' Court*[51] refers to the United Nations Economic Commission for Europe (UNECE) Aarhus Convention Compliance Committee (ACCC) and the wide scope of its provisions when

[50] [2019] EWHC 1211 (Admin), 5 WLUK 225. See also Chapter 11 in this volume on the European Union.
[51] 28 November 2019 (unreported).

granting costs protection to the claimant.[52] This follows earlier judgments on the Convention such as *Austin v Miller Argent (South Wales) Ltd*[53] in 2015 and *Walton v Scottish Ministers*[54] in 2013 in which Lord Carnwath noted (at [100]) that on the issue of common law fairness, and the merits more generally, the court's conclusion had persuasive support from ACCC adding that, while the Convention was not part of domestic law (except when incorporated through European directives), the decisions of the Committee deserve respect on issues relating to standards of public participation.

It is evident from *Walton v Scottish Ministers* that international procedural obligations, such as access to environmental justice, play a crucial role in biodiversity litigation. Moreover, the right of access to justice as a human right in, for instance, the EU legal order, is particularly important in the Aarhus Convention context.[55]

In *Kent*, the challenge was, in broad terms, a review of a magistrates' court decision precluding a private prosecution alleging that the defendant had damaged or destroyed a great crested newt breeding site (a European protected species[56]) contrary to regulation 43(1)(d) and (8) of the Habitats Regulations 2017. The judge in the magistrates' court had unlawfully held that the applicant could not proceed with the prosecution because he had spelt the defendant's name incorrectly and was then time-barred from bringing a fresh prosecution.

3.5 The Role of Environmental Impact Assessment on UK Biodiversity Litigation

Another important area of IBL which has indirect influence is EIA which is found at an international level in Principle 17 of the Rio Declaration and case law.[57] This is transposed in the UK via the EU Habitats Directive 92/43/EC and then the Habitats Regulations 2017 and the obligation to carry out a habitats

[52] The post-order costs judgment of Freedman J has been reported *R (Kent) v Teesside Magistrates' Court* [2020] EWHC 304 (Admin), [2020] Costs LR 195.

[53] [2014] EWCA Civ 1012, [2015] 2 All ER 524.

[54] [2012] UKSC 44, [2012] PTSR 51.

[55] See eg Jean-François Brakeland who notes in 'Access to justice in environmental matters—developments at EU level' that 'the Aarhus Convention is an international instrument that establishes environmental rights as human rights, and that guarantees the respect of those rights through good governance mechanisms and through enforcement procedures open to the public' <https://unece.org/fileadmin/DAM/env/pp/a.to.j/Access_to_justice_in_environmental_matters_oct13.pdf> accessed 13 March 2022.

[56] The great crested newt is also known as *Triturus cristatus* and is listed in Annex 2 to the Habitats Directive 92/43/EEC.

[57] See eg *Pulp Mills on the River Uruguay (Argentina v Uruguay)* (Judgment) [2010] ICJ Rep 14.

assessment for certain activities (also discussed earlier). Principle 17 is also found in a range of EIA provisions such as the Town and Country Planning (EIA) Regulations 2017[58] which transpose Directive 2011/92/EU on the assessment of the effects of certain public and private projects (as amended). And, while there is no express reference to Principle 17 in UK law, EIA and habitats litigation has been extensive over the last twenty-five years with a key area of contention being when and how EIA should be carried on. Importantly, the regulations regard biodiversity as a prominent area for assessment and reference is found, inter alia, in regulation 4(2) providing that:

> The EIA must identify, describe and assess in an appropriate manner, in light of each individual case, the direct and indirect significant effects of the proposed development on the following factors: … (b) biodiversity, with particular attention to species and habitats protected under Directive 92/43/EEC and Directive 2009/147/EC; …

Recent EIA case law focusing on biodiversity includes allegations of both procedural and substantive legality. In *Abbotskerswell Parish Council v Secretary of State for Housing, Communities & Local Government (SSHCLG)*,[59] the High Court held that the Secretary of State had not erred in granting outline planning permission for a major mixed-use development finding that he had the environmental information 'reasonably required' as to the effect of the proposed development on climate change and biodiversity. This was in circumstances where he did not assess in any way the GHG emissions from the proposal and did not provide any indication of the actual effects on the local greater horseshoe bat population, a protected species. The High Court concluded that such an approach was procedurally acceptable and any evaluation not irrational. While in 2020 in *R (Swire) v SSHCLG*,[60] the court held that the Secretary of State had erred in law by concluding that EIA was not required for the redevelopment of a former animal carcass-rendering facility when the Secretary of State was uncertain as to the extent of the site contamination which had previously been used to dispose of cattle infected with bovine spongiform encephalopathy (BSE).[61] In quashing the permission, the judge referred to the 2015 case of *Champion v North Norfolk District Council* in which the Supreme Court warned that using analogous procedures instead of EIA 'would subvert

[58] SI 2017/571.
[59] [2021] EWHC 555 (Admin).
[60] [2020] EWHC 1298 (Admin).
[61] BSE had resulted in the outbreak of Creutzfeldt-Jakob disease (CJD) in humans during the 1980s.

the purposes of the EIA Directive' and that the precautionary principle which underlies the Directive 'implies that cases of material doubt should generally be resolved in favour of EIA'.[62]

In the above cases the parties presented arguments as to the correct application of IBL in its domestic context and, having heard arguments, the court applied that law in its reasoned judgments. It is clear that UK litigants and courts refer to hard law instruments as part of their reasoning, notwithstanding that the underlying principle may derive from soft law. For example, in *Kent* there is a reference to the Aarhus Convention rather than the Rio Declaration.

3.6 Environmental Regulation and Biodiversity

A key area of environmental law and practice that can have a significant influence on biodiversity and be indirectly influenced by IBL is the field of environmental regulation and control through the UK's complex environmental permitting and authorization systems operating across the four nations.[63] The provisions operate through a system of authorizations or permits to pollute granted to operators. A failure to either secure an authorization or permit or to carry on activities in breach of any conditions of a permit/authorization is an offence. The regulatory systems derive from primary or secondary legislation supported by extensive codes of practice and guidance.[64] They are also informed by non-statutory guidance and advice such as the Sentencing Council's environmental offences definitive guideline.[65]

The regulatory provisions are overseen by national public bodies including the Environment Agency, Natural Resources Wales, the Northern Ireland Environment Agency, and the Scottish Environment Protection Agency alongside local authorities. The regulations are enforced by criminal sanctions with significant sentencing options for the criminal courts including unlimited fines and prison for the more serious offences and convictions. The more polluting processes are regulated through an integrated approach to regulation whereby environmental control is managed through a review and protection of all key

[62] [2015] UKSC 52, [2015] 1 WLR 3710, [45] and [51].

[63] Including eg the Environmental Permitting (England and Wales) Regulations 2016 (as amended), the Environmental Authorisations (Scotland) Regulations 2018, and the Environmental Better Regulation Act (Northern Ireland) 2016.

[64] See eg DEFRA, *Waste Duty of Care Code of Practice* (November 2018).

[65] Sentencing Council, 'Environmental Offences: Definitive Guideline' (2014) www.sentencingcouncil.org.uk/wp-content/uploads/Environmental-offences-definitive-guideline-Web.pdf accessed 12 March 2022.

environmental media, that is air, land, and water. The first manifestation of environmental permitting was found in Part 1 of the Environmental Protection Act 1990. This was superseded by legislation to transpose the EU Integrated Pollution Prevention and Control Directive 1999. Any detailed analysis of the environmental authorization and permitting provisions falls beyond the scope of this chapter. However, reviewing some recent case law illustrates the potential biodiversity impacts that arise through the regulatory system and the potential adverse biodiversity impact if there is a failure to enforce those provisions.[66]

In *R v Southern Water*,[67] the defendant was fined a record £90 million (*c.* €100 million) after pleading guilty to thousands of illegal sewage discharges that polluted rivers and coastal waters in South-East England over the five-year period 2010–15. The offences were caused by deliberate failings and causing major harm to protected areas, conservation sites, and oyster beds. In sentencing, Mr Justice Johnson said that the fifty-one offences showed a shocking and wholesale disregard for the environment: for the precious and delicate coastal ecosystems, for human health, and for the fisheries and other legitimate businesses that depend on the vitality of the coastal waters. He added that even adding all the offences together did not reflect the defendant's criminality, because the offences were aggravated by 'persistent pollution of the environment over very many years'.

Similarly, in *R v Foley*[68] the defendant was jailed for two years and three months for illegally disposing of 100,000 tonnes of waste at a former limestone quarry in South-West England. Much of the illegal disposal related to hazardous waste and posing a potential risk to human health, with borehole sampling revealing a high percentage of chopped/shredded plastics, metals, foam and other manmade substances with many being either carcinogenic or ecotoxic. Nearby streams showed an elevated concentration of gases while leachate was breaking out onto the surface of surrounding fields. An application for planning permission at the site had previously been refused by the planning inspector.[69]

Finally, in *R v Bellway*,[70] a criminal case brought under the Wildlife and Countryside Act 1981, a building firm that carried out demolition works at

[66] For further information, see eg www.gov.uk/government/organisations/environment-agency#org-contacts> accessed 13 March 2022; <www.sepa.org.uk/regulations/> accessed 13 March 2022; <https://naturalresources.wales/?lang=en> accessed 13 March 2022; and <www.daera-ni.gov.uk/northern-ireland-environment-agency> accessed 13 March 2022.

[67] 9 July 2021 (unreported).

[68] 8 April 2021 (unreported).

[69] Appeal Ref APP/F0114/A/13/2195706 in November 2013.

[70] 22 December 2020 (unreported).

a site in London that was known to be inhabited by soprano pipistrelle bats, a protected species, was fined £600,000 by Woolwich Crown Court after pleading guilty to the offence.

In essence, while the focus of environmental regulation is on pollution control through permitting and licensing, it often has an important indirect influence in helping to protect biodiversity.

3.7 Private Rights, Human Rights, Nature's Rights?

Other branches of environmental law, such as property rights and human rights, have played a less significant role in biodiversity litigation in the UK, notwithstanding that matters such as human rights have been raised in environmental litigation over the last twenty years.[71] Also, if human rights have been engaged in biodiversity-associated litigation it is often where biodiversity protection measures are alleged to interfere with human rights.[72] The interrelationship between UK human rights and biodiversity protection and enhancement is uncertain and the effectiveness of the human rights provisions as a mechanism for environmental protection is debatable. In *Hatton v UK*,[73] the Grand Chamber of the European Court of Human Rights held that the UK had a 'margin of appreciation' when deciding to increase the number of night flights from Heathrow airport and, in so doing, increasing night-time noise pollution for communities within the locality. A recent example of the English civil justice system grappling with human rights to secure environmental protection is the judgment in *R (Matthew Richards) v Environment Agency*[74] in which the Court of Appeal overturned a declaratory judgment by the High Court that the Environment Agency must work to avoid breaching Article 2 (the right to life) and Article 8 (the right to respect of private and family life and home) of the ECHR by more effectively regulating odours and gas emissions

[71] See eg *Dennis v Ministry of Defence* [2003] EWHC 793(QB) in which the claimants successfully argued that the noise from Harrier jet fighters was a nuisance and also a breach of Art 8 and Art 1, Protocol 1 of the European Convention on Human Rights (ECHR), but where impacts on biodiversity were not a particular concern.

[72] See *R (Countryside Alliance) v AG* [2007] QB 305, where the Court of Appeal held that the enactment of the Hunting Act 2004 introduced in the UK to prohibit fox hunting, deer hunting, hare hunting, and other wild mammals did not breach the claimant's Art 8 right to private life under the ECHR.

[73] [2003] 37 EHRR 611.

[74] [2022] EWCA Civ 26.

including hydrogen sulphide from a landfill site and where the claimant, a five-year-old boy, had severe health and respiratory problems.[75]

Also, while economic interest and investment will very often be a factor in decisions by private and public bodies (including whether to litigate), that investment interest is unlikely to be the driver for biodiversity protection.[76] For instance, where marine, trade, investment, and human rights have been an aspect of biodiversity litigation they have tended to be ancillary or incidental to explicit biodiversity provisions within the claim. For example, in *Sands' Application for Judicial Review*,[77] a key part of the permission being challenged was an investment in a care home and in which the local authority granted permission to build a nursing home within an area of outstanding natural beauty and close to a Site of Special Scientific Interest. In *Sands*, the High Court of Northern Ireland dismissed the claim alleging a breach of, among other things, the EIA and habitats legislation.

Moreover, where biodiversity litigation has potentially collided with matters of investment in English law the courts have sought to disentangle these: in *Network Rail Infrastructure Ltd v Williams*,[78] the Court of Appeal held that encroachment of Japanese knotweed (an invasive species) could amount to a private nuisance but added (at [48]) that:

> The purpose of the tort of nuisance is not to protect the value of property as an investment or a financial asset. Its purpose is to protect the owner of land (or a person entitled to exclusive possession) in their use and enjoyment of the land as such as a facet of the right of ownership or right to exclusive possession.

The Court of Appeal in *Network Rail v Williams* goes on to illustrate the UK common law in action and that the development of the common law through judicial precedent is incremental:

> The decision of the recorder in the present case extends the tort of nuisance to a claim for pure economic loss. Counsel for the claimants did not identify

[75] Further discussion of the interaction of human rights and environmental protection is beyond the scope of this chapter. The Council of Europe provides further information at <www.coe.int/en/web/portal/human-rights-environment> accessed 12 March 2022.

[76] eg in any challenge to a decision relating to a development proposal or project that is alleged to have breached biodiversity laws, there will almost always be an interested party that is concerned about its investment and the loss of, eg, planning permission to proceed with the development or project.

[77] [2018] NIQB 80, [2018] 10 WLUK 642.

[78] [2018] EWCA Civ 1514, [2019] QB 601.

> any case in which a similar decision was reached or, more generally, where the amenity of a property has been held, for the purposes of actionable private nuisance, to include the right to realize or otherwise deploy the value of the property in the financial interests of the owner. Contrary to the view of the recorder, that would not be an incremental development of the common law by way of analogy but a radical reformulation of the purpose and scope of the tort.

One area that may be regarded as having to draw directly upon IBL is the marine environment. This is because of the potentially multiple international interests in the seas and oceans. In this regard, while there has been little direct biodiversity litigation in UK litigation, marine matters have been an underlying concern. For instance, in 2018 in *R (Bancoult) v Secretary of State for Foreign and Commonwealth Affairs (No 3)*[79] the claimant alleged that a Marine Protected Area (MPA)[80] had been created around the British Indian Ocean Territory with an improper motive. that residents of the Chagos Islands had not been properly consulted when creating the MPA, and that information about fishing rights had been improperly prevented from disclosure during the process. The Supreme Court dismissed appeals on the first and second points but found that it was unlawful not to disclose the information on the potential fishing rights. In 2012, in *Hughes v Carmarthenshire County Council*,[81] the Court of Appeal considered matters relating to the Carmarthen Bay and Estuaries European Marine Site which had a range of EU and international biodiversity designations including as a Ramsar site under the Convention on Wetlands (1971).[82] However, the court dismissed the claim which raised concerns about the potential adverse effect that the proposed sewage system of a 550 home development may have on cockle mortality in the designated marine areas. Similarly, in *R (Bruton) v AG to the Prince of Wales*[83] the High Court in

[79] [2018] UKSC 3, [2018] 1 WLR 973.

[80] The definition of a Marine Protected Area by the International Union for Conservation of Nature (IUCN) is: 'Any area of intertidal or sub-tidal terrain, together with its overlying water and associated flora, fauna, historical and cultural features, which has been reserved by law or other effective means to protect part or all of the enclosed environment', see <www.iucn.org/about/work/programmes/pa/pa_what/?4646/Marine-Protected-Areas--Why-have-them/> accessed 13 March 2022.

[81] [2012] EWCA Civ 1509.

[82] Burry Inlet no GB562, covering 6,672 ha, designated under Ramsar criteria 5 and 6. The JNCC general and physical descriptions note that Burry Inlet is a large estuarine complex located between the Gower Peninsula and Llanelli in South Wales. It includes extensive areas of intertidal sand- and mudflats, together with large sand dune systems at the mouth of the estuary. The site contains the largest continuous area of saltmarsh in Wales (2,200 ha). The estuary experiences wide tidal fluctuations (about 8 m) which has the consequence of exposing a large extent of intertidal sediments on a regular basis. These are mostly sandy, but muddy substrates are to be found in more sheltered areas.

[83] [2009] EWHC 1652 (Admin), [2009] Env LR 42.

2010 considered a claim relating to coastal waters and granted permission to proceed with a judicial review challenging the adequacy of an assessment carried out by Natural England on the impact of an oyster farm in a special area of conservation. As can be seen, while marine matters are considered in case law, they tend be driven by the economic interests of the local communities and any potential impact on biodiversity is incidental to the need to avoid harm to socio-economic interests.

Drawing together some strands from the previous discussion it is clear that UK biodiversity litigation arises within the sphere of public rather than private law and that the most common form of challenge is judicial review whereby a decision, act, or omission is 'reviewed' by the court. It is then important to acknowledge Sedley J's comments in *R (Dixon) v Somerset County Council and ARC Southern Ltd*[84] in 1998 (at 121) that:

> Public law is not at base about rights, even though abuses of power may and often do invade private rights; it is about wrongs—that is to say misuses of public power; and the courts have always been alive to the fact that a person or organization with no particular stake in the issue or the outcome may, without in any sense being a mere meddler, wish and be well placed to call the attention of the court to an apparent misuse of public power. . . .

There are occasional instances where private law claims engage with biodiversity, such as *St Helen's Smelting Co* discussed earlier. However, such engagement is uncommon and, to some extent, this is unsurprising. Private law in the UK is essentially about the rights and obligations of individuals and legal persons; and so even when the interference is to, say, property rights such as damages to trees, the concern is the economic consequence of such loss and wider concerns of biodiversity are unlikely to be recognized, at least not explicitly—the property rights claims only recognize direct consequential loss as noted earlier in the 2018 case of *Network Rail v Williams*.

It can also be seen that, in the main, claims tend to be by individuals and/or NGOs with a primary purpose of protecting biodiversity and/or having an ecological interest. This is consistent with other areas of environmental litigation: see, for example, the ClientEarth litigation of 2013 to 2018, including *ClientEarth v SSEFRA*[85] in 2015 and *R (PS) v LB of*

[84] [1998] Env LR 111.

[85] [2015] UKSC 28, [2015] 4 All ER 724. In this case, the UK was found to be in persistent and long-term breach Art 13 of Directive 2008/50/EC on ambient air quality and cleaner air for Europe. The problem of air pollution and breaches of the directive continue in Case C-664/18 *European*

Greenwich[86] on air pollution in 2016 and in 2020 *R (Plan B Earth v Secretary of State for Transport & others*[87] on climate change.

It is important to note that a litigant pursuing a claim must, in almost all instances, have sufficient interest or 'standing' in a particular claim to bring proceedings. This requirement is provided for either by the particular cause of action, such as a claim in private nuisance whereby the claimant must have a proprietary interest in the property or land being materially affected by the nuisance or by the court procedural rules themselves: see, for instance, section 31(3) of the Senior Courts Act 1981 (SCA 1981) which provides that:

> No application for judicial review shall be made unless the leave of the High Court has been obtained in accordance with rules of court; and the court shall not grant leave to make such an application unless it considers that the applicant has a sufficient interest in the matter to which the application relates.

However, it has been settled for some time that the rule on standing is applied taking a wide, purposive approach: see, for example, in *R v HMIP, ex p Greenpeace Ltd (No 2)*[88] in 1994 in which Otton J noted that:

> if I were to deny standing to Greenpeace, those it represents might not have an effective way to bring the issues before the court. There would have to be an application either by an individual employee of BNFL or a near neighbour. In this case it is unlikely that either would be able to command the expertise which is at the disposal of Greenpeace. Consequently, a less well-informed

Commission v UK (2021) ECLI:EU:C:2021:171 [2021] 3 WLUK 56 where the CJEU held that the UK had systematically and persistently exceeded legal limits for nitrogen dioxide (NO_2) pollution in sixteen urban zones since 2010 and failed to take appropriate action to ensure that the exceedance period was as short as possible.

[86] [2016] EWHC 1967 (Admin). In *PS v Greenwich* [2016] EWHC 1967 (Admin), the court dismissed a challenge to the development of a cruise liner terminal on the southern banks of the Thames notwithstanding the significant levels of NO_2 pollution levels that would be emitted in an area already exceeding critical human health levels. Although, subsequent to the judgment, a petition to the European Parliament affirmed that the European Commission would acknowledge the concern in the context of existing sanctions against the UK and the proposal was later abandoned by the London Borough of Greenwich due to air quality concerns.

[87] [2020] UKSC 52. In *Plan B Earth*, the Supreme Court overturned an appeal quashing the decision for a third runway at Heathrow finding that the government did not need to take into account GHG emissions in its policy White Paper and that it could be assumed that the government would have taken this into account.

[88] [1994] 4 All ER 329.

challenge might be mounted which could not afford the court the assistance it requires in order to do justice between the parties....

The remedy that may be available before the court varies depending on the cause of action and the nature of the litigation. There is a wide range of courts, tribunals, appeal bodies, inspectors, and adjudicators that could fall within the scope of biodiversity litigation; most have discrete procedural rules and limits as to what remedies and sanctions could be afforded in finding a breach of any given legislation. For example, the Information Tribunal could, on a finding of unlawful non-disclosure of environmental information, order disclosure and affirming the decision of the Information Commissioner.[89] While a private law claim in, say, nuisance or trespass could include an order for damages to compensate for any harm and an injunction directing either that a particular action is prohibited or that something is required. In *Watson v Croft Promosport Ltd*,[90] the Court of Appeal granted an injunction limiting noisy motor-racing activity alongside compensation for the impact on amenity prior to the injunction having effect. Alternatively, the appeal court may simply direct that the lower court reconsiders the matter; if necessary, by a different judge or tribunal.[91]

However, in the most common and prominent area of judicial review and the associated public law provisions such as statutory review under section 288 of the Town and Country Planning Act 1990, the remedies available to the court are provided for in section 31(1)(a) of the SCA 1981. These include a quashing order which 'quashes' the impugned decision or act,[92] a mandatory order requiring the decision maker to do something or act in a particular way,[93] and a prohibitory order preventing the public body from carrying out particular

[89] See eg *Hemsworth Town Council v Information Commissioner* EA/2017/0120 in which the applicants sought disclosure of a contract for sale of the council's land within which there had been a significant destruction of trees by the proposed buyer and where concerns of land contamination had also been raised.

[90] [2009] 3 All ER 249.

[91] In *Natural England v Warren* [2019] UKUT 300, the Upper Tribunal judge in concluding stated that: 'I have decided that it is not appropriate to constrain the next First-tier Tribunal. The last decision has been set aside. The appeal is to be reconsidered afresh. This decision is binding on the parties and the next tribunal, and it will not be open to either party to re-argue before the First-tier Tribunal any points which this tribunal has decided.'

[92] See eg *R (Croyde Area Residents Association) v North Devon District Council* [2021] EWHC 646 (Admin): ground 2 was based on EIA and resulted in the unintended consent being quashed.

[93] In *ClientEarth*, the Supreme Court considered a CJEU preliminary ruling and made a mandatory order requiring the UK government to prepare new air quality plans under Art 23(1) of the Ambient Air Quality Directive by 31 December 2015.

acts. The court may also under section 31(1)(b) of the SCA 1981 make a declaration which is a formal statement as to whether a particular law applies or grant an injunction, including an interim injunction,[94] which is used to preserve the status quo such to avoid the situation that by the time a particular case is heard at trial the 'damage is done' and substantive concern would be academic because, for instance, the wildlife site that was seeking to be protected had been destroyed.[95] It is generally the case that the quashing order is the most common form of remedy sought in judicial review. Finally, the court does have the discretion to award damages to a claim, although this is exceptional in judicial review and it is very rarely the case in public law environmental litigation (and therefore biodiversity litigation) that an award of damages is sought.[96]

It is important to note that any remedy in judicial review is discretionary and the Court may not grant the order sought by a claimant even if a claim is successful. Contrast this with a private contract or tort claim where damages are an entitlement if a claim succeeds.[97] This discretion has, in part, been placed on a statutory footing by an amendment to section 31(3D) of the SCA 1981 which provides that when considering whether to grant permission to proceed for judicial review a court must refuse permission if it appears: 'highly likely that the outcome for the applicant would not have been substantially different if the conduct complained of had not occurred'. A joint report by the Royal Society for the Protection of Birds (RSPB) and Friends of the Earth[98] concluded that the number of Aarhus Convention claims granted permission to proceed had markedly decreased since April 2016 following the section 31(3D) amendment. The report goes on to add that 'notwithstanding this, Aarhus Convention claims continue to demonstrate a higher success rate at the permission stage when compared to JRs generally'.

[94] See eg the interim injunction granted to prevent ancient tree loss and then subsequently discharged in *Keir v Natural England* [2021] EWHC 1059 (Admin).

[95] In *Devon Wildlife Trust v Teignbridge District Council* [2015] EWHC 2159 (Admin), the High Court claimant NGO challenged the grant of outline planning permission for 230 homes plus employment land use on the alleged failure to comply with the Habitats and EIA Regulations in connection with a European-protected species. The court found that the defendant council had breached the EIA provisions by not adopting an EIA-screening opinion as to whether the proposal was likely to have significant environmental effects and made a declaration to that effect but then concluded that the claim, in substance, failed.

[96] See eg Anna Poole, 'Remedies and expenses in judicial review cases', 2008 9 Scots Law Times (News) 51 at 53.

[97] See for a general discussion, *One Step (Support) Ltd v Morris-Garner* [2018] UKSC 20, [2019] AC 649.

[98] Julia Eriksen, Carol Day, and William Rundle, 'A pillar of justice' (Friends of the Earth and RSPB November 2019) <https://friendsoftheearth.uk/> accessed 13 March 2022.

3.8 The Potential Effects of IBL on Biodiversity Litigation

From the previous analysis it is reasonable to conclude that some of the inchoate rights that flow from the protection and increased obligation on public bodies to, for instance, more fully assess development projects and programmes under the Habitats and EIA Regulations have resulted in increased scrutiny of decision making and also increased biodiversity litigation. However, as is evident from the various unsuccessful challenges to HS2 (the proposed high-speed train line between London and Birmingham),[99] some decisions are politically driven and regardless of the potential environmental costs and significant biodiversity loss they will proceed.[100]

In terms of specific or particular forms of litigation, there is often a crossover between environmental protection regimes and concerns over harm and there does not appear to be a defined distinction between, say, nature and biodiversity; the terms can be used interchangeably. Further, a number of environmental concerns may be raised out of a particular alleged error of law or dispute. For instance, the challenge in *Abbotskerswell v Secretary of State* in 2021 alleged a failure to provide adequate information under the EIA provisions in relation to biodiversity and climate change although the basis for alleged error arose from a single decision. It may often be the case that while a legal challenge has a focus on a particular environmental harm or impact, the consequences of any successful challenge may have a number of environmental effects, including biodiversity.

What does appear to be the case is the apparent increased awareness and acceptance of environmental rights conferred on individuals and organizations flowing from the Rio Declaration and given further effect in UK law under the Aarhus Convention 1998. This is assisted by, for example, the transposition into UK law of those rights by legislation such as the Environmental Information Regulations 2004[101] and the Civil Procedure Rules 1998, Part 45.41–45.45: these were touched upon earlier. While these rights do not extend to non-humans, the opportunity to assert these rights does provide the opportunity for increased indirect access to the courts for nature and non-human species.

[99] *R (HS2 Action Alliance Ltd) v Secretary of State for Transport* [2014] UKSC 3, [2014] 2 All ER 109; *R (Packham) v SST* [2020] EWCA Civ 1004, [2021] Env LR 10; and *R (Misbourne Environmental Protection Ltd) v Environment Agency* [2021] EWHC 3094 (Admin) in which Lieven J dismissed a claim challenging a consent to construct a tunnel which would have impacted on the River Misbourne and a local chalk aquifer.

[100] See eg the permanent destruction of ancient woodland in *Keir v Natural England* (n 94).

[101] SI 2004/3391.

4. A Shift in Biodiversity Litigation

There appears to have been an increased understanding of biodiversity concerns since the introduction of the CBD and the level of argument between the parties is often complex as is clear from the detailed analysis in the 2019 *Canterbury City Council* judgments. However, the general reluctance of the High Court in 1997 to place nature before economic factors and to refuse to grant an interim injunction in *R v Secretary of State for the Environment, ex p RSPB*[102] because the claimant was unable to provide a cross-undertaking in damages to cover the possible economic loss from any delay in the proposed development, was evident twenty years on in *R (Dillner) v Sheffield City Council*.[103]

The tragedy in each case was that if a more purposeful and benign approach to nature had been taken, unnecessary loss to habitats and biodiversity could have been avoided. In the *RSPB* case, and having referred the matter to the Court of Justice of the European Union (CJEU), the Supreme Court ultimately held that when making a special protection area order for Lappel Bank[104] the Secretary of State was not permitted to take into account economic factors in his decision and had therefore acted unlawfully. However, by the time of the final judgment, the developer had concreted over 22 hectares of mudflats that should have been designated with special protection. Similarly, in *Dillner*, by the date of the judgment around 4,000 mature, urban trees in Sheffield had been destroyed with a rolling programme to clear 13,000 trees despite expert evidence suggesting this was unnecessary. As Jeremy Barrell's article 'Tree Benefits' explains:

> Sheffield was widely hailed as one of Europe's greenest cities, but it is rapidly gaining an international reputation as the place where they are felling street trees on an industrial scale. Local democracy seems to be unravelling before an international audience as the wishes of local communities are ignored and healthy trees with decades of life left in them are felled causing significant loss of tree benefits. It is a political problem and it will be for the politicians to find a solution, with issues way beyond the remit for tree experts to resolve. . . .[105]

102 [1997] QB 206.
103 [2016] EWCA Civ 977.
104 Lappel Bank is an area of mudflat on the Medway Estuary (south-east of London) which was an internationally important site for wintering waders and wildfowl.
105 'Tree benefits; the missing part of the street tree cost benefit analysis equation' (ICF Jan 2017) www.charteredforesters.org/2017/02/tree-benefits/ accessed 12 March 2022.

Thus, while a greater understanding of biodiversity appears to be evident in current UK litigation, it does not necessarily follow that biodiversity and nature benefit from this. One of the key concerns is that until the political will and commitment are there to place nature first, then species loss and biodiversity harm will continue to arise at the rate that it does.

In terms of that increased awareness of biodiversity among judges, advocates, and scientists, there are no distinct patterns according to the considered topics of genes, species, ecosystems, access to resources, and benefit sharing found in articles 1 and 2 of the CBD. Rather, the awareness is prompted by judicial decision making which is, in turn, influenced by, for instance, specialist legal opinion or advice from governance bodies such as the Advocate Generals to the CJEU as indicated earlier.

There is an argument that biodiversity litigation may have a strategic as well as a direct value in terms of a claim; although it appears that any strategic use is incidental and *ex post facto*. For instance, the tragedy of the *Lappel Bank* litigation with the developer concreting over a sensitive wild bird site before the courts, and in particular the CJEU, finding that the decision to exclude the site from a proposed Special Protection Area was unlawful did ultimately require action. The ruling left the UK government with an obligation to compensate for the habitat loss in order to maintain the coherence of the Natura 2000 network.[106]

Also, the example of the *Lappel Bank* litigation did provide a clear example of the need for interim injunctive relief to be available without it being prohibitively expensive, something required by article 9(4) of the Aarhus Convention 1998 and now found in amendments to the CPR under Part 25A in April 2013. A recent UK compliance report by the ACCC of 2 September 2021 noted that:

> 64. The Party concerned states that there were 12 applications for interim injunctions between April 2013 and May 2015, 8 of which were granted and in only one order did the claimant give a cross-undertaking for damages. It states that it has no subsequent data on cross-undertakings for damages.[107]

It is evident from the discussion that biodiversity litigation in the UK can reasonably be regarded as public interest litigation. Indeed, it is predominantly so, and the key areas of litigation are within the spheres of judicial review. In that

[106] Case C-44/95 *R v Secretary of State for the Environment* [1997] QB 206.

[107] Report of the Compliance Committee on compliance by the UK, Part 1 (2 September 2021) https://unece.org/environmental-policy/events/Aarhus_Convention_MoP7.

respect, it can reasonably be seen to help to promote broader social change although it is acknowledged that this is not a view shared by everyone[108] and it is unclear how effective it is; with significant species loss throughout the UK continuing apace, the empirical evidence is that biodiversity harm and loss of nature continues. However, it is arguable that, but for the biodiversity litigation, the decline in nature and species loss may have been worse.

With a dualist common law legal system in the UK, and with judicial precedent forming part of that system, it can reasonably be said that biodiversity litigation forms part of the wider notion of biodiversity law. Moreover, it is clear that with the judiciary playing a central role in the constitutional functioning of the UK, including the scrutiny of executive power, litigation by individuals and organizations provides a crucial mechanism for the judicial review of state power. How this litigation influences international law is unclear, although the number of environmental concerns from the UK that are considered by international tribunals and committees suggests that UK litigation certainly informs IBL. This much is evident by the comparatively high level of communications before the ACCC as well as references and enforcement cases before the CJEU.[109]

It is reasonably clear that the greater understanding of biodiversity in the UK legal system correlates to a similar and increasing understanding in the EU. It is less clear whether this, in turn, correlates to the evolution of IBL.

5. Conclusion

It can be seen from this review of UK litigation that the domestic civil courts appear reluctant to disturb public decisions relating to the environment. They are cautious to quash decisions by public bodies and there does not appear to be any inherent environmental empathy or need for protection such as in the 2021 case of *R (Misbourne) v Environment Agency*. The brave new environmental law world anticipated by Sir Harry Woolf (then Lord Justice of Appeal) in his article 'Are the Judiciary Environmentally Myopic?'[110] has yet

[108] See eg Prime Minister Boris Johnson's Economy Speech on 30 June 2020 suggesting that the UK was slow to build homes in Britain because of the 'newt-counting delays in our system'; which was asserted without any evidence or basis and when a previous government in the Letwin Review (2018) had found no fault with the environmental regulation or protection provisions.

[109] To date, at least twenty-three of the 130 communications to the ACCC found to be admissible have related to alleged non-compliance by the UK (close to 18 per cent of all admissible communications). As at 16 October 2017, there were forty-seven signatory states to the Convention: <https://unece.org/> accessed 13 March 2022.

[110] (1992) 4(1) Journal of Environmental Law 1–14.

to materialize within the civil justice system. In contrast, in terms of regulatory litigation and the criminal courts, the sentences being handed down for environmental offences appear to apply the environmental sentencing guidelines consistently and seek to remedy environmental harm.

It is also reasonable to conclude that the influence of IBL is evident in UK litigation, but it is generally indirect, requiring transposition of that law into domestic provision. This is largely due to the nature of the legal justice system in the UK and where it sits within the constitutional structure. Until Brexit, the transposition was obligated by much of the EU environmental legislation and, in particular, to ensure that directives had full effect in the UK. In contrast, if international law has not been transposed in the UK, then under the principle of parliamentary sovereignty, the courts will aim to act consistently with international law but will not be obliged to require the UK public bodies to follow that law (unlike the relationship with the EU). In such circumstances, IBL is persuasive but not binding.

The real impact of Brexit on biodiversity and the wider practice of environmental law, policy, and practice in the UK remains unclear. The divergence of law across the four nations is continuing with Scotland aligning itself with EU law, Wales pursuing what may be seen as an innovative path to sustainability, Northern Ireland tackling with intermittent suspension of its Assembly, and England pressing on with the enactment of the Environment Act 2021. This divergence is progressing at a time when the current government is pursuing ambitions to restrict judicial discretion. Thus, alongside the European Union (Withdrawal) Act 2018 (Relevant Court) (Retained EU Case Law) Regulations 2020[111] conferring power to the UK upper appellate courts to depart from EU case law,[112] judicial scrutiny is proposed to be limited by the Judicial Review and Courts Bill 2020.[113] Whether the Bill imposing restrictions on judicial review will become law is unknown—the prospect of the state seeking to curb the powers of the courts may have a 'chilling effect' on judicial approaches.

Finally, while there has been a delay in replacing the governance and scrutiny role of the European Commission, the Office for Environmental Protection and Environmental Standards Scotland are now in place alongside the Welsh

[111] SI 2020/1525.

[112] The Supreme Court already had this power under the EU (Withdrawal) Act 2018. In accordance with Practice Statement 1966, EU case law will be regarded 'as normally binding, [but] depart from a previous decision when it appears right to do so'.

[113] Bill 152-EN. See eg the widespread concern about the proposals in the lead up to the Bill's publication, eg the Report by the Independent Review of Administrative Law Panel and the responses to the government consultation paper including from the UK Environmental Law Association <www.ukela.org> accessed 12 March 2022.

Environmental Protection Assessor. The Environment Act 2021 has received Royal Assent and many sections are now in force. There is a real opportunity for the UK to meet its aspiration to become an environment world leader. There are encouraging signs with, for instance, the development of guiding environmental principles for all government policymakers and decision takers now underway[114] and the publication of longer term environmental planning (ie over twenty-five years). However, the tensions of devolution must be addressed and the UK as a whole must have confidence to affirm its position on the international stage by setting gold standard policy and law that, for example, goes beyond the EU norms. This will involve placing greater reliance on IBL and embracing its principles. Accepting the tragic state of biodiversity loss and nature's decline will be necessary and the enhancement of biodiversity has to be at the heart of litigation decision making. It is something that is likely to involve a shift in current judicial thinking.

[114] See eg the Scottish Government, 'Guiding Principles: A Consultation on Statutory Guidance' (November 2021) <www.gov.scot> accessed 12 March 2022 and DEFRA, 'Environmental governance consultation on the draft policy statement on environmental principles' (10 March 2021) <www.defra.gov.uk> accessed 10 March 2022.

10

Biodiversity Litigation in the United States

Strong Conservation Laws but Challenges with Enforcement

William J Snape, III

1. Introduction

It is fair to say that the beginning of what is now called US 'biodiversity law' coincided with the dawn of the twentieth century.[1] In May 1900, Congress passed, and President McKinley signed, the Lacey Act, the first US federal wildlife statute. It prohibited, and still prohibits, the interstate transportation of wildlife caught in violation of the applicable state law, with penalties for violators, and has been expanded by Congress over the years to include international law.[2] The Lacey Act was a significant departure from the common law notion that the states, not the federal government, possessed primary jurisdiction over wildlife.[3] Over subsequent decades leading into the 1960s, the US would embark upon a somewhat extraordinary national effort to protect wildlife both inside the country and out.[4]

[1] US forest aficionados will note that the US Forest Service was created in the 1890s 'for the purpose of securing favorable conditions of water flows, and to furnish a continuous supply of timber', 16 USC s 475. In addition, iconic Yellowstone National Park was created in 1872, yet it was not until President Teddy Roosevelt in the early twentieth century that the notion of public lands for nature gained traction. See also Antiquities Act of 1906, 16 USC ss 431–33 (providing the President with authority to declare national monuments to protect important cultural or natural resources).

[2] Lacey Act, 16 USC s 3372 (this statute makes it unlawful 'to import, export, transport, sell, receive, acquire, or purchase any fish or wildlife or plant taken, possessed, transported, or sold in violation of any law, treaty, or regulation of the U.S. or in violation of any Indian tribal law'). Thus, under the Lacey Act, it is unlawful to import, export, sell, acquire, or purchase fish, wildlife, or plants that are taken, possessed, transported, or sold in interstate or foreign commerce involving any fish, wildlife, or plants taken possessed or sold in violation of foreign law. The law covers all fish and wildlife and their parts or products, and plants protected by treaties such CITES, discussed below. Commercial guiding and outfitting are considered to be a sale under the provisions of the Act. In 2008, the Lacey Act was amended to include a wider variety of prohibited plants and plant products, including products made from illegally logged woods, for import.

[3] *Hughes v Oklahoma* (1979) 441 US 322 (affirming broad state trustee powers over native wildlife within its borders).

[4] See Migratory Bird Treaty Act (MBTA), 16 USC ss 703–12; Endangered Species Preservation Act of 1966, PL 89-669.

William J Snape, III, *Biodiversity Litigation in the United States* In: *Biodiversity Litigation*. Edited by: Guillaume Futhazar, Sandrine Maljean-Dubois, and Jona Razzaque, Oxford University Press. © William J Snape, III, 2023.
DOI: 10.1093/oso/9780192865465.003.0010

The apex of federal consensus over wildlife law and policy came in the early 1970s as Congress passed, inter alia, the National Environmental Policy Act (NEPA) (1970),[5] Marine Mammal Protection Act (MMPA) (1972),[6] Endangered Species Act (ESA) (1973),[7] and the Senate ratified the Convention on International Trade in Endangered Species (CITES)[8] in 1975. The ESA implements both CITES and the Convention on Nature Protection and Wildlife Preservation in the Western Hemisphere ('Western Hemisphere Convention').[9] Further, in 1978, the Supreme Court held that a federal agency dam, already partially built, must be enjoined because of a federally listed small fish called the snail darter.[10] However, the election of President Ronald Reagan in 1980 heralded a new era of federal regulatory backlash, including the ESA. Over the past forty years, Republican-led presidential administrations have tried to loosen or weaken endangered species and related biodiversity protections, and Democrat-led presidential administrations have tried, at least nominally, to embrace conservation with various incentive mechanisms.[11]

Congress, the federal branch given lead lawmaking authority, has passed almost no new wildlife or biodiversity legislation this century.[12] Even when the President and Congress are from the same party, gridlock is hard to break. The administration of Donald Trump was the most hostile towards biodiversity and environmental regulation in US history. Although President Joe Biden has a solid conservation record,[13] and selected the first ever Native American to

[5] 42 USC ss 4321 et seq.

[6] 16 USC ss 1361 et seq.

[7] 16 USC ss 1531 et seq.

[8] 12 ILM 1085.

[9] 56 Stat 1354 (1942). The United States, as a party to this treaty, and home to the original Secretariat, possesses the legal authority to call a Western Hemisphere Convention meeting amongst its hemispheric partners and revitalize this important but neglected multilateral agreement. The Western Hemisphere Convention's connections to the CBD and international biodiversity law are inescapable. See eg Keri Lewis, *Negotiating for nature: Conservation diplomacy and the Convention on Nature Protection and Wildlife Preservation in the Western Hemisphere* (Doctoral Dissertation, University of New Hampshire, Durham, Spring 2008) 276. The Convention on Nature Protection as it exists today retains the original spirit of its framers, advancing a comprehensive, flexible, and malleable agreement that laid the foundation for effective nature protection across the Americas.

[10] *TVA v Hill* (1978) 437 US 153.

[11] See Jamie Pang and Noah Greenwald, *Politics of Extinction: The Unprecedented Republican Attack on the ESA* (Center for Biological Diversity 2015).

[12] One of the few things Congress has agreed upon is increased border security in the US. See Public Law 104-208, FY 1997 Omnibus Appropriations Bill (giving authority to the federal government to waive environmental and wildlife law in order to build portions of a 'wall' along the biodiverse rich US–Mexico border, which is, inter alia, prime jaguar habitat).

[13] Senator Joe Biden had a career 83 per cent record on environmental and conservation issues, according to the US League of Conservation voters. By comparison, current Senate Republican leader Mitch McConnell has a career 8 per cent record. 'National Environmental Score Card' <https://scorecard.lcv.org/moc/joe-biden> accessed 14 March 2022.

lead the Department of the Interior,[14] whether his administration has the political strength to address the true nature of the biodiversity crisis in the US is an open question.

This chapter aims to explain what we have learned over the past 150 years in the US, and what the rule of law must accomplish if the US is not to squander its considerable natural splendour. If US wildlife and habitat litigation over the past fifty years is a guide, court action can stem specific injuries to biodiversity, but litigation is generally less successful in advancing proactive long-term conservation. While enforcement of the ESA and related laws in court has led to significant conservation victories, the current system of legal enforcement does not directly address larger biodiversity considerations, and there are some indications that litigation better catalyses conservation action than actually solving embedded biodiversity problems.

2. The Particularities of the United States

2.1 Biodiversity

The United States is one of the more biodiverse countries in the world. The catalogue entitled *Precious Heritage* continues to be among the best overviews of US biological diversity. Here is a cogent summary, edited and abridged, from its current webpage:

> [T]he United States harbors an extraordinary diversity of life, from the lush forests of Appalachia to the frozen tundra of Alaska, and from the Midwest's tallgrass prairies to Hawaii's rainforests. The United States emerges from this assessment as being far richer in species and ecosystems than previously thought, and as a global center of diversity for many life-forms. A surprising number of species are more diverse in the US than anywhere else on Earth. The nation is particularly rich in aquatic life, such as fishes,

[14] The rise of Secretary Haaland gives hope to US conservationists on several fronts. First, she has committed to fully enforce and implement laws such as the ESA. See Melissa Lyttle, 'What You Need to Know About Deb Haaland and the Department of the Interior', *Earthjustice* (15 March 2021) <https://earthjustice.org/brief/2020/what-you-need-to-know-about-deb-haaland-and-the-department-of-the-interior> accessed 14 March 2022. Secondly, she will bring focus to the protection of tribal sacred sites, which frequently have high biodiversity value. See Annette McGivney, 'Biden Administration Pauses Transfer of Holy Native American Land to Mining Firm', *The Guardian* (2 March 2021). Thirdly, her appointment raises larger visionary issues about public lands in the US. See David Treuer, 'Return the National Parks to the Tribes', *The Atlantic* (12 April 2021) <www.theatlantic.com/magazine/archive/2021/05/return-the-national-parks-to-the-tribes/618395/> accessed 14 March 2022.

> turtles, salamanders, and mussels. For example, more fish species are found in a single river, the Tennessee, than in all of Europe. The US also supports a broader array of ecosystems. Several large-scale ecosystems are especially well represented, and the US hosts a large percentage of the world's broadleaf forests, temperate grasslands, and Mediterranean-climate vegetation.[15] One-third of US species are at risk and of conservation concern. Aquatic life is particularly vulnerable; for instance, nearly 70% of the nation's freshwater mussel species and over half of our crayfishes are in trouble. More than 500 U.S. species are already extinct or missing. Of these, at least 100 plants and animals have disappeared forever and are presumed extinct, while another 439 are missing and feared lost. Nearly 60% of the US outside of Alaska has lost most of its natural vegetation, and habitat destruction is the leading threat to U.S. species. Alien species invasions-like zebra mussels and kudzu-are second only to habitat loss as a cause of species declines.[16]

In addition, the US state of Hawaii sadly holds the title of 'extinction capital of the world' with more than 75 per cent of its remaining bird species classified as endangered or already extinct.[17]

2.2 Legal Structure

The US is a democratic republic with a written Constitution. The federal government is made up of three branches, each with spheres of power defined by the Constitution: Congress, which makes the laws, the President and his executive agencies that implement the law, and the court system, which interprets the law. The federal government shares power with the state governments, which possess so-called 'police powers' over the general welfare of their state citizens and residents, though in the case of a conflict, authorized federal law prevails over state law. International treaties must receive the approval of two-thirds of the Senate; when this occurs, international treaties have the same

[15] The US also possesses two global biodiversity 'hotspots': the California Floristic Provence and North American Coastal Plain. See Critical Ecosystem Partnership Fund, 'Explore the Biodiversity hotspots' <www.cepf.net/node/1996> accessed 13 March 2022.

[16] See Bruce Stein, Lynn Kutner, and Jonathan Adams (eds), *Precious Heritage: The Status of Biodiversity in the United States* (OUP 2000). This still current study is now constantly updated online, called NatureServe: available at <www.natureserve.org/products/natureserve-explorerr> accessed 13 March 2022.

[17] See Center for Biological Diversity, *Saving Life on Earth: A Plan to Halt the Global Extinction Crisis* (January 2020) <www.biologicaldiversity.org/programs/biodiversity/elements_of_biodiversity/extinction_crisis/pdfs/Saving-Life-On-Earth.pdf> accessed 14 March 2022.

status as domestic law. However, almost all environmental treaties need domestic implementing legislation.[18]

In addition, the US is not a party to many multilateral conservation agreements such as the Convention on Biological Diversity (CBD).[19] Even when following an international agreement, US courts will grant significant deference and discretion for a federal agency implementing such an agreement.[20] For these structural and political reasons, the US is very much a dualist country with regard to its relationship to international law.

Most biodiversity-related litigation in the US is 'public', meaning a government agency is involved in some manner. This is so for at least three reasons. First, while the ESA and other statutes allow plaintiffs to sue private parties, the vast majority of cases under these laws are against governmental defendants. Secondly, at the federal level, it is virtually impossible to sue on behalf of biodiversity without a congressional statute authorizing such litigation, thus there is no common law for biodiversity at the federal level. Thirdly, even at the state level, where common law is relevant to biodiversity, the state is the lead legal trustee for wildlife within its borders and manages wildlife explicitly for the greater public good.[21] At both the state and federal levels, numerous laws waive 'sovereign immunity' for members of the public to enforce biodiversity-related laws against the applicable governmental entity.[22]

2.3 US Law and 'Biological Diversity'

There is little, if any, US statutory law that protects 'biodiversity' per se.[23] An examination of case law in the US reveals that 'biological diversity' or

[18] See *Greenpeace USA v Stone* (1990) US District Court for the District of Hawaii 748 F Supp 749, 767 (international convention on hazardous waste could not be used to enforce disposal of chemical weapons if there was no implementing law).

[19] 31 ILM 818 (1993).

[20] See *Japan Whaling Association v American Cetacean Society* (1986) 478 US 221 (judiciary would not second-guess a decision by federal agency to find Japan was in compliance with the International Whaling Convention).

[21] See Susan George and others, 'State Endangered Species Acts' in Donald Baur and Ya-Wei-Li (eds), *Endangered Species Act: Law, Policy and Perspectives* (American Bar Association 2021) 345. The role of state and local governments in protecting imperilled species can be summed up with one central fact: state governments traditionally have been the chief stewards of wildlife within their borders.

[22] See Administrative Procedure Act (APA), 5 USC s 702. Other US wildlife statutes, usually pertaining to foreign species, do not create legal rights but provide funding to projects under the African Elephant Conservation Act, Asian Elephant Conservation, Great Ape Conservation Act, Marine Turtle Conservation Act, Rhino and Tiger Conservation Act, and Neotropical Migratory Bird Conservation Act. See <www.fws.gov/program/international-affairs/what-we-do> accessed 28 March 2022.

[23] Only one federal statute even mentions 'diversity'. The 1976 National Forest Management Act, 16 USC s 1604(g)(3)(b), provides for diversity of plant and animal communities based on the suitability of the specific land area in order to meet overall multiple-use objectives. See also US FWS, Policy 601 FW

'biodiversity' is mentioned in only a handful of cases almost all pertaining to the national forest system, which includes the term 'diversity' as a legal marker, but this standard is subjugated to the overall 'multiple use/sustained yield' statutory directive which elevates resource extraction and human recreation above biological diversity.[24] When the term is mentioned, it is usually in passing or because the plaintiff used the term in their pleadings.[25] Still, many US laws at both the federal and state levels protect what is considered to be 'biodiversity', just not by that label; those US laws are discussed and analysed later.

2.4 US Public Lands and Waters

Approximately 28 per cent of land in the US is owned by the federal government on behalf of the American people.[26] Under the Constitution, Congress has the lead power to make rules over these lands.[27] Yet, according to one study, only 12 per cent of the US is in some 'conservation status' meaning that many public lands are used for other purposes.[28] In addition, very little of the 60 per cent of land that is 'private' in the US is in conservation status,[29] making conservation easements and other devices an important tool.

3 (2001) (Biological Integrity, Diversity and Environmental Health on National Wildlife Refuges). In neither instance is biodiversity a controlling legal standard.

[24] See *Sierra Club v Marita* (ED Wis 1994) 845 US District Court of Wisconsin Supp 1317. Despite numerous renowned experts supporting the plaintiffs' claims for protecting biological diversity on Wisconsin national forests, the court found for the agency because of the deferential agency standard provided by 'Multiple Use—Sustained Yield'.

[25] See *1000 Friends of Oregon v Forest Service* (1992) US District Court for the District of Oregon 804 F Supp 104 (plaintiff loses suit where they are in part relying upon the NFMA diversity standard because of deference to federal agency decision); *Wildwest Institute v Kurth* (2017) US Court of Appeals, Ninth Circuit 855 F2d 995 failed challenge to a decision not to list the Joshua tree, which would also protect Mojave Desert biological diversity; *WildEarth Guardians v Salazar* (2011) US District Court for the District of Colorado 834 F Supp 2d 1220 (environmental group loses bid to protect beetle species found in threatened riparian ecosystems in Wyoming, and the judge states in a footnote that Mr Tutchton also alleges that 'the potential extinction of [this beetle], due to the current lack of effective legal protection, harms [him] personally because it represents a loss of biodiversity. Although … this psychic injury may in fact cause Mr Tutchton some degree of harm, the Supreme Court has considered and dismissed similar injuries as insufficient for purposes of the standing inquiry.'

[26] US Congressional Research Service, *Federal Land Ownership: Overview and Data* (21 February 2020) <https://sgp.fas.org/crs/misc/R42346.pdf> accessed 14 March 2022.

[27] US Const Art IV s 3, Cl 2.

[28] Ryan Richards, *Measuring Conservation Progress in North America* (Center for American Progress 2018).

[29] The remaining 12 per cent of US land is owned either by state and local governments or occupied by Native Americans as part of a reservation by the US government.

Four major federal land management agencies administer 606.5 million acres of the land: the Bureau of Land Management (BLM), Fish and Wildlife Service (FWS), and National Park Service (NPS), which reside under the Department of the Interior (DOI), as well as the Forest Service in the Department of Agriculture. A fifth agency, the Department of Defense (excluding the US Army Corps of Engineers, or 'Corps'), administers 8.8 million acres in the US, some of which is scientifically confirmed conservation habitat. The lands administered by the four major land agencies are managed for many purposes, primarily related to conservation, recreation, and development of natural resources, though each agency possesses its own organic statute and set of implementing regulations.[30] These lands are significant reservoirs and migration corridors for biodiversity.[31]

With regard to water, Congress in 1953 enacted the Submerged Lands Act (SLA),[32] which granted the coastal states title to the waters and submerged lands lying beyond the low-water mark out to three nautical miles. This Act also gives states the express power to lease, develop, and manage the natural resources found within their waters, seabed, and subsoil. In the same year as it passed the SLA, Congress further established federal dominion seaward of the coastal state's three nautical mile boundary in the Outer Continental Shelf Lands Act (OCSLA).[33] The US economic exclusive zone is the largest in the world, containing 3.4 million square miles of ocean and 90,000 miles of coastline, and abundant marine biodiversity.[34]

In addition, the US Clean Water Act[35] gives the federal government regulatory primacy over 'waters of the U.S.'.[36] However, while 'navigable waters' is defined by the statute, 'waters of the U.S.' is not, leaving presidential

[30] Forest Service Organic Act of 1897, 16 USC ss 473 et seq; National Forest Management Act of 1976, PL No 94-588, 90 Stat 2949 (codified as amended at 16 USC ss 1600 et seq); Federal Land and Policy Management Act (FLPMA), 43 USC ss 1701 et seq; National Wildlife Refuge System Improvement Act of 1997, PL No 105-57 (codified as amended at 16 USC s 668dd–668jj).

[31] See Bobby Magill, 'America's Best Climate Defense Lies in Public Lands', Scientific American (12 March 2015) <www.scientificamerican.com/article/america-s-best-climate-defense-lies-in-public-lands/> accessed 14 March 2022, noting public lands protect forests, wildlife, and biological diversity as well.

[32] 43 USC ss 1301 et seq.

[33] ibid ss 1331(a), 1332(1).

[34] See US National Ocean and Atmospheric Administration (NOAA), 'The US EEZ: Boundaries of the Exclusive Economic Zones of the United States and Territories' (2006) <https://pubs.usgs.gov/ds/2006/146/basemaps/useez/useezmeta.htm accessed 14 March 2022. The US public has been generally against oil drilling in the US EEZ, eg de facto federal drilling moratoria in the Pacific and Atlantic oceans, and environmental plaintiffs have stalled some but not all projects in the Arctic. See *Center for Biological Diversity v Interior* (2009) 563 US Court of Appeals for the District of Columbia 466.

[35] 33 USC ss 1251 et seq.

[36] US Clean Water Act, 33 USC ss 1311(a), 1344, 1362(12).

administrations from Nixon to Biden to wrestle with the scope and jurisdiction of the Environmental Protection Agency (EPA) and Army Corps in interpreting the meaning of 'waters of the U.S.'.[37] These waters constitute several hundred million acres that could be conserved for biological diversity if Congress so chose.

3. Case Studies

This chapter draws upon over fifty years of federal case history, and over 100 years of statutory history. Three recent empirical studies are here presented to test how these conservation laws are now interpreted by federal courts. These three studies, under three different statutory regimes, are accentuated by the recent administration of Donald Trump, which can be safely characterized by supporters and detractors as 'anti-government'.[38] The basic question asked here is whether political ideology in the executive branch influences litigation over conservation law:

(1) the record of the Trump administration (2017–21) in implementing the inter-agency consultation provision (Section 7)[39] of the ESA, arguably the single most important legal mechanism to prevent biodiversity loss in the US;

(2) a comparison of the records of the Clinton administration (1993–2001), Bush II administration (2001–09), and Trump administration (2017–21) in implementing the NEPA, which requires environmental review of major federal agency actions including those that impact biological diversity or its components; and

(3) the record of the Obama administration (2009–17), Trump administration (2017–21), and Biden administration (2021–present) in litigating private land conservation easements under the US tax code that directly or indirectly impact biodiversity.

[37] Paul Sonderegger and Spenser Owens, 'Waters of the United States' Rule from EPA, Corps May Make Real Estate Development More Easily Achievable and Less Costly' <www.americanbar.org/groups/real_property_trust_estate/publications/ereport/rpte-ereport-winter-2019/_waters-of-the-united-states-rule-from-epa--corps-may-make--real/> accessed 13 March 2022.

[38] See Maggie Haberman, 'Trump, Head of Government, Leans into Antigovernment message', *New York Times* (20 April 2020) <www.nytimes.com/2020/04/20/us/politics/trump-coronavirus.html> accessed 13 March 2022.

[39] 16 USC s 1536(a)(2).

3.1 ESA Consultations

The US ESA might be the strongest and most effective in the world.[40] Section 7 of the ESA may be the most important operating provision of the ESA, aside from the listing of threatened and endangered species themselves,[41] because it forces federal agencies, as well as private parties needing federal agency approval, to 'consult' (ie exchange scientific and technical information) with the US FWS and/or US National Marine Fisheries Service (NMFS) on any federal action that may affect a listed species. Numerous studies of the history of ESA consultation demonstrate that not only does the process result in protection for threatened and endangered species, but it also provides a check into overly expensive or poorly conceived federal actions.[42]

Litigation under Section 7 was particularly intense under the Trump administration because of the political push to expand fossil fuel extraction on US public lands.[43] The Trump administration also attempted to rewrite agency rules by FWS and NMFS, which would have given action agencies[44] more leeway to harm endangered species.[45] In general, unless an action agency simply refuses to consult on its action—for example, building a road, approving a timber sale, leasing oil and gas—scientific and technical determinations by

[40] See J. Berton C Harris and others, 'Conserving Imperiled Species: A Comparison of the IUCN Red List and US Endangered Species Act' (2012) 5 Conservation Letters 64, 64–72. In short, the ESA is arguably the world's most effective biodiversity protection law.

[41] The Trump administration also performed horribly on listing species in need of protection. See Noah Greenwald, 'Lawsuit Seeks ESA Protections for Nineteen Species Left to Languish by Trump', Centre for Biological Diversity (15 April 2021) <https://biologicaldiversity.org/w/news/press-releases/lawsuit-seeks-endangered-species-act-protections-for-19-species-left-to-languish-by-trump-administration-2021-04-15/> accessed 14 March 2022. Long delays in protecting species under the ESA have been a persistent problem for decades. On average, species have waited twelve years for protection during the Act's forty-plus-year history, and at least forty-seven species have gone extinct waiting for protection. Overall, the Trump administration protected only twenty-five species under the ESA—the fewest of any administration since the Act was passed in 1973. In contrast, the Obama administration listed and protected 360 species, and the Clinton administration listed 523.

[42] See Jacob Malcolm and Ya-Wei Li, 'Data Contradict Common Perceptions about a Controversial Provision of the US Endangered Species Act' (2015) 112(52) PNAS 15844, 15844–49. We analyse data on all 88,290 consultations recorded by FWS from January 2008 through to April 2015. In contrast to conventional wisdom about Section 7 implementation, no project was stopped or extensively altered as a result of FWS finding jeopardy or adverse modification during this period.

[43] See Trump Exec Order No 13783 (March 2017) explicitly overturning environmental protections and seeking to expedite fossil fuel extraction, particularly on federal public lands. This EO was overturned by a Biden order on his first day of office, EO 13990 (20 January 2021).

[44] Action agencies are all other federal agencies subject to the ESA. See 16 USC s 1536(a)(2).

[45] The Trump ESA rules were challenged in federal court by multiple parties, and the Biden administration has announced that it is reversing the Trump rules. The same dynamic has played out with Trump NEPA regulations, which the new administration has announced it is suspending.

two expert agencies, FWS and NMFS, usually receive significant deference by the judiciary.[46]

An examination of all ESA consultation litigation during the four years of the Trump administration revealed that the substantive standards of the ESA forced courts to more carefully look at inconsistencies and gaps in the administrative record of the action agency, despite the scientific deference historically given to the services. Over the course of the Trump presidency, plaintiffs prevailed in more consultation cases against the Trump administration (34–24), or 59 per cent for plaintiffs and 41 per cent for the Trump administration. Almost all of the Trump 'wins' were simply because the court deferred to the agency's decision, which is quite frequent in consultation litigation. About six-sevenths of the cases the plaintiffs won were brought by conservation organizations or those with conservation goals, whereas about one-seventh were brought by other entities.

An important aspect of US administrative law was revealed by one ESA legal theme of the Trump era: even when courts expressed doubt that the agency decision was the best decision, they would frequently defer to agency if the decision had a modicum of support in the evidentiary record. For example, in *National Family Farm Coalition v EPA*, the court found that EPA had not made serious enough error to find an ESA violation, despite noting that EPA failed to consider how a new pesticide to target milkweed could harm monarch butterflies.[47] In another case, where a plaintiff tried to compel the Army Corps to reinitiate consultation over the impacts of a dam project on the protected southwestern willow flycatcher and silvery minnow, the court held that the duty to consult only applies with discretionary federal involvement, and given that the Flood Control Act does not provide the Corps with discretion to operate the projects outside flood-control purposes, the Corps thus did not have to engage in consultation with FWS.[48]

By contrast, plaintiffs generally won consultation cases for three primary reasons: (1) the Trump administration made a decision that blatantly did not

[46] See *Defenders of Wildlife v Zinke* (2017) US Court of Appeals of the District of Columbia Circuit 856 F3d 1248. Biological Opinion prepared by FWS to assess the impacts on the threatened desert tortoise from a solar project in Nevada upheld because of the substantial deference that federal courts give to the scientific judgments of the FWS, especially in the face of scientific uncertainty.

[47] (2020) US Court of Appeals, Ninth Circuit 966 F3d 893. Pesticides' impacts upon biodiversity are now understood to be catastrophic, but US agencies have been slow to respond, in large part because of pressure from the chemical industry. See Center for Biological Diversity, 'EPA: Neonicotinoid Pesticides Harm Vast Majority of All Endangered Species' (26 August 2021) <https://biologicaldiversity.org/w/news/press-releases/epa-neonicotinoid-pesticides-harm-vast-majority-of-all-endangered-species-2021-08-26/> accessed 14 March 2022.

[48] *WildEarth Guardians v US Army Corps of Engineers* (2020) US Court of Appeals, Tenth Circuit 947 F3d 635.

comply with the letter of the law; (2) the administration did not use the best science available which is a central standard of the ESA; or (3) political reasons guided decision making with disregard for accepted legal procedure. For instance, *Center for Biological Diversity v Forest Service* did not defer to the FWS's new interpretation of its regulation governing reinitiation of consultation because the regulation's language was deemed to be unambiguous and had been interpreted in a certain way for over twenty years.[49] Given the lack of ambiguity in the rule, the agency had no discretion to change how it interpreted the requirements for reinitiating consultation. Blatant political interference in a legally binding process has also drawn rebuke from the courts. In *Institute for Fisheries Resources v US Food and Drug Administration*, a case about artificially bred salmon, the court found a violation, noting:

> In a strange sequence of events: NMFS and FWS initially urged the FDA to undergo a Section 7 consultation regarding the AquaBounty operations; the FDA took the view that the production of the AquAdvantage salmon 'may affect' endangered salmon, thus triggering the consultation requirement; then FWS prodded FDA to change its 'may affect' determination to a 'no effect' determination, the result being that formal consultation among the agencies would not be required; and thereafter the FDA issued a formal statement that approval of the engineered salmon would have no effect on the endangered species.[50]

3.2 The Intersection of NEPA and 'Biodiversity'

NEPA[51] is the parent of all modern US statutory environmental law. Passed in 1970 after the first Earth Day, it requires that all federal agencies prepare either an environmental assessment (EA) or an environmental impact statement (EIS) if an agency action will affect the 'human environment'. The broad definition of the impacted environment means that biodiversity is definitely covered by it, even though the term 'biodiversity' is not explicitly mentioned.[52] For the purposes of examining the Trump-era use of NEPA to advance or deny biodiversity protection, five general search terms were used to examine NEPA

[49] (2020) US District Court for the District of Arizona 2020 WL 6710944 at 3.
[50] (2020) US District Court for the Northern District of California 499 F Supp 3d 657, 667–68.
[51] 42 USC ss 4321 et seq.
[52] US Council of Environmental Quality, *Incorporating Biodiversity Considerations into Environmental Impact Statement Analysis under NEPA* (January 1993).

litigation: (1) where biodiversity itself was mentioned and impacted;[53] (2) affecting endangered species; (3) affecting migratory birds; (4) affecting federal public lands and wildlife, or (5) affecting marine mammals or fish.[54]

Somewhat surprisingly, the Trump administration did relatively well in its NEPA cases involving 'biodiversity' as defined above. Out of a total of 141 cases falling under our rubric, the Trump administration won ninety-one (64 per cent), while plaintiff groups won fifty (36 per cent).[55] There are two interrelated explanations for these results: (a) NEPA's environmental impact process, unlike the ESA consultation process, is merely procedural and does not possess substantive standards; and (b) as the US judiciary has become more conservative, federal judges are less likely to rule against what they perceived to be 'minor' violations of this largely procedural law.

The most common reason for wins by 'biodiversity plaintiffs' was the result of an agency's failure to take the requisite 'hard look' under NEPA. A good example is *Rocky Mountain Wild v Bernhardt*, which involved an agency proposal for fossil fuel extraction on public lands that was remanded back to the agency to better consider implications to lower level ozone and smog pollution.[56] Another common reason for plaintiff victories was because the court determined that the agency had tried to avoid NEPA altogether. For example, in *Center for Biological Diversity v Ross*, NMFS's issuance of permits for commercial fishing in federal waters off the coast of California was completed without NEPA compliance; the exempted fishing permits here assumed 'that there will be two leatherback sea turtles bycaught, of which one will be a nesting female that will die'. The court ruled that NMFS's decision that this potential death would not have a significant effect on the endangered population was arbitrary and capricious, and that NEPA applied to the action.[57]

In over half of the Trump administration's NEPA/biodiversity wins, the court found the applicable agency had complied with procedural requirements. For example, in *Environmental Defense Center v Bureau of Ocean Energy Management*, the plaintiffs sued a federal agency challenging the

[53] These were mostly cases involving either 'predator control' by the federal government or the 'diversity' standard under NFMA. See eg *W Watersheds Project v USDA APHIS Wildlife Service* (2018) US District Court for the District of Idaho 320 F Supp 3d 1137 (agency should have prepared a full EIS when removing predators of game mammals and listed species).

[54] MMPA, 16 USC ss 1361–407; Magnuson-Stevens Fishery Conservation and Management Act, 16 USC ss 1801–84.

[55] For comparison, see William Snape and John Carter, 'Weakening NEPA: How the Bush Administration Uses the Judicial System to Weaken Environmental Protections' (2003) 33 ELR 10682 (percentage of overall Bush administration wins at 55 per cent vs percentage of overall Clinton administration wins at 74 per cent).

[56] (2020) US District Court for the District of Utah 2020 BL 481223.

[57] (2019) US District Court for the Northern District of California 2019 WC 7020195 at 1.

decision to approve fifty-one permits for offshore fracking operations on the Pacific Shelf.[58] The plaintiffs challenged the finding of no significant impact, arguing that the area of the planned action is home to many endangered species, including the blue whale, but the court disagreed and said the agency had done all that was needed. Other cases resulted in the government's favour because the court ruled that NEPA did not apply at all. In *WildEarth Guardians v FWS*, environmentalists sued the FWS for administering a wildlife export programme for bobcats, gray wolves, river otters, Canada lynx, and brown bears under CITES in violation of NEPA. However, the court held that the agency action was merely 'maintenance of the status quo' rather than an impactful action to any particular species.[59]

3.3 Private Lands and Conservation Easements

Most US environmental laws do not directly regulate private property. Two notable exceptions, controversial as a result, are Section 9 of the ESA and Section 404 of the Clean Water Act, which protects 'wetlands.'[60] Section 9 allows any person to enforce an alleged 'taking'[61] of a listed species, even if that species is on private property, if the property owner does not possess an incidental take permit under Section 10 of the ESA. Similarly, Section 404 allows the Army Corps and EPA to prohibit the filling of wetlands without a permit, though frequently projects can proceed with agreed-upon mitigation. The ESA also possesses incentive programmes for private landowners with listed species on their property.[62]

Because so many important species are found on private property, other tools are often necessary. One prominent legal mechanism is called a conservation easement. Conservation easements in the US are a modern variation of an ancient property law concept. While a traditional easement generally allows a person to 'use another's land' for a specified purpose, conservation easements restrict a landowner from taking certain actions in order to protect a natural resource. Conservation easements exist in many forms, both at the federal and state levels, but the focus here are conservation easements encouraged by

[58] (2018) US District Court for the Central District of California 2018 WL 5919096 at 1.

[59] (2018) US District Court for the District of Montana 342 F Supp 3d 1047.

[60] ESA, 16 USC s 1538; Clean Water Act, 33 USC s 1344.

[61] 50 CFR s 17.3; *Babbitt v Sweet Home Chapter* (2005) 115 S Ct 2407.

[62] See US FWS Landowners and ESA <www.fws.gov/endangered/landowners/index.html> accessed 19 May 2021 (listing numerous mechanisms to aid landowners in conserving imperilled species).

Congress through the enactment of Section 170(h) in the tax code,[63] which allows landowners to claim a federal tax deduction if they donate their easement to a qualifying organization such as a not-for-profit land trust.[64]

To claim a tax deduction under Section 170(h), a landowner must qualify under any of four purposes: (1) outdoor recreation and/or education for the general public; (2) protection of habitat; (3) preservation of delineated open space; and (4) historic preservation. Given the breadth of these categories, not all conservation easements for which a deduction can be claimed are directed at wildlife or biodiversity conservation. However, recent studies have shown that many of these easements possess significant benefits for the protection of biological diversity.[65] According to statistics compiled by the National Conservation Easement Database, which holds data on roughly half of all the country's conservation easements, there are hundreds of thousands (if not more) conservation easements (including but not limited to 170(h) easements) in the US, covering well over 60 million acres and likely more.[66] Further, unlike the federal land estate, land protected by conservation easements continues to increase at a steady rate.

The tax deduction which can be claimed under Section 170(h) is based on the value of the donation, which is based on the highest and best use of the property. In the early 2000s, controversy arose over the total dollars claimed for deductions, as well as the actual conservation benefit of some easements.[67] At the end of the Obama administration, the Internal Revenue Service (IRS) issued Notice 2017-10, which designated certain conservation-easement transactions as 'listed', or suspect: 'some promoters are syndicating conservation easement transactions that purport to give investors the opportunity to obtain charitable contribution deductions in amounts that significantly exceed the amount invested'.[68] Inflated appraisals of these conservation donations, used to create federal tax charitable deductions, are at the heart of the current controversies.[69]

The Trump administration largely followed the Obama scrutiny, perhaps even taking it to a higher level, which was curious given Trump's own allegedly

[63] Internal Revenue Code, s 170(h).

[64] ibid; 26 USC s 170(h). See also Nancy McLaughlin, 'Tax-Deductible Conservation Easements and the Essential Perpetuity Requirements' (2017) 37 Va Tax Rev 1.

[65] See eg William J Snape, III and others, *Conservation Easements as a Tool for Nature Protection* (2021) 171 Tax Notes Fed 875.

[66] See generally Federico Cheever and Nancy McLaughlin, 'An Introduction to Conservation Easements in the United States' (University of Utah College of Law Research Paper No 130 2015).

[67] See eg Joe Stephens and David Ottaway, 'Developers Find Payoff in Preservation', *Washington Post* (21 December 2003) A1.

[68] IRS Notice 2017-10; 2017-4 IRB 544 (23 December 2016).

[69] See eg Adam Looney, 'Charitable Contributions of Conservation Easements' (Brookings Institute 2017) 3.

suspect use of the tax benefits of 170(h).[70] For example, the Trump administration sued some of the syndicates for tax evasion and other crimes.[71] The Trump administration also challenged specific conservation easements in court with mixed success.[72] One recent litigation tactic that has brought the IRS success is a challenge of the 'extinguishment clauses'[73] contained in the conservation easement deed itself. The IRS has based its challenge on the theory that certain changed conditions like 'impossibility'—if not drafted properly in the conservation easement's legal documents—subvert the statutory requirement of 'perpetuity'.[74] Biden Treasury Secretary Janet Yellen has called for the IRS to draft model 'extinguishment clause' language so that conservation easements can continue to be an effective private land conservation tool, at an appropriate price.[75]

4. Analysis

Two conclusions have been drawn thus far:

(1) international law, and specifically international biodiversity law, plays an exceptionally minor role in US biodiversity conservation and in US 'biodiversity legal cases' because the Constitution gives federal 'biodiversity authority' primarily to Congress;[76] and

[70] See eg Bob Lord and Chuck Collins, 'Donald Trump's Abuse of the Conservation Easement Loophole Show How the Tax Code Favors the Ultra-Rich', *Marketwatch* (21 October 2020); Samuel Brunson, 'Trump and Conservation Easements', *Nonprofit Law Prof Blog* (5 October 2020).

[71] Trump's Department of Justice initiated litigation against several alleged participants of syndicated conservation transactions in December 2018. See Joint Committee on Taxation, Report on s 170, p 2, fn 4.

[72] See eg *PBBM-Rose Hill Ltd v Comm'r* (2018) US Court of Appeals, Fifth Circuit 900 F3d 193 (upholding tax court decision to deny charitable contribution on several grounds including valuation); *Champions Retreat Golf Founders v Comm'r* (2020) US Court of Appeals, Eleventh Circuit 959 F3d 1033 (reversing and remanding tax court decision to deny charitable easement donation).

[73] These clauses generally provide for legal remedies if the purposes of the easement become impossible in the future due to unforeseen and unstoppable forces (eg major storms or earthquakes that destroys the resource).

[74] See eg *PBBM-Rose Hill Ltd v Comm'r* (n 72) (faulty extinguishment clause failed perpetuity test); *Coal Property Holdings v Comm'r* (2019) Tax Court 153 TC 126 (faulty extinguishment clause failed perpetuity test).

[75] US Senate Finance Committee, Questions for the Record, Responses by Dr Yellen (21 January 2021) 61.

[76] Further, one could argue that the Bible and other related religious sources are more influential on the federal judiciary than international law. As Holmes Rolston III explained several decades ago, 'Difficult to join though biology and theology sometimes are, they are difficult to separate in their respect for life. Earlier we worried that the processes of creation might be ungodly. But faced with extinction of these processes, biology and theology quickly couple to reach one sure conclusion. For humans to shut down Earth's prolific creativity is ungodly.' Ke Chung Kim and Robert D Weaver (eds), *Biodiversity and Landscapes: A Paradox of Humanity* (CUP 1994) 47–60; Lawrence S Hamilton and

(2) since the early 1970s, with ebbs and flows dependent upon which party controls the executive branch, US domestic litigation pertaining to wildlife and habitat-related laws has significantly driven the political discourse about biodiversity conservation in the US.[77]

4.1 Influence of IBL on US Law

International biodiversity law has generally made a minimal impact on US biodiversity-related litigation. Although this reality appears dark at first glance, the deeper answer is that US 'biodiversity law', while relatively strong and sophisticated, has developed without the term biological diversity, and the US Senate has refused to embrace many international accords with the notable exception of CITES. As a threshold matter, the US has signed but is not a party to the CBD,[78] has not completed a national biodiversity strategy and action plan under the CBD and its Aichi Targets,[79] and indeed barely recognizes 'biodiversity' as a legal term. The vast majority of US cases involving 'biodiversity' (the concept not the term) are based upon congressional statutes and corresponding federal agency rules and decisions on *wildlife and habitat*. Furthermore, the US has also never ratified the UN Convention on the Law of the Sea, the Convention on Migratory Species, or wildlife protection treaties such as the Agreement on the Conservation of Albatross and Petrels.

Historically, the US was a world leader in enacting wildlife protection laws and urging other countries to follow suit. As a top US official stated in 2010:

Ronald J Engel, *Ethics, Religion and Biodiversity: Relations Between Conservation and Cultural Values* (White Horse Press 1993) 40–64.

[77] In the 1980s and 1990s, the spotted owl crisis of the Pacific Northwest received tremendous legal and public attention for the species and its old growth forests, and became a symbol of ESA political battles. See eg *Northern Spotted Owl v Hodel* (1988) US District Court for the Western District of Washington 716 F Supp 479 (remanding back to the FWS their decision not to list the owl under the ESA, which eventually led to the listing of the species). More recently, sage grouse litigation has increased because of the overlap of that species with oil and gas reserves on US public lands. See eg *Montana Wildlife Federation v Bernhardt* (2020) US District Court for the District of Montana 2020 WL 2615631 (rejecting Trump public land decision to increase the permitting of fossil fuel in the habitat of this ESA-candidate species).

[78] CBD (adopted 5 June 1992, entered into force 29 December 1993) 1760 UNTS 79.

[79] President Biden's 2021 plan to conserve 30 per cent of US lands by 2030, however, certainly could become such a target. US Department of Interior, 'Biden-Harris Administration Outlines "America the Beautiful" Initiative' (6 May 2021) <www.doi.gov/pressreleases/biden-harris-administration-outlines-america-beautiful-initiative> accessed 25 March 2022.

> As many of you know, the final negotiations that resulted in CITES were held in Washington, D.C. in 1973. The U.S. has always held CITES in great esteem and we like to keep a special close eye on the progress of this Convention that we helped to launch so many years ago ... representatives from our nations agreed in Washington, D.C. that the stewardship of our fragile planet and the many life-forms that inhabit it was of the utmost importance ... And so it was that CITES ... was established and the U.S. is very proud that we were the first nation to ratify it.[80]

In part because of the US love for wildlife,[81] and in part because CITES is implemented domestically by the ESA, federal courts have been open to holding government actions to the letter of the law.[82] However, where US statutory law is not clear, US courts are much more grudging to provide domestic legal relief based solely on an international agreement. The MBTA is a case in point. Despite the Act's purpose of implementing the four US treaties on migratory birds,[83] and despite its explicit goal of protecting and conserving migratory birds, the statute does not specifically delineate how to enforce the 'take' of migratory birds without a permit, especially as it relates to habitat destruction and 'accidents'. Thus, the MBTA is subject to administrative interpretation and whim.[84]

Although recently retired US Justice Breyer has cogently argued otherwise,[85] most US courts and judges do not rely upon international law to make their decisions. As with international biodiversity law, US law has a primary

[80] Remarks by Ambassador Betty E King, Permanent Representative of the US Mission to the United Nations, On the Occasion of the 35th Anniversary of CITES, Geneva Switzerland (1 July 2010).

[81] See eg Jeremy Bruskotter and others, 'Support for the [ESA] across time and space' (2018) 11 Conservation Letters 1 ('our results show that support for the ESA generally was high—even among those who self-identify with the special interests who sometimes vehemently oppose ESA protections'); Karin Brulliard, 'Americans Love Animals More than They Used to—Even the Scary Ones', *Washington Post* (16 September 2016).

[82] See eg *Defenders of Wildlife v Endangered Species Scientific Authority* (1981) United States Court of Appeals for the District of Columbia Circuit 659 F2d 168, 180.

[83] See eg Convention between USA and Great Britain (on behalf of Canada) for the Protection of Migratory Birds, 39 Stat 1702 (16 August 1916). The US later consummated similar treaties with Mexico, Russia, and Japan.

[84] See eg *NRDC v Interior* (2020) US District Court for the Southern District of New York 478 F Supp 3d 469 (rejecting the Trump administration's attempt to significantly narrow the definition of prohibitive take under the MBTA).

[85] Stephen Breyer, *The Court and The World: American Law and the New Global Realities* (Vintage Books 2015) 284 ('I have written this book in order to show how the interdependence of today's world ... poses considerable challenges for our judiciary ... the need to maintain a rule of law that should spur us on, jurists and citizens, at home and abroad, to understand these challenges and to work at meeting them together.'). But see Stewart Patrick, *The Sovereignty Wars: Reconciling America with the World* (Brookings 2019) 28 ('The tenacity with which Americans cling to sovereignty and resist symbolic incursions on their constitutional prerogatives has had—and continues to have—a profound influence on national political life, US foreign policy, and prospects for international cooperation').

focus on the plain meaning of congressional statutes, which means other forms of soft law—legislative history, past interpretations, and general principles of law—receive considerably less weight.[86] Multilateral agreements on biodiversity have not had a discernible impact on US litigation because only Congress, not an international body, can waive sovereign immunity against the federal government. Less than a dozen reported US cases in total even *mention* any of these treaties, and the majority of those cases only touch on them in an indirect or inconsequential way.

With rare exceptions, US courts rely more on domestic law than international law, and biodiversity litigation is no exception. For example, the CBD has been mentioned, in passing, in a total of two cases in US courts.[87] US courts have also only referred to the Ramsar Wetlands Convention, in passing, twice.[88] US courts have mentioned the World Heritage Convention a grand total of six times, generally without success for the plaintiffs raising it.[89] Additionally, the cases that do refer to those treaties rarely have them as a focal point of litigation, unless they are directly related to a US statute. When it comes to biodiversity issues, US courts tend to focus more on the plain meaning of congressional statutes and typically give general legal principles and non-treaty agreements less weight.

Perhaps the biggest exception of US resistance to international law is trade. In these instances, there exist both domestic statutes such as the Lacey Act and ESA that enforce biodiversity-related trade restrictions,[90] as well as international treaties such as CITES.[91] But even here, there are limits to US interest in trade restrictions, particularly if significant corporate financial interests at

[86] See eg Jonathan Siegel, 'Justice Scalia's Textualist Legacy', *ScotusBlog* (14 November 2017).

[87] See *Edmonds Institute v US Dept of Interior* (2006) US District Court for the District of Columbia 460 F Supp 2d 63; *Petition of the United States, on behalf of Smithsonian Institution* (2019) US District Court for the District of Columbia 2019 WL 3451394 at 1.

[88] See *Friant Water Auth v Jewell* (2014) US District Court for the Eastern District of California 23 F Supp 3d 1130; *Agdaagux Tribe of King Cove v Jewell* (2015) US District Court for the District of Alaska 128 F Supp 3d 1176.

[89] See eg *Students Against Apartheid Coalition v O'Neil* (1987) US District Court for the Western District of Virginia 660 F Supp 333; *Okinawa Dugong v Gates* (2008) US District Court for the Northern District of California 543 F Supp 2d 1082; *Center for Biological Diversity v Export-Import Bank of the United States* (2018) US Court of Appeals, Ninth Circuit 894 F3d 1005; *Wishtoyo Foundation v US FWS* (2020) US District Court for the Central District of California 2020 WL 8409661 at 1.

[90] See eg *United States v Labs of Virginia* (2003) US District Court for the Northern District of Illinois 272 F Supp 2d 764, 770 (finding US importation of wild-caught macaques illegal because the species is protected in Indonesia).

[91] CITES (signed 3 March 1973, entered into force 1 July 1975) 993 UNTS 243, 27 UST 1087. CITES is implemented by the ESA in the US. See eg *Castlewood Products v Norton* (2004) US Court of Appeals of the District of Columbia Circuit 365 F3d 1076 (mahogany import restrictions into the US upheld).

stake.[92] Further, international trade law under the World Trade Organization (WTO)[93], the new version of the North American Free Trade Agreement (NAFTA 2.0),[94] and other bilateral agreements are also implemented by domestic legislation and, thus, generally respected by US courts.[95]

One semi-positive development for the US multilaterally has been the willingness to participate in international agreements in good faith informally. For example, while not a party to the Convention on Migratory Species (CMS), the US has signed some Memoranda of Understanding (MOUs) under the CMS.[96] The main goal of the CMS is to 'facilitate cooperation and communication between member states in conservation efforts of migratory species that travel across international borders'.[97] Although the CMS does not have stringent legal requirements, it operates through smaller agreements that may become more protective over time. Agreements are considered legally binding while MOUs are not. The US is a signatory on the MOU for Pacific Islands cetaceans (whales, dolphins, and porpoises), the MOU for sharks, and the MOU for marine turtles. The US is also considered a Range State for the Agreement on the Conservation of Albatrosses and Petrels and could take additional proactive action via MOUs and other agreements.

4.2 Transboundary Biodiversity Protection

In part because of NAFTA and a long shared history, and in part because US statutes demand it, transboundary biodiversity issues and problems—particularly between and amongst Canada and Mexico—are given slightly

[92] See eg US Congressional Research Service, 'Wildlife, Trade, Covid-19 and Other Zoonotic Diseases' (19 February 2021) ('Trade in wildlife, both legal and illegal, forms a vast economy and has contributed to outbreaks of some zoonotic diseases').

[93] Marrakesh Agreement Establishing the World Trade Organization (adopted 15 April 1994) 1867 UNTS 14.

[94] Agreement Between USA, Mexico, and Canada (entered into force 1 July 2020).

[95] A good example of this is the decades-long 'tuna/dolphin' legal battle between the US and Mexico whereby the US refused to allow full trading privileges for tuna caught by deliberately encircling dolphins with purse seine nets. Despite a 1991 GATT decision against the US and an international agreement that allowed Mexico tuna to gain access to the US, Congress and the relevant agencies modified procedures and quotas on tuna fishing, but refused to change the definition of 'dolphin-safe' tuna, which was enforced by plaintiffs in *Earth Island Inst v Hogarth* (2007) US Court of Appeals, Ninth Circuit 484 F3d 1123. This domestic decision was upheld by the WTO in *United States—Measures Concerning the Importation, Marketing and Sale of Tuna*, WT/DS381 (17 January 2019).

[96] Convention on the Conservation of Migratory Species of Wild Animals, 'United States of America' <https://www.cms.int/country/united-states-america> accessed 26 March 2022.

[97] Christopher Michael Hensz and Jorge Soberón, 'Participation in the Convention on Migratory Species: A Biogeographic Assessment' (2008) 47 AMBIO 739, 745.

higher priority and weight than 'pure' international legal issues.[98] Nonetheless, US legal concepts of standing, causation, and redressability are often used by courts to prevent public interest plaintiffs from suing over US actions that may have an impact on species in Canada or Mexico, or vice versa.[99]

The US-centred approach to international transboundary biodiversity protection is perhaps best captured by *Consejo de Desarrollo Economico de Mexicali, AC v United States*, which was a binational case about water rights, species conservation, and congressional power. Despite the fact that the US unilaterally decided to line the All-American Canal in southern California—which reduced historic water seepage to northern Mexico by the Gulf of California where the Colorado River terminates, harming Mexican residents as well as wildlife species protected in both countries—the US court system was not sympathetic. As a result of a congressional budget rider, it was determined that the project should continue despite clear legal problems with the project.[100]

In fact, unless Congress is specific to the contrary, domestic US laws are presumed not to apply outside the jurisdiction of the US.[101] When US courts do rule for biodiversity-friendly results, it is because a federal agency decision was actually made in the US, and some or all of the impact is either upon the US itself or the global commons.[102]

4.3 Biodiversity's Relationship with Climate Change

The relationship between biodiversity protection and climate mitigation is significant and growing in the US but frequently does not result in either

98 *Trail Smelter* is an early example (US–Canada transboundary clean air dispute) 3 RIAA 1905 (1941). See also Canada–Mexico–US Trilateral Committee for Wildlife and Ecosystem Conservation and Management (known as the Trilateral Committee) established in 1996 via an MOU.

99 See eg *Defenders of Wildlife v Norton* (2003) US District Court for the District of Columbia 257 F Supp 2d (negative US impact on binational Colorado River and Mexico can be ignored).

100 *Consejo de Desarrollo Economico de Mexicali, AC v US* (2007) US Court of Appeals, Ninth Circuit 482 F3d 1157.

101 See *Morrison v National Australia Bank* (2010) 561 US 247, 255 (on the one hand, 'unless there is the affirmative intention of the Congress clearly expressed to give a statute extraterritorial effect, we must presume it is primarily concerned with domestic conditions'; on the other hand, this 'principle represents a canon of construction, or a presumption about a statute's meaning, rather than a limit upon Congress's power to legislate').

102 See eg *Environmental Defense Fund v Massey* (1993) US Court of Appeals for the District of Columbia Circuit 986 F2d 538 (incineration proposal by US National Science Foundation in Antarctica rejected under NEPA because of the negative impacts upon the global commons and US interests); *Friends of the Earth v Mosbacher* (2007) US District Court for the Northern District of California 488 F Supp 2d 889 (US export credit agency must comply with NEPA on decision that occurs in the US and has some environmental impact in the US).

biodiversity protection or climate mitigation in the real world. The most obvious example is the 'threatened' listing of the polar bear under the ESA in 2007, and later upheld by a federal appellate court.[103] While conservationists generally cheered the result, subsequent administrations from both political parties nonetheless limited polar bear protections by refusing to link greenhouse gas (GHG) pollution from other parts of the country (and world) to the melting Arctic habitat of the bear.[104] This same pattern of ESA 'protection' without addressing the GHG sources themselves holds true with many other species.[105] President Biden's executive order on re-engaging domestically and internationally on climate change mentioned 'biodiversity' five times, though not in any regulatory sense.[106]

4.4 The US Judicial System Has Become More Politicized

Touted for its independence, the US federal judicial bench has become much more partisan during this century.[107] Although the Republican–Democrat divide on the environment has existed at least since the Ronald Reagan administration in the 1980s, it appeared to accelerate under the Trump administration.[108] Even without the issue of partisanship or predetermined outcomes, federal courts are reluctant to second-guess scientific determinations (including those related to biodiversity) unless there are factual gaps or inconsistencies in the record of the agency decision at issue.[109] In addition, after

[103] See *In re: Polar Bear ESA Listing and § 4(d) Rule Litigation* (2013) US Court of Appeals for the District of Columbia Circuit 709 F3d 1.

[104] US FWS, Final Rule, 78 Fed Reg 11766 (20 February 2013) ('Under this rule, incidental take caused by activities within the US but outside current polar bear range would not be subject to the takings prohibition').

[105] See eg NMFS, Availability of the Final Recovery Plan for Staghorn and Elkhorn corals, 80 Fed Reg 12146 (6 March 2015). Although this recovery plan details specific ocean temperature and acidification targets and says local, state, regional, national, and international agreements and regulations are necessary to mitigate threats from increasing atmospheric CO_2 concentrations, there is no requirement in the plan to require such action.

[106] See Executive Order 14008, Tackling the Climate Crisis at Home and Abroad (27 January 2021), 86 Fed Reg 7619.

[107] See eg Richard Arenberg, 'The Trumpification of the Federal Courts', *The Hill* (6 January 2020).

[108] See eg William Snape, 'A Pattern of Ruling Against Mother Nature: Wildlife Species Cases Decided by Justice Kavanaugh on the DC Circuit' (2019) 19 Sustainable Dev L & Pol'y 4 (the appendix to this study examined and contrasted three appellate judges' decisions on wildlife: (1) Brett Kavanaugh, nominated successfully for the Supreme Court by Donald Trump who had a pro-wildlife score of 4 per cent; (2) David Sentelle, nominated by Ronald Reagan for the DC Circuit who had a pro-wildlife score of 43 per cent; and (3) Merrick Garland, nominated unsuccessfully by President Obama for the Supreme Court and now US Attorney General under Biden, who had a pro-wildlife score of 54 per cent).

[109] *Mt Graham Red Squirrel v Espy* (1993) US Court of Appeals, Ninth Circuit 986 F2d 1568, 1576 ('this case is a classic example of a factual dispute the resolution of which implicates substantial agency expertise ... When specialists express conflicting views, an agency must have discretion to rely on the

the high-water mark of *TVA v Hill*[110] under the ESA in the mid-1970s, the Supreme Court has generally ruled against wildlife protection over the last several decades when given the opportunity.[111] Mimicking the ideological splits seen at the executive and legislative branches, every Republican nominee to the Supreme Court this century has ties with the Federalist Society, an organization that makes no secret of its desire for a limited federal government and for deregulation across the board, including biodiversity legal protection.[112] In the twenty-first century, seven new justices have been confirmed to the high court, and five have been Republicans with ties to the Federalist Society; the Court now has six Republican justices and three Democratic justices.

4.5 Legal Remedies Available for Biodiversity Loss

What type of remedies are available to address harms to wildlife depend upon both the applicable congressional statute and the entity seeking to enforce it. The two strongest components of ESA enforcement are each bounded by counter-realities in the law. First, while it is true that ESA citizen suit provision, whereby the federal government waives sovereign immunity to allow public interest litigation against offending agencies, is highly effective, the most accepted legal remedy is a remand back to the offending agency to fix (or 'paper over') their original flawed action.[113] Secondly, while it similarly true that the authority of the federal government to bring both criminal and civil cases against ESA violators with a wide range of remedies (including imprisonment, fines, restitution, mitigation, injunction, and property liens),[114] the government very rarely applies the more draconian penalties for habitat- or biodiversity-related infractions.[115]

reasonable opinions of its own qualified experts even if, as an original matter, a court might find contrary views more persuasive').

110 (1978) 437 US 153.

111 *National Association of Homebuilders v Defenders of Wildlife* (2007) 551 US 644 (ESA weakened in conflict of laws case); *Winter v NRDC* (2008) 555 US 129 (marine mammal protections denied); *Summer v Earth Island Institute* (2009) 555 US 488 (no standing to challenge bad Forest Service timber sale decision); *Weyerhaeuser Co v FWS* (2018) 139 S Ct 361 (unanimous Supreme Court vacates and remands ESA 'critical habitat' designation of dusky gopher frog back to the expert agency to better define the term 'habitat'); *FWS v Sierra Club* (2021) 141 S Ct 777 (no public access to species biological opinions under the ESA and Freedom of Information Act).

112 See eg Ann Carlson, 'The Most Anti-Environmental Court in the Modern Era', *The Hill* (3 November 2020).

113 16 USC s 1540(g).

114 16 USC s 1540(a)–(f).

115 There are legal and cultural reasons for this phenomenon. The Fifth Amendment of the US Constitution protects private property, particularly real property, through both the 'due process' clause

One of the few ways public interest lawyers can sue for money damages is under the Clean Water Act.[116] But this is uncommon. Even under statutes with citizen suit provisions such as the ESA, the standards of review and remedies available are steeped in administrative law, not tort law, which means both general judicial deference to agency action and allowance of illegal agency action to be rectified by that same agency.[117] Further, the Supreme Court has recently clamped down on many avenues of aggressive 'biodiversity protection' under the law by raising standing hurdles,[118] and making it much more difficult to gain injunctions against harmful biodiversity projects.[119]

4.6 Volatile Administrative Transitions

So long as Congress is unable to comprehensively act on biodiversity protection, administrative law remains central to biodiversity's fate in the US. This body of US law, while not rudderless, gives new political administrations 'discretion' and 'deference' to implement statutes such as the ESA and NEPA in different ways. For example, while the Trump administration finalized rules that would have reduced protections under both the ESA and NEPA, these rule challenges are all in federal court, and the Biden administration has begun to propose repeals of the Trump rules and issue new rules of its own.[120]

and prohibiting the government from 'taking' property without compensation. 'Taking' includes indirect or regulatory takings such as ESA habitat protections. *Lucas v South Carolina* (1992) 505 US 1003. The Fifth Amendment is also partly why plants get less protection under the ESA on private lands than animals; plants, including trees, generally attach to the underlying property or estate: 16 USC s 1538.

[116] See 33 USC s 1321; see also US Department of Justice, 'Deepwater Horizon Settlement' <www.justice.gov/enrd/deepwater-horizon> accessed 20 June 2022 (BP paid billions of dollars for penalties, damages, and mitigation for the explosion in the Gulf of Mexico, which unfortunately remains a sacrifice zone of sorts for the oil and gas industry).

[117] See eg *Tucson Herpetological Society v Salazar* (2009) US Court of Appeals, Ninth Circuit 566 F3d 870; *Defenders of Wildlife v Norton* (2001) US Court of Appeals, Ninth Circuit 258 F3d 1136. Despite numerous wins and two federal appellate victories by conservation groups over whether the flat-tailed horned lizard should be listed, the FWS has still not listed the species and likely will not for the foreseeable future.

[118] Standing is a threshold judicial concept that requires a plaintiff to prove: (1) actual injury; (2) injury caused by the defendants; and (3) injury remediable by the court. Standing is frequently used to deny otherwise valid claims of illegal behaviour by a public or private defendant. See eg *Lujan v Defenders of Wildlife* (1992) 504 US 555 (standing denied to plaintiffs who alleged injury to US-listed ESA species in foreign countries); *Washington Environmental Council v Bellon* (2013) US Court of Appeals, Ninth Circuit 732 F3d 1131 (climate change injuries not traceable to defendant because of multiple sources of greenhouse pollutants).

[119] The Supreme Court significantly limited the ability to seek injunctions for environmental injury in *Monsanto v Geertson Seed Farms* (2010) 130 S Ct 2743.

[120] See eg Todd Neeley, 'Biden Targets Trump Deregulation of Ag', *Progressive Farmer* (27 January 2021) <www.dtnpf.com/agriculture/web/Ag/crops/article/2021/01/27/biden-administration-set-review-ag> accessed 26 March 2022.

5. Synthesis of Key Findings

First, the US still possesses all the legal authority it needs to protect biological diversity, both at home and abroad. The US legal structure also, for better or worse, gives federal administrative agencies considerable deference and discretion in implementing biodiversity-related laws. Only Congress can make US obligations more definitive and enforceable, either domestically or abroad. When Congress does state clear substantive standards, such as with the ESA, the court results demonstrate a higher success ratio for wildlife and biodiversity. When Congress creates procedural obligations, US courts are increasingly likely to allow *de minimis* violations of statutes such as NEPA. Without private litigation under various US statutes, however, biodiversity protection enforcement would frequently not occur. Over the past decade or two, US litigation to protect 'biodiversity' has become more challenging for a number of interrelated reasons: a more business-friendly judiciary, the associated willingness of courts to reject pro-biodiversity plaintiffs with standing or agency deference arguments, and the overall political gridlock in the US that makes large-scale problem solving of any kind, including biodiversity protection, increasingly difficult.

Secondly, the US must become a better international leader and player on behalf of biological diversity protection. The US possesses significant biological and financial wealth. Thus, the US could not only do a better job of protecting its domestic biodiversity, it could also direct its considerable foreign aid to much more biodiversity-friendly purposes. Despite the US Senate holding the power over treaty ratifications, the President possesses considerable authority to participate in meetings such as at the CBD. The US could also seek to rejuvenate the Western Hemisphere Convention, of which it is a member, as a hemispheric link to the global CBD. The ability to be an effective global partner will also be linked to underlying US legal responses to the biodiversity crisis domestically. Biodiversity litigation may successfully catalyse positive US action, but a much broader political movement is necessary if the objective is to protect large-scale biological diversity in the US and abroad.

6. Conclusion

Current US conservation laws must be preserved and better enforced. However, to take US biodiversity conservation to a point where large-scale and long-term solutions occur, Congress and the executive branch must make biological diversity protection a much higher priority. There is little 'biodiversity litigation' per se in the US because neither Congress nor the executive branch has yet taken bold action in this regard. The US must treat the biodiversity crisis as vigilantly as it does the 'terrorist' crisis. Decades of habitat destruction, pollution, invasive species spread, wildlife exploitation, climate change, population growth, and other human activities have frayed the web of life. With each extinction, natural systems continue to unravel. The drivers of wildlife extinction also undermine the life-support systems of human societies including pollination, water purification, oxygen production, and disease regulation.

The physical, emotional, and spiritual well-being of humans depends on thriving wildlife populations. Wildlife has inspired our histories, myths, and cultures and losing them impoverishes us and leaves the planet a lonelier place for future generations. In addition, every plant and animal species has value in and of itself and deserves the right to continue to exist. Ending the extinction crisis will require leadership from all nations, including the US. The President, without the Senate, can voluntarily participate in multilateral efforts to save biodiversity.[121]

At home, the US must elevate the biodiversity crisis by declaring a national emergency on both climate and the extinction calamities. Since the National Emergencies Act was passed in 1976, every president has declared national emergencies to elevate issues to the highest priority for executive branch agencies to address.[122] It is far past time that a President declares that the global extinction crisis represents a national emergency. Doing so would galvanize public awareness and support for action, as well as unlock specific emergency powers that would otherwise be unavailable to the executive branch to combat extinction.

Bold regulatory and investment actions would also help to reduce the litigation that seeks to enforce existing domestic US standards.[123] For example, President Biden's embrace of 30x30 goals represent a true opportunity for conservation, both domestically and multilaterally. The executive branch could

[121] eg at a recent CBD meeting the Biden administration sent a representative who made a proposal that garnered support from other parties. See Report of the open-ended Working Groupon the Post-2020 Global Biodiversity Framework, CBD/WG2020/3/5 (3 September 2021).

[122] National Emergencies Act, 50 USC ss 1601–51.

[123] The entire point of the ESA 'private attorney general' provision is to empower individuals from the general public to ensure that the provisions of the ESA are followed: 16 USC s 1540(g). That environmental plaintiffs file and win so many ESA cases is not a success story, but a reflection that the federal administrators of the endangered species programme are not doing their jobs the way the law commands.

further clarify that the primary sustainability objective of federal public lands is to protect biodiversity. All this will take shifting significant investment away from war and corporate tax cuts to actually saving and recovering the 1,600 recognized endangered and threatened species in the US, and the hundreds of species on the official candidate list for listing.[124] This is a bold agenda but one worthy of saving life on earth as we know it.

[124] Congress passed a significant piece of spending legislation in summer 2022. The Inflation Reduction Act, P.L. 117–169 (16 August 2022), marks the biggest investment in conservation by the United States this century. In total, $373 billion overall is spent on behalf of energy security, climate change mitigation and adaptation, and biological diversity protection. Of this total, over $1 billion goes to the US Forest Service and US National Park Service each for restoration and maintenance activities, and almost $250 million goes to the US Fish and Wildlife Service for endangered species recovery plans and national wildlife refuge restoration and maintenance. Only time will tell if the benefits touted by Democrats bear fruit, but not one Republican in either chamber of Congress voted for the bill.

11

Biodiversity Litigation Before the Court of Justice of the European Union

A Promising Pathway for Better Enforcement of International Biodiversity Law?

Charles-Hubert Born and Hendrik Schoukens

1. Introduction

During the past decades, the biodiversity crisis has given rise to a growing concern amongst scientists, who suggest that the world is facing a so-called sixth mass extinction event.[1] The plight of biodiversity is not alien to the EU either.[2] While there are some remarkable success stories that merit further consideration, such as the relatively recent recovery of large carnivore species, other studies have unveiled that the populations of so-called common species, such as farmland bird species,[3] have suffered significant losses during the past decades. A majority of EU-wide protected species, such as the European hamster, the Saker falcon, and the Danube salmon, and habitats from grasslands, marshlands, and dunes across Europe, are facing an uncertain future unless more is urgently done to reverse the situation, according to a 2020 report of the European Environment Agency.[4]

This grim outlook stands in sharp contrast with the progressive role the EU often plays in the further development of international biodiversity law (IBL) and policy.[5] As both an active actor and a subject of IBL, the EU has been one

[1] Elizabeth Kolbert, *The Sixth Extinction, An Unnatural History* (Picado USA 2015) 336.
[2] EEA, *State of nature in the EU. Results from reporting under the nature directives 2013–2018*, EEA Report no 10/2020 (2020) 146.
[3] Anna Gamero and others, 'Tracking Progress Towards EU Biodiversity Strategy Targets: EU Policy Effects in Preserving its Common Farmland Birds' (2016) 10(4) Conservation Letters 395.
[4] EEA Report (n 2).
[5] Elisa Morgera, 'The Trajectory of EU Biodiversity Cooperation: Supporting Environmental Multilateralism through EU External Action' in Elisa Morgera (ed), *The External Environmental Policy of the European Union: EU and International Law Perspectives* (CUP 2012) 235–59.

Charles-Hubert Born and Hendrik Schoukens, *Biodiversity Litigation Before the Court of Justice of the European Union* In: *Biodiversity Litigation*. Edited by: Guillaume Futhazar, Sandrine Maljean-Dubois, and Jona Razzaque, Oxford University Press.
 DOI: 10.1093/oso/9780192865465.003.0011

of the major engines of global environmental governance, at many different levels.[6]

Today, the EU is a party to most of the major global and regional (European) international treaties on biodiversity[7]—including the Convention on Biological Diversity (CBD) and, save important exceptions,[8] the most prominent agreements on nature conservation,[9] protection of the marine environment and regional seas,[10] mountain ecosystems,[11] watercourses,[12] and genetic resources.[13] The EU has also ratified the more transversal UN Economic Commission for Europe (UNECE) Espoo Convention on environmental impact assessment in a transboundary context (and its Kyiv Protocol) and the Aarhus Convention on access to information, public participation in decision making, and access to justice in environmental matters.

The EU has implemented its plethora of international obligations in dozens of EU legislative acts—directives and regulations—which are themselves transposed or implemented by Member States through internal legal acts.[14] As a result, IBL often manifests itself within the EU legal order in the guise of EU legal instruments which have implemented its obligations, which makes the

[6] Elisa Morgera, 'Introduction' in Morgera ibid 1.

[7] For an actualized list of the environmental treaties ratified by the EU, see Environment, 'Multilateral Agreements' <https://ec.europa.eu/environment/international_issues/agreements_en.htm> accessed 5 September 2021. For a comment, see Nicholas de Sadeleer and Charles-Hubert Born, *Droit international et communautaire de la biodiversité* (Dalloz 2004) 780.

[8] It is indeed easier to point to the treaties to which the EU is *not* a party amongst which are the Whaling Convention (1946), the Ramsar Convention on Wetlands (1971), the Paris UNESCO World Heritage Convention (1979), the New York UN Watercourses Convention (1997), the ACCOBAMS CMS Agreement (1996), the ASCOBANS CMS Agreement (1992) (signed but not yet ratified by the EU), the EUROBATS CMS Agreement (1991), the Marpol Convention 73/78, and the Carpathian Convention (2003) and its protocols.

[9] Washington Convention on International Trade in Endangered Species of Wild Fauna and Flora (1973) (CITES); Bern Convention on European Wildlife and Habitat (1979); Bonn Convention on the Conservation of Migratory Species (CMS, 1979) and its subsequent Agreement on the conservation of African-Eurasian Migratory Waterbirds (AEWA-CMS).

[10] UNCLOS (1982), OSPAR Convention for the Protection of the Marine Environment of the North-East Atlantic (1992) and its Annex V, Barcelona Convention for the protection of the Mediterranean Sea against pollution (1976) and some of its protocols, Helsinki Convention on the Protection of the Marine Environment of the Baltic Sea Area (1992), Antarctic Treaty (1959), its Protocol on the protection of the environment (1991), and Canberra Convention for the Conservation of Antarctic Marine Living Resources (1980).

[11] Alpine Convention (1991) and some of its protocols, including the Chambéry Protocol to the Convention for the Protection of the Alps on Conservation of Nature and Landscape (1994).

[12] Helsinki UN/ECE Convention on the protection and use of transboundary watercourses and international lakes (1992), Danube (1987), Rhine (1999), and Escaut and Meuse (2000) rivers agreements and conventions.

[13] International Treaty on plant genetic resources, Cartagena Protocol on Biosafety (2000) and Protocol on Liability and Redress to the Cartagena Protocol on Biosafety (2010), Nagoya Protocol on Access to Genetic Resources and the Fair and Equitable Sharing of the Benefits Arising from their Utilization to the CBD (2010).

[14] Martin Hession, 'The Role of the EC in Implementation of International Environmental Law' (1993) 2(4) Review of European Community & International Environmental Law 341–47.

analysis of its use in biodiversity litigation in the EU complex and, inevitably, multilayered. Most often, international biodiversity duties are indirectly enforced through compliance with the existing EU biodiversity legislation, such as the seminal EU Birds and Habitats Directives.[15]

This chapter analyses the role of IBL in the context of biodiversity litigation in the EU legal order, with a particular focus on the litigation before the Court of Justice of the European Union (CJEU). The question of whether and, if so, to what extent, the unique system of multilayered legal protection within the EU contributes to the effectiveness of IBL is the main topic of this chapter.[16]

In Section 2, the status of IBL in the EU legal order and the main legal remedies available within the EU are assessed in the light of the potential for biodiversity litigation. Section 3 addresses the major procedural obstacles to be faced when enforcing IBL at both EU and national levels. Section 4 outlines the main substantive trends in the existing jurisprudence and litigation on biodiversity protection at the EU level so far. In Section 5, the possible future pathways for biodiversity litigation are briefly sketched out by addressing the untapped potential that exists for biodiversity litigation in the supranational EU legal order.

2. The Influence of International Biodiversity Law on the EU Legal Order and Its Enforcement by the CJEU

In order to understand the legal status and impact of IBL within the EU legal order (2.3), it is important to briefly recall the broad outlines of the EU's external competences (2.1) and the role of the CJEU in enforcing its implementation (2.2).

2.1 The EU as an International Actor and a Subject of IBL

As is widely known, the EU is a regional economic integration organization with international legal personality. Since the Treaty on the Functioning of the

[15] Directive 2009/147/EC of the European Parliament and of the Council of 30 November 2009 on the conservation of wild birds (codified version) [2010] OJ L20/7 (hereafter Birds Directive); Council Directive of 21 May 1992 on the conservation of natural habitats and of wild fauna and flora [1992] OJ L206/7 (hereafter Habitats Directive).

[16] Ellen Hey, 'The European Community's Courts and International Environmental Agreements' (1998) 7(1) Review of European Community & International Environmental Law 4–10.

European Union (TFEU) has granted the EU external competences dealing with all external dimensions of its internal policies including environmental protection,[17] the EU is in a prime position to negotiate, conclude, and implement any treaty primarily concerned with the conservation and sustainable use of biodiversity,[18] even in areas that are not yet covered by EU legislation.[19] In areas where competences are shared and in the absence of full harmonization,[20] the European Commission and the Member States are obliged to collaborate when negotiating and concluding international treaties. The latter are referred to as 'mixed treaties'. Since the substance of most biodiversity conservation treaties squarely falls within the scope of the shared environmental competence of the EU,[21] they mostly qualify as mixed treaties.[22]

The extent to which both the EU and the Member States are bound vis-à-vis the third parties to the substantive duties laid out in mixed treaties[23] is often the subject of a specific provision in multilateral treaties. An apt example is offered by the CBD,[24] which explicitly provides the room to adopt a 'declaration of competence' in which the regional economic integration organization is supposed to specify the extent of its competence and that of the Member States. The EU Council adopted such a declaration when the European Community ratified the CBD.[25]

The EU has thus a dual role to play in the context of IBL: on the one hand, as an actor and a subject on the international stage and, on the other hand, as a legislator and as a judge, since it is responsible for implementing and enforcing

[17] Article 191(4) TFEU. See also Arts 3(2) and 216 TFEU.

[18] Provided that the treaty is open to the accession of regional economic integration organizations. Eg the CBD makes the accession of such organizations possible in its art 33. This was not the case with early treaties like CITES, until the entry into force of its Gaborone Amendment in 2013, or the Ramsar Convention. The Court held, however, that 'If the conditions of participation in an international convention exclude conclusion by the Community itself but the area covered by that convention comes within the external competence of the Community, that external competence may be exercised through the medium of the Member States acting jointly in the Community's interest' (Opinion 2/91 (1993) ECLI:EU:C:1993:106, paras 5–6).

[19] Case C-459/03 *Commission v Ireland* (2006) ECLI:EU:C:2006:345 ('MOX' case), paras 94–95.

[20] For a synthetic overview of the external competence of the EU in environmental matters, see Jan H Jans and Hans HB Vedder, *European Environmental Law, After Lisbon* (4th edn, Europa Law Publishing 2012) 64.

[21] Only the conservation of marine biological resources in the field of CFP ranks amongst the exclusive competences of the EU (Art 3(1)(d) TFEU).

[22] Conflicts may arise over the exclusive or shared nature of external competence, as illustrated by the case of the creation of marine protected areas in the Antarctic (Joined Cases C-626/15 and 659/16 *Commission v Council* (2018) ECLI:EU:C:2018:925). See also Case C-370/07 *Commission v Council* (2009) ECLI:EU:C:2009:590 (lack of indication of the legal basis in a Council decision).

[23] Andre Nollkaemper, 'Joint Responsibility between the EU and Member States for Non-Performance of Obligations Under Multilateral Environmental Agreements' in Morgera (n 5) 304–06.

[24] Article 34(2)(3) of the CBD.

[25] Annex B of the Council Decision 93/626/EEC of 25 October 1993 concerning the conclusion of the Convention on Biological Diversity ([1993] OJ L/1).

the relevant international agreements in its own legal order. We focus on the latter role in the subsequent analysis.

2.2 The Judicial Protection System in the EU: A Key to Understanding the Influence of IBL on Biodiversity Litigation in Europe

The EU legal order is to be approached as a concrete manifestation of so-called 'supranational law', since Member States have transferred some competences to EU institutions, which can make binding decisions in their legislative and executive roles. Most prominent in this respect has been the establishment of an independent court system, which has been granted the power to enforce and interpret EU law vis-à-vis Member States.

Judicial control in the EU legal order is exercised at two levels, which is of central relevance for understanding the specific added value of distinct types of biodiversity litigation within the EU legal order.

2.2.1 EU level

At the EU level, the CJEU is tasked with ensuring the uniform interpretation and application of EU law vis-à-vis the EU institutions as well as the Member States, which are mandated to implement and apply the duties in their internal legal order.[26] As 'Guardian of the Treaties', one of the tasks entrusted to the European Commission by Article 17 of the Treaty on European Union (TEU) is to oversee the application of EU law.[27]

In its case law, the CJEU has consistently underlined that the EU legal order is based on the rule of law and aimed at ensuring a complete system of effective judicial protection.[28] This system of complete legal remedies has a two-tiered nature.[29]

Four types of *direct* legal action are provided for by the TFEU to ensure a uniform application of EU law: (1) the infringement procedure—Articles 258 to 260 TFEU—is the principal enforcement mechanism that can be applied by the European Commission against a Member State which is in breach of its

[26] Article 19(1) TEU. Since the Treaty of Lisbon, this expression has covered all European Courts, namely the CJEU, the General Court (formerly the Court of First Instance), and specialized courts (ie the Civil Service Tribunal) (Art 19 TEU).

[27] Article 17(1) TEU.

[28] Case C-565/19 P *A. Carvalho and others* (2021) ECLI:EU:C:2021:252, para 67; Case C-64/16 *Associação Sindical dos Juízes Portugueses* (2018) ECLI:EU:C:2018:117, para 31.

[29] Pål Wennerås, *The Enforcement of EC Environmental Law* (OUP 2007) 368.

obligations under EU law; (2) the action for annulment—Articles 263 and 264 TFEU—is a legal procedure before the CJEU aimed at ensuring the conformity of EU legislative acts, regulatory acts, and individual acts with the superior rules of the EU legal order. An action can be brought within two months of the publication or notification of the contested measure. Applicants are divided into three categories: privileged, semi-privileged, and non-privileged; (3) an action for failure to act—under Article 265 TFEU, any natural or legal person may initiate proceedings before the CJEU claiming that an EU institution has failed to address to that person any act other than a mere recommendation; and (4) the action for damages—under Articles 265 and 266 TFEU—enables individuals or Member States who have suffered damage to obtain compensation from the institution that caused it.

The interim relief before the CJEU and the General Court makes it possible for parties to avoid their positions being irreparably prejudiced pending the main proceedings, which can also be instrumental in environmental cases.[30] A treaty reform from the early 1990s introduced an additional tool for forcing Member States to comply with a decision in infringement proceedings under Article 258 TFEU. Article 260(2) TFEU now offers the CJEU the possibility of imposing a lump sum or penalty payment on the non-compliant Member States.[31] This novel instrument is being increasingly used in the context of compliance with fisheries law[32] and EU environmental law. As to the latter, reference can be made to a decision of 12 November 2019 in which the CJEU held that Ireland had failed to comply with a decision dating back to 3 July 2008, where it was held that Ireland had infringed Directive 85/337 by granting consent for works in the context of the construction of a wind farm without carrying out a prior environmental impact assessment (EIA). As a result, the CJEU ordered Ireland to pay a lump sum of €5 million and a penalty payment of €15,000 per day until the date of compliance with the verdict of 3 July 2008.[33]

As an *indirect* legal action before the CJEU, Article 267 TFEU lays down the preliminary reference procedure, the primary aim of which is to achieve a uniform interpretation of EU law by all domestic courts and to assist in the effective judicial protection of individuals. It is premised on effective cooperation between national judges and the Court of Justice.[34]

[30] Articles 278 and 279 TFEU.
[31] Article 260(2) and (3) TFEU.
[32] Case C-304/02 *Commission v France* (2005) ECLI:EU:C:2005:444.
[33] Case C-261/18 *Commission v Ireland* (2019) ECLI:EU:C:2019:955.
[34] Joined Cases C-261 and 348/08 *Zurita García and Choque Cabrera* (2009) ECLI:EU:C:2009:648, para 36.

Combined, these direct and indirect actions ideally constitute a complete system of legal remedies and procedures to ensure judicial review and provide strong guarantees of effectiveness for EU law in comparison with classic international public law, where lack of effective compliance is often rife.

2.2.2 Member State level

At the level of the Member States, the national courts play a crucial role in enforcing EU rules within the national legal order, if necessary through the prism of the primacy of EU law and direct effect.[35] National courts are therefore increasingly dubbed 'the ordinary courts' for implementing EU law within the legal systems of the Member States.[36] In principle, the mechanism of the preliminary ruling prevents the interpretation of EU law by national courts from diverging from one another. However, one of its inherent weaknesses is that it is dependent on the willingness of the supreme courts of the Member States to comply with their obligation to refer to the CJEU when interpretation questions arise regarding elements of EU law in cases initially brought before.[37] The fact that preliminary reference procedures are often time-consuming might partly explain the reluctance on the part of national courts in this regard.

2.3 The Status of IBL in the EU Legal Order and its Enforcement by the Court as an 'Integral Part' of EU Law

The intersection between international law and the EU legal order is notoriously complex and ambivalent, especially when approached from an outsider's perspective.[38] Already in its nascent case law, the CJEU affirmed the primacy of international law, both customary and conventional, over EU secondary legislation.[39] The EU's commitment to respect international law, both as a player on the international scene[40] and as a party to international agreements,[41] is also reflected in several provisions of the EU Treaties. Several pieces of secondary

[35] Articles 4(3) TEU and 192(4) TFEU.

[36] Opinion 1/09, *Creation of a Unified Patent Litigation System* (2011) ECLI:EU:C:2011:123, ground 80.

[37] Article 267(3) TFEU.

[38] Panos Koutrakos, *EU International Relations Law* (Hart Publishing 2015) 209.

[39] Conventional international law: Case 181/73 *Haegeman* (1974) ECLI:EU:C:1974:41; Case C-405/92 *Mondiet* (1993) ECLI:EU:C:1993:906; Case C-162/96 *Racke* (1998) ECLI:EU:C:1998:293. On customary international law: Case 41/74 *Van Duyn v Home Office* (1974) ECLI:EU:C:1974:133; Case C-286/90 *Poulsen and Diva Navigation* (1992) ECLI:EU:C:1992:453, para 10.

[40] Articles 3(5) and 21(1) TEU.

[41] Article 216(2) TFEU.

biodiversity legislation also recall the primacy of the EU's international commitments in the sphere of environmental law in their preambles.[42]

However, a certain degree of autonomy is still to be observed in the light of the hierarchy of norms that is applicable within the EU legal order. For instance, the primacy of international law does not extend to EU primary law, such as norms enshrined in the TFEU itself, as held by the CJEU in its *Kadi* judgment.[43] Moreover, the applicability of a treaty within the EU is subject to strict conditions set up by the CJEU, which also partly helps to understand the limited potential of biodiversity litigation which is directly based upon provisions of IBL itself.

2.3.1 IBL as an 'integral part' of EU law

As early as 1974, the CJEU clarified the status of international law in the EU legal order. Once an international treaty ratified by the EU enters into force, it constitutes an 'integral part of the legal order of the European Union'.[44] Treaties ratified by the EU are consequently binding on both the EU institutions[45] and the Member States,[46] irrespective of whether the latter have ratified the agreement (or not). As is demonstrated later, even non-binding decisions adopted under the framework set up by such international agreements can be invoked before the CJEU for interpretation purposes.[47] Even a treaty that has been signed but has not yet entered into force must also be taken into consideration by the Member States when drafting their environmental policies, as underscored by the Court in its *Étang de Berre* cases.[48] In this jurisprudence, the Court held that France had not complied with its obligations under the Protocol for the protection of the Mediterranean Sea against pollution from land-based sources.

[42] eg see Art 1.2 of Directive 98/44/EEC of the European Parliament and of the Council of 6 July 1998 on the legal protection of biotechnological inventions; Council Regulation (EC) No 338/97 of 9 December 1996 on the protection of species of wild fauna and flora by regulating trade therein (hereafter CITES Regulation), Art 1(2).

[43] Joined Cases C-402 and 415/05 P *Kadi* (2008) ECLI:EU:C:2008:461; Case T-18/10 *Inuit Tapiriit Kanatami ea* (2011) ECLI:EU:T:2011:419, para 55 and quoted case law.

[44] Case C-181/73 *Haegeman* (1974) ECLI:EU:C:1974:41, paras 3–6; Case C-240/09 *Lesoochranárske zoskupenie (LZ II)* (2011) ECLI:EU:C:2011:125, para 30; Case C-224/16 *Aebtri* (2017) ECLI:EU:C:2017:880, para 50.

[45] Case C-344/04 *IATA and ELFAA* (2006) ECLI:EU:C:2006:10, para 36.

[46] Case C-59/11 *Association Kokopelli* (2012) ECLI:EU:C:2012:447, para 84 and quoted jurisprudence.

[47] Case 30/88 *Greece v Commission* (1989) ECLI:EU:C:1989:422, para 13; Case C-188/91 *Deutsche Shell v Hauptzollamt Hamburg-Harburg* (1993) ECLI:EU:C:1993:24, paras 13–19.

[48] Case C-213/03 *Syndicat professionnel coordination des pêcheurs de l'étang de Berre et de la région (Étang de Berre I)* (2004) ECLI:EU:C:2004:464. The Court referred to this judgment to find France in breach of its obligations, following an infringement action brought by the European Commission (Case C-239/03 *Commission v French Republic* (2004) (*Étang de Berre II*) ECLI:EU:C:2004:598.

Accepting the primacy of international law over secondary EU legislation definitely helps to ensure a better application of the environmental obligations enshrined in IBL at the EU level. In doing so, the CJEU retains the exclusive competence to interpret and monitor the application of ratified treaties of IBL by the EU institutions and the Member States.[49] This jurisdiction extends to mixed agreements (to which both the EU and the Member States are parties).[50] Direct effect, a legal concept that is further explained later, is not a precondition for the CJEU's jurisdiction over a mixed agreement ratified by the EU.[51] By contrast, the existing jurisprudence holds that when the EU is not a party to a treaty and has not 'assumed, under the EEC Treaty, the powers previously exercised by the Member States in the field to which that convention applies', the treaty produces no binding effect whatsoever.[52]

2.3.2 The invalidation of an EU act or decision in relation to IBL

In the context of the previously mentioned legal actions before the CJEU, the latter might be asked to decide whether an EU act or decision complies with IBL. However, this substantive review is possible only if a three-tiered test is passed and, if that is the case, the CJEU will check the validity of EU decisions of secondary law in the light of international norms that are binding upon the EU.

In a first test, the CJEU checks whether the EU is a party to the mixed treaty which is relied upon in the proceedings at hand.[53] However, in its jurisprudence the CJEU has also clarified that codified customary rules of general international law are to be taken into account.[54] Even conventions which have not been ratified by the EU might generate legal effects within the EU. This is the case when the contested acts explicitly aim to incorporate certain rules that are included in a convention to which the EU is not a party. This was illustrated in the CJEU's ruling in the *Nilsson* and *Intertanko* cases, where the Convention on the International Trade in Endangered Species (CITES) and

[49] Case 12/86 *Demirel* (1987) ECLI:EU:C:1987:400, para 7; Case C-741/19 *Republic of Moldovia v Komstroy LLC* (2021) ECLI:EU:C:2021:655, para 23.

[50] Case 12/86 *Demirel* (1987) ECLI:EU:C:1987:400, para 9.

[51] Eve Truilhé-Marengo, *Droit de l'environnement de l'Union européenne* (Larcier 2015) 81.

[52] Case C-379/92 *Peralta* (1994) ECLI:EU:C:1994:296, para 16 (concerning the MARPOL Convention).

[53] Case C-308/06 *Intertanko* (2008) ECLI:EU:C:2008:312, paras 47–52.

[54] Case C-286/90 *Poulsen and Diva Navigation* (1992) ECLI:EU:C:1992:453, paras 9 and 10; Case C-405/92 *Mondiet* (1993) ECLI:EU:C:1993:906, paras 13–15; Case C-162/96 *Racke* (1998) ECLI:EU:C:1998:293, para 45; Case C-308/06 *Intertanko* (2008) ECLI:EU:C:2008:312, para 51.

the United Nations Convention on the Law of the Seas (UNCLOS) played a prominent role.[55]

In a second test, the CJEU analyses whether the 'nature' and the 'structure' (or the 'broad logic') of the treaty prevent it from reviewing the lawfulness of measures adopted by the EU institutions. In doing so, it considers the aim, preamble, and specific wording of the convention. The CJEU found, for instance, that 'the nature and the broad logic' of UNCLOS[56] and the WTO Agreement as well as the TRIPS and TBT Agreements[57] prevented it 'from being able to assess the validity of a Community measure'. Rather unexpectedly, especially given the rather vague wording of the CBD, the CJEU still agreed that this convention could be used as a yardstick for legality reviews as 'unlike the WTO agreement, [it] is not strictly based on reciprocal and mutually advantageous arrangements ...'[58]

The third and final test that needs to be complied with in order to effectively rely upon provisions of IBL before the CJEU addresses the so-called 'direct effect' or the 'direct applicability' of the provisions of the treaty in question. A treaty provision is said to have 'direct effect' if it explicitly provides the possibility for any interested individual to rely on those provisions directly before a judge.[59] Again, this condition provides the CJEU with some leeway in assessing whether an EU act should be reviewed in the light of IBL. As at the time of writing, the CJEU's case law is notoriously ambivalent in this regard. The CJEU's stance is not entirely clear as to the criteria used to establish the 'direct applicability' or the 'direct effect' of a provision of international law. Even more so, the CJEU uses these words interchangeably,[60] which gives rise to further confusion in the legal literature on the topic.[61] In the majority of cases where the notion of direct effect arises, the CJEU resorts to an objective test that is referred to here as the 'direct applicability' test (direct effect in the broad sense), which is passed when, 'regard being had to its wording and to the purpose and

[55] Case C-154/02 *Nilsson* (2003) ECLI:EU:C:2003:590, para 39; Case C-308/06 *Intertanko* (2008) ECLI:EU:C:2008:312, para 52.

[56] Case C-308/06 *Intertanko* (2008) ECLI:EU:C:2008:312, paras 45 and 54–65.

[57] Case C-377/98 *Netherlands v European Parliament and Council* (2001) ECLI:EU:C:2001:523, para 52 (hereafter *Biotech Patients* case).

[58] ibid para 53.

[59] Case C-213/03 *Étang de Berre I* (2004) ECLI:EU:C:2004:464, para 47; Case C-366/10 *ATAA* (2011) ECLI:EU:C:2011:864, para 74.

[60] eg Case C-213/03 *Étang de Berre I* (2004) ECLI:EU:C:2004:464, paras 39–43 ('directly applicable') and paras 45 ('direct effect'); in its *Demirel* case (1987) ECLI:EU:C:1987:400, para 25, the Court did not use the terms 'direct effect' but rather the words 'directly applicable', while referring to the creation of individual rights as a condition for direct effect.

[61] Jan A Winter, 'Direct Applicability and Direct Effect: Two Distinct and Different Concepts in Community Law' (1972) 9 Common Market Law Review 425.

nature of the agreement, the provision contains a clear and precise obligation which is not subject, in its implementation or effects, to the adoption of any subsequent measure'.[62] These criteria are the same as those used to assess the direct applicability of the provisions of secondary EU law, such as an EU directive.[63] The CJEU may take into account the purpose of the treaty to assess its direct applicability,[64] leaving more room for discretion in its appreciation.[65]

Not unsurprisingly, the test of direct applicability often yields a negative result in the context of IBL, as international treaties in this sphere are rarely drafted in 'precise and unconditional' terms. The few provisions of IBL invoked before the CJEU in actions questioning the validity of EU regulations have been disregarded because they were deemed to be imprecise or subject to enforcement measures. The CJEU's refusal to use the provisions of the International Treaty on Plant Genetic Resources for Food and Agriculture as a yardstick for reviewing the validity of the European legislation on the marketing of plants and vegetable seed represents a striking illustration of the limitations for effective biodiversity litigation offered by a restrictive application of the direct effect test.[66]

However, as noted earlier, in its notable decision in the *Biotech Patent* case, the CJEU was persuaded to use the CBD as a legal benchmark when reviewing the validity of EU legislation, without carrying out its usual test explicitly on its wording precision and unconditionality—possibly opening the door for an expansion of the legal effects of IBL in the EU legal order.[67]

As an interim conclusion, it can be postulated that the CJEU has developed a set of flexible criteria to evaluate the precise legal consequences that are attached to international agreements, amongst others those related to biodiversity protection in the EU legal order. Admittedly, this approach leaves ample room for further evolution towards the enhanced effectiveness of IBL,[68] as was also illustrated by the decision in the *Biotech Patent* case. However, it also enables the CJEU to justify its remarkable unwillingness to give effect to some

[62] Case C-213/03 *Étang de Berre I* (2004) ECLI:EU:C:2004:464, para 39. See also *Demirel* (1987) ECLI:EU:C:1987:400, para 14; Case C-344/04 *IATA and ELFAA* (2006) ECLI:EU:C:2006:10, para 39; Case C-308/06 *Intertanko* (2008) ECLI:EU:C:2008:312, para 45; Case C-366/10 *ATAA* (2011) ECLI:EU:C:2011:864, para 74; Case C-59/11 *Kokopelli* (2012) ECLI:EU:C:2012:447, paras 86–92; Joined Cases C-404 and 405/12 P *Stichting Natuur en Milieu* (2015) ECLI:EU:C:2015:5.

[63] Case C-167/17 *Klohn* (2018) ECLI:EU:C:2018:833, para 33.

[64] Case C-213/03 *Étang de Berre I* (2004) ECLI:EU:C:2004:464, para 45. In the same sense, Case C-240/09 *Lesoochranárske zoskupenie* (*LZ I*) (2011) ECLI:EU:C:2011:125, para 44.

[65] Riccardo Pavoni, 'Controversial Aspects of the Interaction Between International and EU Law in Environmental Matters: Direct Effect and Member States Unilateral Measures' in Morgera (n 5) 352.

[66] Case C-59/11 *Kokopelli* (2012) ECLI:EU:C:2012:447, para 86.

[67] Case C-377/98 *Biotech Patents* case (2001) ECLI:EU:C:2001:523, para 54.

[68] Truilhe-Marengo (n 51) 84 (our translation).

seminal instruments of international environmental law, such as Part XII of UNCLOS.[69]

2.3.3 The interpretation of provisions of secondary EU acts and decisions in accordance with international law

Beyond direct reliance on provisions of biodiversity-related international agreements, IBL may also trickle down in the EU legal order in a more incremental manner, for instance by using provisions of international agreements as an interpretation standard when clarifying the precise extent of obligations laid down by EU law.[70] This indirect route is by no means exceptional. For, indeed, the CJEU increasingly relies on international law when interpreting decisions by EU institutions or even Member States, especially if the latter have been enacted to implement a treaty, whether or not the EU is a party, as was the case with CITES until 2015.[71]

As held by Advocate General Kokott in a case concerning the protection of the European hamster, both protected under international law and EU law, 'provisions of secondary European Union law[72] must, so far as possible, be interpreted in a manner that is consistent with the obligations of the European Union under international law'.[73] The CBD,[74] CITES,[75] and its secondary 'soft law',[76] the CMS,[77] the Ramsar Convention,[78] and the Bern Convention[79] have all been referred to by the CJEU or its Advocates General to interpret provisions of EU legislation. Remarkably, the fact that some of these conventions lack direct effect does not preclude the use of IBL as an interpretation standard

[69] This has been criticized by Riccardo Pavoni (n 65) 355.

[70] Koutrakos (n 38) 307.

[71] Case C-510/99 *Tridon* (2001) ECLI:EU:C:2001:559, para 25. See also Case C-169/89 *Gourmetterie Van den Burg* (1990) ECLI:EU:C:1990:227, para 14.

[72] EU secondary law includes all forms of legislation (regulations, directives, decisions) enacted by EU institutions under the EU primary law, ie the Founding Treaties.

[73] See eg the case law reference in the opinion of AG *Kokott* in Case C-383/09 *Commission v French Republic* (2011) ECLI:EU:C:2011:369, para 39.

[74] Case C-377/98 *Biotech Patents* case (2001) ECLI:EU:C:2001:523, paras 53–55: in this case, the Court rejected the Dutch government's argument that Directive 98/44 on the legal protection of biotechnological inventions was contrary to the provisions of the TRIPS Agreement, TBT, and the CBD.

[75] Case C-510/99 *Tridon* (2001) ECLI:EU:C:2001:559, paras 23–27.

[76] See eg Case C-182/89 *Commission v France* (1990) ECLI:EU:C:1990:427 (on the legality of importation permits of Bolivian wild cats in regard to a CITES COP resolution recommending a provisional ban on Bolivian imports).

[77] Case C-88/19 *Alianta pentru combaterea abuzurilor* (2020) ECLI:EU:C:2020:458. The Court referred to Art 1(1)(f) of the CMS to interpret the concept of 'natural range' used in the Habitats Directive (Art 12(1)).

[78] Opinion of the AG in Case C-57/89 *Commission v Germany* (*Leybucht*) (1991) ECLI:EU:C:1991:89, para 36 (about the possibility of reducing the surface of a Ramsar site to build a coastal defence project in the Elms estuary).

[79] Opinion of AG Kokott in Case C-383/09 *Commission v French Republic* (2011) ECLI:EU:C:2011:369, paras 38–39.

pursuant to the CJEU. Even more so, the Court has not refrained from even using soft law instruments to that effect, thereby offering new pathways for progressive litigation strategies in the years to come.[80] For instance, in the *Mondiet* case the Court upheld the validity of an EC regulation forbidding the use of drift nets with, amongst others, a reference to a resolution of the UN General Assembly recommending a moratorium on pelagic drift net fishing.[81]

2.4 The Indirect Influence of IBL Through its Implementation in EU Biodiversity Law

To further implement its international obligations, the EU has developed an extensive—yet notoriously patchy and complex—body of legislation in the form of directives, regulations, and decisions aimed at protecting species and habitats, creating a system of protected areas, improving ecosystems' conservation status, or integrating environmental considerations into local land use policies. This set of environmental directives and regulations while not covering all aspects of biodiversity conservation and sustainable use, is—at least on paper—to be ranked amongst the most ambitious in the world and in many ways goes beyond international binding standards.[82] Most remarkably, some EU legislation covers fields that are governed by international agreements which the EU has not explicitly ratified. This has been the case with CITES (until 2015), the UNESCO World Heritage Convention, and the Ramsar Convention.[83] For instance, some of the sites listed under the two last-mentioned treaties are included in the EU Natura 2000 Network of protected sites, which covers 18 per cent of the EU's land area and more than 8 per cent of its marine territory.[84]

One of the defining characteristics of EU law, in comparison with classic international law, is that it is mostly drafted in binding terms and, in some cases,

[80] Case C-377/98 *Biotech Patents* case (2001) ECLI:EU:C:2001:523, paras 54–55.

[81] Case C-405/92 *Mondiet* (1993) ECLI:EU:C:1993:906, para 21.

[82] Augustin Garcia-Ureta, *EU Biodiversity Law: Wild Bird and Habitats Directives* (Europa Law Publishing 2020) 10.

[83] The CITES Regulation (EC) No 338/97 (1996) reproduces, in stricter terms, the system set up by CITES, although the EU did not become a party to the convention until 2015. As regards the protection of wetlands of international importance under the Ramsar Convention or the protection of sites designated as World Heritage sites under the UNESCO Convention, many sites benefit from the protection under the Natura 2000 regime and the species protection regime. The integrated water resources management regime provided by the Water Framework Directive (WFD, see n 86) encompasses many wetlands under the Ramsar Convention.

[84] 'Natura 2000' <https://ec.europa.eu/environment/nature/natura2000/index_en.htm> accessed 15 March 2022.

sets ecological obligations of result on the part of the Member States. The obligations to maintain or restore, at 'favourable conservation status', natural habitats and species of Community interest and to achieve good (environmental) surface and marine water status on the whole EU territory, as laid down in EU Habitats[85] and Water Framework Directives,[86] can be referred to as the most seminal in this respect.

However, despite its efforts to enforce them, in its Sixth EU Report to the CBD, the European Commission acknowledged that the EU was falling short on its international commitments under IBL.[87] The reasons for this persistent shortcoming are multifold. Beyond some persisting gaps in the EU normative framework itself—on soil protection, for instance—one important reason is the lack of proper and more effective implementation and enforcement of EU biodiversity law at the national level.[88] This finding is underpinned by the fact that the EU Birds and Habitats Directives have featured prominently in infringement proceedings initiated by the European Commission before the CJEU against the Member States during the past three decades.[89] One of the most impactful biodiversity-related cases brought before the CJEU relates to the large-scale economic exploitation of the Białowieża primaeval forest—a UNESCO site—decided by the Polish government and, subsequently, denounced by NGOs to the European Commission.[90]

The latter infringement proceedings are addressed further later in our analysis. At this point, we want to draw attention to the *Caretta caretta* case—infringement proceedings launched by the European Commission against Greece for its failure to protect the breeding sites of the loggerhead turtle (*Caretta caretta*)—that greatly underscored the potency of biodiversity litigation before the CJEU in the specific context of IBL, already back at the turn of the twenty-first century. The endangered turtle species is protected under the Bern Convention (Annex II), CITES (Annex I), and the Bonn Convention (Annex I)—all treaties ratified by the EU. These treaty obligations have been implemented through Article 12 of the Habitats Directive since the species features

[85] Articles 2.2 and 3 of the Habitats Directive.

[86] Article 4.1, a, ii, Directive of the European Parliament and of the Council of 23 October 2000 establishing a framework for Community action in the field of water policy (Water Framework Directive).

[87] EU Commission, EU Sixth National Report to the CBD <https://chm.cbd.int/database/record?documentID=243509> accessed 15 March 2022.

[88] EU Commission, *Fitness Check of the EU Nature Legislation (Birds and Habitats Directives)*, Brussels, 16 December 2016, SWD(2016) 472 final, 96; EU Commission, *Environmental Implementation Review 2019*, 4 April 2019, COM(2019) 149 final, 6.

[89] Garcia-Ureta (n 82).

[90] Case C-441/17 R *Commission v Poland* (2017) ECLI:EU:C:2017:877 (hereafter Białowieża).

in Annex IV, a) of said Directive. Since the 1980s, the Standing Committee of the Bern Convention has spared no efforts to push Greece to step up its marine turtle conservation on the beaches of Zakynthos.[91] With limited results, given the weak compliance regime which is tied to the Bern Convention. In 1995, the Committee closed the case in sheer desperation.[92] Another case concerning the lack of proper turtle conservation action, the *Kyparissia Bay* case, is still pending.[93]

Following complaints from several NGOs, the European Commission initiated infringement proceedings against Greece for its continued refusal to establish an effective protection regime in accordance with the requirements of Article 12(1)(b) and (d) of the Habitats Directive for the loggerhead turtle. Repeated visits to the beach, carried out by the services of the European Commission, underscored the lack of efforts to avoid the intentional disturbance of this vulnerable species and the deterioration of its shrinking breeding sites.

Recognizing that the Bay of Laganas is a 'vital breeding region' for the species, the CJEU held that the legal protection regime of the beaches was insufficient to deal with all the incremental threats to the turtles' breeding site. In its 2002 landmark ruling, the CJEU tackled the conservation failures head on: it clearly went beyond a formal review of the applicable conservation actions that had been put in place by Greece and highlighted that the legal measures taken were in any case ineffective and did not prevent unlawful disturbances and damage due to illegal activities (use of mopeds on the beach, illegal buildings, etc). Consequently, Greece was condemned for breaching its obligations under Article 12 of the Habitats Directive.[94] More than a decade later, Greece was also found responsible for failing to protect the same species in Kyparissia Bay on similar grounds.[95]

This jurisprudence starkly underlines the added value of the supranational nature of the EU judicial protection system to enforce IBL in the EU, especially when compared to the poor results that are often achieved in the 'classic' international sphere, where non-compliance can rarely be effectively tackled. Even if the EU's compliance system is far from perfect—since only a limited number

[91] Recommendation No 9 (1987).

[92] Decision of the Standing Committee (adopted on 3 December 1999).

[93] Recommendation No 174 (2014).

[94] Case C-103/00 *Commission v Greece* (2002) ECLI:EU:C:2002:60. See Charles-Hubert Born, 'L'arrêt Caretta Larratt: Un nouveau souffle pour la protection des espèces d'intérêt communautaire?' (2002) 3 Aménagement-environnement: urbanisme et droit foncier 216–24.

[95] Case C-504/14 *Commission v Greece* (2016) ECLI:EU:C:2016:847. The Court also condemned Greece for violating Natura 2000 rules.

of violations of EU law reach the CJEU and it often takes time before the positive effects are visible on the ground[96]—it still stands out when compared with the ineffectiveness of non-binding compliance schemes under international law, such as the Standing Committee of the Bern Convention. If Member States leave non-compliance scenarios unaddressed, they could face a new infringement procedure, which could lead the CJEU, on second referral, to impose severe financial penalties on said Member State for failure to comply with its first judgment.[97] The prospect of significant financial sanctions undoubtedly constitutes a powerful lever to enforce some of the international obligations included in IBL within the EU legal order.

3. The Available Legal Remedies in the EU Legal Order: Obstacles or Opportunities for Biodiversity Litigation?

Going beyond a theoretical analysis of the distinct legal effects of IBL in the EU, it is also crucial to check how the primacy of IBL can be enforced through courtroom actions. Since the EU as well as its Member States have ratified the 1998 Aarhus Convention, one might expect its system of legal remedies to easily meet the standards set out by its Article 9 on access to justice.[98] However, as at the time of writing this only holds true for biodiversity litigation brought before national courts (3.3), leaving very limited to no room for direct strategic environmental litigation before the EU Courts (3.1 and 3.2).

3.1 Individual Actions Before the EU Courts: No-Go Zone for Biodiversity Litigation?

Many decisions of the EU institutions have a concrete impact on the environment and might effectively go against the international biodiversity commitments of the EU. For instance, the conservation of marine biological resources under the Common Fisheries Policy (CFP) is an exclusive EU competence,[99]

[96] See MEDASSET, T-PVS/Files (2021) 19. Update Report. Follow-up of Recommendation No 9 (1987) on the protection of Caretta fancier in Laganas bay, Zakynthos (Greece).

[97] Article 260 TFEU.

[98] For a critical analysis, see Hendrik Schoukens, 'Access to Justice before EU Courts in Environmental Cases against the Backdrop of the Aarhus Convention: Balancing Pathological Stubbornness and Cognitive Dissonance?' in Christina Voigt (ed), *International Judicial Practice on the Environment* (CUP 2019) 74–119.

[99] Article 3(1)(d) TFEU.

while the European Commission also has wide competence when it comes to the approval of pesticides and genetically modified organisms (GMOs) as well as granting derogations and exemptions for applying air quality standards under EU environmental law.

However, the strict interpretation by the CJEU of the criterion of being 'individually concerned' (one of the two generic criteria to be fulfilled pursuant to Article 263(4) TFEU when pursuing the direct annulments of an EU act or decision), represents an effective restriction on public interest litigation before the EU Courts, especially so in environmental cases where diffuse interests are at stake.[100] In the notable *Plaumann* ruling,[101] which dates back to 1963, the CJEU underscored that in order to be individually concerned by an act, non-addressees need to demonstrate that said act 'affects them by reason *of certain attributes which are peculiar to them or by reason of circumstances in which they are differentiated from all other persons and by virtue of these factors distinguishes them individually just as in case of the persons addressed*'.[102] This formula is still upheld by the CJEU and represents an impossible hurdle to overcome for environmental NGOs and citizens in the context of biodiversity litigation.[103]

During the past decades, several environmental NGOs have tried in vain to challenge this stringent approach to *locus standi* in environmental cases.[104] For instance, in its 2008 ruling in the *WWF-UK* case, in which an NGO claimed that a certain number of fishing quotas set up by the EU Council were not in line with the environmental principles set out in the TFEU, the CJEU declined to rethink its *Plaumann* test in the light of Article 9(3) of the Aarhus Convention, highlighting that international agreements cannot modify primary EU law.[105] The action was dismissed on procedural grounds and no evaluation of the claims on the merits took place. The limited potential for strategic biodiversity litigation at the EU level is further highlighted by the disappointing outcome of the so-called *People's Climate* case, in which thirty-six individuals from ten families from Portugal, Germany, France, Italy, Romania, Kenya, Fiji, and the Swedish Sami Youth Association Saminuorra, argued that

[100] Schoukens (n 98) 46–67.

[101] Case 25/62 *Plaumann* (1963) ECLI:EU:C:1963:17.

[102] See eg Cases T-94/04 *European Environmental Bureau (EEB)* (2005) ECLI:EU:T:2005:425; Joined Cases T-236/ and 241/04 *European Environmental Bureau (EEB)* (2005) ECLI:EU:T:2005:426.

[103] See Diana L Torrens, '*Locus Standi* of Environmental Associations under EC Law—Greenpeace—A Missed Opportunity for the ECJ' (1999) 8(3) Review of European Community & International Environmental Law 336–46.

[104] See Schoukens (n 98) 86–92.

[105] Case C-355/08 *WWF-UK Ltd* (2009) ECLI:EU:C:2009:286. See also Case C-352/19 P *Région de Bruxelles-Capitale v Commission* (2020) ECLI:EU:C:2020:978, paras 25–29.

the EU legislation on greenhouse gas (GHG) emissions was unlawful because it failed to prevent climate change.[106] The claims were ultimately dismissed by the CJEU, reaffirming that the claimants did not pass the *Plaumann* test, not even by invoking potential infringements of their fundamental rights.[107]

Against this rather conservative backdrop, which persistently limits standing in environmental cases before the CJEU in relation to EU decisions, the margin for launching strategic lawsuits in the field of IBL directly before the CJEU understandably remains remarkably slim.

In 2006, though, the EU institutions tried to mitigate the limited access to justice by adopting the so-called 'Aarhus Regulation',[108] which aimed to further implement Article 9(3) of the Aarhus Convention before the EU Courts. The regulation sets up an 'internal review' mechanism, allowing certain environmental NGOs to request the EU institutions to review their own decisions, with a right to appeal before the EU Courts.[109] In the context of biodiversity litigation, reference can be made to the *Mellifera* proceedings, in which an NGO working on the protection of bees submitted to the European Commission a request for an internal review of its approval for the herbicide glyphosate, which is said to have an impact on bee populations. To little avail, since under the terms of the internal review procedure only administrative acts of an individual scope are considered 'reviewable'. Therefore, the European Commission dismissed the request for an internal review on procedural grounds.

The Commission's refusal appeared hardly reviewable in court. Despite some modest successes before the General Court in 2012 in other cases,[110] which held the Aarhus Regulation to be in violation of Article 9(3) of the Aarhus Convention and thereby offered the prospect of more ample effective protection in environmental cases, the CJEU ultimately refused to review the Aarhus Regulation using Article 9(3) of the Aarhus Convention as a benchmark in a landmark ruling in 2015.[111] Also in the *Mellifera* case, the CJEU ultimately held

[106] Case T-330/18 *Armando Carvalho* (2019) ECLI:EU:T:2019:324.

[107] Case C-565/19 P *Armando Carvalho* (2021) ECLI:EU:C:2021:252.

[108] Regulation (EC) No 1367/2006 of the European Parliament and the Council of 6 September 2006 on the application of the provisions of the Aarhus Convention . . . to Community institutions and bodies ('Aarhus Regulation') [2006] OJ L264/13.

[109] See more extensively Hendrik Schoukens, 'Access to Justice in Environmental Matters on the EU Level after the Judgments of the General Court of 14 June 2012: Between Hope and Denial' (2014) Nordic Environmental Law Review 7.

[110] Case T-396/09 *Stichting Natuur en Milieu* (2012) ECLI:EU:T:2012:301; Case T-338/08 *Vereniging Milieudefensie* (2012) ECLI:EU:T:2012:300.

[111] Joined Cases C-404 and 405/12 P *Council and Others v Vereniging Stichting Natuur en Milieu and Milieu and Pesticide Action Network Europe* (2015) ECLI:EU:C:2015:5, para 48; Joined Cases C-401 and

that the contested decision was of a general scope, thereby refusing to proceed to a substantive review of the EU decision.[112] It represents but one recent illustration of the limited leeway for biodiversity litigation before the EU Courts in the context of EU acts and decisions capable of significantly impacting biodiversity.

The CJEU's unwillingness to remove these significant barriers to the internal review procedure was one of the determinative factors that ultimately brought the Aarhus Compliance Committee in 2017 to find the EU to be in violation of the access to justice provisions that are included in the Aarhus Convention.[113] Taking stock of this criticism, the European Commission decided to proceed with a proposal to remedy part of the well-known deficiencies of the Aarhus Regulation in the autumn of 2020.[114] While the Proposal still left some important shortcomings unaddressed, it significantly expanded the material scope of the internal review procedure by including non-legislative acts of general scope. This renders the internal review of decisions in the realm of biodiversity governance more likely in the years to come. A final political agreement on the amended regulation was reached in July 2021,[115] which further opens the door for private citizens to gain access to the internal review procedure, provided that certain criteria are met. The amended regulation was published on 8 October 2021, in the *Official Journal of the European Union*.[116] Most importantly, the amended regulation also allows reviews for acts that do not entail implementing measures. Given that many decisions, such as the approval of pesticides, are often followed up by national implementing decisions, this will probably significantly alter the situation for environmental NGOs for the better, and offer ample opportunities for more effective biodiversity litigation at the EU level.

403/12 P *Council and Others v Vereniging Milieudefensie and Stichting Stop Luchtverontreiniging Utrecht* (2015) ECLI:EU:C:2015:4, para 55.

[112] Case C-784/18 P *Mellifera eV, Vereinigung für wesensgemäße Bienenhaltung* (2020) ECLI:EU:C:2020:630. See also the first decision of the General Court: Case T-12/17 *Mellifera eV, Vereinigung für wesensgemäße Bienenhaltung* (2018) ECLI:EU:T:2018:616.

[113] Communication ACCC/C/2008/32 (Part II) (European Union), adopted on 17 March 2017, paras 93–120.

[114] COM(2020) 642 final.

[115] 'EU throws open courtroom doors for new wave of citizen climate litigations', EURACTIV.com (14 July 2021).

[116] Regulation (EU) 2021/1767 of the European Parliament and of the Council of 6 October 2021 amending Regulation (EC) No 1367/2006 on the application of the provisions of the Aarhus Convention on Access to Information, Public Participation in Decision-making and Access to Justice in Environmental Matters to Community institutions and bodies [2021] OJ L356/1.

3.2 Infringement Proceedings: An Imperfect Instrument Gaining Strength When Pristine Ecosystems Are at Risk?

The supranational nature of the EU legal order is underscored by the existence of a robust compliance scheme which allows the CJEU to address the situations in which a Member State has breached EU law. Since provisions of biodiversity treaties, such as the CBD, that have been ratified by the EU are to be considered part of EU law itself, infringement proceedings can also help to ensure observance of IBL in the EU. The legal teeth of these procedures, which have been highlighted earlier, stand in stark contrast to the lax compliance schemes that exist in the context of international law and render non-compliance more likely in this context.[117] However, whereas private parties, amongst whom environmental NGOs, are allowed to file complaints regarding potential cases of non-compliance with IBL as well as non-application of the EU instruments aimed at implementing those obligations, the European Commission is under no circumstances obliged to open formal infringement proceedings, even if it considers a breach has occurred.[118] Only a limited number of complaints, also in the context of EU nature conservation law, ever end up before the CJEU.

NGOs cannot legally challenge an implicit decision of the European Commission not to take a serious case of violation of EU environmental law before the CJEU.[119] Even political considerations can significantly affect the EU's general infringement policy. This, amongst other things, helps to explain why Finland was taken to the CJEU over its wolf management hunt in 2007[120] whereas Sweden has managed to escape such a fate.[121] As noted by Krämer, this quasi-monopolistic position of the European Commission in bringing cases before the CJEU is to be revised, especially since Member States often enter into political negotiations with the European Commission in order to persuade it not to launch further legal actions.[122]

In the field of EU biodiversity law, including IBL, it is to be noted that the European Commission focused its initial infringement actions on cases in which a Member State had incorrectly or not timely transposed provisions of

[117] COM(2020) 642 final.

[118] See <https://ec.europa.eu/assets/sg/report-a-breach/complaints_en/> accessed 10 March 2022.

[119] See eg Case C-247/87 *Star Fruit Co v Commission* (1989) ECLI:EU:C:1989:58.

[120] Case C-342/05 *Commission v Finland* (2007) ECLI:EU:C:2007:341.

[121] Jan Darpö, 'The Commission: A Sheep in Wolf's Clothing? On Infringement Proceedings as a Legal Device for the Enforcement of the EU Law on the Environment, Using Swedish Wolf Management as an Example' (2016) Journal for European Environmental and Planning Law 270–93.

[122] Ludwig Krämer, 'The Environment before the European Court of Justice' in Christina Voigt (ed), *International Judicial Practice on the Environment* (CUP 2019) 43.

the Birds and Habitats Directives into its domestic legislation.[123] IBL was also involved in some of these court proceedings, since some of the aforesaid provisions also partly implement the CBD and the Bern Convention in the EU legal order.[124] In one case, the Court curiously admitted that provisions of biodiversity treaties ratified by a Member State 'are capable of satisfactorily transposing' specific provisions of the Habitats Directive, provided that the treaty articles are self-executing in the internal legal system of that Member State.[125]

Whereas the European Commission also used to display a remarkable degree of willingness to take up complaints of NGOs regarding non-compliance with the EU Birds and Habitats Directive, it seems to expect the latter to prioritize bringing such cases before the national courts through strategic litigation. Only the more systemic and notorious cases of non-compliance merit the initiation of infringement proceedings. During the past decades, the CJEU has nevertheless been able to condemn Member States over their failure to protect strictly protected species under international law such as the European hamster[126] or, as highlighted previously, the loggerhead turtle.

Interestingly, a significant proportion of the infringement proceedings that have been launched over the past decades have focused on the failure of many Member States to designate a sufficient number of protected sites under both the EU Birds[127] and Habitats Directive.[128] This was a valid strategy, since a designation of being vulnerable is the first and a necessary step for protection regimes to apply in the first place. In some instances, it emerged that overcoming the evidentiary hurdles set up by the CJEU turned out to be relatively strenuous, as was illustrated by the rejection of the infringement procedure regarding the protection of the Iberian lynx in Andalusia, Spain.[129]

More generally speaking, Krämer rightly notes that between 2011 and mid-2017 the European Commission only brought five cases on specific species or habitats before the CJEU,[130] which is a very limited number considering that

[123] ibid 38.

[124] See eg: Case C-6/04 *Commission v UK* (2005) ECLI:EU:C:2005:626; Case C-98/03 *Commission v Germany* (2006) ECLI:EU:C:2006:3.

[125] Case 75/01 *Commission v Grand Duchy of Luxemburg* (2003) ECLI:EU:C:2003:95, paras 95–96 (concerning the 'transposition' of Art 22(c) of the Habitats Directive (on education and general information on the need to protect species) by Art 3(3) of the Bern Convention and art 13 of the CBD).

[126] Case C-383/09 *Commission v France* (2011) ECLI:EU:C:2011:369.

[127] See eg Case C-3/96 *Commission v Netherlands* (1998) ECLI:EU:C:1998:238.

[128] See eg Case C-371/98 *First Corporate Shipping* (2000) ECLI:EU:C:2000:600 (which concerned one particular site, situated in a port area).

[129] Case C-308/08 *Commission v Spain* (2010) ECLI:EU:C:2010:281.

[130] Case C-383/09 *Commission v French Republic* (2011) ECLI:EU:C:2011:369 (European hamster); Case C-404/09 *Commission v Spain* (2011) ECLI:EU:C:2011:768 ('Alto Sil'); Case C-340/10 *Commission v Cyprus* (2012) ECLI:EU:C:2012:143 ('Cypriot grass snake'); Case C-517/11 *Commission*

the Habitats Directive concerns nearly 27,000 protected areas[131] and approximately 1,200 protected fauna and flora species.[132] And, most importantly, apart from one single case related to a Protocol to the Barcelona Convention on the Protection of the Mediterranean against pollution from land-based sources, the European Commission has not taken action enforcing international agreements vis-à-vis Member States.[133]

Yet there exists some reason for modest optimism. When endangered species or habitats are in imminent danger, recent practice seems to illustrate that the European Commission is ready to launch infringement measures, backed up by interim measures in order to avoid further irreparable damage to biodiversity. Arguably, the most powerful and recent example was offered by the European Commission's handling of the case of the protection of the Polish Białowieża Forest, one of Europe's last pristine primaeval forests, which has already been touched upon earlier.[134] In the light of the inclusion of the site in the Natura 2000 Network, numerous environmental NGOs opposed the decision of the Polish government to allow massive logging activities in these vulnerable habitats. Confronted with Polish unwillingness to halt its logging actions, the European Commission did not hesitate to seek interlocutory relief, leading to a first order issued by the President of the CJEU to immediately stop logging in the forest.[135] When subsequently faced with the Polish refusal to obey this order, the CJEU granted the European Commission's application for interim measures. Poland was given fifteen additional days to prove that it had complied with the first Court order to stop logging in Europe's oldest forest or face 'a periodic penalty payment of at least EUR 100 000 per day … until such time as that Member State complies with this order or until final judgment in Case C-441/17 is delivered'.[136] This decision grants significant additional effectiveness to the protection conferred to the site by the UNESCO Convention on World Heritage, since the endangered site was also listed under that international

v Greece (2013) ECLI:EU:C:2013:66 ('Koroneia Lake'); Case C-141/14 *Commission v Bulgary* (2016) ECLI:EU:C:2016:8 ('Kaliakra').

[131] Natura 2000 Barometer, December 2020 (EU-27), *Natura 2000 Newsletter* (July 2021) 8.

[132] Krämer (n 122) 41.

[133] Case C-213/03 *Syndicat professionnel coordination des pêcheurs de l'étang de Berre et de la région and EDF* (2004) ECLI:EU:C:2004:464; Case C-239/03 *Commission v French Republic* (2004) ECLI:EU:C:2004:598.

[134] Another example is related to spring bird hunting practices in Malta forbidden by the Birds Directive: Order, Case C-76/08 R *Commission v Malta* (2008) ECLI:EU:C:2008:252.

[135] Order, Case C-441/17 R *Commission v Poland* (2017) ECLI:EU:C:2017:622.

[136] Order, Case C-441/17 R *Commission v Poland* (2017) ECLI:EU:C:2017:877, para 118.

agreement. However, by and large, such proceedings remain to be treated as the exception, not the rule.

3.3 The National Courts as Ordinary Courts: The Easy Route for Biodiversity Litigation?

In the light of the reluctance on the part of the European Commission to take up a sizeable portion of the complaints submitted by environmental NGOs, having recourse to national court proceedings increasingly constitutes a necessity for any effective biodiversity litigation strategy whatsoever within the EU legal order. Given the supranational characteristics of the EU legal order, which also include the concepts of direct effect[137] and the primacy of EU law,[138] private parties as well as NGOs can rely on directly applicable provisions of EU biodiversity law—including provisions of international biodiversity treaties ratified by the EU—before the national courts. And, most importantly, whereas the EU institutions have vehemently opposed the broadening of *locus standi* for environmental NGOs at the EU level, an opposite approach has prevailed when it has concerned access to the national courts. Even more so, the European Commission has frequently postulated that limited access for environmental NGOs to the EU Court has been largely offset by the dual-track nature of the systems of legal remedies within the EU legal order.[139] And thus broad access in environmental cases to the national courts became the linchpin of a new string of biodiversity-related lawsuits at the domestic level.

This optimistic attitude is not fully reflected in the existing legislative framework since, as at the time of writing, there still does not exist a general directive implementing Article 9(3) of the Aarhus Convention in all sub-domains of EU environmental law.[140] As a result, no explicit provisions guarantee broad access to justice in biodiversity-related cases under EU law, with the exception of such directives as the EIA Directive[141] and the Industrial Emissions Directive.[142] With reference to the Aarhus Convention, however, the case law of the CJEU

[137] Case C-26/62 *Van Gend en Loos* (1963) ECLI:EU:C:1963:1.
[138] Case C-6/64 *Costa* (1964) ECLI:EU:C:1964:66.
[139] Schoukens (n 98) 103.
[140] The Commission adopted a 'Proposal for a Directive of the European Parliament and of the Council on access to justice in environmental matters' in 2003 (COM(2003) 624) but withdrew it in 2014 because of lack of support by Member States.
[141] Article 11(1) of the EIA Directive.
[142] Article 25 of the IED Directive.

has gradually pushed national courts to drop their guard when it comes to the restriction of standing for NGOs in environmental cases.

In its 2009 landmark decision in the *Lesoochranárske zoskupenie I* ('Slovak Brown Bear') case[143], the CJEU clarified that national courts are obliged to apply Article 9(3) of the Aarhus Convention as an interpretation lens when applying national procedural rules.[144] This case law enabled the Slovakian court in effect to grant standing to the environmental NGO at issue in a national dispute regarding compliance with the hunting derogations for the culling of brown bears with Article 16(1) of the EU Habitats Directive. This seminal jurisprudential move was subsequently repeated in yet another Slovakian case, related to a project located in a Natura 2000 site, where once more the importance of effective legal protection in the context of EU biodiversity law was highlighted.[145]

Also in more recent and systemic pollution cases related to the EU Water Framework Directive[146] and the EU Nitrates Directive,[147] both of which are seminal for avoiding further biodiversity degradation in the EU, this progressive rationale towards access to justice prevails and offers new litigation pathways for NGOs at the national level. Even more so, in its 2017 Communication on Access to Justice in Environmental Matters, the European Commission detailed all requirements in the field of effective legal protection that have to be considered by national courts.[148]

In many instances, the decisions of the CJEU have effectively forced national courts to let go of traditional, restrictive approaches and also allow lawsuits launched by environmental NGOs in the field of biodiversity protection.[149] Most notably, the CJEU compelled the German courts to reconsider their well-rooted '*Schutznormtheorie*', under which individuals and environmental NGOs only have standing to invoke legal proceedings that are designed to protect their specific interest, in the light of the Aarhus Convention.[150] In addition, the CJEU has broadened the scope of effective legal protection in environmental cases by also asking courts to carry out a substantive legality

[143] Case C-240/09 *Lesoochranárske zoskupenie VLK I* (2011) ECLI:EU:C:2011:125, paras 45–49.

[144] ibid para 49.

[145] Case C-243/15 *Lesoochranárske zoskupenie VLK II* (2016) ECLI:EU:C:2016:838.

[146] Case C-664/15 *Protect* (2017) ECLI:EU:C:2017:987, para 45.

[147] Case C-197/18 *Wasserleitungsverband Nördliches Burgenland* (2019) ECLI:EU:C:2019:824, para 46.

[148] European Commission, Commission Notice on Access to Justice in Environmental Cases (2017), C(2017) 2616 final.

[149] See eg Case C-263/08 *Djurgården-Lilla Värtans Miljöskyddsförening* (2009) ECLI:EU:C:2009:631.

[150] Case C-115/09 *Trianel* (2011) ECLI:EU:C:2011:289, para 46. See also more recently Case C-137/14 *Commission v Germany* (2015) ECLI:EU:C:2015:683.

review of national decisions that could impact EU-protected nature, such as planning acts or hunting authorizations.[151] For instance, because of the wider standing granted to NGOs in biodiversity-related cases, a Finnish NGO advocating wolf protection was able to convince a Finnish national court to refer interpretation issues regarding the alignment of Finnish wolf management with the derogation clause of Article 16(1) of the Habitats Directive.[152] Recent case law has illustrated that the aforesaid substantive review also covers plans and programmes which Member States are required to adopt, for instance in order to combat air pollution[153] and nitrate impacts.[154] This opens the door for addressing more systemic and accumulated biodiversity-related threats that go beyond the realm of classic, more reactive cases of nature protection, which often focus on the direct destruction of protection sites by project developments or unsustainable hunting practices.

Likewise, the CJEU also pushes for enhanced legal protection in the domestic legal orders in order to prevent irreversible damage to nature since, for instance, it often takes only a few days or weeks to cut down forests or destroy habitats that are located on construction sites.[155] In the context of biodiversity-related cases, the recent case law of the CJEU underscores the importance of the precautionary principle, which is to be observed in the context of the application of the protection regimes set out by the EU Habitats Directive.[156] The latter principle urges the national courts to be very reluctant when dismissing requests for interim measures in cases where serious doubts persist as to the presence of adverse effects on EU-protected nature and thus adds an additional layer of legal protection for endangered biodiversity.

4. Substantive Approaches: Novel Pathways to International Biodiversity Litigation?

A comprehensive overview of the available European and national jurisprudence regarding biodiversity litigation cannot be provided within the limited

[151] See eg: C-127/02 *Waddenzee* (2004) ECLI:EU:C:2004:482, paras 66–70; Case C-137/14 *Commission v Germany* (2015) ECLI:EU:C:2015:683, para 80.

[152] Case C-674/17 *Tapiola* (2019) ECLI:EU:C:2019:851.

[153] Case C-404/13 *ClientEarth* (2004) ECLI:EU:C:2014:2382, para 58; Case C-237/07 *Janecek* (2008) ECLI:EU:C:2008:447, paras 39–46.

[154] Case C-197/18 *Wasserleitungsverband Nördliches Burgenland* (2019) ECLI:EU:C:2019:824, para 46.

[155] Case C-461/10 *Križan* (2013) ECLI:EU:C:2013:8.

[156] Case C-127/02 *Waddenzee* (2004) ECLI:EU:C:2004:482, paras 44 and 58 (Art 6.3); Joined Cases C-473 and 474/19 *Föreningen Skydda Skogen* (2021) ECLI:EU:C:2021:166, paras 38 and 60 (Art 12).

confines of a chapter.[157] Therefore, in this section only the most relevant substantive trends that prevail in the context of biodiversity litigation are outlined, based upon the steady stream of case law from the CJEU, which offers a good overview of the most important biodiversity-related cases at the national level.

4.1 An Effective Ecological Network of Protected Sites where Scientific Input Trumps Economic Considerations

As of today, it is well established that protected sites only produce limited net positive effects if they are merely approached as 'islands' of pristine biodiversity in a sea of impoverished environments. To avoid the risk of 'paper parks', the ecological network approach comes forward as one of the rationales to turn area protection into an effective instrument for biodiversity protection.[158] In this respect, the EU-wide Natura 2000 Network of protected sites, which covers up to 18 per cent of the land territory of the EU Member States,[159] clearly stands out as one of the most progressive pieces of area protection in the world.

This success can partly be linked to the requirement, set out in the EU Birds and Habitats Directives, for national authorities to exclusively rely upon ecological criteria when drafting their designation policies.[160] Despite an almost natural tendency on the side of authorities to ignore ecological evidence as to the eligibility of certain sites for obvious economic reasons, the CJEU has consistently ensured that the rules of the game are respected in this regard, even when the socio-economic stakes are high, as is the case when protected sites are designated in port areas.[161] One of the first illustrations of this progressive jurisprudence was offered by the CJEU's decision in a case focusing on the Santoña marshes in Spain.[162] This jurisprudence creates a very promising pathway for effective and science-based biodiversity litigation for environmental NGOs, especially since the CJEU admitted the use of scientific reports, such as the *Inventory of Important Bird Areas in the European Community* (IBA

157 For a selective yet more comprehensive overview, see Charles-Hubert Born and others (eds), *The Habitats Directive in its EU Environmental Law Context: European Nature's Best Hope?* (Routledge 2015).

158 See Target 11 of the Aichi Biodiversity Targets adopted under the CBD Strategic Plan for Biodiversity 2011–2020, encouraging the parties to conserve important areas for biodiversity through 'effectively and equitably managed, ecologically representative and well-connected systems of protected areas and other effective area-based conservation measures, and integrated into the wider landscapes and seascapes' <https://www.cbd.int/sp/> accessed 21 June 2022.

159 Natura 2000 Barometer, December 2020 (EU-27), *Natura 2000 Newsletter* (July 2021) 8.

160 Article 4(1)(2) of the Birds Directive; Arts 4 and 5 and Annex III of the Habitats Directive.

161 Case C-44/95 *R v Secretary of the State for the Environment* (1996) ECLI:EU:C:1996:297, para 27.

162 Case C-355/90 *Commission v Spain* (1993) ECLI:EU:C:1993:331, para 26.

89), as a benchmark for checking a Member State's compliance with its obligation under the EU Habitats and Birds Directive regarding the designation of protected sites.[163]

It would be incorrect, though, to maintain that the EU judges are treating the IBA documents as quasi-binding documents.[164] The CJEU has indeed indicated that due regard could also be given to other ornithological studies whenever they are objectively verifiable, in order to revise the adequacy of Member States' designation efforts.[165] However, ultimately, the burden of proof seems to rests with the Member States, who have to demonstrate that the non-designation of an ecologically vulnerable site is justifiable in view of other scientific reports.[166] So far, few Member States have succeeded in doing so, which indicates the limited room for allowing economic arguments to override ecological considerations in the context of designation policies.[167]

Even more so, in its recent jurisprudence the CJEU has underlined the flexible and dynamic nature of the selection duties by pointing out that the Member States are required to re-evaluate their designation policies with a view to continuing to monitor results and scientific studies.[168] To be more precise, in its prominent decision in the 2006 *Commission v Austria* case, the CJEU held that '[t]he obligation to classify is not limited by the state of scientific knowledge at any given time'.[169]

Whereas the number of national lawsuits in which authorities are sanctioned for their failure to designate ecologically interesting areas as Natura 2000 sites remains limited, some interesting cases are worth mentioning. For instance, in Belgium, the Council of State held that regional authorities had overstepped the legal designation incumbent upon them by their refusal to propose as a Site of Community Importance a site with a priority natural habitat type threatened by the extension of a landfill.[170] Taking stock of the novel insight regarding the devastating effects of a warming climate, it becomes clear that even sites with relevant restoration potential for future corridors might have to be included in the Natura 2000 Network, as was also highlighted in the CJEU's 2017 ruling in

[163] Case C-3/96 *Commission v the Netherlands* (1998) ECLI:EU:C:1998:238, paras 68–70; Case C-235/04 *Commission v Spain* (2007) ECLI:EU:C:2007:386, paras 23–24. See more extensively: Hendrik Schoukens and Hans Woldendorp, 'Site Selection and Designation under the Habitats and Birds Directive: A Sisyphean Task' in Born (n 157) 37.
[164] Case C-418/04 *Commission v Ireland* (2007) ECLI:EU:C:2007:780, para 52.
[165] ibid paras 53–54.
[166] Schoukens and Woldendorp (n 163) 38.
[167] eg Case C-418/04 *Commission v Ireland* (2007) ECLI:EU:C:2007:780.
[168] Schoukens and Woldendorp (n 163) 51.
[169] Case C-209/04 *Commission v Austria* (2006) ECLI:EU:C:2006:195, para 43.
[170] See Belgian Council of State, No. 94.527 (2001).

the *Leenheerpolder* case.[171] Even sites with limited actual natural values might turn out to be crucial for the survival of threatened species in a world that is getting warmer by the day.

4.2 Precautionary Approaches Ease the Evidentiary Thresholds for Litigation

The lack of scientific consensus on the potential ecological impacts of contested works or activities often presents prominent hurdles to be overcome in the context of biodiversity litigation. In this context, the aforementioned precautionary principle, which is mentioned in Article 191(2) TFEU, is gaining increased relevance in biodiversity-related lawsuits,[172] especially when they concern EU-protected natural habitats and species.[173] A specific reference can be made to the strict interpretation by the CJEU of Article 6(3) of the Habitats Directive, regarding the evaluation of potentially harmful plans and projects in relation to the Natura 2000 Network.[174] When reasonable scientific doubt remains as to the absence of such effects, no authorization can be given for a potentially harmful activity pursuant to the well-known *Waddenzee* rationale, except under the strict conditions of the derogation clause of Article 6(4). In doing so, the burden of proof is gradually shifted to the proponent of a purported plan or activity, thereby relieving potential guardians of nature from the insurmountable task of providing conclusive evidence as regards the adverse effects of certain activities.

Interestingly, the CJEU also used the precautionary principle as a high-water mark when reinterpreting the scope of protection duties—for example, the definition of 'resting places' of protected species[175]—as well as the room for granting derogations under Article 16(1) of the Habitats Directive. As to the latter point, in 2017 the CJEU concluded that wolf management hunting is only legal in the EU when based on scientifically sound evidence as to, amongst other things, the lack of less intrusive means and the risk of putting in jeopardy the remaining populations.[176] Domestic courts are therefore obliged to

[171] Case C-281/16 *Vereniging Hoekschewaards Landschap* (2017) ECLI:EU:C:2017:774, para 33.

[172] The Court of First Instance (actual General Court) held that the precautionary principle is a 'general principle of Community law' (Joined Cases T-74, 76, 83–85, 132, 137 and 141/00 *Artedogan* (2002) ECLI:EU:T:2002:283, para 184).

[173] For a recent overview of the status of this principle in EU law, see Nicolas de Sadeleer, *Environmental Principles* (2nd edn, OUP 2020) esp ch 5.

[174] Case C-127/02 *Waddenzee* (2004) ECLI:EU:C:2004:482, paras 56–59.

[175] Case C-477/19 *Magistrat der Stadt Wien* (2020) ECLI:EU:C:2020:517, paras 34–35 (concerning the European hamster).

[176] Case C-674/17 *Tapiola* (2019) ECLI:EU:C:2019:851, paras 51–54.

meticulously scrutinize the scientific underpinnings of the hunting derogations. A recurring requirement in the context of the preservation duties set out by Article 6(3) of the EU Habitats Directives is the obligation to make sure that appropriate assessments consider 'the best scientific knowledge' in order to enable the competent authorities to conclude with scientific certainty that there will be no adverse effects on the site's integrity.[177]

The practical importance of the precautionary principle for safeguarding the substantive provisions of the EU Nature Directives cannot be understated, especially since it might make or break a biodiversity-related lawsuit. In the aforementioned Białowieża case, one of the strategies of the Polish government to justify its logging activities was to argue that such intrusive actions were needed in order to contain the outbreak of the spruce bark beetle, which was allegedly compromising the forest's future. The Polish government claimed to have science on its side. However, the CJEU was not swayed by this line of argumentation and noted that there was still scientific controversy regarding the most appropriate methods to stop the spread of the spruce bark beetle and thus dismissed the Polish arguments.[178]

Most interestingly, though, the CJEU has also used the precautionary principle to do away with controversial biodiversity offsetting practices which go against the mitigation hierarchy embedded in Article 6(3). In a string of recent court cases, the CJEU refused to consider that project development in which future habitat restoration measures were presented as genuine mitigation measures could be exempted from the appropriate impact assessment required under Article 6(3).[179] One of the main reasons for this strict stance was the finding that the potential positive effects of the future creation of habitats are uncertain and highly difficult to forecast.[180] No borrowing from the future is allowed, seemed to constitute the recurring rationale of the CJEU when interpreting Article 6(3) of the Habitats Directive.

The latter approach yielded practical consequences for project developments. In countries such as Belgium, Ireland, and the Netherlands, it has urged national courts to annul several permits for large-scale infrastructure projects which were justified with reference to uncertain compensation schemes.[181]

[177] Case C-43/10 *Nomarchiaki Aftodioikisi Aitoloakarnanias* (2012) ECLI:EU:C:2012:560, para 115.
[178] Case C-441/17 *Commission v Poland* (2018) ECLI:EU:C:2018:255, para 179.
[179] Case C-164/17 *Grace and Sweetman* (2018) ECLI:EU:C:2018:593, paras 52–56; Cases C-387 and 88/15 *Orleans* (2016) ECLI:EU:C:2016:583, paras 50–56.
[180] Case C-521/12 *Briels* (2014) ECLI:EU:C:2014:330, para 32.
[181] See for an overview: Hendrik Schoukens 'Habitat Restoration Measures as Facilitators for Economic Development within the Context of the EU Habitats Directive: Balancing No Net Loss with the Preventive Approach?' (2017) Journal of Environmental Law 47.

A poignant illustration of the practical importance of this case law of strategic litigation is offered by case law focusing on the excess of nitrogen in Dutch ecosystems. The jurisprudence of the CJEU, which barred authorities from granting permits based upon future emission reductions, led the highest Dutch administrative court to find in 2019 that the Dutch government was breaking EU law by not doing enough to reduce excess nitrogen in vulnerable natural areas (Natura 2000 Network). In the wake of this case law, the Netherlands have been battling a so-called 'nitrogen crisis', which in turn has led to many permit refusals for farm expansion as well as other infrastructure projects affecting the nitrogen deposition levels in nearby EU-protected sites.[182]

4.3 Ecological Integrity as the Ecological Lens to be Used When Litigating Before National Courts?

In addition to a focus on a single species or habitats, effective biodiversity litigation is also to consider the wider picture in times characterized by generic biodiversity losses and unprecedented climate change. The increasing reliance on the concept of ecological integrity (of Natura 2000 sites) in the CJEU's biodiversity case law serves as a useful lever in this regard.[183] In its 2011 landmark decision in the *Sweetman* case, the CJEU concluded that the integrity of a site is adversely affected if the project is liable to prevent the lasting preservation of the constitutive ecological characteristics of a site.[184] Interestingly, the CJEU pointed out that even small-scale interventions could be deemed unacceptable since, when accumulated, they might stand in the way of the much-needed recovery of a Natura 2000 site.[185] This is to be greeted as another progressive jurisprudential strand, especially in view of a so-called 'death by a thousand cuts' scenario where the ecological quality is threatened by an accumulation of small-scale interventions. In the 2019 *Holohan* case, the CJEU also hinted at a more ecosystem-based approach, which entails that even biodiversity that is not explicitly located within the boundaries of EU-protected sites (Natura 2000 Network) enjoys at least some partial protection under EU law.[186]

182 Dutch Council of State (29 May 2019) ECLI:NL:RVS:2019:1764.

183 Ch-H Born, 'Le critère de décision à respecter dans le cadre du régime d'évaluation appropriée des incidences 'Natura 2000' (2017) 4 Amén-Env 262–85.

184 Case C-258/11 *Sweetman* (2013) ECLI:EU:C:2013:220, para 46.

185 ibid.

186 Case C-461/17 *Holohan* (2018) ECLI:EU:C:2018:883, paras 37–40.

When assessing whether or not a planned project puts into jeopardy the ecological integrity of a site, the concept of 'site's conservation objectives' comes to the fore.[187] For now, case law regarding the application of the conservation regime for EU-protected sites demonstrates that the site's conservation objectives are to be treated as binding reference standards,[188] which will be guiding in terms of acceptability of the negative impact of certain projects. Also, when project developments put in jeopardy the achievement of future recovery targets for degraded sites, national courts are required to invalidate permits that authorize further degradation.[189] Interestingly, the CJEU increasingly relies upon conservation biology concepts that are not enshrined in the EU Nature Directives. For instance, in an infringement procedure against France, the CJEU used the concept of species 'population viability' to check the effectiveness of national or regional recovery plans for France's dwindling population of wild hamsters. This strand of jurisprudence provides ample room for future biodiversity litigation focusing on flawed recovery programmes for EU-protected species and habitats before the national courts.[190]

4.4 Hierarchy of Norms: Biodiversity Prevailing over Economic Interests?

It needs little further explanation that the conservation of species and their habitats is prone to significant interference with existing property rights and ongoing industrial or agricultural activities. As a result, biodiversity litigation can be expected to clash more frequently with vested rights attached to existing authorizations or planning decisions in the years to come. The application of general principles of law, such as legal certainty, could hinder national agencies and authorities giving precedence to maintaining ecological integrity over short-term economic interests.

Even so, in its recent rulings, the CJEU seems to have taken a more principled and stricter stance as regards the applicability of nature protection schemes in the face of existing economic rights, which again creates opportunities for more proactive litigation strategies. Most tellingly was the 2016 decision of the CJEU in the *Grüne Liga Sachsen* case, where the CJEU was asked

[187] L Stahl, 'Conservation Objectives' in Born and others (n 157) 56.
[188] Case C-849/19 *Commission v Greece* (2019) ECLI:EU:C:2020:1047.
[189] Case C-127/02 *Waddenzee* (2004) ECLI:EU:C:2004:482, paras 47–54.
[190] Case C-383/09 *Commission v France* (2011) ECLI:EU:C:2011:369, para 24.

to shed light on the legal implications of the continuing adverse effects of an already constructed bridge. In this respect, the CJEU clarified that 'so far as concerns the economic cost of the steps that may be considered in the review of alternatives, including the demolition of the works already completed, ... it must be stated ... that that is not of equal importance to the objective of conserving natural habitats and wild fauna and flora pursued by the Habitats Directive. Therefore, account being taken of the strict interpretation of Article 6(4) of that directive, ... it cannot be accepted that the economic cost of such measures alone may be a determining factor in the choice of alternative solutions under that provision.'[191]

The aforementioned Dutch nitrogen crisis, which pushed the Dutch government to further reduce nitrogen emissions, highlights the potency of the Habitats Directive, if rigorously applied, as an important lever to evolve towards more sustainable farming practices. Most importantly, the CJEU reasoned that Member States cannot use generic conservation actions as a tool for mitigating the nitrogen emissions that are caused by future new project developments.[192] And, as a result, the Dutch government is now required to rethink its industrial farming industry in view of the adverse effects it creates for many degraded EU-protected sites.[193] By restricting the double use of conservation actions as offsets for new degradation, the CJEU makes it easier for environmental NGOs to force authorities to commit to conservation policies that focus on net benefits for endangered biodiversity. This aptly reveals the untapped potential of the EU Habitats Directive in terms of forcing national authorities to rethink existing economic models.

5. Outlook and Perspectives on Biodiversity Litigation in the EU

Having assessed the existing procedural and substantive obstacles as well as the levers for biodiversity litigation in the EU, which significantly overlap with the protection duties under IBL, this subsequent section sketches out the future litigation strategies.

191 Case C-399/14 *Grüne Liga Sachsen eV* (2016) ECLI:EU:C:2016:10, paras 40–46.

192 Case C-293/17 *Coöperatie Mobilisation for the Environment UA* (2018) ECLI:EU:C:2018:882, paras 121–32.

193 See Hendrik Schoukens, 'The Quest for the Holy Grail and the Dutch Integrated Approach to Nitrogen: How to Align Adaptive Management Strategies with the EU Nature Directives?' (2018) Journal for European and Environmental Planning Law 171.

5.1 Linking Biodiversity and Human Rights

As at the time of writing, the majority of the lawsuits launched in the field of biodiversity conservation in the EU are based on national or EU biodiversity legislation. The latter mostly leads to the most frequent successes in the national courts, given that EU law prevails over national law and that national judges, as we have seen, are required to provide effective legal protection in the field of EU environmental law. However, taking account of the emerging science regarding the immediate health benefits tied to biodiversity, future lawsuits might also be partly based upon human rights provisions, either provided for in the EU Charter of Fundamental Rights or reflected in the European Convention on Human Rights (ECHR). For now, the 2005 decision of the European Court of Human Rights (ECHR) in the *Kyrtatos v Greece* case[194] in which the applicants challenged the destruction of a swamp close to their dwellings based upon Article 8 ECHR, is often relied upon as a reminder of the limited potential of human rights in the context of biodiversity-based litigation.

The ECHR ultimately dismissed the suit holding that the applicants had not, according to the Court, 'brought forward any convincing arguments showing that the alleged damage to the birds and other protected species living in the swamp was of such a nature as to directly affect their own rights under Article 8 § 1 of the Convention'. However, the Court nevertheless considered that if the swamp had been 'a forest area in the vicinity of the applicants' house', this might have led to a different outcome. This rather ambivalent excerpt seems to underline the possibility of considering ecosystem services—obvious to anybody in the case of a forest, less in the case of a swamp—as a part of private and family life or 'home' and thus as a possible way to link biodiversity conservation to human rights protection.

Considering the incremental body of science regarding the linkages between biodiversity and public health and, in general, the importance of wetlands and forests as carbon sinks—all important ecosystem services—future human rights-based claims will probably face an even more benevolent reception before international or national courts. Litigation strategies in the field of biodiversity protection can try to replicate the rationale of certain climate change-based lawsuits, such as the notable *Urgenda* case, where the failure to reduce CO_2 emissions was considered to constitute a violation of the right to life (Art 2 ECHR) and the right to privacy and family life (Art 8 ECHR).[195]

[194] ECtHR, *Kyrtatos v Greece*, Application no 41666/98 (2003).
[195] Dutch Supreme Court (2019) ECLI:NL:GHDHA:2018:2591.

5.2 More Strategic Lawsuits Focusing on Systemic Shortcomings?

It is fair to say that, in the past decades, biodiversity litigation in the EU has been mostly characterized by its 'reactive' nature, with an almost exclusive focus on avoiding new harm done by new project developments to biodiversity. However, this piecemeal approach fails to tackle the more systemic failures that arise in the context of biodiversity protection. Against this backdrop, more proactive environmental lawsuits emerge as a tempting alternative pathway. Especially in a context where EU environmental directives lay down an explicit obligation of result, as is the case in the EU Water Framework Directive or the EU Nature Directives, such strategic lawsuits might be worthwhile exploring. The previously analysed rulings of the CJEU in the context of infringement cases have indeed demonstrated that EU judges are willing to scrutinize the substance of national or regional protection programmes in the light of the available science and results on the ground. Such litigation strategies can surely be replicated before the national courts.[196] The specific jurisprudence regarding the Dutch policy on nitrogen reductions underlines the decisive role of the EU Habitats Directive in holding national authorities accountable for their failure to stop the degradation of EU-protected nature. In cases where the EU Habitats Directive is of relevance for the protection of species or habitats, national courts can no longer hide behind the large margin of discretion of national authorities or the *trias politica* argument so as not to adjudicate such cases.

5.3 Restoration-Based Lawsuits as a Novel Court Practice?

During the past decades, the concept of ecological restoration, which underlines the necessity of restoring degraded ecosystems on a large scale back to a better environmental condition, has come increasingly to the forefront of international and EU biodiversity strategies.[197] This begs the question: is it not

[196] See more on this: Schoukens (n 193) 191.

[197] See Target 15 of the 2010 Aichi Biodiversity Targets, aiming at the 'restoration of at least 15 per cent of degraded ecosystems'; European Commission, EU Biodiversity Strategy for 2030, Bringing nature back into our lives, COM/2020/380 final, setting binding targets to restore damaged ecosystems, including the most carbon-rich ones and the improvement of the status or trend of at least 30 per cent of EU-protected habitats and species that are not in a favourable status.

possible to enforce national or regional authorities to implement more restoration actions in the light of the existing legal duties?

Recent research has demonstrated that the existing EU Nature Directives already contain a lot of restoration potential to shift more to restoration-based claims in future litigation strategies.[198] In the past years, some interesting examples of national court proceedings have emerged, in which NGOs focused more on a restoration-based rationale. For instance, in the Netherlands, environmental NGOs have twice succeeded in obtaining court orders compelling national authorities to consider more ambitious recovery programmes for EU-protected species (European hamster,[199] otter[200]) that were at risk of becoming extinct. Also noteworthy is a 2018 ruling of the administrative court of Toulouse, in which France was ordered to step up its recovery actions for the brown bear in the Pyrenees, which serves as a powerful illustration of this new litigation trend. In reaching this conclusion, the court reasoned that the existing efforts were inadequate to reach the so-called 'favourable conservation status'.[201]

5.4 Rights of Nature as a New Paradigm?

In recent years, the emergence of the recognition of the intrinsic rights of nature has come to the forefront in several jurisdictions around the globe.[202] For instance, legislation was passed in New Zealand granting explicit legal personality to rivers and mountains,[203] whereas the Ecuador Constitution explicitly provides clauses 'granting' certain inherent rights to nature, which can be enforced before the national courts. In countries such as Colombia and India, national courts have moved to reassert the intrinsic rights of nature in their decisions.[204] For now, however, this new understanding of the interdependence between man and nature has received little to no attention within the EU legal order. Only at the local (regional) level has it led to the adoption of certain

[198] See more extensively: Hendrik Schoukens, 'Legal Considerations in Operationalizing Eco-Restoration in the European Union' in Afshin Akthar-Khavari and Benjamin J Richardson (eds), *Ecological Restoration Law: Concepts and Case Studies* (Routledge 2019) 167.

[199] Court of 's-Gravenhage (2011) ECLI:NL:RBSGR:2011:BR6099.

[200] Court of The Hague (2013) case no C/09/426350/HA ZA 12-1047.

[201] Administrative Court of Toulouse (2018) case nos 150.1887 and 102320.

[202] See for an overview: Dinah Shelton, 'Nature as a Legal Person' (2015) Vertigo, Hors-Série <https://journals.openedition.org/vertigo/16188> accessed 10 November 2020.

[203] See eg: Te Awua Tupua (Whanganui River Claims Settlement) Act 2017, New Zealand Act No 7, ss 12, 14, and 15.

[204] See eg: Constitutional Court of Colombia, case T-633/16, *Center for Social Justice Studies et al v President of Colombia et al*, Judgment of 10 November 2016.

statutes or ordinances in which the intrinsic rights of ecosystems are recognized. This has happened, amongst others, in one Dutch municipality bordering the Wadden Sea.[205]

So far, however, the EU legal order has not explicitly recognized the rights of nature, which are not explicitly mentioned in the EU Charter of Fundamental Rights. A proposal launched by an environmental NGO to pass an EU directive proclaiming such rights has not yielded any tangible effect so far.[206] Even so, this does not block national courts from holding that, in the light of the existing conservation duties, certain ecosystems or species could be considered as endowed with an intrinsic and enforceable 'right to exist' in a favourable status in Europe, as a result of the justiciability of the corresponding obligations to maintain or restore them in such condition. For instance, in the light of the aforementioned jurisprudence regarding the system of strict species protection, one might envisage litigation strategies aimed at seeking the jurisprudential recognition of the right to exist of endangered species, such as the European hamster or the grey wolf. Some authors posit that strategic litigation focusing on the explicit recognition of the legal rights of protected species might serve as an interesting precursor to developing rights for nature in the EU.[207]

6. Conclusion

On a concluding note, the following three observations can be made when it comes to the potential for biodiversity litigation regarding IBL in the EU legal order.

First, direct references to treaties or soft law instruments in IBL remain relatively rare in the case law of the CJEU, which underlines the limited added value of such legal instruments in a supranational legal order which has implemented most prominent legal duties in more binding legislative instruments, such as the EU Birds and Habitats Directives or the CITES Regulation. At most, the CJEU can be persuaded to use IBL—including soft law—as an interpretation lens when applying EU environmental legislation, in cases where multiple

[205] 'De Waddenzee heeft ook rechten en die horen in de Grondwet te staan' <www.trouw.nl/samenleving/de-waddenzee-heeft-ook-rechten-en-die-horen-in-de-grondwet-te-staan~a874d8b0/> accessed 10 November 2020.

[206] This proposal can be consulted at <www.citizensforeurope.eu/organisation/rights-of-nature-europe> accessed 10 November 2020.

[207] Yaffa Epstein and Hendrik Schoukens, 'A Positivist Approach to Rights of Nature in the European Union' (2021) Journal for Human Rights and the Environment 205.

interpretations exist. The vague wording of most instruments of IBL hinder a more widespread use in future lawsuits, and the same has so far applied to the lack of direct access for NGOs to the CJEU when challenging the legality of EU decisions.

Even so, this grim finding is partly mitigated by the fact that most of the general protection duties included in IBL are explicitly implemented in EU environmental directives. Seminal legal instruments, such as the EU Birds and Habitats Directives, largely cover most of the obligations set out in the biodiversity treaties[208] and, in most instances, expand them to other ecosystems. The supranational nature of the EU legal order, with a prominent role for effective legal protection before national courts and the CJEU (through infringement proceedings), probably serves as one of the most effective compliance mechanisms in the field of IBL. This is further attested to by the wide variety of lawsuits, focusing on the designation of protected sites, species, and recovery, that have popped up during the past decades.

Finally, most biodiversity-related lawsuits still prominently focus on specific cases of destruction of nature, leaving the more systemic challenges to conservation often unaddressed. This chapter argues that more integral litigation strategies, based upon human rights or even the intrinsic rights of ecosystems, are expected to emerge in future jurisprudence. Both the CJEU and the national courts are expected to play an ever more prominent role in enforcing IBL in the EU legal order.

[208] In some cases, however, a biodiversity treaty can contain stricter provisions than the EU legislation. Eg Art 6(b) of the Bern Convention provides protection to the breeding and resting sites of Annex II birds species, while this is not the case in the Birds Directive (Art 5). In these rare cases, invoking the direct effect of the aforesaid treaty in litigation could be fruitful.

12

International Biodiversity Litigation

The Increasing Emphasis on Biodiversity Law Before International Courts and Tribunals

Sandrine Maljean-Dubois and Elisa Morgera

1. Introduction

This chapter is devoted to biodiversity litigation before international courts and tribunals. It will start by reflecting on the idiosyncrasies in this area of international law and defining the scope of the study (Section 2). Section 3 will assess the level of influence of international biodiversity law on international courts and tribunals, with a view to analysing the contribution of international litigation to the effectiveness of international biodiversity law. Section 4 will synthetize our key findings. Section 5 will conclude by identifying possible ways forward.

2. The Idiosyncrasies of the International Context and Scope of the Chapter

In matters relating to the environment, and in particular to biodiversity, states have long shown reluctance towards engaging with international dispute-resolution mechanisms. This trend is even more marked in this field, because the obligations, even those defined in treaties, are often vague, many elements of the environment are perceived as having no market value or a low market value, and also because of the specific nature of environmental damage, which can discourage the initiation of such proceedings.[1] Regarding states' own responsibility, it is worth recalling that the 1996 proposals of the International

[1] Sandrine Maljean-Dubois and Lavanya Rajamani, 'The Present State of Research Carried out by the English-Speaking and the French-Speaking Sections—Report of the Directors of Studies' in Sandrine Maljean-Dubois and Lavanya Rajamani (eds), *Implementation of International Environmental Law* (Martinus Nijhoff 2011) 3.

Sandrine Maljean-Dubois and Elisa Morgera, *International Biodiversity Litigation* In: *Biodiversity Litigation*. Edited by: Guillaume Futhazar, Sandrine Maljean-Dubois, and Jona Razzaque, Oxford University Press.
 DOI: 10.1093/oso/9780192865465.003.0012

Law Commission (ILC) for making states strictly liable for significant transboundary harm proved to be too progressive and that the codification process remains, to this day, partial.[2] Hence, apart from a few cases in which liability can arise from damage,[3] the international responsibility of a state may only be incurred on the basis of an internationally wrongful act (a breach of treaty or customary international law that may be committed through an act or omission). Indeed, states have sought to avoid litigation by laying down rules channelling liability to operators under their jurisdiction (mainly private corporations).[4] This was one of the objectives during the negotiations of the Kuala Lumpur–Nagoya Supplementary Protocol to the Cartagena Protocol to the Convention on Biological Diversity.[5] But the result is rather disappointing from this point of view. The Protocol only addresses responsibility incurred through the transboundary movement of living modified organisms between the forty-nine states that are parties to the Protocol.[6] States have also opted for the implementation of compliance procedures, which can help to resolve disputes, but in a non-adversarial way. Several mechanisms of this kind have been set up by the Conferences of the Parties (COPs) of biodiversity-related conventions with a view to promoting implementation and responding to the underlying causes of delays or non-compliance with international obligations.[7]

[2] Title and texts of the preamble and the draft principles on the allocation of loss arising out of hazardous activities adopted by the Drafting Committee on second reading, 2006, 1. See UN General Assembly Resolution 61/36 (4 December 2006), Allocation of loss in the case of transboundary harm arising out of hazardous activities, commenting on the Principles to the attention of governments.

[3] eg the Convention on International Liability for Damage Caused by Space Objects (open for signature 29 March 1972, entered into force 1 September 1972) 961 UNTS 187.

[4] Convention on Civil Liability for Damage Resulting from Activities Dangerous to the Environment [1993] 32 ILM 1228 (not yet entered into force).

[5] Nagoya–Kuala Lumpur Supplementary Protocol on Liability and Redress to the Cartagena Protocol on Biosafety (opened for signature 15 October 2010, entered into force 5 March 2018) UNTS A-30619.

[6] Sandrine Maljean-Dubois, *Le droit international de la biodiversité* (Brill 2021) 404; Dire Tladi, 'Civil Liability in the Context of the Cartagena Protocol: To Be or Not to Be (Binding)?' (2010) 10 International Environmental Agreements 15.

[7] See eg under the Convention on International Trade in Endangered Species of Wild Fauna and Flora (Resolution Conf 14.3 (Rev CoP18) CITES compliance procedures); the Ramsar Convention on Wetlands of International Importance (Recommendation 4.7: Mechanisms for improved application of the Ramsar Convention; Resolution XIII.11 Ramsar Advisory Missions); the Protocol on Biosafety to the Convention on Biological Diversity (MOP 1 Decision BS-I/7 Establishment of procedures and mechanisms on compliance under the Cartagena Protocol on Biosafety); the Nagoya Protocol on Access to Genetic Resources and the Fair and Equitable Sharing of Benefits Arising from their Utilization to the Convention on Biological Diversity (NP MOP 1 Decision NP-1/4 Cooperative procedures and institutional mechanisms to promote compliance with the Nagoya Protocol and to address cases of non-compliance); the International Treaty on Plant Genetic Resources for Food and Agriculture (Governing body, Resolution 2/2011 Procedures and operational mechanisms to promote compliance and address issues of non-compliance); the Bern Convention on the conservation of European wildlife and natural habitats (28th meeting of the Standing Committee, Strasbourg, 24–27 November 2008, Application of the Convention, Summary of Case files and complaints, Reminder on the processing of complaints and new on-line form, T-PVS(2008)7); the Alpine Convention (COP decision VII/4 Mécanisme de vérification du respect de la Convention alpine et de ses protocoles d'application); the Barcelona

Compliance procedures tend to marginalize traditional dispute-resolution mechanisms, but they do not exclude them, at least in theory.[8]

However, as a result of the growth of international environmental law and the growing awareness of the threats to biodiversity, international case law addressing biodiversity issues has progressively emerged before the International Court of Justice (ICJ), the International Tribunal for the Law of the Sea (ITLOS), the Dispute Settlement Body of the World Trade Organization (WTO DSB), as well as before arbitral tribunals.[9] There are also relevant international disputes in the fields of human rights and investment protection.

Against this background, this chapter deals with a number of judicial bodies, both international and regional, permanent or ad hoc, new and old, with general or specialized jurisdiction, with different judicial authority. Thus, the contexts of claims and the remits to adjudicate disputes are different. However, even if sometimes the data set is too small to draw any final conclusion, we believe that a comparative analysis of this set of cases and decisions sheds light on the relevance of international biodiversity law in international adjudication, including with reference to the complexity and fragmentation of this field of international law.[10] A better understanding of international case law concerning biodiversity could guide domestic courts in their interpretation of international biodiversity law. Even if, in principle, international judgments only have the relative authority of *res judicata*,[11] in practice they have a particular weight. This is especially the case of universal courts, like the ICJ or the ITLOS, but also to some extent of arbitral tribunals. As the ICJ has said, a court 'states the existing law and does not legislate. This is so even if, in stating and applying the law, the Court necessarily has to specify its scope and sometimes note its general trend.'[12] The Court has thus recognized that it has a certain margin of appreciation to participate in the development of international law.

Convention for the Protection of the Marine Environment and the Coastal region of the Mediterranean (COP Decision IG 17/2: Procedures and mechanisms on compliance under the Barcelona Convention and its Protocols).

[8] Martti Koskenniemi, 'Breach of Treaty or Non-Compliance? Reflections on the Enforcement of the Montreal Protocol' (1992) 3 Yearbook of International Environmental Law 1, 129.

[9] For an earlier assessment, see Braulio Ferreira de Souza Dias and Kathryn Garforth, 'Historical Perspectives on the Challenge of Biodiversity Conservation' in Elisa Morgera and Jona Razzaque (eds), *Elgar Encyclopedia of Environmental Law: Biodiversity and Nature Protection* (Edward Elgar 2017) 13–30.

[10] See Chapter 1 in this volume.

[11] See eg Art 59 of the Statute of the International Court of Justice (1945).

[12] *Legality of the Threat or Use of Nuclear Weapons*, Advisory Opinion [1996] ICJ Rep 226, para 18.

For the purposes of this chapter, due to the still low number of international cases addressing biodiversity, we have reviewed the interstate case law and have been able to include all the cases dealing with biodiversity conservation or sustainable use. We have also included in the scope of our study the decisions from regional (African, inter-American, and European) human rights courts and international investment arbitrations that address matters relating to biodiversity conservation or sustainable use.

3. Analysis of International Case Law

Our comparative study of international case law shows that: (1) international biodiversity law has been increasingly invoked before international courts and tribunals; and that (2) courts and tribunals' decisions demonstrate a gradual opening-up to science and uncertainty related to biodiversity conservation and sustainable use. However, despite this openness and the fact that the sources on which decisions are based are various (treaties, customary rules, decisions of COPs, and other secondary law of international organizations), (3) the observable influence of international biodiversity law is still quite limited, even if (4) the possible forms of reparation for harm to biodiversity could permit different litigation strategies at the international level.

3.1 An Increasing Reference to International Biodiversity Law Before International Courts and Tribunals

In the last twenty years, biodiversity issues have been at the heart of various international disputes, and international biodiversity law has been increasingly invoked, whether in terms of treaty obligations or soft law instruments. Two exceptions, however, should be mentioned at the outset. In two cases before ITLOS, one could have expected references to international biodiversity law, but that was not the case. In the *Land Reclamation in and around the Straits of Johor*,[13] there was surprisingly no mention of biodiversity, fauna, flora, or ecosystems, even if the 'significant effects' of the works on the marine environment mentioned were excessive sedimentation, seabed-level changes, and coastal erosion. In the same way, in the *MOX Plant* case, the ITLOS's

[13] *Land Reclamation in and around the Straits of Johor (Malaysia v Singapore)*, Provisional Measures, Order of 8 October 2003 [2003] ITLOS Rep 10.

order on provisional measures only referred to the protection of the marine environment in general, without mentioning biodiversity, fauna, flora, or ecosystems.[14]

3.1.1 Reference to international biodiversity conventions

In conjunction with customary due diligence obligations, international biodiversity treaty law has been increasingly invoked before several international courts and tribunals. For instance, in the *Gabčíkovo-Nagymaros Project* case,[15] before the ICJ, Hungary claimed in its written proceedings a breach of the Convention on Biological Diversity (CBD, Preamble, arts 3, 5, 14, and 22), but also mentioned the Convention on International Trade in Endangered Species of Wild Fauna and Flora (CITES), the Kuwait Regional Convention for Co-operation on the Protection of the Marine Environment from Pollution (1978), the ASEAN Agreement on the Conservation of Nature and Natural Resources (1985), the African Convention on the Conservation of Nature and Natural Resources (1968), and even the UNESCO World Heritage Convention (1972).[16] For its part, Slovakia alleged that Hungary had infringed article 8 of the CBD on conservation in situ.[17] In the *Aerial Herbicide Spraying (Ecuador v Colombia)* case, Ecuador's memorial referred to the CBD (Preamble, art 14) and its Cartagena Protocol, among others.[18] In the *Pulp Mills* case, Argentina alleged breaches of CITES, the Ramsar Convention, and the CBD.[19] In the *Road* case, also before the ICJ, Nicaragua and Costa Rica made cross-allegations of breaches of several biodiversity conventions to which both states were parties: in addition to the CBD (arts 3, 8, 14), also the Ramsar Convention, the 1992 Convention for the Conservation of the Biodiversity and Protection of Priority Wilderness Areas in Central America, the Central American Convention for the Protection of the Environment, the Tegucigalpa Protocol to the Charter of the Organization of Central American States, and the 1990 Agreement over the Border Protected Areas between Nicaragua and Costa Rica (International System of Protected Areas

[14] MOX Plant *(Ireland v United Kingdom)*, Provisional Measures, Order of 3 December 2001 [2001] ITLOS Rep 95.

[15] *Gabčíkovo-Nagymaros Project (Hungary/Slovakia)*, Judgment [1997] ICJ Rep 7.

[16] Memorial of the Republic of Hungary, 2 May 1995 <www.icj-cij.org/en/case/92/written-proceedings> accessed 12 March 2022.

[17] Reply submitted by the Slovak Republic, 20 June 1995 <www.icj-cij.org/en/case/92/written-proceedings> accessed 12 March 2022.

[18] Memorial of Ecuador, 28 April 2009, footnote, 276, see also 283; Reply of Ecuador, 31 January 2011, 20 <www.icj-cij.org/en/case/138/written-proceedings> accessed 12 March 2022.

[19] *Pulp Mills on the River Uruguay (Argentina v Uruguay)*, Judgment [2010] ICJ Rep 14, paras 56, 191.

for Peace [SI-A-PAZ] Agreement).[20] Finally, the *Whaling* case before the ICJ was focused on the interpretation and implementation of the International Convention for the Regulation of Whaling 1946,[21] with parties extensively referring to international biodiversity conventions in their written proceedings (1995 UN Fish Stocks Agreement, CBD, CITES, Convention on the conservation of Antarctic marine living resources, etc).[22]

Regarding interstate arbitration, it is worth mentioning the *South China Sea* arbitration,[23] in which the Philippines alleged breaches of several international treaties by China; namely, the 1982 United Nations Convention on the Law of the Sea, the CBD, the Ramsar Convention, and CITES.[24] The tribunal recalled that China itself had officially stated that, as a state party to the CBD and to CITES, it 'will strictly observe provisions of the conventions and honour her obligations in good faith'.[25]

Before WTO DSB, the CBD and the Convention on Migratory Species (CMS) were invoked, as well as the Protocol concerning Specially Protected Areas and Wildlife to the Convention for the Protection and Development of the Marine Environment of the Wider Caribbean Region in the *Shrimps Turtles* case.[26] The CBD and its Cartagena Protocol on Biosafety were invoked in the *Biotech* case.[27] A combination of conventions on the protection of animals was mentioned in the *Seals* case.[28]

Before the ITLOS, several conventions on marine biological resources have been invoked in addition to the Montego Bay Convention, like the UN Fish Stocks Agreement and the Convention on the determination of the minimal conditions for access and exploitation of marine resources within the maritime

[20] *Certain Activities Carried Out by Nicaragua in the Border Area (Costa Rica v Nicaragua) and Construction of a Road in Costa Rica along the San Juan River (Nicaragua v Costa Rica)*, Judgment [2015] ICJ Rep 665.

[21] *Whaling in the Antarctic (Australia v Japan: New Zealand intervening)*, Judgment [2014] ICJ Rep 226.

[22] See Australia's memorial, paras 4.84 ff, Japan's counter-memorial, paras 6.18 ff <www.icj-cij.org/en/case/148/written-proceedings> accessed 12 March 2022.

[23] Arbitral tribunal constituted under annex VII to the 1982 United Nations Convention on the Law of the Sea between the Republic of the Philippines and the People's Republic of China, Award, 12 July 2016, Permanent Court of Arbitration, para 3.10 <https://docs.pca-cpa.org/2016/07/PH-CN-20160712-Award.pdf> accessed 12 March 2022.

[24] ibid para 828.

[25] ibid para 915.

[26] WTO, *United States—Import Prohibition of Certain Shrimp and Shrimp Products*, AB-1998-4, Report of the Appellate Body [1998] WT/DS58/AB/R.

[27] WTO, *European Communities—Measures Affecting the Approval and Marketing of Biotech Products*, Reports of the Panel [2006] WT/DS291/R WT/DS292/R WT/DS293/R.

[28] European Convention for the protection of animals during transport, Paris [1968] ETS No 65; European Convention for the protection of animals kept for farming purposes, Strasbourg [1976] ETS No 87; European Convention for the protection of animals for slaughter, Strasbourg [1979] ETS No 102; European Convention for the protection of vertebrate animals used for experimental and other scientific purposes, Strasbourg [1986] ETS No 123; European Convention for the protection of pet animals, Strasbourg [1986] ETS No 125.

areas under the jurisdiction of the Member States of the Sub-Regional Fisheries Commission.[29]

Furthermore, international biodiversity law has been addressed before international investment tribunals. In the international investment arbitration *David Aven v Costa Rica*, the Tribunal found that Costa Rica's actions to protect wetlands in an investment area in line with the Ramsar Convention and the CBD were neither arbitrary nor in breach of the investment agreement and obligations to ensure fair and equitable treatment, as environmental damage had been caused by the investor and the host state had acted in accordance with domestic laws and international law.[30] In another investor–state arbitration, an international investor running a nature sanctuary in Barbados lodged a complaint against the government of Barbados for failing to implement its international obligations under the Ramsar Convention and the CBD, which had negatively affected the value of the investment in the sanctuary.[31]

In addition, in its Advisory Opinion on the human right to a healthy environment, the Inter-American Court of Human Rights relied on the CBD to confirm the existence of a treaty obligation to prevent environmental damage and to subject this obligation to a certain degree of severity of the harm that could be caused, by reference to CBD language on 'significant adverse effects on biodiversity',[32] as well as to reaffirm the precautionary principle.[33]

3.1.2 Reference to soft law instruments

In addition to hard law obligations, soft law instruments, or legal tools which normativity is uncertain or contested (such as COP 'decisions'), have also been invoked several times. For instance, in the *Seals* case before the WTO DSB, the European Union and the Panel relied on some recommendations of the Office International des Epizooties, in particular its Guiding Principles for Animal Welfare.[34] Before the ICJ, the *Whaling* case is exemplary of the importance attributed to international soft law, such as the resolutions adopted by the International Commission on the Regulation of Whaling, the importance

[29] Request for Advisory Opinion submitted by the Sub-Regional Fisheries Commission, Advisory Opinion, 2 April 2015 [2015] ITLOS Rep 4.

[30] *David Aven et al v Republic of Costa Rica*, ICSID Case No UNCT/15/3 (Award) (18 September 2018) paras 423, 708 <www.italaw.com/sites/default/files/case-documents/italaw9955_0.pdf> accessed 12 March 2022.

[31] *Peter Allard v Barbados*, PCA Case No 2012-06, Final Award (27 June 2016) para 178 <www.italaw.com/sites/default/files/case-documents/italaw7594.pdf≥ accessed 12 March 2022.

[32] Inter-American Court, Advisory Opinion Oc-23/17 of 15 November 2017, Requested by the Republic of Colombia: *The Environment and Human Rights*, para 134.

[33] ibid para 176.

[34] WTO, *European Communities—Measures Prohibiting the Importation and Marketing of Seal Products*, Reports of the Panel (2013) WT/DS400/R, WT/DS401/R, 25 November 7.408.

of which was extensively discussed by the parties.[35] Even if they are not formally binding, the ICJ has explicitly accepted taking them into consideration in interpreting the 1946 Convention. It considered that:

> Article VI of the Convention states that '[t]he Commission may from time to time make recommendations to any or all Contracting Governments on any matters which relate to whales or whaling and to the objectives and purposes of this Convention'. These recommendations, which take the form of resolutions, are not binding. However, when they are adopted by consensus or by a unanimous vote, they may be relevant for the interpretation of the Convention or its Schedule.[36]

Japan also referred to CBD COP decisions, and in particular the Addis Ababa Principles and Guidelines for the Sustainable Use of Biodiversity (2004) as well as the Plan of Implementation of the World Summit on Sustainable Development,[37] but the Court did not refer to any of them, nor to the CBD.

The Inter-American Court of Human Rights has increasingly engaged with the CBD and its COP decisions to support a mutually supportive interpretation of the international human rights of indigenous peoples and international biodiversity law, notably with regard to three safeguards for the indigenous peoples' rights to land and natural resources (impact assessment, consent, and benefit sharing).[38] This started with the seminal *Saramaka* case,[39] where the Inter-American Court could only rely on a very limited legal basis in international human rights law[40] and therefore relied on the CBD Akwé: Kon Guidelines on socio-cultural and environmental impact assessments.[41] Similar is the case of benefit-sharing guidance included in CBD decisions on protected

[35] ICJ, *Whaling* (n 21).
[36] ibid para 46.
[37] Japan's Counter-Memorial, paras 6.18 ff (n 22).
[38] IACtHR, *The Environment and Human Rights* (n 32) para 44. For a discussion, see Elisa Morgera, 'Under the Radar: Fair and Equitable Benefit-Sharing and the Human Rights of Indigenous Peoples and Local Communities Connected to Natural Resources' (2019) 23 International Journal of Human Rights 1098–139.
[39] IACtHR, *Case of the Saramaka People v Suriname*, Judgment (Interpretation of the Judgment on Preliminary Objections, Merits, Reparations and Costs), 12 August 2008, para 41. See more recently, *The Indigenous Communities of The Lhaka Honhat (Our Land) Association v Argentina*, Judgment of 6 February 2020 (Merits, reparations and costs) paras 248–51, fns 248 and 251.
[40] IACtHR, *Saramaka* (n 39) para 130 and fn 128, para 138 and fn 137.
[41] Akwé: Kon Voluntary Guidelines for the Conduct of Cultural, Environmental and Social Impact Assessment regarding Developments Proposed to Take Place on, or which are Likely to Impact on, Sacred Sites and on Lands and Waters Traditionally Occupied or Used by Indigenous and Local Communities (CBD Decision VII/16C (2004), Annex) paras 46, 56.

areas,[42] which have been identified as relevant by human rights bodies, such as the Committee on the Elimination of Racial Discrimination,[43] to prevent negative impacts from conservation activities on indigenous and tribal peoples' territories. In the 2015 *Kaliña and Lokono* decision, the Inter-American Court was particularly explicit about the need for, and merits of, mutual supportiveness with CBD COP decisions such as the Addis Ababa Principles and Guidelines for the Sustainable Use of Biodiversity and the CBD work programme on protected areas.[44]

3.2 An Increasing Openness to Science and Uncertainty

With biodiversity issues, international courts inevitably have to weigh and adjudicate upon complex scientific and technical issues and to 'focus on the best legal tools to tackle' them,[45] which is quite challenging. Our analysis shows the extent to which international case law has evolved in the last twenty years in this respect.

In its first explicit environmental case, the *Danube dam* case in 1997, the ICJ appeared quite reluctant to enter into scientific considerations. It did not use the term biodiversity, whereas Hungary had extensively referred to it in its written proceedings.[46] The Court kept referring instead to 'natural resources', 'environment', 'natural environment', 'natural processes', or 'nature', in line with the terms of the bilateral treaty concluded by the two states in 1977. In contrast, in the 2015 *Pulp Mills* judgment, the word *biodiversity* is mentioned twelve times.[47]

In its 1997 judgment, the Court did not mention either the precautionary principle, on which the parties were disagreeing. It admitted the possibility of a 'grave peril' for the environment in the long term but, relying on a report from the Hungarian Academy of Sciences, it noted that 'because of the complexity of the ecological processes and lack of the measured data and the

[42] Work programme on protected areas (CBD Decision VII/28 (2004), Annex) [2(1), 2(1)(4)] (while the latter refers to both benefit and cost sharing, the focus on benefit sharing is clarified in CBD Decision IX/18 (2008), preamble para 5).

[43] CERD, Concluding observations on the combined thirteenth to fifteenth periodic reports of Suriname (2015) UN Doc CERD/C/SUR/CO/13-15, para 26.

[44] IACtHR, *Kaliña and Lokono Peoples v Suriname*, Judgment (Merits, Reparations and Costs), 25 November 2015, paras 173–74, 177–78, 181, and 214, fn 247.

[45] Makane Moïse Mbengue and Rukmini Das, 'The ICJ's Engagement with Science: To Interpret or not to Interpret?' (2015) 6(3) Journal of International Dispute Settlement 568.

[46] See eg Hungary's Memorial, 2 May 1994, vol 1, 153, 161–63, 201, 205, 221, 292, 224, 293, 364, 366 <www.icj-cij.org/en/case/92/written-proceedings> accessed 12 March 2022.

[47] ICJ, *Pulp Mills on the River Uruguay* (n 19).

relevant calculations the environmental impacts cannot be evaluated'.[48] Then 'the dangers ascribed to the upstream reservoir were mostly of a long-term nature and, above all, that they remained uncertain'.[49] From this point of view, its conception of risk appeared to be quite outdated, practically leaving no room for uncertainty.[50] Furthermore, when it came to the appreciation of the ecological consequences of the project, it considered the completely opposing views of the parties, and noted that 'both Parties have placed on record an impressive amount of scientific material aimed at reinforcing their respective arguments'.[51] However, the Court found a way not to rule on this point: it stated that, 'The Court has given most careful attention to this material' but 'concludes, however, that … it is not necessary … for it to determine which of those points of view is scientifically better founded.'[52]

On the contrary, in the *Pulp Mills* case, the Court did not hesitate to go into very technical considerations, for instance on the relationship between the discharges from the Orion mill and the malformations of rotifers, or the dioxin found in the sábalo fish or the loss of fat by clams reported in the findings of the Argentine River Uruguay Environmental Surveillance programme.[53]

In the *Whales* case, the ICJ remained cautious, noting for instance that:

> in applying the above standard of review, it is not called upon to resolve matters of scientific or whaling policy. The Court is aware that members of the international community hold divergent views about the appropriate policy towards whales and whaling, but it is not for the Court to settle these differences.[54]

But, in fact, it did consider advanced scientific and technical considerations, for instance to assess if the sample size for statistical examination was reasonable, or if the use of lethal methods responds to a strict scientific necessity.[55] Aware of the fact that it had 'to avoid two main hurdles: limiting its assessment to legal aspects or becoming a judge of science by itself performing the

[48] ICJ, *Gabčíkovo-Nagymaros* (n 15) para 56.
[49] ibid para 55.
[50] Pierre-Marie Dupuy, Verbatim Record 97/6, 69 <www.icj-cij.org/en/case/92/oral-proceedings> accessed 12 March 2022.
[51] ICJ, *Gabčíkovo-Nagymaros* (n 15) para 54.
[52] ibid.
[53] ICJ, *Pulp Mills on the River Uruguay* (n 19) para 262.
[54] ICJ, *Whaling* (n 21) para 69.
[55] ibid paras 172 and 211.

technical analyses', the Court initiated an original approach, adopting a proactive attitude during the cross-examination of experts and explicitly articulating a 'standard of review characterized as "objective" and involving the use of a reasonableness test'.[56] Nonetheless, it has been argued that the Court's method of establishing facts and handling technical and scientific matters could be 'improved, whether through strategic use of existing rules, amendments to those rules or a deeper engagement with fact-finding at the deliberation phase'.[57]

Regarding biotech products and biosafety, the WTO DSB has proven to be unwilling to apply the precautionary principle as an international customary rule, considering that 'since the legal status of the precautionary principle remains unsettled, like the Appellate Body before us, we consider that prudence suggests that we not attempt to resolve this complex issue, particularly if it is not necessary to do so'.[58]

On the contrary, the ITLOS has shown itself to be a pioneer in acknowledging the status of the precautionary principle.[59] The Tribunal's Rules contain provisions to enable the Tribunal to play a proactive role in dealing with expert evidence.[60] In effect, ITLOS did not hesitate to refer to 'best scientific evidence', 'precautionary approach', or even to 'the maximum sustainable yield, as qualified by relevant environmental and economic factors, including the economic needs of coastal fishing communities and the special needs of the SRFC Member States, taking into account fishing patterns, the interdependence of stocks and any generally recommended minimum international standards, whether subregional, regional or global'.[61] Indeed, the ITLOS is developing into a 'transparent, consistent and speedy forum' to adjudicate marine wildlife disputes arising from the United Nations Convention on the Law of the Seas (UNCLOS).[62]

[56] Guillaume Gros, 'The ICJ's Handling of Science in the Whaling in the Antarctic Case: A Whale of a Case?' (2015) 6(3) Journal of International Dispute Settlement 578.

[57] Loretta Malintoppi, 'Fact Finding and Evidence Before the International Court of Justice (Notably in Scientific-Related Disputes)' (2016) 7(2) Journal of International Dispute Settlement 421.

[58] WTO, *Biotech* (n 27) para 7.89.

[59] See in particular *Southern Bluefin Tuna (New Zealand v Japan; Australia v Japan)*, Provisional Measures, Order of 27 August 1999 [1999] ITLOS Rep 280, para 79.

[60] Philippe Gautier, 'Experts before ITLOS: An Overview of the Tribunal's Practice' (2018) 9(3) Journal of International Dispute Settlement 433.

[61] Request for Advisory Opinion submitted by the Sub-Regional Fisheries Commission, Advisory Opinion, 2 April 2015 [2015] ITLOS Rep 4; see also Separate Opinion of Judge Paik, referring to the ecosystem-based approach, 118.

[62] Howard Schiffman, 'UNCLOS and Marine Wildlife Disputes: Big Splash or Barely a Ripple?' (2001) 4 Journal of International Wildlife Law and Policy 257.

3.3 The Limited Influence of International Biodiversity Law on Courts' Decisions

In international litigation, international biodiversity law has not been relied on directly, but rather it has been used to interpret other rules and obligations. Hence, it has exercised an increasing, indirect yet significant influence on courts' decisions.

3.3.1 A limited direct influence

International case law shows no direct influence of international biodiversity law. There are two main reasons for this finding. In some cases, international biodiversity obligations have been considered too vague. In others, they have been set aside as not applicable. In either case, it may not necessarily be due to judges' reluctance, but it may be ascribed to the limitations of international biodiversity law (too vague) or of international law (fragmented). Because of the small data set, it is certainly difficult to draw a definite conclusion. This trend could be reversed in the future, in particular if arguments could be developed about interpretations that narrow the scope and clarify the content of international open-ended obligations (as discussed in the final section).

3.3.1.1 International biodiversity obligations as too vague

The best example is probably given by the *Road* case, in which the ICJ dismissed several allegations of breaches of international biodiversity-related conventions that it considered were too general in their wording. This was the case with the Article 5 of the Ramsar Convention which provides that:

> The Contracting Parties shall consult with each other about implementing obligations arising from the Convention especially in the case of a wetland extending over the territories of more than one Contracting Party or where a water system is shared by Contracting Parties. They shall at the same time endeavour to co-ordinate and support present and future policies and regulations concerning the conservation of wetlands and their flora and fauna.[63]

According to the Court, 'While this provision contains a general obligation to consult 'about implementing obligations arising from the Convention', it does not create an obligation on Nicaragua to consult with Costa Rica concerning a particular project that it is undertaking, in this case the dredging of the Lower

[63] ICJ, *Certain Activities Carried and Construction of a Road* (n 20) para 110.

San Juan River. In the light of the above, Nicaragua was not required under the Ramsar Convention to notify, or consult with, Costa Rica prior to commencing its dredging project.[64]

In the same direction, 'As to the Convention for the Conservation of the Biodiversity and Protection of Priority Wilderness Areas in Central America, the Court sees no need to take its enquiry further, as neither of the two provisions invoked by Costa Rica contains a binding obligation to notify or consult.'[65]

Nicaragua also claimed that Costa Rica was required to carry out an environmental impact assessment under article 14 of the CBD. Here the Court recalled the content of this provision: 'Each Contracting Party, as far as possible and as appropriate, shall: (a) Introduce appropriate procedures requiring environmental impact assessment of its proposed projects that are likely to have significant adverse effects on biological diversity with a view to avoiding or minimizing such effects and, where appropriate, allow for public participation in such procedures.'[66] Then the Court, without any further explanation, 'consider[ed] that the provision at issue *does not create an obligation* to carry out an environmental impact assessment before undertaking an activity that may have significant adverse effects on biological diversity. Therefore, the Court did not establish that Costa Rica breached CBD Article 14 by failing to conduct an environmental impact assessment for its road project.'[67] Admittedly, the obligation contained in article 14 of the CBD ('shall') is qualified by the expression 'as far as possible and as appropriate'. But it has been argued that these qualifications, which are quite common to other international biodiversity-related conventions,[68] should not be interpreted as putting into question the existence of an international obligation, but only as opening up the margin of discretion for different parties to choose different ways to implement the obligation.[69]

[64] ibid para 110 and see also para 172.
[65] ibid para 111.
[66] ibid para 62.
[67] ibid para 164. Emphasis added.
[68] The High Court of Australia (1983) looked at similarly qualified language in the Word Heritage Convention. The court, in that case, held that: 'these articles impose a legally binding obligation that is "real" and "substantive" and could not be read as a mere statement of intention: it was expressed in the form of a command requiring each party to endeavour to bring about the matters dealt with—although there is an element of discretion and value judgment on the part of the State to decide what measures are necessary and appropriate, the discretion only concerns the manner of performance—not the issue of whether to perform or not'. The argument that these qualifications pertain to how the obligations will be implemented, not whether or not they need to be implemented, can be applied by analogy also to the CBD and other international biodiversity-related treaties.
[69] Elisa Morgera, 'Biodiversity as a Human Right and its Implications for the EU's External Action', Report to the European Parliament (2020) <www.europarl.europa.eu/RegData/etudes/STUD/2020/603491/EXPO_STU(2020)603491_EN.pdf> accessed 12 March 2022.

In addition, it has been argued that the recognition of a customary rule to conduct environmental impact assessments implies that a state is under a positive obligation towards potentially affected states to assess harm to biodiversity where that harm extends beyond national borders in relation to impacts on biodiversity, despite the qualified language of the environmental impact assessment obligation under the CBD.[70]

Along similar lines, the statement by the ICJ in the *Pulp Mills* case[71] that 'general international law [does not] specify the scope and content of an environmental impact assessment' demonstrates the Court's disregard for the series of guidelines adopted under the CBD by consensus by 196 parties that detail the content and scope of environmental impact assessments when biodiversity may be at risk.[72]

3.3.1.2 International biodiversity obligations as non-applicable

The best example here is the *Biotech* case before a WTO Panel. In 2003, the United States, Canada, and Argentina requested consultations with the European Communities (EC) on certain measures affecting the approval and marketing of products containing, consisting of, or produced from genetically modified organisms. In the absence of a regulation considered mutually satisfactory, the three countries requested the establishment of a panel to examine the issue. The Panel issued its report in 2006, which was not appealed.[73] The question of particular interest for present purposes was how much weight the Cartagena Protocol, extensively invoked by the EC, would carry in such a configuration. The CBD was also invoked. Would WTO law be interpreted in 'clinical isolation' from these widely ratified texts of international environmental law?

The rejection of the notion of interpretation in 'clinical isolation', as early as the first report of the Appellate Body in the *Gasoline* case,[74] thus showed an openness to external rules. It established that WTO law was not a self-sufficient or self-contained regime, assuming that such regimes exist: WTO law is part of international law—it is not clinically isolated from it—and it is to be interpreted and construed through customary rules of interpretation of international law.

[70] Neil Craik, 'Biodiversity-Inclusive Impact Assessments' in Elisa Morgera and Jona Razzaque (eds), *Elgar Encyclopedia of Environmental Law: Biodiversity and Nature Protection Law* (Edward Elgar 2017) 431–44.

[71] ICJ, *Pulp Mills* (n 19) para 205.

[72] See eg COP Decision VIII/28 (2006), Impact assessment: Voluntary Guidelines on Biodiversity-inclusive Impact Assessment.

[73] WTO, *Biotech* (n 27).

[74] WTO, *United States—Standards for Reformulated and Conventional Gasoline*, WT/DS2/AB/R, Appellate Body Report, 29 April 1996.

However, Article 3:2 of the WTO Understanding on rules and procedures governing the settlement of disputes in itself directly refers only to the rules of interpretation of public international law.[75] Only indirectly or by reference are substantial rules allowed to be taken into account. As to the latter, the rules of interpretation of international law, in particular Articles 31 and 32 of the Vienna Convention on the Law of Treaties,[76] which the Appellate Body has very quickly considered as setting out customary rules, provide for the taking into account of substantive public international law. WTO judges' interpretations must therefore be 'controlled by the normative environment'.[77]

This is the thread of a line of reasoning that the Appellate Body will unwind little by little, not without boldness, in the light of the many markers that the Dispute Settlement Understanding places on its power to develop the law. In fact, its case law has evolved, gradually but clearly, towards taking into account non-WTO rules. Such evolution started from the General Agreement on Tariffs and Trade (GATT 1947), which was much more 'clinically isolated' than WTO law in terms of interpretative practices. For example, it is now established that the WTO Agreements are the primary source of law when considering an international trade dispute, but not the sole source.[78]

But how far should we go in taking into account exogenous rules, other international instruments, and principles? The relationship between WTO rules and other international instruments and principles was one of the key issues raised in the *Biotech* case. Indeed, the EC relied extensively in its defence on other international rules and instruments belonging to the sphere of international environmental and health law, in particular the Cartagena Protocol. For their part, the complainants categorically rejected the relevance of the other international rules and instruments invoked to resolve the dispute, calling on the Panel to stick to the 'covered agreements'; that is, WTO law, internal rules.[79]

In this connection, the principle of systemic integration referred to in Article 31(3)(c) of the 1969 Vienna Convention on the Law of Treaties must lead the interpreter to take 'into account, together with the context ... any relevant rules of international law applicable in the relations between the parties'. In the

[75] WTO, Understanding on rules and procedures governing the settlement of disputes, <www.wto.org/english/tratop_e/dispu_e/dsu_e.htm> accessed 12 March 2022.

[76] Vienna Convention on the Law of Treaties (opened for signature 23 May 1969, entered into force 27 January 1980) 1155 UNTS 331.

[77] ILC, Fragmentation of International Law: Difficulties Arising from the Diversification and Expansion of International Law, Report of the Study Group of the International Law Commission, Finalized by Martti Koskenniemi, A/CN.4/L.682 (2006) 30.

[78] Joost Pauwelyn, 'The Role of Public International Law in the WTO: How Far Can We Go?' (2001) 95(3) The American Journal of International Law 577.

[79] WTO, *Biotech* (n 27).

Biotech case, however, the Panel declined to apply it. It considers that, in order for a treaty rule to be interpreted in the light of another treaty rule, the latter (the Cartagena Protocol) must be applicable to all parties to the former (WTO law).[80] This requirement, which was not met and is only rarely met, arguably means that Article 31(3)(c) essentially allows, in practice, a (WTO) treaty rule to be interpreted in the light of a customary rule. In the Panel's view:

> it is not apparent why a sovereign State would agree to a mandatory rule of treaty interpretation which could have as a consequence that the interpretation of a treaty to which that State is a party is affected by other rules of international law which that State has decided not to accept.[81]

Acknowledging the contrary would represent a great danger to legal certainty. Could it be acceptable for the EC to unravel WTO law by negotiating and concluding the Cartagena Protocol, to which the United States refuses to accede? That would not be 'reasonable', the Panel said.[82] Its report was neither overturned nor subsequently upheld by the Appellate Body.[83] The attempt by the European Union and developing countries to light a counterfire to WTO law by adopting the Biosafety Protocol was therefore futile.[84] Nevertheless, this interpretation is very much criticized in the literature and has been nuanced in other WTO cases.[85]

3.3.2 A clear indirect influence

In its first environmental case, the *Danube dam*, the ICJ evoked the 'new norms and standards' that 'have been developed, set forth in a great number of instruments during the last two decades'.[86] It specified that 'such new norms have to be taken into consideration, and such new standards given proper weight, not only when States contemplate new activities but also when continuing with activities begun in the past'.[87] In other words, these new norms and standards

[80] Joost Pauwelyn, *Conflict of Norms in Public International Law: How WTO Law Relates to Other Rules of International Law* (CUP 2003) 257.
[81] WTO, *Biotech* (n 27) para 7.71.
[82] ibid.
[83] European Communities and Certain member States—Measures Affecting Trade in Large Civil Aircraft, Report of the Appellate Body, WT/DS316/AB/R (18 May 2011) 406. However, the Appellate Body urges caution in such a situation.
[84] According to Hélène Ruiz Fabri, 'Concurrence ou complémentarité entre les mécanismes de règlement des différends du Protocole de Carthagène et ceux de l'OMC?' in Jacques Bourrinet and Sandrine Maljean-Dubois (eds), *Le commerce international des organismes génétiquement modifiés* (Documentation française 2002) 149.
[85] ILC, Fragmentation of international law (n 77).
[86] ICJ, *Gabčíkovo-Nagymaros* (n 15) para 140.
[87] ibid.

were to be taken into account in the interpretation of the 1977 Treaty, since the Treaty itself prescribes an evolutionary interpretation of its own provisions.[88] However the Court was not explicit at all on what these 'new norms and standards' actually were. It did not mention the CBD or other biodiversity-related conventions (except the Convention concerning Fishing in the Waters of the Danube, signed at Bucharest on 29 January 1958[89]). But it did refer in its reasoning to the 'existence of the general obligation of States to ensure that activities within their jurisdiction and control respect the environment of other States or of areas beyond national control is now part of the corpus of international law relating to the environment'.[90] This obligation relates to the environment in general, but it applies *a fortiori* to biodiversity (as an element of the environment). Thus, even if the wording of the Court is vague and not explicit, it uses indirectly international biodiversity law in order to interpret in an evolving way the 1977 Treaty, thus fostering the protection of the environment.

Factual elements and definitions provided by biodiversity regimes are also frequently used by international courts and tribunals. For instance, in the *Road* case, the ICJ considered that the fact that a Costa Rican wetland is on the list of wetlands of international importance of the Ramsar Convention 'heightens the risk of significant damage because it denotes that the receiving environment is particularly sensitive'. Consequently, it found 'that the construction of the road by Costa Rica carried a risk of significant transboundary harm. Therefore, the threshold for triggering the obligation to evaluate the environmental impact of the road project was met.'[91]

In 2015, in the *Kaliña and Lokono* decision, the Inter-American Court of Human Rights was particularly explicit about the need for, and merits of, mutual supportiveness with consensus decisions adopted under the CBD.[92] On that occasion, the Inter-American Court of Human Rights underscored states' obligations to protect, in a manner compatible with their international environmental obligations, indigenous peoples' rights to a dignified life and to cultural identity connected with natural resources on their traditional territories.[93] While these case law developments concern one particular region, the

[88] ibid.
[89] ibid para 18.
[90] ibid para 53, quoting itself in *Legality of the Threat or Use of Nuclear Weapons*, Advisory Opinion [1996] ICJ Rep 241–42, para 29.
[91] ICJ, *Certain Activities Carried and Construction of a Road* (n 20) para 155–56.
[92] CBD, arts 8(j), 10, and 14: IACtHR, *Kaliña and Lokono* (n 44) paras 173–74, 177–78, 181, and 214, making reference to the Addis Ababa Principles and Guidelines for the Sustainable Use of Biodiversity, CBD Decision VII/12 (2004), Annex II and the CBD work programme on protected areas (CBD Decision VII/28 (2004), Annex).
[93] IACtHR, *Kaliña and Lokono* (n 44) paras 181 and 193.

Inter-American Court's line of reasoning has had a visible indirect impact on the African framework on human rights,[94] as well as on global human rights processes.[95]

In the *Shrimps-Turtles* case, the WTO Appellate Body used several biodiversity conventions to interpret the notion of exhaustible natural resources in the GATT 1994:

> The exhaustibility of sea turtles would in fact have been very difficult to controvert since all of the seven recognized species of sea turtles are today listed in Appendix 1 of the Convention on International Trade in Endangered Species of Wild Fauna and Flora ('CITES'). The list in Appendix 1 includes 'all species threatened with extinction which are or may be affected by trade'.[96]

The Appellate Body relied on international environmental conventions and declarations, recalling that they make 'frequent references to natural resources as embracing both living and non-living resources' (quoting UNCLOS, the CBD, the CMS, Agenda 21, etc) to consider that 'exhaustible natural resources' covers not only non-living resources but also living resources.[97] According to the Appellate Body:

> Given the recent acknowledgement by the international community of the importance of concerted bilateral or multilateral action to protect living natural resources, and recalling the explicit recognition by WTO Members of the objective of sustainable development in the preamble of the WTO

[94] Gaetano Pentassuglia, 'Indigenous Groups and the Developing Jurisprudence of the African Commission on Human and Peoples' Rights: Some Reflections' (2010) 3 UCL Human Rights Review 150, 158 with respect to the *Endorois* case. See also African Court on Human and Peoples' Rights, *African Commission of Human and Peoples' Rights v The Republic of Kenya* (26 May 2017) App No 006/2012, para 191.

[95] Independent Expert on Environment and Human Rights, John Knox, *Preliminary Report on the Issue of Human Rights Obligations Relating to the Enjoyment of a Safe, Clean, Healthy and Sustainable Environment*, UN Doc A/HRC/22/43 (2012) para 41 and *Mapping Report*, UN Doc A/HRC/25/53 (2013) para 78; UN Special Rapporteur on the Right to Food, Oliver de Schutter, *Large-scale land acquisitions and leases: A set of minimum principles and measures to address the human rights challenge*, UN Doc A/HRC/13/33/Add.2 (2009) paras 30–33; Special Rapporteur Anaya, A/HRC/21/47 paras 52, 62; UN Expert Mechanism, Indigenous Peoples and Human Rights, *Setting a Framework for Consultation, Benefit-Sharing and Dispute Resolution*, UN Doc A/HRC/EMRIP/2009/5 (2008); and UN Expert Mechanism, *Follow-up report on indigenous peoples and the right to participate in decision-making, with a focus on extractive industries*, UN Doc A/HRC/EMRIP/2012/2 (2012) para 40.

[96] WTO, *Shrimp* (n 26) para 132.

[97] ibid para 131.

> Agreement, we believe it is too late in the day to suppose that Article XX(g) of the GATT 1994 may be read as referring only to the conservation of exhaustible minerals or other non-living natural resources.[98]

In other words, the Appellate Body relied on international biodiversity law to justify an evolutionary interpretation of the GATT 1994. Furthermore, to consider that 'the protection and conservation of highly migratory species of sea turtles, that is, the very policy objective of the measure, demands concerted and cooperative efforts on the part of the many countries whose waters are traversed in the course of recurrent sea turtle migrations', the Appellate Body highlighted that '[t]he need for, and the appropriateness of, such efforts have been recognized in the WTO itself as well as in a significant number of other international instruments and declarations'.[99] Here, it mentioned some provisions of the CBD and the CMS.[100]

The *Biotech* Panel tried to clarify the reasoning of the Appellate Body in the *Shrimps* case. Indeed, the Panel wondered whether 'other rules of international law could be considered by us in the interpretation of the WTO agreements at issue even if these rules are not applicable in the relations between the WTO Members and thus do not fall within the category of rules which is at issue in Article 31(3)(c)'.[101] Indeed, in the *Shrimps* case, as recalled by the EC, the Appellate Body then interpreted the WTO rules (ie the concept of 'exhaustible natural resources' in GATT Art XX) by referring to treaties that were not binding on all parties to the proceedings, including the CBD in support of the US contentions, and although the United States was not a party to it. According to the Panel, the Appellate Body's approach then fell within the framework of Article 31(1) of the Vienna Convention, according to which a treaty shall be interpreted in good faith in accordance with the ordinary meaning to be given to the terms of the treaty in their context and in the light of its object and purpose.[102] This 'ordinary meaning' is 'often determined on the basis of dictionaries'. But, 'in addition to dictionaries, other relevant rules of international law may in some cases aid a treaty interpreter in establishing, or confirming, the ordinary meaning of treaty terms in the specific context in which they are used'.[103] This opens up the selection of instruments and rules to be considered

[98] ibid.
[99] ibid para 168.
[100] ibid.
[101] WTO, *Biotech* (n 27) para 7.90.
[102] ibid para 7.91.
[103] ibid para 7.92.

relevant, including a simple declaration or a treaty not in force between the parties to the dispute. This flexibility is due to the fact that external rules are no longer required 'because they are legal rules, but rather because they may provide evidence of the ordinary meaning of terms in the same way that dictionaries do'.[104] It does not matter if the rules in question are applicable in the relations between the WTO members. What matters then is 'their informative character'. Consequently, 'when a treaty interpreter does not consider another rule of international law to be informative, he or she need not rely on it'. Consideration of other rules of international law is no longer mandatory—as in the case of Article 31(3)(c)—but optional.[105]

In the *Seal* case, the Panel explained that it was persuaded that the evidence 'as a whole sufficiently demonstrates that animal welfare is an issue of ethical or moral nature in the European Union'. Yet, in this evidence as a 'whole', the Panel considered in particular, 'various pieces of legislation and conventions on animal welfare within the European Union and other countries, including Norway and Canada; and various international instruments'.[106]

In the *Tuna* case, the Panel determined that the US dolphin-safe labelling provisions pursued legitimate objectives but without using international biodiversity law (which had been poorly mentioned by the parties). However, the Panel searched for factual information on bycatch in the instruments of regional fisheries organizations, like the Convention for the Establishment of an Inter-American Tropical Tuna Commission or the Western and Central Pacific Fisheries Commission.[107]

The Arbitral Tribunal went the same way in the *South China Sea* arbitration, since it used the definition of ecosystem of the CBD: 'An "ecosystem" is not defined in the Convention [UNCLOS], but internationally accepted definitions include that in Article 2 of the CBD, which defines ecosystem to mean "a dynamic complex of plant, animal and micro-organism communities and their non-living environment interacting as a functional unit"'.[108] In the same way, the fact that some species are listed in CITES Appendices I and II allowed the Tribunal to assert that they are threatened with extinction (the case of all of

[104] ibid para 7.92.

[105] ibid paras 7.90 ff.

[106] See *European Communities—Measures Prohibiting the Importation and Marketing of Seal Products*, Reports of the Panel, WT/DS400/R, WT/DS401/R (25 November 2013) § 7.405, quoted by WTO, *Seal Products* (n 34).

[107] WTO, *United States—Measures Concerning the Importation, Marketing and Sale of Tuna and Tuna Products*, Report of the Panel, WT/DS381/R (16 May 2012) paras 4.237, 4.239.

[108] *PCA Case No 2013-19 in the matter of the South China Sea Arbitration before an arbitral tribunal constituted under annex VII to the 1982 United Nations Convention on the law of the sea, between the Republic of the Philippines and the People's Republic of China*, Award of 12 July 2016, para 140.

the sea turtles found on board Chinese fishing vessels, listed under CITES Appendix I) or threatened (the case of giant clams, listed in Appendix II to CITES and thus 'unequivocally threatened' according to the Tribunal). The Tribunal explained that 'CITES is the subject of nearly universal adherence, including by the Philippines and China, and in the Tribunal's view forms part of the general corpus of international law that informs the content of Article 192 and 194(5) of the Convention'.[109]

In the same vein, international biodiversity law has started to be addressed in a few international investment disputes. In the international investment arbitration of *David Aven v Costa Rica*, the Tribunal found that it is possible (although not in this particular case) for governments to file counterclaims against foreign investors for breach of mandatory rules of environmental protection, including based on international biodiversity treaties which contain *erga omnes* obligations.[110] In the *Peter Allard v Barbados* case, the Arbitral Tribunal did not find that Barbados's efforts to implement international biodiversity conventions amounted to a violation of the terms of the investment agreement, as the obligation of the state to provide the investment with full protection and security standard is of 'due diligence' and 'reasonable care'—not of strict liability.[111] The Tribunal noted that the government took reasonable steps to protect the sanctuary, including by establishing a committee to develop plans for its preservation.[112] On the other hand, the decision has arguably opened the way for future cases in which environmentally minded foreign investors could bring governments before international investment dispute-settlement bodies for not implementing sufficiently international biodiversity law.[113] Notably, the Tribunal indicated that 'consideration of the host States' international [biodiversity] obligations may well be relevant in the application of the standard [of full protection and security to the investor] to particular circumstances'.[114]

Hence, the indirect use of international biodiversity law in order to interpret international rules and obligations has taken various forms in international case law and contributed to foster the protection of the environment.

[109] ibid para 956.
[110] ICSID, *David Aven* (n 30) paras 390, 394, 418, 419, 423, 738–47.
[111] PCA, *Peter Allard* (n 31) paras 178, 190, 198, 230, 238, 243, 244.
[112] '*Peter Allard v Canada*' (1 December 2020) ISDS Blog <http://isdsblog.com/2016/10/13/just-published-peter-allard-v-canada/> accessed 12 March 2022.
[113] ibid.
[114] PCA, *Peter Allard* (n 31) para 244.

3.4 A Wide Array of Remedies

Litigation can pursue different—and sometimes complementary—strategic objectives, going from the reparation for harm to biodiversity to restoration of legality and prevention of future harm. A first consequence when a state is found responsible for a breach of international law is that the internationally wrongful act must cease, if it is still ongoing. Moreover, the responsible state is 'under an obligation to make full reparation for the injury caused by the internationally wrongful act'.[115] This reparation 'takes the form of restitution, compensation and satisfaction, either singly or in combination'.[116]

3.4.1 Repairing harm to biodiversity

Regarding harm to biodiversity, it might in fact be physically impossible to restore the situation *ex ante*. But the ICJ has confirmed that compensation, or satisfaction (or both), may be appropriate forms of reparation, particularly in cases regarding environmental harm where restitution is materially impossible or unduly burdensome.[117] However, it also held that in order to award compensation the Court has to determine 'whether there is a sufficiently direct and certain causal nexus between the wrongful act . . . and the injury suffered by the Applicant'.[118]

Meanwhile, it is worth noting that the ICJ has no difficulty with the notion of compensation for environmental damage. It considered in 2018 that 'it is consistent with the principles of international law governing the consequences of internationally wrongful acts, including the principle of full reparation, to hold that compensation is due for damage caused to the environment, in and of itself, in addition to expenses incurred by an injured State as a consequence of such damage'.[119] Moreover, the ICJ recalled that 'the absence of adequate evidence as to the extent of material damage will not, in all situations, preclude an award of compensation for that damage' and that 'in such case, while the damages may not be determined by mere speculation or guess, it will be enough if the evidence shows the extent of the

[115] ILC, Draft Articles on the Responsibility of States for Internationally Wrongful Acts, with commentaries, in Report of the ILC on its 53rd Session, UN Doc A/56/10 (2001) 31, 126 (art 31).

[116] ibid art 34.

[117] ICJ, *Pulp Mills* (n 19), para 273.

[118] *Ahmadou Sadio Diallo (Republic of Guinea v Democratic Republic of the Congo)*, Compensation, Judgment [2012] ICJ Rep 332, para 14. *Quoted in Certain Activities Carried Out by Nicaragua in the Border Area (Costa Rica v Nicaragua)*, Compensation, Judgment [2018] ICJ Rep 15, para 32.

[119] ICJ, *Certain Activities* (n 118) para 41. See in the same way IACtHR, *The Environment and Human Rights* (n 32) para 72.

damages as a matter of just and reasonable inference, although the result be only approximate'.[120]

3.4.2 Restoring legality and preventing future harm

In some cases, responsibility is not about compensation for a material prejudice but about restoring legality and preventing further harm. From this point of view, it is worth mentioning the decision of the ICJ in the *Road* case, in which the Court found that its 'declaration that Costa Rica violated its obligation to conduct an environmental impact assessment is the appropriate measure of satisfaction for Nicaragua' since that violation of international law had not caused specific damage.[121] An international court can also request the parties to find a solution to their dispute through negotiation and cooperation in good faith.

Admittedly, international biodiversity litigation pursues in general an objective of compensation—triggered *ex post* in relation to damage—but it could evolve in the future, to primarily aim to play a preventive role (*ex ante*), trying to push for concrete action, to press legislators and policymakers to be more ambitious in their approaches to biodiversity protection and sustainable use, and to fill the gaps left by legislative and regulatory inaction (as does climate litigation).[122] For instance, in the *Whales* case, the ICJ observed that:

> JARPA II is an ongoing programme. Under these circumstances, measures that go beyond declaratory relief are warranted. The Court therefore will order that Japan shall revoke any extant authorization, permit or license to kill, take or treat whales in relation to JARPA II, and refrain from granting any further permits under Article VIII, paragraph 1, of the Convention, in pursuance of that programme.[123]

And it added that:

> The Court sees no need to order the additional remedy requested by Australia, which would require Japan to refrain from authorizing or implementing any special permit whaling which is not for purposes of scientific research within the meaning of Article VIII. That obligation already applies to all

[120] ICJ, *Certain Activities* (n 118) para 35, quoting the *Trail Smelter (United States, Canada)* (1938 and 1941) 3 RIAA 1905, 1920.
[121] ICJ, *Certain Activities Carried and Construction of a Road* (n 20) paras 217 and 224.
[122] Regarding climate: UNEP, *Global Climate Litigation Report 2020 Status Review* (2020) 4.
[123] ICJ, *Whaling* (n 21) para 245.

> States parties. It is to be expected that Japan will take account of the reasoning and conclusions contained in this Judgment as it evaluates the possibility of granting any future permits under Article VIII, paragraph 1, of the Convention.[124]

However, the Court's decision essentially led Japan to withdraw from the Whaling Convention[125] and to resume commercial whaling.[126]

4. Synthesis of Key Findings

Our comparative study demonstrates that international biodiversity law plays a growing role in international litigation. Even if courts and tribunals are reluctant to address directly matters of compliance with international biodiversity law, they increasingly rely on it and no longer hesitate to get into scientific concepts, data, and the controversies about biodiversity.

This chapter also shows that international case law has contributed to clarify states' rights and obligations regarding international biodiversity law. This has been particularly significant with regard to the content and legal force of due diligence obligations and principles governing the management of shared natural resources.[127]

Another contribution of international case law has been linking rules with different legal force, from different regimes, favouring a synergistic interpretation of international law, and contributing to improving its consistency and arguably, through that, its effectiveness. While the *South China Sea* arbitration is a perfect illustration of the symbiosis between customary and treaty-based obligations,[128] relevant international case law as a whole illustrates the willingness of international courts and tribunals to contribute to a systemic interpretation of international biodiversity law in itself and with other rules of international law (law of the sea, international trade law, treaty law, etc). The need to develop such an evolutionary interpretation was already clear with regard to the 1977 Treaty in the *Danube dam* case, or to clarify the duty to cooperate in the GATT

[124] ibid para 246.

[125] Statement on Government of Japan withdrawal from the IWC <https://iwc.int/statement-on-government-of-japan-withdrawal-from-t> accessed 12 March 2022.

[126] Sui Phang and Peter Bridgewater, 'Japan Resumes Commercial Whaling—Researchers on How the World Should Respond' (2019) The Conversation <https://theconversation.com/japan-resumes-commercial-whaling-researchers-on-how-the-world-should-respond-119573> accessed 12 March 2022.

[127] See Section 3.3.2.

[128] PCA, *South China Sea* (n 108) paras 941, 948.

1994 in the *Shrimps* case, the duty to carry out an impact assessment in the *Pulp Mills* or the *Road* cases, or the duty to control harvesting of species that are recognized internationally as being at risk of extinction and requiring international protection in the *Shrimps* case or in the *South Sea China* award.

The opinion of Judge Cançado Trindade in the *Whales* case illustrates very well this concern, and the willingness to participate in the ongoing—and very much needed—defragmentation of international law. He emphasized the positive role of international biodiversity-related conventions in this quest, when he noted that 'With the growth in recent decades of international instruments related to conservation, not a single one of them is approached in isolation from the others; not surprisingly, the co-existence of international treaties of the kind has called for a systemic outlook, which has been pursued in recent years. . . . The systemic outlook seems to be flourishing in recent years.'[129]

Furthermore, it is worth mentioning that the engagement with international biodiversity law of the Inter-American Court of Human Rights has led to the identification of minimum levels of protection for the human rights of indigenous peoples under international biodiversity law. These clarifications have been recognized to be of global relevance, beyond the geographical scope of application of the Inter-American regime, as summarized in the 2018 UN Framework Principles on Human Rights and the Environment.[130] For instance, the Inter-American Court indicated that prior environmental and socio-cultural assessments should be prepared by an independent, technically qualified entity with the 'active participation of indigenous communities concerned'.[131] In addition, these assessments must respect indigenous traditions and cultures.[132] This is a key clarification to ensure that indigenous peoples influence the terms of the debate, rather than participate in a process already framed around a predetermined set of development options. Thus conceived, these assessments are expected to contribute to realizing indigenous peoples' right to participate in public affairs.[133]

In addition, the Inter-American Court emphasized states' obligation to deploy effective means to safeguard human rights through judicial organs, and provide the means to execute relevant decisions of public authorities

129 Separate Opinion of Judge Cançado Trindade, para 25.

130 Principle 15.

131 IACtHR, *Kaliña and Lokono* (n 44) para 214.

132 IACtHR, *Saramaka (Interpretation)* (n 39) para 41; IACtHR, *Kichwa Indigenous People of Sarayaku v Ecuador*, 27 June 2012 (Case 12.465) paras 41 and 206; IACtHR, *Kaliña and Lokono* (n 44) para 215; also citing Principle 10 of the Rio Declaration on Environment and Development, UN Doc A/CONF.151/26 (1992) vol 1, Annex 1.

133 IACtHR, *Kaliña and Lokono* (n 44) paras 197, 202–03.

and judgments.[134] Remedies offered by the state should provide a 'real possibility' for indigenous and tribal peoples to defend their rights and exercise effective control over their territory,[135] including through the recognition of legal standing to file administrative, judicial, or other type of action collectively, through their representatives, or individually, taking into account their customs and cultural characteristics. The Court also made reference to guarantees of access to justice that are accessible, simple, and within reasonable time frames; access to technical and legal assistance, ensuring that the community members can be understood in and can understand legal proceedings; and facilitation of physical access to administrative and judicial institutions in the light of geographical distance, elevated costs, or other challenges.[136] Such measures are also expected to respect internal mechanisms for deciding disputes on indigenous issues, which are in harmony with human rights.[137]

5. An Outlook

To conclude, we would like to underline that a better understanding of the range of possible remedies under international law could pave the way for different litigation strategies in the future, including more 'prospective' litigation aimed at inducing substantive compliance rather than providing reparation for injury.[138] The global trend in climate litigation (currently developing at the domestic level) has illustrated how litigation is becoming an emblematic element of contemporary environmental advocacy when the 'weapon' of law is used by citizens and NGOs as a mode of action. Given the traditional reluctance of states to use compulsory international dispute-resolution mechanisms, such a trend should not be expected to arise at the interstate level, for climate change, biodiversity, or other global environmental threats. However, if states do not raise the level of ambition of their national contributions to the Paris Agreement or to the post-2020 global biodiversity framework, litigation could increase in the years to come, not only at the national but also at the international level.

[134] ibid paras 239–40.
[135] ibid.
[136] ibid para 251(3).
[137] ibid, para 251(5).
[138] Geraldo Vidigal, 'Targeting Compliance: Prospective Remedies in International Law' (2015) 6(3) Journal of International Dispute Settlement 462–84.

In particular, this movement could take shape through the request of advisory opinions from the ICJ, or from ITLOS. This would constitute another pathway for an authoritative interpretation of states' rights and obligations. Advisory opinions have no binding force, yet provide an authoritative statement on questions of international law. Vanuatu and other Pacific Island states are exploring this avenue on climate ambition.[139] It appears to be the right time for the Court to clarify the rights and obligations of states on biodiversity as well, as the Inter-American Court of Human Rights has usefully done on the environment and human rights.[140]

From a substantive perspective, the increasing understanding of the interdependence of international human rights law (not only about indigenous peoples, but also everyone's right to health, water, and food, for instance) and international biodiversity law[141] can also be capitalized in future international litigation with a view to arguing the legally binding nature and the clear legal content of international biodiversity obligations that contribute to preventing negative human rights impacts,[142] such as environmental impact assessments.

[139] Tim Stephens, 'See You in Court? A Rising Tide of International Climate Litigation', *The Interpreter* (30 October 2019) <www.lowyinstitute.org/the-interpreter/see-you-court-rising-tide-international-climate-litigation> accessed 12 March 2022.

[140] IACtHR, *Saramaka* (n 39).

[141] Morgera (n 69); Morgera (n 38).

[142] Elisa Morgera, 'Fair and Equitable Benefit-Sharing' in Emanuela Orlando and Ludwig Krämer (eds), *Elgar Encyclopedia of Environmental Law: Principles of Environmental Law* (Edward Elgar 2018) 323–37; Elisa Morgera, 'Dawn of a New Day? The Evolving Relationship between the Convention on Biological Diversity and International Human Rights Law' (2018) 54 Wake Forest Law Review 691–712.

13
Biodiversity Litigation
Review of Trends and Challenges

Guillaume Futhazar, Sandrine Maljean-Dubois, and Jona Razzaque

In the chapters of this book, we have learned a great deal about biodiversity litigation in all its forms. We have seen cases arising in all continents except Antarctica. We have seen jurisdictions where international biodiversity law (IBL) significantly shapes litigation and jurisdictions where the very existence of IBL seems irrelevant in resolving biodiversity disputes. We have seen jurisprudential practices in different legal traditions, common law, or civil law. We have seen disputes in federal states and in unitary ones. Yet, it is fair to say that we still only know a fraction of what the topic entails. This synthesis gathers the key insights from our case studies and aims to answer the questions we raised in Chapter 1 of this volume.[1]

The results of this investigation will be presented here in three steps. First, we will discuss what we learned about the nature of biodiversity litigation; in other words, what it covers and where it takes place. We will then analyse the different forms of influence IBL has on this litigation. After having done so, we will present the different trends of biodiversity litigation we have identified through the case studies and in the literature. To take a step back, we will discuss the concept of biodiversity litigation in a broader context of environmental litigation and climate change litigation. As a conclusion, we will briefly summarize our main findings and the leads for further research.

Before we start this synthesis, a few preliminary comments are in order.

First, given the source material, this synthesis cannot claim to give an exhaustive account of biodiversity litigation. Our case studies should be seen as a first step in a broader investigation that will incorporate many more jurisdictions. As it stands, what this synthesis will provide are trends that need further confirmation with additional studies. Nevertheless, we believe that this first

[1] See Chapter 1.

Guillaume Futhazar, Sandrine Maljean-Dubois, and Jona Razzaque, *Biodiversity Litigation* In: *Biodiversity Litigation*. Edited by: Guillaume Futhazar, Sandrine Maljean-Dubois, and Jona Razzaque, Oxford University Press. © Guillaume Futhazar, Sandrine Maljean-Dubois, and Jona Razzaque, 2023. DOI: 10.1093/oso/9780192865465.003.0013

step in a broader understanding of biodiversity litigation will be a fruitful one, and one that will gain from future research.

Secondly, the source material for this synthesis is predominantly from the global north. This may distort the findings and the reader should be aware of this. Future research, with a stronger focus on the global south will allow us to confirm or infirm the findings of the synthesis.

1. The Characteristics of Biodiversity Litigation

Through the analysis of our contributors, some central features of biodiversity litigation have emerged. We will discuss them along the following lines. We will first address the legal nature of biodiversity litigation (2.1) before diving into the many themes covered by biodiversity litigation (2.2). The third section (2.3) will highlight the scope of biodiversity litigation; that is, its national, international, or transnational reach. Overall, this section will illustrate that while biodiversity litigation is inherently plural, it does seem to follow certain patterns.

1.1 The Different Legal Natures of Biodiversity Litigation

In the chapters of this book, we have seen cases involving states, public institutions, private organizations, and individuals. However, because notions such as 'public' and 'private' may vary depending on the legal system of states,[2] it is difficult to use them as umbrella terms here. Rather, we will categorize cases based on their purpose: remedial or punitive. Within each of these categories, we will highlight the configuration of litigants to understand the dynamic of biodiversity litigation.

1.1.1 Remedial biodiversity litigation

Remedial biodiversity litigation is understood here as litigation that aims at correcting breaches of biodiversity law. The actual remedies, either preventative or reparative, that can be issued in those cases will be addressed in Section 3.3 of this synthesis. We have identified three possible configurations: public

[2] Elisabeth Zoller, *Introduction to Public Law: A Comparative Study* (Martinus Nijhoff 2008); Mark Elliott, Jason NE Varuhas, and Shona Wilson Stark (eds), *The Unity of Public Law Doctrinal: Theoretical and Comparative Perspectives* (Hart Publishing 2018).

vs public, which mostly take place at the international level; private vs public where private actors act as applicants against public institutions; and private vs private.

1.1.1.1 Strictly public litigation

By strictly public, we refer to the cases where only public actors are involved. These cases are commonly found in federal states and at the international level. Although possible in federal states,[3] the case studies for this volume have not highlighted these types of biodiversity-related disputes. In Australia, Brazil, Canada, the UK, or the United States, biodiversity litigation has always involved private and public actors.

Strictly public biodiversity litigation is a logical feature of international disputes. Chapter 12 on international biodiversity litigation has highlighted that biodiversity-related disputes, although rare, are nevertheless a distinct trend in international environmental litigation.[4] The past decade has even seen a rise of such disputes, with well-known examples such as the *Whaling* case[5] or the *Pulp Mills* case[6] before the International Court of Justice. The future may hold more interstate cases on biodiversity as the crisis worsens.

Quantitatively, the most flagrant illustration of strictly public biodiversity litigation is at the European Union level. In Chapter 11 on EU biodiversity, we have seen a wealth of cases, with often innovative approaches concerning scientific considerations and the precautionary approach.[7] Most of these cases were initiated by the European Commission against Member States to implement the numerous rules adopted by the EU institutions.

1.1.1.2 Private actors against public actors

In this subsection, we refer to disputes where states' actions regarding biodiversity are contested by private actors (individuals or NGOs) on several grounds. The first, and most common, ground is when the action is contested because of its alleged illegality with regard to biodiversity-related laws. Such examples are abundant in our case studies, each chapter containing at least one example of a

[3] eg the US Supreme Court has jurisdiction over interstate disputes in accordance with Art III Section 2 of the US Constitution.
[4] See Chapter 12.
[5] *Whaling in the Antarctic (Australia v Japan: New Zealand intervening)*, Judgment [2014] ICJ Rep 226.
[6] *Pulp Mills on the River Uruguay (Argentina v Uruguay)*, Judgment [2010] ICJ Rep 14.
[7] See Chapter 11.

case where the state or its institutions have been sanctioned[8] for their actions that were deemed illegal.

For instance, in South Africa, the Ministry of Agriculture, Forestry and Fisheries saw its decision on total allowable catch declared illegal as it was not based on the best scientific evidence available.[9] In France, hunting permits were cancelled as they were non-compliant with the relevant laws.[10] In Australia, the *Bulga* case saw an association challenge the decision of the Minister for Planning and Infrastructure regarding a large mining project.[11] Similarly, at the international level, the African Network for Animal Welfare sought to suspend a road project in Tanzania before the East African Court of Justice[12] as it breached the 1999 Treaty for the Establishment of the East African Community.[13]

The other types of action of private actors against states or public institutions are rights-based. These actions can fall into two categories: the first one concerning the violation of human rights contained in national constitutions or international instruments, the second concerning the violation of rights and obligations contained in contracts.

The first category contains numerous examples of cases, both national and international, where plaintiffs seek to establish the responsibility of states for having breached human rights.[14] These types of dispute were less frequent in our case studies, but their impacts were resonant.[15] For instance, rights-based disputes are particularly relevant in cases involving indigenous peoples and local communities (IPLC).[16]

The second category manifests itself in investment-related disputes. For instance, this covers cases where actions of states in favour of conservation or

[8] Here we refer to the notion of sanction in a loose sense to convey the idea that a court intervened to halt the activities of public institutions or to impose reparations.

[9] See Chapter 8.

[10] See Chapter 6.

[11] See Chapter 2.

[12] *African Network for Animal Welfare (ANAW) v The Attorney General of the United Republic of Tanzania*, East African Court of Justice Ref no 09 of 2010, 20 June 2014. For an analysis of this case, see James Thuo Gathii, 'Saving the Serengenti: Africa's New International Judicial Environmentalism' (2014) 16 Chicago Journal of International Law 386.

[13] Treaty for the Establishment of the East African Community (signed 30 November 1999, entered in force 7 July 2000) 2144 UNTS 255.

[14] We discuss this trend in more detail in Section 3.

[15] See Chapter 12 on international biodiversity litigation, particularly Section 3.1.2: Inter-American Court of Human Rights (IACtHR), *Case of the Saramaka People v Suriname*, Judgment (Interpretation of the Judgment on Preliminary Objections, Merits, Reparations and Costs) 12 August 2008. The link between human rights and the environment is the topic of numerous publications. See, inter alia, Donald K Anton and Dinah L Shelton (eds), *Environmental Protection and Human Rights* (CUP 2012); John H Knox and Ramin Pejan (eds), *The Human Right to a Healthy Environment* (CUP 2018).

[16] See Chapter 4 on Canada.

sustainable use may hinder the contractual rights of investors. In such configurations, the rights are not used as a tool for environmental protection but rather as a means to hinder environmental policies.[17]

1.1.1.3 Disputes between private actors

Several chapters have highlighted cases where disputes took place between private actors, often NGOs against larger corporations in the context of infrastructure projects. The Green Peafowl Case, in China, showcases a dispute between a local NGO and a larger corporation, the China Hydropower Engineering Consulting Group.[18] In Brazil, a liability case involved a company for its use of endangered species in its advertising.[19]

However, it seems that, in our case studies, strictly private cases are less frequent than the ones involving at least one public actor. Also, though private in nature, these disputes could be described as vertical as the contested actions are often from larger corporations. In contrast, horizontal disputes, between individuals for instance, are not common in biodiversity litigation. Nevertheless, it seems that civil biodiversity litigation, as an additional means of protection of the environment, could gain traction in the upcoming years and is an emerging legal phenomenon that warrants further study.[20]

1.1.2 Punitive biodiversity litigation

Punitive biodiversity litigation refers to cases where a breach of biodiversity law is sanctioned by the court. The purpose of such litigation is to punish a behaviour rather than re-establishing legality. It is therefore in the realm of criminal law where the state or its institutions will act as prosecutor against other actors, mostly private.

Criminal biodiversity litigation is closely linked to the protection of species. As such, poaching and illegal logging is the main type of criminal litigation we

[17] eg *David Aven and others v Republic of Costa Rica*, ICSID Case No UNCT/15/3 (Award) (18 September 2018); as a counter-example, see *Peter Allard v Barbados*, PCA Case No 2012-06, Final Award (27 June 2016). On this topic, see Mariel Dimsey, 'Arbitration and Natural resource Protection' in Shawkat Alam and others (eds), *International Natural Resources Law: Investment and Sustainability* (Routledge 2018) 132; Antony Crockett, 'The Integration Principle in ICSID Awards' in Marie-Claire Cordonier Segger, HE Judge, and CG Weeramantry (eds), *Sustainable Development Principles in the Decisions of International Courts and Tribunals* (Routledge 2017) 539. On the potential of investor–state disputes as a tool for sustainable development, see Godwin Tan and Andrea Chong, 'The Future of Environmental Counterclaims in ICSID Arbitration: Challenges, Treaties and Interpretation' (2020) 9 Cambridge Journal of International Law 176.

[18] See Chapter 5.

[19] See Chapter 3.

[20] See Chapter 6 on France and Chapter 5 on China.

witness.[21] Pollution of protected areas is also a recurring theme. In Chapter 9 covering the UK, we saw an example of criminal fines for acts of illegal sewage discharge in South-East England.[22] In Chapter 8 covering South Africa, we saw cases on Rhino poaching.[23] Criminal biodiversity litigation, though not systematically addressed in the chapters of this volume, appears to be the most common form of litigation across all jurisdictions as criminal laws on wildlife are quite common among states, be they developed, developing, or least developed.[24]

To sum up the legal nature of biodiversity litigation, it appears that there is no fundamental difference with environmental litigation. The same patterns repeat, and unsurprisingly so since biodiversity litigation is a subset of environmental litigation.[25] Also, although not dealt with in our case studies, some jurisdictions leave room for legal pluralism in biodiversity litigation. This is the case, for instance, in Madagascar where custom-based dispute-settlement mechanisms exist and may involve biodiversity-related matters.[26] Further research in other states may shed light on the place of legal pluralism in biodiversity litigation.

1.2 The Themes of Biodiversity Litigation

Given the encompassing nature of biodiversity, biodiversity litigation is unsurprisingly heterogeneous. However, we can discern some trends in this vast ensemble. First, it appears that protected species and areas are common topics in all jurisdictions when it comes to biodiversity litigation. Secondly, the theme of genetic resources and access and benefit sharing (ABS) is also present, but its existence is highly state-dependent. The theme is abundantly litigated in some

[21] For a recent overview of wildlife crimes and their impact, see United Nation Office on Drugs and Crime, *World Wildlife Crime Report* (2020). See also, Giovanni. Broussard, 'Building an Effective Criminal Justice Response to Wildlife Trafficking: Experiences from the ASEAN Region' (2017) 26(2) Review of European Comparative & International Environmental Law 118–27; Melanie Wellsmith, 'Wildlife Crime: The Problems of Enforcement' (2011) 17 European Journal of Criminal Policy and Research 125; Margit Hellwig-Bötte, *Wildlife Crime in Africa—A Global Challenge: Successful Countermeasures Must Involve Local Populations* (Stiftung Wissenschaft und Politik 2014).

[22] See Chapter 9.

[23] See Chapter 8.

[24] As a tool for combatting wildlife crimes, these laws are monitored at the international level and guidelines are often produced to enhance them. See United Nation Office on Drugs and Crime, *Guide on Drafting Legislation to Combat Wildlife Crime* (2018).

[25] We discuss the conceptual implications of biodiversity litigation in Section 4.

[26] On this topic, see Ianjatiana Randrianandrasana, *Le droit de la protection de la nature à Madagascar. Entre centralisme et consensualisme* (L'Harmattan 2018) 331. We wish to thank Randianina Radilofe, who participated in the preparatory workshops for this project, for her insights on this topic.

states and completely absent in others. Thirdly, numerous cases sit at the outer limits of biodiversity litigation, thus challenging the conceptualization of this litigation trend.

It is worth noting that even though aquatic biodiversity litigation is observable in many jurisdictions[27] and at the international level,[28] most contributors in this volume have focused mainly on terrestrial biodiversity litigation. This may indicate an unconscious bias towards a more terrestrial understanding of biodiversity amongst lawyers. This warrants more research and case studies to determine whether this is only a bias in our case studies or an actual trend in biodiversity litigation.

1.2.1 Protecting species and ecosystems: a common thread in all jurisdictions

All the chapters in this volume have addressed the topic of endangered species or protected areas. This is evidently because most states have older laws on these matters. In France or in the United States, such law can be found in the first half of the twentieth century.[29] European countries, through colonialism, have exported their legal system for environmental protection in other states.[30] As recalled in the case study on India in Chapter 7, many rules pertaining to the management of forests are linked to the regulations imposed by the UK as a former colonial power.

In other words, biodiversity litigation often comprises cases on species and areas because these themes are well-established elements of environmental law in many countries, therefore litigation on such aspects has had ample time to develop over the decades. However, as we will see in the next sections of this synthesis, the way in which such cases are dealt with has evolved over time.

A common thread in biodiversity litigation, as made apparent by most case studies, are cases linked to large infrastructure projects, particularly roads,[31] energy infrastructures,[32] and mines.[33] These are illustrations of the inherent friction that human development brings with regard to habitats and species.

[27] See Chapters 8, 2, and 3 on South Africa, Australia, and Brazil respectively.
[28] See Chapter 12.
[29] See Chapter 6 on France and Chapter 10 on the United States (the Lacey Act).
[30] Richard Grove, *Green Imperialism. Colonial Expansion, Tropical Island Edens and the Origins of Environmentalism*, 1600–1860 (OUP 1996); Bhupinder S Chimni, 'International Institutions Today: An Imperial Global State in the Making' (2004) 15 European Journal International Law 1; M Rafiqul Islam, 'History of the North-South Divide in International Law: Colonial Discourses, Sovereignty, and Self-Determination' in Shawkat Alam and others (eds), *International Environmental Law and the Global South* (CUP 2015) 23–49. On the African continent, national laws were influenced by international agreements adopted by the colonial powers. Eg the Convention on the Preservation of Wild Animals, Birds and Fish in Africa (19 May 1900) and the Convention Relative to the Preservation of Fauna and Flora in their Natural State (8 November 1933).
[31] See Chapter 6 on France.
[32] See Chapter 5 on China.
[33] See Chapter 2 on Australia.

In contrast, the question of genetic resources and of access and benefit sharing is a much more recent trend in biodiversity law. Accordingly, its presence in biodiversity litigation is not as widespread.

1.2.2 Genetic resources and access and benefit sharing: a state-dependent trend

Disputes over genetic resources and ABS are relatively less common than ones on protected species and protected areas.[34] As we have seen in the chapters, these disputes can concern the use of genetically modified organisms (GMOs) and their potential impact on human health and biodiversity and the benefits drawn from the exploitation of biodiversity.

On this topic, it appears that the presence of ABS-related disputes is a logical feature of countries where the biodiversity is exploited for commercial purposes.[35] This is the case in India where pharmaceutical companies were compelled by the Uttarakhand High Court to share the benefits of ayurvedic medicine with the local communities who initially had this knowledge.[36] In Brazil in Chapter 3, the question of access to genetic resources was dealt with from a procedural point of view, with a least one case where the court called for the facilitation of such procedures.[37] Interestingly, in this volume, countries with operators that may exploit biodiversity abroad do not showcase ABS-related disputes.[38]

1.2.3 Other themes: the outer limits of biodiversity litigation

With a broad definition of biodiversity litigation,[39] most contributors addressed similar issues. But some explored the limits of what could be considered as biodiversity litigation. For instance, some cases on animal welfare were mentioned in the chapters (eg Brazil, South Africa). Animal welfare and

[34] On the broader topic of access and benefit sharing, see Charles Lawson and Kamalesh Adhikari (eds), *Biodiversity, Genetic Resources and Intellectual Property: Developments in Access and Benefit Sharing* (Routledge 2018); Pia Marchegiani, Elisa Morgera, and Louisa Parks, 'Indigenous Peoples' Rights to Natural Resources in Argentina: The Challenges of Impact Assessment, Consent and Fair and Equitable Benefit-sharing in Cases of Lithium Mining' (2019) 24 International Journal of Human Rights 224–40.

[35] Daniel Robinson, *Confronting Biopiracy: Challenges, Cases and International Debates* (Routledge 2010).

[36] *Divya Pharmacy v Union of India* (Writ Petition) (M/S) No 3437 of 2016. More generally, see Chapter 7 on India.

[37] AI 559568 (TRF3, 21 October 2015) and SLS 1438 (STJ, 9 May 2011).

[38] A case was mentioned in Chapter 6 on France; it was, however, dealt with at the EU level before the European Patent Office.

[39] See Chapter 1, Section 3, 'Any legal dispute at the national, regional or international level that concerns conservation of sustainable use of and access and benefit-sharing to genetic resources, species, ecosystems and their relations.'

animal rights are gaining traction both politically and legally, with more and more laws, cases, and articles appearing every day.[40]

Other approaches can be found in the case studies. The Brazilian case on the illegal use of wildlife images in advertising[41] is not what could be spontaneously described as biodiversity litigation in comparison to the many examples on the impact of infrastructures, but nevertheless it shows that the topic can be far-reaching in unsuspected ways.

The examples of tax related cases in the United States also show that biodiversity litigation can take on an 'immaterial' form, where cases do not directly discuss an impact, or expected impact, on elements of biodiversity.[42]

1.3 The Scope of Biodiversity Litigation: Cases that Stay Within Their National Borders

Even though biodiversity-related disputes may have international implications—with cases concerning migratory species, for instance[43]—it appeared that biodiversity litigation was mainly conceptualized as local litigation. The implications of these cases were often considered within a restricted geographical scope. This, of course, does not apply to interstate international disputes, which, by definition, concern cross-border ecosystems or high sea biodiversity.[44]

Though not mentioned in our case studies, some biodiversity disputes can have legal impacts beyond their national borders. This was the case for the Gibson company, which was found responsible for participating in illegal logging in Madagascar through purchase and importation. The company avoided trial by entering into a criminal enforcement agreement with the US Department of Justice.[45] In France, a civil case was filed in 2021 against the Casino group, specialized in retail, for its contribution to deforestation in

[40] On 4 February 2022, the Constitutional Court of Ecuador admitted that a writ of habeas corpus could have been possible for a woolly monkey. However, the monkey being deceased, the writ was not possible. On this case, see Andreas Gutman, 'Monkeys in their Own Right: The Estrellita Judgement of the Ecuadorian Constitutional Court' (22 February 2022) Verfassungsblog.

[41] REsp 1549459 (STJ, 9 May 2017).

[42] See Chapter 10.

[43] eg an airport project in Portugal is currently being contested on those grounds. The NGO ClientEarth is taking part in the campaign. See <www.clientearth.org/latest/latest-updates/news/portugal-s-proposed-new-airport-would-threaten-thousands-of-protected-birds/> accessed 23 March 2022.

[44] See Chapter 12 on international biodiversity litigation.

[45] See <www.justice.gov/opa/pr/gibson-guitar-corp-agrees-resolve-investigation-lacey-act-violations> accessed 31 March 2022.

Latin America.[46] In Sweden, a court ruled that a company importing teak from Myanmar was in breach of the EU's Timber Regulation.[47] These cases reflect the deterrent role litigation can play in preventing human and environmental rights violations by multinational companies in the global south.[48] With more and more laws being passed or proposed at the national,[49] regional,[50] and international levels[51] to ensure the due diligence of multinational companies—both on the matter of human rights and on environmental considerations—it is likely that the future of biodiversity litigation will be transnational.[52]

Having discussed the different natures of biodiversity litigation, we can now turn to one of the main questions of the project: what is the influence of international biodiversity law on biodiversity litigation?

2. The Influence of IBL

The chapters in this volume have given widely different portraits of the influence of IBL, with jurisdictions where IBL could be deemed as totally irrelevant[53] and other jurisdictions where IBL has been crucial in the context of disputes.[54]

The influence of international law on domestic courts is a well-documented topic.[55] Within this field, there also several analyses on international environmental law and the courts.[56] For this project, we wanted to narrow the focus

[46] See <https://notreaffaireatous.org/actions/action-en-justice-contre-casino/> accessed 31 March 2022. The complaint was based on the 2017 law on the duty of vigilance of corporations. See Loi no 2017-399 du 27 mars 2017 relative au devoir de vigilance des sociétés mères et des entreprises donneuses d'ordre.

[47] Forest Trends, 'Swedish Court Rules Myanmar Timber Documentation Inadequate for EU Importers' (15 November 2016) <www.forest-trends.org/wp-content/uploads/imported/swedish-court-myanmar-timber-pr_final-pdf.pdf> accessed 22 March 2022.

[48] Richard Meeran and Jahan Meeran (eds), *Human Rights Litigation against Multinationals in Practice* (OUP 2021).

[49] eg in France, see Loi no 2017-399 (n 46).

[50] European Commission, Proposal for a Directive of the European Parliament and of the Council on Corporate Sustainability Due Diligence and Amending Directive (EU) 2019/1937, COM (2022) 71 final (2022).

[51] UN Human Rights Council, 'Legally Binding Instrument to Regulate, in International Human Rights Law, the Activities of Transnational Corporations and other Business Enterprise.,' Third draft (2021).

[52] This perspective is already prompting debates amongst practitioners, Zaneta Sedilekova, Nigel Brook, and Wynne Lawrence, *Biodiversity Liability and Value Chain Risk* (Clyde & Co 2022).

[53] See Chapter 10 on the United States.

[54] See Chapter 7 on India.

[55] For recent studies on the topic, see André Nollkaemper and others (eds), *International Law in Domestic Courts: A Casebook* (OUP 2018).

[56] Louis J Kotzé and Caiphas B Soyapi, 'African Courts and Principle of International Environmental Law: A Kenyan and South African Case Study' (2021) 33 Journal of Environmental Law 257; Carl Bruch, 'Is International Environmental Law Really Law?: An Analysis of Application in Domestic

to a specific subset of international environmental law (IEL), namely IBL, to better understand its influence. Also, our focus was not only on national courts but on all courts—national, regional, and international.

Through this analysis, we have observed three types of influence for IBL. The first type of influence is legislative (2.2). These are cases involving laws that have been adopted to implement IBL at the international level. The second influence is interpretative. These are cases where laws are interpreted in the light of IBL (2.3). Finally, the third form of influence is technical and scientific (2.4). These are cases where IBL is used as an element to assess facts in the context of a biodiversity-related dispute. As a preliminary observation, we will explain why the direct influence of IBL, through implementation, is limited (2.1).

Before engaging in the analysis, it is worth mentioning the fact that two IBL instruments stood out particularly in the case studies: CITES[57] and the CBD.[58] Other global conventions were mentioned, such as the Ramsar Convention,[59] the Bonn Convention,[60] the UNESCO Convention,[61] or UNCLOS,[62] but it seemed as if the bulk of IBL in disputes were linked to these two instruments.

CITES may be so often referred to because of its relevance to wildlife crimes, which are a frequent topic of litigation, and also because of its clarity as a legal instrument. Indeed, the CITES appendices system is straightforward, with specific obligations for the species that are listed. The listing system also provides decision makers with information on the status of species.[63] This clarity seems to be favoured by judges who are more comfortable in using this international instrument to complement national laws. With regard to the CBD, its influence may be explained by its place as the conceptual compass of IBL.[64] As

Courts' (2006) 23 Pace Environmental Law Review 423; Daniel Bodansky and Jutta Brunée, 'The Role of National Courts in the Field of International Environmental Law' (1998) 7 Review of European Comparative & International Environmental Law 11; Alan Igleson, *Environment in the Court Room* (University of Calgary Press 2019).

57 Convention on International Trade in Endangered Species of Wild Fauna and Flora (opened for signature 3 March 1973, entered into force 1 July 1975) 993 UNTS 243.

58 Convention on Biological Diversity (opened for signature 5 June 1992, entered into force 29 December 1993) 1760 UNTS 79.

59 Convention on Wetlands of International Importance Especially as Waterfowl Habitat (opened for signature 2 February 1971, entered into force 21 December 1975) 996 UNTS 245.

60 Convention on the Conservation of Migratory Species of Wild Animals (opened for signature 23 June 1979, entered into force 1 November 1983) 1651 UNTS 333.

61 Convention for the Protection of the World Natural Heritage (opened for signature 16 November 1972, entered into force 17 December 1975) 1037 UNTS 152.

62 United Nations Convention on the Law of the Sea (adopted 10 December 1982, entered into force 16 November 1994) 1833 UNTS 3.

63 eg see Chapter 5 on China.

64 See Chapter 1.

a purveyor of principles and concepts for biodiversity law, it can often be used as an interpretative tool for other biodiversity-related norms.

2.1 The Limited Direct Influence of IBL

The direct influence of IBL on biodiversity-related disputes (ie its implementation by judges) is inherently linked to two fundamental aspects. First, the monist or dualist nature of the states bound by IBL and, secondly, the characteristics of IBL itself. In this respect, the question of the influence of IBL is no different from the question of the domestic influence of international law in general. On both these aspects, it seems that the direct influence of IBL is mostly limited.

The distinction between monism and dualism is a tenuous one,[65] but it does bear on whether IBL will have to be translated into national law to have an effect within the legal system. In this volume, monist countries were less represented, but it appeared that IBL was not strikingly more influential in those countries than in dualist ones. For instance, in France, the direct influence of IBL was deemed minimal.

The reason for this lack of direct applicability is due to the way in which IBL was designed. Indeed, at the national level, in monist contexts, IBL is often seen as not being directly applicable since it does not confer rights or obligations to individuals. It is described as a system of obligations that only binds states and is therefore irrelevant to individuals.[66] This diagnostic can be seen in France, but also at the EU level where the examination of international law in disputes is similar.[67] In this context, instruments such as CITES or the Aarhus Convention[68] stand out particularly as they are among the few instruments of IBL that may be directly applicable[69] in the context of disputes.

It would seem at this point that IBL may be more relevant at the international level. But even then, the wording of IBL instruments is fraught with vague,

[65] eg some countries cannot be categorized in one or another frame. See Chapter 5 on China. For a critique of these concepts, see, inter alia, Hisashi Owada, 'Problems of Interaction between the International and Domestic Legal Orders' (2015) 5 Asian Journal of International Law 246.

[66] See Chapter 6 on France.

[67] See Chapter 6 on France and Chapter 11 on the EU.

[68] Aarhus Convention on Access to Information, Public Participation in Decision-Making and Access to Justice in Environmental Matters (adopted 25 June 1998, entry into force 30 October 2001) 2161 UNTS 447. The Aarhus Convention falls into the broader category of international environmental law (IEL) rather than strictly IBL, it is nevertheless crucial for the effectiveness of IBL.

[69] See Chapters 6 and 5 on France and China respectively.

ambiguous, or open-textured terms. Moreover, obligations may sometime be modulated, with expressions such as 'in accordance with its particular conditions and capabilities' or 'as far as possible and as appropriate' that are frequent in the text of the CBD, for instance. In turn, the vagueness of IBL instruments may simply prevent them from having any effect in interstate disputes, as highlighted before the ICJ in the *Road* case between Costa Rica and Nicaragua.[70]

To sum up, the fact that IBL is not generally meant to confer rights and duties to individuals, and is often vague and weakly normative, prevents it from having a significant direct effect on biodiversity litigation. However, as the following discussion indicates, a lack of direct effect does not imply the irrelevance of IBL in biodiversity-related disputes.

2.2 Influence Through Legislation

The rapid development of IBL has played a major role in raising awareness about the importance of protecting nature, wildlife, and finally biodiversity. The evolution of IBL has accompanied changes in national laws. Be it in monist or in dualist states, IBL is frequently transposed to have its full effect at the national level. Most case studies in this volume mentioned legislation that was intended to ensure the transposition of IBL at the national level. India has the 2002 Biodiversity Act, South Africa has the 1998 National Environmental Management Act, France has the 2016 Law on biodiversity. The list could go on. This illustrates that IBL has, at the very least, an obvious legislative impact, which in turn has repercussions for legal disputes. In our case studies, the United States offered a stark contrast as being one of the most reluctant countries to sign or incorporate IBL into its national legislation (notwithstanding CITES).

More than a simple legislative transposition, the case studies in this volume show that the implementation of the CBD has marked a shift in the understanding of biodiversity-related topics. In Canada, the ratification of the CBD has come with a growing awareness of its globally important role in protecting biodiversity and 'is a reality about which Canadian courts and tribunals are becoming increasingly well informed'.[71] In Australia, the ratification of the CBD can be seen as 'an appropriate starting point for considering the

[70] *Certain Activities Carried Out by Nicaragua in the Border Area (Costa Rica v Nicaragua) and Construction of a Road in Costa Rica along the San Juan River (Nicaragua v Costa Rica)*, Judgment [2015] ICJ Rep 665, para 48. See Chapter 12.

[71] See Chapter 4, Section 4.

development of biodiversity law'.[72] On its side, to implement its international obligations, the EU has developed an extensive and ambitious body of legislation aimed at protecting species and habitats, creating a system of protected areas, improving ecosystems' conservation status, or integrating environmental considerations into local land use policies, going in many ways beyond international binding standards.[73] In Brazil, international biodiversity law and governance have motivated the establishment of the Plataforma Brasileira de Biodiversidade e Serviços Ecossistêmicos, based on the model of the Intergovernmental Science-Policy Platform on Biodiversity and Ecosystem Services (IPBES).[74] In the UK, IBL has allowed a less myopic approach to environmental law by some judges. In India, it has influenced the discourse on environmentalism and pushed for the recognition of the rights of indigenous communities and the participation rights of local communities in conservation, propelling discussions on approaches to community-based conservation and locally driven biodiversity conservation that are visible in the Biodiversity Act of 2002.[75]

Because of the importance of national laws as a means of indirect influence, the actual content and design of these laws is crucial. This fact is duly considered within the institutions of IBL and several treaty bodies offer 'model laws' to their parties as a means to ensure a better transposition at the national level.[76] Through this approach, it can be said that IBL regimes are attempting to manage their indirect influence at the national level.

2.3 Influence Through Interpretation

Indirect influence of IBL through the interpretation of other legal rules is one of the most striking elements we have observed in the case studies.

Several cases show that the consequence of the interpretive influence can be significant on the outcomes of biodiversity-related disputes. In the *Shrimp-Turtle* case before the WTO Dispute Settlement Body,[77] the use of

[72] See Chapter 2, Section 2.1.
[73] See Chapter 11.
[74] See Chapter 3.
[75] See Chapter 9.
[76] See eg for the Convention on Migratory Species, Resolution 12 September 2017, Establishment of a Review Mechanism and a National Legislation Programme. For CITES, see Resolution Conf 8.4 (Rev CoP15), National laws for implementation of the Convention.
[77] WTO, *United States—Import Prohibition of Certain Shrimp and Shrimp Products*, AB-1998-4, Report of the Appellate Body [1998] WT/DS58/AB/R. For more detail, see Chapter 12, Section 3.1.1.

IBL was decisive in shaping the arguments of the judges. Had turtles not been considered as an exhaustible resource, the possibility of invoking the exceptions listed in Article XX of the General Agreement for Tariffs and Trade[78] for this species would have been closed off. The impact of IBL as an interpretative tool is also significant before human rights courts.[79] At the national level, we saw examples of national laws being interpreted in the light of IBL instruments in order to annul administrative acts.[80] IBL was essential to the outcomes of these different cases, even though it was not directly implemented.

This interpretative influence of IBL opens the gate to all IBL and not only treaty-based norms or customs. In several examples, we have seen soft law instruments, which are abundant in IBL, take an important place in the arguments of litigants.[81] As mentioned by the WTO Appellate Body, when searching for the 'ordinary meaning' of a word, the judge can refer to dictionaries but also to the 'relevant rules of international law' which may aid a treaty interpreter in establishing, or confirming, the ordinary meaning of treaty terms in the specific context in which they are used. This opens up the selection of instruments and rules that can be considered relevant. This can include a political declaration or even a treaty that is not binding on the disputing parties. This flexibility is due to the fact that, in interpretation, external rules are no longer required 'because they are legal rules, but rather because they may provide evidence of the ordinary meaning of terms in the same way that dictionaries do'.[82] What matters here is more the 'informative character' of a rule than its binding nature.[83]

Climate litigation also exhibits these patterns of indirect influence for international climate law. Indeed, in climate trials, international law is rarely applied directly as a source of positive law. This is either because the legal system is dualist or because the obligations in question are not viewed as self-executing and therefore cannot be directly invoked by individuals.[84] However, the Paris Agreement, alone or in combination with other international obligations, has been successfully used in many cases to interpret

[78] General Agreement on Tariffs and Trade (opened for signature 30 October 1947, entered in force 1 January 1948) 55 UNTS 187.
[79] IACtHR, *Case of Kaliña and Lokono Peoples v Suriname*, Judgment (Merits, Reparations and Costs), 25 November 2015. See Chapter 12.
[80] See Chapter 6 on France.
[81] See Chapters 7, 6, and 12 on India, France, and international biodiversity litigation respectively.
[82] See Chapter 12, Section 3.3.2.
[83] See the *Biotech* case in Chapter 12.
[84] Lennart Wegener, 'Can the Paris Agreement Help Climate Change Litigation and Vice Versa?' (2020) 9 Transnational Environmental Law 24.

domestic rules.[85] In climate-related cases, the courts have carried out several forms of interpretations: systemic, where domestic law is interpreted 'in the light of' all relevant legal elements, but also factual or even moral elements and teleological, where laws are interpreted in consideration of the goal of the climate regime.[86] In doing so, the courts have more discretion in their assessments of whether it is appropriate to use international law, as well as in the choice of sources relied on, which may include unratified treaties or soft law instruments. As interpretative sources, international norm becomes subsidiary, as it is not the implementation of the Paris Agreement that the claimants are asking for. They ask that national policies actually implement the country's international commitments or conform to a consensual standard of conduct.[87]

From this point of view, it is interesting to note that in our case studies, judges have not been asked to scrutinize whether the national laws meet the Aichi Targets. In theory, National Biodiversity Strategy and Action Plans (NBSAPs) and national legislation should be aligned with the Aichi Targets and the Strategic Plan for Biodiversity 2011–2020. In practice, however, national targets are generally poorly aligned with the Aichi Targets, in terms of scope and level of ambition. Of course, the Targets have been adopted by a COP decision, which as such is not legally binding. As a soft law element, the Aichi Targets could nevertheless have been used as an interpretative tool. But that was not the case in any of the case studies, except in India where the NBSAP is seen as a guiding document for executive decision making. It 'functions more like a soft law instrument' where the Biodiversity Act is seen as the harder law for the regulation of biodiversity conservation.[88]

To conclude, it appears that the interpretative influence of IBL is far more impactful than the direct application of IBL. This is due to the fact that indirect influence both eschews monist/dualist distinctions and allows for all norms of IBL to be taken into consideration, both hard and soft ones. However, in the end, this influence is dependent on the willingness of judges to rely on IBL as an interpretative tool.[89]

[85] Kim Bouwer, 'The Unsexy Future of Climate Change Litigation' (2018) 30(3) Journal of Environmental Law 492.

[86] See eg the judgment of the Paris Administrative Court, case Nos 1904967, 1904968, 1904972, and 1904976/4-1, Association Oxfam France, Association Notre Affaire à Tous, Fondation pour la Nature et L'homme, Association Greenpeace France, 'L'Affaire du siècle', Decision dated 14 October 2021.

[87] Bouwer (n 85).

[88] See Chapter 7, Section 2.2.

[89] As a counter-example, see Chapter 10 on the United States.

2.4 Influence Through Evidence

IBL is also used by judges as a tool for assessing the vulnerability of species or habitats. For instance, in China, the Supreme Court judicial policy requires judges to refer to lists formulated by international institutions when determining whether a species is 'precious' or 'endangered', and in particular to Appendices I and II of the CITES which is one of the most cited international treaties before the Chinese courts, alongside the Red List of the International Union for Conservation of Nature (IUCN).[90] In the *South China Sea* arbitration, the Arbitral Tribunal also relied upon the fact that some species were listed in CITES Appendices I and II to assert that they were threatened with extinction (the case of all of the sea turtles found on board Chinese fishing vessels, listed under CITES Appendix I) or threatened (the case of giant clams, listed in Appendix II to CITES and thus 'unequivocally threatened' according to the Tribunal). The Tribunal explained that 'CITES is the subject of nearly universal adherence, including by the Philippines and China, and in the Tribunal's view forms part of the general corpus of international law that informs the content of Article 192 and 194(5) of the Convention' on the law of the sea.[91]

Regarding habitats, French case law gives a good illustration. Here, the listing of an area under the Ramsar Convention on wetlands or the UNESCO World Heritage Convention is indicative of its 'environmental quality' and justifies special protection. This is also the case before the international courts. For instance, in the *Road* case, the International Court of Justice considered that the fact that a Costa Rican wetland was on the list of wetlands of international importance of the Ramsar Convention 'heightens the risk of significant damage because it denotes that the receiving environment is particularly sensitive'.[92] Consequently, it found 'that the construction of the road by Costa Rica carried a risk of significant transboundary harm. Therefore, the threshold for triggering the obligation to evaluate the environmental impact of the road project was met.'[93]

Over time, the IPBES reports could be relied on by plaintiffs and judges, as it is the case for the IPCC reports.[94] This is another lesson from the development of climate litigation. Although the Intergovernmental Panel on Climate Change (IPCC) reports have no legal value, as scientific reports, they have the

[90] See Chapter 5.
[91] See Chapter 12, Section 3.3.2.
[92] See Chapter 12, Section 3.3.2.
[93] *Road* case (n 70) paras 155 and 156.
[94] eg the Urgenda case, Supreme Court of the Netherlands, Judgment19/00135 of 20 December 2019.

advantage of reflecting the global consensus of scientists on the subject, a sort of 'international truth'.[95] The summaries for policymakers that accompany the reports—and which are the parts relied upon in court—also carry particular weight since they are co-approved by scientists and representatives of the states. In the New Zealand *Thomson* case, the court thus noted that 'The IPCC reports provide a factual basis on which decisions can be made.'[96] Furthermore, it held that the government should review its long-term objective every time the IPCC publishes a new report, viewing it as a 'mandatory relevant consideration'.[97]

To conclude on the influence of IBL, it can be said that its influence is greater when not seen as a direct legal tool of immediate application but rather as a catalyst for the evolution and interpretation of other laws, biodiversity-related or not.

Now that the influence of IBL on biodiversity litigation has been explored, we can turn to the trends of biodiversity litigation.

3. The Characteristics of Biodiversity Litigation

The trends identified in the different chapters will be analysed in three steps. First, we will present the actors of biodiversity litigation. Secondly, we will discuss the role of rights discourses in biodiversity litigation. Thirdly, we will question the impacts of biodiversity litigation.

3.1 Actors

The case studies in this volume have highlighted how the role of judges and civil society has evolved regarding biodiversity-related disputes.

3.1.1 The evolving role of judges

The implementation of biodiversity laws at the national level needs to be complemented by an efficient judiciary that people can rely on to resolve disputes. The role of the judiciary to promote environmental conservation was recognized by Agenda 21 (1992) and more recently in the Sustainable Development

[95] Guillaume Futhazar, 'More Than Just a Scientific Report: The Global Assessment on Biodiversity and Ecosystem Services as Scientific and Political Tool' (9 October 2019) Völkerrechtsblog.

[96] eg *Thomson v Minister for Climate Change Issues* [2017] New Zealand High Court 733, para 134.

[97] ibid para 94.

Goals (Goal 16).[98] The functions of a court of law are of great importance to biodiversity conservation—this is, not only as a guardian of the rule of law.[99] Our case studies underline that the judiciary's role in protecting and interpreting constitutional rights (eg rights of nature, collective rights) is also relevant in upholding conservation values. The following discussion focuses on role of judges in applying environmental principles and concepts, their potential role in filling legal gaps, their willingness to engage with scientific expertise, and the role of specialized environmental courts in resolving biodiversity disputes.

3.1.1.1 Judges as innovative problem solvers

A national court's decision can promote the application of environmental principles within the context of IBL in several ways.

By applying an internationally recognized environmental principle, national courts do not only implement it in individual cases. Rather, if implemented with sufficient regularity, these decisions can also have a deterrent effect on or help to shape the future conduct of the legislator.[100] Moreover, through their decisions, national courts can introduce those environmental principles into national law, thereby supplementing or even correcting the work of legislatures. In instances where IBL has not been implemented adequately through national legislation or administrative rulemaking, these court decisions can play a significant role in improving the national legal system. For example, the Indian courts have considered some commonly recognized principles, such as the precautionary principle, the polluter pays principle, the public trust doctrine, and sustainable development, as directly applicable.[101] Although there is no direct application of international law, courts in Australia, for instance, have made reference to principles of CBD and CITES (eg the precautionary principle).[102] In Canada, courts have interpreted the habitat designation obligation as reflecting and embodying the precautionary principle.[103] In cases related to the interpretation of the precautionary principle in Brazil, it is quite common to see reports from different international bodies being used as parameters for the court's decision.[104] Within the EU, the Court of Justice of the European

[98] Para 8.18 of Agenda 21 (1992); Sustainable Development Goal, Goal 16 (Peace, justice and strong institutions).

[99] Denise Meyerson, 'What is a Court of Law?' (2019) 42 University of New South Wales Journal 65.

[100] See Chapter 7 on India: Section 4.1 (*Godavarnam* judgment).

[101] See Chapter 7. Lavanya Rajamani, 'Public Interest Environmental Litigation in India: Issues of Access, Participation, Equity, Effectiveness and Sustainability' (2007) 19(3) Journal of Environmental Law 293; Jona Razzaque, 'Linking Human Rights, Development and Environment: Experiences from Litigation in South Asia' (2007) 18(3) Fordham Environmental Law Review 587.

[102] See Chapter 2.

[103] See Chapter 4.

[104] See Chapter 3.

Union (CJEU) has also used the precautionary principle in relation to habitat creation, restoration measures, or to assess the viability of biodiversity offsetting.[105] The ITLOS plays a similar role and has referred to the precautionary principle in settling marine wildlife disputes arising from UNCLOS.[106]

National judges can also offer guidance for the evolution of judicial practices. In China, this was done through interpreting 'environmental protection' to include biodiversity conservation.[107] However, such guidance may not always benefit biodiversity conservation. While interpreting ecological integrity, we find examples of cases where the courts either take a conservative (in Canada) or a liberal (in the EU) approach. The progressive stance taken by the CJEU underscores that small-scale interventions, when accumulated, can threaten the ecological integrity of an EU-protected site and would be deemed unacceptable.[108] In contrast, according to the Canadian courts, the ecological integrity of national parks may be traded away where other considerations are perceived to be more important. Cases against degradation of national parks through small encroachments have met with little success, with courts deferring to the administrative jurisdiction of the relevant ministers and park authorities.[109]

3.1.1.2 *Judges to fill legal gaps*

Courts are focused on applying and interpreting the law and, if necessary, on filling legislative or regulatory gaps through their decisions. Nevertheless, the courts in democratic states continue to respect the separation of powers and thus do not allow themselves to exert legislative powers through their decisions.[110] Separation of powers ensures that power is not abused in such a way that curtails an individual's liberty. One important aspect of the separation of powers is the role of the judiciary in ensuring that the legislators or the executives do not exceed their authority. Courts come into play in this area when, for example, existing laws need to be reinterpreted and applied, or when they are deemed unfair in their application to specific cases.[111] For

[105] See Chapter 11.
[106] See Chapter 12.
[107] See Chapter 5.
[108] See the *Sweetman* case in Chapter 11, Section 4.3.
[109] See Chapter 4.
[110] Curtis A Bradley and Trevor W Morrison, 'Historical Gloss and the Separation of Powers' (2012) 26(2) Harvard Law Review 412–85; Jeremy Waldron, 'Separation of Powers in Thought and Practice?' (2013) 54 Boston College Law Review 433; Jasmina Nedevska, 'An Attack on the Separation of Powers? Strategic Climate Litigation in the Eyes of US Judges' (2021) 13 Sustainability 8335; Laura Burgers, 'Should Judges Make Climate Change Law?' (2020) 9(1) Transnational Environmental Law 55.
[111] See Chapters 8, 7, and 4 on South Africa, India, and Canada respectively.

instance in China, the Supreme People's Court exercises 'semi-legislative power' and refers directly to lists formulated by international institutions, such as the application of the appendices of CITES in criminal cases that concern endangered species and the Red List of the International Union for Conservation of Nature (IUCN).[112] It is to be noted that, in China, the Penal Code includes reference to such direct application of the CITES appendices, while the IUCN Red List is not referred to in any regulation. The judges' willingness to protect endangered species was seen in the Alexandrine parakeet case when the species was not technically protected under Chinese criminal law.[113]

It is argued that there is nothing unconstitutional about judges putting a check on the executives and filling democratic deficits. However, it could also be argued that such an invasion would be unwise or politically undesirable and might lead to partisan decisions.[114] An important but still unresolved question remains concerning the extent to which judges may go. They are supposed to be bound by statutes and precedents, but societal, political, and economic aspects also play a role in their decisions. Depending on the jurisdiction, there are also limits on the authority of the judges, their role in upholding the rule of law, and how they perceive their duty to interpret and enforce the applicable law. For some critics, judges are ill-equipped to deal with the increasingly political arguments put before them and to come to informed judgments.[115] Judges are allegedly not accountable and not well qualified to take political decisions and may misinterpret the political purpose of the policy expressed in the statute. Then again, the tension between economic growth and environmental protection, and the political and business influence on development decisions, explored in this volume, exacerbate the need for a robust judiciary.

3.1.1.3 *Judges' willingness to engage with scientific expertise*

The collection and synthesis of scientific data and the supporting of scientists in presenting such data is central in biodiversity-related disputes. Experts are more than ever central players for the creation of the necessary link between knowledge and decision making. We also witness a shift in the attitude of

[112] See Chapter 5.
[113] ibid Section 3.1.
[114] See Chapter 10 on the United States.
[115] Peter Gerangelos, *The Separation of Powers and Legislative Interference in Judicial Process: Constitutional Process and Limitations* (Hart Publishing 2009).

judges with regard to scientific and technical elements in biodiversity-related disputes. For instance, at the international level, the ICJ has shown a persistent reluctance to engage with scientific and technical aspects of cases.[116] Its more recent decisions, starting with the *Danube dam* case, show a shift in attitude, later confirmed with the *Pulp Mills* case or the *Whaling* case.[117]

At the national level, the judiciary has been actively seeking and accepting scientific reports to support the claims before the courts.[118] Available scientific reports provide a crucial service that allows litigants to design a litigation strategy, and the courts to offer their opinion supported by scientific studies. Such reports can lead to new sets of scientific data, shape future biodiversity strategy, and can be considered as an indirect impact of biodiversity litigation. Considering the rise in number of such reports at the international level (IPCC, IPBES, Global Biodiversity Outlook, Local Biodiversity Outlook), we may witness in the future a strong influence of such global scientific syntheses on national legal disputes.

National expertise is also crucial, and the judiciary can call upon scientists with data on national and local biodiversity impacts that present a detailed assessment. For example, judges in China use scientific evidence and consult scientists to identify which species of plants or animals have been captured, killed, or traded. This has become more crucial since the link between biosecurity and the Covid-19 outbreak has shown the growing need to have scientific data linking ecological security and public health.[119] Similarly, the critical nature of scientific evidence is reinforced in Canada[120] and cases dealing with GMOs or oil exploration hydraulic fracturing (fracking) in Brazil.[121] Apart from officially appointed experts (panels, witnesses), the practice of amicus briefs[122] is another route to assist the judiciary in dealing with complex biodiversity litigation.

Despite its growing importance in biodiversity-related disputes, expertise may not always have the influence expected. Indeed, Chapter 3 concerning Brazil has shown that the judiciary may not always base its decisions on scientific evidence.

116 Katalin Sulyok, *Science and Judicial Reasoning: The Legitimacy of International Environmental Adjudication* (CUP 2020) 69–117.
117 See Chapter 12.
118 See Chapters 6, 5, and 4 on France, China, and Canada respectively.
119 See Chapter 5.
120 eg Chapter 4, Section 3.1.2 (*Alberta Wilderness Association v Canada* (environment case)).
121 See Chapter 3.
122 See Chapters 3, 8, and 5 on Brazil, South Africa, and China respectively.

3.1.1.4 Judges' role in specialized environmental courts

Specialized environmental courts are emerging in several jurisdictions, as seen in India, China, and Australia. These courts illustrate the growing awareness of the inherent complexity of environmental disputes and of the centrality of experts (eg environmental scientists, expert witnesses).[123] For instance, in Australia and India, the advantages of a specialized environment court are that it brings together both judges and non-lawyer specialists who act as internal experts.[124] Such scientific evidence has been crucial to many cases in Australia—in relation to the application of precautionary principles or to set aside development consent. On the other hand, in Brazil, there is a lack of expertise from judges since there are few specialized sections on environmental issues in the courts.[125] The necessity for specialized environmental courts lies in the fact that such courts and tribunals can act as a 'one-stop hub' for environmental disputes with the availability of technical and scientific expertise, open standing, and effective remedies and enforcement.[126] Our case studies underscore the need for training and dialogue among judges enabling them to share ideas and techniques in view of the diversity and complexity of biodiversity litigation and the limitations of national biodiversity laws. Training in biodiversity-related topics tailored for judges is available; for example, through various programmes run by UNEP and the European Commission.[127] However, bespoke training programmes for judges dealing with complex legal issues surrounding biodiversity conservation is lacking.

3.1.2 The evolving role of civil society

Several elements are relevant to initiate biodiversity litigation: the procedures for going to the courts, the requirements for being a petitioner, and the standing rules. Indeed, standing remains a key issue in allowing petitioners to bring a claim to court. In most biodiversity cases, the litigants/petitioners do not act for personal gain and do not generally have a financial stake in the outcome of the litigation. Rather, the litigants seek to uphold the law, fill the gaps

[123] Brian J Preston, 'Characteristics of Successful Environmental Courts and Tribunals' (2014) 26(3) Journal of Environmental Law 365.

[124] See Chapter 2 on Australia and Chapter 5 on India.

[125] See Chapter 3.

[126] George (Rock) Pring and Catherine (Kitty) Pring, *Environmental Courts & Tribunals: A Guide for Policy Makers* (UNEP 2016).

[127] Academy of European Law and European Commission, Cooperation with National Judges in the field of EU Environmental Law <https://ec.europa.eu/environment/legal/law/judges.html> accessed 22 March 2022. UNEP Training Curriculum on Environmental Law for Judges and Magistrates in Africa: A Guide for Judicial Training Institutions' <www.unep.org/resources/toolkits-manuals-and-guides/training-curriculum-environmental-law-judges-and-magistrates> accessed 22 March 2022.

in the law, or ensure that the government system functions properly. The litigants thus act as a 'watchdog' to keep a check on the executive agencies. It is here that civil society plays a significant role.[128] Our case studies show that, apart from designated public bodies,[129] individuals, groups and NGOs regularly bring proceedings before the lower as well as the higher courts at the national level.

In China, the rising number of NGOs initiating biodiversity litigation has led to public awareness of biodiversity loss.[130] In Australia, NGOs are involved in bringing cases such as the Environmental Defenders Offices and Environment Centre to protect the intrinsic value of biodiversity.[131] Similar examples of NGOs involved in initiating biodiversity cases are found in France, the UK, and South Africa, among others. In the UK, public bodies are responsible for protecting, maintaining, and enhancing biodiversity and have the power to pursue legal action to that end. Individuals and NGOs such as the Royal Society for the Protection of Birds can bring actions to challenge public decision making by judicial review or by pursuing private prosecutions of wildlife crime.[132] In contrast, biodiversity litigation has become more challenging in the United States as courts have raised standing hurdles.[133] Similar standing-related hurdles in the EU stop environmental NGOs from bringing strategic lawsuits in the field of IBL directly before the CJEU, thus leaving the 'quasi-exclusivity' of biodiversity litigation to the EU Commission.

While the Constitution or national laws may determine standing rules, the courts' intention and interpretation may widen these. There are arguments in favour of and against a liberal approach to standing.[134] Liberal standing rules allow legal activists to initiate a claim. This is helpful when the victims are not aware of the violation of their rights and may not have access to adequate information—especially in the global south.[135] More so if the public bodies are not willing to take action (eg to stop a large infrastructure, mining,

[128] Civil society includes citizens, consumers, community groups, farmers, and NGOs.

[129] At the same time, national laws may allow government agencies to bring an action (eg Australia, South Africa, China, Brazil).

[130] In China, NGOs such as Wild China and the Friends of Nature Institute have brought cases. See Chapter 5.

[131] See Chapter 2.

[132] See Chapter 9.

[133] See Chapter 10.

[134] George (Rock) Pring and Catherine (Kitty) Pring, 'Specialized Environmental Courts and Tribunals at the Confluence of Human Rights and the Environment' (2009) 11 Oregon Review of International Law 301.

[135] Jona Razzaque, 'Information, Public Participation and Access to Justice in Environmental Matters' in Erika Techera and others (eds), *Routledge Research Handbook on International Environmental Law* (Routledge 2020) 58–72.

or oil exploration project). However, to protect themselves from a multitude of claims, courts are required to be cautious as to who should be granted standing. For example, abuse of standing is not uncommon in the field of public interest litigation[136] and strategy such as 'green lawfare' in Australia has the potential to delay development projects.[137]

The discussion on standing rules emphasizes the importance of procedural rights such as access to justice. Strong substantive rights (eg right to a healthy environment, discussed in Section 3.2.1) supported by procedural rights—right to information, participation, and access to justice—can help civil society to engage in biodiversity conservation. Procedural rights promote fairness by allowing civil society to be part of the decision-making process, and empowerment by enabling them to take an active role in decisions affecting biodiversity. The CBD and its protocols underscore the importance of public participation in biodiversity decisions.[138] Since the 1992 Rio Declaration, there has been a tremendous development of procedural rights at the international, regional, and national levels.[139] For example, the Aarhus Convention and the Escazu Convention[140]—both regional treaties—elaborate on procedural rights in environmental matters. Our case studies show that the Aarhus Convention is relevant in biodiversity litigation dealing with access to environmental justice and environmental impact assessments (EIAs).[141]

Many deficiencies in public participation processes can be traced to weaknesses in legal and institutional frameworks—for example, weak EIA laws, restricted access to information on biodiversity decisions, lack of meaningful consultation, and expensive court processes.[142] For example, biosafety laws in many countries of the global south do not include any provision on access to information or participation.[143] Such legal deficiencies lead to limited civil society engagement in the biodiversity-related decision-making process. Moreover, many energy, mining, and large infrastructures projects are often

136 Michael G Faure and Angara V Raja, 'Effectiveness of Environmental Public Interest Litigation in India: Determining the Key Variables' (2010) 21(2) Fordham Environmental Law Review 239–93.

137 Similar examples can be found in India. Though the actual negative impact of green lawfare might sometimes be exaggerated. On this matter, see Chapter 2 on Australia.

138 Article 14(1)(a) of the CBD, Art 23 of the Cartagena Protocol, Art 12(2) of Nagoya Protocol.

139 Human Rights Council, Report of the Independent Expert on the Issue of Human Rights Obligations Relating to the Enjoyment of a Safe, Clean, Healthy and Sustainable Environment, A/HRC/25/53 (30 December 2013).

140 Regional Agreement on Access to Information, Public Participation and Justice in Environmental Matters in Latin America and the Caribbean (opened to signature 4 March 2018, entered into force 22 April 2021) <www.cepal.org/en/escazuagreement> accessed 9 March 2022.

141 See Chapters 11, 9, and 6 on the EU, the UK, and France respectively.

142 Razzaque (n 135).

143 Lalanath de Silva, 'Public Participation in Biodiversity Conservation' in Elisa Morgera and Jona Razzaque (eds), *Biodiversity and Nature Protection Law* (Edward Elgar 2017) 468.

planned and implemented without free, prior and informed consent, and such lack of access to information and consultation with affected IPLC results in more resource conflicts[144] and litigation.

Even with weaknesses in procedural rights, civil societies are actively engaged in biodiversity negotiations, and playing a major role in sharing knowledge and information, designing litigation strategies, and suggesting remedies.[145] The scale of global biodiversity degradation has led to the proliferation of regulation at all levels of governance and challenges traditional accounts of law as a state-centered and cohesive concept. Law is no longer the privilege of a single actor—the state. Instead, we witness the transformation to a new plural setting that involves a wide range of non-state actors. In the context of biodiversity litigation, the collaboration between local communities, NGOs, scientists, and academics is invaluable, especially in the context of overfishing, hunting, terrestrial- and marine-protected areas, and wildlife crime.

3.2 Rights Discourses in Biodiversity Litigation

In this subsection, we will explore how the language of rights has been used in biodiversity litigation and has been framed in different contexts. More specifically, we intend to understand the place of humans, nature, and rights in the disputes that relate to biodiversity. We will first examine the human right to a healthy environment before turning to non-human rights.

3.2.1 Human rights

Here, we will consider cases where damages (likely to occur or which has already occurred) to biodiversity or breaches of biodiversity law were considered as a breach of human rights.

Human rights can be a tool for the conservation, sustainable use of biodiversity, and equitable sharing of benefits.[146] Numerous cases show how damage to the environment has been reconceptualized as an infringement of human rights.[147] These cases tend to multiply as the right to a healthy environment becomes more widespread, the culmination of this trend being in October 2021

144 See the *Niyamgiri* case in Chapter 6, Section 4.1 on India. Examples of such conflicts are found in the *Environmental Justice Atlas* (2018) <https://ejatlas.org/> accessed 21 March 2022.

145 See examples in Chapters 4, 7, and 9 on Canada, India, and the UK respectively.

146 UN Human Rights Council, Report of the Special Rapporteur on the issue of Human Rights Obligations Relating to the Enjoyment of a Safe, Clean, Healthy and Sustainable Environment, A/HRC/34/49 (2017).

147 See Chapter 4 on Canada and Chapter 7 on India.

with formal recognition at the UN level.[148] For instance, the regional courts for human rights all have examples of cases linking the environment with human health.[149] However, at the national level, the connection between human rights and the environment is not systematic. For instance, in Australia or France, biodiversity litigation seems to be disconnected from any discourse on rights.

From this multitude of cases, different conceptions of the connection between human rights and the environment appear. For instance, before the European Court of Human Rights, the protection of biodiversity will have to be linked directly to (potential) harm to humans.[150] Contrastingly, the Inter-American Court of Human Rights considers that the protection of the environment in its own right, irrespective of a potential human damage, is entailed in the right to a healthy environment.[151]

Within the categories of human rights, the rights of IPLC are worth mentioning for their impact on biodiversity litigation.[152] As recalled by the IPBES in its Global Assessment, 'at least a quarter of the global land area is traditionally owned, managed, used or occupied by indigenous peoples'. Within those areas 'nature is generally declining less rapidly in indigenous peoples'.[153] Moreover, the socio-cultural diversity of IPLC is correlated to the surrounding biodiversity. These elements highlight the specific link that exists between IPLC and biodiversity and warrants a dedicated regime for the protection of their rights. Several countries thus acknowledge a specific legal status to IPLC. We can mention, for instance, the Plurinational State of Bolivia which has a strong constitutional emphasis on IPLC.[154]

The recognition of IPLC specific rights can influence the outcomes of biodiversity-related disputes. For instance, in Canada, a road project was contested on several legal bases, for environmental reasons and for its potential impact on sacred grounds.[155] In this case, the impact on sacred land had a greater effect in halting the project than environmental considerations. In the chapters

[148] Resolution of the UN Human Rights Council 48/13, The Human Right to a Safe, Clean, Healthy and Sustainable Environment (18 October 2021).

[149] See Chapter 12 on international biodiversity litigation.

[150] The ECtHR provides a fact sheet with a summary of all relevant cases on environmental matters. See ECtHR Press Unit, Environment and the European Convention on Human Rights (fact sheet, January 2022).

[151] Inter-American Court, Advisory Opinion Oc-23/17 of 15 November 2017, Requested by the Republic of Colombia: *The Environment and Human Rights* 134.

[152] Sandra Díaz and others (eds), *Summary for Policymakers of the Global Assessment Report on Biodiversity and Ecosystem Services of the Intergovernmental Science-Policy Platform on Biodiversity and Ecosystem Services* (IPBES 2019).

[153] ibid 14.

[154] Bolivia (Plurinational State of) Constitution of 2009, Arts 30, 31, 32.

[155] See Chapter 4.

of this volume, we have seen that the rights of IPLC had a particular place in the legal system set up for the conservation and sustainable use of biodiversity.[156]

But human rights are not only conservation tools. It is worth mentioning that they can also hinder biodiversity conservation measures. For instance, Chapter 6 on France, we saw that hunters have claimed an alleged right to hunt to protest administrative decisions for the management of game. Chapter 9 covering the UK also highlighted the fact that human rights are sometimes invoked before the courts to challenge biodiversity conservation measures.

3.2.2 Non-human rights

Non-human rights, understood here as the recognition of the rights of nature as a whole, some of its components, or individual animals, has gained considerable traction over the past decade.[157] The idea of conferring rights on nature or its elements in order to better protect it or them, to reinforce the effectiveness of environmental law, has been seen as a remedy for many of the difficulties in implementing environmental law.[158] Originally very controversial,[159] this idea is beginning to be translated into positive law with the recognition of the rights of non-human living entities, individually (an animal) or more often collectively (an ecosystem).[160] Interestingly, these recent developments are strictly national and are spreading in a horizontal manner. On this topic, international law is mostly silent, a spectator so to speak.[161] With regard to animals, international law is far more concerned with welfare.[162]

None of our case studies directly addressed biodiversity litigation that involved non-human rights. However, such cases are carefully monitored and numerous examples can be mentioned. For instance, in India, several rulings

156 See Chapter 7 on India and Chapter 12 on international biodiversity litigation.

157 Guillaume Chapron, Yaffa Epstein, and Jose Vicente Lopez-Bao, 'A Rights Revolution for Nature: Introduction of Legal Rights for Nature could Protect Natural Systems from Destruction' (2016) 363 Science 1392; David R. Boyd, *The Rights of Nature: A Legal Revolution that Could Save the World* (ECW Press 2017); Christopher Rodgers, 'A New Approach to Protecting Ecosystems: The Te Awa Tupua (Whanganui River Claims Settlement) Act 2017' (2017) 19 Environmental Law Review 266; Anne Peters, 'Liberté, Égalité, Animalité: Human–Animal Comparisons in Law' (2016) 5 Transnational Environmental Law 25; Saskia Stucki, 'Towards a Theory of Legal Animal Rights: Simple and Fundamental Rights' (2020) 40 Oxford Journal of Legal Studies 533.

158 See n 157.

159 Christopher D Stone, 'Should Trees have Standing? Towards Legal Rights for Natural Objects' (1972) 45 Southern California Law Review 450; Marina Brilman, 'Environmental Rights and the Legal Personality of the Amazon Region' (24 April 2018) European Journal of International Law: Talk, Blog of the European Society of International Law.

160 Nathalie Rühs and Aled Jones, 'The Implementation of Earth Jurisprudence Through Substantive Constitutional Rights of Nature' (2016) 8(2) Sustainability 174.

161 Though authors are calling for a strengthened role of international law in order to promote non-human rights, see Anne Peters, *Animal in International Law* (Brill 2021) 421–531.

162 See eg the work of World Organization for Animal Health.

acknowledged the legal personality of rivers, or even of the entire animal kingdom.[163] In Latin America, cases on the legal personality of rivers can be found,[164] and the legal personality of nature as a whole is even explicitly recognized in the constitution of Ecuador.[165] Similarly, in New Zealand, the Whanganui River has been considered as a legal person since March 2017.[166] In its 2017 Advisory Opinion, the Inter-American Court of Human Rights took note of the current trend of recognizing legal personality for nature and rights to nature, not only in court decisions but also in constitutional provisions.[167]

It may very well be that the topic of non-human rights is what sets biodiversity litigation apart from other forms of environmental litigation as it highlights a mix between philosophical, political, and scientific considerations in our understanding of the environment. However, even though these cases attract their fair share of attention, this might create a distortion in how we envision biodiversity litigation. In most countries, and at the international level, the very notion of non-human rights remains foreign. This does not prevent biodiversity litigation from taking place and from innovative approaches to sprout.

3.3 Impacts

The biodiversity regime broadly aims at conservation, sustainable use, and access and benefit sharing. To reach its goals, this regime relies on national policies and laws, which are supposed to be designed and implemented in accordance with NBSAP. However, it is clear that these goals are far from

[163] On rivers, see High Court of Uttarakhand at Nainital, *Mohammed Salim v State of Uttarakhand & others* (Writ Petition) (PIL) No 126 of 2014, 20 March 2014. On animals, see High Court of Punjab and Haryana at Chandigarh, CRR-553-2013, 31 May 2019, para 29, 'The entire animal kingdom including avian and aquatic are declared as legal entities having a distinct persona with corresponding rights, duties and liabilities of a living person. All the citizens throughout the State of Haryana are hereby declared persons in loco parentis as the human face for the welfare/protection of animals.' This judgment follows the path established in Supreme Court of India, *Animal Welfare Board of India v A Nagaraja & others*, Civil Appeal No 5387 of 2014, 7 May 2014.

[164] Corte constitucional, República de Colombia, Sala Sexta de Revision, T-622, 10 November 2016; Corte Suprema de Justicia, Sala de Casacion Civil, STC 4360-2018, Radicacion No 1101-22-03-000-2018-00319-01, Bogotá, 5 April 2018.

[165] See Constitucion De La Republica Del Ecuador Decreto Legislativo 0, Registro Oficial 449 de 20 October 2008, Ultima modificación: 13 July 2011, Art 71 recognizes the rights of Pacha Mama. This article has had repercussions in disputes, see *Wheeler v Director de la Procuraduria General Del Estado de Loja*, Juicio No 11121-2011-0010; and República del Ecuador Asamblea Nacional, Comisión de la Biodiversidad Recursos Naturales, Acta de Sesión No 66; Louis J Kotzé and Paola Villavicencio Calzadilla, 'Somewhere Between Rhetoric and Reality: Environmental Constitutionalism and the Rights of Nature in Ecuador' (2017) 6(3) Transnational Environmental Law 401–33.

[166] Te Awa Tupua (Whanganui Claims Settlement) Act 2017, Public Act no 17, 20 March 2017.

[167] Inter-American Court, Advisory Opinion Oc-23/17 (n 151).

being reached. For instance, most of the Aichi Targets have not been met, and the future prospects for biodiversity are pessimistic.[168] In this context, where both international and national initiatives seem to be unfit for purpose, it is likely that more cases will be initiated in the courts. This opens up a space to assess the impacts of such litigation at various levels of governance. This also begs the question: can biodiversity litigation meaningfully contribute to the effectiveness of biodiversity law?[169] In reality, biodiversity litigation is often about trade-offs and competing interests. The result of the balancing exercise is, however, uncertain and will vary from one country to another. Remedies available to the courts and how these are implemented also vary widely.

3.3.1 Biodiversity litigation balancing competing interests

Biodiversity litigation recognizes the multiple components of biodiversity protection and underscores their interlinkages. For instance, themes such as protected areas, forest rights, and indigenous peoples' rights highlight the obvious ties between conservation and sustainable use. Unsurprisingly, disputes on indigenous peoples' rights will concurrently address conservation issues.[170] In sum, biodiversity litigation often amounts to a balance between several elements or interests, as illustrated by our case studies.

Courts had to balance different environmental, social, and economic interests, and recognize trade-offs. Biodiversity cases in India highlight the marginalization of forest dwellers and indigenous people due to exclusionary conservation practices. Cases on infrastructure development in the UK and France show how the judiciary is balancing such competing interests that can ultimately lead to biodiversity degradation.[171] Cases involving mining in the Great Barrier Reef in Australia and the protection of endangered species and coal mining in the protected areas in South Africa evidence the trade-offs involved in biodiversity conservation decisions.[172] Yet, it appears that the success of the courts in halting large infrastructure projects is uneven. As highlighted in several chapters, economic interests prevail, and the intervention of the courts fails to put a stop to such unsustainable projects.[173]

168 Sandra Diaz and others, 'Pervasive Human-Driven Decline of Life on Earth Points to the Need for Transformative Change' (2019) 366(6471) Science.

169 Here understood as all laws related to biodiversity, at all levels—national, regional, international.

170 See Chapter 4 on Canada.

171 See Chapters 6 and 9 on the UK and France respectively.

172 See Chapters 2 and 8 on Australia and South Africa respectively.

173 See Chapters 2, 6, and 9 on Australia, France, and the UK respectively.

In this context of trade-off, courts' decisions in biodiversity litigation may have varying impacts that are linked to the available remedies or how their decisions may resonate within society.

3.3.2. The remedies of biodiversity litigation

A failure to design a coherent biodiversity law or policy at the national level undermines biodiversity conservation and governance. On this matter, the impacts of biodiversity litigation can be seen, first, in better monitoring and enforcement of national biodiversity laws. For example, in India, the judiciary has asked the legislatures to formulate new strategies, create monitoring committees, and demanded periodic reports from public agencies.[174] The effective enforcement of national biodiversity laws is also challenged through cases involving wildlife crime. Despite intense worldwide efforts, the illegal wildlife trade still represents a major threat to endangered species. Pursuing cases involving the illegal wildlife trade through the criminal justice systems[175] and regular monitoring can lead to more effective law enforcement responses.[176] Secondly, biodiversity litigation highlights the need for a synergistic link between biodiversity law and other areas of biodiversity response—such as human rights,[177] intellectual property rights,[178] trade law,[179] criminal law,[180] investment law,[181] and conservation with a transboundary impact.[182]

At the national level, monetary compensation and injunctive relief remain the two most common forms of remedy in biodiversity litigation.[183] For example, in the UK, a wide range of bodies can deal with biodiversity-related issues and remedies differ depending on in which forum the matter was challenged. It is possible to have compensation, an injunction, or a reconsideration of the matter by a lower court with different judges or a differently constituted tribunal.[184] In Brazil, fines are applied to companies that have not shared the benefits related to the economic exploitation of genetic resources.[185] In China,

[174] See Chapter 7.
[175] See Chapters 9, 5, 8, and 3 on the UK, China, South Africa, India, and Brazil respectively.
[176] UNODC, *World Wildlife Crime Report: Trafficking in Protected Species* (2016).
[177] See the *Saramaka* case in Chapter 12, Section 3.1.2.
[178] See Chapter 7 on India.
[179] See Chapter 10 on the United States and, eg, the *Seals* case before WTO in Chapter 12, Section 3.1.2.
[180] See Chapter 8 on South Africa and Chapter 3 on Brazil.
[181] See Chapter 12 on international biodiversity law.
[182] See Chapter 10 on the United States.
[183] See examples in Chapters 4, 2, 7, 9, and 3 on Canada, Australia, India, the UK, and Brazil respectively.
[184] See Chapter 9.
[185] See Chapter 3.

public interest litigation cases include the removal of waste and reparation for ecological damage. In the United States, while a wide range of remedies including imprisonment, fines, restitution, mitigation, injunctions, and property liens are available, the application of such remedies in biodiversity cases is limited. At the international level, the ICJ has confirmed that compensation is an appropriate form of reparation, 'particularly in cases regarding environmental harm where restitution is materially impossible or unduly burdensome'.[186]

In addition, restoration is another option that plays a central role in returning the ecosystem to baseline conditions (eg restoration of ecological integrity of national parks in Canada). The UN Decade on Ecosystem Restoration (2021–30) underscores the urgency of ecosystem restoration to mitigate biodiversity as well as the climate crisis. Ecosystem restoration can help to reverse some biodiversity losses and address the societal and cultural goals set in international agreements (eg CBD, UNFCCC, UNCCD) and commitments (eg Aichi Biodiversity Targets, SDGs). Through ecological restoration, ecological integrity can be reinstated by recovering the structure (eg species composition, and soil and water properties) and functional properties (eg productivity, energy flow, nutrient cycling) of an ecosystem.[187] Ecological restoration often builds on efforts to remediate and rehabilitate ecosystems.[188] Cases from the Netherlands, France, and India reveal the courts' willingness to apply a restoration-based rationale.[189] For example, following the Erika oil spill case in France,[190] restoration and clean-up activities were explicitly added to the Environmental Code with the 2016 Law on Biodiversity, Nature and Landscape.[191] In Brazil, civil solidary liability[192] is an example whereby priority is given to the complete restoration of the damage. In making a determination of compensation in *Costa Rica v Nicaragua (Compensation)* case, the International Court of Justice stated that 'damage to the environment, and the consequent impairment or loss of the ability of the environment to provide

[186] See Chapter 12, Section 3.4.1.

[187] Afshin Akhtar-Khavari and Benjamin J Richardson, 'Ecological Restoration and the Law: Recovering Nature's Past for the Future' (2017) 26(2) Griffith Law Review 147.

[188] eg in the EU, Directive 2004/35/EC on Environmental Liability with Regard to the Prevention and Remedying of Environmental Damage [2004] OJ L143/56.

[189] See Chapter 11 on the EU. For India, see *Narmada Khand Swabhiman Sewa v Madhya Pradesh*, Original Application No 144/2013, NGT Judgment, 1 October 2014.

[190] Danai Papadoupolou, 'The Role of French Environmental Associations in Civil Liability for Environmental Harm: Courtesy of Erika' (2009) 21(1) Journal of Environmental Law 87–112.

[191] Elise Buisson and others, 'Promoting Ecological Restoration in France: Issues and Solutions' (2018) 26(1) Restoration Ecology 36–44.

[192] Solidary civil liability means that any person, natural or legal, that has caused, directly or indirectly, damage to the environment will be jointly and severally liable to repair or indemnify the damage. Objective and joint civil liability is provided for in arts 3°, IV and 14, § 1° of Law 6.938/1981.

goods and services, is compensable under international law.'[193] The Court assessed the restoration costs, as well as the value attributed to the impairment of goods and services prior to recovery.[194] However, restoration as a remedy remains complicated in practice as illustrated by the determination of baselines for restoration (eg what is the baseline condition?) and the complexity of some restoration activities.[195]

In order to reduce the problem with expenses related to a case, the court can make a cost order that does not inhibit the litigants from enforcing their environmental rights. The purpose of a cost award should not be mainly punitive or compensatory and its primary focus must be to allocate the cost of litigation equitably. This practice is evidenced in public interest environmental litigation,[196] and the same argument can be applied in favour of a general exception for the costs rule in biodiversity litigation. Biodiversity cases are often brought in the broader public interest whereby the case helps to bring clarity to the law, thus reducing the need for future litigation. Examples of such cost orders favourable to litigants in biodiversity cases protecting the public interest are found in South Africa and India.[197] In such circumstances, the courts either did not make any cost order or the cost and the expenses of the cases were ordered to be paid by the respondents (eg the state as the respondent was asked to pay the costs of the case).

3.3.3 Biodiversity litigation and the public

Finally, is there any lasting or significant impact of biodiversity litigation on public behaviour? If a court's decision influences people's behaviour, this could demonstrate remarkable effectiveness of these decisions in the fight against biodiversity destruction. Although the impact of climate change litigation in the context of social movements is visible,[198] the social influence of biodiversity litigation has not yet been comprehensively assessed. In the context of climate change, the influence of courts on society and politics cannot be denied.[199]

[193] *Certain Activities Carried Out By Nicaragua in the Border Area (Costa Rica v Nicaragua)*, Compensation, Judgment [2018] ICJ Rep 15, para 42.

[194] ibid para 53.

[195] James Bullock and others, 'Restoration of Ecosystem Services and Biodiversity: Conflicts and Opportunities' (2011) 26(10) Trends in Ecology & Evolution 541–49.

[196] Jona Razzaque, *Public Interest Environmental Litigation in India, Pakistan and Bangladesh* (Kluwer 2004), 229–66.

[197] ibid 246. Also, Chapter 8 on South Africa.

[198] Joana Setzer and Rebecca Byrnes, 'Global Trends in Climate Change Litigation: 2020 Snapshot' (Grantham Research Institute on Climate Change and the Environment and Centre for Climate Change Economics and Policy, London School of Economics and Political Science, 2020), 13–14.

[199] Laura Burgers, 'Should Judges Make Climate Change Law?' (2020) 9(1) Transnational Environmental Law 63.

Although the direct effects of court decisions on public behaviour are difficult to establish, certain indirect influences of the courts' decisions in climate litigation are evidenced in the increased level of public awareness, media attention, and public activism.[200] Collaboration and networking among vulnerable groups can empower them to protect their rights. Indeed, the increasing level of global biodiversity destruction needs to influence people's behaviour and values.[201] Initiatives such as 'one meat-free day a week'[202] or 'flight shame'[203] and social marketing strategies (eg TV ads) coupled with educational campaigns are common strategies to change consumer behaviour,[204] although evidence on the effectiveness of such initiatives is lacking. Therefore, if we take lessons from climate change, socio-political events such as biodiversity summits or protest actions by activists may promote these changes in people's behaviour. Thus, a court decision can have a strong impact on the population, as it is accepted more widely by society as an authoritative interpretation of the law.

Finally, beyond the diversity of approaches and cases studied in this volume, what could be the added value of this new concept of biodiversity litigation?

4. The Added Value of the Concept of Biodiversity Litigation

With this edited collection, our intention was to explore a sub-field of environmental litigation that focuses on biodiversity and to conceptualize it as a distinct field. To this end, it is interesting to observe how climate change litigation has become a theme in its own right and determine whether the same could

200 Anke Wonneberger and Rens Vliegenthart, 'Agenda-Setting Effects of Climate Change Litigation: Interrelations Across Issue Levels, Media, and Politics in the Case of Urgenda Against the Dutch Government' (2021) 15(5) Environmental Communication 701.

201 Liisa Varumo and others, 'Perspectives on Citizen Engagement for the EU Post-2020 Biodiversity Strategy: An Empirical Study' (2020) 12(4) Sustainability 1532.

202 Ruben Sanchez-Sabate and Joan Sabaté, 'Consumer Attitudes Towards Environmental Concerns of Meat Consumption: A Systematic Review' (2019) 16(7) International Journal of Environmental Research and Public Health 1220.

203 'The Guardian View on 'Flight Shame': Face it- Life Must Change', *The Guardian* (17 January 2020) <www.theguardian.com/commentisfree/2020/jan/17/the-guardian-view-on-flight-shaming-face-it-life-must-change> accessed 22 March 2022.

204 Matthias Lehner, Oksana Mont, and Eva Heiskanen, 'Nudging—A Promising Tool for Sustainable Consumption Behaviour?' (2016) 134 Journal of Cleaner Production 166; Kerry Waylen, Philip McGowan, and EJ Milner-Gulland, 'Ecotourism Positively Affects Awareness and Attitudes but not Conservation Behaviours: A Case Study at Grande Riviere' (2009) 43(3) Environmental Science 343.

be said about biodiversity litigation. Moreover, what influence could climate change litigation have on biodiversity litigation?

4.1 Biodiversity Litigation as a Stand-Alone Field: Lessons from Climate Litigation

Recognizing 'biodiversity litigation' as a concept could help to bring more attention to an environmental crisis that is overshadowed by climate change. It is well established that climate and biodiversity are interlinked and that climate change will have an impact on biodiversity.[205] However, even if we were to tackle climate change effectively in the near future, it would not necessarily mean that biodiversity would be significantly preserved. Indeed, biodiversity is often on the losing end of environmental efforts.[206] In other words, promoting the concept of biodiversity litigation could help to keep this priority afloat while we are also focusing our efforts on climate change mitigation and adaptation.

As a starting point, we defined 'biodiversity litigation' in Chapter 1 as *any legal dispute at the national, regional or international level that concerns conservation of, sustainable use of and access and benefit-sharing to genetic resources, species, ecosystems and their relations.* However, it must be said that biodiversity litigation does not yet have a strong 'legal identity'. On the one hand, it is basically a relabelling of part of environmental litigation. On the other hand, it is often difficult to differentiate biodiversity cases from other environmental cases. The biodiversity component is generally only one among many others, like economic development, human rights, indigenous peoples' rights, etc.

We could, however, say the same for climate litigation, which has nevertheless emerged as a specific field of dispute, even if there are still debates on its exact scope.[207] How can we explain this difference? One reason could be that biodiversity litigation has a much longer history and is linked to well-established but distinct legal fields: urban planning, waste management, protected areas, to name a few. In contrast, climate litigation is a recent trend which has grown exponentially and has been publicized as such. Except for

[205] IPBES, IPBES–IPCC cosponsored workshop Biodiversity and Climate Change Scientific Outcomes (IPBES 2021).
[206] Sandrine Maljean-Dubois, *Le droit international de la biodiversité* (Brill 2021).
[207] Jacqueline Peel and Hari M Osofsky, *Climate Change Litigation: Regulatory Pathways to Cleaner Energy* (CUP 2009).

'charismatic megafauna',[208] public awareness is higher for climate issues than for biodiversity. Therefore, it may be harder to promote the use of the concept of biodiversity litigation in a field where legal habits are deeply entrenched.

Additionally, in climate litigation, judges are seen as—and are becoming—key actors in the global effort to tackle climate change. The Paris Agreement is more in the spotlight than the CBD. The international climate regime has given rise to an international network of activist lawyers working for associations and forming, with a committed academic community, an international 'epistemic community' at the service of climate. Climate change litigation has initiated an international dialogue by judges, even in legal systems where such an approach might be uncommon. Judges know the worldwide publicity that climate rulings enjoy. They also know that their decisions will be analysed and commented on well beyond their own national borders and that they may in turn inspire courts in other countries. In comparison, biodiversity cases are, in nearly all cases, framed as local, or sometimes national, cases. They have remained 'insular'. The idea that a threat to biodiversity is a global one is not usually found before the courts.

Measurable in quantitative as well as qualitative terms, the growing role of international law before domestic courts has been confirmed by more general studies They link this development to the normative expansion of international law and to the increasing interdependence of states in the context of globalization.[209] The increased presence of international law is also the direct consequence of the growing openness of states to international law.[210] All this is leading national courts to think 'outside the "Westphalian" box' marked by the lack of permeability between the international and national spheres.[211] Many academics have called for this, asking national courts to play a much more important role as instruments for safeguarding the international legal order, by taking into account 'meta-national' considerations, beyond short-term national interests.[212]

208 Andrew C Mergen, 'Lessons from the Polar Bear Listing Litigation' (2015) 29(3) Natural Resources & Environment 30; Natalie Klein and Nikolas Hughes, 'National Litigation and International Law, Repercussions for Australia's Protection of Marine Resources' (2009) 33 Melbourne University Law Review 182.

209 Yuval Shany, *National Courts as International Actors: Jurisdictional Implications* (International Law Forum of the Hebrew University of Jerusalem Law Faculty, Research Paper, No 22-08, 25 October 2008) 5.

210 Jean d'Aspremont, *The Systemic Integration of International Law by Domestic Courts, in the Practice of International and National Courts and the (De-)Fragmentation of International Law* (Hart Publishing 2014) 143.

211 Stephane Beaulac, *Westphalia, Dualism and Contextual Interpretation: How to Better Engage International Law in Domestic Courts* (EUI Working Paper, MWP 2007/03) 4.

212 Antonio Cassese, 'Remarks Theory of "Role Splitting" (dédoublement fonctionnel) in International Law' (1990) European Journal of International Law 230.

Taken as a whole, these phenomena illustrate how the processes of normative and judicial intertwining, very well described as early as 2013 by Mireille Delmas-Marty, are capable of 'creating a movement that makes it possible, under certain conditions, to integrate and reconcile the multiple constraints of systems—national and international—which were initially based on different models'.[213] National courts thus become 'organizers of clouds', to use her beautiful metaphor.[214]

Vague international law, as is most of IBL, can gain legal clarity through the intervention of national courts, which make up for the lack of an international control mechanism. Through their interpretation of states' international commitments, which go well beyond international environmental law, national courts can connect, harmonize, bring together, and even hybridize international and national norms, with the various courts mutually inspiring each other across borders.[215] National courts, through their cascading decisions, could thus be one of the keys to better combine, on the one hand, international commitments and national regulations and, on the other hand, international ambition and state action. The urgency is obvious, as shown by the first IPBES report, published in 2019.

To summarize, there is no formal reason why the concept of biodiversity litigation could not be used as a parallel to the concept of climate litigation. This would simply entail a reframing and a relabelling of existing judicial practices. Doing so could open the door to creative legal thinking, by relying on novel concepts and principles. We also believe that such a concept is also relevant for scholarship in environmental law. As highlighted by Elisabeth Fisher, environmental law is characterized by its rapid and continuous growth. This in turns calls for the development of concepts and frames that allow for a more rigorous description of the field.[216] The notion of biodiversity ligation can serve such a purpose by adding more clarity to the quasi-boundless notion of environmental litigation. Moreover, should the notion become more widespread, this would in turn reshape the debates around courts and the environment and lead to other relevant ideas and propositions.[217]

[213] Mireille Delmas-Marty, *Le pluralisme ordonné. Les forces imaginantes du droit (II)* 63 (authors' translation).

[214] ibid.

[215] ibid.

[216] Elizabeth Fisher, 'Environmental Law as "Hot" Law' (2013) 25 Journal of Environmental Law 347.

[217] As argued by Daniel Bonilla Maldonado in Ole W Pedersen (ed), *Perspectives on Environmental Law Scholarship* (CUP 2018) 41–59.

4.2 Climate Litigation, an Inspiration for the Future Development of Biodiversity Litigation?

Climate litigation could be an inspiration for the development of biodiversity litigation, potentially creating new reflexes in both claimants and judges. Various elements point in this direction.

First, strategic biodiversity disputes are more frequent. Following the same patterns at play in the field of climate change, the cases try to address what is perceived as a failure on the part of public authorities or companies. They also encourage public authorities or companies to take stronger measures to protect biodiversity, to implement more ambitious policies, to obtain compensation for damage suffered, to stop a project potentially harmful, etc. Representing this tendency, a new French case initiated by the Ligue de Protection des Oiseaux, an NGO specializing in the conservation of birds, consists in civil proceedings against Bayer and Nufarm for their alleged responsibility in the decline of field birds due to the effect of the pesticides these companies produce.[218] A similar case has been brought in Costa Rica where the Supreme Court ordered a scientific study that may lead to a ban on pesticides that harm pollinating insects.[219] Furthermore, in the future biodiversity litigation risks could also become a new concern for companies. Following the model of climate lawsuits, with increasing attention being paid to the impacts of companies on biodiversity, there are 'new physical, regulatory, market and reputational risks—all of which are compounded by the hyper-connectivity of global value chains'.[220] As with climate, litigation risks can arise from breaches of due diligence along the value chain, or failure to disclose those risks adequately or accurately.[221]

Another factor of mutual influence that could lead to an increasing role of international law, may be that the same NGOs are engaging in climate and biodiversity litigation, with increasing experience in the use of international law and mutual inspiration. For instance, in China, the Friends of Nature Institute, the very same NGO that first advocated for climate change litigation, has also sued enterprises over biodiversity causes.[222] Similarly, in France, it is the NGO 'Notre affaire à tous', which is involved in several climate cases, that has initiated

[218] See Chapter 6.

[219] Boya Jiang and others, *10 Landmark Cases for Biodiversity* (ClientEarth 2021), 12–13 <www.clientearth.org/media/upvbjd4p/10-landmark-cases-for-biodiversity.pdf> accessed 25 March 2022.

[220] See Sedilekova and others (n 52) 3; Isabella Kaminski, 'Legal Eagles: How Climate Litigation is Shaping Ambitious Cases for Nature', *The Guardian* (16 March 2022).

[221] Sedilekova and others (n 52) 4.

[222] See Chapter 5, Section 4.

the previously mentioned Pollinis case.[223] Treaties like the Aarhus Convention or the recent Escazu Regional Agreement play, or can play, a major role here, in setting procedural obligations on access to information, participation, and access to justice and thus having the potential to serve as a catalyst for biodiversity litigation.

Such an inspiration could be reinforced by the future adoption of the Post 2020 Global Biodiversity Framework which could fuel biodiversity litigation in the same way as the Paris Agreement has fuelled climate litigation in recent years. Incorporating the reference to the new Strategic Plan on Biodiversity into their legal arguments could be of added value for the plaintiffs and give more weight to their demands, judging by the evolution of climate litigation in which references to international law are usually a booster. Judges could then work on reconciling the global objectives and targets with—clearly inadequate—national policies, as they do in climate litigation.

Mutual influence could also be favoured by the increasing linkages between biodiversity and climate change issues. If the two topics have been kept separate thus far, we are now witnessing an increasing interplay between climate change claims and biodiversity claims. There are more and more disputes over the consequences of climate policies on biodiversity (development of renewable energy vs habitat conservation, biofuel production vs deforestation). Climate change and biodiversity are not always competing interests.[224] In some cases, biodiversity claims have even strengthened climate change litigation.[225] In others, biodiversity litigation has been influenced by climate change.[226] As nature-based solutions to climate change come under the spotlight and as climate change drives the biodiversity crisis, climate and biodiversity litigation will undoubtedly become increasingly entangled and difficult to separate either practically or conceptually.[227] In this sense, provided that we recognize the trade-offs and synergies of the co-benefits associated with their implementation, nature-based solutions could potentially contribute to the achievement of several SDGs, 'by promoting the delivery of bundles of ecosystem

223 See Chapter 6, Section 1.

224 See eg in India the case *We the People v Union of India* in Chapter 7, Section 6; Australia with prominent cases involving Australian biodiversity that have been brought to address the impacts of mining.

225 Australia, Brazil (the ADPF 708); Joana Setzer and Lisa C Vanhala, 'Climate Change Litigation: A Review of Research on Courts and Litigants in Climate Governance' (2019) 10(3) Wiley Interdisciplinary Reviews: Climate Change e580.

226 Andrew C Mergen, 'Lessons from the Polar Bear Listing Litigation' (2015) 29(3) Natural Resources & Environment 30.

227 Arie Trouwborst, 'International Nature Conservation Law and the Adaptation of Biodiversity to Climate Change: a Mismatch?' (2009) 21(3) Journal of Environmental Law 419.

services together generating various social, economic and environmental co-benefits'.[228]

For all these reasons, biodiversity litigation could be a growing part of the 'conservation law toolkit' in the future, and IBL could become a major tool for a more proactive and creative judiciary. Admittedly, IBL has been criticized as being founded on anthropocentric and utilitarian legal–political ontologies, thereby blocking the path to 'a more hopeful system of global ecological law and governance based on the "rights of nature" that might be able to honour the intrinsic value of the biosphere as a rich, agentic, and communicative whole, fundamental to the Earth's survival'.[229] If there is some truth in that assertion, our case studies show that it has to be nuanced. In raising awareness, as a purveyor of concepts, as an element of evidence, IBL has advanced the cause of biodiversity. Even if it has not actively promoted the 'rights of nature' and ecocentric approaches, and must certainly evolve from this point of view, it has not blocked their entry into—at least some—domestic laws.[230]

5. The Way Forward

What have we learned about biodiversity litigation?

First, biodiversity litigation is evidently influenced, in varying degrees, by international biodiversity law. The most important influence of IBL, both in terms of frequency and in terms of impacts, is its indirect influence, particularly as an interpretative tool.

Secondly, biodiversity litigation has evolved over the years to exhibit certain patterns. It is a form of litigation where the involvement of NGOs and IPLC is crucial and where judges have progressively become more open to science and expertise. Rights discourses have shaped biodiversity litigation in an uneven way, some jurisdictions being open to them and some focusing on environmental law only.

Thirdly, biodiversity litigation can be a tool for the effectiveness of biodiversity law in general. It offers a wealth of remedies and can shape popular opinion

[228] Eulalia Gómez Martín and others, 'Using a System Thinking Approach to Assess the Contribution of Nature-based Solutions to Sustainable Development Goals' (2020) 738 Science of the Total Environment 139693.

[229] Anthony Burke, 'Blue Screen Biosphere: The Absent Presence of Biodiversity in International Law' (2019) 13(3) International Political Sociology 333–51. See also Usha Natarajan and Kishan Khoday, 'Locating Nature: Making and Unmaking International Law' (2014) 27(3) Leiden Journal of International Law 573–93.

[230] See eg Chapter 7 on India.

through symbolic cases. This is, however, highly dependent on non-legal elements, such as the strength of the rule of law in states or the actual willingness of governments to preserve biodiversity.

Fourthly, it appears that 'biodiversity litigation' does not yet have an identity as strong as 'climate litigation'. Nevertheless, the cases studies in this volume and the available literature show that there is some merit in welcoming 'biodiversity litigation' as a staple of environmental law. We believe that this will open the door for more creative legal thinking when dealing with biodiversity-related disputes and refine the discourses around environmental litigation.

There is, however, so much more left to do on the topic. In this volume we have examined a mere fraction of a vast ensemble of cases. By engaging in more case studies, we hope to participate in making the concept of biodiversity litigation a common notion of environmental law. Indeed, as we conclude this project, we see initiatives and studies springing up around the globe.[231]

[231] See eg the website of Conservation Litigation <www.conservation-litigation.org/> accessed 28 March 2022; Jacob Phelps, Carole Adaire Jones, and John A Pendergrass, 'Liability for Environmental Harm as a Response to the Anthropocene' in Michelle Lim (ed), *Charting Environmental Law: Futures in the Anthropocene* (Springer 2019); Jacob Phelps and others, 'Environmental Liability Litigation could Remedy Biodiversity Loss' (2021) 14(6) Conservation Letters e12821; Sedilekova and others (n 52); Achiba Gargule, *Beyond the Institutional Fix? The Potential of Strategic Litigation to Target Natural Resource Corruption* (Targeting Natural Resource Corruption, Topic Brief, February 2022, U4-CMI, 2022).

APPENDIX

Key Multilateral Biodiversity Treaties—Status of Case Study Countries and the EU

[Signature: S; Ratification: R; Accession/Approval/Approbation: A; Not a Party: X]

Multilateral Biodiversity Treaties	Australia	Brazil	Canada	China	EU	France	India	South Africa	UK	USA
International Treaty on Plant Genetic Resources for Food and Agriculture (2001)	R	R	R	X	A	A	R	X	R	R
Convention on Biological Diversity (1992)	R	R	R	R	A	R	R	R	R	X
Convention on the Conservation of Migratory Species of Wild Animals (1979)	A	A	X	X	A	R	R	A	R	X
Convention on International Trade in Endangered Species of Wild Fauna and Flora (1973)	R	R	R	A	A	A	R	R	R	R
Convention for the Protection of the World Cultural and Natural Heritage (1972)	R	A	R	R	X	A	R	R	R	R
Convention on Wetlands of International Importance especially as Waterfowl Habitat (1971)	A	A	A	A	X	R	A	S	R	R

Multilateral Biodiversity Treaties	Australia	Brazil	Canada	China	EU	France	India	South Africa	UK	USA
International Plant Protection Convention (1951)	R	R	R	A	A	R	R	R	R	R
International Convention for the Regulation on Whaling (1946)	R	A	X	A	X	R	A	R	R	R

Source: This table has been created based on the information available at the United Nations Treaty Collection (https://treaties.un.org/).

Index

For the benefit of digital users, indexed terms that span two pages (e.g., 52–53) may, on occasion, appear on only one of those pages.

Tables and figures are indicated by *t* and *f* following the page number